The Coptic Encyclopedia

Editors and Consultants

The Coptic Encyclopedia

Aziz S. Atiya
EDITOR IN CHIEF

Volume 5

Macmillan Publishing Company
NEW YORK
Collier Macmillan Canada
TORONTO
Maxwell Macmillan International
NEW YORK · OXFORD · SINGAPORE · SYDNEY

Macmillan Publishing Company
866 Third Avenue, New York, NY 10022

Collier Macmillan Canada, Inc.
1200 Eglinton Avenue East, Suite 200, Don Mills, Ontario M3C 3N1

Library of Congress Catalog Card No.: 90-23448

Printed in the United States of America

printing number
1 2 3 4 5 6 7 8 9 10

Library of Congress Cataloging-in-Publication Data

The Coptic encyclopedia / Aziz S. Atiya, editor-in-chief.
p. cm.
Includes bibliographical references and index.
ISBN 0-02-897025-X (set)
1. Coptic Church—Dictionaries. 2. Copts—Dictionaries.
I. Atiya, Aziz S., 1898– .
BX130.5.C66 1991 90-23448
281′.7′03—dc20 CIP

The preparation of this volume was made possible in part by a grant from the National Endowment for the Humanities, an independent federal agency.

Photographs on pages 567, 736, 754, 755, 790, 791, 876–878, 1284, 1311, and 2168 are reproduced courtesy of the Metropolitan Museum of Art. Photography by the Egyptian Expedition.

J

(continued)

JOHN, SAINT, Bishop of Armant (feast day: 7 Kiyahk). According to the SYNAXARION of Upper Egypt, John's parents, who were citizens of the town of Armant (Hermonthis), practiced the trade of carpentry. His elder brother Pisentius withdrew to the monastery of Ṭūd. The excellence of the Christian religion having become clear to him, Pisentius had himself baptized with his brothers John and Patermutius. Immediately afterward John became a monk on the mountain of Armant. One day when he experienced a carnal temptation, John rolled himself in the briars until his whole body was bruised by the thorns and appeared as if lacerated. When he returned to the monastery, the holy abbot named Pisentius said to him, "Welcome to the young, adolescent Ethiopian: behold! because of your patience, your constancy, and your firmness of spirit which you have shown in the thorns, God will entrust to you the episcopate of the town of Armant."

Shortly afterward, the inhabitants of the town asked Pisentius to become their bishop. He refused, and delivered to them his brother John, whom they accepted and brought to Alexandria to be consecrated bishop there.

On his return, John baptized a number of idolators who lived in Armant. He wished to build a church, but the idolaters came to destroy the building. His miracles converted a number of pagans, who had themselves baptized. He refused presents under the pretext of ordination.

One day on coming down from his episcopal cell, he saw some men hanging by the arms because of their refusal to pay taxes, and said, "Who has dared to hang up the image of God?" He was told that the prefect had given the order. Immediately he went to the prefect's residence, and by his insistence succeeded in being ushered in at a time when the prefect was having a meal. The prefect asked, "Why do you dare to thrust yourself into my house?" The bishop replied, "I have been a carpenter, and if your door has been damaged I can repair it; but the image of God, if it is broken, you will never restore as it was before."

The prefect replied, "The sovereign demands of us the appointed taxes; it is not possible for us to remit anything whatever to anyone." The bishop said to him before leaving, "Let them go, and I myself will pay for them." The magistrates respected him, and did not dare to commit an injustice.

The mention of the pagans who were converted leads one to place his episcopate in the pre-Islamic period. The Moir-Bryce diptych published by W. E. CRUM (1908 and 1926, Vol. 1, pp. 135f.) contains two Johns; that is why we cannot determine the period at which this John lived.

BIBLIOGRAPHY

Crum, W. E. "A Greek Diptych of the Seventh Century." *Proceedings of the Society of Biblical Archaeology* 30 (1908):255–65.

———. *Monastery of Epiphanius at Thebes,* Vol. 1. New York, 1926.

RENÉ-GEORGES COQUIN

JOHN OF ANTIOCH,

a fifth-century bishop of Antioch who was the chief supporter of NESTORIUS, patriarch of Constantinople, in the Nestorian controversy over the nature of Christ. To resolve the controversy, which set Nestorius against Saint CYRIL I, patriarch of Alexandria, Emperor Theodosius II ordered the Council of Ephesus to be convened in 431. The council, under the presidency of Cyril, was inaugurated 22 June, before the arrival of the Syrian bishops under the leadership of John of Antioch, the main sympathizer with Nestorius. By the time the Syrian delegation reached Ephesus, the council had already approved the doctrine of the Virgin as THEOTOKOS, condemned Nestorianism (which opposed the doctrine), and deposed Nestorius. Consequently, John of Antioch, together with his Syrian bishops and a number of other dissenting bishops, convened a rival council that confirmed Nestorius and his teaching and excommunicated Cyril. But their decisions were never sanctioned by the imperial authority, and the problem between John and Cyril remained unsolved until 433, when a compromise was reached whereby Nestorianism was finally rejected and the *Theotokos* accepted. John died in 441.

BIBLIOGRAPHY

Chadwick, H. *The Early Church,* pp. 194–200. Harmondsworth, 1967.

D'Alès, A. *Le Dogme d'Ephèse.* Paris, 1931.

Fliche, A., and V. Martin, eds. *Histoire de l'église,* Vol. 4, pp. 163–96. Paris, 1939.

Frend, W. H. C. *The Monophysite Movement,* pp. 1–49. Cambridge, 1972.

Hefele, C. J., and H. Leclercq. *Histoire des conciles,* Vol. 2, pt. 1, pp. 287–377. Paris, 1908.

Kraatz, W., ed. *Coptic Acts of Council of Ephesus.* Texte und Untersuchungen 26, no. 2. Leipzig, 1904.

AZIZ S. ATIYA

JOHN THE BAPTIST, FEAST OF COMMEMORATION OF SAINT.

See Festal Days, Monthly.

JOHN THE BAPTIST, SAINT,

in the New Testament the forerunner of the Messiah (feast day: 30 Ba'ūnah). He is called *Ioannes ho Baptistes* because in Matthew 3:6–11 he prepares for the coming of Christ by administering the baptism of conversion and penance. His origin and mission are described in Luke 1:5–80 as parallel to those of Jesus Christ.

Life

John is the son of Zechariah, of priestly family, and Elizabeth, and his birth is considered miraculous because of the old age of his parents. Tradition situates the event in ʿAyn Kārim, a small village some 4 miles (about 7 km) west of Jerusalem. Luke 1:80 states that the child dwelt in the desert until the day of his manifestation to Israel, which might suggest that he had some relation to the Essene movement based in Qumran, although John the Baptist differs from the Qumran community in that his message was open to all. He appears preaching and baptizing on the banks of the Jordan in the fifteenth year of the reign of Tiberius Caesar (A.D. 28–29). When Jesus goes from Nazareth to receive John's baptism, John recognizes him and proclaims him the Messiah (Mt. 3:1–12). In his preaching John censures the behavior of Herod Antipas, which leads to his own imprisonment, and beheading at the request of Herodias, niece of Herod, who receives his head on a platter. John's body is recovered by his disciples and buried (Mt. 14:3–12).

The Gospels show John the Baptist as Elijah restored to life (Mt. 11:14, 17:10–13; Mk. 9:13), applying to him the passage of Malachi 2:23. Although he is inferior to Jesus and at the service of the latter's mission (Mt. 3:11–12; Jn. 1:8, 30–31), he is greatly praised by Jesus as the greatest of those born of woman (Mt. 11:9–11; Jn. 5:35). John's preaching to the whole of Israel is an invitation to repentance and the radical conversion of men in preparation for the coming of the Kingdom and the Messiah (Lk. 3:7–9, 16–17). A group of disciples gathers around him, some of whom will later follow Jesus (Jn. 1:35–51), whereas others seem to continue John's movement parallel to that of Christ (Acts 18:24; 19:1ff.).

John is also praised by Flavius Josephus, who adds that he died in Maqueronte (Josephus *Antiquities* 18. 5. 2). The apocryphal gospels add new data to his life. Some state that his conception took place 9 October and his birth 5 June. The *Protogospel of James* of the second or third century, based on Matthew 23:35, confuses Zechariah the father of John the Baptist with Zechariah the prophet, son of Berechiah, a confusion that continues in a large part of later literature. This same apocryphal gospel relates the legendary flight of Elizabeth with the child from the persecution of Herod, and the miracle whereby the rock opens up and hides mother and child from their pursuers. The Qur'ān mentions him (19 and 21), and so John the Baptist and his parents became popular figures in Islamic literature.

Cult

The cult of John the Baptist was widely extended throughout the church at the end of the fourth century, almost certainly through the influence of the monks, who saw in him a perfect model of asceticism, and also because of the continual discoveries of relics of the saint. Numerous churches were dedicated to John the Baptist in Palestine during the Byzantine period, located in 'Ayn Kārim and especially in Sebaste (in Samaria), the place to which the disciples, according to tradition, removed his body. Churches were soon erected in the West also. It is sufficient to mention Saint John Lateran in Rome and the church in Ravenna consecrated by Saint Peter Chrysologus. From the fourth century at least, the Greeks celebrated 7 January as the feast of the day after the baptism of Jesus. This date was changed by the Nestorians and Armenians. The West, at least from the time of Augustine, celebrated the birth of John the Baptist on 24 June, corresponding to the celebration of the birth of Jesus on 25 December, whereas the beheading was commemorated on 29 August, perhaps corresponding to the date of the dedication of a church in his honor in Sebaste or the translation of relics.

There are abundant traditions of relics of John the Baptist and places where they are preserved. Saint JEROME, Rufinus of Aquileia, and Theodoretus coincide in stating that the body of John the Baptist was buried and venerated in Sebaste. According to Theodoretus, the tomb was profaned in the time of JULIAN THE APOSTATE, in the fourth century, the body burned and the ashes scattered to the winds. Rufinus, however, states that some monks were able to save the bones and send them to Patriarch ATHANASIUS I of Alexandria. Some scholars, such as Sozomen in the fifth century, claim that the head of John the Baptist, having been removed from Alexandria, was sent to Constantinople by order of the Emperor Valens in the fourth century. Others, such as Dionysius Exiguus in the sixth century (PL 67 pp. 420–32) state that it was taken from the Holy Land to Emessa by two monks.

Place in the Coptic Church

In the Coptic church John the Baptist is the most venerated biblical character after Jesus and the Virgin Mary. His cult was highly popular in Egypt and many churches were dedicated to him. There are eight feasts related to him in the calendar of the Coptic church: (1) 2 Tūt commemorates the death of Zechariah and recalls the childhood of John the Baptist; (2) 26 Tūt commemorates the annunciation by the archangel Gabriel to Zechariah of the birth of John; (3) 18 Bābah commemorates the death of the patriarch THEOPHILUS OF ALEXANDRIA who built the shrine for the relics of John the Baptist; (4) 11 Tūbah marks the baptism of Jesus by John the Baptist in the Jordan; (5) 16 Amshīr marks the death of Elizabeth, recalling John's birth; (6) 30 Amshīr recalls the discovery of John the Baptist's head; (7) 2 Ba'ūnah recalls the discovery of his bones; and (8) 30 Ba'ūnah celebrates his birth.

On the translation and permanence of the relics of John the Baptist in Alexandria, Coptic historical tradition, contained in the *History of the Church of Alexandria* (Orlandi, 1968) and in the HISTORY OF THE PATRIARCHS, draws on a tradition along the lines of Rufinus of Aquileia and is briefly as follows. In the times of Julian the Apostate, the relics of John the Baptist were in danger of being destroyed by fire in Sebaste (or Jerusalem) when the emperor ordered the Christian tombs, discovered during the reconstruction of the Temple, to be burnt. Some Christians were able to save them and send them to Athanasius, who placed them in the baptistery of Alexandria. Athanasius declared his intention of building a martyrium to John the Baptist in the place occupied by the garden of his parents. Theophilus heard of this, and when he succeeded Athanasius as archbishop of Alexandria, he built the martyrium over the ruins of the Sarapion, which had been destroyed by the monks. The relics were then removed to the martyrium.

Place in Coptic Literature

Coptic literature is full of references to John the Baptist in encomia, doxologies, and magic texts. Among the encomia there is a Sahidic fragment attributed to Theophilus of Alexandria, probably genuine, *De aedificatione Martyrii Ioannis Baptistae* (Orlandi, 1969, pp. 23–26). This fragment contains an account of the translation of the bones of John the Baptist and of the prophet Eliseus to Alexandria and the intent of Athanasius to build the martyrium, a project he was unable to complete. The text probably continues with the building of the church by Theophilus, as narrated in the fragments of a Sahidic encomium (van Lantschoot, 1931, pp. 235–54). Also preserved is an untitled homily in Sahidic that might have belonged to CYRIL I, patriarch of Alexandria (Rossi, 1887, fasc. 3, pp. 53–65; for the attribution to Cyril, see Orlandi, 1971, p. 181). The fragments of this homily narrate the martyrdom of John the Baptist and largely coincide with another encomium attributed to THEODOSIUS I, patriarch of Alexandria, in Sahidic and preserved in several manuscripts (Kuhn, 1966, Vols. 33 [text] and 34 [translation]). This encomium is divided into three parts: the birth of John the Baptist, the baptism of Jesus, and John's martyrdom. John is said to have his throne in the seventh heaven by the side of the Holy Trinity.

A homily preserved in Bohairic, by an unknown author, is dependent on these Sahidic works and narrates the martyrdom (De Vis, 1922, pp. 1–52). An encomium attributed to PROCLUS OF CONSTANTINOPLE has also been preserved in Sahidic Coptic (Rossi, 1887, pp. 65–82). It is independent of the works mentioned and is concerned in particular with the burial of John the Baptist's head. A further encomium in Sahidic is attributed to Saint JOHN CHRYSOSTOM (Budge, 1913, pp. 128–145 [text]; pp. 335–51 [translation]; see also the improved translation in German by W. Till, 1958, pp. 322–32). This work is of great interest because of the apocalyptic traits it contains. As his field of action, John the Baptist is assigned to the third heaven, to which he carries the souls dedicated to him in a golden ship, freeing them from rivers of fire. The discovery of relics of John the Baptist is also narrated in other Coptic works, for example, in "*Gesta Gessi et Isidori*" (Steindorff, 1883, pp. 137–58). There are besides many other fragments, probably from homilies on the birth of Christ or liturgical texts, that mention John the Baptist and his glory in heaven (Till, 1958, pp. 311–21; Orlandi, 1971, p. 181).

Coptic literature concerning John the Baptist contains the marvelous accounts proper to apocryphal literature and attributes to the saint new miracles, such as his appearance to a wealthy young woman, who, when she is about to marry, consecrates herself to virginity (van Lantschoot, 1931, p. 239). But above all, his role as prophet and forerunner of the Messiah is stressed, together with his glorification in heaven. Thus in the *Panegyric on John the Baptist* by Theodosius of Alexandria (Kuhn, 1966) it is stated that in the visitation of Mary to Elizabeth, John, in an imaginary conversation with his mother, asks her to allow him to leave her womb in order to adore his Lord and the mother of his Lord. When he realizes that the moment of his birth has not yet arrived, he asks Elizabeth herself to adore Jesus and Mary (Kuhn, 1966). The voice crying in the wilderness (Mt. 3:3ff.) is interpreted as the voice of the archangel Gabriel, who sends John the Baptist to prepare the way of the Lord. When John, acknowledging his unworthiness, refuses to baptize Jesus, the latter tells him that he has already baptized John through his mother Mary's greeting when he was still in Elizabeth's womb. A curious feature is that John the Baptist is compared in dignity with Adam, insofar as the latter was not the son of man but created directly by God, and he is even called the second Adam. Finally, attention is drawn to the fact that a confession of trinitarian and Christological faith is seen in the letters that make up the name of John the Baptist.

BIBLIOGRAPHY

Bartina, S. "Juan el Bautista y su teologia en un Deletreo copto." *Boletin de la Asociación española de Orientalistas* 8 (1972):208–212.

Budge, E. A. W., ed. *Coptic Apocrypha in the Dialect of Upper Egypt*. London, 1913.

Kuhn, K. H., ed. "A Coptic Panegyric on John the Baptist Attributed to Theodosius Archbishop of Alexandria." *Le Muséon* 76 (1963):55–57.

______. "Three Further Fragments of a Panegyric on John the Baptist Attributed to Theodosius, Archbishop of Alexandria." *Le Muséon* 88 (1975):103–112.

______, ed. *A Panegyric on John the Baptist Attributed to Theodosius, Archbishop of Alexandria. CSCO* 268, 269, *Scriptores Coptici* 33, 34. Louvain, 1966.

Lantschoot, A. van. "Fragments coptes d'un panégyrique de St. Jean-Baptiste." *Le Muséon* 44 (1931):235–54.

Orlandi, Tito, ed. and trans. *Storia della Chiesa di Alessandria.* In *History of the Church of Alexandria,* Vol. 1, lines 307–327. Milan, 1968.
______. "De aedificatione Martyrii Ioannis Baptistae." *Revista degli Studi Orientali* 44 (1969).
______. "Un frammento copto di Teofilo di Allessandria." *Revista degli Studi Orientali* 44 (1969):23–26.
______. "Teodosio di Allessandria nella letteratura copta." *Giornale Italiano di Filologia* 23 (1971): 181–82.
______. "Les papyrus coptes du Musée égyptien de Turin." *Le Muséon* 87 (1974):121.
Rossi, F., ed. *I Papyri copti del Museo Egizio di Torino, trascritti e tradotti,* Vol. 1, fasc. 3, pp. 53–82. Turin, 1887.
Steindorff, G., ed. *"Gesta Gessi et Isidori." Zeitschrift für ägyptische Sprache und Altertumskunde* 211 (1883).
Stramare, T., and A. Cardinali. "Giovanni Battista." *Bibliotheca Sanctorum,* vol. 6, pp. 599–624. Rome, 1965.
Till, W. "Johannes der Täufer in der koptischen Literatur." *Mitteilungen des deutschen Archeologischen Instituts Kairo* 16 (1958):310–32.
Vis, H. de. *Homélies coptes de la Vaticane,* Vol. 1. Copenhagen, 1922.

GONZALO ARANDA PEREZ

JOHN CALYBITES, monk in Early Christian Rome noted for his great asceticism (feast day: 4 Amshīr). The story of his life is known in Greek (Bibliotheca Hagiographa Graeca 868–69) and has come down in Sahidic in only one codex (British Library, Or. 6783,6).

The text belongs to the category of individual stories, that is, those not linked to a CYCLE. Such stories could have Greek origins, as seems to be the case here, or they could be Coptic in origin.

The author of the codex presents himself as a contemporary of John, who he says was the son of a magistrate of Rome, educated by Christian parents. A monk of the *akoimetai* ("sleepless ones") persuades him to become a monk. He then has his parents buy a Gospel decorated in gold (hence his Coptic name, translated "John of the Golden Gospel") and leaves home secretly, to their despair. After he has become a monk among the *akoimetai,* the devil leads him into apathy, so that he returns to find his parents. On the way home he gives his clothes to a poor man; for this reason his parents do not recognize him, and he spends a year as a beggar at the entrance to their house. They give him food without knowing him and even make him a small hut (*calybe*—hence his name in Greek) close to the door of the house. After ten years of very hard ascetical practice, he has a vision announcing his death. He reveals himself to his parents by mentioning the golden Gospel and then dies.

BIBLIOGRAPHY

Budge, E. A. W. *Coptic Martyrdoms . . . in the Dialect of Upper Egypt.* London, 1914.
Muyser, J. "Saints étrangers honorés dans l'Eglise copte. L'Eglise de S. Jean le possesseur de l'Evangile doré à Naqadah." *Collectanea Christiana* 7–8 (1954):11–18.

TITO ORLANDI

JOHN CHRYSOSTOM, SAINT (c. 347–407), patriarch of Constantinople and doctor of the church (feast day: 13 November in the East, 13 September in the West). John Chrysostom was born in Antioch, where he studied law and theology. For some years he devoted himself to monastic life, part of the time as a hermit. He was a deacon under the bishop Flavian, who ordained him a priest in 386 and appointed him to preach. His name Chrysostom means "golden-mouthed." He was made patriarch of Constantinople in 398 against his will.

Chrysostom's stern moral stance and tactless efforts to reform the corrupt court and city led to conflict with the empress Eudoxia and with Saint THEOPHILUS, patriarch of Alexandria, who was jealous of him. Theophilus took the occasion of Chrysostom's having received the Tall Brothers, Origenist monks from Egypt, to have him condemned for Origenist views at the Synod of the Oak in Chalcedon in 403. The synod, through the intervention of the empress, had him deposed and exiled to the Caucasus, where he died in 407.

This article will concentrate on Chrysostom's important position in Coptic literature. It is surprising that despite his conflict with Theophilus, he was enthusiastically taken up by Coptic tradition, both as an author of homilies and as a saint. This process was achieved without compromising the position of Theophilus. In fact, the earliest Coptic sources and those that are most authoritative concerning Chrysostom omit his relations with Theophilus, attributing the cause of all his tribulations to Eudoxia. Thus a Coptic history of the church defines him as a "wise man of God, full of faith, wisdom and charity," and after a long account of his literary works it attributes his misfortunes solely to his dispute with the wicked Eudoxia. The text of the so-called *Memoirs of Dioskoros* (Johnson, 1980, pp. 88–90) speaks in similar terms.

In the Coptic translation of the *Vita Epiphanii episcopi Salaminae,* however, the relations between Theophilus and John Chrysostom are brought out. The homily, *De hora mortis,* attributed to Saint CYRIL THE GREAT, albeit spurious and late, is also aware of this episode, although it speaks of a post mortem reconciliation of the two bishops. The feeble echo of the vicissitudes of the life of John Chrysostom and his death in exile gave rise at a later date in the seventh century in the period of the CYCLES to a series of fictional texts attributed to him or concerning him, which will be examined separately below.

A list of the authentic works by Chrysostom that have survived in Coptic translation follows.

From his monastic period there are Epistle 2 *ad Theodorum,* and the Epistle *ad Stelechium* (fragment, Vienna, *Papyrussammlung,* ed. Orlandi 1974).

Of his homilies, those in Sahidic are especially important. These are *Excerpta* from the homilies on the Epistle to the Hebrews (fragments from DAYR ANBĀ SHINŪDAH); *In Ioseph, In Susannam* (Clavis Patrum Graecorum 4566–67; Museo Egizio, Turin, Cat. 63000, cod. 8, 15–25, ed. Rossi, 1887–1892, Vol. 2, pp. 20–37; British Library, Or. 5001, ed. Budge, 1910, pp. 46–57); *De Davide et Saul 3* (Clavis Patrum Graecorum 4412.3; Museo Egizio, Turin, Cat. 63000, cod. 8, 26–39, ed. Rossi, Vol. 2, pp. 38–47); *In Petrum et Heliam* (Clavis Patrum Graecorum 4513; fragment from Dayr Anbā Shinūdah, ed. Devos, 1975–1976); *De Chananaea* (Clavis Patrum Graecorum 4529; British Library, Or. 5001, ed. Budge); *De Nativitate* (Clavis Patrum Graecorum 4657; Pierpont Morgan Library, New York, C6, ed. Crum, 1915); *In Matt. 12:4 (exeuntes Pharisaei)* (Clavis Patrum Graecorum 4640; Museo Egizio, Turin, Cat. 63000, cod. 6, 74–91, ed. Rossi, Vol. 1, pp. 54–70); *De Pentecoste* (Clavis Patrum Graecorum 4536, unpublished fragment from Dayr Anbā Shinūdah).

Many others are found in Bohairic (especially in the Vatican Library, Coptic 57; but also in other codices of Saint Macarius; cf. Hebbelynck and Van Lantschoot, 1937, 1947), but these are probably a translation deriving from the Sahidic, and even if some are translated directly from the Greek, it would not seem possible that they could go back to the fifth and sixth centuries, as is the case for the Sahidic.

Other homilies, however, are not only certainly spurious but were also most probably composed directly in Coptic no earlier than the mid-sixth century. Leaving aside for now the Cycle of Chrysostom (see below), seven works are listed.

De Resurrectione (Pierpont Morgan Library, New York, M595; unpublished) speaks of the normal episodes referring to the Resurrection, dwelling principally on two points of interest: the calculation of the chronology of Jesus' stay in the tomb and the moment of the Resurrection, and an "autobiographical" episode concerning a certain Eutychus, who died when Chrysostom had been a bishop for two years.

After the first part of *In Iohannem Baptistam* (British Library, Or. 7024, ed. Budge, 1913, pp. 128–45; fragment from Dayr Anbā Shinūdah), which has the normal character of an Encomium, a report is given of what the author is said to have found in a precious book from the Apostles' library in Jerusalem concerning the honors accorded to John the Baptist in heaven.

After a normal prologue for *In Raphaelem Archangelum* (British Library, Or. 7022, 6806A, ed. Budge, 1915, pp. 526–33; fragment from Dayr Anbā Shinūdah), an "autobiographical" episode is introduced in which Arcadius has the oratory of Raphael built. This is followed by the account of the miracles that occurred in the oratory.

In Quattuor Animalia (Pierpont Morgan Library, New York M612; Berlin, *Papyrussammlung* Pl1965; fragment from Qaṣr Ibrīm) is one of the texts concerning the enthronement of angelic creatures (cf. similar texts concerning MICHAEL, RAPHAEL, etc.). Pseudo-John is said to have found this text in a book of the library of the Anastasis of Jerusalem (dialogue between Jesus and the disciples prior to the Resurrection).

In Luke 7:37 "De Peccatrice" (Pierpont Morgan Library, New York, M; ed. Yassa, 1958–1960) is a simple exegesis of the passage relating the sinful woman's anointing the feet of Jesus.

In Michaelem et Latronem (Bohairic manuscript in the Vatican Library, Coptic 58, ed. Simon, 1934, pp. 217–42 and 1935, pp. 222–34) is a list of the feasts dedicated to Michael in the course of the liturgical year, and related miracles and apparitions.

In Heliam Prophetam (Bohairic manuscript in the British Library, ed. Budge, 1893, pp. 355–404) is a simple compilation of biblical passages referring to Elijah.

Finally, the Cycle dedicated to John Chrysostom, which belongs to a special type of production of

Coptic texts (cf. CYCLES), to be dated about the seventh century, is a series of texts derived from Chrysostom's life and divisible into two parts: (1) his activity in Antioch and Constantinople in the period in which he was elected bishop; and (2) his tribulations related to the conflict with Eudoxia (Theophilus is not mentioned) and his exile.

Concerning the first part the creation of a fictitious figure is of particular interest. This is DEMETRIUS OF ANTIOCH, who is said to have ordained John Chrysostom a priest. It is impossible today to see what purpose was served by substituting the historically true Flavian by this Demetrius. In any case, some homilies were even attributed to him, and at least one was attributed to Chrysostom himself: *In Victorem* (manuscript of Dayr Anbā Shinūdah, ed. Bouriant, 1893), in which he himself recounts his ordination and translation to Constantinople.

Concerning the second part, we find principally a kind of biography of Chrysostom (fragment from Dayr Anbā Shinūdah), in which, after undergoing various sufferings in Thrace, he converts the local population to Christianity. In this work, mention is already made of a certain Anthimos, who, according to the homily *In Michaelem* attributed to EUSTATHIUS OF THRACE, became bishop of Thrace; Eustathius was his successor in that see. The same area is dealt with in a homily attributed to PROCLUS OF CONSTANTINOPLE, *In XXIV Seniores*.

BIBLIOGRAPHY

Bouriant, U. "L'éloge de l'apa Victor fils de Romanos." *Mémoires publiés par les membres de la mission archéologique française au Caire* 8 (1893):145–268.

Budge, E. A. W. "On the Fragments of a Coptic Version of an Encomium on Elijah the Tishbite, Attributed to Saint John Chrysostom." *Transactions of the Society of Biblical Archaeology* 9 (1893):355–404.

______. *Coptic Homilies.* London, 1910.

______. *Coptic Apocrypha.* London, 1913.

______. *Miscellaneous Coptic Texts.* London, 1915.

Campagnano, A.; A. Maresca; and T. Orlandi. *Quattro omelie copte: Vita di Giovanni Crisostomo, Encomi dei 24 Vegliardi, Encomio di Michele Arcangelo di Eustazio di Tracia.* Testi e documenti per lo studio dell'antichita, serie copta 60. Milan, 1977.

Crum, W. E., ed. and tr. *Der Papyruscodex Saec. VI–VII der Phillippsbibliothek in Cheltenham. Koptische Theologische Schriften.* Schriften der wissenschaftlichen Gesellschaft in Strassburg 18. Strasbourg, 1915.

Devos, P. "Deux feuillets coptes sur Pierre et Elie." *Oriental Library Publications* 6, 7 (1975–1976):185–204.

Hebbelynck, A., and A. van Lantschoot. *Codices coptici vaticani barberiniani borgiani rossiani.* Rome, 1937, 1947.

Orlandi, T. *Papiri copti di contenuto teologico.* Mitteilungen aus der Papyrussammlung der Österreichischen Nationalbibliothek 9. Vienna, 1974.

Rossi, F. *I papiri copti del Museo Egizio di Torino,* 2 vols. Turin, 1887–1892.

Simon, J. "Homélie copte inédite sur S. Michel et le Bon Larron, attribuée à S. Jean Chrysostome." *Orientalia* 3 (1934):217–242; 4 (1935):222–234.

Yassa, 'Abd al-Masīḥ. "A Discourse by St. John Chrysostom on the Sinful Woman in the Sa'idic Dialect." *Bulletin de la Société d'Archéologie Copte* 15 (1958–1960):11–39.

TITO ORLANDI

JOHN CHRYSOSTOM, SAINT, CANONS OF.

See Canons of Saint John Chrysostom.

JOHN COLOBOS, SAINT.

[*This entry consists of two parts:* Coptic Tradition *and* Arabic Tradition.]

Coptic Tradition

John Colobos, the Little or the Dwarf (fourth and fifth centuries), is one of the most striking figures among the desert fathers. He is known principally from the APOPHTHEGMATA PATRUM and from a Life in the form of a panegyric composed in Coptic by Zacharias, the bishop of Sakhā in Lower Egypt, at the end of the seventh century. This Life adds certain extra information to the data in the apothegms, the value of which it is difficult to assess with any precision. Some of the apothegms also should be handled with caution. In the fourth century there were many monks in Egypt bearing the name John, and it is not easy to be sure of the establishment of the role each played. The episode regarding the piece of wood that was watered for three years as an act of obedience should, according to Saint John CASSIAN, be attributed to JOHN OF LYCOPOLIS. On the other hand, we should certainly keep the identification of John Colobos with the John described as "the Little," who was a disciple of Ammoes (PG 65, cols. 125–28) mentioned by EVAGRIUS in his treatise *On Prayer* (PG 79, col. 1192).

According to Zacharias (*Annales du Musée Guimet,* p. 324), this John, also called the "Theban," was a native of the village of Tesi in the region of Oxyrhynchus (known today as al-Bahnasā). From his youth he sought to serve God continually, without any preoccupation, like the angels. He must have come to SCETIS in the middle of the fourth century. He found the abbot Ammoes a rough and austere master who did not stint when it came to humiliating and rebuffing him. When Ammoes became incapacitated, John cared devotedly for him for twelve years, without ever receiving the least thanks. It was only just before he died that Ammoes praised his disciple, saying to the old men who were present, "He is an angel, not a man" (PG 65, col. 240B).

When in his turn John had become one of the "elders," he led a solitary life "in a pit," that is, in one of those narrow, deep natural caves in the environs of the Wādī al-Naṭrūn, doubtless at the site where later the monastery bearing his name was to be erected. His holiness, his humility, and his discernment ensured that his influence would be an extraordinary one: "Who is John that by his humility he had all Scetis hanging on his little finger?" And yet we do not know the names of any of his disciples. We know only, through Theodore the Studite, that ARSENIUS, on arrival at Scetis, was subjected by John to a humiliating test (PG 99, col. 852). Moreover, from the way in which POEMEN speaks of him, it may be conjectured that he himself had profited from John's teaching (PG 65, col. 340, no. 74). In the apothegms there is no indication that John was a HEGUMENOS and a priest as Zacharias claims. However, he was a spiritual father renowned and appreciated, always available to welcome the brethren who came to consult him. He was also able to be severe on occasion, to ensure that the claims of God and the requirements of silence were respected during meals and work alike. At such times he could even let his spirited temperament run away with him to the point of finding it difficult to master his temper. Sometimes his thoughts were so fixed on God that he could not turn away from meditating to deal with the things of this world.

His concern to "win" souls was such that he had no hesitation in going to a prostitute to convert her, and succeeded so well that he saw his convert ascend to heaven by the very next night. Recorded in an apothegm, the story may have shocked some monks of former days, but it filled Saint Theresa of Lisieux with enthusiasm (*cf.* Regnault, 1983).

John Colobos had to leave Scetis for good when raiders made an incursion into the region, doubtless in 407 (Evelyn-White, 1932, pt. 2, p. 158). He withdrew to the Clysma area where he seems to have died on 17 October 409 and his remains were brought back to Scetis on 22 August 804 (Evelyn-White, Vol. 2, p. 294). The monastery of Saint John, the ruins of which are now almost entirely covered with sand, is located roughly 2 miles (3 km) to the southeast of that of DAYR ANBĀ BISHOI. In Upper Egypt, to the south of Minyā, in the village which still bears his name—DAYR ABŪ ḤINNIS—near the ancient Antinoopolis, there existed another monastery dedicated to John, going back possibly to the sixth century. This could be where John Colobos led a hermit's life before going to Scetis. This monastery at least proves that the cult of John spread rapidly as far as the Thebaid. The saint is mentioned in the Coptic Synaxarion under 17 October and sometimes also under 22 or 23 August.

We may regard the apothegms on John Colobos as a particularly noteworthy synthesis of desert spirituality. There is nothing hard and fast or systematic, nor is there any abstract development, but rather a series of live pictures interspersed with maxims of great lucidity, the outcome of rich experience. According to Poemen, John cultivated every virtue and encouraged his disciples to do likewise, giving them a whole list which perhaps did not pass his lips as it stands all at once, but must nevertheless be a good reflection of his teaching, since we find most of its elements scattered among the other apothegms. All the essentials are there, from ascetic toil practiced with "endurance" to the heights of humility and the fear of God. Its basis was "the love of God" and "winning one's neighbour" "with every fervour of soul and body." To this end a constant struggle is necessary against the fleshly passions, by means of dieting restrictions; and against bad thoughts, by means of watchfulness, *hesychia* (quietness), and the opening up of the soul (Poemen 101). Every monastic observance has its place in this list: prayer and manual work, nocturnal watches, hunger and thirst, cold and nakedness, troublesome impositions, and so forth, but the accent is laid on the spiritual side with the words "soul," "heart," and "spirit" cropping up several times. Keeping what matters most is "spiritual *hesychia.*" Spiritual combat is necessary because it is the condition for progress, but still more necessary is the action of the Spirit to produce a variety of foliage and fruits in each person.

In John Colobos, mystical allusions are always unobtrusive. Whereas Zacharias' account abounds in visions, the apothegms record only three and do so very soberly. John certainly was a great contemplative, but doubtless it was not he who spoke of "contemplation." In his youth he had dreamed of angelic carefreeness and later he had already enjoyed here on earth the company of the angels. He had asked God to free him from his passions and had obtained his request, but he had learned that perfection consists rather in endurance and humility.

BIBLIOGRAPHY

Acta sanctorum octobris, Vol. 8, pp. 39–59. Brussels, 1853.

Arras, V. *Collectio monastica.* CSCO 238–239.

Budge, E. A. W., trans. *The Paradise or Garden of the Holy Fathers,* 2 vols. London, 1907.

Clédat, J. "Notes archéologiques et philologiques." *Bulletin de l'Institut français d'Archéologie orientale* 2 (1902):41–70.

Cotelier, J. B., ed. *Apophthegmata Patrum.* PG 65, 204–220. Paris, 1864. Supplementary items were published by J. C. Guy, *Recherches sur la tradition grecque des Apophthegmata Patrum,* pp. 23–24. Brussels, 1962.

Delehaye, H., ed. *Synaxarium Constantinopolitanum,* col. 208, 57. Propylaeum ad Acta SS. Novembris. Brussels, 1902.

Draguet, R. "A la source de deux apophtegmes grecs (Migne: *Patrologia Graeca* 65, Jean Colobos 24 et 32)." *Byzantion* 32 (1962):53–61.

______. *Les formes syriaques de la matière de l'histoire Lausiaque.* CSCO 399, p. 240. Louvain, 1978.

Evagrius. *On Prayer.* PG 79, col. 1192.

Evelyn-White, H. G. *The Monasteries of the Wadi'n Natrūn.* Part 2, *The History of the Monasteries of Nitria and of Scetis.* New York, 1932. Part 3, *The Architecture and Archeology,* ed. W. Hauser. New York, 1933.

Freire, J. G. *Commonitiones sanctorum Patrum,* pp. 313–15. Coimbra, 1974.

Grebaut, S., ed. *Synaxaire éthiopien.* PO 9, pp. 418–22.

Guy, J. C. "Jean Colobos ou Le Petit." In *Dictionnaire de Spiritualité,* Vol. 8, cols. 390–92. Paris, 1974.

Martin, M. *La Laure de Der-al-Dik à Antinoè,* pp. 3–5, 66–69. Bibliothèque d'Etudes Coptes 8. Cairo, 1971.

Meinardus, O. *Christian Egypt: Ancient and Modern.* Cairo, 1965.

Nau, F. "La version syriaque de l'histoire de Jean le Petit." *Revue de l'Orient Chrétien* 17 (1912): 347–89; 18 (1913): 53–68, 124–36, 283–307; 19 (1914): 3–57.

Regnault, L. "Le vrai visage d'abba Jean Colobos à travers ses apophtègmes." Cahiers d'Orientalisme 3, pp. 225–34. Geneva, 1983.

Sauget, J. M. *Bibliotheca sanctorum* 6, cols. 666–69. Rome, 1965.

Theodorus Studitae S. *Laudatio S. Arsenii,* PG 99, cols. 852–53.

Zacharie. "Vie de Jean Colobos." In *Annales du Musée Guimet* 25, ed. E. Amélineau, pp. 316–410. Paris, 1894.

LUCIEN REGNAULT

Arabic Tradition

The Arabic version of the Life of John Colobus by Zacharias of Sakhā (Göttingen codex Arabic 114, sixteenth century, fols. 110r–150r) has not been published. There is a much older translation into Syriac, made in 936 and preserved in a series of Syriac manuscripts in the British Museum. The edition and translation were provided by F. Nau in *Revue de l'Orient chrétien* from 1912 to 1914. Some interesting facts emerge from this long text. First, the name of John Colobos is not mentioned, except in the title. In the passage about the visit to Theophilus, the text conforms with the panegyric which is attributed to him in Sahidic. There are, therefore, grounds for asking if the Bohairic Coptic text has not inserted an independent story into the panegyric of Zacharias of Sakhā of which only the Sahidic fragments remain.

Doubtless also through Arabic channels comes the Ethiopic reference for 29 Nahasé (5 September) which tells of the difficulties in moving the remains of John Colobos from Clysma, then in Chalcedonian hands, to the convent of Saint Macarius (DAYR ANBĀ MAQĀR) of Scetis in the year A.M. 520/A.D. 805.

This transference was without doubt mentioned in his Life, hitherto better known. It is rather strange that in the Ethiopic SYNAXARION (PO 9, pp. 418–22), the commemoration of this event took place on the same day as the Nativity of our Lord as well as the martyrdom of Saint Athanasius of Clysma whose Chalcedonian legend places this celebration on exactly the same date. His tomb was identified among those of the desert fathers including John Colobos. However, the Arabic Synaxarion merely states under 20 Bābah that the remains of Saint John Colobos were transferred to Minyā.

BIBLIOGRAPHY

Amélineau, E. *Histoire des monastères de la Basse-Egypte.* Paris, 1894.

Baumstark, A. *Geschichte der syrischen Literatur,* p. 283, n. 8. Bonn, 1922.

Crum, W. E. *Der Papyruscodex saec. VI–VII der Philipps-bibliothek in Cheltenham.* Strasbourg, 1915.

Nau, F. "La version syriaque de l'Histoire de Jean le Petit." *Revue de l'Orient Chrétien* 17 (1912):347–89; 18 (1913):53–78, 124–33, 282–307; 19 (1914):33–57.

Orlandi, T. *Storia della chiesa di Alessandria,* Vol. 2. Milan, 1970. pp. 102–104.

Till, W. "Ein sahidischer Bericht der Reise des Apa Johannes nach Babylon." *Zeitschrift für die neutestamentliche Wissenschaft* 37 (1938):230–39.

MICHEL VAN ESBROECK

JOHN OF EPHESUS, Monophysite writer of a history of the church in the Syriac language. He was born around 516 in Amida in northern Mesopotamia. He lived until at least 585, the last observable date in his history. In 542 the emperor JUSTINIAN appointed John a missionary to Asia, Caria, Phrygia, and Lydia, where in four years he converted some 70,000 persons to Christianity and caused ninety-eight churches and twelve monasteries to be built for them. In 558 he became bishop of Ephesus.

Only the third part of John's tripartite church history is extant. References in this extant portion indicate that the first two parts of the work covered the time from the reign of Julius Caesar to the sixth year of the reign of JUSTIN II (571). The third portion, divided into six books, deals with the period between 571 and 585. The work is an important source for the struggle between Chalcedonians and Monophysites in the sixth century. His *Lives of the Eastern Saints* is a prime authority for the lives of the Monophysite leaders and for Monophysite missions during the sixth century.

BIBLIOGRAPHY

Ball, C. J. "Joannes (160)." In DCB 3, pp. 370–73. Repr. New York, 1974.

Ashbrook, S. A. *Asceticism and Society in Crisis: John of Ephesus and the* Lives of the Eastern Saints. University of California Press, 1990. Includes bibliography.

RANDALL STEWART

JOHN, HEGUMENOS OF SCETIS (c. 585–675), born at Jepromenesin (Shubrā Mansinā) in the nome of Arwāṭ and a monk at the age of eighteen. It is not known when and why he came to Scetis (Wādī al-Naṭrūn). He was three times made prisoner by the Maziques in the course of their raids in the area. When the imperial officer came in the name of the governor of Egypt to demand the submission of the monks to the Tome of Leo in 631, John had gone off to the inner valley to hide the church's sacred vessels, and it was there that the barbarians made him prisoner for the third time (Evelyn-White, 1932, pp. 275–78).

Some years later he met ṢAMŪ'ĪL OF QALAMŪN, and it seems that John was only released at the time of the ARAB CONQUEST OF EGYPT (Van Cauwenbergh, 1914, pp. 87–88, 110–12).

He appears to have become hegumenos of Scetis about 641. He took part in the translation of FORTY-NINE MARTYRS OF SCETIS (de Ricci and Winstedt, 1910, p. 348). He assisted the patriarch BENJAMIN I in the restoration of the monastery of Scetis, although his name does not appear in the book of the consecration.

He is known as the master of several saints and important personages and shared with them his hermitage of Bajīj outside the enclosure of the monastery of Saint Macarius (DAYR ANBĀ MAQĀR).

BIBLIOGRAPHY

Cauwenbergh, P. van. *Etude sur les moines d'Egypte.* Paris and Louvain, 1914.

Evelyn-White, H. G. *The Monasteries of the Wadi 'n Naṭrūn.* Part 2, *The History of the Monasteries of Nitria and Scetis.* New York, 1932.

Ricci, S. de, and E. O. Winstedt. "Les quarante-neuf vieillards de Scété." *Notices et extraits de manuscrits de la Bibliothèque nationale et autres bibliothèques* 39, pp. 323–58. Paris, 1910.

RENÉ-GEORGES COQUIN

JOHN JEJUNATOR. *See* John IV the Faster, Saint.

JOHN KĀMĀ, SAINT (feast day: 25 Kiyahk). The ninth-century John Kāmā was born in the village of Jebromounonson in the nome of Sais, in the Delta. This village name has not survived, but it could be identical with Shubrā Wasīm in the *markaz* (district) of Kom Ḥamādah in the modern province of Beheirah. He is said to have been very pious in his youth and to have contracted an unsoiled marriage, having persuaded the spouse chosen for him not to consummate the matrimonial union.

Guided by an angel, he went to SCETIS, where he became the disciple of a certain Apa Teroti, a name not unknown in Coptic literature, who lived in a hermitage dependent on DAYR ABŪ MAQĀR. Teroti assigned him a habitation and taught him the rules concerning the divine office.

After a certain time spent under the jurisdiction of Teroti, he was moved by a vision and arrived at the monastery of JOHN COLOBOS (the Small). An angel ordered him at the same time to found a new monastery, to which his name would remain attached.

The Virgin Mary is said to have later appeared to him, promising him that a church would be built in her name and that the walls of the new monastery would never be destroyed. In token of these promises, the Virgin is said to have delivered to him three coins on each of which was inscribed a cross (the Muslims then dominated Egypt), pieces that were still preserved in the diaconia of the monastery at the time when the life was composed.

The virtues of John Kāmā attracted numerous disciples. The life speaks of three hundred. For them, the saint wrote canons and rules. A place of reunion, probably a church, was built to shelter the synaxis of the nocturnal psalmody, which appears to have been publicly celebrated at this period. The Life mentions the names of his principal disciples: Shenute, Mark, Colluthus, the deacon George, Antony, and another George. After the establishment of the new monastery, John Kāmā was ordained priest.

He seems to have had a particular devotion to Saint Athanasius, who is said to have appeared to him in a vision. He is supposed to have introduced the mention of his name in hymns.

At the injunction of an angel, he is said to have undertaken a journey to Upper Egypt, but this may have been to camouflage his flight before the barbarian invaders during the sack of 817. He is said to have ordered his disciple Shenute to hold his place at the head of the community during his absence.

Warned by an angel of his approaching end, he was smitten by a sudden fever, in the course of which he addressed a last sermon to his monks.

According to Evelyn-White (1932, p. 306, n. 4), the name Kāmā is sometimes written with an X, which would make it a proper name, and sometimes with a K as if it were an adjective, meaning "the Black" in Coptic and thus indicating that he was indeed black.

BIBLIOGRAPHY

Budge, E. A. T. W. *The Miracles of the Blessed Virgin Mary and the Life of Ḥanna.* London, 1900.

______. *One Hundred and Ten Miracles of Our Lady Mary.* London, Liverpool, and Boston, 1923.

Davis, H., ed. *The Life of Abba John Khamé.* PO 14, pp. 315–72. Paris, 1920.

Evelyn-White, H. G. *The History of the Monasteries of Nitria and Scetis,* pt. 2, *The Monasteries of the Wadi 'n Natrun.* New York, 1932.

RENÉ-GEORGES COQUIN

JOHN OF LYCOPOLIS, SAINT, so called from the name of the town of ASYŪṬ in Upper Egypt, on the West bank of the Nile, where he was probably born in the first or second decade of the fourth century, and not far from which he died at the end of 394 or beginning of 395. This was a little before or after the death of Emperor Theodosius I (d. 395), with whom his name was often associated. He was an ascetic and recluse of renown, whose fame as a prophet and also a healer spread well beyond the Thebaid, reaching its peak in his closing years. His role as a strict recluse in a cave that he himself adapted, did not prevent his communicating through a little window with visitors—all male—whom he received on Saturdays and Sundays. Information about him comes chiefly from the evidence of two famous visitors who came to see him a few months before he died.

The first, a spokesman for "seven foreign brethren" who had come from Jerusalem, is the anonymous author of the HISTORIA MONACHORUM IN AEGYPTO. John takes up the first and longest chapter (65 paragraphs) of this well-known Greek work, which at the beginning of the fifth century was translated into Latin with some personal additions by Rufinus of Aquileia. It was, however, censured by Jerome in his Epistle 133 ad Ctesiphontem, for the placing of John—*quem et catholicum et sanctum fuisse non dubium est*—at the beginning of the collection, to gain easier acceptance for the "heretics" who followed.

The second author, who journeyed eighteen days from the Kellia, was the Galatian PALLADIUS, a future bishop of Helenopolis, as foretold by John. Twenty-five years later Palladius recorded in chapter 35 of the *Historia lausiaca* an interview he had with John, assisted by a local interpreter named Theodorus. Chapter 35 became one of the largest texts in that work.

Rather than contrasting their accounts, it is better to establish any links there may have been between them, while respecting their specific characters.

In the *Historia Monachorum in Aegypto* John is aged ninety, forty years of which he has spent as a recluse. There is nothing on his earlier life, as priority is given to his spiritual conversation with the Seven for three days in succession. The very day they left him, John announced to them that "the letter relating to Theodosius' victory over the tyrant Eugenius" had just arrived. This was at the time of the important battle of the River Frigidus on 5–6 September 394.

In the *Historia lausiaca,* John is seventy-eight years old, forty-eight years of which have been spent as a recluse and eighteen with the "gift of prophecy." In his youth he had learned the trade of a carpenter while his brother was a dyer. From ages twenty-five to thirty he was trained in "various monasteries."

He read men's hearts, knew hidden things, present and to come, predicted natural events such as Nile floods and harvests, as well as personal occurrences. The two predictions most often recalled are the intimations of victory he arranged to have passed on to Theodosius when that emperor had consulted him on the matter of the usurpers Maximus (388) and Eugenius respectively.

Maximus and Eugenius are mentioned in the Latin supplement added to Eusebius' *Historia ecclesiastica* by Rufinus of Aquileia, for whom the gift granted to John is merited through the piety of Theodosius.

John CASSIAN recorded (*Institutiones coenobiticae* 4. 23 and *Collationes* 24. 26) that the "abbot" John owed to his virtue of obedience both his "prophetic charisma" and the trust he enjoyed "even among the kings of this world," despite the "extreme obscurity" of his origins. Cassian, according to the confidences recorded in *Historia Monachorum in Aegypto* (1. 21), recalls that John was not immune from the nocturnal wiles of the devil but makes him furthermore a paragon of obedience when he was a novice. He attributes to him, among other exploits, the watering of a dried-up stick for a whole year in a spirit of submission to the Lord (*Institutiones coenobiticae* 4. 24–26).

Through Rufinus, Augustine learns of the double "prophetic reply" to Theodosius (*De Civitate Dei* 5. 26) and is emphatic about the gift of discerning spirits, which he attributes to John. Augustine regrets being unable to ask this man about certain problems, since he had shown himself "in a dream" to the wife of a *tribunus* (*De cura gerenda pro mortuis* 17, 21).

Eucherius of Lyons is scarcely more explicit (*De laude heremi* 27), while in his *Chronicon,* Prosper of Aquitaine records the prediction of the victory on the Frigidus on the exact date.

Among the Greeks, the *Historia Ecclesiastica* of Sozomen (6. 28, 1; 7. 22, 6–8) gives more information than that of Theodoret (5. 24, 1–2), and of John's role at the time of the above-mentioned victory known both to George the Monk (*Chronicon, Tenbrev,* p. 589) and to George Cedrenus (*Historiarum Compendium* 1, *Corpus scriptorium historiae Byzantinae,* p. 568).

John exercised the gift of healing by the use of holy oil. Perhaps the secret of his gifts resides in John's remark to the Seven (*Historia Monachorum in Aegypto* 1. 28): "He who has been judged worthy of some partial knowledge of God . . . also attains knowledge of all the rest; he sees the divine mysteries for God himself shows them to him; he foresees things to come, he has revelatory visions like those of the saints, he accomplishes miracles, he becomes the friend of God and obtains from God whatever he asks him for."

Among John's visitors, apart from the two already named, were the following: (1) those of unknown name: a *stratēlatēs,* a *tribunus* (and his wife, see above), a *praipositos* and a *sugklētikos,* each with his wife (*Historia Monachorum in Aegypto* 1. 2, 4–9, 10, 12); (2) the *hēgemōn* of the region of Lycopolis, known by name only—Alupios (*Historia Lausiaca* 35. 5–6); (3) others known from elsewhere: (a) Eutropios, the "praepositus sacri cubiculi," the messenger of Theodosius to John before the battle of the Frigidus, a detail owed to Sozomen (*Historia Ecclesiastica* 7. 22, 7), which permits the understanding of two passages of the poet Claudian (*In Eutropium* 1. 311–12; *aegyptia . . . somnia protratosque . . . tyrannos; Libri* II *praef.,* 39; (b) Evagrius of Ponticus and Ammonius "Parotes," who probably also both came from the Kellia two months after Palladius. There is attestation to their conversation with John in at least four passages of the *Antirrhetikos* of Evagrius (2. 36; 5. 6; 6. 16; 7. 19); (c) the abbot Bessarion and his disciple Doulas (*Apophthegmata* 159, Bessarion 4); (d) Poemenia, a "servant of God" and relative of Theodosius, known both from the last paragraph of the Palladius reference and from the life (preserved in Syriac) of Peter the Iberian, in which it is said that she had the Church of the Ascension built on the Mount of Olives at Jerusalem.

With Poemenia it is possible to move from the Greco-Latin tradition about John to Coptic tradition, which, in fact, tells about the woman visitor to

Lycopolis, who had the benefit of a cure and a prophecy from John, then left for Jerusalem.

There did exist at least four Sahidic codices from the White Monastery (DAYR ANBĀ SHINŪDAH) with abundant material on John. Unfortunately, only thirty or so damaged leaves survive out of the several hundreds they contained. However, there are enough for us to be able to make out two types of hagiographic literature: a life or series of lives, beginning with a reproduction and translation of the references in *Historia Monachorum in Aegypto* and *Historia Lausiaca,* on to John's role at the time of the COUNCIL OF CHALCEDON in 451 (codices A, B, D); an Encomium that begins with a proemium and also ending with the Council of Chalcedon (codex C). This Encomium can probably be found again in part in the references in the Coptic Synaxarion in its Coptic version for 21 Hātūr and in its Ethiopic version for 21 Ḥedār (17 November). In both types there are various accounts of the same stories, unknown in the Greco-Latin sources. For example one is the episode, which may be historical, of John's intervention on behalf of his native town when it was under threat of extermination by Theodosius as a reprisal for murders occurring after a sporting contest between rival factions. Historically the best is doubtless intermingled with the worst. It is probable that the renown that cast an aura around the "prophet" John even before his death was exploited by overzealous disciples of the archimandrite SHENUTE to glorify their master, as well as by partisans of the deposed patriarch DIOSCORUS in order to discredit the Council of Chalcedon. Mockery has been made of chronology to the point of making John, who had been dead for more than half a century, into a contemporary of the emperor Marcianus (450–457) who is supposed to have consulted John to this end, as his distant predecessor had done on another matter. There is an echo of this consultation of the solitary of Asyūṭ, mentioned by name in the Syriac *History of Dioscorus, Bibliotheca Hagiographica Orientalis* 257, by the Pseudo-Theopistos. The Ethiopic SYNAXARION gives John's death age as 125. It could be said that the voluntary recluse was a victim of his own notoriety. From the standpoint of history, the loss of these Coptic documents is regrettable and deplorable.

The question of the writings claimed as John's need not detain us long. I. Hausherr, who has done more than anyone to reestablish the truth on the point of the writings claimed as John's, expressed himself thus: "How is it that none of the numerous documents about him breathes the slightest word about a literary activity?" also declaring that "The Seer of the Thebaid is a perfect orthodox saint and who had written nothing" (*Aux origines . . . ,* pp. 500, 508). And even less did he write in Greek than in any other language, since John needed an interpreter to converse with PALLADIUS. It was only wrongly and belatedly, and with never a mention of Lycopolis, that works attributed to his name are actually those of a namesake, John the Solitary, a Syriac author whose identity is at present the subject of considerable debate.

The essence of John's personality has been best defined by Hausherr. "No reputation as a *contemplative* ever excelled that of the 'seer' and 'prophet' of the Thebaid" (1938, p. 498). All his spirituality is contained in his instruction to the Seven with the striking portraits of the three monks facing Temptation in their three different ways (32–58). This entire instruction can be summed up as a pressing invitation to purity of intention.

No wonder, therefore, that the only two apothegms that concern him should be two extracts from this instruction: "The abbot John of the Thebaid said: 'A monk must above all have humility. . . .'" (*cf. Historia Monachorum in Aegypto* 1. 59); and "The abbot John, the one of the cave, said: 'My children, pursue quietude, exercising yourselves always in contemplation so that in your prayers to God you may keep your minds pure. . . . The contemplative who has withdrawn from activity into knowledge is better and greater . . . free from every care, he stands near to God, and no conflicting thought drags him back. Such a man passes his life with God, his commerce is with God, as he celebrates God in endless hymns'" (*cf. Historia Monachorum in Aegypto* 1. 62–63).

In conclusion, the *Historia Monachorum in Aegypto* (1. 13, 18) and the *Historia Lausiaca* (8, 10, 11) agree in giving the nonagenarian recluse a playful character and a smiling countenance.

BIBLIOGRAPHY

Devos, P. "La 'servante de Dieu' Poemenia . . ." *Analecta Bollandiana* 87 (1969):189–212.

———. "Fragments Coptes de l'Historia Monachorum in Aegypto; S. Jean de Lyco et la Tentatrice." *Analecta Bollandiana* 87 (1969):417–41.

———. "Feuillets coptes nouveaux et anciens . . ." *Analecta Bollandiana* 88 (1970):153–87.

———. "S. Jean de Lycopolis et l'empereur Marcien." *Analecta Bollandiana* 94 (1976):303–16.

———. "De Jean Chrysostome à Jean de Lycopolis." *Analecta Bollandiana* 96 (1978):389–403.

Frankenberg, W. "Evagrius Ponticus." *Abhandlungen der königlichen Gesellschaft des Wissenschaften zu Göttingen, Philologische-historische Klasse,* Vol. 13, no. 2. Berlin, 1912.
Guy, J.-Cl. "Jean de Lycopolis." In *Dictionnaire de spiritualité ascétique et mystique,* Vol. 8, cols. 619–620. Paris, 1932.
Hausherr, I. "Aux origines de la mystique syrienne: Grégoire de Chypre ou Jean de Lycopolis?" *Oxford Classical and Philosophical Monographs* 4 (1938):497–520.
———. "Jean le Solitaire (Pseudo Jean de Lycopolis), Dialogue sur l'âme . . ." *Oxford Classical and Philosophical Monographs* 120 (1939).
———. "Un grand auteur spirituel retrouvé: Jean d'Apamée." *Oxford Classical and Philosophical Monographs* 14 (1948):3–42.
Muyldermans, J. "Un texte grec inédit attribué à J. de L." *Recherches de science religieuse* 41 (1953):525–30.
Peeters, P. "Une Vie copte de S. Jean de Lycopolis." *Analecta Bollandiana* 54 (1936):359–81.
Regnault, L. *Les Sentences des pères du désert, Collection alphabétique.* Sable-sur-Sarthe, Abbaye Saint-Pierre de Solesmes, 1981.
Sauget, J.-M. "Giovanni di Licopoli." *Bibliotheca Sanctorum* 6, cols. 818–22.
Till, W. "Koptische Heiligen- und Martyrerlegenden." *Orientalia Christiana Periodica* 102 (1935): 138–54; 108 (1936):137–40.

PAUL DEVOS

JOHN OF MAYUMA, sixth-century bishop who wrote an anthology of miraculous tales. John of Mayuma was a monk from the Monastery of Bayt Rufina, whence the name John Rufus, by which he is also known. He succeeded Peter the Iberian as bishop of Mayuma near Gaza in Palestine.

Around the year 515, John composed a collection of *plerophoriae* (anecdotes and brief episodes) of a miraculous nature that were meant to testify to the orthodoxy of the Chalcedonians. The majority of these stories were already in existence and, indeed, had been incorporated in various other compilations and texts. However, the anthology of John of Mayuma was the most widespread, and so by antonomasia it gained the title *Plerophoriae,* by which it is known today.

The original version was certainly written in Greek, but only a few fragments of it have survived. Two complete manuscripts, however, exist in a Syriac translation (Nau, 1912). In Coptic there are only fragments coming from three codices and a fourth manuscript, which we might designate as a "personal" concoction. Two of these fragmentary codices are in Sahidic (Pierpont Morgan Library, New York, C13, ed. Crum, 1913; National Library, Vienna, K2502, ed. Orlandi, 1974) and contain an anthology similar to the Syriac translation, though their numberings are different. Hence, these two codices have many omissions, additions, and a different order for the episodes. The third Coptic codex is in Bohairic (Coptic Museum, Cairo, S. Macar. 12(6)), and it probably contained only those events referring to the life of TIMOTHY II AELURUS, some of which agree with episodes in John's *Plerophoriae.* The fourth manuscript (4925 [University of Michigan], ed. Orlandi, 1974) has some excerpts from a collection very similar to the Syriac translation, as well as some additional episodes.

BIBLIOGRAPHY

Crum, W. E., ed. *Theological Texts from Coptic Papyri,* pp. 62–64. Oxford, 1913.
John Rufus. *Plérophorie.* PO 7, pt. 1, ed. F. Nau. Paris, 1912.
Orlandi, T. *Papiri copti di contenuto teologico,* pp. 110–17. Vienna, 1974.
———. "Un frammento delle Pleroforie in copto." *Studi e Ricerche sull'Oriente Cristiano* 2 (1979):3–12.

TITO ORLANDI

JOHN OF NIKIOU, seventh-century bishop of Nikiou in the Prosopite nome, in the southwest Delta—a place already known in the third century B.C. All that we know of his life is contained in the HISTORY OF THE PATRIARCHS. In the *History* he is present at the death of the patriarch JOHN III of Samannūd in 689 and at the election of his successor, ISAAC, in 690, accompanying him to the court of the governor, ʿAbd al-ʿAzīz. He was general overseer of the monasteries under Simon (693–700) until he was deposed for beating to death a monk who had raped a virgin. Since his *Chronicle* does not extend beyond that date, his death may be assigned to some time shortly after A.D. 700.

John's *Chronicle* survives in an Ethiopic version made from a lost Arabic version. Views have been divided about how the text was written. H. Zotenberg, the first editor, believed that the original text was written partly in Greek and partly in Coptic, according to the source used. Some claim that it was written totally in Greek; others that it was entirely in Coptic. Yet it is unlikely that, as a leading

Monophysite bishop, John would have composed his work in the language of the Melchites, and T. Nöldeke pointed to traces of Coptic in the Ethiopic translation. Considering the absence of any reference to the *Chronicle* in Byzantine literature, it becomes almost certain that the original language was Coptic, although John drew upon Greek writers plentifully.

The Ethiopic version is badly mutilated, especially the material on the first half of the seventh century, for which John provides valuable contemporary evidence. The work, which is prefaced by a summary, presents some problems. From chapter lxv the summary and text disagree numerically as well as in content.

The purpose is to chronicle the whole history of the human race from Adam, including references to Egypt and sections on early Roman history, as well as on Hellenistic history. A full, though brief, account of the reigns of the Roman emperors focuses on those who persecuted the Christians. As the Empire becomes Christianized, details increase about both secular and religious matters, although much of the information is untrustworthy. John is dependent, indirectly, no doubt, on Malalas and, for ecclesiastical matters, on the ecclesiastical historian Socrates. For the reign of Justinian, John gives (chap. xcii, 20–21) the histories of Procopius and Agathias credit for being the authoritative studies on the Vandalic and Persian wars.

From the reign of Maurice through the events leading to the accession of Heraclius and the subsequent Arabic invasion of Egypt, John assumes the role of a contemporary authority of major importance. Unfortunately, his text for this period, particularly the account of the Arabic conquest, is corrupt, full of lacunae, and dislocated. The lacuna in the relevant chapters (cvii-cxxii to the end) omits completely the years 610–640. Thus the history of the Sassanid conquest, occupation, and evacuation of Egypt and the preliminary phases of ʿAmr's operations before his investment of Babylon have been omitted. Despite the difficulty of interpreting the chapters about the later stages of the conquest (chaps. cxi–cxxi; see ARAB CONQUEST OF EGYPT), his narratives assume pride of place over the Arab chroniclers in instances where they disagree on fundamental points.

The style of the *Chronicle*—as it appears in translation from Ethiopic—is simple, naive, and disjointed in places. Nevertheless, it carries conviction by its detail, even when the sequence is confused either by the author or by the intermediaries between him and the surviving Ethiopic version.

BIBLIOGRAPHY

Butler, A. J. *The Arab Conquest of Egypt and the Last Thirty Years of Arab Dominion.* Oxford, 1902.

Caetani, Leone. *Annali dell'Islam,* vol. 3, Milan, 1905–1926.

Charles, R. H. *The Chronicle of John, Bishop of Nikiu.* London, 1916.

Nöldeke, T. In *Göttingische Gelehrte Anzeigen* 1 (1881):587–94; 2 (1883):1364–71.

Zotenberg, H. "Mémoire sur la chronique byzantine de Jean, évêque de Nikiou." *Journal asiatique* 7, 10 (1877):451–517; 12 (1878):245–347; 13 (1879):291–386.

P. M. FRASER

JOHN OF PAKE (feast day: 19 Baramhāt), hermit of the fifth or sixth century who does not appear in the Synaxarion but who is well known from inscriptions of monasteries. It is probable that he was considered a saint by the monks. As the inscriptions show, he was no doubt a native of Pake, a village to the north of Minyā in Middle Egypt.

BIBLIOGRAPHY

Crum, W. E. "Fragments of a Church Calendar." *Zeitschrift für die neutestamentliche Wissenschaft* 73 (1938):23–32.

Drew-Bear, M. *Le nome Hermopolite. Toponymes et sites.* American Studies in Papyrology 21. Missoula, Montana, 1979.

RENÉ-GEORGES COQUIN

JOHN OF PARALLOS, SAINT (c. 540–610/620) (feast day: 19 Kiyahk), bishop of Parallos in lower Egypt, who was one of the most important Egyptian churchmen and theologians of his time. John of Parallos (Burullus in Arabic) vigorously opposed heresy in his writings and as an active participant in church politics; possibly he was valued adviser to DAMIAN, patriarch of Alexandria. He was probably born about 540 in a respected clerical family of Lower Egypt. Like his parents he was recognized for his charity. After their death he used his inheritance to build a hospice, where he himself cared for the sick and wandering. A monk who visited him in his hospice persuaded him to relinquish all he owned and follow an ascetic life. Accordingly, he became a monk in the Monastery of DAYR ANBĀ MAQĀR (Monastery of Saint Macarius) in Scetis under the hegumenos Daniel. Later he became an anchorite as a better way to confront the devil. He was probably ordained in 576 by PETER IV, patriarch of Alexandria.

We can reconstruct John's activities from his writings, as well as from the Copto-Arabic SYNAXARION. Undoubtedly he knew Greek and Coptic, and perhaps Syriac. Standing firmly against every heresy, he did not share the Coptic inclination to search for instruction in unorthodox books or in the Egyptian Gnostic quest to decipher God's secrets not found in the Bible. Rather, he labored arduously against any book encompassing doctrines or revelations additional to those recognized as orthodox. He investigated monastery libraries and burned virtually every such book that he found.

He wrote a Homily about the archangel Michael in which he condemned the heretical books read in the orthodox churches in the Coptic (Sahidic) language. He mentioned five such heretical books, among them *The Institution of Saint Michael.* He supported the teachings of the Bible, denying later revelations about the creation of angels, *The Institution of Saint Michael,* and the fall of Satan. In a similar manner, he decried teachings about ABBATON, the angel of the dead. *The Institution of Saint Michael,* however, survived in Sahidic and Fayyumic versions, written in the second half of the eighth century, which were discovered in the Monastery of Saint Michael at Sōpehes on the southwestern border of the Fayyūm.

As a theologian of strict orthodoxy, John influenced seven groups of Christians who were following unorthodox doctrines to return to the official faith. He also grappled with two visionary monks who claimed to have been inspired by the archangel Michael and the Prophet Habakkuk and who were able to mislead many of the faithful. Nevertheless, he found opponents not only in the strong Syrian colony in Lower Egypt but also in his own circles.

Other bishops did not follow his teachings, nor did all of the patriarchs (e.g., JOHN III in the seventh century).

Other writings by John include works about the Resurrection and the Last Judgment, as well as about the verses of the Psalms, "the Lord shall rejoice in His works" and "who has dealt bountifully with me is the Lord" (Ps. 104 [103]:37 and 116 [114]:7). He composed other treatises on the holy and orthodox faith; on the right faith; and thirteen anathemas on the *Confessio patrum* (against Christological errors; taken out of a book entitled *Tartīb al-Kanīsah* [Order of the church]). He left a life of the Holy Virgin Damiana. All these works are extant in Arabic or Ethiopic translations. The originals were, of course, Coptic.

John of Parallos played a major part in the dogmatic controversy between DAMIAN, patriarch of Alexandria, and Peter of Kallinikon in Syria, where he stayed for four months, helping Damian. It is possible that he contributed to the redaction of Damian's treatises sent to Syria.

BIBLIOGRAPHY

Lantschoot, A. van. "Fragments coptes d'une homélie de Jean de Parallos contre les livres hérétiques." *Miscellanea Giovanni Mercati* 1, offprint with own pagination. Studi e Testi 121, pp. 1–31. Vatican City, 1946.

______. "Un texte palimpseste de Vat. Copte 65." *Le Muséon* 60 (1947):261–68.

Müller, C. D. G. *Die alte koptische Predigt* (*Versuch eines Überblicks*), pp. 102–103, 150–56, 300–349. Darmstadt, 1954.

______. "Einige Bemerkungen zur ars praedicandi der alten koptischen Kirche." *Le Muséon* 67 (1954):231–70.

______. "Die koptische Kirche zwischen Chalkedon und dem Arabereinmarsch." *Zeitschrift für Kirchengeschichte* 75 (1964):271–308.

______. "Aufbau und Entwicklung der koptischen Kirche nach Chalkedon 451." *Kyrios* 10 (1970): 202–210.

Wüstenfeld, H. F. *Synaxarium, das ist, Heiligen-Kalender der Coptischen Christen,* pp. 187–89. Gotha, 1979.

C. DETLEF G. MÜLLER

JOHN THE PRESBYTER, author to whom a Coptic version of the life of Saint PISENTIUS, bishop of Qifṭ (Coptos), dating from the mid-seventh century is attributed. The text has reached us in only one codex (British Museum, London, Or. 7026, Budge, 1910, pp. 75–127).

The Life of Pisentius is made up of miraculous episodes; these do not always appear in the same order in the different versions and may sometimes have additions or omissions—in some cases homiletic passages.

De L. O'Leary (1930) identifies four versions: one in Sahidic Coptic, attributed to John the Presbyter; one in Bohairic Coptic, attributed to MOSES OF QIFṬ; and two in Arabic, one shorter than the other. O'Leary also gives a careful summary of the versions. The text is clearly based on a preexisting collection of episodes, so that it is later than the version attributed to Moses of Qifṭ.

The main feature of the version attributed to John the Presbyter is that it has the form of a real homily, with an added prologue, conclusion, and personal reflections by the author. These are of an encomiastic or moral nature, inserted between episodes or groups of episodes. The most interesting sections are the prologue (which also discusses the literary justification for the work), a digression on Jacob, another on Moses, to whom Pisentius is compared, and a third on the oratorical skill of Pisentius.

BIBLIOGRAPHY

Budge, E. A. W. *Coptic Homilies in the Dialect of Upper Egypt.* London, 1910.

O'Leary, De L. *The Arabic Life of S. Pisentius.* PO 22, 3. Paris, 1930.

TITO ORLANDI

JOHN RUFUS. *See* John of Mayuma.

JOHN SABAS (fl. c. 550), Nestorian ascetic who spent a long time as a hermit and at an advanced age was the founder and principal of a monastery. His writings consist of letters, short sermons, and a compendium on the spiritual life called *Ru'ūs al-Ma'rifah* (Chapters of Understanding). Despite his Nestorian faith, these writings made him greatly esteemed in Jacobite and Monophysite circles, so that he became known as the "spiritual elder," almost as a legendary character.

BIBLIOGRAPHY

Wright, W. *A Short History of Syriac Literature.* London, 1894.

VINCENT FREDERICK

JOHN OF SHMŪN, sixth- and early seventh-century bishop of Shmūn and writer of two Coptic works in praise of Saints MARK and ANTONY. There is no other evidence about him in Coptic literary tradition except for a passage by the historian SĀWĪRUS IBN AL-MUQAFFA' and John's own mention in one work of his contemporary, DAMIAN, patriarch of Alexandria.

John's encomium of the Evangelist Mark (ed. Orlandi, 1968, with an Italian translation) consists of a prologue, which praises the great figures of Egyptian Christianity; a paraphrase of episodes concerning Paul, Barnabas, and Mark from the Acts of the Apostles; legendary relations between Mark and Peter; Mark's deeds in Alexandria, according to apocryphal accounts; and an exhortatory conclusion.

John's encomium of Antony (Pierpont Morgan Library, New York, M579, fols. 72–87; ed. Garitte, 1943, with Latin translation) consists of a prologue; the praises of Antony, which go on at considerable length; and an exhortatory epilogue.

John does not give a real biography of the saint being praised, as would be indispensable in a later period. Nevertheless, both works show an excellent capacity for construction and for the organization of content. The rhetorical style is florid and often very complex, in line with the taste of that time, which was distantly derived from that of the "second sophistic" style.

From his works, John's most marked characteristic appears to be a burning nationalism, which is also obviously the basic reason for the choice of the subjects of these two homilies. At the time of Damian, in fact, the Coptic church tended to be closing in upon itself and to view Egypt as a privileged region that alone was capable of preserving orthodoxy against almost all the rest of the Christian world.

From the literary viewpoint, one can observe John's participation in the argument about the appropriateness of reopening discussion of subjects already treated by the great Greek fathers of earlier times. In the late sixth and early seventh centuries, Coptic was becoming established as the language for everyday use (from the popular to the scholarly) within the church; at the same time, texts in Greek could no longer be trusted from the theological viewpoint.

BIBLIOGRAPHY

Garitte, G. "Panégyrique de Saint Antoine par Jean évêque d'Hermopolis." *Orientalia Christiana Periodica* 9 (1943):100–134, 330–65.

Orlandi, T. *Studi Copti. 1. Un encomio di Marco Evangelista. 2. Le fonti copte della Storia dei Patriarchi di Alessandria. 3. La leggenda di S. Mercurio.* Testi e documenti per lo studio dell'antichità 22. Milan, 1968.

TITO ORLANDI

JOHN THE SHORT. *See* John Colobos, Saint.

JOHN AND SYMEON, fourth-century martyrs in Egypt. They are the subject of the Passion of John and Symeon, a Coptic work that survives in only one Bohairic manuscript of the ninth century (Hyvernat, 1886–1887, pp. 174–201). The Passion belongs to the late literary pattern defined by T. Baumeister as *"koptischer Konsens,"* the repetitive treatment of the Egyptian theme of "indestructible life" (see HAGIOGRAPHY). It is related to the cycle of Julius of Aqfahṣ (see MARTYRS, COPTIC) and for certain legends to the Antiochene Cycle of BASILIDES (see CYCLES).

The Passion opens in Kenemoulos, a village in the Panau district of Egypt, where live old Moses and his wife, Helen, who are childless. Moses makes a vow to John the Baptist to build a sanctuary, and the latter promises him a son who will become a martyr. John is born, and when he is eleven he becomes a shepherd for his cousin Symeon. After performing a first miracle, he comes back home and learns the Bible by heart. During a visit by the bishop, John shows his knowledge and is therefore made presbyter. He performs some more miracles. When John's parents die, Symeon comes to live with him. Then other miracles follow, among them one for an imperial Roman officer. When the daughter of the emperor Quintilian falls ill in Antioch, the officer's advice is to call John. He is miraculously taken to Antioch, where he cures the girl, and then is miraculously returned to Egypt. Then the Passion reports the episode of Nicomede, the son of the king of Persia, who had been captured in war—a story typical of the Basilidian cycle. After Diocletian, successor to Quintilian, rejects Christianity John and Symeon go to Alexandria in order to confess their faith. They are imprisoned by the prefect Armenius. Before Julius of Aqfahṣ they are tortured and put to death. Julius saves their bodies and writes their Passion.

BIBLIOGRAPHY

Baumeister, T. *Martyr Invictus. Der Märtyrer als Sinnbild der Erlösung in der Legende und im Kult der frühen koptischen Kirche.* Münster, 1972.

Hyvernat, H. *Les Actes des martyrs de l'Egypte tirés des manuscrits coptes de la Bibliothèque Vaticane et du Musée Borgia.* Paris, 1886–1887.

TITO ORLANDI

JONAH. *See* Biblical Subjects in Coptic Art.

JONAH, FAST OF. *See* Fasts.

JOORE, martyr in fourth-century Egypt. Joore was presumably venerated on 10 Kiyahk. The uncertainty springs from the fact that the text of his Passion has survived in only one codex, which is in Sahidic dialect and is mutilated toward the end (Egyptian Museum, Turin, Cat. 63000, 1).

The text obviously belongs to the genus of "epic" Passions (see HAGIOGRAPHY), but certain fairly archaic features of both language and narrative organization indicate that it should be placed among the older ones, written (in Greek or Coptic) in about the fifth century.

The text begins with the arrival at Shmin of an unnamed Roman prefect in the reign of the emperor Diocletian. On the day on which the Christians who refuse to make sacrifice to the emperor are to be judged, five soldiers go to the town of Jinjeb and meet Joore, a shepherd who admits that he is a Christian. They try to capture him, but he manages to escape. They then take two of his animals. Joore returns and recovers the animals by force, wounding three of the soldiers. When the prefect hears of this, he threatens the *komarches* (village leader) of Jinjeb, who takes Joore in custody. Although Joore manages to escape once again, he is recaptured and imprisoned. In prison the other Christians encourage him to martyrdom. There follows a debate with the prefect that lasts into the evening and includes various episodes and discussions, after which the text ends.

BIBLIOGRAPHY

Rossi, F. "Un nuovo codice copto del Museo Egizio di Torino." *Atti Accademia dei Lincei,* ser. 5, 1 (1893):3–136.

TITO ORLANDI

JOSEPH, secretary of Apa SHENUTE (feast day: 30 Tūt). This saint is not in the SYNAXARION of the Copts, but he was celebrated at the monastery of Apa Shenute in Akhmīm, as the *typika* (liturgical manuals) coming from this monastery witness. He is also mentioned in the Life of Shenute in Coptic and Arabic versions (CSCO 129, pp. 32–33).

We know nothing about this person. It is possible that he was also a doctor (according to the Arabic version of the Life of Shenute, where he is called al-Hakīm, a term that in the Middle Ages signified a doctor).

BIBLIOGRAPHY

Amélineau, E. *Monuments pour servir à l'histoire de l'Egypte chrétienne aux IVe et Ve siècles.* Mission archéologique française au Caire, Mémoires 4. Paris, 1888.

Crum, W. E. *Catalogue of the Coptic Manuscripts in the Collection of the John Rylands Library.* Manchester, 1909.

Leipoldt, I., and W. Crum. *Sinuthii archimandritae Vita et opera omnia.* CSCO 41.

Pleyte, W., and P. A. A. Boeser, eds. *Manuscrits coptes du Musée d'Antiquités des Pays-Bas à Leide.* Leiden, 1897.

RENÉ-GEORGES COQUIN

JOSEPH, STORY OF. *See* Biblical Subjects in Coptic Art.

JOSEPH OF BISHWĀW, SAINT, a monk from Qift who lived with Saint ELIAS OF BISHWĀW (feast day: 5 Hātūr). He was the son of parents who were important in this village. His father being already dead, his mother called him to her deathbed. Joseph said to her, "Why are you forsaking me?" She replied, "I am entrusting you to Jesus Christ, my Lord. He will not forsake you, and will never be far from you." According to the SYNAXARION, he had several brothers, the eldest of whom received him into his home and took care of him.

God, his first tutor, suggested to him that he cross the river and withdraw into the cave of Saint ELIAS OF BISHWĀW. He there found the book of the prophet Elias and began to read in a very sweet voice, which caused Saint Elias to say, "May this young man remain here and spend the feast of Easter with us, that we may hear him read!"

Joseph returned to the town, and Anbā Elias had a vision in which he received a palm that bore fruits in the place where he was. Joseph answered the call of the Lord Jesus Christ. He abandoned the world and embraced the monastic life. He asked his brothers for his share of the inheritance, which they gave him, some 120 gold denarii, not counting the furniture of the house. His brothers said, "What will you do with it? Do not squander it—leave it with us to keep safe." He answered, "You do not need it." He distributed it to the poor and needy, the widows and the orphans.

Crossing the Nile, he became a monk in the mountain of Benhadab. He fell sick, and said to himself, "If I recover and regain my health, I will live with Saint Elias." This was done, and he did not leave Saint Elias until his death. He applied to himself the gospel saying, "It is enough for the disciple to be as his master, and the servant as his lord" (Mt. 10:25). He applied himself to asceticism, consuming neither bread nor olives. He contented himself with berries and gave himself up to strict fasting. He spent the greater part of the night in prayer, to the point that he fell ill, spitting blood. But one night as the brethren surrounded him, Jesus came to heal him. He then resumed his asceticism to the point of becoming so thin that his skin adhered to his bones. Allowing himself no rest, he fell sick again, and died at the age of thirty-three.

BIBLIOGRAPHY

Graf, G. *Catalogue de Manuscrits arabes chrétiens conservés au Caire.* Studi e Testi 63. Cairo, 1934.

Troupeau, G. *Catalogue des manuscrits arabes, première partie: manuscrits chrétiens,* Vol. 1. Paris, 1972.

RENÉ-GEORGES COQUIN

JOSEPH THE CARPENTER, saint and spouse of the Virgin Mary and foster father of Jesus Christ (feast day: 26 Abīb).

Biblical Accounts

In the New Testament Joseph is mentioned in the accounts of the birth and childhood of Jesus (Mt. 1–2; Lk. 1–2) and also in Luke (3:23, 4:22) and John (1:45, 6:42) as the father of Jesus. He belonged to the tribe of Judah and the family of King David (Mt. 1:2–16; Lk. 3:23–34), and in the Gospels he is the link that joins Jesus to that lineage. The Gospels differ in the name given to Joseph's father in the genealogies of Jesus. According to Matthew 1:16 it is Jacob; according to Luke 3:23 it is Heli. The different explanations for this divergence remain in the realm of hypothesis. For Julius Africanus in the third century, Jacob and Heli were brothers, and on the death of Heli, Jacob married his widow in accordance with the Levitical law. Saint Augustine suggested that Heli had adopted Joseph, who was the son of Jacob. Heli could also have been the father of Mary. Since she was the only child, on her marriage the family rights of Heli would have passed to Joseph. The Gospels tell us nothing of the birthplace of Joseph, but ancient Christian writers suggest three possibilities: Jerusalem, Bethlehem, and Nazareth. The evangelists call Joseph *ho tekton* (artisan). The Coptic, Syriac, and Ethiopic versions take him to be an artisan who works with wood, a carpenter; the Latin versions take him to be an artisan who works with iron, *faber.* Greek writers generally call him a carpenter.

The Gospels relate that Mary was already betrothed to Joseph when she received the annunciation of the angel (Mt. 1:18; Lk. 1:27). From the text of Matthew it appears that the situation was that of the formal promise of matrimony, the first stage in a Jewish marriage, which was completed by leading the bride to the husband's house. In such a situation it is unlikely that Joseph would have accompanied Mary on her journey to the hill country of Judea to visit Elizabeth (Lk. 1:39). On observing the signs of Mary's motherhood before they lived together, Joseph, a just man, decided to put her away privately (Mt. 1:19). In a dream he then received the revelation of the mystery that had been worked in Mary and voluntarily accepted the mission of paternity that God commended to him (Mt. 1:24–25). As legal father by divine vocation, Joseph gave the child the name Jesus and took care of the Holy Family. In the Gospel of Matthew, we are told that Joseph had further divine revelations about the journey to Egypt and the return to Nazareth (Mt. 2:13–19). According to Luke, Joseph accompanied his spouse, Mary, who is the protagonist of the events (Lk. 2:4–5; 16:48). Since there is no direct mention of Joseph during the public life of Jesus, it can reasonably be supposed that he had already died.

Apocryphal Accounts

Joseph logically appears in apocryphal literature, which has had a great influence on artistic representations. Joseph appears above all in the apocryphal gospels of the birth of Mary and the childhood of Jesus. The oldest of this series is the so-called *Protogospel of James,* dating from the second century (Tischendorf, 1876, pp. 1–48), the main idea of which is to defend the honor and virginity of Mary in the narration of the antecedents of Mary and her husband Joseph. The latter, an old widower with children, is given the task of looking after Mary by the high priest after a meeting of the widowers of Jerusalem in which a dove appears from Joseph's staff and flies over his head (chap. 9). When Mary is found to be with child, the high priest suspects Joseph and submits both of them to the test of drinking the bitter waters. They come through the test unharmed and their innocence is acknowledged (chaps. 15–16). Such a presentation of Joseph clarifies the New Testament references to the brethren of Jesus (Mt. 12:46; Mk. 3:31; Jn. 2:12; Acts 1:14), since these would be children of a previous marriage of Joseph; the perpetual virginity of Mary is also protected. *The Gospel of Pseudo-Matthew* is dependent on the *Protogospel of James.* In this sixth-century work (Tischendorf, 1876, pp. 50–105), episodes from the childhood of Jesus are narrated. Equally dependent on the *Protogospel* is the *De nativitate Mariae* (ninth century; Tischendorf, 1876, pp. 113–21), which eliminates such themes as the first marriage of Joseph and the test of the bitter waters and clarifies other themes such as the true marriage of Joseph and the Virgin.

The apocryphal gospels of the childhood of Jesus have the prime aim of showing the divinity of the child and contain many anecdotes on the relationship between Joseph and Jesus. Thus the *Gospel of Pseudo-Thomas,* which dates from the second century (Tischendorf, 1876, pp. 140–75), gives an account of the miracle worked by Jesus when He causes some clay pigeons to take flight after having been scolded by Joseph for making them on the Sabbath (chap. 2). Joseph scolds Jesus and pulls His ears, when he cannot understand the child's behavior (chap. 5), and he tries in vain to find a teacher suitable for Jesus (chap. 14). Along the same lines is the so-called *Arabic Gospel of the Childhood,* also known in Syriac (ed. from Latin version in Tischendorf, 1876, pp. 181–209), which includes details of the journey to Egypt and the return to Nazareth. This apocryphal work includes the tradition of the stay of the Holy Family in Maṭariyyah, a town some 6 miles (9 km) northeast of Cairo near the ancient Heliopolis. There Jesus caused a spring to flow in which Mary washed His robe, and the balmy perfume of the sweat filled the whole region (chap. 24). However, this tradition is not included in the twelfth-century *Churches and Monasteries in Egypt.*

The apocryphal *History of Joseph the Carpenter* has also been preserved in Coptic. Previously it was known only in the Arabic version, edited by G. Wallin in 1727 and translated into Latin by C. Tischendorf, 1876, pp. 309–336, and in the Latin version of 1522 by Isidoro de Isolano. E. Quatremère in 1808 and G. Zoëga in 1810 drew attention to the existence of Bohairic and Sahidic versions. Both texts were edited by E. Revillout (1876, pp. 28–70) and P. de Lagarde (1883); new Sahidic fragments were edited by F. Robinson (1896) and L. T. Lefort (1953). The Bohairic manuscript is from the Monastery of DAYR ANBĀ MAQĀR (Saint Macarius). The Sahidic fragments of two manuscripts are from DAYR ANBĀ SHINŪDAH (the White Monastery). The original of this apocryphal work, undoubtedly in Greek, though some think in Sahidic, dates from the fifth or sixth century or even earlier. In its present form it is a discourse by Jesus to the Apostles describing the death of His father Joseph, "the blessed old carpenter." Chapters 2–11 describe the life of Joseph and are heavily dependent on the apocryphal works concerning the Nativity. Chapters 12–31 describe the death of Joseph, emphasizing his fears at its approach and the help he is given by Jesus and Mary. These chapters are the most original part of the book and are similar in style to the apocryphal works on the death of Mary.

The way in which this History of Joseph begins leads to the conclusion that in its present form it was written to be read in the liturgy in the Coptic monasteries on the feast of Saint Joseph. Some modern scholars (G. Klameth, S. Morenz) see in the date of this feast, on which the beginning of the flooding of the Nile was celebrated, a point of similarity between the accounts of the death and burial of Joseph and the Osiris myths. But such a hypothesis is not sufficiently well founded, since the basic motif in the history of Joseph is the death of Joseph, whereas the motif of the myths is the resurrection of Osiris. Although certain expressions tainted with gnosticism can be found in the *History of Joseph*, its contents are substantially orthodox and suppose a well-developed doctrine of the Trinity, judgment after death, the immortality of the soul, the angels, and even (according to G. Giamberardini) the sacraments. On the other hand, it contains apocryphal information concerning the life of Joseph, such as that he was from Bethlehem, was married for the first time at the age of forty, remained married for forty-nine years, and was a widower for a year. He then took the Virgin into his care and two years later they were married. He died at an advanced age when Jesus was eighteen. By his first marriage Joseph had four sons and two daughters called Assia and Lida. In Bethlehem Joseph registered Jesus before his birth (chap. 7). The *History of Joseph* also includes the tradition of the death of the prophets Elijah and Enoch at the hands of the Antichrist (chap. 31), as is narrated in the *Apocalypse of Elijah*.

An interesting feature of the *History of Joseph* is that it is the oldest indirect witness to a feast in honor of Saint Joseph, leading to the conclusion that the Christians of Egypt were the first to celebrate it.

The figure of Joseph is, of course, closely linked in the traditions of the Coptic church to the journey of the Holy Family to Egypt. On this subject it is sufficient to note, among the homilies in Arabic, that of Zakariyyā of Sakhā, in which the reasons for the journey are given for the first time: to purify Egypt of idolatry, to fulfill the prophecies of the Old Testament, and to shower blessings on Egypt. In two homilies by Cyriacus of al-Bahnasā there is mention of the Holy Family's stay in Bisūs for four days and of a Book of Joseph, in which the saint wrote an account of his life. Many places in Egypt lay claim to the residence there of Joseph and the Holy Family, for example, Cusa and Hermopolis in the Thebaid (Meinardus, 1963). In the apocryphal *Vision of Theophilus*, preserved in Syriac (ed. Mingana, 1929), it is recalled that near Cusa Jesus took Joseph's staff and planted it in the ground as a witness of His arrival there, and that immediately the staff began to sprout.

Cult of Saint Joseph

The cult of Saint Joseph received its first explicit witness in the West in the eighth century (Central Library, Zurich, Rh 30.30) with a feast celebrated on 20 March. From the tenth century the different calendars and martyrologies place the feast on 19 March, and the first witnesses to public devotion are found in the twelfth century. This devotion became more widespread in the West through the activities of the Premonstratensian, Servite, Franciscan, and Carmelite orders, and the figure of Saint Joseph grew in esteem and became the object of theological reflection to such an extent that Pope Pius IX on 8 December 1870 declared Saint Joseph patron of the Roman Catholic Church (feast day since 1955: 1 May). Saint Joseph is acknowledged as having a divine mission and a singular holiness below that of Jesus and Mary alone. In the East the feast of Saint Joseph is mentioned in the ninth-century calendars of the Palestinian monastery of Saint Sabas (feast day: first Sunday after Christmas).

The commemoration of the parents of Jesus is joined to that of the Nativity and is celebrated the day after or on the preceding Sunday.

The Coptic church has used a proper office for Saint Joseph since the Middle Ages. It is placed after that of John the Baptist, but before that of the Apostles. In the SYNAXARION of the Coptic church of Alexandria, written about 1425, the feast of 26 Abīb is preserved. The feast to celebrate the stay of the Holy Family in Egypt is joined to the feast of the consecration of the churches of those places in which they are supposed to have resided. There are signs of a feast celebrated on 26 Amshīr, which could be the betrothal of Joseph and Mary. The most theological consideration of Joseph before the modern period is by Ibn Al-Ṭayyib al Mashriqī (1403) in a Commentary on the Gospel of Matthew.

At present the devotion to Joseph is not of particular importance among the Copts, and his feast and office are celebrated only in the monasteries. Some connect the forty-three days of fasting in Advent to a fast of the same length by the Virgin before she gave birth in Bethlehem because Joseph had insulted her (Giamberardini, 1966, pp. 47–48). The Jerusalem Copts celebrate the appearance in 1954 of the Virgin Mary, the Infant Jesus, Joseph, and the angels in Saint Antony's College, next to the Church of the Holy Sepulcher (Meinardus, 1970, p. 267).

BIBLIOGRAPHY

Battista, A., and B. Bagatti. *Edizione critica del testo arabo della Historia Iosephi Fabri Lignarii e ricerche sulla sua origine.* Jerusalem, 1978.

Giamberardini, G. *San Giuseppe nella tradizione copta.* Cairo, 1966.

Klameth, G. "Über die Herkunft der apokryphen 'Geschichte Josephs des Zimmermanns.'" *Angelos* 3 (1930):6–31.

Lefort, L. T. "A Propos de 'L'Histoire de Joseph le charpentier.'" *Le Muséon* 66 (1953):201–223.

Legarde, P. de. *Aegyptiaca,* pp. 1–37. Göttingen, 1883.

Meinardus, O. F. A. *In the Steps of the Holy Family from Bethlehem to Upper Egypt.* Cairo, 1963.

———. *Christian Egypt Faith and Life.* Cairo, 1970.

Michel, C., and P. Peeters. *Evangiles apocryphes I,* 2nd ed., pp. 194–245. Paris, 1924.

Mingana, A. "Vision of Theofilus, or the Book of the Flight of the Holy Family into Egypt." *Bulletin of the John Rylands Library* 13 (1929):383–425.

Morenz, S. *Die Geschichte von Joseph dem Zimmermann, übersetzt, erlautert und untersucht.* Texte und Untersuchungen zur Geschichte der altchristlichen literatur 56, no. 1. Berlin, 1951.

Révillout, E. "Apocryphes coptes du Nouveau Testament." *Etudes égyptologiques* 7 (1876):28–70.

Robinson, F. *Coptic Apocryphal Gospels.* Texts and Studies 4, no. 2. Cambridge, 1896.

Santos, A. de. *Los Evangelios Apocrifos,* pp. 358–78. Madrid, 1956.

Stramare, T., and M. L. Casanova. "Giuseppe, sposo di Maria." *Bibliotheca Sanctorum,* Vol. 6, pp. 1251–92. Rome, 1965.

Tischendorf, C., ed. *Evangelia Apocrypha,* 2nd ed. Leipzig, 1876.

GONZALO ARANDA PEREZ

JOSEPH OF TSENTI, SAINT.

The life of Joseph is summarized in the recension of the SYNAXARION from Upper Egypt at the day of his death, 5 Hātūr (Basset, 1907, pp. 283–86; Forget, 1954, Vols. 47–49, pp. 295–96 [text]; 78, 1953, pp. 120–21 [trans.]).

A native of Fāw, Joseph was an only son. His parents reared him with the child of neighbors named Patasius. When the two children had grown up, they went to the monastery of Tsenti founded by Saint PACHOMIUS of Tabennēsē and asked to be received as monks. Joseph decided to live as a recluse and established himself in the mountain of Tsenti (al-Aṣāṣ) in the nome of QIFṬ.

His friend Patasius was the first to die, after predicting his own death. Joseph accomplished miracles and also built a church in the name of the apostles where Patasius was buried. The church was situated, according to the *Synaxarion,* "in a cave in the mountain." Nothing more is known of Joseph of Tsenti than what is recorded in the *Synaxarion.*

This Joseph of Tsenti should not be confused with another saint, JOSEPH OF BISHWĀW, who lived and died on the mountain of Tsenti to the west of Qifṭ, more precisely in the southern part called al-Bishwāw (the Persea). Joseph of Bishwāw is mentioned in the *Synaxarion* only within the notice devoted to his master ELIAS OF BISHWĀW. His name is written "Yusāb" in the *Synaxarion,* but Winlock and Crum have shown that this is a transliteration of the Coptic way of writing Joseph.

BIBLIOGRAPHY

Winlock, H. E., and W. E. Crum. *The Monastery of Epiphanius at Thebes,* 2 vols. New York, 1926. Reprinted 1973.

RENÉ-GEORGES COQUIN

JOSEPHUS FLAVIUS, famous Jewish historian of his people, who wrote in Greek during the second half of the first century A.D. As he reports in his autobiography, through his father Matthias he was a member of the priestly family of Jehoiarib (cf. 1 Chr. 24:7), which rose to high-priestly rank. Moreover, through his mother he was a descendant of the royal house of the Hasmonaeans/Maccabees, and was thus, as he emphasizes, of royal blood. In accordance with his lineage and his father's social position, he received an excellent education. For a noble Jewish boy in Jerusalem at that time, this included intensive study of the religion and history of his people, as well as a comprehensive introduction to Hellenistic culture, which imparted a knowledge of the important parts of classical Greek literature in its original language and of the basic rules of rhetoric. Naturally, in view of the importance of the high-priestly families in the Sanhedrin, the central body for Jewish self-administration, correct information concerning the position of the Jews in all parts of the Roman Empire was also included.

Josephus probably never participated in the priestly activities in the Temple. Rather, when he was old enough, he likely went into the service of the Sanhedrin. However, in 64 he traveled to Rome on a diplomatic mission, in order to effect the release of some priests whom the procurator Felix (52–60) had arrested, presumably for political reasons, and had sent to Rome for judgment by the emperor. Josephus resolved this difficult issue quickly and completely, and thereby earned the confidence of the Jewish authorities in his political abilities. Thus in 66, as one who held the moderate political views of the Pharisees, he received the task of restraining the rebels in Jerusalem, who were pressing toward open conflict with the Romans. After he failed in this attempt, the remaining official authorities in Jerusalem sent him to Galilee to secure peace and order there at least. He failed again, but after various difficulties was named commander of the regular Jewish forces in Galilee. After a total defeat in 67 he was captured under very curious circumstances by the Romans. Handed over to Vespasian, the commander of the Roman forces, in the presence of Vespasian's son Titus, Josephus predicted Vespasian's elevation to caesar and emperor. Vespasian therefore granted him his life and kept him in his company, though as a captive.

After Nero's death in 68 and Vespasian's enthronement in 69, Josephus was released and from then on called himself Josephus Flavius as a sign of his connection to the new imperial family. Vespasian attached him to the suite of Titus, his son and successor (79–81), who was appointed to bring the Jewish war to an end. During the siege of Jerusalem in 70, Josephus tried repeatedly, but in vain, to persuade the rebels to surrender and especially to preserve the Temple from destruction. After the city's capture he lived in Rome, now a Roman citizen and a distinguished member of the Flavian court, especially during the reign of Domitian (81–96), who valued the company of scholars. Josephus probably died in Rome; the date and the exact circumstances are not known.

During Vespasian's lifetime Josephus composed the history of the Jewish war, probably in Aramaic. This first edition, which is lost, was followed by a final edition in Greek, which he prepared with the assistance of good stylists for the general Hellenistic public. His further works are the history of the Jewish people from the beginnings to the outbreak of the Jewish war (*Antiquitates Judaicae*), designed for educated non-Jews; an autobiography (*Vita*); and a learned discussion on contemporary anti-Semitism (*Contra Apionem*). Probably he wrote and published all these works during Domitian's reign.

In the course of its social and spiritual reorganization after 70, Jewry lost all contact with the literary work of Josephus for many centuries. Deficiencies of language may have hindered the reading of the Greek texts. It is, however, much more likely, based on Josephus' reports on his life and actions during the war, that in leading Jewish circles there was the conviction that he was a deserter and a traitor to his nation. In any case, his works were ignored until the tenth century. But then they appear as historical sources of a popular Hebrew book with the title *Josippon*, which narrates the history of the Jewish people up to the destruction of Jerusalem by the Romans in 70. Obviously the unknown author used one of the Latin translations of Josephus' works, which—except for this autobiography—had been made in the church since the fourth century. Today Josephus and his works are a favorite subject of Jewish scholarship.

Surely the Latin translations reflect the reputation that the works of Josephus gained in the old Western Christian church. Similar popularity is attested by the partial texts of Josephus in Syriac and Slavic, which are not translations, strictly speaking, but reworkings with an explicitly Christian orientation. There is no Coptic translation. During the Middle Ages the works of Josephus were a favorite part of reading matter in the Western church, no less so than the works of the fathers of the church. This is astonishing, in view of the fact that early Christianity plays virtually no part in the works of Josephus, although he certainly knew of it both in his native country and in Rome. He reports in *Antiquitates* on the work and fate of John the Baptist, and on the violent death of James the brother of Jesus, "the so-called Christ." However, he mentions them not for their own sake but because their fate exposes the men who did away with them. There is also a remark concerning a certain Jesus, the so-called Testimonium Flavianum. However, because Jesus is there called the Christ without qualification, its genuineness is disputed, and today it is generally viewed as having been at least revised by Christian hands.

BIBLIOGRAPHY

Feldman, L. H. *Josephus and Modern Scholarship (1937–1980).* Berlin and New York, 1984.
Rengstorf, K. H., ed. *A Complete Concordance to Flavius Josephus,* 4 vols. Leiden, 1973–1983.
Schreckenberg, H. *Bibliographie zu Flavius Josephus.* Leiden, 1968.
———. *Bibliographie zu Flavius Josephus: Supplementband mit Gesamtregister.* Leiden, 1979.

KARL HEINRICH RENGSTORF

JOSHUA. *See* Old Testament, Arabic Versions of the.

JOVIAN (c. 332–364), Roman emperor who restored orthodox Christianity to its official status after its deposition by JULIAN THE APOSTATE. Jovian was born in Moesia, Illyria, in the Balkans, to a military officer, Count Varronius. Jovian was an officer in Julian's army when Julian died fighting the Persians in 363 and the troops hailed him as emperor. The situation of the Roman army in Persia was perilous, and Jovian was forced to conclude a disastrous peace with Shapur II in order to save his forces from destruction. On July 1, 363, he surrendered the five provinces east of the Tigris River that Galerius had captured in 298, the frontier cities of Nisibis and Singara, and all Roman influence in Armenia. It was a "necessary but ignoble peace" (Eutropius *Breviarium* 10. 17).

Jovian restored Christianity as the official religion of the empire, but he seems also to have issued an edict allowing all his subjects freedom of conscience except for practices of magic (Themistius *Oratio* V). The chi-rho symbol, a stylized, abbreviated form of the name "Christ" in Greek, was restored to the coinage, and some of the privileges taken away by Julian were restored to the church. In particular, immunities from taxation were restored to the clergy, as well as their allowances in kind (*annona*), and stipends were to be paid once more to widows and virgins.

On his way to Antioch in September, Jovian met ATHANASIUS, exiled bishop of Alexandria, and together they rode into Antioch. It was one of Athanasius' great triumphs. The angry critic of the emperor Constantius, who had deposed him, became a loyal imperial subject once more. Jovian formally restored him to his bishopric and, equally important, invited him to draw up a statement of the faith. This is preserved as Athanasius' *Letter* 56. Petitions by Athanasius' opponents in Alexandria were dismissed by the emperor with indignation.

While the Nicene Creed was now established as orthodox and Athanasius' tenacity had been vindicated, it was not possible to bridge the differences between him and Melitius, bishop of Antioch, who represented the "New Nicene" party (see MELITIAN SCHISM). Melitius agreed with the HOMOOUSION position on the nature of Christ, but a council over which he presided on 5 October 363 added the gloss "the Son is born of the substance of the Father, and in respect of substance is like him" (Socrates Scholasticus *Historia ecclesiastica* 3. 25; cf. Sozomen *Historia ecclesiastica* 6. 4). Melitius and Athanasius remained out of communion with each other.

Jovian left Antioch in November and progressed slowly toward Constantinople. He stopped at Tarsus, where he paid his respects at Julian's tomb, before moving north to Ancyra, where on 11 January 364 he promulgated an edict abrogating Julian's restrictions on Christian teachers of the classics (*Codex Theodosianus* 13. 3. 6). Thence he reached Dadastana, on the borders of Bithynia and Galatia, on 16 February. The night was cold, and a charcoal brazier was brought into the emperor's room. Next morning he was found dead, suffocated by its fumes.

Socrates had a high opinion of Jovian and believed that in his good sense and moderation his reign showed the highest promise. His contemporary Ammianus is more noncommittal. Jovian appears to have been a competent rather than an inspired soldier, moderately educated, and a convinced Christian. A bluff good humor and general goodwill carried him through the crises of his short reign. His reign is important in the history of Egyptian Christianity for its unequivocal support for the theology of Athanasius. It assured the bishop of Alexandria's prestige and authority as spokesman for orthodoxy and enhanced the standing of Alexandria as "the city of the orthodox."

BIBLIOGRAPHY

Wirth, G. "Jovian, Kaiser und Karikatur." In *Vivarium. Festschrift Theodor Klauser zum 90. Geburtstag,* pp. 353–84. Jahrbuch für Antike und Christentum, Ergänzungsband 11. Münster, 1984.

Wordsworth, J. "Jovian." In *DCB* 2, pp. 460–65. Repr. New York, 1974.

W. H. C. FREND

JUDAS CYRIACUS, SAINT, second-century bishop of Jerusalem associated in legend with the discovery of the cross. In connection with Judas Cyriacus we must distinguish history from legend. EUSEBIUS OF CAESAREA is the earliest witness that Judas was the fifteenth bishop of Jerusalem, after James, the brother of the Lord. But Eusebius himself was astonished that there were thirteen bishops between 107 when Symeon died at 120 years of age, and 135, when Judas became bishop. It is clear that Eusebius has harmonized independent sources. His note on Symeon is borrowed from Hegesippus, that on the third bishop, Justus Barsabas, from Papias, and that on the first non-Jewish bishop of Jerusalem, Mark, from Aristo of Pella. The historical Judas may have lived later, and it is very likely that the period of his episcopate occurred a century later, since there were both a Judeo-Christian hierarchy and a Gentile hierarchy.

Judas Cyriacus is at the center of the legends of the discovery of the cross. These developed as early as the fourth century. They consist basically of three connected versions, of which only one has come down to us in Coptic in a sufficiently accurate form. But the other two, fragmentary accounts have nevertheless had much influence on the characterization of Judas Cyriacus in more than one Coptic literary text. From these texts, his person has to be taken as a symbol of the growing autonomy of Jerusalem from Byzantium.

The three legends of the discovery of the cross that were woven around the person of Judas Cyriacus appear in almost all languages of the Christian East, including, of course, Coptic.

The discovery of the cross by Saint Helena starts with the vision of Constantine on the shores of the River Danube in the seventh year of his reign. Following the promise of victory as a result of the vision of the cross, Constantine receives baptism at the hands of Eusebius of Rome and sends his mother, Helena, to the Holy Land on a kind of pilgrimage. The discovery of the cross is supposed to take place in the 233rd year of the Resurrection. That fact might be the last vestige of the actual life of Judas as bishop of Jerusalem. Helena questions the Jewish dignitaries about their traditions and the whereabouts of the cross. Judas, himself Jewish, refuses to point out where the cross is hidden, and consequently is thrown into a pit for seven days. Emerging from the pit, he recites a long prayer in Hebrew, the earth trembles, and the holy relics of the crucifixion appear. The corpse of a young man lying near the three crosses revives when that of Jesus is presented to him. The devil appears to Judas and tells him that he will suffer martyrdom for his treasonable action. At this point, Helena baptizes Judas under the name of Cyriacus and obtains for him the title of bishop of Jerusalem from Eusebius of Rome.

The second legend is that of the martyrdom of Judas Cyriacus under JULIAN THE APOSTATE. The Greek legend in its best form is still unpublished, but the corresponding Coptic version was edited by I. Guidi (1904) from the Vatican Coptic codex 62. Different from the Greek text and other versions, this manuscript introduces the Passion of Judas Cyriacus under Julian with the account of the discovery of the cross by Helena. This may explain the nonexistence of the text in Coptic. The other known texts in Greek and Syriac recount the occasion of the questioning of Judas by Emperor Julian the Apostate and how Judas reveals his identity, recalling his consecration as bishop by Eusebius of Rome when Helena came to Jerusalem. The martyrdom presents Judas Cyriacus along with his mother, Anna, and a magus, Admon, who suffer martyrdom with him. An unpublished Greek text (Sinai, Gr. 493) gives the exact date of the martyrdom as 25 May 362, the month of Artemisius.

The third legend in which Judas Cyriacus figures exists only in Syriac. It has been incorporated into the *Doctrina Addai* in two sixth-century manuscripts. In this legend, Protonike, the wife of Emperor Claudius, witnesses the miracles of Simon Cephas (Peter) in Rome and believes in Christ. With her two daughters and her son, she goes to James, the Lord's brother and bishop of the town, and asks to see Golgotha, the cross, and the tomb. As the holy places are held by the Jews, she summons the priests Onias ben Hannan, Guedalla ben Kajapha, and Judas ben Ebedshalom to lead her to what she seeks. Scarcely has she reached the three crosses when her daughter dies suddenly. Thanks to the Lord's cross, which becomes identified through that incident, she revives. Protonike goes back to Rome and incites Claudius to issue an edict against the Jews. As a consequence, the Jews, under Trajan, stir up persecution against Symeon, the second bishop of Jerusalem, and the cross is taken by Niketas and buried at a depth equivalent to the height of twenty men. There, according to Eusebius, it remained during the reigns of thirteen bishops until it was found by Judas for the second time.

Such are the Greek and Syriac legends; all three complement one another. But the Coptic tradition is apparently earlier than the Greek form, which begins with the vision of Constantine on the Danube. This episode is intended to blacken the memory of Constantius the Arian, to whom CYRIL OF JERUSALEM had dedicated a letter in 351 on the occasion of the battle of Mursa, in which Constantius II was victorious at the Danube. By bringing this vision back to 312 (Constantine's seventh year), the anonymous apologist places all the enemies of Christianity out of reach of the shame of apostasy. This composition undoubtedly dates from about 400. In fact, the legend of Saint Helena is known by Saint Ambrose in 395 in connection with the death of Theodosius the Great. In Rufinus, at the beginning of the fifth century, Macarius is actually the bishop of the discovery of the Cross. In Socrates and Sozomen, it is always Macarius who is bishop of Jerusalem.

The originality of the Coptic tradition is plain in the panegyric on the cross, attributed to Cyril of Jerusalem, published from a London manuscript by E. A. Wallis Budge in 1915 and A. Campagnano from the Pierpont Morgan Library in 1980.

The origin of this first discovery is easy to find. It had to be explained why the cross had been buried the first time. Moreover, under Claudius, Helena of Adiabene, who was Jewish, traveled to Jerusalem and offered gold utensils for the Jerusalem temple. Of the family of Berenice (Protonike), this Helena was Christianized on account of the second Helena in order better to justify direct dependence on James of Jerusalem. Note that the date 233, as it paradoxically remained in the Greek legend, might correspond to the person of Judas. In any case, the Latin legend of the discovery, which is very old, still mentions the death of Macarius before the nomination of Judas Cyriacus.

Graf (1944, vol. 1, p. 244) gives some details of an Arabic version of the discovery by Helena in Bibliotheca Hagiographica Graeca 395. His data are confined today to a single manuscript, the scattered parts of which belong to a Sinaitic manuscript dated 950. The portion dealing with the discovery of the cross is in a manuscript at Leiden (Oriental Arabic manuscript 14238, fol. 40), as well as in the fragments scattered in two manuscripts (Mingana Arabic 149, 1, and Mingana Arabic 94, fols. 3, 2 and 4). More recent is a sixteenth-century codex in the National Library, Paris (Arabic codex 281, fols. 342–49; Troupeau, 1972, vol. 1, p. 250, n°.27.G., and Graf, 1944), which quotes several other manuscripts.

The Sinaitic manuscript of 950 includes the legend of Cyriacus within the Arabic framework of the dormition of the Virgin in six books, today in the pages preserved at Bryn Mawr College.

BIBLIOGRAPHY

Budge, E. A. W. *Miscellaneous Coptic Texts in the Dialect of Upper Egypt,* pp. 220–26. London, 1915.

Campagnano, A. P. *Cirillo di Gerusalemme. Omelie copte sulla passione, sulla croce et sulla vergine.* Testi e Documenti per lo Studio dell'Antichità, Serie Copta 65, pp. 76–148. Milan, 1980.

Esbroeck, M. van. "L'Opuscule 'sur la croix' d'Alexandre de Chypre et sa version géorgienne." *Bedi Kartlisa* 37 (1979):102–132.

______. "Remembrement d'un manuscrit sinaïtique arabe de 950." *Orientalia Christiana Analecta* 218 (1982):135–47.

Guidi, J. "Textes orientaux inédits du martyr de Judas Cyriaque, évêque de Jérusalem, II. Texte copte." *Revue de l'Orient chrétien* 9 (1904):310–32.

Levison, W. "Konstantinische Schenkung und Silvester-Legende." *Miscellanea Bransesco Ehrle* 2 (1924):159–247.

Troupeau, G. *Catalogue des manuscrits arabes,* Vol. 1. Paris, 1972.

M. VAN ESBROECK

JUDGES. *See* Old Testament, Arabic Versions of the.

JUDGMENT, LAST, belief in a final reckoning after the resurrection of the dead, when God will judge men and reward them for their deeds.

There are copious references to the Last Judgment in both Old and New Testaments: Ecclesiastes 11:9, 12:14; Isaiah 3:13; Matthew 10:15, 11:22, 24; Luke 10:12; Acts 17:31; Hebrews 9:27; 2 Peter 2:9, 3:7; 1 John 4:17. Many of the early fathers of the church treated the subject of the Last Judgment. According to Polycarp of Smyrna, "Whoever perverts the saying of the Lord for his own desires, and says that there is neither resurrection nor judgment, such a one is the first-born of Satan. Let us, therefore, leave the foolishness and the false teaching of the crowd, and turn back to the word which was delivered to us in the beginning" ("[Second] Letter to the Philippians," in Jurgens, 1970–1979, Vol. 1, p. 29).

Saint JOHN CHRYSOSTOM stated, "Let us therefore take courage at His love of mankind and let us be diligent in showing repentance before that day arrives which will preclude our benefiting from repentance. Now everything depends on us; but then He alone who judges will be master of the sentence" ("Homilies on the Gospel of Matthew," in Jurgens, 1970–1979, Vol. 2, p. 111).

Saint Augustine equally affirmed that "just as there are two regenerations, of which I have already spoken above, one according to the faith, which is accomplished now and through Baptism; and the other according to the flesh, . . . so too are there two resurrections: a first one, which takes place now and is of souls; . . . and the second resurrection, which takes place not now, but is to be at the end of time, and which is not of souls but of bodies, and which, through the last judgment, will send some to the second death and others to that life in which there is no death" ("The City of God," in Jurgens, 1970–1979, Vol. 3, p. 103).

In contrast to the Roman Catholic church, the Coptic church preaches one last and general judgment, which will take place after the Second Coming of Christ (Mt. 24:30; Lk. 21:27; 1 Thes. 4:17), and following the general resurrection (Mt. 25: 31–46; 1 Thes. 4:16; Heb. 6:2). It will be a universal judgment, of sinners and pious alike, of the whole man, both body and soul simultaneously. This is attested by the sayings of the early fathers. Thus, Tertullian wrote, "We say, first of all, that it must be believed that the judgment of God is full and perfect, in such a way that it is final and therefore perpetual; and that it is just, since it is not less severe with some than with others; and that, full and perfect, it is worthy of God, since it is in keeping with His patience. It follows, then, that the fullness and perfection of the judgment consists in nothing else than in its representing of the interests of the whole man. Since the whole man is comprised in the union of both substances, he must appear in both; for it is necessary that he who passed through life in his entirety be judged in his entirety" ("The Resurrection of the Dead," in Jurgens, 1970–1979, Vol. 1, p. 149).

[*See also:* Hades; Paradise.]

BIBLIOGRAPHY

Cullmann, O. *Christ and Time.* London, 1951.
Ḥāfiẓ Dāwūd. *Al-Disqūliyyah aw Taʿālīm al-Rusul,* 2nd ed., pp. 123–124. Cairo, 1940.
Jurgens, W. A., trans. *The Faith of the Early Fathers.* 3 vols. Collegeville, Minn., 1970–1979.
Mīkhāʾīl Mīnā. *ʿIlm al-Lāhūt,* Vol. 2, pp. 225–32. Cairo, 1936.
Morris, L. *The Wages of Sin.* London, 1955.
———. *The Biblical Doctrine of Judgement.* London, 1960.

ARCHBISHOP BASILIOS

JULIAN (d. after 518), bishop of Halicarnassus who was a leader of MONOPHYSITISM. Because he was opposed to the orthodox view of the nature of Christ declared at the Council of CHALCEDON, Julian was deposed from his see in Halicarnassus (modern Bodrum, Turkey) and fled to Alexandria, a center of monophysitism. There he became the leader of the religious party known to its opponents as Julianists, or Aphthartodocetae (supporters of the doctrine of incorruptibility, *aphtharsia,* of the body of Christ), or Phantasiastae (supporters of the teaching of a merely phenomenal body of Christ). In fact, Julian taught that the body of Christ "was free of corruption from the moment of union" rather than from the Resurrection only. In the days of His flesh Christ was free from the "corruption" that infected all flesh; for as the Son of Man, he was *homoousios* (consubstantial) with Adam before the Fall, not with man in his present fallen state. Inevitably, this doctrine seemed to suggest analogies with the DOCETISM of an earlier century, a heretical view that the humanity of Christ, especially His body, was "apparent" rather than real. Julian was refuted by other opponents of Chalcedon, notably the moderate Monophysite SEVERUS, patriarch of Antioch, against whom Julian wrote four works. A large series of fragments of these in Syriac and Greek have survived. Some of his letters also have been recovered.

BIBLIOGRAPHY

Bardenhewer, O. *Geschichte der altchristlichen Literatur,* Vol. 5, pp. 2–6. Repr. Darmstadt, 1962.

Draguet, R. *Julien d'Halicarnasse et sa controverse avec Sévère d'Antioche sur l'incorruptibilité du Christ.* Louvain, 1924. Fragments in Syriac and Greek.

———. "Pièces de polémique antijulianiste." *Le Muséon* 44 (1931):255–317; 54 (1941):59–89.

Jugie, M. "Julien d'Halicarnasse et Sévère d'Antioche." *Echos d'Orient* 24 (1925):129–66, 256–85.

Sanda, A., ed. *Severi Antijulianistica.* Beirut, 1931.

MARTINIANO PELLEGRINO RONCAGLIA

JULIAN, EVANGELIST. According to the *Ecclesiastical History* of John of Ephesus, the first Christian missionary to work among the Nubians was a Monophysite priest named Julian. He had earlier accompanied the Coptic patriarch THEODOSIUS I in his exile in Constantinople, and through him had become imbued with a zeal to convert the Nubians. In pursuit of this goal, Julian went to see the Byzantine empress Theodora, who was sympathetic to the Monophysite cause; from her he received an official commission to preach the gospel in the northern Nubian kingdom of NOBATIA. However, the emperor Justinian, the husband of Theodora, ordered instead that a Melchite mission be dispatched to Nobatia. When Theodora heard of this plan she connived with officials in Egypt to delay the departure of the Melchites, with the result that Julian arrived first on the Nubian scene. According to John of Ephesus, he was ardently received by the Nobatians and soon achieved the conversion both of the king and of his subjects. Julian remained in Nobatia for two years, after which his missionary efforts were carried on by Theodore, bishop of Philae. The final conversion of Nobatia was completed by LONGINUS between 569 and 575.

[*See also:* Nubia, Evangelization of.]

BIBLIOGRAPHY

Adams, W. Y. *Nubia, Corridor to Africa,* pp. 441–42. Princeton, N.J., 1977.

Gadallah, F. A. "The Egyptian Contribution to Nubian Christianity." *Sudan Notes and Records* 40 (1959):38–43.

Monneret de Villard, U. *Storia della Nubia cristiana,* pp. 61–64. Orientalia Christiana Analecta 118. Rome, 1938.

Vantini, G. *Christianity in the Sudan,* pp. 38–40. Bologna, 1981.

WILLIAM Y. ADAMS

JULIAN, SAINT, eleventh patriarch of the See of Saint Mark (180–189). He held the office for ten years during the reigns of emperors Marcus Aurelius and Commodus. He was laid to rest on 8 Baramhāt next to the remains of Saint Mark in the Church of Bucalis at Alexandria.

BIBLIOGRAPHY

Atiya, A. S. *History of Eastern Christianity.* Millwood, N.Y., 1980.

AZIZ S. ATIYA

JULIAN THE APOSTATE (332–363), Roman emperor who attempted to restore the classical pantheon. Julian was born in Constantinople, son of Julius Constantius and Basilina. With his half-brother Gallus, he survived the massacre that claimed many of the relatives of Emperor Constantine I on 9 September 337, including their father and elder brother. Julian was, however, removed from the capital, and his early education took place under the supervision of Bishop Eusebius of Nicomedia and the eunuch Mardonius, the latter nominally a Christian but also an admirer of the classics. On Mardonius' death, Emperor Constantius II, Julian's cousin, ordered the brothers' removal to Macellum, a distant imperial estate in Cappadocia (modern Turkey). There Julian studied the classics but, with Gallus, moved closer to Christianity. He was baptized and became a lector and a pupil of Bishop George of Cappadocia (later bishop of Alexandria). In 348 the two princes were recalled to Constantinople, where Julian came into contact with Libanius and other pagan philosophers; thenceforth the pagan classics held his devotion. In 351 Gallus was created caesar, and Julian found greater opportunity to travel. Journeys to Ephesus, Pergamum, and Troy irrevocably committed him to the mystical form of Neoplatonism, to which he adhered for the remainder of his life.

Gallus failed in his function as caesar, and in November 354 Constantius had him executed. This act, coupled with the suspicion that Constantius had been behind the murder of his father in 337, alienated Julian from the emperor. Nevertheless, he had to bide his time. In the same month he found himself accused of abetting anti-imperial activities and was summoned to the imperial court at Milan, but he was saved from Constantius' anger by the empress. He was allowed to go to Athens, where he came into contact with BASIL THE GREAT and his friend GREGORY OF NAZIANZUS, who retained a vivid, if unfavorable, memory of Julian (Gregory *Oratio* 5.23). For Julian it was a happy period in which he was able to visit famous pagan shrines in Greece and finally to renounce Christianity, at least mentally.

In less than a year, however, Julian was back in Milan. Germanic invasions along the Rhine frontier required urgent attention. From a life of study and philosophic debate, he found himself at age twenty-three created caesar (6 November) and sent to Gaul to command the disorganized and demoralized Roman forces. To the surprise of all, Julian, ably assisted by Constantius' generals, proved himself a leader and a sound strategist. In three campaigns (356–358) he completely cleared Gaul and the Rhineland of invaders, winning a decisive victory at Strasbourg in August 357.

Meanwhile, war had broken out with Persia in the east. Constantius needed reinforcements and requested them from Julian's armies. The troops refused to leave Gaul. Early in 360 they revolted and declared Julian emperor, much against his will. For the next eighteen months, Julian was involved in negotiations designed to avoid a civil war, but they failed. He made a triumphant march through the western and Balkan provinces of the empire, but a decisive battle with Constantius was avoided by the latter's death in Cilicia in November 361. Julian entered Constantinople in triumph on 11 December.

During the next twenty months the new emperor feverishly attempted to put the clock back a generation, by restoring worship of Greco-Roman gods as the religion of the empire. Some of Julian's measures were all to the good. The corrupt and noxious crew of court spies and eunuchs with which Constantius had surrounded himself was summarily expelled, and the former emperor's episcopal advisers were replaced by pagans, mainly philosophers. Julian attempted to restore the senate in Constantinople as a center of authority; some excessive taxes on cities were remitted; in the countryside, justice was made more certain by restoring itinerant magistrates (*judices pedanei*), and an adequate low-value coinage on the lines of the *follis* of the tetrarchy was instituted. On the reverse side of these new coins, however, was the sacred bull Apis and the inscription *Securitas Republicae*. The choice was unfortunate, for few would accept that the safety of the state depended on a bull.

Julian began his religious reformation by recalling all those bishops and clergy whom Constantius had exiled, in the cynical belief "that no wild beasts are such enemies to mankind as are most Christians in their deadly hatred of one another" (Ammianus Marcellinus, 22.5.4). In North Africa and in Alexandria his beliefs were justified. On 24 December 361, a mainly pagan mob had lynched Bishop George of Alexandria. After a short interregnum, during which Julian wrote a mild rebuke to the Alexandrians for their violent behavior (*Letter* 21), ATHANASIUS I, who had been deposed in favor of George, was allowed to return to his episcopal city (21 February 362).

Julian's attempt to restore paganism was hopeless from the start. Though the Celtic provinces of the empire were very largely pagan, in the wealthiest and most important areas, including Egypt, worship of the traditional deities had been giving way increasingly to Christianity. His attempt to organize paganism in a form imitating the Christian hierarchy failed to catch on, as did his effort to instill a sense of purpose and practice of charitable action among the pagan priests. As he admitted to Arsacius, high priest of Galatia (*Letter* 22), "the Hellenic religion does not yet prosper as I desire." Christian benevolence to strangers, care of the graves of the dead, and the pretended holiness of their lives had done most to increase atheism (i.e., Christianity). Julian was to find out the truth of this for himself at Antioch in 362–363.

Julian so far had confined himself to administrative measures, to rescinding privileges conferred on Christian clergy by Constantius (Sozomen *Historia ecclesiastica* 5.15), to exhortation and admonishment of his correspondents to return to the gods (*Letter* 41, to the citizens of Bostra), and to the unconditional restoration of temple property taken over by Christians to the former owners. There were, however, two exceptions. Athanasius, who had managed to proselytize in favor of Christianity at Alexandria and to hold an important church council in the summer of 362, was once more exiled as a "bad man" (*Letter* 46).

More important was Julian's effort to curb Christians who were teaching the pagan classics. On 17 June 362, he ordered that, before teaching, all professors must obtain a license from their city council countersigned by himself. There was nothing in this about Christians, but they later did not receive licenses, on the pretext of their not being sufficiently sincere in their work (*Codex Theodosianus* 13.3.5; cf. Julian, *Letter* 42). Six months later he went further, forbidding Christians to teach the liberal arts (Bidez, 1930, p. 263). Though consistent with his policy of favoring paganism and restoring it as an integrated force in education and worship, this act dismayed Julian's friends. For Ammianus it was something that "should be passed over in eternal silence" (*Res gestae* 25.4.20; cf. 22.10.7), and Christians were too firmly entrenched in the educational system throughout the East to be seriously inconvenienced, at least in the short term.

By this time, the summer of 362, Julian had established his headquarters in Antioch, preparing for what he hoped would be a final reckoning with Persia. On two counts his romanticism played him false. First his effort to restore paganism in Antioch only provoked ridicule and discontent among the populace and involved the emperor in an undignified squabble with local satirists (recorded by Julian in his *Misopogon* ["the Beard-Hater"]). Second, instead of a well-prepared, limited campaign to retake ground lost by Constantius in 359–360 and secure for the empire a defensible frontier on the Tigris with Persia—which, as events showed, was within his power—he aspired to emulate Alexander the Great and conquer Persia outright. It was an impossible dream. Beginning his campaign on 5 March 363, Julian won a series of brilliant victories on his march down the Euphrates toward Ctesiphon. There, like others before and after him, he was checked. Fatal miscalculations (or perhaps an act of treachery) caused him to retire up the east bank of the Tigris; and with the river behind them, his forces were counterattacked by the Persians. Even so, Julian might have made good his retreat by virtue of the superior fighting ability of his troops. But on 26 June he was wounded by a spear thrown from an unknown hand. The wound proved fatal, and he died around midnight on 26 June 363.

Christians were to claim that the emperor's death was due to the hand of God. By the sixth century, the credit for his death had been given to the Cappadocian martyr Mercurius, supposedly a general who had suffered for his Christian faith under Emperor Decius in the third century. This story became current in Egypt, and the HISTORY OF THE PATRIARCHS records how Mercurius was sent by God to punish Julian for his apostasy, and that he struck the emperor through the head with his lance. The *History* records Basil the Great as the source of this account, though placing it under the episcopate of Athanasius. A document found in the cathedral of Qaṣr Ibrīm in Nubia shows a further development of the legend, in which Athanasius himself and Saint PACHOMIUS are the central figures. Pachomius has a vision of Mercurius, who tells him how he struck down the "enemy of God," Julian, and this he relates to Athanasius (Frend, 1986). Pachomius had, of course, long been dead at the time; but the version of the legend, repeated on a fresco from the cathedral at Faras, shows the desire of the Coptic and Nubian churches to associate Athanasius with Julian's destruction. In addition, it demonstrates the role of the Byzantine military saints in the protection of the Christian religion and, in the case of Nubia, the national identity of the Christian Nubian kingdoms.

BIBLIOGRAPHY

Athanassiadi-Fowden, P. *Julian and Hellenism, an Intellectual Biography*. Oxford, 1981.

Baynes, N. H. "The Death of the Emperor Julian in Christian Legend." *Journal of Roman Studies* 27 (1937):22–29.

Bidez, J. *La Vie de l'empereur Julien*. Paris, 1930.

Borries, E. "Julianos (Apostata)." In *Real-Encyclopädie*, Vol. 19, cols. 26–91. Stuttgart, 1917. Also Supplement, Vol. 8, cols. 755–756, no. 141.

Bowersock, G. W. *Julian the Apostate*. London, 1978.

Browning, R. *The Emperor Julian*. Berkeley, Calif., 1976.

Frend, W. H. C. "Hero of a Lost Cause." *The Rise of Christianity*, chap. 17. Philadelphia and London, 1984.

______. "Fragments of an Acta Martyrum from Qasr Ibrim." *Jahrbuch für Antike und Christentum* 29 (1986):66–70.

Glover, T. R. *Life and Letters in the Fourth Century*. New York, 1925.

Malley, J. *Hellenism and Christianity*. Analecta Gregoriana 210. Rome, 1978.

W. H. C. FREND

JULIUS OF AQFAHṢ. *See* Martyrs, Coptic.

JULLIEN, MICHEL MARIE (1827–1911), French Jesuit missionary. He served in Egypt from 1880 to 1886. After an interlude of ten years in Syria, he returned in 1896 to Egypt, where he remained until his death. He was a member of the Institut d'Egypte, a founder of the first Coptic-Catholic seminary at Ṭahṭā (1899), and the initiator of the modern pilgrimage to the Virgin of Maṭariyyah, a church dedicated in 1904 to the Holy Family. His writings, which detail his explorations and researches on ancient Christian Egypt, have remained very useful: *L'Egypte, souvenirs bibliques et chrétiens* (1899) and *Sinaï et Syrie, souvenirs bibliques et chrétiens* (1893). Also there are some precious articles on the condition of Coptic monasteries in Upper Egypt at the turn of the nineteenth century in *Missions catholiques* (October 1894, June 1901, June 1902, April–June 1903).

BIBLIOGRAPHY

Martin, M. "Notes inédites du P. Jullien sur trois monastères chrétiens d'Egypte: dêr Abou Fâna, le couvent des 'Sept-Montagnes' et dêr amba Bisâda." *Bulletin de l'Institut français d'Archéologie orientale* 71 (1972):119–28.

Munier, H. "Les Monuments coptes d'après les explorations du P. Michel Jullien." *Bulletin de la Société d'Archéologie copte* 6 (1940):141–68.

MAURICE MARTIN, S.J.

JUNKER, HERMANN (1877–1962), German Egyptologist and Coptologist. He studied for the Catholic priesthood at Trier and then at Berlin with Egyptology as his major. He joined the University of Vienna in 1907. He was also involved in the foundation of the Institute of Egyptology and African Studies at Vienna University (1923), served as director of the German Archaeological Institute in Cairo (1929), and became professor of Egyptology at Cairo University. Junker was primarily an archaeologist, epigraphist, and "field man."

His excavations were all related to dynastic Egypt, and his colossal output is mainly in the field of Egyptology. Nevertheless, he made a number of significant contributions to Coptic studies.

BIBLIOGRAPHY

Dawson, W. R., and E. P. Uphill. *Who Was Who in Egyptology*, pp. 154–55. London, 1972.

Kammerer, W., comp. *A Coptic Bibliography*. Ann Arbor, Mich., 1950; repr. New York, 1969.

AZIZ S. ATIYA

JUSTIN I (c. 450–527), Byzantine emperor who worked for orthodoxy and the reunion of Rome and Constantinople. He was born about 450 in Bederiana (in modern Yugoslavia). Of peasant stock, he followed his father into the Roman army, fighting with distinction against the Isaurian rebels in 498, the Persians from 502 to 505, and the rebel general Vitalian in 514. He became captain of the imperial guard.

On the death of Emperor Anastasius on 8 July 518, Justin was proclaimed emperor. It soon became clear that his religious policy would be radically different from the anti-Chalcedonic stance (see CHALCEDON, COUNCIL OF) of his predecessor. In this Justin was following popular opinion in Constantinople, parts of Syria, and Jerusalem, which increasingly demanded the unequivocal assertion of the canonical status of the Council of Chalcedon, the removal of the Monophysite patriarch SEVERUS OF ANTIOCH from his see, and the restoration of communion with Rome broken by the ACACIAN SCHISM in 482. The first two demands were easily met. Regarded by the sixth-century historian Theodorus Lector as a "blazing zealot" on behalf of Chalcedon, Justin had Severus deposed as early as 20 July.

Ending the Acacian Schism took longer, since Pope Hormisdas was determined to use the situation to gain every possible advantage for the papacy. Between 7 September 518, when Justin informed the pope of his steps to end the conflict (*Collectio Avellana*, nos. 143, 146), and 28 March 519, when patriarch John, of Constantinople, signed the papal letter, tortuous negotiations took place (see Vasiliev, 1950, pp. 166ff). The papal legates who arrived in the capital on 25 March insisted that the price of ending the schism must be the condemnation not only of Acacius patriarch of Constantinople (471–489), but also of his four successors and the emperors ZENO and Anastasius. The weak handling of the negotiation by Patriarch John allowed the papacy to gain a tactical victory over the claims of Constantinople, which caused lasting bitterness in the East. However, Justin himself had directed the course of the negotiations (*Collectio Avellana*, no. 161), and kept supreme authority in ecclesiastical (as opposed to doctrinal) matters in his hands. He did not intend to see his patriarch humiliated, and John was the first patriarch of Constantinople to use the later much disputed title "ecumenical patriarch." All the anathemas except that directed against Acacius were quickly allowed to lapse.

Justin had intended the return of the ecclesiastical situation to the status quo before Acacius and the consequent reunion of Rome and Constantinople. On 7 September 518, Justin's nephew, the already powerful Count JUSTINIAN (who later became emperor), had written to Hormisdas, informing him that his presence in Constantinople was awaited "without delay." There was no question in the emperor's mind of subjecting his own authority or that of his patriarch to the papacy. He was concerned, as Zeno had been, with the religious unity of the empire, except that he saw this unity not in terms of Zeno's HENOTICON but in terms of the canonical status of the four ecumenical councils and the unity of Rome and Constantinople, the Old and New Rome.

Between 521 and 523 Justin took stern measures to enforce the new ecclesiastical order. In Asia Minor, Syria, and Mesopotamia, some fifty-five bishops were expelled (the names of fifty are listed in the *Chronicon ad annum 846 pertinens*, pp. 171–173), including strong anti-Chalcedonians such as Philoxenus of Maboug and John of Tella. Such massive uprooting of clergy supported by a strong current of religious loyalties in the East made the establishment of an anti-Chalcedonian hierarchy inevitable. During Justin's reign the first tentative steps were taken toward the formation of the Monophysite church, independent of Byzantine orthodoxy.

In Egypt, however, Justin's measures had little effect. According to Zacharias Rhetor (*Historia ecclesiastica* 8.5), "the see of Alexandria was hardly disturbed, and Timothy succeeded Dioscorus [in 517] and he neither retired nor accepted the synod [of Chalcedon] in the days of Justin." Alexandria became a haven for anti-Chalcedonian exiles, including Severus and the bishop JULIAN OF HALICARNASSUS. The Egyptian church remained united against the *Tome* of Pope LEO I and Chalcedon, as Severus justly claimed (Severus *Select Letters* 8.11).

In one important particular, also, Justin showed that the major interests of the empire overrode ecclesiastical policy. In the early years of the sixth century, missions known collectively as those of the Nine Saints had arrived in Ethiopia, preaching an anti-Chalcedonian faith and practicing a monastic order based on the Pachomian Rule. By Justin's reign, Ethiopia and its dependent territory of Yemen were in the anti-Chalcedonian camp. Yemen, however, was also an area where Roman and Persian influences clashed; and in 523, when war broke out between the Yemeni Jews supported by Persia and the Christians, Justin supported the Christian cause. The defense of Najran and the massacre of Christians that resulted from its fall in 523 were avenged by an Ethiopian army supplied and victualed by Justin, using TIMOTHY III, patriarch of Alexandria, as his intermediary with the Ethiopian court. Christianity was not threatened again in Yemen until the reign of Justin II in the late sixth century.

In 526, the final year of his reign, Pope John I visited Constantinople as an emissary of Theodoric the Ostrogoth. The Pope was permitted to crown the emperor, but otherwise the preeminence of the patriarch in the imperial capital was maintained (see Vasiliev, 1950, pp. 212–21).

Justin's short reign had an importance disproportionate to its length. His policies showed that the Latin-speaking provinces still counted in the empire. The unity of the two Romes and the canonical status of Chalcedon were affirmed as the cornerstones of imperial ecclesiastical policy. There could be no return to the anti-Chalcedonian policy of Emperor Anastasius. Alexandria and the Coptic Christians were left on the sidelines, and Alexandria was to find that its claim to be "the city of the orthodox" could be sustained only outside the orbit of Byzantine and Latin Christianity.

BIBLIOGRAPHY

Frend, W. H. C. *The Rise of the Monophysite Movement*, 2nd ed., chaps. 6, 8. Cambridge, 1979.

Moberg, A. *The Book of the Himyarites*. Lund, 1924.

Ryckmans, J. *La Persécution des chrétiens humyarites au sixième siècle*. Istanbul 1956.

Shahîd, I. "Byzantium in South Arabia." *Dumbarton Oaks Papers* 33 (1980):23–94.

Vasiliev, A. *Justin the First*. Dumbarton Oaks Studies 1. Cambridge, Mass., 1950. Contains full bibliography of source and secondary material.

W. H. C. FREND

JUSTIN II (d. 578), Byzantine emperor who lost territory in war and shifted from toleration of MONOPHYSITISM to persecution. Justin was a nephew of the emperor JUSTINIAN and was married to Sophia, the niece of Justinian's wife, THEODORA I. He held the post of *curophlates* (palace administrator). When Justinian died in 565 the succession was a matter of speculation, for he had left no son and no clear instructions. As the choice of the Senate and John III Scholasticus, patriarch of Constantinople, he secured the succession over the claims of Justin son of Germanus without difficulty though not without ill feeling (Evagrius, 1898). A heavy investment in propaganda is evident from the Latin panegyric of the court poet Corippus, written shortly after Justin's accession (Corippus, 1976). Corippus claimed that Justinian had named Justin on his deathbed (perhaps an addition in 566, in view of opposition to Justin) and laid great stress on his relation to Justinian. There were also claims of support for Justin by the patriarch Eutychius and the stylite Symeon the Younger.

Justin's reign began well enough with attempts at reconciliation with the Monophysites. He restored those exiled by Justinian and attempted to win agreement with the Monophysites by issuing an edict aimed at their concerns and calling a meeting at Callinicum. His efforts were rejected, however, and he turned to persecution in the early 570s. Many bishops were again exiled. After the loss of Dara in Mesopotamia to the Persians in 573, he went mad. In 574 he made Count Tiberius caesar in an affecting speech in which he asked forgiveness from God and the people for his errors. John of Ephesus was certain that his madness was a punishment for the persecution of the Monophysites.

Justin's reign was remarkable for the prominence of the empress Sophia. According to JOHN OF EPHESUS, she tried hard to gain control when Justin became ill and largely succeeded for a time. She was featured with the emperor on coins and was named coruler in legal documents. Evidently conscious of the prestige of being Theodora's niece, she seems to have had strong religious inclinations herself. She is represented by Corippus as expressing public devotion to the Virgin Mary and as linking with Justin in sending a fragment of the True Cross to Poitiers. Nevertheless, she was finally ousted from power by Tiberius, who was made augustus before Justin's death in 578.

BIBLIOGRAPHY

Bury, J. B. *History of the Later Roman Empire from Arcadius to Irene II.* London, 1899.

Cameron, A. *Continuity and Change in Sixth-Century Byzantium.* London, 1981.

Frend, W. H. C. *The Rise of the Monophysite Movement.* Cambridge, England, 1972.

AVERIL CAMERON

JUSTINIAN (c. 482–565), Byzantine emperor. Originally given the name Petrus Sabbatius, he took the name Justinian upon being adopted by his uncle Justin, whom he later succeeded as emperor (1 August 527). Justinian's reign was marked by extensive legal reform, successful military incursions against the Vandals and the Goths, vast architectural undertakings, and an intense but unsuccessful attempt to unite the Chalcedonians and Monophysites.

Justinian believed that Rome had been a great nation, and he felt it was his task to restore its preeminence. A major thrust of this restoration took the form of a renovation of the Roman legal system. On 7 April 529 a commission headed by Justinian's legal expert, Tribonian, produced the first CODEX JUSTINIANUS, a revision and expansion of Theodosian's Code. The *Institutes,* based on the legal text compiled by the second-century Roman jurist Gaius, was published in 533. The *Digest,* consisting of codified excerpts of the classical jurists, followed on 16 December 533, and a second, revised edition of the Codex Justinianus, on 16 November 534. Subsequently Justinian added to, and modified, these constitutions through more than 150 *Novellae.* Together these works established a single code of law incorporating all of the constitutions back to the time of the emperor Hadrian (117–138).

Another aspect of Justinian's restoration unfolded in battles against the barbarians, who had encroached on the empire's borders. On the eastern frontier he was forced to fight a lengthy and inconclusive war with the Persians. Although a treaty arranged in 532 was designed to end this war, fighting broke out again in 540 and continued with intermittent truces until a new treaty was compacted in 562. Fortunes in North Africa were more salubrious. On 13 September 533, Justinian's troops, led by Belisarius, defeated the Vandals at Ad Decimum. On the next day, they captured Carthage. The Vandal kingdom was dismantled quickly and efficiently. ARIANISM fled before the incursion of Catholicism. Belisarius next turned his attention to Italy, where he conducted successful campaigns against the Ostrogoths during the years 535–540; Justinian's general Narses finally subdued the Ostrogoths completely in 553. Meanwhile, in 551, a major portion of Visigothic Spain was conquered.

Throughout the empire Justinian not only renovated older buildings and aqueducts but also erected churches, monasteries, and fortresses. The most notable achievement of this building campaign was the cathedral of Hagia Sophia in Constantinople. After five years of construction, the church, which was built after the plan of a Greek cross with an octagonal dome, was dedicated on Saint Stephen's Day 537.

In an attempt to establish orthodoxy and harmony throughout the empire, Justinian enacted legislation against the major heresies of his day, such as Nestorianism, Eutychianism, and Apollinarianism. In 529 he closed the Academy of Athens, thus ridding the empire of its last outpost of pagan intellectualism. But Justinian was thwarted in his boldest religious undertaking, for despite his diligent efforts, he was unable to close the rift between the Monophysites and Chalcedonians. When he failed in his attempt to unite the two sides in acceptance of the Theopaschite formula "one of the Trinity suffered in the flesh" and when a series of meetings between the two groups in 532 and early 533 did nothing to reduce the tension, Justinian ratified the banishment imposed by a home synod on the Monophysite leader Severus in 536.

Next he tried to reintroduce Origenism, but this attempt to provide a Christological concept acceptable to both sides also failed, and in 543, Justinian condemned ORIGEN, a move that resulted ultimately in the loss of many of that churchman's works. The next approach involved removing from the pacts of the Council of CHALCEDON those points most offensive to the Monophysites. Accordingly, sometime between 543 and 546, Justinian issued an edict condemning the Three Chapters—that is, the writings of THEODORUS OF MOPSUESTIA, THEODORET's work against Cyril's *Twelve Anathemas,* and the *Christological Letter* of Ibas of Edessa. However, at the Fifth Ecumenical Council, convened on 5 May 553 in the secretariat of Hagia Sophia, the edict won scant support, and it also failed to bridge the gap between the two groups.

Justinian's inability to bring religious unity to the empire may have been indicative of a failure to establish peace at home. THEODORA, Justinian's wife, was a strong and active supporter of the Monophysites. Often working behind the scenes without Justinian's knowledge, she arranged shelter for Monophysite clergy who had been exiled; encouraged the mission of JACOB BARADAEUS to Syria, where he ordained a large number of Monophysite priests; and promoted Monophysite missions to Nubia. The historian Procopius, who left one of the best records of Justinian and his accomplishments, felt her actions had a decidedly divisive influence on the empire.

Justinian died in 565, leaving the empire larger and better equipped with legal codes, trade relations, and architectural splendors than it had been at his accession, but overextended, open to attack by the Slavs and Lombards, and the Monophysite schism involving Egypt and Nubia without prospect of settlement.

BIBLIOGRAPHY

Barker, J. W. *Justinian and the Later Roman Empire.* Madison, Wis., 1966.

Browning, R. *Justinian and Theodora.* London, 1987.

Cameron, A. *Procopius.* London, 1985.

Downey, G. A. *Constantinople in the Age of Justinian.* Norman, Okla., 1960.

Frend, W. H. C. *The Rise of the Monophysite Movement.* Cambridge, 1979.

______. *The Rise of Christianity,* pp. 527–65. Philadelphia, 1984.

Rubin, B. *Das Zeitalter Justinians.* Berlin, 1960.

RANDALL STEWART

JUSTUS, sixth patriarch of the See of Saint Mark (122–130). He held the office during the reign of Emperor Hadrian. He was laid to rest on 12 Ba'ūnah next to the remains of Saint Mark in the Church of Bucalis at Alexandria.

AZIZ S. ATIYA

JUSTUS, SAINT, martyr in fourth-century Egypt. Justin is related to the Antiochene cycle concerning the family of the Roman general BASILIDES (see CYCLES). His Passion was presumably written later, when the descriptive elements of the cycle were already much developed and the kinships among people were very elaborate. The Passion was handed down through two quite different redactions, in two incomplete codices both dated to the ninth century: one in Sahidic (Winstedt, 1910, pp. 188–99) and the other in Bohairic (White, 1926, pp. 78–82). The more complete text is in Sahidic. A version similar to the Bohairic exists in Ethiopic (Pereira, 1955, pp. 73–98).

The title of this text mentions, in addition to Justus, his wife, Stephanou, his daughter, Sophia, and the son of Basilides, the martyr Eusebius. The text begins with the apostasy of the Roman emperor DIOCLETIAN, briefly explained in the Bohairic version by the treason of the Antiochene bishop, who returns Nicomedes, the captured son of the king of Persia, to the Persians in exchange for money. Diocletian asks the heathen priests what he must do. They order him to make sacrifices and persecute the Christians. Many people refuse to obey his edict. Here the character of Justus is introduced, the son of the emperor before Diocletian, who was a friend of Basilides. The text also reports the well-known late legend that Diocletian was an Egyptian called Agrippidas.

In the Sahidic version Justus and Eusebius confess their faith in front of Diocletian in Rome. In the Bohairic version Justus comes with Apoli and Theoclia. Diocletian sends them all to the prefect Armenius in Egypt, who in turn sends them to the south to the prefect Arianus. The Sahidic manuscript is interrupted here, while the Bohairic text reports the martyrdom of Justus and Eusebius under Arianus.

BIBLIOGRAPHY

Pereira, M. E. *Acta Martyrum.* CSCO 37–38, *Scriptores Aethiopici* 20–21. Louvain, 1955.

White, H. G. *New Coptic Texts from the Monastery of Saint Macarius.* New York, 1926.

Winstedt, E. O. *Coptic Texts on Saint Theodore the General, Saint Theodore the Eastern, Chamoul and Justus.* London and Oxford, 1910.

TITO ORLANDI

K

KAFR AYYUB. *See* Pilgrimages.

KAFR AL-DAYR. *See* Pilgrimages.

KAHLE, PAUL ERIC (1923–1955), British Coptologist of German extraction. He was the son of Professor Paul Ernst Kahle, the eminent Orientalist. His family fled to England from Hitler's Germany in 1938. He held the Laycock Studentship in Egyptology at Worcester College, Oxford, for the years 1948–1954, during which he studied under Battiscombe George Gunn. He was elected to the Lady Wallis Budge Fellowship at University College, Oxford, in 1954. He published a large collection of literary and documentary material from the monastery of Dayr al-Balayzah, at Asyūṭ in Upper Egypt, arriving at important conclusions regarding the distribution of Coptic dialects: *Bala'izah: Coptic Texts from Bala'izah in Upper Egypt* (2 vols., Oxford, 1954). He died at Charlbury, Oxfordshire.

BIBLIOGRAPHY

Dawson, W. R., and E. P. Uphill. *Who Was Who in Egyptology,* p. 155. London, 1972.

M. L. BIERBRIER

KAHYOR. *See* Monasteries of the Middle Ṣa'īd.

KALABSHA. *See* Talmīs.

KALAMON. *See* Dayr Anbā Ṣamū'īl of Qalamūn.

KALLILEION. *See* Anointing.

KAMIL MURAD. *See* Murad Kamil.

KANEBO. *See* Museums, Coptic Collections in.

KARABACEK, JOSEPH VON (1845–1918), Austrian Orientalist. He became privatdocent for paleography and numismatics of Islamic peoples at the University of Vienna in 1869, was made professor extraordinary in 1874, was professor ordinary of history of the East and related subjects from 1885 to 1915, and served as prefect of the Court Library from 1899 to 1917. The library is indebted to him for much of its preeminent collection of ancient texts. In 1893, Karabacek was able to acquire for Vienna around ten thousand Coptic, Greek, and Arabic papyri that had been found in the Fayyūm in 1877–1880. His cooperative efforts with Theodor Graf were beneficial to him in his purchases for the library, outlined in *Die Theodor Graf'schen Funde in Ägypten* (Vienna, 1883) and *K.-k. österreichisches Museum: Katalog der Theodor Graf'schen Funde in Ägypten* (Vienna, 1883). The editions of Arabic texts that he had prepared were continued and published by Adolf Grohmann.

BIBLIOGRAPHY

Loebenstein, H. "Vom 'Papyrus Erzherzog Rainer' zur Papyrussammlung der österreichischen Nationalbibliothek. 100 Jahre Sammeln, Bewahren, Edieren." *Festschrift zum 100 jährigen Bestehen der Papyrussammlung der österreichischen Natio-*

nalbibliothek: Papyrus Erzherzog Rainer. Vienna, 1983.

Österreichisches biographisches Lexikon, 1815–1950, Vol. 3, pp. 228–29. Graz and Cologne, 1965.

MARTIN KRAUSE

KARANIS, an ancient Egyptian farming village that was a lively center of Christianity in the third, fourth, and fifth centuries. It was north of the Fayyūm some 20 miles (30 km) from Arsinoë, the metropolis of Arsinoë Nome. Excavations have supplied only mute evidence of village life, in the form of Coptic textiles and Roman coins. But a large number of papyri, about 5,000 documents, from the third century B.C. to the fifth century A.D. give a good picture of daily concerns: they include Egyptian texts found at Karanis and Greek Christian texts from the nearby village of Soknopaiou Nesos, which disappeared at the end of the third century. Ten of the papyri from Soknopaiou Nesos, written later than the third century, could have been found in the neighborhood of Karanis.

Situated not far from the ancient Egyptian religious center of Nilopolis in the Fayyūm and Soknopaiou Nesos, Karanis itself had a temple of the crocodile god Peisouchos attended by numerous clergy—fifty-four priests and fifty *pastophori* (priests of a lower class). Demotic Egyptian was still written and spoken there in the second and third centuries.

Christianity, however, took root there early. In the middle of the third century, according to *The Archive of Aurelius Isidorus* (hereafter referred to as *P. Cair. Isid.*), some inhabitants gave their sons Christian names. Petros, born about 250 or earlier, father of Polion, did not know how to write in Greek (Boak and Youte, 1960, 81. 3. 31; also Preisigke et al., 1915–1983, 7676). Johannes, born about the same time, was a gymnasiarch and could write in Greek (*P. Cair. Isid.* 114. 1. 15; 115. 2. 8). Paulos was born about 290–300 (*P. Cair Isid.* 77. 30). These men were among those tenants who held an average of about 25 acres (10 hectares), which put them into the best-endowed part of the population.

We have no archaeological evidence of a church or monastery, but repeated mention by the papyri of the presence of deacons in the fourth century proves the existence of a church community. These deacons shared the life of the region. One of them, Amaeis, fulfilled his obligation for work on the embankments (Browne, 1970, 595. 5. 10). Another, Aion, paid a land tax that placed him a little below the average in the list of taxpayers in which he appears (Brower, 1975, 12. 651. 4). Still another, Antoniaos, was in the company of a monk, Isak, in the fields around the village. This is the first use of the word "monk" in the papyri (Bagnall, 1979, 12. 171. 15). Isak came to the help of Isidoros, son of Ptolemaios and father of the Paulos previously mentioned.

This Isidorus, a descendant of a Roman soldier and himself a Christian, had been exasperated at seeing a cow owned by two villagers lay waste his harvest. In conformity with Roman law (Oxyrynchus Papyrus 2704), he seized the offending animal for confiscation and sale at auction for the benefit of the treasury (*P. Cair. Isid.* 78; Rees, 1959, p. 92). The cow's owners attacked and beat him. Through the intervention of the deacon and the monk, the wounded man was rescued and the cow restored to its owners.

In the fourth century, the gradual drying of the periphery of the Fayyūm made agricultural life precarious. Karanis, whose cultivated land extended down from the little cliff on which the village was built, was close to the canal leading the flood waters from the Nile as far as Soknopaiou Nesos. The safeguarding of the water supply was a collective matter for the men of Karanis representing the state authorities.

In the fifth century the clergy of Karanis had responsibility for the water supply. A Greek document dated 20 May 439 (Preisigke et al., 1915–1983, 14. 11357), the last of those that have come down to us from Soknopaiou Nesos, is an official writing that shows twelve priests and five deacons playing the role formerly played by the elders of the village. They undertook to watch over the use of the water under the control of the prefect through the agency of a *numerarius* ("accountant"). In this arrangement the village scribe writes for those priests and deacons "who do not know how to write" (that is, write Greek); in fact, they no doubt knew Coptic, as the use of a fourth- or fifth-century Coptic biblical text found at Karanis tends to prove. In the early sixth century, well before the Arab conquest in 641, Karanis became extinct. (Browne, 1979, p. 2).

BIBLIOGRAPHY

Bagnall, R. *Fourth Century Documents from Karanis*. Missoula, Mont. 1979.

———. "Religious Conversion and Onomastic Change in Early Byzantine Egypt." *Bulletin of the*

American Society of Papyrologists 19 (1982):105–123.
Boak, A. E. *Karanis, Topographical and Architectural Report of Excavations during the Seasons 1924–1928.* Ann Arbor, Mich., 1931.
Boak, A. E., and H. C. Youte. *The Archive of Aurelius Isidorus.* Ann Arbor, Mich., 1960.
Bonneau, D. "Un Règlement de l'usage de l'eau au Ve siècle de notre ère." Hommages Serge Sauneron 2, pp. 3–23. Cairo, 1979.
Browne, G. M. *Documentary Papyri from the Michigan Collection.* Toronto, 1970.
______. *Michigan Papyri* XII. Toronto, 1975.
______. *Michigan Coptic Texts.* Barcelona, 1979.
Geremek, H. *Karanis. Communauté rurale de l'Egypte romaine au IIe–IIIe siècle de notre ère,* pp. 41–52. Warsaw, 1969.
Haelst, J. van. *Catalogue des papyrus littéraires juifs et chrétiens.* Paris, 1976.
Husselman, E. M. *Karanis: Topography and Architecture.* Ann Arbor, Mich., 1979.
Judge, E. A. "The Earliest Use of Monachos for 'Monk' (*Youtie* 77) and the Origins of Monasticism." *Jahrbuch für Antike und Christentum* 20 (1977):72–89.
Modrzejewski, J. "Ulpien et la nature des animaux." *Accademia Nazionale dei Lincei* 373, no. 1 (1976):1177–99.
Preisigke, F.; F. Bilabel; E. Kiessling; and H. A. Rupprecht, eds. *Sammelbuch griechischer Urkunden aus Ägypten.* Published in various places, 1915–1983.
Rees, B. R. *Greek Papyri in the Collection of W. Merton,* Vol. 2. Dublin, 1959.

DANIELLE BONNEAU

KARARAH. *See* Qarārah.

KĀRIMĪ GUILD, one of the most important guilds of merchants in the history of the Middle East. It conducted extensive trade between the East and the West at the end of the Middle Ages, including the Kārimī commerce in spices, jewelery, and precious stones, from the Far East to the coast of the Mediterranean Sea, via the Red Sea and the Eastern Desert of Egypt and the Nile Valley. Its centers were in QŪṢ, Cairo, Alexandria, and Damietta.

It is still difficult to trace the origin of the Kārimī. However, the first reference to these merchants goes back to the tenth century, and particularly to the Fatimid epoch in Egypt. Though the first names among the membership of the guild are Muslim and Jewish, there is no doubt that Copts were also represented among them.

Even though the earliest roots of the Kārimīs are still enveloped in mystery, and though the detection of the names of Coptic merchants among the Kārimī guild is still difficult, it is known that the last participation of the Copts coincided with the beginning of the Crusades and a change in Egypt's commercial policy during the reign of the Ayyubids, which made it incumbent upon this guild to be Islamic and its members Muslims.

Perhaps the last notable Copt of this guild was the Kārimī merchant Abū al-Majd ibn Abī Ghālib ibn Sāwīrus, who lived in the closing years of the Fatimid dynasty and the opening years of Ayyubid rule in the reign of Ṣalāḥ al-Dīn (1171–1193). He died less than two years before the Ayyubid sultan al-Kāmil (1218–1238) came to power. Abū al-Majd had endowed his enormous wealth, amounting to 17,000 dinars, to charity after he, as a layman, was selected to become the seventy-fourth patriarch of the Coptic Church, under the name of JOHN VI (1167–1189).

BIBLIOGRAPHY

Labib, S. Y. *Sozial und Wirtschaftsgeschichte. Handelsgeschichte Ägyptens im Spätmittelalter (1171–1517).* Wiesbaden, 1965.

SUBHI Y. LABIB

KARM AL-AKHBĀRIYYAH, a small settlement from the late Roman period in the Mareotis, about 5 miles (8 km) northeast of Abū Mīnā. The place contains only a few buildings, among which were also some agricultural structures such as cisterns and a wine press. Excavations so far have been limited to the church and its immediate ancillary buildings, to which also belongs a small court adjacent on the north side. The church is a small, short basilica of the usual form with an apse in the east but no apse side rooms (*pastophoria*). The north main entrance is adorned with an outer prothyron. On the west there is a later annex like a narthex, which, however, can be entered only from inside the church. North of this lies the baptistery.

The special significance of this church lies in the paintings once contained in it, which reveal a high artistic standard. Unfortunately these are completely destroyed, and could be recovered only in the form of numerous small, painted-plaster fragments strewn over the floor of the church. It will take years of work before a reassembling of the fragments can be completed.

BIBLIOGRAPHY

Grossmann, P. "Kirche am Karm al-Akhbarīya." *Mitteilungen des Deutschen Archäologischen Instituts—Abteilung Kairo* 26 (1970):75.

Müller-Wiener, W. "Die Kirche im Karm al-Akhbarīya." *Archäologischer Anzeiger* (1967):473–80.

PETER GROSSMANN

KARNAK IN THE CHRISTIAN PERIOD.

The temple at Karnak formed an immense complex of buildings dedicated to the worship of Amon. Today the oldest known remains go back to the Eleventh Dynasty (about 2100 B.C.) and occupy the central core known as the Court of the Middle Kingdom. From this core the temple continued to develop, principally toward the west in the direction of the Nile and toward the south, but also toward the east. This development, realized in a succession of hypostyle halls and of courts separated by enormous pylons, was only completed at the end of the Ptolemaic era. All the great pharaohs of the New Kingdom and of the Late Period contributed to this extension, sometimes usurping the monuments of their predecessors, altering them, or occupying their places. Simultaneously with these constructions, the precincts of Amon continued to grow, enclosing a large number of minor buildings.

With the decline of the pharaonic civilization, the complex became set in the situation in which we see it today. The domain of Amon then covered 30 hectares, of which eight were built over. It was in these abandoned and partly ruined monuments that the Christian population established itself from the fourth century, remaining no doubt until the eighth, after which it gradually declined. We find this situation in all the other great Theban temples. The Christians made great use of unbaked brick in their constructions, at the same time taking advantage of the existing stone walls.

Saint John the Baptist depicted on the fourth column on the eastern side in the festival hall of Tuthmosis III at Karnak. *Courtesy A. Sadek.*

The great festival hall of Tuthmosis III in Amon's Temple, Karnak. *Courtesy A. Sadek.*

From the nineteenth century down to the middle of the twentieth, archaeological excavations aiming chiefly at investigation of the pharaonic monuments gradually caused the disappearance of the Christian remains considered of minor importance, and what survives today consists of a few architectural elements in stone, either displaced (columns, lintels) or in situ in the ancient walls (niches, traces of ceilings, etc.). The relative height of the elements in position allows us to determine the level of the floors and the height of the ceilings in the Christian installations.

An OSTRACON from Karnak mentions a church, "the holy sanctuary of Apa Stephanos in the town of Apé." The Djeme papyri discovered at Madīnat Hābū mention a "monastery of St. Sergius" and a "monastery of Papnoutios in Apé." Archaeological investigations have allowed the conclusion that there were at Karnak at least three churches and three monasteries, although we cannot identify them with the monuments mentioned above.

A monastery was constructed on either side of the first pylon on enormous masses of unbaked brick, the remains of ramps abandoned after serving for the construction of the pylon. We can see, on either side of each tower, traces of the insertion of a regular series of wooden beams representing two or three stories. The pylon has transverse passages that served originally to attach the flagstaffs. Access to these corridors was gained by flights of steps cut in the Christian period, which allowed a passage through the towers of the pylon. There was thus a relation between the buildings on the east and on the west. Two niches in the form of conches have been hollowed out in the east face of the south tower.

The second known monastery was situated in the courtyard between the seventh and eighth pylons. It, too, is marked by the insertion of beams for two upper stories, in the eighth pylon, and by a row of fifteen niches forming as many cupboards, which were equipped with wooden doors and shelves. The latter are generally thought to be linked with a refectory or a library. Remains of stone walls, a staircase, and shafts of columns were still in this court in 1922. They have now been removed.

A third monastery that occupied the court between the ninth and tenth pylons seems to have been destroyed by a fire. Here have been found shafts of columns, capitals with acanthus leaves, and decorated door lintels in sandstone or limestone, material deriving from the demolition of the temples. Excavation has yielded oil lamps, statuettes in terracotta, stelae, stands for water jars, and so forth. A niche adorned with a conch cut in the south face of the west tower of the ninth pylon proves that these installations were raised about 15 feet (8 m) above the ancient ground level.

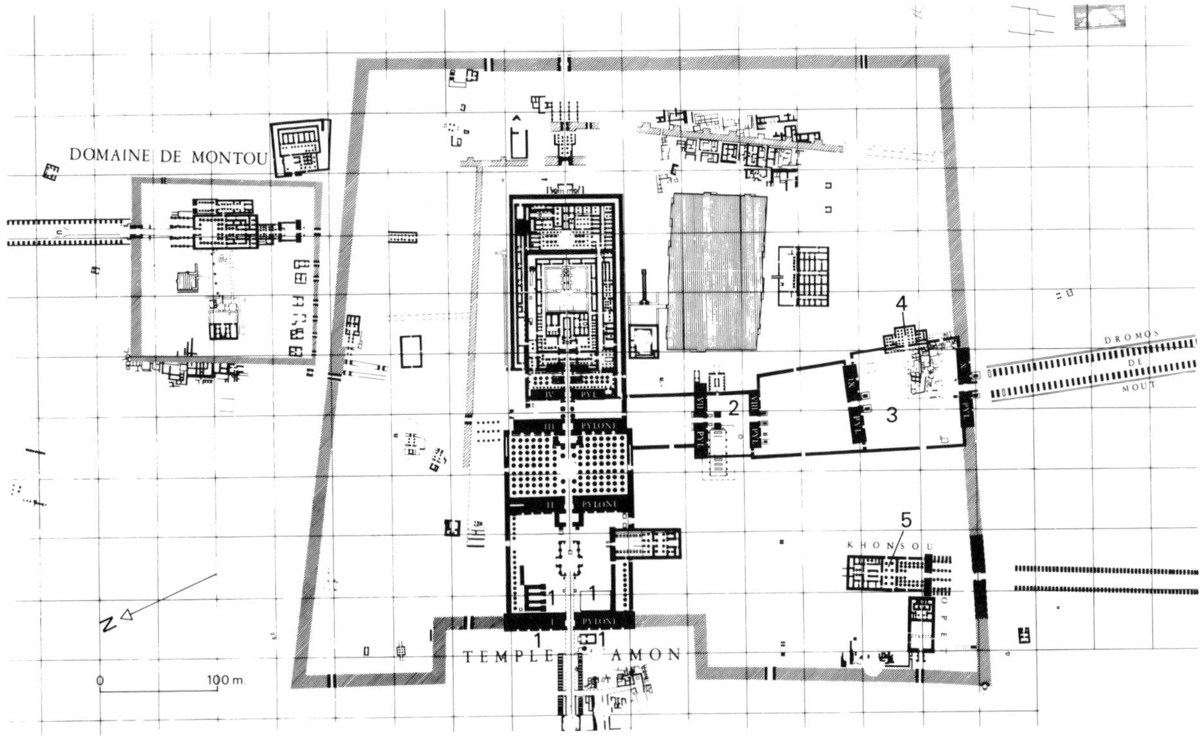

Plan of the Christian remains at Karnak. **1**: monastery constructed on either side of the first pylon. **2**: the second known monastery, between the seventh and eighth pylons. **3**. the third monastery, between the ninth and tenth pylons. **4**. church connected with the third monastery. **5**. hypostyle hall. *Courtesy French-Egyptian Center of the Temples of Karnak.*

The three churches of which it has been possible to find traces were all installed directly on the floors of the pharaonic monuments. We can imagine that others may have existed, built higher up near the level of the known monasteries.

The church built in the so-called edifice of Amenophis II has left practically no traces apart from the defacement of the pharaonic scenes in the hypostyle hall and some mortises under the capitals of the columns at the entrance. A few lamps and statuettes were found there. However, the name that this monument still bears, "al-Kanīsah" (the church), confirms the presence of Christian worship there. The church was oriented east–west. It was no doubt connected with the third monastery mentioned above.

Recent investigations, still unpublished, in the temple of Khonsu have refuted the assumption that a church was established there on a north–south axis, the principal axis of the temple. It was, in fact, in the hypostyle hall that this church was situated, on an east–west axis. The alterations necessitated by its installation involved the blocking of a door to the east, the construction of a sanctuary, the reuse as an altar of a pharaonic barkstand, the installation of an ambon, and the use of a room to the northwest perhaps as a baptistery.

The enclosure at Karnak may have contained several hamlets, identified today by remains of pottery: in its southeast corner and near the temple of Ptah, in its northwest corner, and to the northwest of the temple of Khonsu. In association with this last hamlet, there must have been an oratory or sanctuary on the roof of the temple of Opet, where there remains a niche with a conch cut into the wall.

One of the two great subsidiary complexes of Karnak, the enclosure of Montu to the north, contains no Christian traces, and the other, the enclosure of Mout to the south, has not yet yielded any.

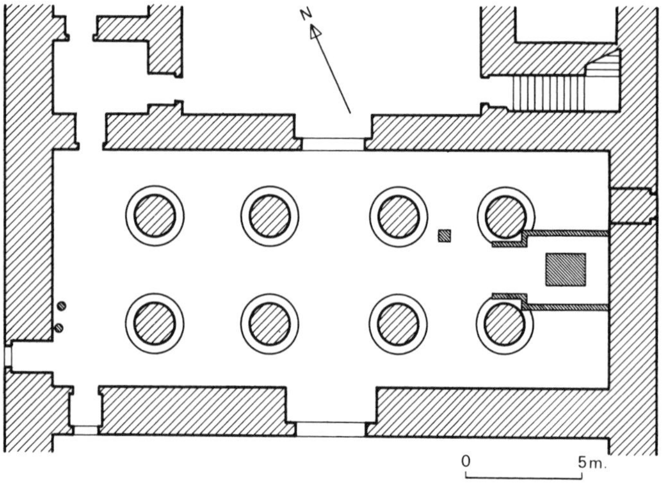

Remains of the church in the hypostyle hall of the temple of Khonsu, Karnak. *Plan after F. Laroche-Traunecker. Courtesy Peter Grossmann.*

BIBLIOGRAPHY

Anus, P., and R. Saʿad. "Fouilles aux abords de l'enceinte occidentale à Karnak." *Kemi* 18 (1968): 229–39.

Coquin, R.-G. "La christianisation des temples de Karnak." *Bulletin de l'institut français d'archéologie orientale* 72 (1972):168–78.

Jullien, M. "Le culte chrétien dans les temples de l'ancienne Égypte." *Les Études* 92 (1902):237–53.

Munier, H., and M. Pillet. "Les édifices chrétiens de Karnak." *Revue de l'Égypte ancienne* 2 (1929): 58–88.

Pillet, M. *Thèbes, Karnak et Louqsor.* Paris, 1928.

JEAN JACQUET

KASSA ASRATE STELE, Ras (1918–1974), Ethiopian nobleman, vice-president, then president of the Senate (1957–1964), governor of Eritrea (1964–1971), and president of the Crown Council. He led several missions to Egypt, mainly in 1958 and 1959, to negotiate the demands of the Church of Ethiopia for independence from the Coptic church in Egypt. He was murdered with many others by the revolutionary regime that came to power in 1974.

MIRRIT BOUTROS GHALI

KAUFMANN, CARL MARIA (1872–1951), German priest and archaeologist. His discovery and excavation of ABŪ MĪNĀ (1905–1907) places him among the founders of Christian archaeology in Egypt. He also explored in the Fayyūm and in Middle Egypt. His writings include several publications on Christian archaeology and on excavations and findings at Abū Mīnā, as well as various literary works. His autobiography is *Allah ist gross* (Freiburg, 1950).

BIBLIOGRAPHY

Baumstark, A. *Karl Maria Kaufmann. Skizze eines deutschen Gelehrtenlebens.* Leipzig, 1937.

PETER GROSSMANN

KAYSĀN IBN ʿUTHMĀN IBN KAYSĀN, tenth-century Melchite physician of Miṣr. He is mentioned in the *History of Physicians* by Jamāl al-Dīn ibn al-Qifṭī (d. A.H. 646/A.D. 1248). Ibn Abī Uṣaybiʿah does not devote a section to him, but he mentions him in passing when speaking of his brother, the physician Abū al-Ḥasan SAHLĀN IBN ʿUTHMĀN. The brief section by Ibn al-Qifṭī may be translated: "Kaysān ibn ʿUthmān ibn Kaysān Abū Sahl was an Egyptian Christian physician, who lived in Egypt at the time of al-Muʿizz [341–365/953–975] and al-ʿAzīz [365–386/975–996]. He had a solid reputation, and was well known for his capacity to cure. He was in the service of the palace, where he had an honored place. He died on the sixth day of Shaʿbān of the year 378, while he was living at the palace, at the time of al-ʿAzīz." This date corresponds to 19 November A.D. 988. He was thus a contemporary of SĀWĪRUS IBN AL-MUQAFFAʿ, the Coptic bishop of al-Ashmūnayn.

Ibn Abī Uṣaybiʿah records that Kaysān was buried at DAYR AL-QUṢAYR, the monastery of Saint Arsenius overlooking the small town of Ṭurah, about 10 miles (15 km) south of Cairo.

BIBLIOGRAPHY

Ibn Abī Uṣaybiʿah. *ʿUyūn al-Anbāʾ fī Ṭabaqāt al-Aṭibbāʾ*, ed. Nizār Riḍā, p. 549, ll. 2–7. Beirut, 1965.

Jamāl al-Dīn . . . ibn al-Qifṭī. *Tārīkh al-Ḥukamāʾ*, ed. Julius Lippert, pp. 267–68. Leipzig, 1903.

KHALIL SAMIR, S.J.

KEEP (Arab., *jawsaq*), multistoried tower with defensive capabilities. It has strong walls and in most cases there is no entrance at ground level. The entrance lies at the second-floor level, and is reached by means of a drawbridge that can easily be taken in or drawn up into the keep when danger threatens. This accounts for the fact that a keep of this kind is always connected with a staircase tower, which is physically separated from it. A second staircase was required inside the tower.

In the way it is built and the purpose it served, this kind of keep is basically different from the so-called watchtower or burg of the late-Roman border defense system, a large number of which are known in the western oases and in which small troop units were stationed. The keeps in civilian settlements were used for passive defense only, and to some extent served as a protective haven of retreat for the inhabitants when danger threatened. They were particularly advantageous in isolated settlements. If appropriate precautions were made with regard to provisions and water supply, the inhabitants of a keep of this kind would be in a position to sustain a long siege. Thus the keep was employed quite early in monastery construction and most notably is a predominant feature of the hermit colonies (lauras). The Greek monasteries on Athos are also provided with corresponding towers.

This kind of keep is first mentioned within the context of a monastic community in the Ammonius narrative (dated between A.D. 373 and 381) that deals with the tower of the lauras at Mount Sinai (Mayerson, 1980, pp. 137–40). Of course, keeps of this kind were in existence at a much earlier period. G. Welter (1954, pp. 87–93) describes several Hellenistic towers similarly constructed on the island of Chios. They differ only in certain details. Large numbers of keeps, especially from the Roman imperial period, are also known from Syria (Butler, 1919) and Palestine (Negev, 1973), among which the latter show a kind of stairway matching Egyptian examples. Other famous examples are the keeps built by Herod in Jerusalem, the impregnability of which is stressed frequently in Josephus (*De bello Judaico* 5.4, 3–5; 5.5, 8; 5.18.4).

The oldest keeps at least partially preserved on Egyptian soil were discovered in the great laura of KELLIA on the western edge of the Delta and are to be dated with certainty to the first half of the fifth century. The ground plan is divided by two inner separating walls running at right angles to each other into four large room units of approximately the same size, one of which contained the staircase. In addition to the staircase, smaller keeps generally have only a single room, or besides that only a very small side chamber. A somewhat larger room plan, in which the staircase and three additional rooms are arranged along a central corridor, is contained in the keep of hermitage No. 44 of Qusūr ʿIzeila in Kellia (Mission suisse, 1983, Vol. 2, pl. 42), evidently deriving from the sixth or seventh century. The further development of the keep also belongs to this same form of ground plan. An almost identical disposition of the rooms is still apparent in the much later keep (1130–1149) of DAYR AL-MUḤARRAQ (Monneret de Villard, 1929, pp. 28–33). This plan also underlies the large keeps in the Wādī al-Naṭrūn. In the keep of DAYR AL-BARĀMŪS only the proportions are varied and the inside corridor extended, to make place for extra rooms. The latest towers are the towers of DAYR ANBĀ BISHOI and DAYR ANBĀ MAQĀR. In the first upper story both towers contain a church with three altars. To accommodate them, the ground plan of the towers had to be extended east of the inner corridor by a depth of two rooms. Neither tower is to be dated before the middle of the thirteenth century (Grossmann, 1982, p. 215).

The water supply in the keep was vitally important in the event of a siege. The oldest examples in the Egyptian lauras evidently did not always have immediate access to a watering place. Apparently, at first an indoor supply of water was not regarded as a matter of urgency. In the Ammonius narrative, pilgrims attacked on Mount Sinai needed only one day in the shelter of the tower to recuperate (Mayerson, 1980). Still, in the period of the patriarch SHENUTE I (858–880) the monks in the Kellia had to leave their towers to fetch water (*History of the Patriarchs,* Vol. 2, pt. 1, p. 60 [English trans.]). On the other hand, the keep of Dayr al-Baramūs in the Wādī al-Naṭrūn, which unfortunately has not yet been dated, was already provided with a well that could be reached by an underground passageway (Evelyn-White, 1933, Vol. 3, p. 233). The same arrangement might also have been available in the very old keep of DAYR ANBĀ ṢAMŪ'ĪL OF QALAMŪN. The later keeps in the Wādī al-Naṭrūn even have wells within the keep walls.

There is no uniformity in the question of access to the keep. While in the oldest examples of keeps known to us from the different colonies of hermits, entrance was effected only on the second floor, this detail was in a strange way occasionally disregarded in the keeps found in the cenobite monasteries. Thus the keep found immediately in front of the south door of the church of Dayr Anbā Bishoi in Suhāj can be entered at ground-floor level through a wide door (Grossmann, 1974–1977, pp. 323–25). The extensive keeplike lodging complex in DAYR ANBĀ HADRĀ in Aswan also had an entrance on ground level. Apparently the securing of the keep entrance was not regarded as very important by the large number of monks in the cenobite monasteries. The early keeps of the Nabataeans are also provided with ground floor entrances.

BIBLIOGRAPHY

Butler, J. C. *Syria.* Publications of the Princeton University/Expedition Division II. Architecture. Leiden, 1919.

Evelyn-White, H. G. *The Monasteries of the Wādī 'n Naṭrūn,* Vol. 3, *The Architecture and Archeology.* New York, 1933; repr. 1973.

Grossmann, P. "Sohaj." *Archiv für Orientforschung* 25 (1974–1977):323–25.

———. *Mittelalterliche Langhauskuppelkirchen und verwandte Typen in Oberägypten,* pp. 213–15. Glückstadt, 1982.

Ibrahim Hajjāj. "Introduction in Coptic Defence Architecture" (in Arabic). Dissertation, Cairo, 1984.

Mayerson, P. "The Ammonius Narrative: Bedouin and Blemmye Attacks in Sinai," pp. 133–48. In *The Bible World, Essays in Honor of Cyrus H. Gordon,* ed. G. Rendsburg. New York, 1980.

Mission suisse d'Archéologie copte de l'Universite de Genève, under the direction of R. Kasser. *Survey archéologique des Kellia (Basse-Egypte), rapport de la campagne 1981.* Louvain, 1983.

Monneret de Villard, U. *Deyr el-Muḥarraqah,* pp. 28–35. Milan, 1929.

Negev, A. "The Staircase Tower in Nabataean Architecture." *Revue biblique* 80 (1973):364–83.

Orlandos, A. K. Μοναστηριακη ἀρχιτεκτονική, pp. 134–37. Athens, 1958.

Walters, C. C. *Monastic Archaeology in Egypt,* pp. 86–99. Warminster, 1974.

Welter, G. "Von griechischen Inseln." *Archäologischer Anzeiger* (1954):48–93.

PETER GROSSMANN

KEIMER, LUDWIG (1893–1957), a German Egyptologist. Keimer was a professor at Cairo University, where he became vice president of the Egyptian Institute. He earned doctorates from the universities of Münster (1922) and Würzburg (1922, 1924). His most influential mentor, G. Schweinfurth, wrote the preface to Keimer's first Egyptological work, *Die Gartenpflanzen im alten Ägypten,* 2 vols. (Hamburg, 1924).

A bibliography of his publications appeared in the first part of Keimer's *Etudes d'égyptologie* (Cairo, 1940). Biographies were published by J. Leclant in *Archiv für Orientforschung* 18 (1957–1958):488–89; and by B. van de Walle in *Chronique d'Egypte* 33 (1958):66–78, 235, the latter of which includes a bibliography for the period 1940–1957.

S. KENT BROWN

KELLIA. [*This entry consists of the following articles:*
History of the Site
French Archaeological Activity
Swiss Archaeological Activity
Egyptian Archaeological Activity
The Churches
Epigraphy
Paintings.]

History of the Site

The Kellia is one of the most important and most celebrated monastic groupings in Lower Egypt. Its location long remained uncertain. In 1935 Omar Toussoun wrongly believed he had discovered its ruins near the northwest extremity of the Wādī al-Naṭrūn. It was the exact location of the ancient Nitria by H. G. Evelyn-White (1926–1933, Vol. 2, p. 1932) in the Delta that made it possible to identify the site of the Kellia, which the ancient texts situate between Nitria and Scetis. This identification, already proposed by A. F. C. de Cosson in 1937, was definitively established in 1964 by A. Guillaumont. The site is at the entrance to the Libyan desert, some 11 miles (18 km) south of al-Barnūjī, the ancient Nitria, two miles beyond the Nūbāriyyah canal.

A foundation story reported in the APOPHTHEGMATA PATRUM makes plain the link that existed between Nitria and the Kellia. The new habitat was founded by AMMON, on the advice of Saint ANTONY, for those monks who wished to live in a greater solitude than at Nitria. The monks, who lived in cells scattered in the desert, practiced a semi-anchoritism: on Saturdays and Sundays they all assembled at the church, celebrating the liturgy or *synaxis* together and sharing a meal taken in common. According to PALLADIUS, nearly 600 monks were living in the Kellia at the end of the fourth century. The priest-monk who officiated at the church exercised a certain authority over them all, particularly a spiritual authority; he was assisted for serious matters by a council formed from the oldest. The best-known priest of the Kellia at the end of the fourth century was MACARIUS ALEXANDRINUS. Within this fairly loose organization, the monks could group themselves into "fraternities," the most widely known of which is the one that gathered around EVAGRIUS and AMMONIUS. This was the community of monks considered as Origenists, against whom a disciplinary expedition was directed at the beginning of 400, under the orders of the patriarch THEOPHILUS (385–412). Among the monks who were then forced into exile, and who were later able to return to the Kellia, was Apa ISAAC, who when he became priest of the Kellia added a hostelry to the church for passing strangers and for sick monks, as was already the case in Nitria. At this period there was still only a single church in the Kellia.

The ecclesiastical dissensions that arose in the course of the fifth century following the Council of CHALCEDON were the cause of other troubles and more serious divisions among the monks of the Kellia. As we learn from an apothegm under the name of Phocas, it was necessary to build another church, in order that Chalcedonian and anti-Chalcedonian monks might each have their own. As this apothegm also shows, it was in the course of this century that the cells, while remaining hermitages, tended to become grouped into monasteries, the most remote being gradually abandoned. This was probably to escape the dangers to which the monks were exposed by the incursions of the nomads, who devastated Scetis several times during the fifth century.

Important evidence about the Kellia in the seventh century is furnished by the *Book of the Consecration of the Sanctuary of Benjamin*, an account of a journey of the patriarch BENJAMIN I (622–661) to the Wādī al-Naṭrūn to consecrate the new church of the DAYR ANBĀ MAQĀR in the winter of 645–646 or 646–647 (Coquin, 1975, p. 59). During this journey, as narrated by his companion, the priest AGATHON (Benjamin's successor), the patriarch stopped for two days with the monks of the Kellia, some of whom thereafter guided him on the road to the Wādi al-Naṭrūn. This text, preserved in Coptic and in Arabic, has been summarized by SĀWĪRUS IBN AL-MUQAFFA' in his HISTORY OF THE PATRIARCHS; in the Coptic text the Kellia is called ⲛⲓⲣⲓ (niri), "the cells," which is the translation of the Greek name. The corresponding term in the Arabic text of Sāwīrus is *al-Munā*, which is probably a transcription of the Greek *moné*, a synonym of *kellion*. It is in fact under this appellation of al-Munā that the Kellia is mentioned in Arabic authors. According to the same work, Benjamin had already visited al-Munā in 631. When fleeing before the Melchite patriarch Cyrus, he went first to the Wādī al-Naṭrūn and then to Upper Egypt. The same work affirms elsewhere that it was thanks to the patriarch Benjamin that "the reconstruction was undertaken of the monasteries of the Wādī Habīb [Wādi al-Naṭrūn] and al-Munā," which had been destroyed in unknown circumstances in the period of the patriarch DAMIAN (569–605) or his successor ATHANASIUS (605–616).

The same *History of the Patriarchs* informs us about the Kellia in the course of the eighth century. It is related that under the patriarch ALEXANDER II (705–730), John, bishop of Sais, charged by the Muslim governor with collecting the taxes due from the Christians, came to al-Munā, where he won back to orthodoxy the Gaianite and Barsanuphian monks who were there, proof that the divisions which arose in the Coptic church during the sixth century had a lasting effect among the monks of the Kellia, as among those of Scetis (Evetts 1904–1909, vol. 3, pp. 62–63).

The evidence concerning the ninth century leads one to think that in this period the monasteries ceased to be inhabited. This is affirmed by Ya'qūbī (d. 900), who knew the sites. In the eleventh century, Bakrī, probably using a much earlier source, says that the site was covered with imposing ruins, where, however, some monks were still living. In the fifteenth century al-Maqrīzī makes no mention of the Kellia or of al-Munā, proof no doubt that the ruins of the monasteries were already covered by the sands.

These ruins have survived to our time. Unfortunately the site is on the way to being completely destroyed, in consequence of the works of irrigation and of extending the arable land undertaken since before 1964 by the Service of Agrarian Reform. To the destruction thus caused must be added the damage effected by the construction in 1977 of a railway line from Tanta to Alexandria, crossing the site from one side to the other (Guillaumont 1981, pp. 195–98).

ANTOINE GUILLAUMONT

French Archaeological Activity

At the time of the discovery of the site of the Kellia in the spring of 1964 following the investigations conducted by A. Guillaumont, it had the appearance of a scattering of *koms* (Arabic, hillocks), the result of the collapsing of the vaults and walls and the progressive leveling of the constructions as a whole. Those in the center had offered greater resistance, and the sand had gradually filled the empty spaces. Some elements of the materials had come to the surface again in such a way as to form a solid crust, giving to each hermitage the appearance of a nipple. Sometimes a building was so greatly leveled that it was not marked by any elevation. These *koms* extend in an east–west direction over more than 7 miles (12 km) and in a north–south direction over about 2 miles (3 km). The majority of them were grouped in agglomerations that in the Arab period received designations compounded of the word *qaṣr* (pl., *quṣūr;* from the Latin *castrum,* fortification).

The Institut français d'Archéologie orientale carried out a first campaign in March–April 1965 on *kom* 219 of Quṣūr el-Ruba'īyāt, with the collaboration of the University of Geneva. Since the site is immense, it later appeared more advantageous to divide the groups of *koms* between the two institutions. Of more than 1,500 listed in 1972 (Kasser), about 900 remained still intact after the beginning of the works of the agrarian reform (1964). The Swiss mission was to devote its efforts to the eastern part: Quṣūr el-Izeila (al-'Uzaylah), Quṣur el-'Abīd, Quṣūr 'Īsā, to which R. Kasser (1969) later added two groups found further to the southeast: Quṣūr el-Higeila (al-Ḥijaylah) and Quṣur el-'Ireima (al-'Uraymah). The French institute would work on the western sector: Quṣūr el-Ruba'īyāt and Qaṣr Waḥeida (al-Waḥaydah).

Between 1966 and 1968 the French institute accomplished an exhaustive topographical survey of Quṣūr el-Ruba'īyāt (later published in Daumas-Guillaumont, 1969). From 1965 to 1968 and then after an interruption due to the state of war in Egypt, from 1979 to 1984, it cleared eleven *koms* of types varied both in their dimensions and in their plans, which we may classify as follows:

Type A. Hermitages of Small Dimensions

For a single occupant. This kind of hermitage appears to have been rather rare in the Kellia, or at least there are only a few examples. One of them bears the number 166 in the survey of Quṣūr el-Ruba'īyāt, and measured only 50 by 40 feet (15 by 12 m) in its primitive state and then about 72 by 40 feet (22 by 12 m) in its second phase. It could have had only a single inhabitant, for it had only a single oratory and a single storeroom, even in its second stage. Of the two other rooms, one to the east of the oratory was reserved for manual work, as is shown by some cavities in which bones of camels or cattle are wedged about 1 foot (0.30 m) from the ground, four of them symmetrically arranged opposite to one another. In the first phase of occupation there was neither well nor kitchen nor latrine. The pottery collected, dating probably from the last occupation, gives a general dating to the sixth and seventh centuries. This would show that alongside very developed hermitages, in which the hermits grouped together, there were entirely isolated hermits who lived the anchorite life as the texts describe it.

For two or even three occupants. Five *koms* of this type have been cleared at the western extremity of Quṣūr el-Ruba'īyāt, to which must be added the small primitive hermitage found included in a later extension of *kom* 167. These hermitages have a surrounding wall measuring on the outside between 50 and 65 feet (15 and 20 m) wide (north–south) and 65 to 100 feet (20 to 30 m) long (east–west). Their plan is rather varied, but in the habitations placed to the west we can clearly distinguish two (sometimes three) cells: that of the elder containing three rooms, the oratory in the northwest corner, and two chambers of which one gives access to a small storeroom, the whole being closed by an entrance door with a bolt. The cell for the disciple (or disciples) is situated to the south of the first one, and most often contains only two rooms, one of them an oratory. Large rooms, apparently communal, are set to the east of these two (or three) cells: in front of the elder's cell, a hall with two bays accessible from the courtyard by a door (in the oldest hermitages the north bay of this hall was appropriated for artisanal work and appears to have been converted into a reception lobby). To the east of the disciple's cell are placed the kitchen (which contains a bread oven) and a room which could have served as a pantry. The purpose of the other large rooms, to the south and also against the north wall, remains unknown. The well was dug in the southeast corner of the courtyard and surrounded by one or several basins from which channels ran, no doubt irrigating a vegetable garden. One of these channels often ended in a basin on the outside of the surrounding wall. This wall encloses the whole hermitage, including the courtyard, but its original height is difficult to estimate. Latrines are constructed against the south wall, sometimes the east. In several small hermitages, no gateway has been brought to light.

Type B. Hermitages of Medium Dimensions

Their surrounding wall, rectangular as in the preceding type, measures on the outside 80 to 90 feet (25 to 28 m) by 80 to 130 feet (25 to 40 m). In Quṣūr el-Ruba'īyāt, such hermitages are the *koms* bearing the numbers 88, 167 (in its final extension), and 171. One characteristic of this type is the multiplication of the habitation units: up to five in the three *koms* cleared by the French institute. The very large dimensions of the halls are another feature; the largest, which is always the oratory of the elder's cell, reaches 23 by 23 feet (7 by 7 m), whereas in the preceding hermitages it did not exceed 13 by 13 feet (4 by 4 m). Moreover, the decoration becomes very rich, with imitations of sculpture (capitals and columns), in fine materials like marble, and mural paintings which can hardly be the work of the hermits alone. The plan is distinguished from type A by the addition of large rooms, including a habitation unit, against the north wall and even the south wall, where we sometimes notice an assembly room (chapel, or perhaps refectory). We also see towers of refuge appearing in these hermitages (*kom* 88) in the south. The water installations are more extensive and complicated, and there is an entrance gateway in the surrounding wall, on the east side, sometimes also—at least in an early phase—in the north wall.

Type C. Hermitages of Very Large Dimensions

A single example of this type has been cleared, in Quṣūr el-Ruba'īyāt, *kom* 219. It seems to have been occupied by some ten hermits, and probably represents the most developed stage of the Kellia hermitages. Its dimensions, 145 by 195 feet (45 by 60 m), are imposing. It is difficult to specify the limits of each cell, but we find here the same elements as in the hermitage of type A: the elder's apartment in the northwest and disciples' cells to the south of it. However, these last (about ten) are lodged almost everywhere. As in type B, a large hall, here against the south wall and originally of three bays, may have served as a chapel. This hermitage may have been Gaianite, by reason of two inscriptions, no doubt down to the conversion of these schismatics by John of Sais in the eighth century. Excavations have shown the evolution of this hermitage, starting with a building of type B, by progressive extension to the final stage.

Type D. Center of Communal Services

The site in question is Qaṣr Waḥeida to the southwest of Qusūr el-Ruba'īyāt, cleared in 1967–1968. This is not a hermitage, for we have found neither the plan nor the constitutive elements such as individual oratories or chambers with store room, but on the contrary, buildings which to all appearance served the inhabitants of a cluster of hermitages. This is clear from the presence in particular of two churches in juxtaposition, the apse of the one being backed on to the west wall of the other. Each is of basilical plan, with a sanctuary in three parts and three aisles separated by pillars or columns (only the bases were still in place). The altar of the small church, to the west—the older—was square in form, and the north annex of the sanctuary was occupied by a baptistery with steps to east and west, as well as an aperture for emptying at the bottom of the piscina. The large church had a circular altar on small columns, but did not possess a baptistery. In each an ambo was backed against the south side of the sanctuary, with three steps to give access to it. There was a kind of peristyle on the south face of the large church, and a marble fountain-basin was placed to the right of the entrance door under this peristyle, probably for the washing of hands (and perhaps face) before the synaxis. A cistern constructed in the northwest corner of the small church collected the rain water, for unknown use. The large church fell out of favor at some period and was transformed into a cemetery. This complex of communal services also included inside a surrounding wall a very large hall with three aisles, no doubt a hostelry, with a kitchen adjoining and different rooms in juxtaposition, and also a refuge tower. A second tower of the same type had been built, backing on to the surrounding wall but on the outside and in proximity to the first. The independent staircase that gave access to the first floor was, it seems, common to the two towers. Water installations around two wells allowed the irrigation of the gardens.

This series of French excavations on the site of the Kellia was of limited character compared to the exceptional extent of the agglomerations. Still, by reason of the very diversity of the *koms* cleared, it nonetheless brought confirmation of information supplied by historical sources, and also new data. The inhabitants of the Kellia were hermits, not cenobites, living an almost autarchic life within their hermitages. They assembled only on Saturday and Sunday for the eucharistic synaxis in the communal church. However, the archaeological data show that this primitive ideal was gradually weakened. With larger numbers in the same hermitage, the hermits regrouped behind walls and with the possibility of taking refuge in a tower. The churches multiplied, sometimes even within the hermitages. It appears that life became less eremitic and less harsh. All the same, some appear to have remained faithful to the unwritten rule of the earliest times.

RENE-GEORGES COQUIN

Swiss Archaeological Activity

The Swiss mission in Coptic archaeology from the University of Geneva carried out its activities in the Kellia on three different and complementary levels. Between 1965 and 1971 (with extensions down to 1978), it accomplished a topographical survey of the site of the Kellia as a whole, covering more than 49 square miles (126 square km). The east, north, and west parts have been published (Kasser, 1972). This survey sought to locate all traces of ancient constructions showing on the surface of the ground, either from remains still standing or from the presence of the debris of buildings or of terra-cotta. More than 1,500 Coptic buildings were rapidly recorded on the general plan (*koms* still well preserved or already leveled by the works in progress for agricultural development). In the areas affected by the agricultural works, hundreds of buildings were leveled toward 1964 to half the height of their elevation. In the fields not yet under cultivation, morning dew marked on the ground the outline of the walls, through spots of dampness which lasted for several hours. A rapid survey of these traces was undertaken in 1967, although archaeological analysis was not possible. This enabled the publication in 1972 (Kasser, 1972, fols. 24–27) of a relatively detailed plan of the agglomerations of monasteries of Quṣūr ʿĪsā (about 550 buildings) and Quṣūr el-ʿAbīd (about 30 buildings). If the exact organization of these monasteries cannot always be seen, these plans give an excellent account of the dimensions of the dwellings, their orientation, and some internal developments.

The ever increasing constraints of agriculture stirred the mission into searching for methods of archaeological and architectural investigation, which could be applied to groups of *koms* still intact, without requiring complete excavation of all the structures. The end in view was to compile a plan of the buildings and analyze their internal development through the relative chronology of the architectural additions. These investigations were fulfilled by a superficial clearing of the *kom*, bringing to light only the upper part of the walls preserved. The functions of certain areas, the nature of the pictorial decoration, and the presence of inscriptions were ascertained by more or less extensive soundings at various points.

Methodical collection of the pottery in terms of its conformity in surface and an examination of its architectural reuse provided a dating, sometimes approximate, for all the constructions and their modifications. Application of this procedure to the whole of the agglomeration of Quṣūr el-ʿIzeila (al-ʿUzaylah) in a single excavation campaign in 1981 produced the essentials of the data required, with practically no damage to the substance of a sometimes fragile architecture. Detection by this method of particularly interesting buildings or structures allowed their methodical exploration in the course of later campaigns planned to this effect. This method of analysis was applied in 1982 to a group of fifty-five *koms* of the Quṣūr el-Ruba'īyāt, a group including several buildings of very large dimensions. In this area, where destruction was considerable between 1982 and 1985, these investigations made possible the detection of the particularly remarkable architectural ensembles. Excavation of various items whose function had been identified allowed the preservation of pictorial and decorative material of great importance.

The topographical work and the surface analyses carried out by the Swiss mission between 1964 and 1985 have brought to light numerous points of interest in the site, some of which have been the objects of partial or complete archaeological excavation.

The longest, most thorough, and most complete investigations have had as their object a particularly large and complex *kom* (Quṣūr 'Īsā 1), where it was hoped to find chronological and typological references reflecting the history of the site as a whole. The discoveries made in this very special building, rich in a long history, have supplied the essential basis for the chronology of the pottery of the Kellia, a tool for dating and analysis indispensable for any further study. Apart from this special case, in the face of the immensity of site and the abundance of the problems posed, the investigators of the Swiss mission have been very selective in choosing their objectives. The results are sufficiently conclusive to provide the state of our archaeological knowledge in the areas explored and an appreciation of the physical factors that conditioned the various forms of monastic settlement in the Kellia.

Site of the Kellia: Geological and Geographical Criteria

The monastic site of the Kellia was founded in a desert milieu, a quarter of the distance between Nitria and Scetis. The occupation developed on a strip running from northwest to southeast, parallel to the edge of the Delta and thus remaining at an altitude less than 33 feet (10 m) above sea level. In the most southerly low-lying area, one could easily reach the table of fresh water by digging a well. Desert conditions became established in the final Pleistocene period, shaping the site in undulating dunes on an axis from north and northwest to south and southeast. This formation was later hardened by a saline upsurge linked to a pre-Neolithic climatic variation. In the Coptic period the isolated hermitages, and later the agglomerations, were founded for preference in the low-lying areas, to take advantage of the proximity of the water table while escaping the notice of distant neighbors.

In a vast area, one could thus find all the requisite conditions for raising isolated constructions in a desert milieu, where one could live and even cultivate a soil that was fertile if it was suitably watered.

Construction Materials

The only construction material available on the site is the alluvial and briny sand that can be extracted from the subsoil at any point. Moistened with water and molded in the trenches from which it was dug, it takes on the consistency of a thick concrete, which allows the making of crude molded bricks, which dry almost without shrinkage. No vegetable or mineral additions have been observed. The bricks are bound together by a mortar of briny mud of the same provenance. The massive brickwork was placed directly on the sandy ground. Sometimes the buildings were slightly hollowed out in the subsoil.

The roofing of the buildings of the Kellia is very original. By far the majority have a system of graduated vaulting, mounted without any shoring. Hyperbolic or semicircular arches, built of unbaked brick wedged with shards of pottery, were piled up against the support of a backing wall. The density of the local bricks and the weak adhesiveness of the mud mortar limit the slope of the vaulting to a maximum of 45 degrees. The vaults were formed by two sets of brickwork supported on the opposing walls of the room and overlapping one another at their junction in the center. The general appearance is that of a very low vault resting on the backing walls. The rooms are for the most part rectangular, and are then covered by elongated and flattened domes. Spans of more than 23 feet (about 7 m) have been observed.

There was a less common system reserved for important buildings (churches, reception halls). Four spherical triangles forming a pendentive were established simultaneously by the graduated vaulting technique, resting on the corners of the room. In the new angles resulting from their junction, four new spherical triangles were set in place, and the process continued until the dome was completely closed. To roof an elongated room with two bays, the springs of the two neighboring vaults were supported on a median arch resting on two pillars. The rooms making up the buildings were added one to another as need required, and the vaults mutually buttressed one another.

Hinged wooden doors furnished with bolts ensured the closing of the entrances. Windows with sloping frames or loop holes pierced in the vaults supplied light and ventilation. A very large number of niches was contrived in the walls.

The walls were plastered with clay-mortar, then washed with white lime or coated with lime mortar. Like the baked bricks, the few hewn stones and the wood, this last material was entirely imported from the Delta. The floors and sometimes the plinths were carefully covered with lime cement mixed with crushed baked brick. The upper part of the walls and the vaults were generally washed with lime, and this was the foundation for painted decorations and inscriptions.

Unbaked brick being very susceptible to humidity, the outer curves of the vaults were rendered watertight by layers of clay, and sometimes lime-mortar. Installations connected with water (wells, basins, latrines) were constructed of baked brick and coated with lime or mortar mixed with chips of bricks.

Wood was rare, reserved for the frames and flaps of doors, shelves in some niches, or sets of shelves, and the recovered pottery was abundantly used in construction. Amphorae and pots were sunk into the floors and the walls (there is controversy about their function: acoustic vases, drains, niches, hiding-places?). Piping was made of amphorae placed end to end. The bricks of the vaults were wedged with the aid of countless shards of pottery.

Typology of the Monastic Habitation

The traces of the most ancient constructions observed in the Kellia were discovered in the *kom* Quṣūr ʿĪsā 1 in the form of very small rooms deeply excavated in the subsoil and roofed by graduated vaults made of small bricks (17 × 14 × 7 cm). These constructions belong to the second half of the fourth century at the earliest.

These shelters must scarcely have risen above the surface of the desert, and were entered by a short flight of steps, through a door sheltered from the prevailing winds. The use of lime mortar is not attested during this early period. Some niches are fitted into the walls, and there is a kind of cylindrical silo or hiding place sunk into the floor of most of the rooms; its function remains unknown. There is evidence that benches or bunks were placed along the walls, in the form of brickwork uprights that could support planks or a wooden panel. The progressive addition of similar rooms, sometimes interconnected, shows that several people lived together in a complex of a gradually expanding type, although no specific organization is apparent.

At the beginning of the fifth century, a southern addition displays the first features of an architectural model that was to have a considerable development in the history of the site of the Kellia. This is a chamber with a silo and a bench-bed, with an important niche in the east wall adorned with a painted cross. It connects with a smaller secondary room. Here we find lime mortars and bricks of a large size, and the first indication of the enclosure of the building by a wall delimiting a courtyard with a well. A first church is associated with this building.

Traces of craft and culinary activity have been noticed outside the dwelling, in the courtyard. The complex of Quṣūr ʿĪsā 1 stands apart from the other buildings excavated at the Kellia through the construction of three churches of large dimensions, dating to the fifth to seventh centuries. The adjoining constructions—such as enclosures, courtyards, and chambers—had functions quite certainly linked to the service of the churches, and are not the most characteristic of the current monastic habitation.

The investigations carried out by the Swiss mission between 1965 and 1984 in various zones of the site and particularly in Quṣūr el-ʿIzeila in 1981 (surface analysis of 120 buildings of an agglomeration) have allowed us to grasp the recurrent characteristics of the monastic habitation current in the sixth and seventh centuries, and the way in which the hermitages developed through progressive increase in the effective strength of the community around the cell of some elder. If the plans of the buildings dated to the fifth century are rare and variable, a model often repeated appeared from the sixth century on: one described by de Cosson (plan A) when he identified the site of the Kellia in a 1937 article (pp. 247–53) in which he presents the essentials of the west building of a hermitage which he briefly excavated at Quṣūr el-Rubaʿīyāt. The French excavations have cleared and analyzed several of these constructions in detail.

The great majority of the buildings examined, with few exceptions, present common characteristics which attest the presence of several successive and effective barriers between the outside world and the monk. The mutual relationships of the occupants of the same hermitage and between them and visitors could be very subtly controlled by the use of numerous doors.

For individual retreat, the hermit had in the first monastic times his primitive cell. Later in Kellia the cell developed into a chamber, still simple, with whitewashed walls pierced with niches and furnished with a leaved door. The oratory niche was placed in the east wall of a large room communicating with the cell in the northwest corner of the hermitage. Described as an oratory, this room was distinguished by its decorated niches, ventilation sky-lights, windows, pictorial decorations, and inscriptions. There was sometimes another small unfurnished room opening upon it, lit by small windows but without a store room, in which one could shut oneself away in the same manner as in the "monk's chamber." No archaeological evidence—and no inscription—has made it possible to determine its function. This first group of rooms, with an optional passage in front of them, always formed a separate apartment, closed off by a leaved door. This door opened on a circulation and service area, the core of which was a hall with two bays. The northern part sometimes showed traces of artisanal activity (weaving or the making of mats). In the east wall of the southern part, which was a reception hall, the entrance door of this main block opened on to the courtyard. To the south, one passed through a pantry, then into the kitchen. In the Kellia this was invariably a room with earthen walls blackened by smoke. A vault raised above, fitted with vents, took the place of a chimney over one or more hearths arranged against the wall on a raised bench. There was also a bread oven of a somewhat cylindrical shape placed vertically or obliquely; this had a removable cover. Beside the kitchen we very often find a chamber with a storeroom identical to the monk's chamber. The person who lived there evidently had some function in relation to the kitchen, with use of the vestibule and control of the entrance door and the courtyard space. The principal resident or elder thus ordinarily had at his service a subordinate perhaps charged with managing part of the contacts with the outside world and probably also with stewardship.

The garden-courtyard is the fourth enclosure of the hermitage. In the southeast corner of the enclosure are the latrines, which run off to the outside. In the same sector a well of baked bricks is surrounded by basins and drainage channels, probably for artisanal use, the surplus water from which could irrigate a few planted areas. The entrance gate to the hermitage opens in the south enclosing wall, sometimes in the east. Visitors could be received in a room which formed a vestibule or gatehouse. Outside the hermitage at some distance from the gate was a rubbish heap where kitchen waste, building rubbish, and broken pottery were thrown.

The hermitages rarely preserved this structure throughout their history. Apartments or other buildings, either separate from the elder's dwelling or communicating with it, were installed one after the other inside the enclosure and along its length. We can recognize them in general rooms that have the same functions and decoration as the apartment in the northwest: a chamber with a store room, an oratory, a reception room, sometimes a kitchen. We can thus observe the successive installation of up to five apartments in the larger hermitages.

Another architectural solution in response to the increase in the strength of the small community was to knock down some of the enclosing walls and extend the enclosure in one or two directions in order to install more or less important blocks of buildings. The growth of the hermitages was effected through successive additions of monastic dwellings, and it is only rarely that we observe demolitions and reconstructions on the same site. Thus the vast majority of the hermitages of the Kellia from the sixth to the eighth centuries reproduce a very restricted number of very closely related plan types, which are carried out in a more or less spacious or luxurious manner according to the means of the residents. Each hermitage had its own internal evolution, yet in obedience to principles that appear to have been the rule.

Amid the apparently multiple and variable architectural forms which the monastic habitation may take in the secondary apartments, certain constants stand out which no doubt reflect important aspects of the monastic organization. The cell or monk's chamber with its indispensable store room remains the most remote and private place in every residence. In front of the cell are one or more rooms, one of which always has in its east wall an oratory niche. This arrangement allows the association of the functions of this room with those of the oratory in the elder's apartment. The separation of the functions of the rooms, however, appears in a less rigid fashion in the secondary apartments. New architectural solutions, combining the functions with one another, make clear the probable hierarchical difference between the elder and other occupants.

The Two-Bay Hall

The most remarkable construction in the secondary blocks of buildings is the hall with two (sometimes three) bays, a juxtaposition of rooms communicating through a wide arcading that recalls the vestibule in the principal apartment. The bays are amply lit by openings or windows. This room becomes the largest in the hermitage, with direct access to the courtyard through one or several leaved doors.

The eastern niche with its special decoration is very rarely lacking. Kitchens with or without a pantry are often clearly associated with the two-bay halls, which thus suggests a possible function as a refectory, although the oratory niche is, nevertheless, not absent. As in many of the oratories, the floor of these halls sometimes has blocks of stone set in the smooth lime cement, or carpets painted on the floor in front of the oratory niche.

The development of two-bay halls in the developed hermitages is a remarkable phenomenon in the Kellia. The oratory niche here takes on an increasing importance, and in some cases is replaced by a third eastern bay in which all the characteristics of the choir of a sanctuary are sometimes brought together. We note in particular the presence of an altar. These chapels or monastery churches were the object of frequent transformation or modification; these imposing constructions required either the extension of the primitive enclosure or profound modification of the ancient main building. Five buildings of this type have been discovered among the 120 hermitages of the agglomeration of Quṣūr el-ʿIzeila. They may be attributed to the second half of the seventh century in the same way as the basilica attached to a conventional hermitage, excavated in 1968 at Quṣūr ʿĪsā (no. 366 bis northwest).

The Towers

The towers are important constructions that appear sporadically in the second half of the seventh century and particularly in the northern half of the agglomeration of Quṣūr el-ʿIzeila (19 towers in a total of 120 hermitages). Their substructures are very thick and carry high walls which one finds collapsed in compact masses at the foot of the foundations. Access was by an independent staircase and a movable gangway leading to an upper floor door pierced in the tower. The base of the towers contains only storerooms, hiding places, and flights of internal stairs. The tower is most often backed on to the enclosure wall of the hermitage, or on the outside in such a way that access is possible from the top of the wall and the roofs of the hermitage, and this in proximity to the entrance gates.

No tower in the Kellia has been sufficiently preserved to show the arrangement of the upper stories. Piping and water outlets attest the presence of latrines.

The towers are generally associated with hermitages which have been extended or enlarged, or include important annexes (double-bay halls, refectories, or churches).

The existence of a much earlier tower has been attested in the complex of the churches of Quṣūr ʿĪsā: subsequent to the building of the second church and built outside, a tower measuring 26 by 30 feet (8 by 9 m) at its base was erected toward the apse or choir of the church. Access was by an independent staircase and a removable bridge. In contrast with the towers of the seventh century, this construction was set up in the center of the monastery and not on the enclosing wall.

Special Buildings

A building of about 260 feet (80 meters) square was erected on the southern edge of the agglomeration of Quṣūr el-ʿIzeila (nos. 141–42). The building comprises a simple enclosure wall, in the interior of which nineteen identical and contiguous rooms are aligned on the north, with a door and two niches. This vast whole was probably an enclosure for commercial functions, an interpretation reinforced by the presence of numerous fragments of amphorae.

The Complex of the Churches of Quṣūr ʿĪsā 1

A *kom* situated at the southern limit of the agglomeration of Quṣūr ʿĪsā was the subject of methodical excavation from 1965 to 1968 and 1976 to 1977 by the Swiss mission from the University of Geneva. It became apparent that this complex was quite exceptional among the hundreds of *koms*. It was in operation during the entire history of the Kellia, or nearly so, and three churches have been brought to light. Both in its structure and in its content the building presents numerous analogies with that of Qaṣr Waḥeidah partly explored by the French mission. A first nucleus is formed by very small cells half buried in a thoroughly desert milieu, described above (second half of the fourth century). At the end of the fourth century and the beginning of the fifth, a church was built (33 by 26 feet [10 by 8 m]), and this was included in an ensemble of rooms already well organized in a rectangle of 65 by 90 feet (20 by 28 m) with a courtyard and a central well.

Through the addition of rows of rooms and adjoining constructions, this complex thereafter underwent a practically continuous extension. At the end of the fifth century we find there a second church 55 by 33 feet (17 by 10 m) of basilical plan, with a nave of six columns. A cistern collects the rain water from the roofs. A high tower adjoins outside the apse or choir of the church. An enclosing wall of about 176 by 169 feet (54 by 52 m) with its northwest and southwest corners rounded, surrounds the whole, and the principal entrance is on the east.

In the sixth century the enlargement continued through the addition of a southern wing with a new well, and later by a simultaneous extension of the enclosure to the north and east. A final phase of major works, which caused important changes in the plan of the monastery, is dated to the beginning of the seventh century. A western extension of the enclosure brought its dimensions to about 250 by 234 feet (77 by 72 m). The buildings of the fourth and fifth centuries were razed and filled up. A spacious church 72 by 39 feet (22 by 12 m) of basilical plan (nave with 16 columns) was erected on the site of the first church. The two basilicas then function simultaneously, opening on a central court bounded on the west by a columned portico. Several living and service rooms open on to it. There is also a large hall, the roof of which is supported by three middle columns. This was no doubt a guest hall or refectory, opening at once onto the portico, the kitchens, and the back courts, which themselves open to the outside through service doors. The principal entrance to the enclosure on the east remains in operation.

At the end of the seventh century the aspect of the site changed. All the peripheral buildings fell suddenly out of favor; the vaults collapsed for want of maintenance, the courtyards and the ruins were completely covered with sand. All that survived was the two basilicas strengthened by buttresses of mud bricks, the central court, and probably the old tower. The openings of the portico were walled up and a kitchen was installed in a corner of the colonnade.

On the outside, a large cemetery extends to the north, east, and south of the churches in the ruins of the ancient buildings. The tombs are oriented east and west, with the head to the west. The definitive disaffection took place before the middle of the eighth century.

The complex of Quṣūr ʿĪsā 1 throughout its history displays its permanent peculiarity. Situated on the margin of a very large agglomeration which probably developed in the sixth to the eighth centuries, it is a center where one finds buildings essentially intended for the service of the churches (courtyards, reception rooms, refectories, kitchens, etc.). Series of rooms suitable for forming residences, such as we observe everywhere else in the hermitages of the Kellia, are exceptional, which indicates that the permanent residents were, no doubt, few in number.

The decline of Quṣūr ʿĪsā 1 and its churches may be explained by a profound change in the cultic habits of the monks of the Kellia, which occurred in the course of the second half of the seventh century. The churches outside the agglomerations of the sixth and seventh centuries, in which the community gathered from the fourth century on, were abandoned to the advantage of places of worship integrated into the hermitages themselves, like the chapels and churches observed at Quṣūr el-ʿIzeila, which even attain to the dimensions of genuine basilicas (Quṣūr ʿĪsā, 366 bis northwest).

The Development of the Agglomerations

One single agglomeration of the Kellia (Quṣūr el-ʿIzeila) was the subject of a full-scale analysis during the 1981–1984 project of the Swiss mission. The results of this analysis allow us to suggest a model for the development of the site, which is probably equally valid for the other parts of the Kellia.

The cells of the primitive type, from the fourth and fifth centuries, are known only at Quṣūr ʿĪsā 1. We do not know the distribution of these small half-buried constructions, but toward the beginning of the sixth century, in contrast, hermitages of a simple plan, with an enclosure, are distributed in very scattered fashion at the low points on the map of the Kellia. The density is that of the numerous small constructions, of generally unknown type and date, which are strewn over the site outside the later agglomerations, without any particular concentration and invisible one from another. It is likely that this distribution is in the spirit of the initial stage.

In the course of the sixth century we witness at Quṣūr el-ʿIzeila, on the contrary, a concentration of the buildings in a great depression. Variants appear in the typology of the hermitages, where the annexed apartments were multiplied. We can thus distinguish arrangements conceived for a single resident or for an elder and his disciple.

According to the simple systems which were to prove their worth during nearly two centuries (seventh and eighth), we witness on the one hand successive developments of apartments within the existing enclosing wall, and on the other hand new foundations of hermitages which reinforced the density and thus created veritable agglomerations of buildings more or less contiguous and of diverse orientation, separated by rubbish heaps.

In the seventh century, very specific additions modified the character of certain portions: towers and places of worship or assembly appear in the developed hermitages.

The buildings excavated in the principal agglomerations, Quṣūr al-Ruba'īyāt and Quṣūr 'Īsā, confirm this scheme of development and indicate that the extreme concentration of the agglomerations occurred in the seventh and eighth centuries. The great isolated buildings situated to the south of these zones and giving shelter to churches for community use (Quṣūr 'Īsā 1 and Qaṣr Waḥeidah) played a role up to the middle of the seventh century, the date at which they were practically abandoned or transformed into cemeteries.

DENIS WEIDMANN

Egyptian Archaeological Activity

Independently of the French and Swiss archaeological investigations in the Kellia, the Egyptian Antiquities Organization has also carried out important excavations on this site, principally along the line of the Tanta–Alexandria railway under construction (some thirty *koms* at Quṣūr al-Ruba'īyāt, in addition to several sites cleared in collaboration with the Swiss mission). This work has gone on since 1977, when the increasing pace of destruction obliged all the available institutions to concentrate their efforts on the western part of the Kellia, which no means of protection was going to save from rapid annihilation. The working out of the results of these excavations has not yet reached a stage at which a full account can be given.

DENIS WEIDMANN

The Churches

In the general area of the Kellia a not inconsiderable number of churches has so far been identified. Several of these were conceived as independent buildings, while others had clearly the character of later annexes to buildings already in existence (hermitages). Moreover the churches so far found belong to very distinct types that are discussed below according to their typology and topography.

Quṣūr 'Īsā South 1 had three churches; they did not, however, all exist at the same time.

The older north church came into being shortly after 400 and is therefore the oldest church so far identified in the Kellia. It has a short but relatively wide single-aisle naos, which was evidently roofed over by a tier of beams running east and west. The sanctuary consisted at first of a single rectangular altar room. However, while the construction was still in process, two additional side rooms were added on the two sides. The one on the south was connected by a narrow passage with a subterranean hiding place.

The south church belongs to the end of the fifth century and is a fully developed church building with a three-aisle naos and three-part sanctuary, the middle room of which contains the altar and the northern side room, a baptistery. The entrance lies on the north side and is provided with a covered porch, necessary because of the frequent winds in the desert area. A small platform extending to the left serves as substitute for a narthex. In general, this church is only a modest building with very unbalanced proportions.

The later north church stands directly above the older north church, which accordingly had ceased to exist. In its architectural development, it goes a step further than the south church and is provided with a western return aisle. The sanctuary is again tripartite, but shifted slightly to the north from its axis in order to make room for a staircase to the roof, accommodated at the south end. This church was built in the early seventh century.

Qaṣr al-Waḥaydah is the most important place in Quṣūr al-Ruba'īyāt and in many respects comparable to the complex of Quṣūr 'Īsā South 1. Here two churches have so far been discovered.

The west church is almost the exact counterpart of the south church in Quṣūr 'Īsā South 1. It too consists of a very simply proportioned three-aisle naos with three-part sanctuary, in the north room of which the baptistery was again accommodated. The round piscina itself has the canonical form with steps on west and east. The entrance to the church is in the middle of the south wall.

The east church corresponds to the later north church of Quṣūr 'Īsā South 1, but is some years older. Its naos was originally divided for its whole length into three aisles with a weakly stressed central aisle. In a later change of the position of the columns, the central aisle was widened and space created at the west end for a return aisle. The southern apse side room contains an additional table, which probably served for the preparation of the sacrifice of the mass. At the southern entrance to the church an exonarthex was later added, in the form of a roofed vestibule (Andreu, Castel, and Coquin, 1980, pp. 347–68).

In Quṣūr ʿĪsā *kom* 58,85/19,46, the great church dates from the seventh century and was a later addition on the north side of a hermitage already frequently extended. The three-aisle naos has a western return aisle, and its rear third is divided by the insertion of two quatrefoil pillars into two sections of unequal length. The longer front section exhibits in the middle on both sides a fairly large intercolumniation, which was presumably intended to indicate a transverse axis. Whether the outer walls contained niches relating to this can no longer be determined. In the sanctuary the side sections are separated from the altar by simple rows of columns while the northern side room has a bench running round the walls.

In Quṣūr el-ʿIzeila, hermitage 14 (55,42/20,14), the church is built onto the south side of an already existing hermitage. The naos consists of two domed bays one behind the other, which were linked together by a wide transverse arch. The sanctuary consists of a simple transverse room with a large niche in the east wall. Later the room was divided into three sections by the building of two arches. Traces of an altar base are not to be seen. Pottery finds allow a dating of the church to the middle of the seventh century.

In Quṣūr el-ʿIzeila, hermitage 16 (55,40/20,12), the church is built into the northeast corner of an already existing hermitage. The naos, as with the preceding church, is composed of two domed bays. The sanctuary shows an asymmetrical division of the rooms, with a main room corresponding to the breadth of the naos and in the middle of it the altar. On the north side a small side area is separated by three arcades and has a bench running round it, while a second actual side room adjoins on the southern outer side and is itself connected with a rear staircase. Chronologically the church belongs to the second half of the seventh century.

In hermitage 19–20 (55,60/20,12–14), the church is in the latest annex to the hermitage, lying wholly to the south, and like the other examples has a naos composed of two bays. The sanctuary originally consisted of three separate rooms. Later, however, the dividing walls were broken through to form large connecting openings. Behind the altar room, under the staircase adjoining there was a hiding place, which elsewhere is not common. The building of the church is to be set even before 630.

In hermitage 45 (55,70/19,20), the church is on the south side of a frequently extended hermitage, and like the other two examples consists of two bays set one behind the other. The sanctuary is adorned with several paintings, and is divided by large arches into three openly linked sections. On the floor a special area is marked out by paintings, in the middle of which a portable altar was presumably to be set up in case of need. The building of the church can be dated to the middle of the seventh century.

In Quṣūr ʿĪsā, *kom* 59, 35/18,83, the place where several marble pillar fragments were found points to a church of several aisles that once stood on this spot. The building itself was completely destroyed through the canal works in this area.

PETER GROSSMANN

Epigraphy

Identification of the Site

By the Kellia we understand the "presumed site of the Kellia," given that no inscription, mural or otherwise, giving explicitly the name of the site has yet been found in situ. The amphora shard with the inscription *ενκλησιασ κελλιων*, enklēsias kelliōn (Egloff, 1977, p. 11), could be an argument in favor, but the object may have been found on the site quite by chance (an amphora sent from one place to another with the name of the sender). Other abbreviated inscriptions in the form *εκ* on amphorae or potsherds can only be resolved into *εκ* (*κλησιασ*), and for this reason cannot constitute evidence for the identification of the site.

The Inscriptions of the Kellia

In the interior of the hermitage inscriptions can be found everywhere. For the most part they are in the vestibules, the passage leading to the oratory, and the oratory itself. Inside the rooms they are placed at the will of the scribe. For preference, the parts of the wall at eye level were inscribed, and thereafter, as need might be, the rest of the available surface. For the inscriptions of the important monks, choice was made of the surface above the passages or the niches (or their background), each surface with a good plaster to ensure the survival of the inscription. The Arabic inscriptions (in black or graffiti) are found on the outside of the walls on the rosy mortar dado (in Pompeian red) where there are practically never any Coptic or Greek inscriptions.

Bases for Inscriptions

Inscriptions were written on clay plaster covering brick made of sand, on limewash laid directly on clay plaster, on plaster cross-bars prepared for the inscriptions of important monks, on plaster whether whitewashed or not, and on marble. The majority of the inscriptions are painted with red ocher (with a calamus or brush); some are traced in black ink or charcoal, or else scratched with a pointed implement. In one case a Coptic funerary stela has been found in chalky limestone with engraved letters painted with red ocher (Kasser, 1972, p. 82b, fig. 33).

Decoration of the Inscriptions

The inscriptions may or may not be set in a frame. The frames sometimes imitate the *tabulae securiclatae* of the Greco-Roman inscriptions, but the number of handles (sometimes as many as eight) proves that their primitive function was forgotten. The frames may be decorated with stylized palmettes or rope patterns or take the form of two columns on the capitals of which there is an arch—a form known in the decoration of the lists of the canons in the gospel manuscripts of the late empire and high Middle Ages (cf. Nordenfalk, 1938). The influence of manuscript decoration is visible (stylized coronis and obelus, decorative upper lines, etc.; see Cramer, 1964, Vol. 10, pp. 13, 18–20). We may observe the transition from the ☧ (initial or final; the Constantinian monogram), which could be understood as ☥ (a Christianized ankh), to the cross by way of the ⳨ (symbol for ⲥⲧⲁⲩⲣⲟⲥ stauros).

Paleography

Alongside calligraphers (uncial hands of various types) and professional scribes (cursives approaching the epigraphic capital, Coptic and Byzantine cursives that are also found on the economic and juridical papyri of the period), there are unskilled hands, the work of monks who hardly knew how to write or were semiliterate. In some inscriptions cryptography is used.

Language of the Inscriptions

Coptic, in the Bohairic dialect, is the language of the majority of the inscriptions (almost the oldest monuments of this dialect). Greek very badly written appears rather rarely, and may be contaminated by the use of Coptic words. The Arabic inscriptions were for the most part traced after the Kellia had been abandoned by the monks.

Content of the Inscriptions

The major part of the inscriptions of the Kellia consists of the obituary mementos of the monks, which are fairly uniform in form. In the interior of the hermitage the monks could copy one another for certain invocations or particular expressions, which thus become characteristic for a given monastery. The names in the Kellia are typically biblical or Coptic. Sometimes the name of a historical personage—a patriarch of Alexandria or emperor of Byzantium—is intercalated, or the name of the invader ravaging Egypt at the period.

The dated inscriptions may serve as chronological benchmarks (if the archaeological context permits) for the decoration, and the latest constitute a *terminus post quem* for the construction of the hermitage (or of the addition in which they were found).

A series of inscriptions (the majority in Greek) accompany the decorations (cross with invocations, representations of the saints, or others). Some consist of reading notes (name of a personage or quotation from the Bible or the apocrypha), or lists of pilgrims who have visited a hermitage, with pious invocations. In one case a long prayer to Christ has been found (Daumas and Guillaumont, p. 99). The poorly legible inscriptions on pottery have not yet been sufficiently studied.

Some hieroglyphic inscriptions were also found in the Kellia, on pharaonic blocks reused in the Coptic constructions (Kasser, 1972, 82b, 126b–27a, in a hydraulic installation: 444/82).

A relative chronology of the epigraphy in the Kellia shows the following: oldest site, Quṣūr ʿĪsā; intermediate, Quṣūr el-ʿIzeila (sixth to eighth centuries); and latest, Quṣūr el-Rubaʿīyāt (seventh-eighth to twelfth centuries).

JAN STANISLAW PARTYKA

Paintings

The majority of the rooms in the Kellia were decorated. In the simplest cases, only the base was painted in dark red, and occasionally a band of geometric motifs—most often monochromatic—

surmounted it. A dark stripe framed the doors, windows, and niches, and marked the corners of the rooms.

The monks' vestibules and oratory displayed the richest and most varied decor. The walls were covered with various patterns (triangles, braids, foliated interlacing, intertwinings, leafy scrolls, vine scrolls, succulents, pomegranates). Various animals were also depicted. Horses were legion: there were also stags, camels, giraffes, lions, and hares. Birds appeared in equal abundance, with peacocks, doves, partridges, and parrots being the most frequent. They were pictured alone or in association with other motifs, notably the cross. Many boats were also to be seen, either merely sketched with large rapid brush strokes, or painted with a great abundance of detail. Though often only ornamental, when a boat decorated the interior of a niche, it assumed a clear eschatological meaning.

The most frequent motif at Kellia, however, is the cross. Contrary to what is seen at the monasteries of Saqqara and BĀWĪṬ, where crosses were rarely pictured, at the Kellia they are found everywhere. Protective symbols, they appear near passageways or upon restorations to be attributed to divine grace. As ornaments, they were repeated constantly upon the walls. As cult objects, they decorated the central wall of the eastern niche in the oratory. Indeed, as at Saqqara, the eastern wall had both secondary niches and a principal one, larger and more important than the others, before which offerings were made.

Kellia doubtlessly offers the widest range of crosses of every kind: Greek, Latin, pattées, potent, botonées, or with scalelike decoration. They rise up amid plants or birds. They stand majestically upon a platform. Processional crosses have a long staff. They are sometimes simple, even monochromatic, sometimes adorned with gems, garlands, small bells, and censers. Many times a medallion decorates the intersection of the arms, with a medallion bearing the bust of Christ in one case.

Secular scenes have been discovered at Kellia, such as a river and a feminine figure reminiscent of Isis, half reclining as in ancient classical iconography.

But Christian scenes are becoming increasingly apparent: monks, anonymous saints, as well as Saint Menas between his camels, and Saint Tatania, cavaliers, warrior saints on foot, and *maiestas Domini.*

In contrast to what has been discovered at Bāwīṭ and Saqqara, these personages do not seem to have a specific location in the buildings. However, in one oratory niche there is a composition quite similar to that at Saqqara, with a *maiestas Domini* depicted in a conch, and saints and monks on the walls; but the Virgin—always present at Saqqara—has not yet been found here.

As at Bāwīṭ and Saqqara, painting served to evoke the use of precious materials and to imitate the appearance of stone when applied to architectonic elements.

MARGUERITE RASSART-DEBERGH

BIBLIOGRAPHY

Andreu, G.; G. Castel; and R.-G. Coquin. "Sixième campagne de fouilles aux Kellia, 1979–1980, rapport préliminaire." *Bulletin de l'Institut français d'archéologie orientale* 80 (1980):347–68.

Andreu, G., R.-G. Coquin et al. "Septième campagne de fouilles aux Kellia (avril 1981), rapport préliminaire." *Bulletin de l'Institut français d'archéologie orientale* 81 (1981):159–88.

Chitty, D. J. *The Desert a City.* Oxford, 1966.

Coquin, R.-G. *Livre de la consécration du sanctuaire de Benjamin. Introduction, édition, traduction et annotations.* Cairo, 1975.

Coquin, R.-G. et al. "Huitième campagne de fouilles aux Kellia (avril 1982), rapport préliminaire." *Bulletin de l'Institut français d'archéologie orientale* 82 (1982):363–77.

Cosson, A. F. C. de. "The Desert City of El Muna." *Bulletin de la Société royale d'archéologie d'Alexandrie* 31 (1937):247–53.

Cramer, M. *Koptische Buchmalerei.* Recklinghausen, 1964.

Daumas, F. "Les fouilles de Kellia, 1965–66." *Comptes rendus de l'Académie des inscriptions et belles-lettres* (1966):300–309.

______. "Les fouilles de Kellia, 1966–67." *Comptes rendus de l'Académie des inscriptions et belles-lettres* (1967):438–51.

______. "Les fouilles de Kellia, 1967–68." *Comptes rendus de l'Académie des inscriptions et belles-lettres* (1968):395–408.

______. "Les Fouilles de l'Institut français d'archéologie orientale de 1959 à 1968 et le site monastique des Kellia." *Zeitschrift der deutschen morgenländischen Gesellschaft,* Suppl. I, XVII, *Deutscher Orientalistentag* (1968):1–7.

______. "Les fouilles de Kellia, 1968–69." *Comptes rendus de l'Académie des inscriptions et belles-Lettres* (1969):496–507.

Daumas, F. and A. Guillaumont, et al. *Kellia I, kom 219.* Cairo, 1969.

Egloff, M. *Kellia, la poterie copte, quatre siècles d'artisanat et d'échanges en Basse-Égypte.* Geneva, 1977.

Evelyn-White, H. G. *The Monasteries of the Wadi 'n Natrūn,* Vol. 3, pt. 1: *New Coptic Texts from the Monastery of Saint Macarius;* pt. 2: *The History of the Monasteries of Nitria and of Scetis;* pt. 3: *The Architecture and Archaeology.* New York, 1926–1933.

Guillaumont, A. "Le Site des Cellia (Basse Egypte)." *Revue archéologique* (1964):43–50.

———. "Premières fouilles au site des Kellia (Basse Egypte)." *Comptes rendus de l'Académie des inscriptions et belles-lettres* (1965):218–25.

———. "Une inscription sur la 'prière de Jésus.'" *Orientalia Christiana Periodica* 34 (1968):310–25.

———. "Histoire des moines aux Kellia." *Orientalia Lovaniensia Periodica* 8 (1977):187–203.

———. "Le Site des Kellia menacé de destruction." In *Prospection et sauvegarde des antiquités de l'Egypte.* Cairo, 1981.

Hyvernat, H. *Album de paléographie copte.* Osnabrück, 1972, repr. of 1888 edition.

Jarry, J. "Description des restes d'un petit monastère coupé en deux par un canal d'irrigation aux Kellia." *Bulletin de l'Institut français d'archéologie orientale* 66 (1968):147–55.

Kasser, R. "Exploration dans le désert occidental, Qouçoūr Hégeila et Qouçoūr 'Ereima." *Kēmi* 19 (1969):103–10.

———. "Sortir du monde, réflexions sur la situation et le développement des établissements monastiques des Kellia." *Revue de théologie et de philosophie* 109 (1976):111–24.

Kasser, R., et al. *Kellia 1965, topographie générale, mensurations et fouilles aux Qouçour 'Īsā et aux Qouçoūr el-'Abīd, mensurations aux Qouçoūr el 'Izeila.* Geneva, 1967.

Mission suisse d'Archéologie copte de l'Universite de Genève, under the direction of R. Kasser et al. *Survey archéologique des Kellia (Basse-Egypte), rapport de la campagne 1981.* Louvain, 1983.

Slane, W. MacGuckin, baron de, ed. *Description de l'Afrique septentrionale* by Abou Obeid-el Bekri. Algiers, 1911.

Toussoun, O. *"Cellia" et ses couvents.* Memoires de la Société royale d'archéologie d'Alexandrie, Vol. 8, pt. 1. Alexandria, 1935.

Wilson, R. McL., ed. *The Future of Coptic Studies.* Leiden, 1978.

KELLS, BOOK OF. *See* British Isles, Coptic Influences in the.

KENYON, FREDERIC GEORGE (1863–1952), English scholar and administrator. After his studies in Oxford, he entered the British Museum as an assistant in the Department of Manuscripts. In 1898 he was named assistant keeper of manuscripts, and in 1909, director. He held this post until 1930. He edited Volumes 1 (1893), 2 (1898), and 3 (1907, with H. I. Bell) of *Greek Papyri in the British Museum* and many books on the text of the Greek New Testament, notably *The Text of the Greek Bible: A Student's Handbook* (London, 1937; 2nd ed., 1949). After his retirement, he worked on Chester Beatty's collection of biblical papyri, cataloged in *The Chester Beatty Biblical Papyri* (8 vols., London, 1933–1941).

BIBLIOGRAPHY

Bell, H.I. "Frederic George Kenyon." *Dictionary of National Biography,* pp. 576–78. London, 1971.

MARTIN KRAUSE

KEYS. *See* Metalwork, Coptic; Woodwork, Coptic.

KHĀ'ĪL I, forty-sixth patriarch of the See of Saint Mark (744–767). Khā'īl, or Michael, was a simple monk and presbyter of the Monastery of Saint Macarius (DAYR ANBĀ MAQĀR) in WĀDĪ AL-NAṬRŪN. When THEODORUS, his predecessor, died, the congregating bishops together with the clergy of Alexandria and the archons of the Coptic community selected an episcopal delegation to go to the governor at al-Fusṭāṭ (Old Cairo) to ask permission to select a new patriarch. This was granted by Ḥafṣ ibn al-Walīd al-Ḥaḍramī on the condition that they bring the candidate for an audience before the consecration. The delegates seized this opportunity to complain of the harshness of Ḥafṣ's predecessor, Abū al-Qāsim, who doubled the KHARĀJ tax and extorted a lot of money from the people at a time when the country's resources were depleted by famine and pestilence and the Nile was low. The delegation left for Alexandria with Ḥafṣ's approval, but without securing relief from Abū al-Qāsim's imposts.

For several days, deliberations in Alexandria could not procure unanimity on a name until, following a dream, a deacon came forth with the suggestion of Khā'īl, the monk of Saint Macarius, as the worthy candidate. So the bishops proceeded to Wādī Habīb and came back with Khā'īl, whose consecration took place after his introduction to the governor. In the meantime, the benign caliph Hishām (724–743) was succeeded by al-Walīd ibn Yazīd (743–744), who abused his power in Egypt by recruiting slave labor to build a new city in his name. But he was killed by his successor, Ibrāhīm (744), who released the enslaved workmen and, in anticipation of introducing new reforms, appointed a rival governor better acquainted with the administration of the country. But Ibrāhīm was forced to flee to Damascus, and Ḥafṣ resumed the governorship with the promise of relieving the Copts who embraced Islam from the poll tax or JIZYAH. Tempted by this proposition, 24,000 Copts abjured their faith and apostatized to Islam, and some of them became Islamic soldiers, while Khā'īl, the patriarch, helplessly watched this calamitous event.

Ḥafṣ was pursued by a new governor, Hawtharah, who burned him alive and killed most of his supporters and confiscated all their property. This cruel action gave the people of Egypt a breathing space. According to the HISTORY OF THE PATRIARCHS, "he loved the Orthodox; and as he resided at Wasim with all his army for three years he used to consult the Father Abba Moses about the salvation of his soul."

In the meantime, fighting continued among the Muslims everywhere until Marwān II (744–750) seized the reins of the caliphate. In his household he had a Chalcedonian by the name of Theophylact, a goldsmith by profession, who prevailed upon the caliph to make him Chalcedonian patriarch of the Greeks, in opposition to the Coptic Orthodox Khā'īl. Though relative peace persisted in Egypt for five years, a new governor, of Islamized Jewish extraction, 'Abd al-Malik ibn Mūsā ibn Nāṣir, overran part of western Egypt and entertained much hatred for the Copts. He encouraged Theophylact, now Chalcedonian patriarch under the name of Cosmas, to reclaim some Byzantine churches that had been appropriated by the Copts after the Arab conquest of Egypt, including the famous cathedral of Saint Menas (Abū Mīnā), built by Emperor Arcadius in Mareotis. This led to a heated debate between Khā'īl and Cosmas. Saint Menas was an Egyptian martyr of the third century, and though the Chalcedonians tried to prevail by bribery, apparently the eloquence and the logic of the Coptic patriarch in the end won this battle of wits. During the time the Chalcedonians tried to restore the unity of the two churches, with subsequent prolonged discussions between the two parties, general attention was drawn away from religious dialogue by a pestilence. But the government resumed its quest for extraordinary financial imposts from both patriarchs. The Coptic patriarch was constrained to ask permission to go to Upper Egypt to collect funds, with which he could quench the thirst of the rulers for gold.

Another incident of international character seems to have worsened the situation of Khā'īl. He was led to interfere in a conflict between the king of Nubia and his bishop. After a long exchange of letters between the king and the Patriarch, the governor of Egypt became aware of the situation and seized Khā'īl and placed him in prison. He was charged with going beyond his jurisdiction in meddling with international matters over the head of the governor. The king, Cyriacus, took arms and invaded Egypt with a hundred thousand horsemen, as well as a hundred thousand camels. The Nubians are said to have reached the precincts of Miṣr, and the governor was constrained to free the captive patriarch and urge him to go to the king and induce him to withdraw from Egypt. This he did, and for the time being the patriarchal conflict with the administration was ameliorated.

Later, the governor laid a heavy hand on Lower Egypt, extorting extraordinary imposts from the people, so that the Bashmurites rebelled against the Muslims and slew many of them (see BASHMURIC REVOLTS). Consequently, in 749 Marwān II arrived in Egypt with a tremendous army to chastise the rebels, but he could not reach them for they were safely entrenched behind the marshes of the delta. Thus, he seized the patriarch, accusing him of complicity with the Bashmurites and imprisoning him with "a mass of iron to his feet" (*History of the Patriarchs*). Numerous members of the clergy were put to flight. The patriarch was abused and flogged by his captors, who threatened him with decapitation. But he was saved from murder by the feeling among the Muslims that this would bring no good. It was a time when the Umayyads were fighting the Abbasids, who are called Khurasanians in the *History of the Patriarchs*, and they entertained the idea of flight to Nubia, where the Coptic patriarch was highly honored. So, if they hurt Khā'īl, that might make them unwelcome in their southern refuge. Marwān was cornered in Egypt and decided to burn Miṣr to deprive the Abbasid invaders of a shelter. He also sent his men to destroy the fields that might supply his enemies with provisions. But the Abbasids managed to reach al-Fusṭāṭ before this and ultimately were able to cross the Nile, whereupon Marwān and his company took flight, leaving behind them Patriarch Khā'īl and his bishops, whom they had incarcerated. With Marwān's disappearance, the persecuted Coptic clergy and the patriarch regained their freedom from the new masters.

A new governor, Abū 'Awn, took the reigns of power in Egypt. He seemed to be more sympathetic toward applying only the just *kharāj* tax to the Copts. The patriarch spent the remainder of his reign in relative peace under Abū ʿAwn. The *History of the Patriarchs* (Vol. 1, part 3, pp. 402–403) describes his character in the following terms: "Now our father Abbā Khā'īl was sweet in speech, beautiful in countenance, perfect in stature, decent in his attire, well-formed and dignified; and his words were like a sword against the rebellion, and his teaching was like salt to people of virtue and modesty. And the hand of God was with him in those hardships which he endured through ʿAbd al-Malik." After a reign of nearly twenty-four years, he died, and his body was interred with the bodies of the holy fathers buried in Alexandria.

BIBLIOGRAPHY

Atiya, A. S. *History of Eastern Christianity*. London, 1968.

Cambridge History of Islam, 2 vols., ed. P. M. Holt, Ann K. S. Lambton, and Bernard Lewis. Cambridge, 1970.

Hitti, P. K. *History of the Arabs*. London, 1946.

Lane-Poole, S. *History of Egypt in the Middle Ages*. Paris, 1925.

SUBHI Y. LABIB

KHĀ'ĪL II, fifty-third patriarch of the See of Saint Mark (849–851). Khā'īl succeeded YŪSĀB I without encountering opposition from the bishops, the clergy, and the Coptic archons. He was well known to them for his sanctity and his profound knowledge of the Holy Scriptures. Originally, as a simple deacon, he had acted as scribe and assistant to Yūsāb, and it was in that capacity that the Alexandrians first became acquainted with him. In due course, he pleaded with the patriarch to release him from his local duties and to permit him to go to the wilderness of Wādī Habīb in the Western Desert. Consequently, he entered the monastery of Saint John (Dayr Anbā Yuḥannis) and concentrated on prayers and further studies. He became widely known for his scholarship in all religious matters. When the delegation from Alexandria came to fetch him for consecration, he resisted, but they eventually forced him to accompany them to the city, where he was consecrated on 24 Hātūr.

His reign was rather brief and uneventful, for he occupied the throne of Saint Mark for only one year and five months. His contemporary caliph was al-Mutawakkil (847–861) of the Abbasid dynasty, who enjoined the governor of the country to press the patriarch for immediate payment of his heavy taxes. Thus, the main problem facing him was the permanent and vexatious imposition of increasing annual taxation, which he, nevertheless, seems to have rendered to the satisfaction of the Islamic administration. He was a man of frail physical stature, and the weighty duties of the patriarchal office seem to have been too much for him to bear. In the second year of his reign, he went back to Wādī Habīb to celebrate Easter with the monks, following an established custom of previous patriarchs. There he fell seriously ill and died. He was buried in the Monastery of Saint Macarius (DAYR ANBĀ MAQĀR).

AZIZ S. ATIYA

KHĀ'ĪL III, fifty-sixth patriarch of the See of Saint Mark (880–907). Khā'īl succeeded SHENUTE I shortly after his death. Little is known about his life before or after he took the monastic vow except that he was a man of virtue and that he was penalized by one of his bishops, the occupant of the diocese of Sakhā. He was a contemporary of Aḥmad ibn Ṭūlūn (870–881) at the outset of his patriarchate. Khā'īl happened to be at the village of Danūshar within the episcopate of Sakhā, near the modern city of Disūq in the Gharbiyyah province (Amélineau, 1893, p. 143), for the consecration of a new church in the name of Ptolemeus the Martyr. Apparently the bishop was absent from the liturgy of consecration, and the patriarch proceeded with the performance of that function. Then the bishop arrived and protested against action in his absence, and he took the sacramental utensils and threw them away, which was regarded as a mortal sin, for which the patriarch deposed him. Viciously, the bishop went to Aḥmad ibn Ṭūlūn to complain about Khā'īl and to declare that the patriarch had immense wealth. Ibn Ṭūlūn, being in dire need of funds for his impending military expedition to Palestine, summoned Khā'īl and demanded money from him, which he did not have. Consequently, the patriarch was arrested and incarcerated. On hearing this, two Coptic scribes of Ibn Ṭūlūn's administration, Bisūs and Abraam, went to the vizier, Aḥmad ibn al-Maridānī, and pleaded with him to intercede with the sultan on behalf of patriarchal freedom. Ibn Ṭūlūn freed the patriarch on the stipulation that he would pay 10,000 dinars in a month and another 10,000 within four months. The first amount was levied from ten bishops, but the second sum was not paid because Ibn Ṭūlūn died in the field during the interval and was succeeded by his son Khumārawayh (881–896), who was more lenient toward his Christian subjects and chose to forget about the second installment. Little beyond this minor episode is mentioned in the HISTORY OF THE PATRIARCHS, save some miraculous and legendary tales. According to the same source, however, simony (CHEIROTONIA) had to be revived to help in payment of state financial imposts. The patriarch died on 21 Amshīr in the reign of al-Muktafī (904–908).

BIBLIOGRAPHY

Amélineau, E. *Géographie de l'Egypte à l'époque copte*. Paris, 1893.

Lane-Poole, S. *History of Egypt in the Middle Ages*. London, 1901.

———. *The Mohammadan Dynasties*. Paris, 1925.

SUBHI Y. LABIB

KHANDAQ, AL-,

KHANDAQ, AL-, ancient small village on the outskirts of Cairo northeast of the city. There is some uncertainty about its name. One possibility emerges when one extrapolates from three different accounts of the martyrdom of Saint APOLI. The end of the Coptic martyrdom indicates that a memorial church was to be built in which his body would be entombed. Later a flourishing town named Pesenetai sprang up at the site. Another version of the martyrdom relates that after some time the body of Apoli was transferred from Pesenetai to a place named Psobt-m-p-hoi. W. E. Crum (1907, p. 291) and H. G. Evelyn-White (1926, p. 92, n. 5) deduced that this Psobt-m-p-hoi was the Coptic name of al-Khandaq from the fact that the Arabic SYNAXARION gives al-Khandaq as the name of the place where the body of Apoli was kept for a time. That Psobt-m-p-hoi means "the wall of the moat" and al-Khandaq means "the moat" adds strength to the deduction.

Another name presented by the medieval list of Egyptian churches and monasteries is Shats, which stands as the Coptic equivalent of al-Khandaq. The available evidence does not point to an obvious answer to this puzzle, but among the possible solutions are the following: al-Khandaq may have been known in Coptic as Psobt-m-p-hoi at an earlier period and as Shats in a later era; Psobt-m-p-hoi may have been a village, in which the body of Apa Apoli was kept for a time before it was brought to al-Khandaq, which was known in Coptic as Shats.

Al-Khandaq was a bishopric by the middle of the eleventh century when Bishop George joined with a number of others in an attempt to drive Patriarch CHRISTODOULUS (1047–1077) from office.

[*See also:* Dayr al-Khandaq.]

BIBLIOGRAPHY

Amélineau, E. *La Géographie de l'Egypte à l'époque copte*. Paris, 1893.

Crum, W. E. "Hagiographica from Leipzig Manuscripts." *Proceedings of the Society of Biblical Archaeology* 29 (1907):289–96, 301–307.

Evelyn-White, H. G. *The Monasteries of the Wadi 'n Natrun*, pt. 1. New York, 1926.

Timm, S. *Das christlich-koptische Ägypten in arabischer Zeit*, pt. 3, pp. 1082–87. Wiesbaden, 1985.

RANDALL STEWART

KHARA'IB AL-NĀMŪS. *See* Dayr al-Nāmūs.

KHARĀJ,

KHARĀJ, a tax imposed on property and districts rather than on individual persons. The exact meaning of the word is "land yield," signifying the harvest produced by a given territory. It was originally paid in kind as in the preceding Byzantine system of taxation. P. Schwartz (1916) has attempted to establish the thesis that the Arab system was inherited from the Arabs' Byzantine predecessors. Linguistically *kharāj* is a corruption of the Greek *choregia*, and both words are identical in their practical usage. With the passing of time, payment in kind was considered to be impractical and was replaced by its equivalent in currency. In later centuries the tax became a somewhat unlimited impost on farmers, who gradually became more and more like slave laborers on land owned theoretically by the conquering Muslim community as *fay'* (Qur'ān 59:6–7), signifying that all goods, chattels, and land should be secured from unbelievers without fighting. Hence the proceeds of all such property must be ceded to the state.

Legally, the governors in Egypt had a free hand in the imposition of the *kharāj* on the inhabitants of all villages. The governors often imposed such massive levies as to leave the Coptic farmers without the slightest share of what the land produced, a situation that eventually led to their migrating to neighboring towns in search of a livelihood. As can be seen from the histories of certain medieval patriarchs, the migration movement became so strong that whole territories became fallow, a state that alarmed the rulers because of the loss of *kharāj*. Consequently, the government issued firm decrees to stop migration and ordered the return of the migrants by force to their original homes.

In the Abbasid period, the legal particulars of the *kharāj* were codified by jurists such as Abū Yūsuf Ya'qūb and, later, Mawardī and others. However, the *kharāj* as land tax became obsolete as more and more Christian inhabitants converted to Islam and thus automatically became liable to tithing (*'ushr*) and *zakāt* instead of *kharāj*. The *kharāj* eventually fell into disuse.

It is noteworthy, however, from the HISTORY OF THE PATRIARCHS that additional irregular taxes were imposed by the governors of Egypt on every Coptic pope after his consecration, and the beleaguered patriarch had to ask for special dispensation to tour the country to collect the requested impost, so that he would be left to occupy the throne of Saint Mark in relative peace. Such extraordinary financial measures became customary for each pope at his accession.

BIBLIOGRAPHY

Becker, C. H. "Die Entstehung von 'Ushr- und Kharāj-Land in Ägypten." *Zeitschrift für Assyriologie* 18 (1904–1905):301–319.

Fagnan, E. Abou Yousof Ya'koub. *Le Livre de l'impôt foncier.* Paris, 1921.

Gaudefroy, D. *Le Monde musulman et byzantin jusqu'aux croisades.* Paris, 1931.

Schwartz, P. "Die Herkunft von arabisch 'Kharāj' (Grund) Steuer." *Der Islam* 6 (1916):97ff.

Wellhausen, J. *Das arabische Reich und sein Sturz.* Berlin, 1902.

Ye'or, Bar. *The Dhimmi: Jews and Christians Under Islam,* trans. from French, David Maisel, Paul Fenton, and David Littman. Rutherford, Calif., and London, 1985.

AZIZ S. ATIYA

KHARTOUM. *See* Sudan, Copts in the.

KHIRBAT AL-FILŪSIYYAH, a fortified town at the east end of the Sabkhat al-Bardawīl (the ancient Lake Serbonis), with the seat of a bishop from A.D. 359 (Munier, 1943, p. 7). Since it was a harbor town and because of its position close to the most important military and caravan route linking Egypt and Palestine from Pelusium (Faramā) via Rhinokorua (al-'Arish) to Gaza (Josephus *De bello Judaico* 4. 661; also Gardiner, 1920, pp. 99ff.), at least from Roman times it had a significant mercantile importance. At the beginning of the sixth century it was developed into a strong fortress. It was destroyed by the Persians (619), but under Arab rule was rebuilt on a somewhat different site, using much material (*spolia*) from the old site. The final destruction presumably resulted from the earthquake of 1302.

During the excavations in the region of the former town, whose ruins extend over an area of several square miles, parts of the camp from late antiquity as well as two churches were discovered. Both churches belong to the basilica type, and are provided with an atrium, which is seldom the case elsewhere in Egypt.

In the town area in the neighborhood of the late Roman camp, the south church is the larger of the two and has on the west side of the atrium several separate rooms and a cistern (wrongly regarded as a baptistery). The naos shows the usual division into three aisles with a western return aisle and a three-room sanctuary. In the apse there was a synthronon and in front of it the bema with vestiges of the cancelli. The altar seems to have been covered by a ciborium. Each of the two apse side rooms had a semicircular niche in the east wall. According to the excavation report (Clédat, 1916, p. 24), the setup of the church was of a remarkable uniformity. It may therefore be dated to the first half of the sixth century.

The north church in the harbor area is substantially smaller, and appears to have had an entrance only on the west. Access was through a tribelon from the atrium into the narthex, and then through three further doors into the three-aisle naos. There is no return aisle. The sanctuary as usual is divided into three rooms, and here also the apse is equipped with a synthronon. In front of the apse is the bema surrounded by cancelli, with the altar in the middle. A peculiarity of this church is a small triconch added to the apse at the back, which in its east conch contains a recess with a flight of steps ascending in front of the east wall, and therefore practically unusable. The excavators have no explanation to offer. Whether it is an arbitrarily formed baptistery, as conjectured by A. Khatchatrian (1962, p. 84), remains uncertain.

[*See also:* Architectural Elements of Churches.]

BIBLIOGRAPHY

Clédat, J. "Fouilles à Khirbet el-Flousiyeh." *Annales du Service des Antiquites de l'Egypte* 16 (1916):6–32.

Gardiner, A. H. "The Ancient Military Road Between Egypt and Palestine." *Journal of Egyptian Archaeology* 6 (1920):99–116.
Khatchatrian, A. *Les baptistères paléochrétiens.* Paris, 1962.
Leclercq, H. *Dictionnaire d'archéologie chrétienne et de liturgie* 13 (1937):54–70.
Munier, H. *Recueil des listes épiscopales de l'église copte.* Cairo, 1943.
Nussbaum, O. *Standort des Liturgen am christlichen Altar vor dem Jahre 1,000.* Bonn, 1965.
Vincent, H. "Un type de baptistère byzantin." *Revue biblique* 21 (1922):583–89.

PETER GROSSMANN

KHIRBITAH, town located on the western edge of the Egyptian Delta about 3 miles (5 km) southwest of Kom Hamādah in the Beheirah Province. In Greek the town was known as Andropolis.

Coptic sources from the pre-Arabic period do not mention Christians or churches in Khirbitah, but the fact that the town was a bishopric within a few decades of the ARAB CONQUEST OF EGYPT suggests that it had been an important center of Christianity even earlier. Records indicate that Bishop Jacob from Khirbitah was one of those present when Patriarch JOHN III died in 686.

Khirbitah was still a bishopric in the eleventh century as evidenced by the attendance of Bishop Theodorus from Khirbitah at the election of Patriarch CYRIL II in 1078 and at a synod in Cairo in 1086 (Munier, 1943, pp. 26, 28).

BIBLIOGRAPHY

Munier, H. *Recueil des listes épiscopales de l'église copte.* Cairo, 1943.
Timm, S. *Das christlich-koptische Ägypten in arabischer Zeit.* Wiesbaden, 1985.

RANDALL STEWART

KHIZĀNAH (Arabic), storeroom or warehouse. In Egyptian monastery architecture it also has the meaning of a hiding place. In some sources the same hiding place is called in modern Arabic *makhba'*. They are to be found in almost all monasteries, and in part probably also served as archives. Their main function was, however, as places where objects of value such as liturgical utensils could be left in case of danger, while the inhabitants of the monastery took flight. Accordingly they are usually provided with a secret entrance. In the church of the monastery of Shenute at Suhāj (White Monastery) three have so far been identified, under the two side chambers of the east conch and under the southern (westward) ascent of the north staircase, one of which is mentioned by Abū al-Makārim. In each case the secret entrance is located in a wall niche, the bottom ledge of which consisted of a thick stone slab and could be moved sideways in the stonework leaving the way down open. The *khizānah* in the north wall of the church of Sitt Maryam at DAYR AL-SURYĀN (Grossmann, 1982, p. 206) can be entered through the cover of one of the wall niches in the northern sanctuary. Several *khizānah*s, with sometimes very complicated entrances, were found in some of the monks' dwellings in the great laura of KELLIA. They seem to have been added by some of the hermits for use when they had to go on a journey, but this was not the rule. Other monks left everything accessible. Finally in the Melchite and Maronite churches *khizānah* means sacristy (Arabic, *sakristiyyā*) as well as tabernacle to keep the remains of the communion (Graf, 1954, p. 42).

BIBLIOGRAPHY

Graf, G. *Verzeichnis arabischer Kirchlicher Termini.* Louvain, 1954.
Grossmann, P. *Mittelalterliche Langhauskuppel-Kirchen und verwandte Typen in Oberägypten.* Glückstadt, 1982.
Kasser, R., et al. "Survey archéologique des Kellia (Basse-Égypte)." *Rapport de la campagne 1981.* Louvain, 1981.

PETER GROSSMANN

KHŪRUS. *See* Architectural Elements of Churches.

KIRCHER, ATHANASIUS (1602–1680), German Jesuit. In 1630 he became professor of philosophy, mathematics, and Oriental languages at Würzburg, and from 1635 to 1643 he was professor of mathematics at Rome. His endeavors to decipher Egyptian hieroglyphics bore no fruit but aroused interest in ancient Egypt. His Coptic studies, *Prodromus Coptus sive Aegyptiacus* (1636) and *Lingua Aegyptiaca Restituta* (1643), were successful.

BIBLIOGRAPHY

Chaine, M. "Une Composition oubliée du P. Kircher en l'honneur de Peiresc." *Revue de l'orient chrétien* 9 (1933–1934):196–206.

Dawson, W. R., and E. P. Uphill. *Who Was Who in Egyptology.* London, 1972.
Janssen, J. "Athanasius Kircher 'égyptologe.'" *Chronique d'Egypte* 18 (1943):240–47.

MARTIN KRAUSE

KISS OF PEACE (Greek, *aspasmos*), a greeting exchanged among the clergy and the congregation during the Divine Liturgy as a token of pure love and communion of spirit. The *aspasmos* dates back to the apostolic age. In his epistles Saint Paul repeatedly referred to the "holy kiss," as in Romans 16:16, 1 Corinthians 16:20, 2 Corinthians 13:12, and 1 Thessalonians 5:26. Saint Peter described it as a "kiss of charity" in 1 Peter 5:14. CYRIL OF JERUSALEM (c. 315–386) prescribed the essential spiritual nature of the kiss of peace: "Do not think that this kiss is like that which friends are accustomed to give one another when they meet. This is not such a kiss. This kiss unites the souls together and destroys all resentment. This kiss is a sign of union of souls" (1955, no. 23, p. 153). Saint Augustine called it a "sign of peace" and added that "the outwardly shape of the lips expresses what is in our hearts" (PL 38, col. 1101a). Its intrinsic quality was stressed by THEODORUS OF MOPSUESTIA: "By this kiss people make a kind of profession of the unity and charity which they have among themselves. It is not fitting for those who form one body in the church that anyone of them should hate any of his brothers who are sharing in the faith."

The introduction of the *aspasmos* in the Coptic liturgy directly after the Prayer of Reconciliation signifies, in the words of Saint Paul, that God "reconciled us to Himself and gave us the ministry of reconciliation" (2 Cor. 5:18). Accordingly the celebrant says, "And make us all worthy, O Lord, to greet one another with a holy kiss," to which the deacon responds, "Pray for perfect peace, for love, and for the holy *aspasmos* of the Apostles." Then the congregation sings the *aspasmos* hymn that starts with the words "Rejoice, O Mary the handmaiden and mother." For this reason the Prayer of Reconciliation was named the Prayer of the *Aspasmos* in some old euchologia; the verbal greeting accompanying it was "Christ is between us," to which the response was "He is and will be" (Gogol, 1934, p. 36).

At first the Kiss of Peace was a real kiss exchanged by the faithful in the church, but in time it became a movement in which four hands enfold in a mutual greeting with two palms touching, as is practiced now. The thirteenth-century Coptic writer IBN SIBĀʿ described it as a kiss on the right cheek, reciprocally given and received, followed by a handshake.

The Kiss of Peace is also given at certain points during church services. At the start of the liturgy, having made a prostration toward the east before the altar, the celebrant bows to his fellow priests, embraces them, and asks for their absolution and prayers on his behalf. In the presence of the patriarch, metropolitan, or bishop during the liturgy, a priest takes the incense box to him and then kisses the cross and his hand. When he has passed the incense to his fellow priests, they embrace as a sign of peace and love. After the Liturgy and preceding the dismissal, the priests embrace, as do the members of the congregation. Following the completion of the sacraments of baptism and anointing with the holy chrism, the priest and the faithful embrace the person baptized, who has become a member in the body of Christ. The Constitutions of the Holy Fathers (1951–1959, p. 483) laid it down that following the consecration of a bishop, "he be placed in his throne, in a place set apart for him among the rest of the bishops, they all giving him the Kiss in the Lord."

The kiss is not permitted on the Wednesday and Thursday of HOLY WEEK, in memory of the treacherous kiss of Judas Iscariot who betrayed Christ (Mt. 26:48; Mk. 14:44; Lk. 22:48).

BIBLIOGRAPHY

Gogol, N. V., ed. *La Divine liturgie,* trans. T. Belpaire. Namur, 1934.
Ibn al-ʿAssāl, al-Ṣafī. *Kitāb al-Qawānīn.* Repr. Cairo, 1927.
Ibn Sibāʿ Yūḥannā ibn Abī Zakarīyā. *Kitāb al-Jawharah al-Nafīsah fī ʿUlūm al-Kanīsah,* ed. Viktūr Manṣūr. Cairo, 1902. Latin version *Pretiosa Margarita de scientiis ecclesiasticis,* trans. Vincent Mistrīḥ. Cairo, 1966.
Malatī, T. Y. *Christ in the Eucharist,* Bk. 5. Alexandria, 1973.
Yūḥannā Salāmah. *Al-La'ālī' al-Nafīsah fī Sharḥ Ṭuqūs wa-Muʿtaqadāt al-Kanīsah.* Cairo, 1909.

ARCHBISHOP BASILIOS

KLÉBER, JEAN-BAPTISTE (1753–1800), French general who joined the FRENCH EXPEDITION to Egypt in 1798. For a time he was military governor of the province of Alexandria and then of Damietta; after the departure of Napoleon, he succeeded him in the supreme command of the French Oriental Army.

As governor of Alexandria, Kléber tried to remain neutral regarding the different religious groups. But he could already see that the leaders of the non-Muslim minorities showed more loyalty to the French than the Muslims. His positive impression concerning the non-Muslim population of Egypt grew stronger during his stay at Damietta, because of the cooperation of the former leaseholder of the customs tax farm of the port, a Syrian Christian, and of the head of the Greek Orthodox community.

When Kléber became supreme commander, he was confronted with enormous financial problems. The pay for the soldiers was in arrears and there was no cash in the treasury. Napoleon had left the collection of the taxes to a great extent in the hands of the Copts under the direction of JIRJIS AL-JAWHARĪ. Kléber was conscious of the disadvantages of this system, but he believed that he could not dispense with the services of the Copts. He tried to reduce the irregularities by more closely controlling and reducing the Coptic administrative machinery. But the scarcity of money induced him to grant the Coptic bureaucracy and its tax collectors more independence and to give them financial premiums in the form of bonuses for the year 1800. Since these measures failed, he tried force, with threats and arrests, to make the demanded sums of money available.

Kléber's attitude to the Muslim people was cooler, more objective, and more formal than Napoleon's. He dealt with the Muslim leaders respectfully, and he promised to protect and respect Islam as the religion of the majority. But inwardly he was convinced that the Muslims, in spite of their reverence to the French, clung to their religion and only waited for a propitious moment to come down upon their foreign enemy. His skepticism was corroborated during the preparations of the evacuation and throughout the insurrections that followed the annulment of the treaty of al-'Arish. As a punishment, Kléber inflicted enormous levies on the Muslim population of the seditious towns. Thus, his relationship to the Muslim leaders remained cold and rather hostile for some time. Only the threat of a new Turkish attack moved him to hold out the hand of reconciliation to the *'ulemas* (Muslim religious leaders).

After the Muslim revolts in Cairo and other places, Kléber gave up his neutrality toward the different religious groups and openly used the support of non-Muslim minorities. He transferred the police supervision in Cairo and its surroundings to the auxiliary troops, which were mainly recruited from Greek Christians. The collection of the punitive levies inflicted on the Muslims was handed over to the Coptic YA'QŪB, the former secretary of Sulaymān Bey and later intendant of General Desaix, who was granted wide-reaching powers. With his help, a Coptic auxiliary of 600 soldiers was also established, the so-called COPTIC LEGION, of which Ya'qūb was appointed commander. Ya'qūb replaced Jirjis al-Jawharī as native adviser and confidant to the French. Moreover, Kléber made use of the mood among the non-Muslim population to reinforce the existing Greek auxiliaries and to create two new companies of Syrian Christians.

After the reconquest of Egypt, Kléber once more gave the collection of taxes entirely to the Copts, but the upper level of the Coptic administrative machine was put directly under the control of the French financial administration.

Kléber granted compensation to the Christian minorities, which had suffered losses of life and property during the Muslim insurrections. He also closed his eyes to the chicanery the Muslims were subjected to by the Christians as revenge for their suffering. However, a month after the recapture of the capital, he stopped these actions, announced a reconciliation between the French and the Muslims, and promised a policy more considerate of the interests of the Muslim population. Kléber was not able to realize this plan of internal peace between the different religious groups in Egypt. On 14 June 1800, he was murdered by a Muslim from Aleppo, whom officers of the grand vizier had hired. General Menou succeeded him as supreme commander of the French Oriental Army.

BIBLIOGRAPHY

La Jonquière, C. E. L. M. de Taffanel. *L'Expédition d'Egypte, 1798–1801*, vols. 1–5. Paris, 1899–1906.

Motzki, H. *Dimma und Egalité. Die nichtmuslimischen Minderheiten Ägyptens in der zweiten Hälfte des 18. Jahrhunderts und die Expedition Bonapartes (1798–1801)*. Bonn, 1979.

Pajol, C. P. V. *Kléber—Sa vie, sa correspondance*. Paris, 1877.

Rigault, G. *Le Général Abd-allah Menou et la dernière phase de l'expédition d'Egypte (1799–1801)*. Paris, 1911.

HARALD MOTZKI

KOM ABŪ BILLŪ. *See* Tarnūṭ.

KOM NAMRŪD, early Christian anchorite settlement on the edge of the desert, northwest of Samālūt, part of which has been uncovered by the Egyptian Antiquities Organization. As in Kellia, the hermitages consist of rectangular buildings situated well away from each other, with a walled courtyard and a small living area in one corner that was often extended on different sides at a later period. The ground plans of the houses, however, differ from the examples at KELLIA. Almost in the center of the area is a church that was built partly on an older hermitage and was constructed along the lines of a basilica. Early Christian *spolia* were used for the columns. The sanctuary of the church consists of an apse with a wide but short forechoir and two rectangular side rooms. The southern side room is narrowed a little on the south and east sides in order to make room for a staircase. Inserted in the wall work on both sides of the apse curve are two small rooms probably intended as hiding places (KHIZĀNAH).

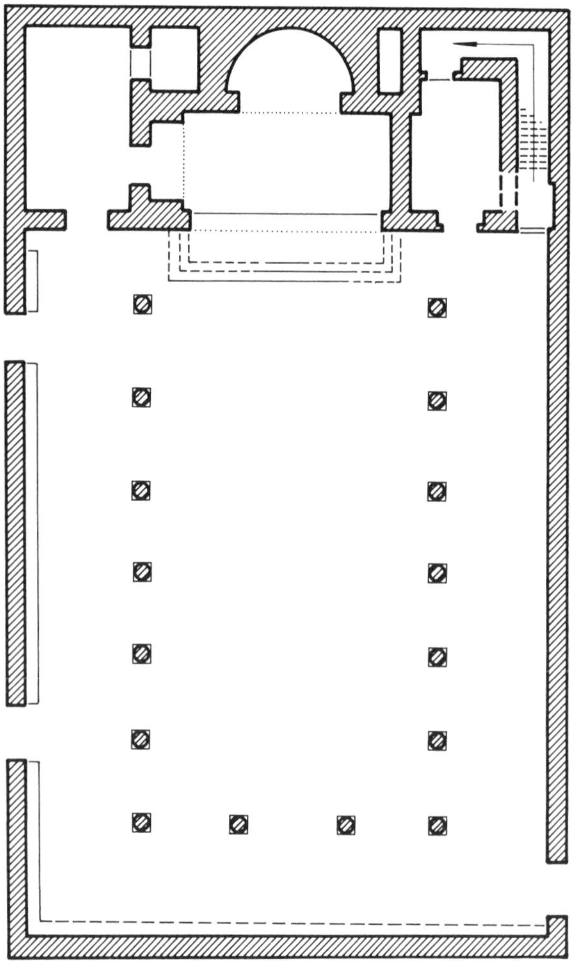
Plan of the church at Kom Namrūd.

[*See also:* Architectural Elements of Churches.]

PETER GROSSMANN

KOM OMBO, a town on the east bank of the Nile, and the only one of any size between the Nile narrows at Jabal al-Silsilah and Aswan. It is also important from the point of view of trade, since here the caravan route from the Sudan leads into the Nile Valley. The double-celled temple from the Ptolemaic period, dedicated to the crocodile god Suchos and the falcon god Haroeris, must be regarded as its most important monument. In the area of this temple, and still within its enclosure wall, some pedestals of columns from late antiquity were found to the northwest of the actual temple building, and these are generally regarded as elements from a church. A somewhat larger base was still in situ. The only surviving capital is a reused late imperial capital.

East of this stands a simple dwelling house of the early Christian period, in which all kinds of church furnishings were found. Some connection between this building and a church is therefore very natural.

BIBLIOGRAPHY

Barsanti, A. "Rapport sur les travaux de consolidation exécutés a Kom Ombo." *Annales du Service des Antiquités de l'Egypte* 15 (1915):173–74.

Gutbub, A. "Kom Ombo." In *Lexicon der Ägyptologie,* Vol. 3. Wiesbaden, 1980.

Kees, H. "Omboi 2." In *Realencyklopädie für protestantische Theologie und Kirche* 18 (1939):346–49.

PETER GROSSMANN

KOM AL-RĀHIB, village about 6 miles (10 km) northwest of SAMĀLŪT. The ruins of a large monastery containing a garden of palm trees, a cistern, a church, and monks' cells have been discovered there (Johnson, 1910–1911, p. 13).

In the neighborhood, an ancient cemetery has yielded up a very fine funerary STELA (Arif, 1906, pp. 113–14).

M. Ramzī (1953–1954, 1963, Vol. 2, pt. 3, p. 236) identifies Kom al-Rāhib with the ancient Pergoush and the Dayr Anbā Bakhūm, but there is nothing to support this identification.

BIBLIOGRAPHY

Arif, S. "Découverte d'une tombe chrétienne près de Samallut." *Annales du Service des antiquités de l'Egypte* 7 (1906):111–13.

Johnson, J. de M. "Graeco-Roman Branch, Excavations at Atfieh." In *Archeological Report 1910–1911*, ed. F. L. Griffith, pp. 5–13 and pl. 6–8.

Ramzī, M. *Al-Qāmūs al-Jughrāfi lil-Bilād al Miṣrīyyah*, 3 vols. in 6 pts. Cairo, 1953–1968.

RENÉ-GEORGES COQUIN
MAURICE MARTIN, S.J.

KOPTOS. *See* Qifṭ.

KRAJON AND AMUN, SAINTS, martyrs in fourth-century Egypt (feast day: 25 Abīb). Some fragments of the original Passion have survived in Bohairic in the Coptic Museum, Cairo, and the University Library, Leipzig (Evelyn-White, 1926, pp. 105–113). The text belongs to the Cycle of ARIANUS (see CYCLES) and seems to be of the seventh to eighth century, inspired by the more highly fictionalized style of this later period. According to the summary of their Passion in the Copto-Arabic SYNAXARION, it had a twofold focus: their martyrdom at SCETIS and the translation of their remains to Alexandria. The remaining text fragments explain that Krajon and Amun are two thieves who are friends; they are converted and become monks at Scetis. Krajon then goes to Pshati (Nikiou) and meets the emperor. After a missing section, we find Amun in dispute with the prefect Arianus at Antinoopolis. Arianus sends him to the prefect Culcianus in Alexandria, where he meets many holy confessors in prison.

BIBLIOGRAPHY

Baumeister, T. *Martyr Invictus. Der Märtyrer als Sinnbild der Erlösung in der Legende und im Kult der frühen koptischen Kirche.* Münster, 1972.

Evelyn-White, H. G. *New Coptic Texts from the Monastery of Saint Macarius.* New York, 1926.

TITO ORLANDI

KRALL, JAKOB (1857–1905), Austrian Egyptologist and Coptologist. He was educated in Trieste, Athens, and the University of Vienna (1879–1880). He then studied Egyptology at the Collège de France and at the Louvre. He was appointed extraordinary professor at Vienna University (1890), ordinary professor (1897), and full professor (1899). He was a corresponding member of the Vienna Academy from 1890. He made many important contributions to Egyptology and to Coptic studies.

BIBLIOGRAPHY

Dawson, W. R., and E. P. Uphill. *Who Was Who in Egyptology*, p. 160. London, 1972.

Erman, A. "Joseph Krall." *Zeitschrift für Ägyptische Sprache und Altertumskunde* 42 (1905):86.

Kammerer, W., comp. *A Coptic Bibliography.* Ann Arbor, Mich., 1950; repr. New York, 1969.

AZIZ S. ATIYA

KRESTODOLU I. *See* Ethiopian Prelates.

KRESTODOLU II. *See* Ethiopian Prelates.

KRESTODOLU III. *See* Ethiopian Prelates.

KUENTZ, CHARLES (1895–1978), French Egyptologist. He was a professor in France; then he became successively a member, secretary, and director of the Institut français d'Archéologie orientale du Caire (1919–1953). He was also director of research at the Centre national de la Recherche scientifique in Paris (1953–1965).

BIBLIOGRAPHY

Trad, M. "Bibliographie de Charles Kuentz." *Bulletin de l'Institut français d'Archéologie orientale* 79 (1979):5–16.

Vercoutter, J. "Charles Kuentz (1895–1978)." *Bulletin de l'Institut français d'Archéologie orientale* 78 (1978):1.

RENÉ-GEORGES COQUIN

KÜHNEL, ERNST (1882–1964), German scholar. He was director of the Islamic Department of the Berlin Museum (1931–1951); professor at the University of Berlin (1935–1954); consultant to the Textile Museum in Washington, D.C.; and member of many academies. He worked in all branches of Islamic art, notably on the connection between Coptic and Islamic art, especially textiles. His major works are *Late Antique Coptic and Islamic Textiles* *of Egypt,* with W. F. Volbach (London, 1926); "La Tradition copte dans les tissus musulmans" (*Bulletin de la Société d'archéologie copte* 4, 1938, pp. 79–89); "Koptische Kunst im islamischen Ägypten" (in *Koptische Kunst, Christentum am Nil: Catalogue of the Exhibition in the Villa Hügel, Essen, May–August 1963,* Essen, 1963, pp. 153–56); and "Nachwirkungen der koptischen Kunst im islamischen Ägypten" (in *Christentum am Nil. Internationale Arbeitstagung zur Ausstellung "Koptische Kunst" Essen, Villa Hügel, 23.–25.7.1963,* Recklinghausen, 1964, pp. 257–59).

BIBLIOGRAPHY

Ettinghausen, R. "In memoriam Ernst Kühnel." *Madrider Mitteilungen* 6 (1965):215–36.

Kühnel-Kunze, I. "Aus der Welt der Islamischen Kunst." In *Festschrift für Ernst Kühnel zum 75. Geburtstag am 26.10.1957.* Berlin, 1959.

MARTIN KRAUSE

KULA AL-HAMRA, AL-. *See* Hermitages, Theban.

KURUM AL-TUWAL. *See* ʿAmriyyah.

KUSH, EMPIRE OF. Roman Egypt was bordered on the south by the empire of Kush, whose territory extended from Lower Nubia at least as far southward as the confluence of the Blue and White Niles. The empire was ruled for nearly a thousand years by descendants of the "Ethiopian" pharaohs of the Twenty-fifth Dynasty, who maintained a pharaonic-style state in their own country long after they had ceased to rule Egypt. Their earliest capital was at Napata, near the Fourth Cataract of the Nile. Later, as the empire expanded southward, the capital was shifted to the more southerly city of Meroë. From here the Kushite rulers maintained diplomatic relations with the Ptolemaic and Roman rulers of Egypt, and Meroë was visited on occasion by Greek and Roman envoys.

The people, or at least the rulers of Kush, spoke a language called Meroitic. Although a considerable number of texts survive, the language has not been deciphered, and it is thus not certain who the Kushites were or whence they originated. Their language does not appear to be related either to ancient Egyptian or to any of the Nubian dialects (see NUBIAN LANGUAGES AND LITERATURE) spoken more recently in the Sudan.

Around 350 the empire of Kush finally disintegrated through a combination of internal weakness and barbarian inroads. Most of its territory was taken over by Nubian-speaking groups (see NUBIANS) who moved into the Nile Valley from areas further to the west. The Nubians established three kingdoms of their own in the old territories of Kush: NOBATIA in the north, MAKOURIA in the middle, and ʿALWĀ in the south, around the confluence of the Blue and White Niles. Nobatia, though located far from Meroë, inherited and carried on more of the ancient traditions of Kush than did the two more southerly kingdoms.

In the middle of the sixth century all three Nubian kingdoms were converted to Christianity (see NUBIA, EVANGELIZATION OF). The medieval civilization that subsequently developed, and that is now recognized as one of the high points in Sudanese cultural history, was a blend of Christian influences and of older traditions inherited from the empire of Kush.

BIBLIOGRAPHY

Adams, W. Y. *Nubia, Corridor to Africa,* pp. 246–381. Princeton, N.J., 1977.

Arkell, A. J. *A History of the Sudan, from the Earliest Times to 1821,* pp. 110–73. London, 1955.

Shinnie, P. L. *Meroe.* New York, 1967.

WILLIAM Y. ADAMS

KUTLAH AL-WAFDIYYAH, AL-. *See* Political Parties.

KYRIAKOS MĪKHĀʾĪL. *See* Mīkhāʾīl, Kyriakos.

KYRIE ELEISON, Greek for "Lord, have mercy." According to Saint JEROME (c. 342–420) and Saint GREGORY OF NAZIANZUS (329–389), it is one of the traditions entrusted by the apostles to the church. The petition is used extensively throughout the Psalms. It is also mentioned by Jesus Christ in the parable of the Pharisee and the publican (Lk. 18:13) and appears in various places in the Gospels, used by different persons asking Christ for mercy (Mt. 9:27, 15:22, 20:30; Mk. 10:47; Lk. 18:38).

The term *Kyrie eleison* or its equivalent in other languages is widely used in all church prayers, of which the following instances deserve mention:

1. at the beginning of the prayers of the CANONICAL HOURS.
2. in the annual and Kiyahk psalmodia, particularly in the petition said toward the end of the service.
3. at the beginning of evening prayer and morning prayer, where the priest starts the petition of mercy before the Gospel petition; the deacon and the congregation respond by saying the *Kyrie eleison* three times.
4. many times during the Divine Liturgy and as a special intercession.
5. in the Liturgy of Saint Gregory.
6. said by the congregation when the priest reads the petition of the FAST during morning prayer in the Fast of Jonah and in the Great Lent.
7. many times during the performance of the sacraments.

ARCHBISHOP BASILIOS

KYRILLOS. *See* Ethiopian Prelates.

KYRILLUS. *See* Cyril.

KYROLLOS. *See* Cyril.

L

LABIB, CLAUDIUS. *See* Iqlādiyūs Labīb.

LABIB, SUBHI YANNI (1924–1987), professor of Near Eastern history at the Christian-Albrechts University of Kiel.

He was born at Tanta (Egypt), and received his education at the University of Alexandria. In 1961 he obtained a doctorate from Hamburg University.

His active academic service included the posts of chief cataloger at the University of Alexandria Library from 1947 to 1954, lecturer in Arabic at Hamburg University from 1961 to 1978, and professor of Near Eastern History at Kiel University from 1979 until his death in 1987. He was also a history professor at the University of Utah from 1970 to 1974. Besides numerous articles, he wrote and edited some major volumes in German and Arabic, including *Handelsgeschichte Ägyptens im Spätmittelalter* (Wiesbaden, 1965) and al-Turkumānī's *Arabic Chronicle* (Cairo, 1986).

YOUSSEF FARAG

LABIB ḤABACHI (1906–1984), Egyptologist. He was born at al-Manṣūrah, capital of the province of Daqahliyyah, and died in Luxor.

He took an interest in Coptic studies from his earliest days. His first publication in Arabic was a book in 1929 on the Coptic monasteries of the Eastern Desert. Although his education and active career in the Department of Antiquities led him to become one of the foremost Egyptologists of modern times, he never lost interest in Coptology.

He was one of the earliest graduates of the newly established Institute of Egyptology in Cairo University in 1928, and joined the Department of Antiquities in 1930 where he spent thirty years, during which time he covered practically all the Egyptian inspectorates and became thoroughly acquainted with all antiquities. He also studied the Egyptian collections in the leading museums of the world. The Oriental Institute of Chicago University selected him as consultant to its Nubian expedition in 1960. In 1981, on the occasion of his seventy-fifth birthday, a festschrift was dedicated to him by German institutes, a 531-page volume containing seventy contributions by Egyptologists from twelve nations. His bibliography, numbering approximately 170 titles, shows occasional contributions in the field of Coptology. He became a member of the board of directors of the Society of Coptic Archaeology in 1976.

BIBLIOGRAPHY

Ḥabachi, L. *The Obelisks of Egypt.* New York, 1977.

Ḥabachi, L., and Z. Tawaḍrūs. *Fī Saḥarā' al-'Arab wa-al-Adyirah al-Sharqiyyah.* Cairo, 1929.

Trad, M. "Bibliography of Labib Habashy." *Bulletin of the Society of Coptic Archaeology* 28 (1986).

MIRRIT BOUTROS GHALI

LABLA. *See* Monasteries of the Fayyūm.

LABOR CONTRACTS. *See* Law, Coptic: Private Law.

LACARON, SAINT, martyr in fourth-century Egypt (feast day: 14 Bābah). His Passion has come down in a complete codex in Bohairic in the Vatican Library (Coptic 68, fols. 1–15) (Balestri and Hyvernat, 1908, Vol. 1, pp. 1–23). The text is that of one of the late Coptic Passions from the period of the CYCLES and can be dated to the eighth century. It deals with the period of persecutions under DIOCLETIAN. The Roman prefect ARIANUS comes to Asyūt and orders sacrifice to the gods. Lacaron, a soldier, refuses and, after the usual arguments, is put in jail. The text then describes the usual episodes of torture, miraculous healings, sudden conversions—of a magistrate and the torturers themselves—and other visions and heavenly interventions. It includes an account of the archangel Michael's gathering up the various pieces of Lacaron and restoring them to life. In the end Lacaron is killed, after converting and baptizing the soldiers around him.

BIBLIOGRAPHY

Balestri, I., and H. Hyvernat. *Acta Martyrum.* CSCO 43, 44. Paris, 1908.

Baumeister, T. *Martyr Invictus. Der Märtyrer als Sinnbild der Erlösung in der Legende und im Kult der frühen koptischen Kirche.* Münster, 1972.

TITO ORLANDI

LACAU, PIERRE (1873–1963), French Egyptologist. Working in all fields of Egyptology, he also published Coptic biblical and apocryphal texts: "Textes de l'Ancien Testament en copte sahidique" (*Recueil de travaux* 23, 1901, pp. 103–124); *Fragments d'apocryphes coptes* (1904); *Textes coptes en dialectes akhmimique et sahidique* (1908); and "Fragments de l'Ascension d'Isaie en copte" (*Le Muséon* 59, 1946, pp. 453–67).

BIBLIOGRAPHY

Daumas, G. *Bulletin de l'Institut français d'Archéologie orientale* 62 (1964):231–35.

Dawson, W. R., and E. P. Uphill. *Who Was Who in Egyptology.* London, 1972.

MARTIN KRAUSE

LA CROZE-VEYSSIERE, MATHURIN (1661–1739), Huguenot historian and linguist. He wrote no less than four dictionaries (Armenian, Coptic, Slav, and Syriac). His correspondence with P. E. Jablonski and David Wilke, *Lacroze, Mathurin Veyssière de, Thesauri Epistolici Lacroziana* (ed. J. L. Uhlius, 3 vols. Leipzig, 1742–1746), has many references to Coptic. After his death, his manuscripts passed into the hands of Th. Hirsch and C. E. Jordan (1881, pp. 504–506), whose brothers sold the Armenian and Coptic dictionaries to the University of Leiden, where the manuscript of the Coptic dictionary is still kept (Codex 431 B). C. Scholtz, the brother-in-law of Jablonski, asked his pupil C. G. Woide to copy this manuscript. Woide also made a copy for himself. This dictionary was published in 1775 in Oxford by Scholtz and Woide (Kammerer, 1950, no. 289). La Croze's dictionary was based on copies of Coptic manuscripts that Jablonski had given to him of the New Testament, the liturgies of Basil and Gregory, and the psalter of the Old Testament published in 1663 by Petraeus (ibid., no. 852). J. F. CHAMPOLLION, who composed a Coptic lexicon, made use of La Croze's dictionary.

BIBLIOGRAPHY

Hirsch, T., and C. E. J. Jordan. *Allgemeine deutsche Biographie,* Vol. 14. Berlin, 1881; 2nd ed., Berlin, 1969.

Kammerer, W., comp. *A Coptic Bibliography.* Ann Arbor, Mich., 1950; repr. New York, 1969.

"La Croze." In *Orientalia Neerlandica,* pp. 71–74. Leiden, 1948.

Quatremère, E. *Recherches critiques et historiques sur la langue et la littérature de l'Egypte.* Paris, 1808.

MARTIN KRAUSE

LADEUZE, PAULIN (1870–1940), Belgian theologian and ecclesiastical historian. Ladeuze joined the faculty at the University of Louvain at the age of twenty-eight. He was a founding member of *Revue d'histoire ecclésiastique* and succeeded his teacher, Msgr. Hebbelynck, as head of the theology department and eventually as rector of the university. Both his dissertation and his subsequent teaching and publishing careers focused on Coptic studies.

A biography was published by L.-T. Lefort in *Le Muséon* 53 (1940):151–53.

S. KENT BROWN

LADLES AND SPOONS. *See* Metalwork, Coptic.

LAGARDE, PAUL ANTON DE (1827–1891), German Orientalist. He was a pupil of M. G. Schwartze, became professor in Göttingen in 1869, and published many texts of the Old Testament: *Der Pentateuch koptisch* (1867); *Psalterii Versio Mem-*

phitica (1875); *Psalterium, Job, Proverbia Arabice* (1876); and "Bruchstücke der koptischen Übersetzung des ATs" (*Abhandlungen der Gesellschaft der Wissenschaften zu Göttingen* 24, 1879, pp. 63–104). His New Testament texts include *Acta Apostolorum Coptice* (1852); *Epistulae Novi Testamenti Coptice* (1852); and *Catenae in Evangelia Aegyptiacae quae Supersunt* (1886). His apocryphal texts are in *Aegyptiaca* (1883).

BIBLIOGRAPHY

Rahlfs, A. "P. de Lagardes wissenschaftliches Lebenswerk im Rahmen einer Geschichte seines Lebens." *Mitteilungen des Septuaginta-Unternehmens der Gesellschaft der Wissenschaften in Göttingen.* Göttingen, 1928.

Schaeder, H. H. "P. de Lagarde als Orientforscher." *Orientalistische Literaturzeitung* 45 (1942):1–13.

MARTIN KRAUSE

LAḤN (plural *alḥān*), Arabic translation of Coptic ⲏⲭⲟⲥ, adopted from Greek *ēkhos*, a term used in Coptic liturgical books and manuscripts to specify the music to be sung to a given text. Sometimes translated into English as "air," "tone," "melody," or "mode," it refers basically to either a certain melody or melody type that is readily recognized by the people and known by a specific, often descriptive name, such as *Laḥn al-Faraḥ* (. . . of joy) and *Laḥn al-Ḥuzn* (. . . of sorrow). Two leading *Alḥān* to be cited as melody types are ADĀM and WĀṬUS. *Laḥn* may have some affinities yet to be elucidated with the Byzantine *echos* and the Arabic *maqām*. For a more complete discussion, see MUSIC: DESCRIPTION OF THE CORPUS, and MUSIC: HISTORY.

MARIAN ROBERTSON

LĀLIBALĀ. This small and isolated community set deep in the Simyen Mountains of central Ethiopia is one of the most remarkable Christian religious centers in Africa. Within the confines of the town are no fewer than eleven monolithic churches, hewn from the native red sandstone of the Ethiopian Plateau. Tradition attributes them all to Emperor Lālibalā of the Zagwé dynasty (1181–1221), who had his capital here and for whom the town is named. Modern scholarship suggests, however, that the churches were made over a considerable period of time, from the reign of Lālibalā to sometime in the fourteenth century.

Among monolithic monuments, the churches of Lālibalā have sometimes been compared to the great rock temples of Abu Simbel in Egypt and to the shrines at Petra in Jordan. They are unique in that they are not cut into cliff faces but are hewn downward from the level plateau surface. For seven of the churches, a wide and deep trench was first cut downward so that it surrounded a monolithic mass of stone, into which chambers, doors, and windows were then hewn. Each church thus gives the impression that it is standing in the bottom of a pit, the rooftop being level with the surrounding ground. However, four of the Lālibalā churches are "grotto churches." They are not completely freestanding but are surrounded by a trench on only one, two, or three sides.

The largest of the Lālibalā churches, called Medhane Alem (savior of the world), measures 112 × 80 feet (34 × 24 m) and is 37 feet (11 m) high. It has a simple rectangular plan comprising a central nave flanked by two aisles on either side, all of equal width. There is a small narthex chamber at the west end, and at the east a wide rectangular sanctuary area flanked by smaller sacristies. The nave and aisles are separated from each other by imitation colonnading (actually hewn from the monolithic rock), and there was originally a colonnade running around the exterior of the building as well. Many of the other churches at Lālibalā are also rectangular, but they have only one aisle on either side of the nave and do not have a narthex. Typically there is a centrally placed door in the west wall, giving directly onto the nave, and additional doors in the north and south walls. The church of Biet Maryam (house of Mary) has projecting porches at the north, south, and west, hewn from the same stone mass as the body of the church.

One of the most spectacular of the Lālibalā churches is Biet Giorgios (house of George), which has the shape of a perfect equilateral cross. It is two stories in height, but the interior consists of only a single very tall chamber.

A distinctive feature of all the Lālibalā churches is their elaborate exterior decoration, using alternating advanced and recessed panels, ranged either horizontally or vertically. This is a very ancient tradition in Ethiopian architecture, visible also in the monuments of Axum and traceable ultimately to South Arabian influence. There are many variations in the paneling scheme on each individual church, and no two of the buildings are closely similar in their decoration. Doorways and windows are especially decorated; windows frequently have an arched top or are cut in the shape of a cross or

Church of Bieta Gheorgis. Lālibalā, Ethiopia. Eleventh century. *Courtesy Pierre du Bourguet.*

swastika. Additional paneled decoration is found on the roofs of many churches. Interiors are lavishly adorned with carved scrollwork, geometric and floral friezes, and effigies of saints set in shallow niches. The decoration of the Lālibalā churches has sometimes been attributed to Egyptian Coptic artisans, but this has not been historically proved.

There are at least a dozen other rock churches in the immediate vicinity of Lālibalā, and scores of others throughout northern Ethiopia. Their exact number is still unknown, but a survey in 1966 discovered the existence of three dozen such churches that had never previously been seen by outsiders. It is generally conceded, however, that the churches at Lālibalā are unmatched in the elegance of their decoration.

Before 1960 Lālibalā was accessible only by muleback, and was reported to be three days' travel from the nearest road. In 1960 a landing strip was constructed in the valley below the town, and regular air service was inaugurated in the dry season. A network of primitive roads leads to the town and to some of the nearby rock churches, and the area has become a significant tourist attraction. Extensive renovation was carried out in some of the Lālibalā churches in the years after 1967.

BIBLIOGRAPHY

Barriviera, L. B. "Le Chiese in roccia di Lalibela e di altri luoghi del Lasta." *Rassegna di Studi Etiopici* 18 (1962):5–76; 19 (1963):5–118.

Bidder, I. *Lalibela.* Cologne, 1959.

Buston, D. "The Christian Antiquities of Northern Ethiopia." *Archaeologia* 92 (1947):22–34.

Findlay, L. *The Monolithic Churches of Lalibela in Ethiopia.* Cairo, 1944.

Gester, G. *Churches in Rock.* London, 1970.

Jäger, O. A. *Antiquities of Northern Ethiopia,* pp. 103–118. Stuttgart, 1965.

Monti della Corte, A. A. *Lalibelà.* Rome, 1940.

WILLIAM Y. ADAMS

LAMPS. *See* Ceramics, Coptic; Glass, Coptic; Metalwork, Coptic.

LANGUAGES, COPTIC. *See Appendix.*

LAQQĀN (pl. laqqānāt), Coptic designation for the mandatum tank, which on Maundy Thursday and on the feast day of Peter and Paul (5 Abīb) is used for the ceremony of the foot washing. It is a small basin sunk slightly into the floor in the western part of the nave. It is covered with a wooden lid when not in use. In older examples made from

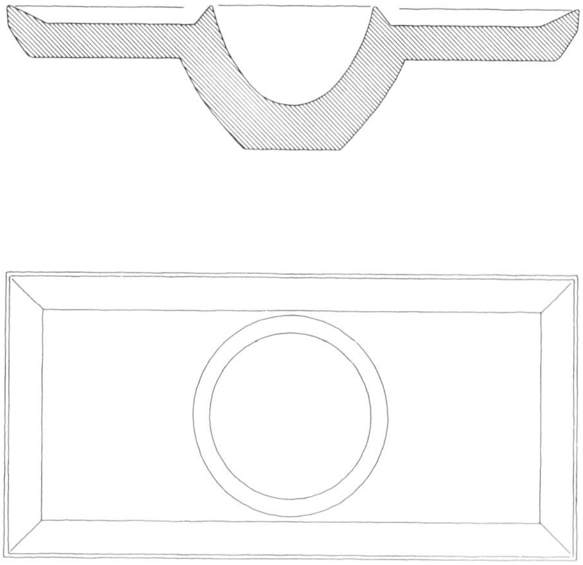

Lid of a mandatum tank, or *laqqān:* elevation and plan. *Courtesy Peter Grossmann.*

light-colored marble, the form of the lids is strikingly uniform. Lids usually consist of a rectangular stone slab with a high rim, in the middle of which is a round conical hollow also provided with a raised rim. In the churches of Old Cairo such as Saint Mercurius in DAYR ABŪ SAYFAYN and Abū Sarjah there are also some lids with an octagonal shape and polychrome marble inlays, which probably date to the Mamluk period.

When *laqqānāt* began to be used is still not clear. They are unknown in the early Christian period. There is no church known from this period in which there are any remains or even traces of their existence. On the other hand, the ceremony was mentioned as early as the seventh century. Probably at that time portable basins were employed.

BIBLIOGRAPHY

Assfalg, J., ed. and trans. *Die Ordnung des Priestertums, Tartīb al-Kahanūt; ein altes liturgisches Handbuch der Koptischen Kirche*. Cairo, 1955.

Burmester, O. H. E. "Two Services of the Coptic Church Attributed to Peter, Bishop of Bahnasā." *Le Muséon* 45 (1932):235ff.

______. *The Egyptian or Coptic Church*, pp. 256–63. Cairo, 1967.

Evelyn-White, H. G. *The Monasteries of the Wādī 'n Naṭrūn*, Vol. 3, p. 21. New York, 1933; repr. 1973.

PETER GROSSMANN

LAQQĀNAH, town located in the Egyptian Delta about 7 miles (11 km) east of Damanhūr in the Beheirah Province. Laqqānah was a bishopric by 1145 when Bishop Ya'qūb al-Qāri' of the town was one of a number of men who attempted to make Yūnis ibn Kadrān patriarch. In 1257 Bishop John of Laqqānah was present at the consecration of the holy CHRISM, and in 1299 Bishop John (perhaps the same man) of Laqqānah and Damanhūr was present at the same event (Munier, 1943, pp. 35–36). AL-MAQRĪZĪ wrote in the late fourteenth or early fifteenth century that there was a church of JOHN COLOBOS in Laqqānah.

BIBLIOGRAPHY

Munier, H. *Recueil des listes épiscopales de l'église copte*. Cairo, 1943.

Timm, S. *Das christlich-koptische Ägypten in arabischer Zeit*. Wiesbaden, 1985.

RANDALL STEWART

LASCARPIS. *See* Ya'qub, General.

LAST SUPPER. *See* Christ.

LATROCINIUM. *See* Ephesus, Second Council of.

LATSON, APA (feast day: 17 Ba'ūnah). There is reference to this saint in the SYNAXARION of the Copts at 17 Ba'ūnah and in the notice devoted to Saint PALAMON at 30 Ṭūbah. W. E. Crum (1926, Vol. 1, p. 114) thinks that the two names refer to the same person, although he is called Talāsūn in the Life of Saint Palamon at 30 Ṭūbah. His Life, written by his disciple PHILOTHEUS, is preserved in a manuscript in the Coptic Museum, Cairo (History 469, fol. 314). Arabic fragments of the Life are preserved in the British Library (Or. 5650, 69, 70).

Latson was a native of al-Bahnasā (OXYRHYNCHUS). While still a child, he one day heard the passage from Matthew (16:25–26), "Whoever would save his life will lose it, and whoever loses his life for my sake will find it." He withdrew to the mountain of SCETIS, where an angel appeared to him, enjoining him to go and find Saint ISIDORUS, who would give him the monastic habit. If we are to believe Crum's hypothesis, he left Scetis and was the confidant and friend of Saint Palamon.

One of the manuscripts of the Synaxarion recounts that, having received from the dying abbot of a monastery the confession of his sins, he wished to apply the Gospel text, "Greater love has no man than this, that a man lay down his life for his friends" (Jn. 15:13). He therefore attempted several times to kill himself, but each time was brought back to life by Christ or an angel. Finally, Christ announced to him that the soul of the abbot had been reduced to nothing, since it could neither be retained in hell because of the penances of Saint Latson, nor admitted into heaven because of its own sins.

The mention of Saint Isidorus at Scetis at the beginning of this notice seems to indicate that Saint Latson lived at the end of the fourth and the beginning of the fifth centuries.

BIBLIOGRAPHY

Winlock, H. E., and W. E. Crum. *The Monastery of Epiphanius at Thebes*, Vol. 1. New York, 1926.

RENÉ-GEORGES COQUIN

LAURA, term that seems to have originated in Palestine, where it described a range or group of cells around a common center, including a church, a bakery, and various communal services, where the hermits gathered on Saturday and Sunday, bringing the fruit of their labors and leaving again with their bread for the week. Since the Greek word *lavra* means a narrow street or alley, one thinks of what is suggested by the Arabic word *sūq*, that is, a narrow street lined with booths, a kind of market where the hermits brought their work together and went off to their cells with the product of their week's work (see D. J. Chitty, 1966, index, p. 203).

Consequently the Greek term appears to have had two meanings. First, it designated several monasteries of cenobites, grouped around a common center including a church, a hostelry, and a bakery; it seems indeed that the young monks were grouped there while waiting to be assigned to the different monasteries that formed the laura. The only laura that answers to this meaning of the word seems to have been that of the ENATON, west of Alexandria. We may note that in Palestine the word appears to have taken this sense. If it was applied to monasteries near Alexandria, it seems to have been by strangers and fairly late (before the fourth century it does not appear to have been used): narratives attributed to DANIEL OF SCETIS (Clugnet, 1900, p. 61) or journey of John Moschus (PG 87, cols. 3029, 3032, etc.), for whom *lavra* signifies simply monastery.

Second, it designated a group of hermitages around common buildings, one of them a church. This appears to be the primitive sense, at least in Palestine. No Egyptian text seems to use the word in the same way. It has come about that, for convenience, it is used in this sense, but it should be known that texts do not so use it when referring to Egypt. If we read it in some texts, this is the work of non-Egyptians who transpose to Egypt the realities they know.

BIBLIOGRAPHY

Chitty, D. J. *The Desert, a City*. London, 1966.
Clugnet, L. "Vie et récits de l'abbé Daniel de Scété." *Revue de l'Orient chrétien* 5 (1900):49–73, 254–71.
Crum, W. E. *A Coptic Dictionary*. Oxford, 1939; 2nd ed., 1962.
Lampe, G. W. H. *A Patristic Greek Lexicon*, p. 794. Oxford, 1961.
Moschus, John (Ioannis Moschi). *Patrum Spirituale*. PG 87. Paris, 1860. French trans. M. J. Rouet de Journel. *Le pré spirituel*. Sources chrétiennes 12. Paris, 1946.

RENÉ-GEORGES COQUIN

LAURA OF KALAMON. *See* Eikoston.

LAW, COPTIC. By "Coptic law" we understand the particularities of legal practice evidenced in documents written in the Coptic language, from roughly the sixth to the ninth century (Steinwenter, 1955; Schiller, 1932a, 1957, 1971a). The substance of the law is found in the combination of Greek, Coptic, and Arabic documents, but the present treatment rests largely on the Coptic evidence. The notion of "law" (ⲛⲟⲙⲟⲥ, nomos) in Coptic documents embraced customary rules, Hellenistic institutions, and somewhat distant echoes of late Roman imperial legislation (Steinwenter, 1957; Schiller, 1971b). What functioned as a source of law was what we see operative in the documents themselves.

Private Law

Law of persons. The birth of a natural person was often, but not always, registered (Crum, 1926, nos. 99–100). The person came of age at fourteen (cf. *P. Lond.* V 1554.8). His or her status could be "free" (Till, 1951), "slave," or "dedicated person" (Steinwenter, 1921; MacCoull, 1979a).

Marriage was often accompanied by a contract respecting the parties' property (cf. MacCoull, 1979b); divorce also was signaled by a contract (Crum, 1902, no. 130; Crum, 1926, no. 161, *P. Cair. Masp.* II 67153, 67154, 67155), both parties having the right to remarry or to choose the monastic life. (Incompatibility was often cited; there was no inflexible church teaching on indissolubility.)

Four kinds of matrimonial property are known: ⲥⲭⲁⲁⲧ (skhaat, gift from the groom), ϣⲉⲗⲉⲉⲧ (sheleet, gift from the bride), ⲣⲟⲙⲡⲉ ⲛ̄ⲟⲩⲱⲙ (rompe nouōm, literally "year of eating," probably support payments), and ⲛⲟⲩϩⲣ ⲉⲃⲟⲗ (nouhr ebol, probably movable household goods). These perhaps derive from older Egyptian categories and correspond to the fourfold terminology found in the Byzantine papyri of ἕδνα, προίξ, ἀναλώματα and σκευή (hedna, proiks, analōmata, and skeuē), after the old terminology of φερνή/παράφερνα, phernē/parapherna, passed out of use.

As for juristic persons, according to one theory both the ⲕⲟⲓⲛⲟⲛ (koinon) of a village and the ⲇⲓⲕⲁⲓⲟⲛ (dikaion) or governing board of a monastery could be conceived of as juristic persons, as they acted subjectively in transactions and executed business (Steinwenter, 1930; cf. 1953); but the concept was not fully developed.

Law of things. The Byzantines divided property into ⲁⲕⲓⲛⲏⲧⲟⲛ (akinēton, land, buildings, trees), ⲕⲓⲛⲏⲧⲟⲛ (kinēton, articles), and ⲁⲩⲧⲟⲕⲓⲛⲏⲧⲟⲛ (autokinēton, animals) obtained. Ownership of property was indicated by ⲣ̄ϫⲟⲉⲓⲥ (r̄joeis, or *dominium*, κυριεύειν, [kyrieuein]) and ⲁⲙⲁϩⲧⲉ (amahte, or *possessio* the right to use, improve, and pledge, and to alienate (sell, give, bequeath) the property. Churches and monasteries, or parts thereof, could be the private property of an individual, a practice at variance with imperial law.

Regarding inheritance (Till, 1954), both ecclesiastics and lay persons could make wills, called ⲇⲓⲁⲑⲏⲕⲏ(-ⲁⲓ), diathēkē(-ai). Both relatives and nonrelated persons, and both church bodies and individual ecclesiastics, could inherit. The principal heir was usually obliged to bury the testator, offer liturgies for his or her soul, and pay outstanding debts. Disinheritance was known (Crum and Steindorff, *Koptische Rechtsurkunden des achten Jahrhunderts*, 68, 71, 67; Crum, 1905, or British Museum 445; cf. *P. Cair. Masp.*, III, 67353v). A great many Coptic legal cases involved disputes over the division of an inheritance; they were usually settled by arbitration (see below, under civil procedure), the agreements reached being incorporated in a ⲇⲓⲁⲗⲩⲥⲓⲥ (dialysis) document (e.g., Crum and Steindorff, *Koptische Rechtsurkunden des achten Jahrhunderts*, 35, 37, 44).

Law of obligations. The usual document of a loan is an ⲁⲥⲫⲁⲗⲉⲓⲁ (asphaleia), in which the debtor acknowledges receipt of money or goods and promises to repay with or without interest (e.g., Crum and Steindorff, *Koptische Rechtsurkunden des achten Jahrhunderts*, 64; cf. Crum, 1902, no. Ad. 17). Loans were often repayable at harvest time; a money loan could be repaid in kind, or with interest in kind. Loans in kind are most often of basic agricultural commodities (grain, wine, often payable in Mesore at the grape harvest; oil); they can include provision of a money fine in case of default, or payment in money (cf. Bagnall, 1977). On receipt of payment the creditor made acknowledgement to the debtor in an ⲁⲡⲟⲇⲉⲓⲝⲓⲥ (apodeiksis). Both creditors and debtors are found in both clerical and lay status.

The usual name for a document of sale (Boulard, 1912) of immovable property is ⲡⲣⲁⲥⲓⲥ (prasis), the operative verb being ϯ ⲉⲃⲟⲗ (ti ebol). Transfer of ownership was effected by the drawing up and signing of the document of sale. The seller could be one representative of several co-owners (e.g., Crum and Steindorff, *Koptische Rechtsurkunden des achten Jahrhunderts*, 1; Schiller, 1932b, no. 7). For the sale of movable property terminology is looser, and practices appear to have varied from district to district (regionalism in Coptic law would repay further study).

Leases of land were either yearly (ⲙⲓⲥⲑⲱⲥⲓⲥ, misthōsis) or heritable (ⲉⲙⲫⲩⲧⲉⲩⲥⲓⲥ, emphyteusis) (Comfort, 1937), the latter favored by monastic and ecclesiastical landlords (MacCoull, 1989). The contract of lease could be drawn up by either the lessor or the lessee; in the former case the boundaries, the length of term, and the amount of rent (ⲡⲁⲕⲧⲟⲛ, ϣⲱⲙ, ⲫⲟⲣⲟⲥ [pakton, shōm, phoros]), in money, in kind, or in both, are specified. In the latter case the rent can be called either ϣϭⲟⲣ (shcor), of a one-year ⲙⲓⲥⲑⲱⲥⲓⲥ (misthōsis), or ⲡⲁⲕⲧⲟⲛ/ⲫⲟⲣⲟⲥ (pakton/phoros), of an ⲁⲥⲫⲁⲗⲉⲓⲁ (asphaleia) for several years (Schiller, 1932a, pp. 278–79). Penalties could be exacted for nonpayment of rent. Many rent receipts are preserved (ⲁⲡⲟⲇⲉⲓⲝⲓⲥ, -ⲉⲓⲥ [apodeiksis, -eis]). The ⲉⲙⲫⲩⲧⲉⲩⲥⲓⲥ (emphyteusis) or heritable lease could be framed by either party (Crum, 1905, or British Museum 1014–1015; Crum, 1909, or Rylands 174). In this case, the rent, called ⲡⲁⲕⲧⲟⲛ (pakton), was payable in money, in kind, or in both.

The main types of labor contracts (Till, 1956) are ⲥⲩⲙⲫⲱⲛⲟⲛ (symphōnon), drawn up by either employer or employee, often in two copies; ⲗⲉⲃⲉⲕⲉ (lebeke) (a title for the hired person), simple hiring for wages by a community; ⲉⲡⲓⲧⲣⲟⲡⲏ (epitropē), usually for agricultural services; and ⲡⲁⲣⲁⲙⲟⲛⲏ (paramonē), an apprenticeship contract with provision for support of the learner. There are also many documents and letters embodying a simple commission or charge on a party to perform some service for a second or third party; they are probably not legal contracts in the narrow sense.

For deposits (ϩⲩⲡⲟⲑⲏⲕⲏ/ⲕⲉⲓⲥⲑⲁⲓ [hypothēkē/keisthai], ⲁⲣⲏⲃ [arēb], ⲉⲩⲱ [euō]), either the whole of an individual's property (e.g., Crum, 1905, or British Museum 1039 and elsewhere) or specific articles (e.g., Crum, 1926, no. 95) could be pledged. The receiver of the pledge obtained *possessio* at the time of transfer, but *dominium* only in the case of nonredemption (e.g., Crum, 1902, no. 183).

Surety (**ϵⲅⲅⲩⲏ** [engyē], **ϣⲧⲱⲣϵ** [shtōre]; Till, 1950–1957) could be given in the case of a public or a private obligation. Most public surety is for taxes (Steinwenter, 1920, p. 4) or for performance of the compulsory services exacted by the Arab government (as seen in the Aphrodito documents in *P. Lond.* IV). Private surety is often found; the document of **ϵⲅⲅⲩⲏ** (engyē) served to entitle one to go surety for the one requesting it (cf. Crum and Steindorff, *Koptische Rechtsurkunden des achten Jahrhunderts,* 115). Such action occurs in connection with loans, sales, labor contracts, and leases. There are also ecclesiastical sureties, in which one cleric guarantees that another will carry out his office (Crum, 1902, nos. 31–33, and many more; cf. Steinwenter, 1931).

Agency is an obligation usually embodied in a clause of a document of one of the types mentioned above (**ϵⲓⲣϵ ⲙ̄ⲡⲣⲟⲥⲱⲡⲟⲛ**, eire mprosōpon, literally "make" someone's face or persona; see San Nicolo, 1924). Also in this category are many examples of a simple request, in letters or other private documents, that one party bring money or goods to a third; these seemingly were not regarded as legally binding. Numerous other sorts of contracts are loosely designated **ϩⲟⲙⲟⲗⲟⲅⲓⲁ** (homologia) or **ϵⲅⲅⲣⲁⲫⲟⲛ** (engraphon), and treat of joint ventures (e.g., Crum and Steindorff, *Koptische Rechtsurkunden des achten Jahrhunderts,* 55), often agricultural (Crum, 1902, no. 304). Occasionally they deal with barter, but this situation is hard to distinguish from sale or loan (Crum and Steindorff, *Koptische Rechtsurkunden des achten Jahrhunderts,* 7, 24, and elsewhere).

Most recorded donations (**ⲇⲱⲣϵⲁⲥⲧⲓⲕⲟⲛ**, dōreastikon) (Horwitz, 1940) were made to monasteries or churches; they were of land, children, or, in one case, one's self (Crum and Steindorff, *Koptische Rechtsurkunden des achten Jahrhunderts,* 104). Some donations were made in fulfillment of a will (Crum, 1902, 135) or a promise, or for the repose of a soul (*donatio mortis causa;* Crum and Steindorff, *Koptische Rechtsurkunden des achten Jahrhunderts,* 106).

Not many penalties for nonfulfillment of obligation are recorded, but they could be secular or religious (cf. below, on oaths).

Public Law

The elements of continuity and change in late antique Egypt as a province first of the Byzantine empire and then of the caliphate are well documented (*P. Cair. Masp.* I-III; *P. Lond.* IV-V; Rémondon, 1953; Rouillard, 1928; Hardy, 1932), but a synthesizing study remains to be made. Here we can treat only what is known from Coptic documents dealing with public obligations, almost all from the Arab period.

The inhabitant of Egypt was affected most directly and most often by the requirements of taxation. Taxes were levied in money (the poll tax or **ⲁⲛⲁⲣⲓⲥⲙⲟⲥ/ⲇⲓⲁⲅⲣⲁⲫⲟⲛ** [andrismos/diagraphon], the land tax or **ⲇⲏⲙⲟⲥⲓⲟⲛ** [dēmosion], properly so called; and the **ⲇⲁⲡⲁⲛⲏ** [dapanē]; see Bell's preface to *P. Lond.* IV); and in kind (the grain **ϵⲙⲃⲟⲗⲏ** [embolē], formerly for the provisioning of Constantinople). Usually the Arab governor (**ⲥⲩⲙⲃⲟⲩⲗⲟⲥ**, symboulos) ordered the pagarch (sometimes through the *dux*) to draw up a list or register (**ⲕⲁⲧⲁⲅⲣⲁⲫⲏ**, katagraphē) of taxable persons and properties. Individual local tax collectors were obliged to pay out of their own pockets the quota of the entire pagarchy if others' contributions fell short of the total quota. Monks and ecclesiastics were taxed (cf. Kahle, Vol. 2, 1954, nos. 290–304). Many tax receipts are preserved from these village collections (esp. Crum, 1902; Stefanski, 1952). The form of receipt seems to vary slightly from place to place; most are dated only by the indiction, and contain a simple declaration by the collector that he has received the sum assessed.

"Fugitives" (*φυγάδες*, phygades) were those who had fled from their own place of enrollment, usually to escape taxes. Numerous documents from the Umayyad period exist ordering the return of fugitives (e.g., in *P. Lond.* IV and *P. Russ. Georg.,* IV). In connection with this situation we encounter the so-called **ⲗⲟⲅⲟⲥ ⲙ̄ⲡⲛⲟⲩⲧϵ** (logos m̄pnoute, Schiller, 1935a; Till, 1938) and the *σιγίλλια* (sigillia) or safe-conduct passes.

Oaths in Coptic legal documents have been treated and classified by E. Seidl (1935; cf. Till, 1940). Of interest for social history are oaths on the monastic habit, on relics or icons, and in churches (especially on the Gospels).

Legal Procedure

It has been contended (Schiller, 1969) that owing to the divisions after Chalcedon, the Coptic-speaking population in late Byzantine and early Umayyad times had no recourse whatever to public tribunals and settled all disputes by private means, usually arbitration (Schiller, 1968; 1971a). Our principal sources for this sort of proceeding are the

Budge Papyrus (Schiller, 1968), *P. Lond.* V, 1709, and *P. Cair. Masp.* III (67353r). It may be that, lacking further evidence, to claim that all references to judicial bodies in Coptic documentary practice are merely commonplaces of the notariate without factual referents is somewhat exaggerated. In addition to the sources for arbitration, we have evidence for the judicial activities of pagarchs and bishops (cf. the clauses contrasting ⲁⲣⲭⲟⲛⲧⲓⲕⲟⲛ/ⲉⲕⲕⲗⲏⲥⲓⲁⲥⲧⲓⲕⲟⲛ [arkhontikon/ekklēsiastikon]: Crum and Steindorff, *Koptische Rechtsurkunden des achten Jahrhunderts,* 5, 24, 48, 98, 107; Schiller, 1932b, 1; MacCoull, 1989b). Authority was principally seen to reside in the village ⲗⲁϣⲁⲛⲉ (lashane, headman) and the body of ⲛⲟϭ ⲛ̄ⲣⲱⲙⲉ, (noc nrōme), or *μείζονες* (meizones, formerly the *protocometai;* Steinwenter, 1920). Still at issue is the question of the extent to which Hellenistic-Coptic Egypt received and conformed to the Justinianic law and later *Novellae* (Schiller, 1971b). In actual praxis, conformity seems to have been minimal; the world of Coptic law is a world of its own.

In civil procedure, the claims and counterclaims were usually brought to an arbiter (the operative verb is ⲁⲓⲥⲱⲧⲙ̄/ⲁⲛⲥⲱⲧⲙ̄ [aisōtm̄/ansōtm̄, I/we have heard]). If his decision was accepted, the plaintiff drew up a document of ⲁⲙⲉⲣⲓⲙⲛⲉⲓⲁ (amerimneia, release) after the defendant had obeyed the ruling. All parties could join in drawing up a ⲇⲓⲁⲗⲩⲥⲓⲥ (dialysis, see above). We have no records of Coptic criminal trials as such, except for measures taken against tax evaders (see above) and the occasional intervention of a bishop (e.g., Crum, 1902, 336; but cf. *P. Mich.* XIII 660–661, a murder case, sixth century). Penalties included fines, imprisonment, and church sanctions (Schiller, 1935b, pp. 30–31).

The interpenetration of Coptic civil and canon law is a practically virgin territory. We have very few early sources, and again norms must be inferred from actual practice. No codifications were made in the classical period treated in this article.

BIBLIOGRAPHY

Greek papyri are, by universally accepted convention, cited according to J. F. Oates, et al., *Checklist of Editions of Greek Papyri and Ostraca*, 3rd ed., Atlanta, 1985. The standard work is Steinwenter, A. *Das Recht der koptischen Urkunden. Handbuch der Altertumswissenschaft,* Vol. 10, pt. 4, no. 2. Munich, 1955. The Djeme documents (as a group) are found in Till, W. C. *Die koptischen Rechtsurkunden aus Theben übersetzt.* Österreichische Akademie der Wissenschaften, Philosophisch-historische Klasse, *Sitzungsberichte* 244.3. Vienna, 1964.

Bagnall, R. S. "Prices in 'Sales on Delivery.'" *Greek, Roman and Byzantine Studies* 18 (1977): 85–96.

Boulard, L. *La vente dans les actes coptes.* Paris, 1912.

Comfort, H. "*Emphyteusis* Among the Papyri." *Aegyptus* 17 (1937):3–24.

Crum, W. E. *Coptic Ostraca from the Collections of the Egypt Exploration Fund, the Cairo Museum and Others.* London, 1902.

______. *Catalogue of the Coptic Manuscripts in the British Museum.* London, 1905.

______. *Catalogue of the Coptic Manuscripts in the John Rylands Library.* London, 1909.

______. *The Monastery of Epiphanius at Thebes.* New York, 1926.

Hardy, E. R. *The Large Estates of Byzantine Egypt.* New York, 1932.

Horwitz, I. *The Structure of the Coptic Donation Contract.* Philadelphia, 1940.

Kahle, P. E. *Bala'izah,* 2 vols. London, 1954.

MacCoull, L. S. B. "Child Donations and Child Saints in Coptic Egypt." *East European Quarterly* 13 (1979a):409–15.

______. "A Coptic Marriage-Contract in the Pierpont Morgan Library." In *Actes du Congrès international de papyrologie,* Vol. 2. Brussels, 1979b.

______. "Patronage and the Social Order in Coptic Egypt." *Egitto e storia antica* (1989):447–52.

______. "ⲧⲩⲡⲟⲥ in Coptic Legal Papyri," *Z Sav Kanon* 75 (1989b):408–11.

Remondon, R. *Papyrus grecs d'Apollonos Ano.* Cairo, 1953.

Rouillard, G. *L'administration civile de l'Egypte byzantine,* 2nd ed. Paris, 1928.

San Nicolo, M. "Das ⲉⲓⲣⲉ ⲙ̄ⲡⲣⲟⲥⲱⲡⲟⲛ als Stellvertretungsformel in den koptischen Papyri." *Byzantinische Zeitschrift* 24 (1924):336–45.

Schiller, A. A. "Koptisches Recht." *Kritische Vierteljahrschrift für Gesetzgebung und Rechtswissenschaft* 25 (1932a):250–96.

______. *Ten Coptic Legal Texts.* New York, 1932b.

______. "The Coptic ⲗⲟⲅⲟⲥ ⲙ̄ⲡⲛⲟⲩⲧⲉ Documents." In *Studi in memoria di Aldo Albertoni,* Vol. 1. Padua, 1935a.

______. "Koptisches Recht." *Kritische Vierteljahrschrift für Gesetzgebung und Rechtswissenschaft* 27 (1935b):18–46.

______. "Coptic Documents." *Zeitschrift für vergleichende Rechtswissenschaft* 60 (1957):190–211.

______. "The Budge Papyrus of Columbia University." *Journal of the American Research Center in Egypt* 7 (1968):79–118.

______. "The Courts Are No More." In *Studi di onore E. Volterra,* Vol. 1. Milan, 1969.

______. Introduction to W. E. Crum and G. Steindorff, *Koptische Rechtsurkunden des achten Jahrhunderts aus Djeme (Theben),* 2nd ed. Leipzig and Hildesheim, 1971a.

———. "The Fate of Imperial Legislation in Late Byzantine Egypt." In *VIII Congresso internazionale diritto comparato.* Brussels, 1971b.

Seidl, E. *Der Eid im römisch-ägyptischen Provinzialrecht,* Vol. 2. Munich, 1935.

Stefanski, Elizabeth, ed. *Coptic Ostraca from Medinet Habu.* Chicago, 1952.

Steinwenter, A. *Studien zu den koptischen Rechtsurkunden aus Oberägypten.* Studien zur Paläographie und Papyruskunde 19. Leipzig, 1920.

———. "Kinderschenkungen an koptische Klöster." *Zeitschrift der Savigny-Stiftung, Kanonistische Abteilung* 42 (1921):175–207.

———. "Die Rechtsstellung der Kirchen und Klöster." *Zeitschrift der Savigny-Stiftung, Kanonistische Abteilung* 50 (1930):1–50.

———. "Die Ordinationsbitten koptischer Kleriker." *Aegyptus* 11 (1931):29–34.

———. "Über einige Bedeutungen von *ius* in den nachklassischen Quellen." *Jura* 4 (1953):124–248.

———. "ΝΟΜΟϹ in den koptischen Rechtsurkunden." In *Studi in onore di A. Calderini e R. Paribeni,* Vol. 2. Milan, 1957.

Till, W. C. "Koptische Schutzbriefe." *Mitteilungen des Deutschen Archäologischen Instituts* 8 (1938):71–146.

———. "Zum Eid in den koptischen Rechtsurkunden." *Zeitschrift für ägyptische Sprache und Altertumskunde* 76 (1940):74–79.

———. "Die koptischen Bürgschaftsurkunden." *Bulletin de la Société d'archéologie copte* 14 (1950–1957):165–226.

———. "ⲉⲗⲉⲩⲑⲉⲣⲟⲥ: Unbescholten." *Museon* 64 (1951):251–59.

———. *Erbrechtliche Untersuchungen auf Grund der koptischen Urkunden.* Österreichische Akademie der Wissenschaften, Philosophisch-historische Klasse, *Sitzungsberichte* 229.2. Vienna, 1954.

———. "Die koptischen Arbeitsverträge." *Eos* 48, 1 [Symbolae Raphaeli Taubenschlag dedicatae] (1956):273–329.

LESLIE S. B. MACCOULL

LAW OF OBLIGATIONS. *See* Law, Coptic: Private Law.

LAW OF PERSONS AND FAMILY. *See* Law, Coptic: Private Law.

LAW OF THINGS. *See* Law, Coptic: Private Law.

LAYING-ON OF HANDS. The laying-on, or imposition, of a bishop's hands on a person's head on the occasion of his nomination to the priesthood or diaconate is a rite first mentioned in the Old Testament and has been practiced in the church ever since the apostolic age.

Before the Ascension of Christ, He appeared to the disciples while they were meeting behind locked doors, and insufflating them, He gave them the gift of the Holy Spirit, by which they could grant or withhold forgiveness. In their turn, the apostolic fathers ordained others as bishops, priests, or deacons by laying their hands on them. In this way, they appointed the first deacons, including Stephen (Acts 6:6). When Saint Paul and Saint Barnabas ordained elders in churches, following prayer and fasting, they did this through the laying-on of hands. The Greek term used in Acts 14:23 is *cheiratonesantes,* which appears in various English translations as "chose," "appointed," or "ordained" and originally meant "laid their hands on them."

When Saint Paul ordained Timothy bishop of Ephesus and Titus bishop of Crete, he did so by laying his hands on them. This is confirmed by his words to Timothy, when he wrote to exhort him to stir into flame the gift of God "which is in thee by the laying on of thy hands" (2 Tm. 1:6). In an earlier epistle he had warned Timothy not to be overzealous in the laying-on of hands in ordination, lest he incur responsibility for other people's misdeeds (1 Tm. 5:22).

The APOSTOLIC TRADITION stipulates the imposition of hands as part of the process of ordaining bishops: "Let the bishop be ordained after he has been chosen by all the people. When someone pleasing to all has been named, let the people assemble on the Lord's Day with the presbyters and with such bishops as may be present. All giving assent, the bishops shall impose hands on him, and the presbyters shall stand by in silence. Indeed all shall remain silent, praying in their hearts for the descent of the Spirit. Then one of the bishops present shall, at the request of all, impose his hand on the one who is being ordained bishop" (Hippolytus, 1970, Vol. 1, p. 166).

The same provisions are made in the Constitutions of the Holy Apostles: "Concerning the ordinations of presbyters, . . . when thou ordainest a presbyter, O bishop, lay thy hands upon his head, in the presence of the presbyters and deacons, and pray" (1951, p. 491). The same procedure is recommended in the ordination of deacons.

According to al-SAFĪ IBN AL-'ASSĀL, "the Bishop

shall be installed on a Sunday, with the approval of all the congregation, both the people and the clergy testifying for him. The bishops who are present shall lay their hands upon him, saying, 'We lay our hands on this servant who has been chosen for God, in the name of the Father, the Son, and the Holy Spirit, to be installed to an upright rank, for [the service of] the One Church of God, which is without blemish'" (1927, pp. 32–33).

From Acts 8:14–17, it seems that the act of laying-on of hands was a requisite for receiving the Holy Spirit. Thus, having heard that in Samaria there were converts who had accepted the word of God and been baptized but had not been visited by the Holy Spirit, the apostles sent Peter and John to pray for them, asking that they might receive the Holy Spirit. When Peter and John laid their hands upon them, their mission was fully accomplished.

Acts 9 relates that when Saint Paul in the course of his voyages came to Ephesus, he found a number of converts and wanted to ascertain from them whether they had received the Holy Spirit when they became believers. They replied that they had not even heard of the Holy Spirit and that they had been baptized according to John's baptism. Paul therefore baptized them into the name of Christ, and when he had laid his hand on them, the Holy Spirit came upon them, and they spoke in different tongues and prophesied.

The Power of Healing through the laying-on of hands was demonstrated by Christ on various occasions, as when He was at Nazareth (Mk. 6:5), at Bethsaida (Mk. 8:23–25), and at Capernaum (Lk. 4:40–41), and again when He healed the crippled woman who was also possessed by a spirit that left her enfeebled for eighteen years (Lk. 13:12–13).

This power was given to the disciples in Christ's final commandment: "Go into all the world and preach the gospel to the whole creation. . . . In my name they will cast out demons . . . they will lay their hands on the sick; and they will recover" (Mk. 16:15–18).

The Acts of the Apostles records various instances of this miraculous healing. Saul of Tarsus regained his sight when Ananias was commanded by the Lord to go to the house of Judas in Damascus and ask for a man from Tarsus named Saul and lay his hands on him to restore his sight (Acts 9:10–12). Later on, having himself become a powerful tool in the hands of God, Paul laid his hands on the father of Publius, the chief magistrate of the island of Malta, and cured him and others of their physical ailments.

BIBLIOGRAPHY

Mīkā'īl Mīnā. *'Ilm al-Lāhūt* (The Study of Theology), Vol. 2. Cairo, 1936.

William Sulaymān Qilādah. *Kitāb al-Disqūliyyah, Ta'alīm al-Rusul* (The Didascalia). Cairo, 1979.

ARCHBISHOP BASILIOS

LEAD COLLARS. *See* Alexander II.

LEASES. *See* Law, Coptic: Private Law.

LEATHER BINDINGS. *See* Book Binding.

LEATHER RESTORATION. *See* Art Preservation.

LEATHERWORK, COPTIC.

The importance and craftsmanship of Coptic leatherwork is well attested. Yet, despite the extraordinary climatic conditions of Egypt, which had a paramount role in preserving ancient artifacts and particularly those made of organic material otherwise prone to disintegrate, only rare samples of leatherwork have been preserved except for the bookbindings.

Among the more frequent finds, sandals, which are scattered in various museums throughout the world, are most common. Some sandals were found in graves. The overwhelming majority are open sandals, with a sole and strips on the top to hold the feet.

Less usual is the flat shoe, with a covered upper surface (*Koptische Kunst, Christentum am Nil*, 1963, p. 290–92 no. 228). The decoration may be openwork, exploiting colorful effects from different shades of leather or sometimes painted.

Few pouches have been preserved, and a fragment with an interesting decoration may belong either to a pouch or to a saddle. Most of the techniques used for the decoration of such items are similar to those encountered in the major field of leatherwork, for which our information is the widest—that of BOOKBINDING.

BIBLIOGRAPHY

History of Bookbinding 525–1950. The Walters Art Gallery. Baltimore, 1957.

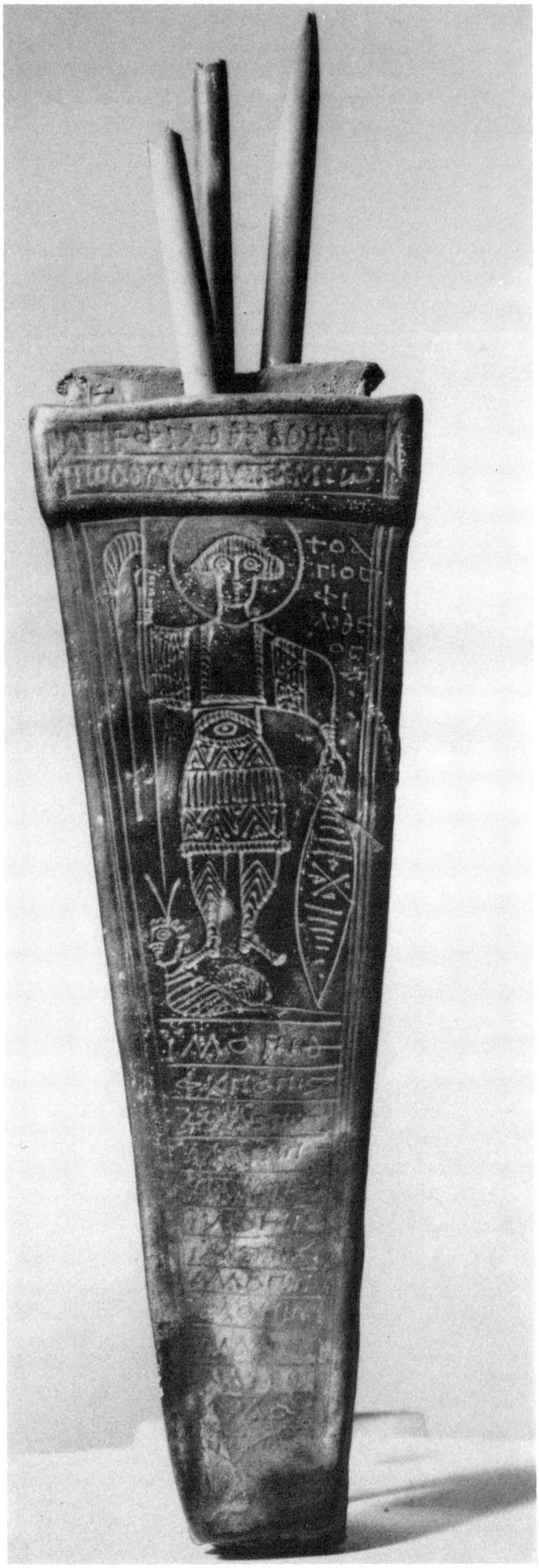

Koptische Kunst, Christentum am Nil. Villa Hügel, Essen, 1963.

MYRIAM ROSEN-AYALON

LECTERN, a four-legged wooden or metal bookstand, about 50 inches (125 cm) in height, on which the Bible and other liturgical books are placed for reading. It is often in the form of an eagle with outstretched wings. The lower part is customarily used as a storage container for books and musical instruments employed in the services, such as cymbals and triangles.

There are two lecterns in every Coptic church. These lecterns are often adorned with geometric designs and sometimes inlaid with ivory carvings. The finest example is to be found in the old Cathedral of Saint Mark at the district of al-Azbakiyyah in Cairo. It had earlier belonged to al-Mu'allaqah Church in Old Cairo and may date to the tenth or eleventh century. A covering of silk or some rich material is sometimes placed on the *manjaliyyah* in such a way that it covers the sloping desk and hangs halfway down the front.

The two lecterns always stand in the choir area before the *haykal* (sanctuary) door. The one at the north side faces east and is used for singing the lessons in Coptic. The other lectern, at the south side, faces west and is used for reading the lessons in Arabic. Occasionally, there is only one lectern, but the bookrest in this case is usually double and revolves on a central column. The north side of the choir is considered the proper place for a single lectern.

To the left of the person reading at each lectern usually stands a tall candelabrum on which the censer is hung when not in use.

The principal purpose of the lectern is to support the books of the biblical liturgical lessons, that is, the lectionaries for the whole year, for Lent, and for Holy Week. It is also used for reading the Apocalypse (on Holy Saturday), the SYNAXARION, the Homilies, the PSALMODIA, the DIFNĀR, the ṬURŪḤĀT (see ṬARḤ), and the biblical lessons in other priestly offices such as matrimonial or burial services.

It is also normally used as a pulpit for sermons, though a sermon by the patriarch or a bishop is delivered from his own seat.

Pen case with representation of Saint Philotheus. Leather (the case) and reeds. Length: 23.5 cm. *Courtesy Louvre Museum, Paris.*

At the beginning of Holy Week, the lecterns and candelabra are moved from the choir into the nave of the church and the lecterns are covered with black cloth. All the lessons are then sung or read at these lecterns in the nave, except those of the morning offering of incense and the Divine Liturgy on Maundy Thursday, which are read from a lectern in the choir area. At the twelfth hour of Good Friday the lecterns and candelabra are returned to their places in the choir area.

[*See also:* EUCHOLOGION STAND and LITURGICAL INSTRUMENTS.]

BIBLIOGRAPHY

Burmester, O. H. E. *The Egyptian or Coptic Church,* pp. 20, 27. Cairo, 1967.

Butler, A. J. *The Ancient Coptic Churches of Egypt,* Vol. 2, pp. 65–68. Repr. Oxford, 1970.

Graf, G. *Verzeichnis arabischer kirchlicher Termini.* CSCO 147, p. 108. Louvain, 1954.

Ibn Sibāʿ Yūḥannā ibn Abī Zakarīyā. *Kitāb al-Jawharah al-Nafīsah fī ʿUlūm al-Kanīsah,* ed. Viktūr Manṣūr. Cairo, 1902. Latin version *Pretiosa Margarita de scientiis ecclesiasticis,* trans. Vincent Mistrīḥ, p. 349. Cairo, 1966.

EMIL MAHER ISHAQ

LECTIONARY, set of four books containing the readings for the various liturgies of the Coptic church. Different lectionaries existed according to different rites in Upper and in Lower Egypt; it was only with the coming of the printing press (see CYRIL IV) that a certain uniformity evolved among the Coptic churches in the whole of Egyptian territory.

In the beginning, for the reading of a passage from the Psalms, the whole Psalter was used, and for a section from the Gospels, a book containing the whole Gospel of Matthew or Mark or Luke or John, with an index indicating to the reader at what point he was to begin and end. At a second stage, it appeared more practical to consign to a special book, the lectionary, those passages that could be properly read on the different feasts and celebrations, drawn from the various biblical books. This multivolume book—for it rapidly grew beyond a single volume—was given the name *kata meros,* probably from the Greek, signifying "in parts," which does indeed indicate its content. The indexes previously in use continued to circulate—we still have manuscripts—but they do not give the sections to be read in full, only the beginning and end of each lection, which could be a source of confusion.

The lectionary in use today was printed for the first time in 1900–1902. Information will be found in Ḥannā Malak's study (1964) about the publication of each volume, both for the Orthodox and for the Catholic Copts. The original term, no doubt Greco-Coptic, has given rise to the Arabic transliteration *qaṭamārus* according to the vocalization adopted. As in the ancient manuscripts, there are two editions, one bilingual with the two texts, Coptic and Arabic, in parallel columns, the other with the Arabic text only.

We may add one point that is important for the history of the calendar of the feasts celebrated in various places. The lectionary consists of two principal elements. It supplies, of course, the passages from the Old and above all the New Testament that ought to be read at an office or mass; and before these biblical sections, it includes a rubric mentioning the feast or the saint, the whole forming a precious calendar, for the SYNAXARION itself is a literary work, reflecting the personal researches of its authors. Moreover, the Synaxarion has been remodeled several times, and thus does not render an account of the actual usage of each church. These calendars, at least some from the environs of Cairo, and also some of the most ancient, have been studied or published and translated into French by François Nau (1913). Some date from the twelfth century, well before the oldest manuscripts of the Synaxarion. As for the choice of the biblical pericopes, or passages, it is examined at least for the annual lectionaries by U. Zanetti (1988).

The commentaries on the lectionary are also important, as they provide a kind of spiritual commentary on the lections made at each celebration.

Four lectionaries are used in the Coptic church on various occasions through the year: the annual *qaṭamārus,* the Great Lent *qaṭamārus,* the Pascha *qaṭamārus,* and the Pentecost *qaṭamārus.*

The Annual *Qaṭamārus*

This includes the readings assigned for all Sundays and weekdays through the year, with the exception of those collected separately in the three other lectionaries.

Far from being gathered at random from the various books of the Bible, the Gospel readings for the Sunday liturgy are methodically arranged and coordinated so that the Gospel lections for the four Sundays of every month in the Coptic calendar combine to present a particular theme. The themes of the twelve months are planned to correspond with the beginning and end of the year, the establishment and consummation of the church, and the creation and termination of the world. These themes become apparent when the subjects of all four Sundays of a given month are examined as one unit, as follows: (1) Tūt: the love of God the Father for mankind; (2) Bābah: the authority of Christ and His power of purifying souls and bodies; (3) Hātūr: the word of the Gospel, its blessings and rewards; (4) Kiyahk: the nativity of Jesus Christ; (5) Ṭūbah: the grace and blessings of salvation; (6) Amshīr: spiritual nourishment; (7–9) Baramhāt, Baramūdah, and Bashans: during the months in which the church observes Great Lent and celebrates Easter and Pentecost, the Gospel readings are closely related to fasting, prayer, and repentance; (10) Ba'ūnah: the fellowship of the Holy Spirit; (11) Abīb: Christ's authority imparted to His disciples; and (12) Misrā: the consummation of the church.

Each of the above-mentioned themes is fully expounded through the readings apportioned for every Sunday. Thus, in Tūt, the first month of the year, the general theme of which is the portrayal of God's love for mankind, the lections are designed to reflect the following constituent elements: *first Sunday* (Lk. 7:28–35): the wisdom of God the Father as revealed in sending John the Baptist to pave the way for Christ; *second Sunday* (Lk. 10:21–28): the manifestation of the gospel of Jesus Christ; *third Sunday* (Lk. 19:1–10): the promise of salvation given to those who, like Zacchaeus, are willing to accept it; and *fourth Sunday* (Lk. 7:36–50): Christ's mercy and compassion toward sinners.

Two further points are worthy of note in the general framework of lections. First, when a month contains a fifth Sunday, its reading is invariably taken from Luke 9:12–17, which relates the miracle of feeding the five thousand.

Second, since all twelve months of the Coptic Calendar have thirty days each, accordingly, should the remaining five or six days (known as *al-Nasi*) include a Sunday—the final Sunday of the year—its Gospel reading is taken from Matthew 24:3–35, in which Christ talks to His disciples about various warnings of the imminent end of the world and the birth pangs of the new age.

Weekday readings, on the other hand, are selected and arranged to harmonize with the life story of the saint or saints being commemorated on each day, as recorded in the Synaxarion. On certain occasions, such as the feast day of a particular saint, the reading refers to another day in the calendar on which an analogous saint is commemorated. Thus, 24 Bābah, 9 Kiyahk, and 23 Ba'ūnah are the feast days of Saint Hilarion, Saint Bīman the Confessor, and Saint Abanūb the Confessor, respectively. On each of these days the readings refer to 22 Ṭūbah, the feast day of Saint Antony, the father of monasticism.

Closely related to the Gospel reading of the Divine Liturgy are the two other readings assigned for the service of the raising of incense for the evening and for the morning. For instance, to fit in with the readings apportioned for the liturgy of the first Sunday of Tūt—the theme of which is God's wisdom—the Gospel for the evening service is taken from Matthew 11:11–19, and for the morning service from Matthew 21:23–27. The theme of the former reading is God's mercy, and of the latter God's justice, mercy and justice being the woof and warp of God's wisdom.

Similarly, on the third Sunday of Ṭūbah, where the Gospel reading (Jn. 3:22–36) promises eternal life to those who believe in Christ the Savior, we find that the two preceding readings for the evening and morning services (Jn. 5:1–18 and Jn. 3:1–21) refer, respectively, to purification from sin and renewal through baptism.

This system is slightly modified during the months of Bābah, Hātūr, Ba'ūnah, Abīb, Misrā, and the last two Sundays of Bashans, when the story of the Resurrection is read every time from a different gospel in the morning service of incense raising. On the first Sunday it is Matthew 28:1–20, on the second Mark 16:2–8, on the third Luke 24:1–12, and on the fourth John 20:1–18.

Readings from the Pauline and Catholic Epistles and Acts are also closely interrelated and bear directly upon the Gospel of the day and its Psalm-versicle, thereby helping to provide an integrated message that the church offers day by day to the faithful, as seen from the following example.

On 17 Hātūr the church celebrates the feast day of Saint John Chrysostom. A close look at the contents of this day's readings will reveal a common thread. The Gospel (Jn. 10:1–16) speaks of the Good Shepherd and His care for the flock. It is preceded by the Psalm-versicle 73:17, 23, 24: "Thou dost hold my right hand, thou dost guide me with thy counsel, and afterward thou wilt receive me to glory." The Epistle to Timothy lays down the pastoral duties of a presbyter to his congregation (2 Tm. 3:10; 4:1–22), and in the Catholic Epistle (1 Pt. 5:1–14), the key verse is "Tend the flock of God that is your charge." Likewise the reading from the Acts centers upon the responsibility of the shepherds: "Take heed to yourselves and to all the flock, in which the Holy Spirit has made you guardians, to feed the church of the Lord which he obtained with his own Son" (Acts 20:28).

Great Lent *Qaṭamārus*

This lectionary comprises readings assigned for the three-day fast of Jonah and the seven-week fast preceding Easter, known as Great Lent.

For the fast of Jonah, the lections are all centered upon the idea of salvation through belief in the resurrection of Jesus Christ, as foreshadowed by Jonah. The four chapters of the book of Jonah are spread over the three days (Monday, Tuesday, and Wednesday) and are read before the Gospel of the morning service, which is followed by a relevant sermon.

The main theme of all Great Lent lections is spiritual fortitude. In the first four weeks special emphasis is laid upon the aspects of such fortitude, and in the remaining three weeks, upon its fruits and benefits.

A major feature of worship in Lent is that, with the exception of Saturdays and Sundays, the church commands full abstinence from all food and drink —not just from foodstuffs including animal fat—till the end of the Divine Liturgy of the ninth canonical hour, that is, three o'clock in the afternoon. During the other five days of the week, from Monday to Friday, the evening service does not include the offering of incense or Gospel reading, but lections for the morning raising of incense contain particular prophecies chosen from the Old Testament.

The Pascha *Qaṭamārus*

This includes lections apportioned for the Holy Week. Here again the readings from both the Old and the New Testament are particularly correlated to focus the various events that took place in the life of Jesus Christ throughout Holy Week.

The Pentecost *Qaṭamārus*

The lections for Pentecost cover a period of seven weeks starting with the Monday that follows Easter Sunday. The readings assigned for each week form a coherent unit the theme of which is closely related to the Sunday Gospel.

Pentecost may be divided into two main sections: The first forty days follow the resurrection and end with the ascension, during which Christ appeared to the disciples. It is particularly significant that the first Sunday in this period is named after Thomas and is also referred to as "New Sunday." Lections are centered upon the theme of belief in Jesus Christ. The last ten days culminate in the descent of the Holy Spirit, the theme being the promise of the Holy Spirit given to the disciples (Acts 1:4–8).

[*See also:* Holy Week; Lent; Pentecost.]

BIBLIOGRAPHY

Bānūb ʻAbduh. *Kunūz al-Niʻmah li-Maʻūnat Khuddām al-Kalimah fī Sharḥ Anājīl al-Sanah al-Tūtiyah Ḥasab Tartīb wa-Muʻtaqad al-Kanīsah al-Qibṭiyah al-Urthūdhuksiyyah,* Vol. 1, Cairo, 1952; Vol. 4, 1958; Vol. 5, 1962; Vol. 6, 1965.

Malak, Hanna. "Les Livres liturgiques de l'église copte." In *Mélanges Eugène Tisserant,* Vol. 3, pt. 2. Studi e Testi, Vol. 233, pp. 1–35. Vatican City, 1964. Lectionaries are dealt with on pp. 9–12.

Nau, François. *Les Ménologes des evangéliaires coptes-arabes.* PO 10, pt. 2. Paris, 1913.

Yūḥannā Salāmah. *Kitāb al-Laʼālī al-Nafīsah fī Sharḥ Tuqūs wa-Muʻtaqadāt al-Kanīsah,* Vol. 2, pp. 297–99. Cairo, 1909.

Zanetti, Ugo. *Les Lectionnaires coptes annuels—Basse Egypte.* Publications de l'Institut orientaliste de Louvain 31. Louvain-la-Neuve, 1988.

ARCHBISHOP BASILIOS
RENÉ-GEORGES COQUIN

LEDA. *See* Mythological Subjects in Coptic Art.

LEFORT, LOUIS THÉOPHILE (1879–1959), Belgian Coptologist and Orientalist. He was born at Orchimont and studied at the Jesuit College at Namur and the Petit Séminaire at Bastogne before going to the University of Louvain in 1901. Then he studied under Alfred Wiedemann at Bonn. He became professor and honorary president of the Oriental Institute of the University of Louvain; he was also director of the journal *Le Muséon* (cf. "Mélanges L. Th. Lefort," *Le Muséon* 59, 1946), in which most of his immense output in the field of Coptic studies was published. He died at Louvain.

BIBLIOGRAPHY

Dawson, W. R., and E. P. Uphill. *Who Was Who in Egyptology.* London, 1972.

Kammerer, W., comp. *A Coptic Bibliography.* Ann Arbor, Mich. 1950; repr. New York, 1969.

AZIZ S. ATIYA

LEGAL PROCEDURE. *See* Law, Coptic.

LEGAL SOURCES, COPTIC. The sources for coptic law are legal documents in Greek, Coptic, and Arabic. The reason for this is that several languages were in use in Egypt in this period, as is shown also by the fact that the Egyptian civil lawyers drafted Greek and Coptic documents at the same time, while Copts who demonstrably did not understand Greek nevertheless had a Greek will drawn up (Kenyon and Bell, I, 77). The Greek and Coptic formularies, however, also lived on in the Arabic documents drawn up for former Christians converted to Islam. This has been shown for the sale of immovable and residential property through investigations undertaken by Frantz-Murphy. Further comparison of documents will enlarge this picture.

The nature of the sources requires that the Coptic legal historian know the three languages mentioned or—if he or she is concerned only with the period before the Arab conquest—Greek and Coptic only. This requirement was met by the two legal historians who have left fundamental works on Coptic law: A. A. SCHILLER, who also edited Coptic legal documents, and A. STEINWENTER. To date no legal historians have been able to continue their work in the field of Coptic law. It is therefore important to follow the path begun by Till and to translate Coptic documents that belong together into modern language groups and so make them accessible to legal historians who have either an inadequate knowledge of Coptic or none at all.

Till translated the Coptic labor contracts, security documents, marriage contracts (cf. his essay on alimony claims), and letters of safe-conduct. The legal historian Liebesny has contributed an essay on the last group of documents. Till concerned himself with the Coptic parallel documents and expressed his views on the oath in Coptic legal documents and on the Coptic stipulation clause. Following the pattern of Kreller's investigations into marriage law in the Greco-Egyptian papyrus documents, Till examined the statements of the Coptic documents on marriage law and presented all the published legal documents from Thebes to the legal historians for evaluation in a German translation. Schiller and Steinwenter assessed the material thus made available (cf. the literature mentioned in LAW, COPTIC). Till's services are not diminished by the fact that since the appearance of his work, further documents of this group have become known and have enriched our knowledge. As an example we may refer to the group of marriage documents: the document called no. 3 by Till has since been edited afresh by Kahle (Vol. 2, pp. 566–71) as no. 152. Two further Coptic marriage documents from al-Ashmūnayn were edited in 1953 by Balogh and Kahle along with a document of divorce. Montevecchi put together the Greek marriage and divorce documents in 1936, and they were treated afresh in 1955 by Taubenschlag. Till's 1948 work overlooked that published by Abbott (1941) on Arabic marriage contracts among the Copts, which included two tenth-century marriage documents of Copts who "belong to the lower clergy-families."

BIBLIOGRAPHY

Abbott, N. "Arabic Marriage Contracts Among Copts." *Zeitschrift der deutschen morgenländischen Gesellschaft* 95 (1941):59–81.

Balogh, E., and P. E. Kahle. "Two Coptic Documents Relating to Marriage." *Aegyptus* 33 (1953):331–40.

Frantz-Murphy, G. "A Comparison of the Arab and Earlier Egyptian Contract Formularies, Part 1: The Arabic Contracts from Egypt (3d/9th–5th/11th Centuries)." *Journal of Near Eastern Studies* 40 (1981):203–25.

Kahle, P. E. *Bala'izah. Coptic Texts from Deir el-Bala'izah in Upper Egypt,* 2 vols. London, 1954.

Kenyon, F. G., and H. I. Bell, eds. *Greek Papyri in the British Museum,* 5 vols. London, 1893–1917.

Kreller, H. *Erbrechtliche Untersuchungen auf Grund der graeco-aegyptischen Papyrusurkunden.* Leipzig and Berlin, 1919.

Liebesny, H. "Rechtsgeschichtliche Bemerkungen zu den koptischen Schutzbriefen." *Mitteilungen des Deutschen Instituts für ägyptische Altertumskunde in Kairo* 8 (1938): 127–14.

MacCoull, L. S. B. "Coptic Marriage-Contract." In *Actes du XVe Congrès international de papyrologie,* Vol. 2. Brussels, 1979.

Montevecchi, O. "Ricerche di sociologia nei documenti dell'Egitto greco-romano II. I contratti di matrimonio e gli atti di divorzio." *Aegyptus* 16 (1936):3–83.

Schiller, A. A. "Introduction." In *Koptische Rechtsurkunden des achten Jahrhunderts aus Djême (Theben),* 2nd ed. Repr. Leipzig, 1971.

Steinwenter, A. *Das Recht der koptischen Urkunden.* Munich, 1955.

Taubenschlag, R. *The Law of Greco-Roman Egypt in the Light of the Papyri 332 B.C.–640 A.D.,* 2nd ed., pp. 101ff. Warsaw, 1955.

Till, W. C. "Koptische Schutzbriefe, mit einem rechtsgeschichtlichen Beitrag von H. Liebesny."

Mitteilungen des deutschen Instituts fur ägyptische Altertumskunde in Kairo 8 (1938):71–146.

———. "Zum Eid in den koptischen Rechtsurkunden." *Zeitschrift für ägyptische Sprache und Altertumskunde* 76 (1940):74–79.

———. "Die koptischen Eheverträge." In *Österreichische National Bibliothek, Festschrift Josef Bick*. Vienna, 1948.

———. "Die koptische Stipulationsklausel." *Orientalia* n.s. 19 (1950):81–87.

———. "Koptische Parallelurkunden." In *Studi in onore di Vincenzo Arangio-Ruiz*, Vol. 4. Naples, 1952.

———. *Erbrechtliche Untersuchungen auf Grund der koptischen Urkunden*. Österreichische Akademie der Wissenschaften, Philosophisch-historische Klasse, *Sitzungsberichte* 229.2. Vienna, 1954.

———. "Die koptischen Arbeitsverträge." *Eos* 48, 1 [Symbolae Raphaeli Taubenschlag dedicatae] (1956):273–329.

———. "Die koptischen Bürgschaftsurkunden." *Bulletin de la Société d'archéologie copte* 14 (1958):165–226.

———. *Die koptischen Rechtsurkunden aus Theben (Übersetzung)*. Österreichische Akademie der Wissenschaften, Philosophisch-historische Klasse, *Sitzungsberichte* 224.3. Vienna, 1964.

MARTIN KRAUSE

LEGION. *See* Army, Roman.

LEGRAIN, GEORGES (1865–1917), French Egyptologist. At first he studied art and architecture in Paris under Jean-Léon Gérôme, Auguste Choisy, Léon Heuzey, and Edmond Pottier, and Egyptian archaeology and philology under Paul Pierret and Eugène Révillout at the Louvre. He went to work for the Institut français d'Archéologie orientale in Cairo in 1892. Although he concentrated his activities on Egyptology and Egyptian sites, he had time for interest in the modern Copts and Coptic folklore.

BIBLIOGRAPHY

Dawson, W. R., and E. P. Uphill. *Who Was Who in Egyptology*. London, 1972.

Kammerer, W., comp. *A Coptic Bibliography*. Ann Arbor, Mich. 1950; repr. New York, 1969.

AZIZ S. ATIYA

LEIPOLDT, JOHANNES (1880–1965), German theologian and Coptologist. He studied theology and Egyptology, mainly Coptic, under Georg Steindorff at Leipzig. He was professor of New Testament studies in Leipzig (1916–1954), where he taught S. Morenz, among other notable scholars. He also published Coptic nonliterary (*Koptische Urkunden*, Berlin, 1904–1905, with A. Erman) and literary texts (*Sinuthii Archimandritae Vita et Opera Omnia*, Paris, 1906–1913) and wrote the biography of Shenute (Leipzig, 1903).

BIBLIOGRAPHY

Dawson, W. R., and E. P. Uphill. *Who Was Who in Egyptology*, p. 172. London, 1972.

MARTIN KRAUSE

LEMM, OSKAR EDUARDOVICH VON (1856–1918), Russian Coptologist. He was educated at Alexandrewski Lyzeum in St. Petersburg. In 1877 he went to Germany to study at Leipzig University. He published *Ägyptische Lesestücke mit Schrifttafel und Glossar* (Leipzig, 1883). From 1887 to 1891 he lectured at the Oriental Faculty of St. Petersburg on Egyptian, Coptic, and Semitic languages. His principal published works on Coptic are: *Bruchstücke der sahidischen Bibelübersetzung nach Handschriften der kaiserlichen öffentlichen Bibliothek zu St. Petersburg* (Leipzig, 1885); *Koptische apokryphe Apostelacten* (St. Petersburg, 1890–1892); *Zwei koptische Fragmente aus den Festbriefen des heiligen Athanasius* (Berlin, 1899); *Der Alexanderroman bei den Kopten. Ein Beitrag zur Geschichte der Alexandersage im Orient* (St. Petersburg, 1903); *Das Triadon, ein sahidisches Gedicht mit arabischer Übersetzung* (St. Petersburg, 1903); *Sahidische Bibelfragmente*, 3 vols. (St. Petersburg, 1890–1907); *Die Thalassion-Legende bei den Kopten* (Leipzig, 1912); *Bruchstücke koptischer Märtyrerakten* (Petrograd, 1913); *Koptische Miscellen* 1–148 (1907–1915), reprinted from *Bulletin de l'Académie impériale des sciences de St. Petersburg* (Leipzig, 1972); *Zu einem Enkomium auf den hl. Viktor* (Leipzig, 1911); *Kleine koptische Studien* 1–58 (repr. Leipzig, 1972).

BIBLIOGRAPHY

Kammerer, W., comp. *A Coptic Bibliography*. Ann Arbor, Mich., 1950; repr. New York, 1969.

Ricci, S. de. "Les Etudes coptes en Russie et les travaux de M. von Lemm." *Revue archéologique*, ser. 4, 2 (1903):302–318.

Turaev, B. A. "Les Pertes récentes de l'orientalisme en Russie." *Recueil de travaux relatifs à la philo-*

logie et à l'archéologie égyptiennes 39 (1921):111–12.

AZIZ S. ATIYA

LENORMANT, CHARLES (1802–1859), French Egyptologist and numismatist. He accompanied J. F. CHAMPOLLION to Egypt (1828); his journal of the journey through Egypt was posthumously published in 1861. He was professor of Egyptian archaeology at the Collège de France (1848). Several of his many publications deal with Egyptology and were of great value in their time. His contributions to Coptic studies may be found in *A Coptic Bibliography* (Kammerer, 1950, 1969).

BIBLIOGRAPHY

Carré, J.-M. *Voyageurs et écrivains français en Égypte*. 2 vols. Cairo, 1932.
Dawson, W. R., and E. P. Uphill. *Who Was Who in Egyptology*. London, 1972.
Kammerer, W., comp. *A Coptic Bibliography*. Ann Arbor, Mich., 1950; repr. New York, 1969.

AZIZ S. ATIYA

LENT. *See* Fasts.

LEO I THE GREAT (c. 400–461), pope who asserted uncompromisingly the primacy of the papacy, opposing both the doctrinal and ecclesiastical claims of Alexandria, represented by the patriarch DIOSCORUS I. He also helped to defend Rome against threatened attack by the Huns. He is regarded as a doctor of the church and saint in the Roman Catholic church (feast day: 10 Nov.) and as a saint in the Orthodox church (feast day: 18 Feb.).

Leo was an Italian, if not a Roman, by birth. Perhaps he is to be identified with the "acolyte Leo" who brought letters from the deacon Sixtus (afterward Pope Sixtus III) to Aurelius, Augustine, and other African bishops in 418 (Augustine, *Letters* 191, 194.1). If so, his date of birth would be about 395. Under Pope Celestine I he was deacon and, according to Gennadius (*De viris illustribus* 61), he was archdeacon of Rome. In the doctrinal struggle between CYRIL I, patriarch of Alexandria, and NESTORIUS on the nature of Christ, he was on the anti-Nestorian side, according to Cassian (*De incarnatione*, praefatio) and the recipient of a letter from Cyril urging him not to sanction the promotion of Juvenal of Jerusalem to patriarchal status. This is his first recorded contact with Alexandria, and it was a friendly one.

Leo continued to be influential during the pontificate of Sixtus III, and in 439 Prosper Tiro records in his *Chronicon* his warning against readmitting former Bishop Julian of Eclanum to the church, on the grounds that he had not recanted his Pelagian errors. In 440 Leo was head of a diplomatic mission to Gaul, to heal the breach between the general Aetius and the pretorian prefect Albinus, when Sixtus died in mid-August. The Roman church waited for him to return to consecrate him pope on 29 September 440.

The first five years of Leo's pontificate were occupied mainly with problems of the church in Rome and the West. His early letters and sermons denounce the heretical views of Manichees, Priscillianists, and Pelagius (see PELAGIANISM). In these works he makes it clear that he regards himself, as bishop of Rome, to be a mouthpiece of Peter. It was this "power that lives and his authority that prevails in his See" (*Sermon* 3.3). In 445, the Western emperor, Valentinian III, pronounced that in the provinces under his rule, "whatever the authority of the Apostolic See has enacted, or may hereafter enact, shall be the law for all." Bishops summoned for trial before the bishop of Rome would be compelled to attend. Though Valentinian's edict was aimed at settling a dispute between Hilary, bishop of Arles, and the pope, it set a precedent for papal supremacy in the Western church throughout the Middle Ages.

The position of the papacy in the East, however, was to be vastly different. Dioscorus I succeeded his uncle, Cyril, as patriarch of Alexandria in June 444. The first contacts between him and Leo were friendly enough, with Leo offering some well-meant if patronizing advice, as if counseling an inexperienced subordinate. He told Dioscorus that he should not hesitate to celebrate the liturgy twice on the same day if necessary, and gave instructions on how to ordain clergy according to the proper procedure. Leo was not the only bishop of that time to misjudge Dioscorus.

Leo does not appear to have had an agent in the imperial capital, Constantinople, and the ever-increasing complications of the dispute between Flavian, patriarch of Constantinople, and the monophysite-minded archimandrite EUTYCHES passed him by. When the crisis erupted in the winter and spring of 448–449, he was on the sidelines and surprised at the fuss. Eutyches had written to him in 448 deploring the revival of "Nestorianism," and Leo had replied on 1 June, thanking him for his solicitude. After his condemnation by the synod at Constantinople on 22 November, Eutyches had included Leo among the senior ecclesiastics to whom he appealed against his sentence. Breakdowns in communication between Rome and Constantinople prevented Flavian's report of the synod's proceedings from reaching Rome. Leo was irked by what appeared to be Flavian's neglect and failed to give his colleague in Constantinople timely support. It was exactly a month from 13 May, when he received his summons to the "Robber Council" that the Eastern emperor had convoked at Ephesus, to his dispatch of his letter to Flavian on 12 June, affirming in uncompromising terms the doctrine of the two natures of Christ. This letter, number 28, has become known to history as the *Tome* of Leo.

Leo's object was to steer between the teachings of Nestorius and of Eutyches on the basis of accepted doctrine in the West. Christ was to be recognized in two natures, the properties of each nature being present in the other (the COMMUNICATIO IDIOMATUM). Although Leo sent similar letters to the emperor's sister, Pulcheria, and to the council via his legate, the *Tome* was for the time being ineffective. It arrived too late to help Flavian; and, not unreasonably, Dioscorus, who presided at the council, which opened on 8 August, considered that the emperor's letters and the issue between Flavian and Eutyches should be judged first. The *Tome* was not refused a reading but was placed far down the agenda. Before it was reached, Eutyches had been acquitted of heresy, and Flavian had been condemned for disturbing the good order of the church and seeking to add to the Nicene Creed (by teaching the recognition of two natures in Christ). He was declared deposed. The papal legate, the deacon Hilarius (later pope), and Julius, bishop of Puteoli, were grossly insulted. It was perhaps fortunate that the *Tome* had not been read, for the prevailing mood of the council would have led to its condemnation and its author's excommunication.

So long as Emperor Theodosius II lived, Alexandria was the "city of the orthodox," and a Monophysite interpretation of Cyril's theology was the faith accepted by Eastern Christendom. In Flavian's place was Dioscorus' trusted deacon and representative in the capital, Anatolius. Despite great activity and many expostulations, there was little that Leo could do to alter matters. On 28 July 450, however, Theodosius died as the result of a hunting accident. Everything changed overnight. The new ruler, Pulcheria, and the elderly Thracian officer Marcian, whom she married on 25 August, were intent on restoring relations between Constantinople and Rome. In the ensuing months Leo was brought round to the idea of a new council, and Anatolius was weaned from his dependence on Dioscorus. On 23 May 451, Pulcheria and Marcian summoned an ecumenical council to meet at NICAEA in September. The location was changed to CHALCEDON and the date changed to 8 October, but the terms of reference suited Leo. The new council was "to end the disputations and settle the true faith more clearly and for all time."

Leo had had last-minute hesitations before accepting the emperor's invitation. In the event, the council had elements both of triumph and of setback for him and the Roman see. The *Tome* was accepted as orthodox. Leo's formulation that "two natures are united without change, without division and without confusion in Christ" found its place in the final Christological definition; but his legates failed to prevent the council from agreeing with Canon 28, which placed Constantinople on a par with the Roman see except for the "primacy of honor" reserved to the latter. Also, the *Tome* was accepted only because the bishops, in their willingness to please the emperors and their readiness to rid themselves of Dioscorus, were prepared to affirm with acclamation that "Cyril and Leo taught alike." The priority, however, was Cyril's.

For the remainder of his pontificate, Leo was occupied in long, drawn-out disputes with the imperial court and Eastern episcopate that were designed to safeguard the Chalcedonian definition from all attempts to reinterpret it or undermine its authority, and at the same time to deny the validity of Canon 28 of the council. Thus, in March 453, Leo branded those who questioned the binding character of the definition as "Eutychians" and heretics. On 21 June 453, in response to Marcian's request to him, as "archbishop of Rome," that he ratify all the decrees of the council, Leo stated his reservations regarding Canon 28. Previously he had told Anatolius that while Constantinople might be a royal city, nothing could make it into an apostolic see, and this remained his position.

Marcian died on 26 January 457, and his successor, Emperor Leo I, respected the decisions of Chalcedon. However, supporters of Dioscorus (who had died in 454) consecrated a former presbyter of Cyril's, TIMOTHY II "the Cat," as patriarch (16 March). Twelve days later his rival, Proterius, who had been appointed at the Council of Chalcedon and was loyal to its decrees, was murdered (Maundy Thursday, 28 March).

The events that followed led to a culmination of Leo's difficulties in the East. Despite his protests, he had not been able to prevent Anatolius from "promoting" the deacon Aetius, who had been secretary at the Council of Chalcedon, to the rank of presbyter in charge of unpleasant duties connected with the cemeteries of the capital. Nor, in the same year (453), had he kept Anatolius from consecrating the patriarch of Antioch and hence demonstrating his position as senior bishop in the East. In July 453, the death of Pulcheria had robbed Leo of an important supporter in Constantinople. Now, he failed to have the murderers of Proterius punished. Despite frantic activity in important and well-argued letters, dispatched on 1 September 457, the future of Timothy was decided by the emperor and the bishops of the East. A "plebiscite" involving some 1,600 bishops came out overwhelmingly against Timothy in early 458 and vindicated Chalcedon's value at least as a disciplinary council that also formally protected the rights of the see of Constantinople against all comers.

In 458 and 459, Leo attempted to justify the papal attitude toward Chalcedon. The emperor forwarded Leo's letters to Timothy, whose reply that he was prepared to condemn Eutyches, as well as the *Tome* of Leo and the Council of Chalcedon, defined the attitude of the anti-Chalcedonian (later, monophysite and Coptic) church in Alexandria from thenceforth (Zacharias Rhetor *Historia ecclesiastica* 4.6). The emperor was, however, dissatisfied with Timothy's reply, and he had Timothy arrested and removed from Alexandria at the end of 459. Leo had the satisfaction of seeing the line of Chalcedonian patriarchs continued in Alexandria by TIMOTHY SALOFACIOLUS ("little white turban") in the spring of 460. He showed some independence from Rome, and one of Leo's last acts was to protest the inclusion of Dioscorus on the diptychs containing the names of those to be remembered at the celebration of the Eucharist in his church. His last recorded letters, sent on 22 August 461, were also to Timothy. He died on 10 November of that year.

Leo's life and achievement must be assessed against his actions in both the West and the East. In the West he enabled the papacy to emerge as the one authoritative and stabilizing force in a period of crisis and confusion resulting from the invasion of Attila the Hun and constant movements of the Germanic peoples in the former provinces of the Western empire.

In the East, however, he was less successful, and his effect on the Coptic church was wholly negative. Anti-Chalcedonian (and later, monophysite) opinion was not alienated from the Roman see as such; Pope Julius I was believed by SEVERUS OF ANTIOCH, on the strength of Apollinarian forgeries, to have favored the "one nature" Christology. The *Tome* of Leo, however, was associated with the Council of Chalcedon as an impious and heretical document. "Cursed be the Council. Cursed be the *Tome* of Leo"—the outcries of the populace of Antioch at the time of Severus' enthronement as patriarch on 6 November 518 (John of Beit-Aphthonia, *Life of Severus*, p. 111)—were typical of reactions in the East. In Egypt, condemnation of the *Tome* figured, with the abrogation of Chalcedon, as the basic requirement in every negotiation between the Coptic-Monophysite church and the imperial authority. For the Coptic church Leo and Cyril did not teach alike, and no one has convinced its adherents that they did.

BIBLIOGRAPHY

Batiffol, P. "Léon le Grand." In *Dictionnaire de théologie catholique*, Vol. 9, pp. 218–301. Paris, 1926.

Dvornik, F. *Byzance et la primauté romaine*. Paris, 1964.

Frend, W. H. C. "Eastern Attitudes to Rome During the Acacian Schism." In *Studies in Church History*, ed. D. Baker, Vol. 13, pp. 69–81. Oxford, 1976.

Hofmann, P. "Der Kampf der Päpste um Konzil und Dogma von Chalkedon von Leo dem Grossen bis Hormisdas (451–519)." In *Das Konzil von Chalkedon*, ed. A. Grillmeier und H. Bacht, Vol. 2, pp. 13–94. Würzburg, 1953.

Jalland, T. G. *The Life and Times of St. Leo the Great*. London, 1941.

Pickman, E. M. *The Mind of Latin Christendom*, pp. 589–616. London, 1937.

W. H. C. FREND

LEONTIUS OF TRIPOLI, SAINT, martyr in the early fourth century in Syria (feast day: 22 Abīb). The Coptic tradition has preserved in translation two documents about Leontius, a Passion and a panegyric. The two texts fill the first seventy-five pages of a Codex 585 in the Pierpont Morgan Library, New York, dating from the ninth century and analyzed by G. Garitte. They are related to a wide collection of texts about Leontius in many forms and languages. Their content is described here, followed by an assessment of each in the light of the Greek, Syriac Arabic, and Georgian parallels.

The Coptic Passion

The Passion opens with Leontius "the Arabian" living in the time of persecution by the emperor Maximian. The decree of persecution is received by the proconsul Julian in Tripoli, in Syria. The angel of the Lord appears to Publius, a noble and rich man who has received the young orphan Leontius into his home. When Publius and Leontius come to the tribunal to bear witness to their faith, the hostile judge threatens punishment. Leontius is scourged, beaten with lashes, has salt rubbed into his wounds, and is burned on his sides with lamps, but the archangel Michael comes to cure him. Leontius then professes his faith in a dialogue with Julian and refuses to sacrifice to the emperor. Leontius is then rolled upon iron spikes, struck in the face with thongs until all his teeth are broken, and cast into boiling sulfur and lead; again Michael descends to heal him. Leontius throws earth into Julian's face and has his tongue slit, but Michael once again descends to cure him. The proconsul then prepares a cauldron of sulfur, bitumen, and tallow until its boiling makes a great noise, but scarcely has Leontius entered into it when the brew is transformed into cool water, so that the tallow sticks to his body like wax. Leontius then defies Asclepius, god of healing, by healing a paralytic whom the god cannot relieve. Finally the proconsul gives an order for the beheading of Leontius and Publius. Their last prayer is received by the archangel Michael. Leontius' blood is collected to work healings. The corpses, left by order as prey for wild beasts, are protected by the angels, and the Christians come by night to bury them with honor.

This Coptic Passion is the longest of those relating to Leontius. The common motifs of Coptic HAGIOGRAPHY are present in abundance, in particular the frequent descents of the archangel Michael. This type of narrative has all the marks of an imaginary story without any actual documentation. None of the Greek documents (Bibliotheca Hagiographica Graeca 986–87d) know anything of Publius, but they associate Leontius with two soldiers whom he converts, Hypatius and Theodule, who suffered with him under the judge Hadrian much earlier (first century) in the time of Vespasian. The Coptic Passion probably owes its origin to the foundation of a church of Saint Leontius at Daphne in 507, following the destruction of a synagogue. For Daphne received its theater under Vespasian, and the cult of Leontius must have replaced an older cult. The Syriac Passion and the corresponding Georgian Passion both presuppose a lost Greek Palestinian model. Leontius there is Greek, not an Arab as he is according to the statement of Theodore the Oriental (Bibliotheca Hagiographica Orientalis 1163) inserted in the title of the Coptic Passion. Probably there is some connection with the sanctuary of Leontius in the Hauran. In the Syriac and Georgian Passions, Leontius is judged with Publius under Diocletian and Maximian by the tribune Philocrinus and then by the judge Firmilian. Publius is sent to the prefect Eumenius at Tyre but dies on the journey. Leontius, who has been set free, is rearrested and scourged with branches of thorny citron, then plunged into the sea, after which he dies. His body is taken up by Joannia, who in clothing it for burial takes an image of his face and prays for her husband, Maurus, who is imprisoned near the emperor in Rome. Maurus is, in fact, set free, dines with the emperor, and on his return to Tripoli is led by a stranger who disappears before he reaches the city. When his wife shows him the icon of Leontius, he recognizes the features of his guide. This final episode in the Syriac and Georgian texts has migrated into one of the Greek Passions published in 1964 by F. Halkin and into an unpublished Arabic Passion (Sinai Arabic manuscript 406, fols. 183–89, dated from 1264). This Arabic Passion describes Maudûs (a version of Maurus) as close to Diocletian. Leontius has no companion, and his judge is called Tîfârius (perhaps a version of Firmilianus).

The Coptic Panegyric

The Coptic Panegyric is the most striking historical piece of all the texts in praise of Leontius. It may be contrasted with two Syrian panegyrics delivered by SEVERUS OF ANTIOCH, on June 513 and 514 (homilies 27 and 50 in the great collection of 125 of Severus' homilies). The Coptic work, which has several paragraphs in common with homily 27, appears to have been delivered at Tripoli, near the saint's sanctuary, whereas the Syriac homilies were given in Daphne. The Coptic work, which is much longer than the Syriac, contains a paragraph in which Severus recalls his youth as a student of Roman law in Beirut and how he was converted in the very church of Saint Leontius in Tripoli. This episode was probably deleted from the Syriac homily because Severus' enemies, who considered his pagan origin a detraction, used it against him. The

Coptic Panegyric also recounts a story of the martyrdom according to the statements of an old man whom Severus himself once met. This story emphasizes the torment of the cauldron in which the boiling tallow is transformed into wax, which in Severus' time was still used for the healing of the sick. Three etiological miracles are linked to the story and testify beyond doubt to the experience of an eyewitness in 488, the probable date of the conversion of Severus.

The corresponding Syriac passage, at the point of passing to the testimony, says that Leontius had no need of a scribe to write his Passion with all the flowers of rhetoric because the saint himself wrote it with the cures that continued to be performed at his tomb. This important affirmation is interpreted by G. Garitte (Garitte, 1968, pp. 425–26) as if no Passion yet existed in 513. But it may be rather a question of the lofty style of rhetoric, for Severus' reflection indicates that in his period Passions were necessary for more than one saint. However that may be, in the fifth century the church at Tripoli received some distinguished visitors, such as Melanie the Younger and Peter the Iberian. It would probably be wrong to deny the existence of the martyrdom or the documentary value of the simplest text, the Syriac Passion.

BIBLIOGRAPHY

Garitte, G. "La Passion copte sahidique." *Le Muséon* 78 (1965):313–48.

———. "L'Homélie copte de Sévère d'Antioche." *Le Muséon* 79 (1966):335–86.

———. "La Passion syriaque." *Le Muséon* 61 (1968):415–40.

Halkin, F. "Passion et miracle posthume de saint Léonce martyr à Tripoli en Phénicie." *Analecta Bollandiana* 82 (1964):319–40.

MICHEL VAN ESBROECK

LEPSIUS, KARL RICHARD

LEPSIUS, KARL RICHARD (1810–1884), German Egyptologist. He was born at Naumburg an der Saale and educated at the universities of Leipzig, Göttingen, and Berlin, where he continued his studies of archaeology and Egyptology. His efforts in the field of Coptology were very limited and confined to a few minor works, listed in *A Coptic Bibliography* (Kammerer, 1950, 1969). He died in Berlin.

BIBLIOGRAPHY

Dawson, W. R., and E. P. Uphill. *Who Was Who in Egyptology*. London, 1972.

Kammerer, W., comp. *A Coptic Bibliography*. Ann Arbor, Mich., 1950; repr. New York, 1969.

AZIZ S. ATIYA

LE QUIEN, MICHEL

LE QUIEN, MICHEL (1661–1733), French church historian. He was born in Boulogne-sur-Mer and completed his studies in Paris. Then, at the age of twenty, he entered the Dominican order. He specialized in patristic studies with a concentration on Eastern Christendom. He compiled a tremendous mass of materials for his major project, entitled *Oriens Christianus* (3 vols., Paris, 1740). He published a prospectus of that work in 1722, but the work itself was published posthumously. His edition of the *Works of Saint John Damascene* in 1712 remains a standard one. The accumulated material on the Eastern patriarchates, though not without shortcomings, is one of the most complete records on the subject.

BIBLIOGRAPHY

Leclercq, H. "Le Quien." In *Dictionnaire d'archéologie chrétienne et de liturgie*, Vol. 8, 2. Paris, 1907–1953.

AZIZ S. ATIYA

LEROY, JULES

LEROY, JULES (1903–1979), French historian of Christian iconography of the anti-Chalcedonian churches. He was master of research at the Centre national de la Recherche scientifique in Paris. He studied with A. Grabar and worked on the miniatures of Syriac, Ethiopian, and Coptic manuscripts, as well as on Coptic mural paintings.

BIBLIOGRAPHY

Coquin, R.-G. "L'Abbé Jules Leroy (1903–1979)." *Bulletin de l'Institut français d'archéologie orientale* 80 (1980):5–15.

RENÉ-GEORGES COQUIN

LETRONNE, JEAN ANTOINE

LETRONNE, JEAN ANTOINE (1787–1848), French archaeologist and classical scholar. He was born in Paris. He became keeper of national archives (1840) and took a prominent interest in the deciphering of hieroglyphics by J. F. CHAMPOLLION and Thomas Young. He made a few contributions to Coptic studies. He died in Paris.

BIBLIOGRAPHY

Dawson, W. R., and E. P. Uphill. *Who Was Who in Egyptology*. London, 1972.

Kammerer, W., comp. *A Coptic Bibliography*. Ann Arbor, Mich., 1950; repr. New York, 1969.

AZIZ S. ATIYA

LETTER OF AMMON. The two most important manuscripts that have transmitted the text of the first Greek Life of Pachomius to us, the *Florentinus* and the *Atheniensis*, have also preserved the text of a document known as the *Epistula Ammonis*. It is a letter addressed by a bishop called Ammon to a certain Theophilus and is followed in the manuscripts by a response from the latter.

The texts of the letter and of the answer were first published by Papenbroech in 1680 in his ACTA SANCTORUM (Bollandus, 1643) and again by F. Halkin in 1932 in his *Sancti Pachomii Vitae Graecae*, according to the *Florentinus* manuscript. Halkin published the version of the *Atheniensis* manuscript in 1982.

No translation of this text appeared before the two published in 1982: one by A.-J. Festugière, following the *Atheniensis* manuscript (with footnotes indicating the divergent readings of the *Florentinus* manuscript), and the other by A. Veilleux, following the *Florentinus* manuscript but taking into account the readings of the *Atheniensis* manuscript.

From the details given in the letter itself, we know that Ammon, born to pagan parents in Alexandria, was converted to Christianity at the age of seventeen and went to Pbow as a monk in 352, six years after the death of PACHOMIUS OF TABENNĒSĒ, when THEODORUS OF TABENNĒSĒ was at the head of the Pachomian *koinonia* (community). He spent three years there in the house of the Alexandrian brothers and then transferred to NITRIA, where he spent many years before becoming a bishop. His letter is a kind of panegyric of Theodorus, for whom he developed a great admiration during the three years he spent at Pbow. It is accompanied in the manuscripts by a response from a certain Theophilus and was published by Papenbroech under the title *Epistula Ammonis Episc. ad Theophilum Papam Alexandriae*. But since the lemma of the *Florentinus* manuscript has no mention of Theophilus and that of the *Atheniensis* manuscript speaks of "a certain Theophilus," it is far from certain that the addressee of the letter was really the archbishop of Alexandria.

The authenticity and the historical value of Ammon's letter, generally acknowledged by historians, was radically questioned by L. T. LEFORT (1943), whose conclusions were in turn rejected by P. PEETERS (1946) and especially by D. J. Chitty (1954).

Ammon knew Theodorus personally and heard about him from various people, especially from two monks called Ausonius and Elourion. Although he wrote some forty years after leaving the THEBAID, Ammon seems to have had a very good memory for dates, and his letter is extremely useful in reconstructing the chronology of early Pachomian monasticism. But the fact that he lived for a long time at Nitria after only three years at Pbow and that he wrote his letter so many years later certainly explains that his terminology and even his preoccupations (e.g., the possibility of forgiveness of sins committed after baptism) are not particularly Pachomian. Of Theodorus and the other Pachomians he has remembered not so much their virtues and their graces of prayer as their gift of prophecy and their miracles.

BIBLIOGRAPHY

Bollandus, *Acta sanctorum*. Antwerp, 1643. Continued by J. B. Carnendet, G. Henschenius, D. Papenbroech. Venice, 1734; Paris, 1863.

Chitty, D. J. "Pachomian Sources Reconsidered." *Journal of Ecclesiastical History* 5 (1954):38–77.

Halkin, F. *Sancti Pachomii Vitae Graecae*. Subsidia Hagiographica 19. Brussels, 1932.

———. *Le Corpus athénien de saint Pachôme avec une traduction française par A.-J. Festugière*. Cahiers d'orientalisme 2. Geneva, 1982.

Lefort, L. T. *Les Vies coptes de saint Pachôme et de ses premiers successeurs*, pp. li–lxii. Bibliothèque du Muséon 16. Louvain, 1953; repr. 1966.

Peeters, P. "Le Dossier copte de S. Pachôme et ses rapports avec la tradition grecque." *Analecta Bollandiana* 64 (1946):258–77.

Veilleux, A. *La Liturgie dans le cénobitisme pachômien au IVe siècle*, pp. 108–111. Studia Anselmiana 57. Rome, 1968.

———. *Pachomian Koinonia*, Vol. 2, *Pachomian Chronicles and Rules*. Cistercian Studies 46. Kalamazoo, Mich., 1981.

ARMAND VEILLEUX

LETTER OF PETER TO PHILIP, a Gnostic Christian tract, probably from the second century. The only manuscript that we have of this treatise is the Coptic translation of the original Greek. The Coptic text (NAG HAMMADI LIBRARY VIII. 2) recounts a Gnostic version of Pentecost, the descent of the Holy Spirit that gave birth to the Christian church. To some extent, the treatise parallels Luke 24 and the first chapters of Acts and may well share a common tradition.

The central message is the emphasis on the soteriological value of the simple act of proclaiming the gospel. The words of the apostles when they preach are actually inspired by the Holy Spirit. For example, when Peter is first filled with the Spirit, he gives voice to the sacred creed:

Our illuminator Jesus came down and was crucified.
And he wore a crown of thorns.
And he put on a purple robe;
And he was crucified upon a cross;
And he was buried in a tomb;
And he rose from the dead.

Pentecost fulfilled the promise made by Christ when he appeared on the Mount of Olives before the disciples in order to convey to them the importance of the missionary activity about to begin. He explains how the cosmos came into being and in it mankind, which harbors a spiritual self that must be awakened and set on the path to freedom in the spiritual world in which there is no death (see GNOSTICISM). Trying to prevent the escape of the disciples and others like them are the archons (cosmic powers) created by the Arrogant One (the Demiurge). So far there is nothing new in this version of the myth about the fall and redemption of the spirit. However, the disciples want to know what weapons they can use to combat the archons and not be destroyed. They learn that the archons' fight is against the "inner person," that is, the spiritual self, and that they can be countered successfully by girding the inner person with the power and understanding that come from the Holy Spirit.

In other words, the Holy Spirit grants to the disciples the spirit of understanding (*pneuma epistēmēs*), empowering them to heal and to spread the saving knowledge about Christ. Armed thus, the disciples (now apostles) are able to overcome the enemy; for the Spirit's activity strengthens them both physically and spiritually and reveals to them the way out of the cosmos. The fight is for the spiritual man, and the appropriate defense is described here in terms of spiritual gifts.

Pentecost is clearly the birthday of the Christian community, but in this text it is set within a framework of ongoing revelation. The structure of the work rests on four sacred events, or divine epiphanies, each in a different setting. In the first, the disciples travel to the Mount of Olives, where, in response to their petitions, Christ appears to them in the forms of light, a voice, thunder, and lightning. In the second, on the road back to Jerusalem, the voice is heard once again. In the third the disciples arrive at the Temple in Jerusalem, where they experience (first Peter and then all of them) the coming down of the Holy Spirit, which fills them with its power to preach and to heal. The fourth epiphany takes place after Pentecost and after the first period of Christian missionizing, when Jesus appears to the disciples in order to give them his blessing.

Thus, the *Letter of Peter to Philip* reflects a view according to which the disciples' experience of ongoing revelation is a guiding factor in the development of the Christian church. The risen Christ appears more than once, both before and after the descent of the Spirit at Pentecost. Nothing in the text suggests an end to such epiphanies.

The account given in the *Letter of Peter to Philip* varies in numerous ways from that of the author of Luke and Acts. For example, in Acts, the event of Pentecost takes place in some unspecified location among a crowd of anonymous Jews; here, Pentecost takes place in the Temple and involves only Peter and *his* disciples. The opening lines, which recount Peter's invitation to Philip to join him and the other disciples in order to prepare together for the coming mission (from which derives the manuscript's title), may be a polemical statement. In Acts 8:4ff. and 14ff., we read that Philip converted many to Christ but that he himself had not yet received the Holy Spirit, for Peter and John are sent to finish his work for him. Whereas Philip had only baptized others in the name of the Lord Jesus, Peter and John are able to transmit the Spirit through the laying on of hands. Perhaps the Gnostic text was written in a Christian community that traced its origins to Philip's missionary activity and wished to emphasize his participation in the original, spirit-giving event of Pentecost.

BIBLIOGRAPHY

Bethge, H.-G. "Der sogenannte 'Brief des Petrus an Philippus': Die Zweite 'Schrift' aus Nag-Hammadi-Codex VIII eingeleitet und übersetzt vom Berliner Arbeitskreis für koptisch-gnostische

Schriften." *Theologische Literaturzeitung* 103 (1978):161–70.

Koschorke, K. "Eine gnostische Pfingstpredigt: Zur Auseinandersetzung zwischen gnostischem und kirchlichem Christentum am Beispiel der 'Epistula Petri ad Philippum' (NHC VIII, 2)." *Zeitschrift für Theologie und Kirche* 74 (1977):323–43.

______. "Eine gnostische Paraphrase des johannischen Prologs: Zur Interpretation von 'Epistula Petri ad Philippum' (NHC VIII, 2) 136,16–137,14." *Vigiliae Christianae* 33 (1979):383–92.

Luttikhuizen, G. P. "The Letter of Peter to Philip and the New Testament." In *Nag Hammadi and Gnosis*, pp. 96–102. Nag Hammadi Studies 14. Leiden, 1978.

Ménard, J. E. *La Lettre de Pierre à Philippe*. Quebec, 1977.

______. "La Lettre de Pierre à Philippe: sa structure." *In Nag Hammadi and Gnosis*, pp. 103–107. Nag Hammadi Studies 14. Leiden, 1978.

Meyer, M. W. *The Letter of Peter to Philip: Text, Translation, and Commentary*. Society of Biblical Literature Dissertation Series, no. 53. Chico, Calif., 1981.

Perkins, P. "Peter in Gnostic Revelation." In *Society of Biblical Literature 1974 Seminar Papers*, Vol. 2, pp. 1–13. Cambridge, 1974.

Wisse, F. "The Letter of Peter to Philip." In *The Nag Hammadi Library in English*. San Francisco, 1977.

BEVERLY MOON

LIBANIUS (c. 314–395), Antiochene sophist and rhetorician, and a champion of pagan classical literature. He was an admirer and supporter of the apostate emperor JULIAN, but he also numbered among his friends and students the Christians JOHN CHRYSOSTOM, BASIL THE GREAT, and THEODORUS OF MOPSUESTIA. As a young man Libanius spurned the teachers in Antioch and steeped himself in the Greek classics. At about the age of twenty-two, he went to Athens, where he studied for four years. He later taught and lectured in Constantinople and Nicomedia, where he first became acquainted with Julian, the young emperor-to-be. He spent the last half of his life in his beloved Antioch.

The voluminous works of Libanius, which provide much valuable information on political, social, and economic affairs in the eastern portion of the Roman Empire, include rhetorical exercises, declamations, orations, an apology of Socrates, a life of Demosthenes, an autobiography, and a collection of letters that includes correspondence with ATHANASIUS, GREGORY OF NYSSA, John Chrysostom, and the emperor Julian.

BIBLIOGRAPHY

Foerster, R. *Libanii Opera*, 12 vols. in 13. Bibliotheca Scriptorum Graecorum et Romanorum Teubneriana. Hildesheim, 1963. Reprint of 1903–1923 edition.

Liebeschuetz, J. H. W. G. *Antioch: City and Imperial Administration in the Later Roman Empire*. Oxford, 1972.

Pack, R. *Studies in Libanius and Antiochene Society Under Theodosius*. Menasha, Wis., 1935.

RANDALL STEWART

LIBERAL CONSTITUTIONAL PARTY. *See* Political Parties.

LIBERAL EGYPTIANS PARTY. *See* Political Parties.

LIBRARIES. In pre-Christian times there were libraries in the temples of Egypt. From the Hellenistic period the library of Alexandria is particularly well known. It once sheltered 700,000 scrolls, but in 48–47 B.C. it fell victim to a conflagration. A second library of Alexandria, located at the Serapeum, was destroyed in A.D. 391 during the storming of the Serapeum.

When Egypt was Christianized, other libraries in addition to Alexandria were set up, above all in the chief centers of the bishoprics of Egypt and later also in the monasteries. Of these, despite the dry climate, which is favorable to the preservation of libraries, only remnants have survived. The library of the archbishop of Alexandria was particularly large. It served also for the theological instruction at the CATECHETICAL SCHOOL. In the time of ORIGEN it was the model for the library of Jerusalem, and after his banishment from Alexandria (231), Origen built up an important library in Caesarea on the model of the library in Alexandria.

An impression of the number of books in a church is afforded by the inventory list of the Church of Theodorus in Hermopolis, which mentions thirty-one books without naming the titles (Crum, 1909, no. 238, pp. 112–14). According to Crum (1905, XII, no. 5), the Coptic manuscripts of Turin may have belonged to a church in Thinis (Abydos).

On the evidence of the literary sources, the libraries of the Egyptian monasteries were especially large. The Rule of PACHOMIUS required that those entering the monastery not only should learn Bible texts by heart but also should learn to read. Every monastery contained a library, from which during weekdays a monk could borrow a book to read in his cell. In the evening he had to lay it on the windowsill, in order that the superior's representative might count the volumes and lock them up for the night (Leipoldt, 1962, pp. 210ff.). No list has survived of the books in the monasteries of Pachomius.

Under SHENUTE, too, the monks had to learn to read. In a room situated to the north of the great apse of the church of the White Monastery (DAYR ANBĀ SHINŪDAH), inscriptions were found on all four walls that name the titles of books, sometimes with the number of copies of the book concerned. From this, Crum concluded that the monastery library was located in this room (1904, p. 552; 1909, pp. Xff.). According to the inscriptions (Crum, 1904, pp. 564ff.), the New Testament books were on shelves on the north wall, those of the Old Testament on the south wall, the homiletic and historical books on the east wall, and the biographies on the west wall. Of the four Gospels there were more than a hundred copies; of the Life of Pachomius, twenty; and of the Life of Shenute, eight.

Individual biographies of Pachomius, the founder of monasticism, and of his successors HORSIESIOS and THEODORUS OF TABENNĒSĒ are mentioned, as well as of Abraham of Pbow. Alongside Shenute his successor BESA appears, as well as a series of other monks: PISENTIUS OF COPTOS, JOHN COLOBOS, Apa Apollo, Apa Elias, SAMUEL OF QALAMŪN, and others. It is not known from what period the inscriptions come. There are dated inscriptions from the twelfth and thirteenth centuries. The period when the monastery flourished extends down to the thirteenth century. Of the oldest manuscripts, which were written on papyrus, none has survived. Even of the early parchment codices, which replaced papyrus in the sixth and seventh centuries, only scant remains are preserved. On the evidence of the colophons, manuscripts were given as gifts to the library of the White Monastery by other monasteries (e.g., in the Fayyūm) and by private persons.

At the beginning of the eighteenth century, the first leaves of manuscripts from this library came to Europe, initially in the collection of Cardinal Borgia, and then through C. G. Woide and H. Tattam to Oxford. R. Curzon also brought manuscripts from his travels in Egypt. In 1883 G. Maspero bought all the manuscripts that remained in the monastery library. These are now in Paris (cf. Hyvernat, 1933).

Parts of manuscripts or individual pages are today divided among the libraries of many countries. In addition to Egypt (Cairo) these include Italy (Naples, Rome, and Venice), Great Britain (London, Manchester, Oxford), France (Paris), Austria (Vienna), Russia (Leningrad, Moscow), the Netherlands (Leiden), Sweden (Stockholm), Germany (Berlin), and the United States (Ann Arbor). W. E. Crum, O. von Lemm, H. Hyvernat, L. T. Lefort, and others began the task of reconstructing the original codices. Other scholars, among whom D. W. Young and T. Orlandi should especially be mentioned, have continued the work more recently.

In the libraries of older monasteries there were Greek as well as Coptic codices. This is shown by a monastery manuscript list deriving from the Fayyūm (Crum, 1892, p. 50). It includes the writings of the New Testament in several copies, both in Greek and in Coptic, the Psalter in both languages, lectionaries, and a series of theological books. Some of the codices were of papyrus, some of parchment. There is a further book list in Turin (Crum, 1926, Vol. 1, p. 205 and n. 3).

The works of Origen and DIDYMUS, written in Greek, that were found in 1941 in the monastery of Arsenius at Ṭurah also came from a monastery library (Koenen and Müller-Wiener, 1968, p. 48 and n. 14).

The library of DAYR APA PHOIBAMMON is designated in child donation documents (see DONATION OF CHILDREN) as the place where such deeds were to be deposited (e.g., *Koptische Rechtsurkunden*, no. 89, l. 36). While we have no information about the number of the manuscripts kept in it, a part of the monastery archives has survived. From the neighborhood of this important monastery comes a library catalog (cf. Coquin, 1975) of the period about 600, written on a large limestone ostracon, from the otherwise little-known monastery of Elias (Crum, 1926, Vol. 1, p. 113). It enumerates in three sections some eighty titles with a statement of the writing material. For the most part it is a question of papyrus codices, occasionally with the addition "new." Parchment codices are in the minority. The ostracon, bought from a dealer in Luxor and published by U. Bouriant, was discussed in detail by Crum along with the remains of literary texts found in Thebes (1926, Vol. 1, pp. 197–208). His arguments are in part to be corrected in accordance with the new edition by R.-G. Coquin, who emended errors in the first edition. In addition to the books of the Old and New Testaments, sometimes in two or more examples, the following are mentioned: LECTIONARIES, church canons, a book about the birth of the Lord and the feast of Epiphany, the life of Mary, books about JOHN THE BAPTIST, works of the monastic fathers PACHOMIUS and Shenute, the church fathers ATHANASIUS and CYRIL I (the Great), biographies of and encomia on monks (Pachomius, Shenute, Apa THOMAS THE ANCHORITE, etc.), martyrs (Archbishop Peter of Alexandria, Apa Epithymites, etc.) and church fathers (EPIPHANIUS, BASIL THE GREAT), two books about burials, and a medicine book (see PAPYRI, COPTIC MEDICAL).

From a later period come two manuscript discoveries from two monastery libraries. These are, first, the find of fifty-six codices from the monastery of the archangel MICHAEL, situated at Sopehes in the Fayyūm, which passed almost completely to the Pierpont Morgan Library. They were written between 820 and 920 in the Fayyūm and were published in facsimile by Hyvernat in 1922. The extant library (complete inventory in Hyvernat, 1922) contains, in addition to books of the Old and New Testaments, lectionaries, homilies, and an antiphonary. The sermons are traced back to archbishops of Alexandria (PETER I, ATHANASIUS I, TIMOTHY I, THEOPHILUS, CYRIL I, DIOSCORUS I, JOHN III), to bishops of other, non-Egyptian cities (CYRIL OF JERUSALEM, JOHN CHRYSOSTOM of Constantinople, DEMETRIUS OF ANTIOCH, SEVERUS OF ANTIOCH, Basil the Great of Caesarea, SEVERIAN OF JABALAH) and of Egyptian dioceses (Macarius of Antaiopolis, Constantine of Lycopolis, Stephen of Herakleopolis), and abbot Shenute of Atrīb.

Among Passions of martyrs are those of COLLUTHUS, COSMAS AND DAMIAN, Cyprian, Elias, MERCURIUS, PHOIBAMMON OF PREHT, and both THEODORUS STRATELATES and Orientalis, as well as the miracle stories of Saint MENAS and Phoibammon. The biographies deal with the apostle John, the protomartyr Stephen, and the monks and hermits Antony of Kome, Apollo, ARCHELLIDES, LONGINUS and Lucius, ONOPHRIUS, PHIB, and SAMŪ'IL OF QALAMŪN. The installation of the archangels GABRIEL and Michael is also dealt with, as is the death of the patriarch ISAAC.

The codices of the monasteries at Idfū were written somewhat later, from 974 to the twelfth century, above all those of the Mercurius monastery, which were bought in Egypt in 1907 by R. de Rustafjaell and passed to the British Museum, where they were published by E. A. W. Budge between 1910 and 1915. As the titles of Budge's publications show, these are biblical and apocryphal writings, homilies, and passions.

From the Middle Ages come the surviving libraries of the monasteries of the Wādī al-Naṭrūn, which were investigated by H. Evelyn-White in 1920–1921. The older libraries were destroyed mainly through the inroads of the bedouin in the years 408, 434, 444, and 817. That of the Macarius monastery (DAYR ANBĀ MAQĀR) must have been particularly important, since the emperor annually provided money for it, and in the middle of the sixth century the patriarch transferred his seat to this monastery. The library surviving from the Middle Ages fell into decay about the middle of the fourteenth century, and its dispersal began in the seventeenth century. J. S. Assemani brought valuable books to the Vatican; Huntington to the Bodleian Library in Oxford; Tattam's books passed to the John Rylands Library in Manchester; and K. von Tischendorf brought codices to Leipzig and Cambridge, to mention only the most important European travelers, before Evelyn-White brought the remains of the most important manuscripts that had remained in the *qaṣr* to the Coptic Museum in Cairo. The fate of the library of the Syrian monastery (DAYR AL-SURYĀN) is dealt with by Evelyn-White (1926–1933, Vol. 2, pp. 439–58), as is that of the smaller monasteries (Vol. 1, 1926, pp. 270–74). For the reconstruction of the libraries of the monasteries of the Wādī al-Naṭrūn, all the codices brought to European libraries must be taken into consideration, as well as the remnants that still remain.

BIBLIOGRAPHY

Bouriant, U. "Notes de voyage." *Recueil de travaux* 11 (1889):131–38.

Budge, E. A. W. *Coptic Homilies in the Dialect of Upper Egypt Edited from the Papyrus Codex Oriental 5001 in the British Museum.* London, 1910.

______. *Coptic Apocrypha in the Dialect of Upper Egypt.* London, 1913.

______. *Coptic Martyrdoms, etc., in the Dialect of Upper Egypt.* London, 1914.

______. *Miscellaneous Coptic Texts in the Dialect of Upper Egypt.* London, 1915.

Coquin, R.-G. "Le catalogue de la bibliothèque du couvent de Saint Elie 'du rocher.'" *Bulletin de l'Institut français d'Archéologie orientale* 75 (1975):207–239.

Crum, W. E. "Coptic Papyri." In *Medum*, ed. Flinders Petrie, p. 50. London, 1892.

______. "Inscriptions from Shenoute's Monastery." *Journal of Theological Studies* 5 (1904):552–69.

______. *Catalogue of the Coptic Manuscripts in the British Museum.* London, 1905.

______. *Catalogue of the Coptic Manuscripts in the Collection of the John Rylands Library, Manchester.* Manchester, 1909.

______. *The Monastery of Epiphanius at Thebes,* p. 1. New York, 1926.

Crum, W. E., and G. Steindorff. *Koptische Rechtsurkunden des Achten Jahrhunderts aus Djême (Theben).* Leipzig, 1912. Repr. 1971.

Evelyn-White, H. *The Monasteries of the Wadi 'n Natrun,* 3 vols. New York, 1926–1933.

Hebbelynck, A. "Les manuscrits coptes-sahidiques du 'Monastère Blanc.' Recherches sur les fragments complémentaires de la collection Borgia." *Le Muséon,* n.s. 12 (1911):91–154; n.s. 13 (1912):275–362.

Hyvernat, H. *Bibliothecae Pierpont Morgan codices coptici photographice expressi,* 56 vols. in 63 facsimiles. Rome, 1922.

______. "Introduction au Porcher, E., Analyse des manuscrits coptes 131^{1-8} de la Bibliothèque nationale, avec indication des textes bibliques." *Revue d'Egyptologie* 1 (1933):105–116.

Koenen, L., and W. Müller-Wiener. "Zu den Papyri aus dem Arsenioskloster bei Turā." *Zeitschrift für Papyrologie und Epigraphik* 2 (1968):42–63.

Leipoldt, J. "Pachom." *Bulletin de la Société d'archéologie copte* 16 (1962):191–229.

Lemm, O. von. *Koptische Miscellen.* St. Petersburg, 1914. Repr. Leipzig, 1972.

Lucchesi, E. *Répertoire des manuscrits coptes (sahidiques) publiés de la Bibliothèque nationale de Paris.* Cahiers d'Orientalisme 1. Geneva, 1981.

Orlandi, T. "Un codice copto del 'Monastero Bianco.'" *Le Muséon* 81 (1968):351–405.

______. "Un projet milanais concernant les manuscrits coptes du Monastère Blanc." *Le Muséon* 85 (1972):403–413.

______. "Realizzazioni e projetti del corpus dei manoscritti copti litterare." In *Atti del XVII Congresso internazionale di papirologia, Naples 1983,* Vol. 2. Naples, 1984.

Rustafjaell, R. de. *The Light of Egypt. From Recently Discovered Predynastic and Early Christian Records,* 2nd ed., pp. 101–138. London, 1910.

Young, Dwight W. "Observations on White Monastery Codices Attested in the University of Michigan Library." In *Atti del XVII Congresso internazionale di papirologia, Naples 1983,* Vol. 2. Naples, 1984.

MARTIN KRAUSE

LIBYA. *See* Pentapolis.

LIGHTING EQUIPMENT. *See* Metalwork, Coptic.

LINEN. *See* Textiles, Coptic: Yarns.

LINGUISTICS, COPTIC. *See Appendix.*

LINTELS. *See* Woodwork, Coptic.

LITERATURE, COPTIC. National literatures are defined not only by the language in which they are written but also by ethnic and cultural affinities that bind their authors. That is why we may distinguish an American literature in English from British literature or a Latin-American literature in Spanish from Spanish literature. The literature in the Coptic language is unusual because it should be considered as part of a wider literature that includes patristic Greek literature and Christian Arabic literature written in Egypt. This article will examine Christian literature written in the Coptic language from the second century till the eleventh century, by which time Coptic had been virtually superseded by Arabic. We shall exclude magical and medical texts, though the most ancient of them may be considered the first examples of Coptic writing.

The Beginnings

The origins of Coptic literature are problematic because the documentation is scant. Nevertheless, since the Greek language predominated in Egypt for some time before and after the beginning of the Christian era, we can assume that Greek literature was at the base of Coptic literature, affecting its development in both content and style. In fact, at the beginning, Coptic texts, particularly biblical and Gnostic texts, were merely translations of Greek originals. Since the Bible and Gnostic texts are treated in separate articles, we will deal with them here only to place them in relation to the general development of Coptic literature.

For some time, many scholars assumed that the first people to accept the necessity and convenience of making translations into Coptic were the Gnostics and that Alexandria was the place for their production. This assumption was made because the most ancient Coptic manuscripts contain either biblical or Gnostic(izing) texts. But neither of these ideas is supported by documented proof.

Other scholars have indicated monastic groups as the place for the translating and missionary activity as their purpose. According to this view, it seemed necessary to make the texts of the new Christian religion spreading through Egypt comprehensible to those who did not understand Greek.

This view may be partially true, but the formation and use of the Coptic language appear so complicated, given the acceptance of an enormous number of Greek words and the importance of Greek syntax, that the "practical" purpose of translation does not seem to hold. Other purposes should be considered, namely, the effort to revive a national Egyptian culture long since in decline though never completely dead and a wish to interpolate the content of the new religious spirit into the ancient Egyptian tradition.

It is generally inferred from some passages in the Life of Antony by Saint ATHANASIUS I and in the rules of Saint PACHOMIUS that the Coptic translation of at least some books of the Bible (above all the Psalms and the New Testament) was used in the official church at least by the beginning of the fourth century. In fact, we possess many biblical codices from that period. The biblical translations had a continuous tradition until the end of the Coptic culture. The texts found in later codices, though sometimes different, are often very close to those found in the ancient ones. This similarity indicates that already by the fourth century translation was done at a high level and probably was the work of learned and responsible people. The fact that we also find manuscripts of "wild" translations, especially in dialects other than Sahidic, is only natural and in no way contradicts the preceding statement. All these problems remain open for further study.

Gnosticizing texts, however, and those of generally moral character accompanying them (see NAG HAMMADI LIBRARY) are no longer found in later manuscripts and are written in a less accurate language, possibly indicating that they were produced and read in different religious groups (also Christian) that later disappeared or changed their mind, probably under constraint.

The same groups that produced biblical translations seem also to have produced translations of a small number of "patristic" texts, such as some homilies by MELITO OF SARDIS, and some apocryphal works such as *Apocalypsis Heliae*, *Visio Isaiae*, *Acts of Paul*, and *Epistula Apostolorum*. They might point to contacts with Asiatic circles, rather than the Alexandrian school, and therefore to an origin in the Nile Valley rather than Alexandria.

The first person who might have written (or rather dictated) originally in Coptic was Saint ANTONY, a hermit in the desert in the second century. We have a collection of his seven letters, existing in Latin (from a lost Greek original), in Georgian, and in Coptic (some fragments). But whether the Coptic text as we now have it is the original one or a translation from the Greek is not known.

Another person who might have written in Coptic is HIERACAS OF LEONTOPOLIS, a fascinating figure in the beginning of Egyptian monasticism and Christian culture. According to Epiphanius of Salamis (*Panarion* 67. 1 and 3), he was well acquainted with both Egyptian and Greek science and wrote a biblical exegesis and nine Psalms in both Coptic and Greek. He was a professional scribe and therefore may have been a central figure in the formation of the Coptic language, script, and literature. He was probably a follower of ORIGEN in his exegetical (allegorical) methods, which he expanded into Gnostic ideas. All this fits into the frame of the beginning of Coptic literature, but nothing more than this can be said at present.

The first original author of whom we are well informed by historical documents and some extant works is Saint PACHOMIUS, a fourth-century abbot. Until a few years ago, we could speak of the literary achievements of the Pachomian communities only on the basis of general deductions rather than with much concrete evidence. From Pachomius himself in the Coptic language, we had but a few fragments of his rule and other texts of doubtful authenticity. This situation was radically changed in 1972 by the identification of the Coptic text of some of Pachomius' letters and of letters of his successors Saint THEODORUS OF TABENNĒSĒ and Saint HORSIESIOS.

The fundamental questions about the authenticity of the text of Pachomius' letters and its original language are not yet completely clarified, but we may make three observations. First, such an ancient text, attributed with precision to only one particularly noted author, may well be considered genuine, at least until some other documentation is found that proves the contrary. Second, the peculiar form of transmission of the text (scrolls were often used, rather than the usual codex) points to something special in the Coptic tradition. Third, as to the original language, everything leads us to believe that the letters were indeed written in Coptic.

The works of Pachomius and his immediate successors, therefore, represent the oldest original Coptic texts with true literary characteristics. Their content and form (especially in the letters of Pachomius) are rather problematic, mainly because of the alphabet used. Also, there is difficulty in understanding the general meaning, because the text was formed of a sequence of biblical quotations and short connecting sentences, without a real structure.

In fact, it is possible that, though Pachomius and his successors accepted the function of some kind of writing in Christian monastic spirituality, they rejected the rules of literature formed in the Greek rhetorical tradition and accepted by other Christian authors writing in Greek or Latin.

Shenute

The initial step toward accepting the common rules of literature when producing Coptic texts was taken by Saint SHENUTE, fifth-century abbot of Atrīb, later known as the famous Dayr Anbā Shinūdah (the White Monastery) of Upper Egypt. He has rightly gained wide renown among both his contemporaries and modern scholars as the most important author of Coptic literature. But the documented evaluation of his works apart from a generic appreciation is very difficult for many reasons.

The manuscripts containing his works were conserved almost exclusively in the library of his monastery, from which they were sorted only in fragments, and it was as fragments that they became known as, through the years, they reached various parts of Europe and America.

The first portions arrived in Italy in the eighteenth century (Borgia and Nani collections, now in Rome, Naples, and Venice). In 1888 came the important discovery of the remains of the White Monastery library. Most of the find was taken to Paris, while smaller portions went to Leiden, London, Vienna, and elsewhere. The work of editing began rather quickly, and the extensive publication of texts began in 1903, by E.C. AMÉLINEAU, C. F. J. WESSELY, and J. LEIPOLDT, and W.E. CRUM.

The manner in which Shenute's work was edited is not satisfactory, though it was justified by the poverty of technical and practical means available at the time. The scholars worked mainly on one collection, rarely trying to put together fragments of the same work from different collections. So Amélineau limited himself to the Borgia fragments, merely transcribing and translating them in haste without indicating any internal structure or the general meaning of the pieces. Wessely limited himself to transcribing the fragments at Vienna, with no translation or critical work.

Leipoldt, whose research dates from 1908–1913, concentrated on the Paris collection. Unlike Amélineau, Leipoldt (working with the help of Crum) sought out fragments in which a title or some other indication permitted him to characterize and thereby organize them. But he was unable to achieve much beyond a collection of excerpts that are generally brief and all in all among the least significant examples of Shenute's thinking. Also, although he did seek out parallel codices in other collections, he omitted the essential task of putting these fragments in the original order of the codex from which they were taken. So it happens that he published, under different numbers and titles, fragments from the same work.

In the meantime, P. LADEUZE, who worked in the University of Louvain, published a fundamental monograph on Shenute. His research was the result of historical criticism by Catholic scholars; it was sound in philology but somewhat lacking in a more liberal approach. Unfortunately, he could not avail himself of the texts published by Amélineau and by Leipoldt and Crum. So his work was severely criticized by liberal Protestants, especially A. Harnack and his collaborators.

The basic monograph about Shenute remains the one published by Leipoldt, who proposed the first historic evaluation of Shenute's works. Although he was too severe in his judgment of Shenute as writer, theologian, and ecclesiastical leader, he did try to reconstruct the figure of Shenute in the frame of the Egyptian church and monasticism of his times. However, owing to a lack of sympathy toward monastic life in general, and toward that of Shenute and Egypt in particular, his evaluation of the man and writer remained unkind and hardly objective.

In attempting any analysis of Shenute, we must admit that there are still very few codices, either complete or partially complete, that give a satisfactory idea of the transmission of his works. But we may mention at least three: one at the Louvre, the other two at the Institut français d'Archéologie orientale in Cairo. They demonstrate that the works of Shenute were gathered into *corpora*, with titles and remarks, which are useful in placing them in some historical context.

The remaining work to be done on the remnants of the Shenute codices depends on the basic task of reconstituting the White Monastery library. This work is beginning to yield some results that add to the theory that places the Gnosticizing codices discovered at Nag Hammadi (see NAG HAMMADI LIBRARY) in a monastic setting of Upper Egypt and that have reawakened an interest in Shenute, which had become somewhat dormant.

About the historical figure of Shenute, one of the first problems to be examined is that of his relation to Pachomian monasticism. The common belief was that Shenute and his community remained basically Pachomian, except for some reforms of the rules. Four facts, however, seem to contradict this idea. First, there are two different traditions about the participation of Copts at the first Council of EPHESUS as helpers of the patriarch CYRIL I: the Pachomian tradition centered on the monk VICTOR OF TABENNÊSÊ and the Shenutean centered on Shenute himself. Second, at the time of the Chalcedonian crisis, the Pachomians remained faithful to the imperial authority, even at the cost of losing some of their archimandrites, while the followers of Shenute persisted in their loyalty to the anti-Chalcedonian patriarchs descending from DIOSCORUS I and thus held to a more genuinely Egyptian culture. Third, although Shenute's works (and those of BESA, his successor) were in a sense introduced into a literary tradition created by Pachomius, Shenute followed Pachomius only insofar as they both wrote in Coptic. As to the content, form, style, and quantity, there is great divergence in their writings. While Pachomius did not especially want to be a literary figure, Shenute sought not only to use the language per se but also wished to make it a means of literary expression completely individual and highly developed. Fourth, although the documentation today is yet anything but abundant, we find differences in theology also. Whereas Shenute shows clear examples of an anti-Origenist stand (with all that this implies also for Gnosticizing texts), there is no such evidence for the Pachomians, because the evidence in the various Lives of Pachomius should be considered suspect. From what appears in the dossier of AGATHONICUS OF TARSUS, we have reason to believe that even the Origenist doctrines of EVAGRIUS PONTICUS might have been accepted by some of the first Pachomian communities.

This fourth point leads to the question of Shenute's theological background. Although Leipoldt harshly denied it, we can now read at least two works in which Shenute showed that he was not only abreast of the doctrinal currents of his own time but also knew how to discuss them in an original way, securely and ably. First, we have a work published by L. T. Lefort that treats the well-known issues of the Incarnation and transubstantiation, especially against the Nestorian heresy. We also have a text, recently reconstructed from many fragments, that discusses problems pertaining to the Origenist controversy of the beginning of the fifth century, as well as some popular Gnostic ideas—found in the codices from Nag Hammadi—about the creation, the preexistence of the soul, apocryphal literature, Christology, prayer, and angels.

We know today that Shenute was a highly educated person. He knew the Greek language and Greek literature, not only ecclesiastical but also classical; he knew theology and was interested in many subtle questions of ethics and physics, which he treated in a manner characteristic of his times. His influence on Coptic literature is due not only to his vast production but also to the work of translation that he fostered and supervised, as it seems, in his monastery. It is very probable that much of the material to be examined in the next section was produced there.

Translations of the Fourth and Fifth Centuries

Apart from the works of Shenute, and possibly of some unfamiliar authors such as Saint PAUL OF TAMMA, Coptic literature of the fourth and fifth centuries consists mostly of translations. Except for the language, this literature is not in itself very interesting for scholars, who would prefer to analyze the authors' original thought and style; this is one of the reasons why the study of Coptic literature is generally neglected. In fact, we shall see that there are many original texts that are disguised as translations and that therefore did not attract the attention of scholars. They belong in any case to the later period (of the CYCLES).

What is interesting about the translations of the fourth and fifth centuries is the peculiar choice of material made by the Coptic translators. Whereas we generally possess systematic translations of *corpora* of the most important Greek authors in Syriac, Armenian, Georgian (and later in Arabic and Ethiopic), in Coptic the situation is entirely different. In vain we look for basic texts such as the Armenian translation of Irenaeus, or the Syriac translation of the works of SEVERUS OF ANTIOCH, not to mention the most important homiletical, theological, and historical works of the church fathers of the time.

The Coptic preference was rather for the minor production of those fathers such as individual Homilies preserved in Greek (if at all) in secondary collections, often changing their attribution for accidental reasons—such as errors in manuscript transmission or the interests of some collector.

In fact, it seems evident that during this period the Copts chose texts for translation without considering the name of the author very seriously. It is even possible that in the beginning texts circulated anonymously, only to have an author assigned to them later on. An example is the homily on the Canaanitish woman, by Saint JOHN CHRYSOSTOM, whose attribution in Coptic to EUSEBIUS OF CAESAREA, "the historiographer," is explicable only by its initial allusion to the church and his history.

Another reason leading us to think that the author per se was of little importance to the Copts is the fact that the Egyptian writers—including the venerated bishops of Alexandria—were quite unfairly treated when it came to the choice of material for translation. So for the homilies treating the problem of the Nestorian heresy, PROCLUS OF CONSTANTINOPLE was chosen rather than Cyril himself. A large place was reserved for JOHN CHRYSOSTOM, because of the great literary fame that spread his texts into Egypt, notwithstanding the bad relations between him and the patriarch THEOPHILUS OF ALEXANDRIA.

The material selected for translation seems to have been chosen chiefly according to the requirements of a special section of Egyptian society, the monastic groups. Many of the translations treated spiritual problems peculiar to Egyptian MONASTICISM. Apart from that, the criterion for selection seems to have been whatever the "normal" market was offering, a market geared more for popular consumption than for the demands of any "official" level. Accordingly, the needs of pleasing simply educated people were also considered.

As to literary genre, the texts chosen for translation may be divided into two basic groups: the homilies of the church fathers and the martyrdoms (or lives) of saints. For most of these texts we have the Greek original (though, as we have said, the attribution may vary in Greek and in Coptic); others have no corresponding Greek text, but their style and content make it sufficiently evident that they were translated from the Greek. All relevant information about the translations of individual authors or hagiographical works is found in their respective entries. Therefore we shall simply mention now the names of the church fathers: ATHANASIUS I, BASIL THE GREAT, CYRIL I of Alexandria, CYRIL OF JERUSALEM, EPHRAEM SYRUS, EPIPHANIUS OF SALAMIS, Jerome the Presbyter, JOHN CHRYSOSTOM, GREGORY OF NAZIANZUS, GREGORY OF NYSSA, PALLADIUS, Proclus of Constantinople, SEVERIAN OF GABALA, SEVERUS OF ANTIOCH, THEODOSIUS I, THEOPHILUS OF ALEXANDRIA.

There are also the APOCRYPHA (others than those mentioned above), the APOPHTHEGMATA PATRUM, and the canonical literature, which are treated in their particular articles.

In order to determine an approximate date of the translations, we can set as a limit after which the translation must have been produced the date of the original in Greek, but never a useful limit before which it must have been produced: no Coptic or Greek text contains any data about this question. Information might be inferred from the date of the manuscripts, if they were not too late (from the ninth century on) to be of any use. We would set these translations around the fifth century, because it is logical to assume that they were made of works of contemporary interest and not too ancient. From this viewpoint it is significant that most of the authors translated fit into a span of time between Athanasius and Saint JEROME (c. 330 to 420); later authors of the fifth century, such as Theodosius I and Severus of Antioch, are justifiable exceptions.

The Sixth Century

The vicissitudes and final decisions of the Council of CHALCEDON (451) determined at once an ecclesiastical crisis and the detachment of most of the Egyptian church from the "international" Christianity supported by the emperors of Byzantium. This crisis also produced cultural effects, but they were not felt until the beginning of the sixth century, when the events following the exile of Theodosius I from Alexandria put an end to hopes not only for a reconciliation between the patriarchates but also for developing a normal ecclesiastical life in Egypt, maintaining beliefs and hierarchy different from those officially approved by the imperial (pro-Chalcedonian) crown. This is probably the moment when Greek began to be perceived as the language of the oppressors and the patristic Greek ("international") culture was looked upon with suspicion as the vehicle of false dogmas and misleading historical information. It was at this time that Egypt really sensed the need to build a historical and spiritual culture, one typically Egyptian (therefore Coptic), in opposition to that of the imperial, Greek-speaking church.

However, we must not think that the question of language became a central problem all at once. The change was probably quite a slow process, which began with a determination to be different from the Byzantine culture, proceeded to a rejection of anything coming from Byzantium—and therefore in Greek—and eventually brought about a refusal even to use the Greek language at all.

Nevertheless, it is clear that during this lengthy period Greek was still used, for traditional reasons and in relations with Christian sects having beliefs similar to those of Egypt, especially the church in Syria. In fact, for the texts under discussion, it is extremely difficult to differentiate between those translated into Coptic from Greek and those originally conceived in Coptic. The literature of the "international" Christian culture of this period, using the Greek language, is enormously rich in theological treatises written by both Chalcedonian and anti-Chalcedonian writers in defense of their confessions. The names of John the Grammarian of Caesarea and Leontius of Byzantium are prominent on the Chalcedonian side, and those of Severus of Antioch and Julian of Halicarnassus on the other. This kind of literature was not translated into Coptic, probably because interested people preferred to read such works directly in the original language.

We mention here the most important sixth-century works that we have in Coptic, whether original or translations; more information will be provided in articles on these works. First is the *History of the Church* in two parts. The first is a translation, with some changes, of Books 1 through 7 of the *Ecclesiastical History* of Eusebius. The second part recounts the events from PETER I of Alexandria down to TIMOTHY II AELURUS (early fourth to late fifth century); this is an original composition, compiled from many different sources ranging from internal chronicles of the Alexandrian see to historical or literary narrations and simple hagiographical legends.

Another interesting work is the Panegyric of Macarius of Tkow (see DIOSCORUS I), in which the events surrounding the Council of Chalcedon and the life of Dioscorus are narrated. In fact, it is actually a compilation of at least three different texts of historical or autobiographical nature. An anonymous Life of Athanasius, written on the basis of semihistorical documents, also belongs to this period. Its tendentious and hagiographical aims prevail over the facts.

The same mixture of history and legend is to be found in many other texts recounting the lives of such figures as Severus of Antioch, the famous monk JOHN OF LYCOPOLIS, and DIOSCORUS (different from the text cited above). Of a more polemic character were the "plerophories," a series of little stories collected by JOHN OF MAYUMA to prove the thesis of the anti-Chalcedonians.

In this period the collections of the "acts" of the three great ecumenical councils were probably also redacted; in Coptic they differ somewhat from the Greek and Latin texts. The material related to Nicaea went in Coptic under the title "Canons of Hippolytus," and comprised the *credo*, the *gnomai*, the DIDASCALIA, and other minor texts. The acts of Ephesus were centered around the monk Victor of Tabennēsē, who does not appear in the Greek and Latin collections.

Finally, a number of texts relate the lives of the great monks (mainly archimandrites) of this period, in which history, legend, facts, and miracles are all mixed together. Among these are accounts of ABRAHAM OF FARSHŪT, MATTHEW THE POOR, Moses of Balyanā, and many others of importance and interest. Similar hagiographies appeared later in such works as the Panegyric of Apollo of Pbow by STEPHEN OF HNĒS and the Life of Ṣamū'īl of Qalamūn by ISAAC OF QALAMŪN.

Late Sixth Century and Early Arab Period

We have one example of the literary activity of Saint DAMIAN, patriarch of Alexandria, a homily on Christmas, fragments of which are preserved in two papyrus codices of the seventh and eighth centuries. This indicates that, though probably preached in Greek (it is difficult to conceive the Syrian Damian speaking Coptic), the homily was immediately translated into Coptic. The same was done for his well-known *Synodicon* and for a partially lost work entitled *Kerygmata* (Proclamations), of uncertain character.

Other Egyptian writers of this age surely wrote directly in Coptic, although they all depended on the tradition of rhetoric and faith of the Greek-speaking ancient church of the fourth century. These were the bishops of the most important towns of the Nile Valley, a fact that confirms the continued vitality of these communities as cultural and ecclesiastical centers. It is quite probable that a town such as Shmun, the ancient center of the Thoth-Hermes cult, had never completely lost the memory of its earlier importance.

The author whose life is best affirmed is Saint PISENTIUS, bishop of Coptos (Qifṭ). We have not only two different lives of him—one written by Moses of Qifṭ, his successor, and the other by JOHN THE PRES-

BYTER (in the style of the previous "plerophoric" lives of monks)—but we have also part of his personal archives, found in the monastery of DAYR EPIPHANIUS at Luxor. His only complete work to be preserved is an encomium of Onophrius.

CONSTANTINE, bishop of Asyūṭ, specialized in panegyrics. He wrote two for Athanasius, two for the martyr Claudius, and another for the martyr George. We have an account of his life from the Arabic Synaxarion, but it is fragmentary and does not say much concerning his activities. From his works we understand that he tried to help Bishop Damian in his efforts to reform the organization of the Egyptian church and to improve the morals of the people, which had deteriorated through the long difficulties of the previous century. Constantine was also one of the strong champions of Egypt, which he saw as the nation destined to preserve the true church, with its own dogma and ethics, despite the often denounced tendency of the people toward sin.

JOHN OF SHMŪN was another author with strong nationalistic feelings. His two main works are panegyrics of the two figures representing for him the most important phases of Egyptian Christianity: Saint MARK the Evangelist and founder of the Egyptian church, and Saint Antony, the founder of the anchoritic life. Egypt is always foremost in his thoughts, and, as many passages in these homilies testify, he skillfully defends the right, his own and that of his fellow men of letters, to produce works in Coptic.

John, bishop of Parallos in the Delta region, wrote a special treatise against the apocryphal and heretical books still surviving in the Egyptian church. And RUFUS OF SHOTEP, who seems to have been a close friend of Constantine of Asyūṭ, wrote the last preserved example of exegetical activity before the Arab invasion of 642 in a commentary on the Gospels of Matthew and Luke.

These authors may have witnessed the Persian invasion of the years 619–627, and some probably lived to see the Arab invasion. In any event, at the beginning of the Arab era the most important personalities in the Egyptian church were still able to produce works more or less openly. Thus, from the patriarch BENJAMIN I we possess a long homily on the miracle of Cana and a short passage of the panegyric of Shenute. Benjamin's successor, the patriarch AGATHON, wrote a homily in which he narrated episodes about Benjamin's consecration of a church in honor of MACARIUS THE EGYPTIAN. He probably also composed a panegyric of Benjamin. Another patriarch, JOHN III, wrote a panegyric of MENAS (whose sanctuary in the Mareotis desert was still attracting masses of pilgrims), and composed a theological treatise in the form of *erotapokrisis* ("questions and answers"), which seems to have been finally redacted by one of his priests. At the same time, Saint Menas of Pshati, bishop of Nikiou, described the life of the patriarch ISAAC (686–689) and wrote a panegyric of the martyr MACROBIUS of Pshati. ZACHARIAS, bishop of Sakhā, left two homilies of exegetical content, and possibly a Life of Saint JOHN COLOBOS. The twelfth-century patriarch MARK III wrote the last Coptic homily to have a known author (which was merely an adaptation of a homily by Epiphanius of Salamis).

The style of all these writers is rather similar, reminiscent of the typical canons of that Greek literary movement of the second to fourth centuries known as the "second sophistic," a movement that influenced all the great preachers of the Christian church. What we most appreciate is the ability of all these men to write and speak a Coptic language that is perfectly capable of expressing any concept desired. This is the first time that this occurred, for neither the translations of the Bible nor those of the homilies and martyrdoms of the fourth and fifth centuries reflect a language that has at last become so independent and sufficient in its syntactical and stylistic elements. Only Shenute (and Besa after him) approached this level.

The Seventh and Eighth Centuries: The Period of the Cycles

The attribution of the many texts mentioned below to this later period of Coptic literature will undoubtedly arouse both surprise and suspicion: surprise because the works we will treat are generally ascribed—according to the manuscripts' *inscriptiones*—to authors of the fourth and fifth centuries, and they describe events and problems of this earlier period; suspicion, that we might have used such a simple expedient merely to collect texts of doubtful origin and attribute them to a single late period and one homogenous literary school.

Our reasoning can be explained. First, the writings examined below have already been recognized for the most part as having false titles. Furthermore, the real problem of their chronology has never been posed because scholars somehow believed them to be translations from Greek. We have observed, however, that many pseudepigraphous texts of Coptic literature can be collected and reassembled by noting certain historic episodes and personages that appear in diverse works; these works constitute a pseudo-historic substratum that sustains the narration of the various events. It is evident that the episodes they describe are historically false and could not have been invented in the earlier period. Whoever compiled these texts and whoever read or listened to them might have had a vague memory of events from this previous period, but they really understood neither the mentality of the time nor its normal, everyday affairs.

The basic train of the narrations and the accompanying considerations correspond to objectives entirely different from those appropriate to the earlier era. These aims were, first of all, propagandist and addressed to different segments of the populace. For those within the church, the purpose was to strengthen the people's faith in the Coptic church tradition and to reinforce and elevate their moral sentiments and behavior. For those outside the church, the purpose was to affirm the existence, antiquity, and orthodoxy of the doctrine of the Coptic church in comparison with those Christian sects separated from it. A second raison d'être for these works was the need to defend Christian doctrine in the face of the rival Jewish and Islamic religions. Third, we can perceive a motive of providing spiritual entertainment, for these texts are filled with descriptions of the most attractive, wondrous, and grim events imaginable, all related in a most pompous and lavish style.

In codices that transmit these works to us in a unified form, the possibility of such combination and assembly of these diverse texts does indeed exist. Thus, we have concluded that these works were conceived at once by single authors or groups of authors adhering to similar criteria in a period very much later than that to which the texts have been assigned. We feel justified in grouping these problematic texts according to various predominant events or personages that form a unifying theme and we have called these groups CYCLES.

Often these cycles were produced by using preexisting works, modified to fit the aim of the redactor and assembled, when necessary, with other original extracts written for the purpose. This is why, within the homilies assigned to this period, there appear extracts from old translations of genuine texts of the church fathers dating from the fourth and fifth centuries. The critical work in this regard is, for the most part, yet to be done and, we believe, rich in possibilities.

The redaction of each cycle presents its own special problems as to the various personages, events, and texts involved. All the Cycles, however, had as a point of departure one or more authentic works or else certain episodes already famous in the tradition of the Coptic church. But, despite what was said earlier about the chronology and the production of these Cycles, there remain, nevertheless, two major problems: that of their literary basis and that of the causes for their "creation." That such a phenomenon should happen sporadically in a given literature may be natural and also serve some purpose, but that it should occur on such a grand scale with so few "honest" examples demands an explanation.

The tradition behind this production is not difficult to trace. We can call attention to the previous hagiographers' school of the fourth century (mentioned above), whose task was precisely to produce texts that would appear to come from the hand of another (perhaps that of a secretary or some other witness present at the trials and deaths of the martyrs). After all, it is logical to think that the Copts writing in the seventh century might have remembered some of these bygone authentic texts. Also, many works written during the period following Chalcedon furnished excellent precedents whose doubtful historical authenticity would not have passed completely unnoticed after one century.

More difficult is the investigation into the causes that might have determined or suggested such a literary posture. In fact, a number of different causes probably coalesced to produce these Cycles, causes that we will seek out while limiting ourselves to objective proofs.

The first evidence is that these writers extracted from the literary tradition names of great authors along with accompanying memoirs. At the same time, they avoided the genuine works, which, in our opinion, the Egyptians of the seventh and eighth centuries must have still been able to obtain in Greek. In fact, it seems that these writers actually tended not only to replace but also to demolish the authentic texts.

This phenomenon may be explained by seeing it in the perspective of the theological situation of the post-Chalcedonian period. "Coptic" theology was basically simple (at least so it seems in the theological excerpts of the homilies) and sought to assume a distinctly popular character. Seen from this point of view, all the homilies of the fourth and beginning of the fifth centuries became suspect because they contained a trinitarian and above all Christological theology that could have seemed confusing to Coptic listeners (and probably even to the more educated clergy). Clearly diophysite phrases were easy to identify in these early texts, but by subtle arguments they could be reduced to "orthodoxy," and thus be put in accord with Monophysite Coptic thinking. Such activity seemed to occur specifically in the monastic societies, which, after the long period of the post-Chalcedonian crises, were fashioning the fundamentals of Coptic culture, and thus substituted more acceptable texts for the old patristic ones.

It also seems that the prominent authors of this period were not free, and did not feel free, to publish works under their own names, perhaps because they sought to give greater authority to their writings by attributing them to a venerated author of antiquity. Then, too, at the beginning of the seventh century particularly, a contrary movement was born: authors strained to produce "in first person" more modern works, meant especially as substitutions for the writings of the ancient church fathers. In fact, had these two opposing movements been free to express themselves openly, the situation might have been quite different and the number of both kinds of texts would be more or less equal, rather than a predominance of pseudepigraphical texts.

Another cause for this kind of literary production may have been the changed taste of the public. Although the liturgical traditions of the church were maintained nearly intact, the social climate was changed. First of all, the triumph of Christianity throughout the Mediterranean world had driven the masses away from such forms of popular entertainment as the circus and theater and had pushed them to seek substitutes within the church. Thus there arose, among other things, mass pilgrimages to the major sanctuaries and the propagation of miraculous stories, which contained various trimmings. Second, the Arab invasion forced the faithful to restrict themselves to ecclesiastical matters, making the church the very fulcrum of life in a broad sense that included all occasions for entertainment. Therefore, the homilies—whether delivered for the general liturgy or for the feasts of particular saints—had to satisfy this need and expectation for diversion.

The Ninth to the Eleventh Centuries: The Period of Decline

After the anonymous and even clandestine flourishing of the cycles, the final decline for Coptic literature began during the ninth to the eleventh centuries. There was literary activity in this period, for old material still useful for some special purposes was reassembled and rearranged, but no original production has been discovered. The Arabic language was slowly but surely submerging Coptic, both as the administrative and everyday language and as the vehicle for the transmission of Christian culture. Further, continued political troubles and increasingly difficult relations between the Coptic and Islamic communities recommended the use of a single, common language to avoid an isolation that could only damage the conquered community.

In the Egyptian Middle Ages, the center of Christian life was the monasteries, which tended to arrange all extant, valid, and vital texts according to their specific use and rationale. Since the texts were to be read during the *synaxeis* (part of the liturgy preceding the Eucharist), they had to be copied in books set aside for that purpose, with clear titles to identify them and the proper occasion for their delivery. These were the homilies or the so-called Synaxaria (to use the terminology of the Eastern church), in which all kinds of old texts assumed a similar shape: that of a homily, or at most, the life of a saint. Even texts that originally had been treatises were recast as Homilies by this school. The feasts of the saints were the occasion for a more extensive collection of texts, which consisted of (1) the martyrdom or *vita*, more often in the enlarged form of the seventh and eighth centuries' redaction than in the original fifth-century or sixth-century one; (2) an encomium, which could again contain a homiletic form of the martyrdom or *vita;* and (3) a series of miracles, with references to the grace that could be obtained in the sanctuaries of the saints involved.

Texts that originally differed from these genres were simply and often naively rearranged in order to fit them. A new title and a few lines of introduction sufficed to accomplish this purpose; the titles usually mentioned the author (not necessarily the true one), the relevant parts of the contents (i.e., relevant for that epoch—generally there was no reflection of the actual subject), and the supposed liturgical occasion for pronouncing the text.

Indeed, with the exception of the oldest Coptic texts (fourth and fifth centuries), in the Nag Hammadi Library, BODMER PAPYRI, or MADĪNAT MĀḌĪ, most of the texts from which we derive our knowledge of Coptic literature were compiled or copied in the ninth to the eleventh centuries. The codices, although used for practical, liturgical purposes, were also venerated as luxury objects and a means to obtain divine grace. They were produced not for the individual but rather for the community and thus depended on the common taste of the time. In summary, their shape derives from the school of this period, which provided the final liturgical systematization of Coptic literature.

Of course, the important monasteries were depositories of the manuscripts so arranged. One thinks above all of the White Monastery in the south and DAYR ANBĀ MAQĀR (Monastery of Saint Macarius) in the north. From them radiated the culture on which all Coptic ecclesiastical life was based. This situation continued for the next few centuries, though in the Arabic language. Soon Coptic almost disappeared, first as the language for sermons, then also as the language for the rest of the liturgy. The manuscripts remained in half-forgotten rooms or caves, deteriorating little by little from dust, humidity, animals, and age until Western travelers and manuscript hunters rediscovered them, and renewed interest led to the removal of many from the native monasteries to libraries around the world.

In conclusion, we should bear in mind that this last systematization in the ninth to the eleventh centuries was the principal cause for the very low esteem hitherto accorded to the texts of Coptic literature, for they have appeared at first glance as something boringly uniform, without those differentiations in character and age that can offer guidelines for the historical appreciation of a given literature. Therefore, the historian should first recognize in this final stage of Coptic literature the last activity of Coptic writers—an activity of redaction, choice, and systematization, not creation. Then, by means of these late texts, the historian may trace stratifications to recover the older stages of the literature. For, if it is true that Coptic writing is consistent in quality and subject matter, being almost exclusively religious, its products are in fact diverse in character, content, and style.

BIBLIOGRAPHY

Amélineau, E. C. *Oeuvres de Shenoudi.* Coptic text with French translation. Paris, 1907–1914.

Bardy, G. *La Question des langues dans l'église ancienne.* Paris, 1948.

Baumstark, A. *Die christlichen Literaturen des Orients.* Sammlung Göschen 527, 528. Leipzig, 1911.

Bohlig, A. "Koptische Literatur." In *Die Religion in Geschichte und Gegenwart,* Vol. 4, cols. 8–11.

Bourguet, P. du. "Bref tableau de la littérature copte." *Boletin AEO* 5 (1969):175–81.

Crum, W. E. "Inscriptions from Shenoute's Monastery." *Journal of Theological Studies* 5 (1904): 552–69.

Dawson, W. R. "Early Christianity in Egypt. The Literature of the Coptic Period." *Asiatic Review,* ser. 2, 17 (1921):342–51.

Doresse, J. "Littérature copte." In *Encyclopédie de la Pléiade. Histoire des Littératures,* Vol. 1, pp. 769–79. Paris, 1956.

Elanskaja, Alla I. "Koptskaja literatura." In *Folklor i literatura narodov Afriki: Sbornik statej,* pp. 18–27. Moscow, 1970.

Gaselee, S. "The Native Literature of Christian Egypt." *Transactions of the Religious Society,* ser. 2, 33 (1915):21–45.

Guillaumont, A. "Copte (littérature spirituelle)." In *Dictionnaire de Spiritualité,* Vol. 1, cols. 2266–78. Paris, 1952.

Hyvernat, H. "Coptic Literature." In *The Catholic Encyclopedia,* Vol. 5, cols. 350–63 and Vol. 16, cols. 27–31. New York, 1907–1912.

Kasser, R. "Réflexions sur l'histoire de la littérature copte." *Le Muséon* 88 (1975):375–85.

Krause, M. "Koptische Literatur." In *Lexikon der Ägyptologie,* Vol. 3, cols. 694–728. Wiesbaden, 1979.

Ladeuze, P. *Etude sur le Cénobitisme Pakhomien pendant le IVe siècle et la première moitié du Ve siècle.* Louvain, 1898.

Lefort, L. T. "Littérature bohairique." *Le Muséon* 44 (1931):115–35.

______. "La Littérature égyptienne aux derniers siècles avant l'invasion arabe." *Chronique d'Egypte* 6 (1931):315–23.

Leipoldt, J. "Geschichte der koptischen Litteratur." In *Geschichte der christlichen Litteraturen des Orients,* ed. P. Brockelmann et al., pp. 131–82. Leipzig, 1907; reprint Leipzig, 1976.

Morenz, S. "Die koptische Literatur." In *Handbuch der Orientalistik,* ed. B. Spuler, Vol. 1, 1.2, pp. 239–250. Leiden, 1952; 2nd ed., pp. 239–50. Leiden, 1970.

Müller, C. D. G. *Die alte koptische Predigt. Versuch eines Überblicks.* Berlin, 1954.

______. "Einige Bemerkungen zur 'Ars Praedicandi' der alten koptischen Kirche." *Le Muséon* 67 (1954):231–70.

______. "Koptische Redekunst und griechische Rhetorik." *Le Muséon* 69 (1956):53–72.

______. "Was können wir aus der koptischen Literatur über Theologie und Frommigkeit der ägyptischen Kirche lernen?" *Oriens Christianus* 48 (1964):191–215.

______. "Koptische Literatur." In *Kleines Wörterbuch des christlichen Orients,* ed. J. Assfalg and P. Kruger, pp. 205–208. Wiesbaden, 1975.

Nagel, P. "Der Ursprung des Koptischen." *Altertum* 13 (1967):78–84.

O'Leary, De L. E. "Littérature copte." In *Dictionnaire d'archéologie chrétienne et de liturgie,* Vol. 9, pt. 2, pp. 1599–1635. Paris, 1907–1939.

Orlandi, T. *Elementi di lingua e letteratura copta.* Milan, 1970.

______. "Patristica copta e patristica greca." *Vetera Christianorum* 10 (1973):327–41.

______. "The Future of Studies in Coptic Biblical and Ecclesiastical Literature." In *The Future of Coptic Studies,* pp. 1–22. Coptic Studies 1. Leiden, 1978.

______. "Coptic Literature." In *The Roots of Egyptian Christianity,* pp. 51–81. Philadelphia, 1986.

Quaegebeur, J. "De la préhistoire de l'écriture copte." *Orientalia Lovaniensia Periodica* 13 (1982):125–36.

Roberts, C. H. *Manuscript, Society and Belief in Early Christian Egypt.* Oxford, 1979.

Roncaglia, M. P. "Littérature copte et patristique (I et II s.)." *Al Machriq* 58 (1964):607–618.

______. "Essai d'histoire de la littérature copte des origines à la fin du IIIe siècle." *Al Machriq* 61 (1967):103–133.

______. "La Littérature copte et sa diffusion en Orient et en Occident (essai)." In *Actes du 8e Congrès de l'Union européenne des Arabisants,* pp. 219–42. Aix-en-Provence, 1978.

Schmidt, C. "Übersicht über die vornicänische Literatur (einschliesslich der Apokryphen) in koptischer Sprache," In *Geschichte der altchristlichen Literatur bis Eusebius,* ed. A. von Harnack, Vol. 1, pp. 918–24. Leipzig, 1893.

Till, W. C. "Coptic and Its Value." *Bulletin of the John Rylands Library* 40 (1957):229–58.

Wessely, Karl. *Griechische und koptische Texte theologischen Inhalts,* Vols. 1–5. Leipzig, 1909–1917.

TITO ORLANDI

LITERATURE, COPTO-ARABIC. Coptic literature per se, a subject treated elsewhere, is confined to the writings in the Coptic language during the early centuries of medieval Egyptian history when that language was the spoken language of the people as well as their only written instrument. After the ARAB CONQUEST OF EGYPT in the seventh century, the use of Coptic survived in the administrative structure of the government for some decades. Gradually, bilingual documents appeared in which Coptic and Arabic were used in parallel columns, mainly for clarification of administrative affairs to the Arab governors, who did not understand any Coptic. Then in the year A.H. 85/A.D. 705, the Muslim administration of the country decreed that Arabic be exclusively used in all administrative offices and all accounts. This revolutionary decision led ultimately to the establishment of Arabic as the accepted official language in the country—at the expense of Coptic. The state functionaries found it necessary to be proficient in the language of the conquerors in order to retain their positions in the administration as tax collectors and scribes. The Copts were very able linguists and soon mastered Arabic. In time, however, Arabic became preponderant in daily life and Coptic declined steadily, until sometime in the later Middle Ages it became defunct. As early as the tenth century, however, we begin to find works written in Arabic by noted Coptic personalities.

Two major works written in classical Arabic appeared in that period. The first was a book of chronicles, *Kitāb al-Tawārīkh,* by Sa'īd ibn al-Biṭrīq (877–940), known as Eutychius, Melchite patriarch of Alexandria. The other was *Tārīkh Baṭārikat al-Iskandariyyah al-Qibṭ,* the famous history of the Coptic patriarchs, begun by SĀWIRUS IBN AL-MUQAFFA', bishop of Ashmūnayn. Although the Coptic language was still the spoken language of Egypt at the time, it is obvious from these works that the authors became proficient in their knowledge of classical Arabic, and their works marked the beginnings of a vast Copto-Arabic literature, which eventually became an established discipline among the Copts in medieval and modern times.

Sa'īd ibn al-Biṭrīq wrote another book, also in Arabic, entitled *Al-Jadal bayn al-Mukhālif wa-al-Naṣrānī,* a polemical treatise in which he defended Christianity against non-Christians and tried to justify his Melchite creed against the predominant non-Chalcedonian orthodoxy of the Coptic people. But his historical work, *Kitāb al-Tawārīkh,* which he addressed to his brother 'Īsā, remains his major contribution. He intended thereby to cover the whole span of world history from Adam to his own day. Apparently, he covered the period of Islamic history to the Abbasid caliphate of al-Rāḍī (934–940). From this point his work was continued by Yaḥyā ibn Sa'īd al-Anṭākī on a more massive scale covering most of the rest of the Abbasid period from the caliphate of al-Muttaqī (940–944) to the caliphate of al-Ẓāhir (1225–1226). We must remember that Yaḥyā spent a great many years in Egypt and that he included in his accounts, beside Islamic episodes, a considerable amount of external history including the Christian patriarchates of the Eastern provinces. His work may be treated here on the periphery of Copto-Arabic letters.

On the other hand, the strictly Coptic native

product is the HISTORY OF THE PATRIARCHS by Bishop Sāwīrus ibn al-Muqaffa', who was a much more prolific writer in the Arabic language. He is credited by Kāmil Sāliḥ Nakhlah with the composition of some thirty-eight works. Though many of the works of Sāwīrus have been lost, others of particular importance have survived. Apart from the monumental biographical history of the patriarchs, he wrote a treatise in refutation of Sa'id ibn Biṭriq's Melchite attack on Coptic orthodoxy. His work on the ecumenical councils, entitled *Kitāb al-Majāmi'*, has survived in toto. Most of the other works deal with theological subjects of the highest importance, such as the Incarnation of Jesus, a book on the first principles of the Christian faith prepared for the vizier Quzmān ibn Mīnā, commentaries on several biblical texts, traditions and liturgies of the Coptic church, a treatise on heresies, another on fasts and feasts, and a multitude of other works on purely religious and moralistic subjects. On the margin of religious studies, he wrote also in Arabic on such subjects as psychology and psychic medicine, and several brochures on educational matters as well as a discussion of Arabic proverbs. In a word, he seems to have inaugurated a substantial amount of Copto-Arabic literature. It is thought that other, unknown treatises composed by him have been lost. On the whole, the contributions of Sāwīrus to this field are still open for further inquiry.

The compilation executed by Sāwīrus ended with the biography of his contemporary, Pope SHENUTE I (858–880). He depended on a certain Bidayr al-Damanhūrī who later became bishop of Tānīs, Buqayrah al-Rashīdī, and Yu'annis ibn Zakīr, as well as Tidrā or Tadrus of Minūf, in assembling his material from original Coptic sources.

His work was continued by later compilers, of whom the first was the above-mentioned bishop of Tānīs, Anbā Mikhā'il, who appears to be responsible for the biographies of KHĀ'IL III (880–907) to SHENUTE II (1032–1046).

Afterward, this monumental work was continued by other writers in Arabic. These included Mawhūb ibn Manṣūr ibn Mufarrij for the period 1069 to 1079, followed by Yuḥannā ibn Sā'id ibn Mīnā al-Qulzumī for the period from 1092 to 1128. The patriarch MARK III (1167–1189) is known to have written about three of his predecessors, from 1131 to 1167.

Ma'ānī Abū al-Makārim ibn Barakah ibn Abū al-'Alā' covered the period from 1131 to 1167, and Anbā Yūsāb, bishop of Fuwwah, the period from 1224 to 1261. The rest of the work was filled out by anonymous contributors until we reach the modern period, where the name of a certain *hegumenos*, 'Abd al-Masīḥ, emerges in the seventeenth century. After him, the most famous name in the Arabic literature of the Copts is that of 'ABD AL-MASĪḤ ṢALĪB AL-MASŪ'DĪ, a monk of Dayr al-Baramūs.

In subsequent centuries, the Coptic literary heritage in Arabic kept multiplying in all manner of disciplines, sometimes by the pen of Islamized Copts who apostatized in order to retain their high positions in the administration of the country, but mainly by great writers of the highest merit among the Copts themselves who dealt with purely Coptic subjects.

One of those who converted to Islam in the twelfth century is the author of a rare text of the highest importance entitled *Kitāb Qawānin al-Dawāwīn*, written in the year 1209. The author, who was a distinguished Copt and a minister of state in the Ayyubid dynasty and who converted to Islam to keep his high position, was al-As'ad ibn al-Muhadhdhab ibn Zakariyyā ibn Qudāmah ibn Mīnā Abū al-Makārim ibn Sa'īd Abū al-Malīḥ. Since his Islamization he has been known as IBN MAMMĀTĪ, the Arabic corruption of the Coptic "Mahometi." He was a Christian native of the city of Asyūṭ. Apparently he descended from a well-known Coptic family, his father being a contemporary of BADR AL-JAMĀLĪ and the caliph al-Mustanṣir Billāh (1035–1094), for whom he attained the dignity of chief scribe of the *diwan*, a position his son al-As'ad inherited toward the end of Fatimid rule in the caliphate of al-'Āḍid (1160–1171). The caliph laid a heavy hand of persecution on the Copts and forced al-As'ad to apostatize. Consequently he was promoted to an even higher position at the head of the *diwan* of the army, which he retained under Ṣalāḥ al-Dīn (Saladin; 1169–1193) and his son al-'Azīz 'Uthmān (1193–1198). Ibn Mammātī presumably wrote his book for the later Sultan al-'Azīz, mainly as a record of all the provinces and districts of Egypt. He supplemented it with a statement of taxation for each province or district in four volumes, of which only one has survived, since all financial statements were regarded as confidential and restricted to the state records. The work as it stands, however, is a tremendous mine of information, not only in the field of the historical geography of Egypt but also on the agricultural calendar of the Nile Valley. The details contained in it are closely associated with the Coptic agricultural reckonings, which indicate the author's familiarity with the Coptic calendar of the martyrs.

Ibn Mammātī's life has been detailed by Ibn Khallikān in his work *Wāfiyāt al-Aʿyān*, as well as al-ʿAynī's *ʿIqd al-Jumān*, al-Maqrīzī's *Khiṭaṭ*, and Yāqūt's *Irshād al-Arib īlā Maʿrifat al-Adīb*. All seem to be in full agreement about his stature in the administration of Egypt and on his literary excellence. He is known to have written a number of other works besides *Qawānīn al-Dawāwīn* and to have composed a fair amount of poetry, quoted by his biographers, on literary as well as political subjects. A few lines quoted by al-Maqrīzī sound like an appeal by a Muslim on behalf of the Copts and the imposition of restrictions on the type of dress they wear. Ibn Mammātī died in Aleppo in 1209. His death was lamented by the poets of his time in obituary poems that indicate his unusual place in twelfth-century Egypt.

Contemporary with Ibn Mammātī, a Coptic priest named ABŪ AL-MAKĀRIM was busy assembling materials of a similar geographical nature between 1177 and 1204. But this time the author concentrated on a purely Coptic subject. The title of his book in Arabic is *Tārīkh al-Kanā'is wa-al-Adyurah* (The Churches and Monasteries of Egypt and Neighboring Countries). It is interesting to remark that its unique manuscript, now deposited in the National Library in Paris, was purchased in Egypt by the traveler J. VANSLEB in 1674 for the pitifully small price of three piasters. This Arabic text was owned by ABŪ ṢĀLIḤ THE ARMENIAN, whose name was inscribed on the manuscript. Owing to the importance of its contents, it attracted Western scholars and was first published at Oxford in 1895 by B. T. A. Evetts mistakenly ascribed to Abū Ṣāliḥ the Armenian; in 1969 the English translation was republished. A Coptic monk of Dayr al-Suryān, Ṣamū'īl al-Suryānī, issued a new edition (1984) of this invaluable work. The text is a complete listing of the churches and monasteries of Egypt, classified under provinces and cities as they stood in the twelfth century. The author, Abū al-Makārim, attempted to use classical Arabic, but his peculiar style indicates beyond doubt that he could have been a Coptic-speaking native using a foreign language. Though his Arabic style is full of peculiarities that must have been current among the Copts of that period, the contents are of the highest importance for Coptic annals and historical geography of Egypt in the Middle Ages.

In the thirteenth century, and specifically under the Ayyubid dynasty, Arabic Christian literature flourished and its products multiplied. The most eminent authors of that period were members of the family of AWLĀD AL-ʿASSĀL. Their life and work mark the peak of productivity in the Coptic families whose members occupied eminent scribal positions in the Egyptian administration. They are known to have resided in the famous Coptic district of Ḥārit Zuwaylah, with its historic churches, in Cairo. Most eminent among them for his contributions was al-ṢAFĪ IBN AL-ʿASSĀL, whose name is associated with the great jurisprudential compilation entitled *al-Majmūʿ al-Ṣafawī*, in which the author assembled all the available materials concerned with two wide subjects from the orthodox point of view. The first was the question of religion and Coptic orthodox religious tradition; the second comprised all the items of civil jurisprudence, to which he applied the rules of classical Islamic works on this subject. The first section consists of many chapters and deals in the first instance with the position of the patriarch, who is the equivalent of the imam or caliph in Islamic society. The capital difference is that the Muslim position is both religious and civil, whereas the patriarchal dignity is restricted to the religious surveillance of the Coptic community. The civil section of this work treats the material life of individuals within the context of biblical and orthodox traditions. Details of contractual conditions for sales, rentals, witnesses, and the like are surveyed in more or less the same system as the Islamic *fiqh* (works of jurisprudence). Other subjects such as inheritance are treated from the orthodox outlook, which varies from the Islamic system, in which, for instance, the female inheritance is estimated as half the male, contrary to the Coptic, in which the two sexes are equal. Moreover, in marital relations, divorce is not permitted except within the restricted condition of adultery. Numerous other legal and fiscal items are surveyed in this comprehensive work. Al-Asʿad ibn al-ʿAssāl is known to have composed some Arabic poetry on subjects treated by him, including a long iambic poem (*urjūzah*) on the subject of inheritance among the Coptic Christians.

One of the greatest contributions of the AWLĀD AL-ʿASSAL family in the field of religion was the translation of the New Testament into Arabic, which they based on Coptic, Greek, and Syriac original languages, with which they were thoroughly acquainted. A copy of their original translation of the four Gospels, signed by Jirjis Abū al-Faḍā'il ibn Luṭfallāh, is dated A.M. 1057. This is available at the patriarchal library in Cairo and is a true reproduction of the autographed original by al-Asʿad Abū al-Faraj Hibatallāh himself.

Members of the family of Awlād al-ʿAssāl have

also become famous for their exquisite Arabic penmanship, which became known to posterity as the As'adī style of Arabic writing. Among al-Ṣafī's legacy are a series of religious homilies or orations in which he extemporized eloquent pronouncements in rhymed Arabic equal in beauty to any similar texts known in Islamic literature. The Awlād al-'Assāl left behind them a number of other works on religious questions including a significant treatise entitled *Nahj al-Sabīl fī al-Radd 'alā man Qadaḥa al-Injīl*, a kind of literary defense against those who deprecated the Gospels. Apparently they were highly proficient in their knowledge of the Coptic language, for they compiled a Coptic-Arabic dictionary as well as a grammar of the Coptic language.

During the same century, other Coptic writers distinguished themselves by their works in Arabic, including Jirjis ibn al-'Amīd, known as Ibn al-Makīn, a scribe in the Ayyubid military *diwan*, who wrote a considerable universal history concentrating on Muhammadan dynasties. The first section of that work reviews world history to the reign of the Roman emperor Heraclius and the spread of Christianity. The second section is devoted to Islamic history from the time of the prophet Muḥammad to the reign of al-Ẓāhir Baybars (1260–1277). This history was supplemented by another Copt named al-Faḍl ibn Abī al-Faḍā'il under the title *Al-Nahj al-Sadīd, wa-al-Durr al-Farīd fīmā ba'd Tārīkh ibn al-'Amīd*. AL-MAKĪN IBN AL-'AMĪD left another work entitled *al-Ḥāwī*, comprising a defense of the Christian faith and a commentary on sections of the Gospels.

To the same century and of considerable renown in Copto-Arabic literature belongs another writer, ABŪ SHĀKIR IBN AL-RĀHIB, also known as Abū al-Karam ibn al-Muhadhdhab, the son of a leading Coptic scribe, who retired from the sultan's service and, after losing his wife, became a monk and was nominated priest of the historic Church of Abū Sarjah. His son Abū Shākir became a deacon of the Church of Our Lady known as al-Mu'allaqah in 1260. He was a contemporary of Popes CYRIL III (1235–1243) and ATHANASIUS III (1250–1261) as well as GABRIEL III (1268–1271) and JOHN VII (1262–1293). He may have also survived to the reign of THEODOSIUS II (1294–1300). Ibn al-Rāhib distinguished himself during those patriarchates by his prolific writings in Arabic, which showed his vast knowledge in theology, the exact science of Coptic astronomy, and the history of his church. His literary heritage included the following works: (1) *Kitāb al-Burhān*, on theological subjects and Coptic traditions in fifty-two chapters; (2) *Kitāb al-Shifā fī Kashf ma-Istatara min Lāhūt al-Masīḥ wa-Ikhtafā*, a treatise on the divinity of Jesus Christ; (3) *Kitāb al-Tawārīkh*, on the definition of the Coptic epact and the major feasts of the Coptic church in fifty-one chapters; (4) *Kitāb al-Tārīkh*, a succinct universal history from the creation to his day; (5) *Kitāb al-Majāmi'*, a survey of the ecumenical councils; and (6) *Uṣūl Muqaddīmat Sullam al-Lughah al-Qibṭiyyah*, a *scala* and introduction in Arabic to the Coptic language and Coptic grammar.

His compilation of the patriarchal biographies and the computations of the dates of the patriarchs is considered the most invaluable source in this connection on account of his meticulous astronomical and mathematical knowledge.

Next in succession to Abū Shākir ibn al-Rāhib, we have an equally distinguished name in Copto-Arabic literature, al-As'ad Abū al-Barakāt, better known as IBN KABAR. He lived until the opening decades of the fourteenth century and his work marked the peak of the golden age of Coptic belles lettres. He descended from a wealthy Coptic family and received all the education available at his time, thus becoming conversant with Coptic as well as with classical Arabic. In addition he was proficient in Greek, Hebrew, and Syriac. He occupied a high scribal position in the government administration, but decided to retire in the year 1283, even before the sultanate of the Baḥrī Mamluk al-Ashraf Khalīl ibn Qalāwūn, who declared that he wanted no Christian in his administration. In 1300, he was unanimously nominated by the Coptic archons as priest of the important Church of Our Lady known as al-Mu'allaqah in Old Cairo. He was a contemporary of the patriarchs John VII, Theodosius II (1294–1300), JOHN VIII (1300–1320), and JOHN IX (1320–1327). His theological acumen and vast knowledge of Coptic religious traditions are evident in the array of his encyclopedic works, comprising the following items: (1) *Kitāb Miṣbāḥ al-Ẓulmah fī Īḍāḥ al-Khidmah*, a kind of encyclopedia of Coptic religious knowledge and traditions in twenty-four sections with numerous supplements. This is undoubtedly the most comprehensive record of Coptic jurisprudence. In it he meticulously discussed every detail imaginable concerning the church, ending up with a history of the patriarchs from Saint Mark to Pope MARK IV, the eighty-fourth patriarch in 1363; (2) a collection in eloquent classical Arabic style of fifty-one miscellaneous obituaries, orations, and epistles; (3) the *Sullam* or *Scala*, a comprehensive lexicon of all available Coptic terms and their Arabic equivalents, classified in thirty-two chapters; (4)

Kitāb Jalā' al-'Uqūl fī'Ilm al-Uṣūl, in eighteen chapters, on theological problems comprising a detailed account of Christian beliefs and doctrines, from the oneness of godhead to the Trinity and the Lord's incarnation. This work is sometimes identified with a similar text by Ibn al-'Assāl under the title *Tiryāq al-'Uqūl fī Ilm al-Uṣūl* (On the mysteries of the Christian faith), also associated with Buṭrus al-Sadamantī; (5) a polemical work in refutation of Jewish and Islamic attacks on Christianity, of which a single manuscript is preserved in the Vatican Library, still unpublished; (6) *Risālat al-Bayān al-Azhar,* written in refutation of the arguments in behalf of the doctrine of predestination.

Even after his retirement from government service, Ibn Kabar continued to assist his superior and friend, the Baḥrī Mamluk amir Rukn-al-Dīn Baybars-Jashankīr (1308–1309), in the compilation of a historical treatise on Islamic history entitled *Zubdat al-Fikrah fī Tārīkh al-Hijrah.* This is ascertained by two famous Muslim historians, Abū al-Mahāsin Yūsuf ibn al-Maqarr and al-Maqrīzī.

From the above statements, it may be deduced that Ibn Kabar's work stands at the peak of Copto-Arabic literary accomplishment. The last years of his rich life were spent in complete seclusion away from the eyes of persecutors of the Copts, and it must be assumed that he spent those years in concentrated revisions of his vast literary products. The date of his death is known with certainty to be 15 Bashans A.M. 1040/10 May A.D. 1334.

Yuḥannā ibn Zakariyyā IBN SIBĀ', who was a contemporary of Ibn Kabar, produced a work on the same subject as *Misbāḥ al-Ẓulmah* (Lamp of Darkness); the work is more modest, but worthy of a citation nevertheless. Little is known about Ibn Sibā' except that he lived in the latter part of the thirteenth and the first part of the fourteenth century. In fact nothing is known about him beyond the fact that he wrote a work entitled *Al-Jawharah al-Nafīsah fī'Ulūm al-Kanīsah,* the annotated text of which has been edited with a Latin translation by Vincentio Mistrīḥ under the title *Pretiosa Margarita de Scientiis Ecclesiasticis* (Cairo, 1966). The work begins with a biblical introduction to the nativity of Jesus Christ in twenty-two chapters. This is followed by a summary of the rise of Christianity in ten chapters. In the rest of the book, consisting of eighty chapters, he deals with Coptic traditions and gives a meticulous display of the Coptic church offices and officers from the deacon and the archdeacon to the presbyter and the HEGUMENOS, to the bishops, the archbishops, and the patriarch. Ibn Sibā' goes into every detail of the liturgical offices and the ecclesiastical instruments. Several chapters are devoted to the feasts and fasts of the church with a concentration on Holy Week and the Easter season. Later chapters deal with the burial offices and the sacrificial offerings for the souls of the deceased. He records the patriarchal duty of assembling all the priesthood every week for a moralistic homily. The patriarch is also supposed to keep an eye on his flock and to follow their increase or decrease numerically. The last chapters define the meanings of the ringing of the church bells during the liturgical celebration.

The steady decline of the Coptic language during the later Middle Ages had the inevitable effect of the rise of a new form of Copto-Arabic literature. The above-mentioned works from the tenth century onward reached their peak in the works of authors of the thirteenth and fourteenth centuries. Parallel to the Arabic translation of the Gospels, we should not overlook the other purely religious works, hitherto employed in the liturgies of the church in Coptic. It was gradually becoming necessary for the Coptic hierarchical authorities to translate some of the Coptic literature into Arabic so that the congregation, who had started to speak Arabic as a substitute for the spoken Coptic, could understand it. It is difficult to fix a precise date for this translation, but we can safely assume that it must have taken place in the later medieval period, at least parallel to the translation of the Gospels. This formed a class of Copto-Arabic letters that has been the subject of numerous studies in the area of theology and ecclesiology. Here we must be content with quoting such literature as *Kitāb al Khūlājī al-Muqaddas,* edited by ḤABĪB JIRJIS and sung throughout Coptic Christendom. Other works, such as *Kitāb al-Ṭurūḥāt wa-al-Abṣāliyyāt,* which contains songs of the church edited by Qummuṣ Bākhūm al-Baramūsi and 'Iryān Faraj, are a sample of Coptic religious literature generally published in both Coptic and Arabic. Perhaps the Coptic versions are used only in the monasteries. But the Arabic is used as much as needed by the priests within their churches.

On the whole, we must regard the age of Ibn Kabar and Awlād al-'Assāl, together with these liturgical texts, as the golden age of Copto-Arabic literature. Perhaps the work of Ibn Sibā', despite the importance of his endeavor, should be considered as the inception of the decline precipitated by the advent of Ottoman rule.

With the dawn of modern history and the subjection of Egypt to the Ottoman yoke in 1517, Egypt seems to have gradually lost its intellectual flair among both Muslims and Copts. Whereas a faint ray of sunshine kept flickering in the ancient fortress of Muslim education at al-Azhar University, Coptic education became restricted to the primitive *kuttāb* (*scriptoria*) affiliated with the churches under the supervision of the Coptic cantors (sing. *'arīfs*, pl. *'irfān*), who were generally blind and offered only limited religious instruction. Assistants conducted programs of reading and writing of liturgical texts, as well as intensive courses in practical mathematics and accounts in order to prepare the candidates for scribal offices and tax collection in the government. The Copts could not attend al-Azhar University for a higher education in jurisprudence, advanced grammar, logic, and prosody on a religious basis, though the Hanifite sect raised no objection in principle to the admission of Copts. The period of nearly four centuries until the advent of the French occupation in 1798–1802 proved to be one of the darkest in Egyptian annals.

We must thus cross from Ibn Kabar's age to modern history to discover any real awakening of Copto-Arabic literature. The seeds of modern education were sown among the Copts by Pope CYRIL IV (1853–1861), known as the "Father of Reform," who devoted his attention to the establishment of schools with teaching staffs of high quality. His example was followed by a number of Coptic benevolent societies such as the TAWFĪQ COPTIC SOCIETY, and Coptic schools sprang up, not only in Cairo and Alexandria but also in most provincial towns in Lower and Upper Egypt. A number of the graduates of these schools even managed to attend al-Azhar University under borrowed and rather anomalous names. These included Mīkhā'īl 'Abd-al-Sayyid, who later established the daily newspaper *al-Waṭān;* Tadrus Wahbī, the eminent Coptic educator; and the journalist Jindī Ibrāhīm, who among Muslims was known as Shaykh Ibrāhīm al-Jindī. The three became leading stars in Copto-Arabic literature, and all memorized whole sections of the Qur'ān, which they quoted frequently in their written works.

In the meantime, numerous Copts attended study circles held privately by the rector of al-Azhar, the famous Shaykh al-Islam Muḥammad 'Abdū, who did not object to their participation but welcomed it. The Coptic poet Francis al-'Itr, who was the son of a well-known Coptic priest, was a regular participant in Shaykh Muḥammad 'Abdū's study circles throughout the year 1902.

In this way, Coptic literary scholarship and Coptic education in general gave birth to a new class of young people with literary tendencies that became evident in Coptic literary creativity and in Coptic journalism. The old Coptic newspapers *al-Waṭan* and *Miṣr* became the forum in which the literary products of the age were amply demonstrated.

The educational reform movement was extended to female instruction and the liberation of women from past traditional restrictions. Here perhaps the Copts were pioneers, though the national leader of this movement in Egypt happened to be a progressive Muslim by the name of Qāsim Amīn. This movement found outspoken supporters in the poetry of noted Coptic poets of the day, especially Naṣr Lūzah al-Asyūṭī, who sang its praise in delicate Arabic poems as early as the first decades of the twentieth century. In the provinces, poets such as 'Ayyād Bishāy followed suit. Numerous poems are quoted by the historian of Coptic literature, the Muslim Muḥammad Sayyid Kīlānī, in *Al-Adab al-Qibṭī* (1962). Somewhat obscure Coptic poets such as Basṭā Bishāy, Riyāḍ Ghubriyāl, Rufā'īl Nakhlah, and in particular the better known Naṣr Lụzah al-Asyūṭī have written poetry to commemorate progressive educational events among the Copts.

The reform movement in general education found its echo in the Coptic religious institutions, where the CLERICAL COLLEGE slumbered until one of its students, Malạti Sarjiyūs, eloquently attacked its stationary status and pleaded for its reform. A long poem by Ibrahīm Ḥunayn al-Bibāwī was published in Kilāni's *al-Adab al-Qibṭī*. It supports Boutros Pasha's position against the retrogressive attitude of Pope Cyril V.

Hitherto the Copts seemed to act as a separate community within the body politic of the Egyptian nation and prided themselves on their direct descent from the pharaohs. This separatist tendency was intensified as a reaction to the rising movement toward universal Islamic unity, which the Copts regarded as antinationalistic. This tendency reflected itself in the Coptic press and became the origin of the movement that led to the COPTIC CONGRESS OF ASYŪṬ to fight for equal rights for the Copts, who felt barred from principal administrative positions in the state. In the early twentieth century a campaign reviling the Copts by Shaykh 'Abd al-Azīz Jāwīsh, the editor of the leading Muslim daily newspaper *al-Mu'ayyad*, resulted in a counterattack in the Coptic daily *al-Waṭan*, where Jāwīsh was accused of being a foreign meddler of Tunisian extraction. Well-meaning Muslims and Copts, however, repudiated this wave of hatred among segments of the same nation, and poets on both sides preached brotherhood and love and unity. On the Islamic side, we read pacifying poetry by ʿAbd al-Raḥmān Shukrī and Maḥmūd Ramzī Nāzim, and on the Coptic side, by ʿAwaḍ Wāṣif and Ibrāhīm Ḥunayn. These were even joined by noted Coptic politicians such as WISSA WASSEF and Murqus Ḥannā. The literature of both Muslim and Coptic poets is quoted by Kilānī (pp. 80–84).

This situation was not helped by the assassination of Boutros Ghālī on 21 February 1910, which precipitated a new wave of tearful literature. Lamenting the murder of an illustrious Coptic prime minister, Coptic versifiers poured out their hearts in poems of bitter grief, tinging this literary stage with sorrowful eloquence (Kilānī, pp. 145ff.). The battle of words was resumed with vehemence on the pages of the dailies *al-Mu'ayyad* and *al-Waṭan*.

An avalanche of literary output reflected the universal support of the Coptic people for the principles for which the COPTIC CONGRESS OF ASYŪṬ (1911) stood. Kīlāni (pp. 106–113) quoted Coptic poets who explicitly praised the just requests of their coreligionists. These included Būlus al-Shammāʿ, Riyād Ghubrīyāl, Naṣr Lūzah al-Asyūṭi, Tadrus Wahbī, Ibrahīm Ḥunayn, and Zakī Wāṣif. The Coptic press overflowed with articles from the pens of eminent journalists and politicians. The Muslim reaction in holding a parallel meeting known as the EGYPTIAN CONFERENCE OF HELIOPOLIS, counterpart to the Asyūṭ Coptic Congress, is interesting but outside the scope of this article.

The Copts were pleased by the death of the British Commissioner, Sir Eldon Gorst, who sympathized with the Muslim majority against the Coptic minority. But Coptic hopes were not raised by the appointment of Lord Kitchener as his successor. A ray of hope appeared on the Egyptian political horizon when U. S. President Theodore Roosevelt visited Egypt. He spoke out for constitutional liberties and the American conception of equality among all citizens irrespective of their faith or color. The Copts were unreserved in their literary praise of the American president. Riyāḍ Ghubriyāl published a long poem in praise of Roosevelt. In fact, the Roosevelt visit to the Near East and his outspoken pronouncements seem to have sparked a budding movement toward nationalistic aspirations that blossomed in the 1919 revolution under the leadership of SA'D ZAGHLŪL, who managed to bring Muslims and Copts closer together in the ensuing battle for independence.

The Wafd party of Zaghlūl was composed of Muslims and Christians on an equal basis, and the nearest person to Saʿd Zaghlūl was a young and eloquent Copt, MAKRAM ʿEBEID. Though the British instituted a new policy of protecting the minorities through the declaration of 28 February 1922, this protection was refused by the Copts. This time there was complete unity of purpose, and while the Muslims preached independence in churches, the Copts attacked the British occupation in mosques. Qummuṣ Sarjiyūs delivered memorable orations at al-Azhar mosque, where he was applauded by the Muslim *ʿulema'*. This new development on the Egyptian scene generated a new phase in Coptic literature in which poets spoke out for the total and undiminished independence of Egypt, together with a multitude of writers who professed national unity. The leading Coptic poet, Naṣr Lūzah al-Asyūṭī, recited verses glorifying the unity of the crescent and the cross. Poetic obituaries were unrestrained in their glorification of Saʿd Zaghlūl on his death in 1927. The Coptic literature inspired by Saʿd's death included significant poetry by Naṣr Lūzah al-Asyūṭī, Qusṭandī Dawūd, Philip ʿAṭallah, and others (Kilānī, pp. 167–78).

The problem after the realization of independence for Egypt was a constitutional one, on which the Copts held varying opinions. Some wanted the representation of the Copts to conform to their numerical percentage, while others thought that Copts and Muslims should stand before the electorate without religious distinction. The latter party won the day. This problem has become acute with the emergence of fundamentalist Muslims.

The Copts, with the exception of the 1919 revolution, tended to look upon themselves as a separate nation with its peculiar trials and tribulations, its own aspirations, its feasts and traditions and customs. They looked upon themselves as the pure Egyptian stock and professed their pharaonic lineage. This becomes evident in works on Coptic history, best represented in the brilliant Arabic *History of the Coptic Nation* by YA'QŪB NAKHLAH RUFAYLAH. Numerous other works by authors old and new, such as Tawfīq Iskārūs and Ramzī Tadrus and many others, concerning famous Copts in the nineteenth and twentieth centuries, follow the same line of thought. This has also been recognized as an established fact by some Western authors such as S. H. Leeder (1918).

After many years of comparative stagnation, reform was pioneered by Pope Cyril IV, the "Father of Coptic Reform." His life was commemorated in poems by Iskandar Quzmān, Ibrāhim Ḥanna ʿAṭāyā, and others. Obituary literature commemorated Coptic celebrities such as Boutros Ghālī (Pasha) and Yūsif Sulayman (Pasha) (Kilānī, pp. 183–84).

On the whole, Coptic literature bears the impression of religiosity and Christian compassion, and reverence for the church. This appears clearly in a number of poems by Rufā'īl Nakhlah, Naṣr Lūzah al-Asyūṭī, Iskandar Quzmān, and Mikhā'īl Manṣūr (Kilānī, pp. 192–98). Sometimes, Coptic literary writers are constrained by certain circumstances to use Islamic dicta. One such is Tadrus Wahbī's poem on the occasion of the return of Khedive Abbas II (1892–1914) from pilgrimage to Mecca; another is his felicitation to the same prince at the Bairam Muslim feast (Kilānī, pp. 199–201). With its numerous bifurcations or aberrations, Coptic belles lettres have genuine qualities of originality, creativity, and superb Arabic style. Coptic poetry has varied in its tendencies from age to age, reflecting the feelings of the people in a given set of circumstances and calling for the expression of certain specific emotions. The education of each poet left its indelible mark on his poetry. Though it is difficult to place Coptic poets in the same high category as Aḥmad Shawqī or Ḥāfiẓ Ibrāhīm, they retain for themselves a place of honor, modest but appreciable and respectable.

Finally, the work on Coptic literature by Kilānī (pp. 205–231) ends with a poetic selection assembled from the literary products of a number of noted Coptic poets, hitherto dispersed in many journals and Coptic daily newspapers, supplemented with succinct notes on their biographies.

BIBLIOGRAPHY

Abū al-Makārim. *Tārīkh al-Kanā'is wa-al-Adyurah*, 4 vols., ed. Samū'īl al-Suryānī. Cairo, 1984 (older edition under Abū Ṣāliḥ al-Armanī, ed. B. T. A. Evetts).

Atiya, A. S., ed. *Kitāb Qawānīn al-Dawāwīn by ibn Mammātī*. Cairo, 1943.

Eutychii Patriarchae Alexandrini Annalium (facsimile). Oxford, 1654. Arabic text ed. L. Cheikho, B. Carra de Vaux, and H. Zayyat. In CSCO 50–51. *Scriptores Arabici* 6–7. Beirut, 1904–1909.

Ibn Kabar. *Miṣbāḥ al-Ẓulmah fī'Īḍāḥ al-Khidmah*, 2 vols., ed. Samir Khalil. Cairo, 1971.

Kāmil Ṣāliḥ Nakhlah. *Kitāb Tarīkh wa-Jadāwil Baṭārikat al-Iskandariyyah al-Qibṭ*. Cairo, 1943.

Leeder, S. H. *The Modern Sons of the Pharaohs*, London and New York, 1918; repr. New York, 1973.

Muḥammad Sayyid Kilānī. *Al-Adab al-Qibṭī-Qadīman wa-Ḥadīthan*. Cairo, 1962.

Ya'qūb Nakhlah Rufahlah. *Kitāb Tārīkh al-Ummah al-Qibṭiyyah*. Cairo, 1899.

AZIZ S. ATIYA

LITHAZOMENON AND SAINT PETER'S BRIDGE, two monasteries west of Alexandria, no doubt fairly near the city. The name Lithazomenon indicates a stony terrain. The first attestation is toward the middle of the fifth century (Orlandi, 1975, pp. 82–83), but it is not stated whether there was already a monastery there. At the end of the sixth century or beginning of the seventh, John Moschus, in company with Sophronius, visited the Thessalonian monk Abbā Palladius. Moschus adds further on that he knew at Alexandria the pious Syrian reader Zoilus, a scribe by profession, who later on was buried at the Lithazomenon, in the monastery of the same Abbā Palladius.

The monastery of Saint Peter's Bridge was home to John the Soldier. The life of this holy man was curiously divided between asceticism and the inevitable basket-making, on the one hand, and the barracks, on the other.

Drescher (1949) was unable to determine which was the water-course crossed by the bridge nearby. As for the name, it seems that it relates to the patriarch PETER I (300–311), the "hieromartyr" executed under DIOCLETIAN. Several sources, in fact, testify that his martyrium was set up outside the walls, west of the city. This reliquary church, which survived until after the ARAB CONQUEST OF EGYPT, characteristically bore the name Western (al-Gharbiyyah; Basset, 1907, Vol. 11, pp. 758–59). There is little doubt, in our eyes, that Saint Peter's Bridge drew its name from that of the nearby martyrium. That a monastery should have been established in the locality is only natural.

One of the manuscripts of the Life of THEODORA OF ALEXANDRIA (National Library, Paris, Arabe 1454; Wessely, 1889, p. 30) gives the Apostle Peter and not the archbishop of the same name as the person to whom the martyrium was dedicated. This is certainly an error, and besides, other manuscripts (Paris, Arabe 1468 and 1506) are content with "Saint Peter" (Wessely, pp. 29, 30).

BIBLIOGRAPHY

Calderini, A. *Dizionario dei nomi geografici e topografici dell'Egitto greco-romano*, 3 vols. in 8. Milan, 1966–1980.

Drescher, J. *Bulletin de la société archéologique d'Alexandrie* 38 (1949):13–15.
Orlandi, T., ed. *Vite dei monaci Phif e Longino.* Milan, 1975.
Wessely, K. *Die Vita s. Theodorae. Fünfzehnter Jahresbericht des k. und k. Staatsgymnasiums in Hernals.* Vienna, 1889.

JEAN GASCOU

Pastoral staff. *Courtesy Coptic Museum, Cairo.*

LITURGICAL INSIGNIA. Just as the crown and scepter are part of the regalia reflecting the majesty of a monarch, the liturgical insignia serve as emblems of the authority and dignity of the clergy during the celebration of the Divine Liturgy, reflecting the majesty of God.

Pastoral Staff

A pastoral staff is a long ornamental stick carried by a patriarch or a bishop. It is surmounted by a cross on a small orb between two inwardly curved serpents. This staff is symbolic of the victory of the Cross, as well as the pastoral care expected of a good shepherd. The serpents are an illustration of the words of Christ with reference to Moses' brazen serpent, when He spoke of His imminent crucifixion, "And as Moses lifted up the serpent in the wilderness, so must the Son of Man be lifted up, that whoever believes in Him may have eternal life" (Jn. 3:14–15).

The pastoral staff is usually carried before a patriarch or a bishop during processions. It has a red silk sash hanging down from its upper curves.

Cross, Pectoral

A pectoral cross is worn by the clergy (as well as pious Christians, both men and women) as an insignia and distinguishing mark, giving the clergy spiritual power and protection.

The custom of wearing pectoral crosses seems to have been widespread during the early centuries of Christianity. Saint Macrina, sister of Saint GREGORY OF NYSSA (335–395), is said to have always worn a cross. Saint JOHN CHRYSOSTOM used to encourage every believer to carry a cross and take pride in so doing, as if wearing a crown.

Cross, Processional

A large cross mounted on a pole is carried by a deacon at the head of a procession during feasts, celebrations, and other special occasions. The crossbearer is followed by two other deacons, each carrying a fan, and then by the rest of the deacons, all holding banners.

Eusebius gave a description of a processional cross designed by Constantine the Great, on which were engraved the initial letters of the name Jesus Christ. It was carried at the head of the army when it went to battle.

On one side of the processional cross there is usually the picture of the Crucified Christ, and on the other side, the Risen Christ.

Cross with Tapers

Allegorically, the cross with three lit tapers symbolizes the fact that Christ, who was crucified on the cross, is the light of the world and that He has called believers out of the darkness into His glorious light (1 Pt. 2:9).

It is used on several occasions. At the evening and morning services, following the creed, the officiating priest holds a cross with lit tapers at the entrance to the sanctuary *(haykal)* and says the prayer of God, have Mercy on Us. He silently makes the sign of the cross on the congregation three times and then turns to the east and prays, "O God, have mercy upon us, establish Thy mercy unto us, have compassion on us, hear us, bless us, keep us, help us, take away Thy anger from us. Visit us with Thy salvation and forgive us our sins." To this, the congregation responds *Kyrie eleison* three times. At the morning service of the two Feasts of the Cross (17 Tūt and 10 Baramhāt), after the above-mentioned prayer, the clergy and deacons make a circuit round the church with the cross with tapers and then resume the service. At the morning service of Palm Sunday, again after the above-mentioned prayer, they make three circuits round the altar with the cross with tapers, singing the *Kyrie eleison*, and then stand at the entrance of the *haykal* and sing the hymn of ϵⲩⲗⲟⲅⲏⲙⲉⲛⲟⲥ. Then they make a circuit round the church and resume the service.

Miter

The miter (see also LITURGICAL VESTMENTS) is a representation of the golden crown worn by each of the twenty-four elders seen ministering to God in heaven by Saint John the Divine (Rev. 4:4). It is also symbolic of the authority given by the Lord to His high priest (2 Cor. 10:8), by which a patriarch becomes the steward of the secrets of Christ (1 Cor. 4:4).

BIBLIOGRAPHY

Matta al-Miskīn. *Ḥayāt al-Ṣalāh.* Cairo, 1968.

Mattā'ūs, Bishop. *Rūḥāniyat Ṭaqs al-Quddās fī al-Kanīsah al-Qibṭiyyah al-Urthudhuksiyyah*, 2nd ed. Cairo, 1980.

ARCHBISHOP BASILIOS

LITURGICAL INSTRUMENTS. The liturgical instruments of the Coptic church, as well as everything worn or used during the services, must be consecrated by the patriarch or a bishop as part of the general process of CONSECRATION.

Basin and Ewer

A basin and ewer are usually placed on a low wooden stand at the northern side of the ALTAR; they are used to wash the priest's hands during the Divine Liturgy.

The basin and ewer are usually of silver, brass, or bronze, and are entrusted to the deacon on ordination. When all communicants have partaken of the Holy Communion, the deacon pours water from the ewer over the church vessels until the priest makes sure of their proper ablution. He then pours water into the palms of the priest, who says the following prayer: "O Angel of this Sacrifice ascending up on high with this hymn of praise, remember us before the Lord, that He may forgive us our sins." The priest then insufflates the water, casts it up into the air before the altar, wipes his own face with his hands, and then touches his fellow priests.

It is also usual for the priest to take the ewer into his left hand, pass down the middle aisle of the church, and sprinkle the water over the congregation in the form of aspersion before praying the final blessing and dismissal (see 'Abd al-Masīḥ, 1902).

Candelabrum

A candelabrum is a large ornamental candlestick. It appears in various forms and is usually made of bronze, iron, copper, or silver. It is placed inside the SANCTUARY (*haykal*) or outside, next to the ICONOSTASIS.

In some churches one candelabrum stands at the north end of the altar and another at the south, meant to represent the two angels who appeared inside the Holy Sepulcher, one at the head and the other at the foot of the place where the body of Christ had lain. It is also common to see in some churches two candelabra outside the *haykal* screen, representing the Old and New Testaments.

The use of the candelabrum was originally commanded by God to Moses as part of the furnishings of the Tabernacle (see Ex. 25:31–40, 37:17–24; Nm. 8:1–4).

Censer

The censer is a metal bowl about 5 inches (12 cm) in diameter, in which incense is added to the glowing coals. To it are attached three chains, each measuring about 22 inches (54 cm) in length, which end with a small domelike lid and a hook. Small spherical bells are sometimes attached to the three chains.

In the Old Testament the censer was a receptacle carried by hand, to be filled with live coals from the altar (Nm. 16:46). Censers used in the Tabernacle of the Congregation were made of bronze (Ex. 27:3, 38:3), whereas those used on the altar, as well as the censer which was taken by the chief priest to the *sanctum sanctorum* on the day of atonement, were made of pure gold (1 Kgs. 7:50; 2 Chr. 4:22).

God commanded Moses to make an altar on which exclusive sweet incense was burnt by Aaron every morning (Ex. 30:7). The perfume of incense thus came to be symbolical of prayer and the presence of God. Hence the added significance of Solomon's words "While the king was on his couch, my nard gave forth its fragrance" (Sg. 1:12).

In Christian worship the offering of incense continued to have the same importance, and the censer acquired an essential symbolic significance in the Coptic liturgy. The censer that bears live coals and sweet-smelling incense became an analogy for the Blessed Virgin Mary, who bore the Savior of the world. Reference is made to this particular relationship at certain points in the liturgy, as when, following the Prayer for the Absolution of Ministers, the congregation sings the Hymn to the Virgin: "This is the censer of pure gold, containing the ambergris, that was entrusted to the hands of Aaron the Priest, raising incense upon the altar." On fast days the following section is chanted: "The Virgin is the gold censer, our Savior is its ambergris. She gave birth to Him Who has saved us and forgiven our sins." Throughout the Fast of Lent the following verse is chanted: "You are the pure gold censer, containing the Blessed Live Coals." In the PSALMODIA, the Sunday THEOTOKIA include similar instances of the Virgin-censer analogy.

The Ethiopian liturgy contains the same analogy in the prayer that the priest says while offering incense before the icon of the Virgin: "You are the gold censer which bore the Live Coal Fire. . . . Blessed be He Who was incarnated of you, Who offered Himself to His Father for incense and acceptable offering." Standing outside the iconostasis, the priest also says, "The censer is Mary; the incense is He Who was in her womb, Who is fragrant; the incense is He Whom she bore, He came and saved us, the fragrant ointment, Jesus Christ."

Censer. Bronze. *Courtesy Coptic Museum, Cairo.*

Open censer with handle. Bronze. Ahnāsyah (Thebes). Fifth century. *Courtesy Coptic Museum, Cairo.*

The offering of incense was widely practiced right from the beginning of the Christian era. Some ecclesiastical commentators, however, have expressed doubt as to the validity of this belief, perhaps because of the scant references made to the use of incense in the writings of the early fathers of the church. This may be attributed to the fact that many details of Christian worship and church mysteries were intentionally unrecorded, lest they be misused by heretics, and were therefore only verbally entrusted to believers.

Nevertheless, the use of incense may be inferred from several sources. The HISTORY OF THE PATRIARCHS supplies clear evidence of the use of censers and incense in the postapostolic age. When the congregation raised objections against DEMETRIUS I (189–231) as the twelfth patriarch of the See of Saint Mark on the grounds of his being a married man, he demonstrated his chastity by pouring glowing coals from the censer onto his garment in front of the congregation without being burned (Manassā Yūḥannā, 1983, p. 23).

From the Revelation to John, it can be inferred that the censer was used in a way different from the earlier Jewish usage: "And another angel came and stood at the altar with a golden censer; and he was given much incense to mingle with the prayers of all the saints upon the golden altar before the throne; and the smoke of the incense rose with the prayers of the saints from the hand of the angel before God" (Rev. 8:3–4). The next chapter speaks of the twenty-four elders "each holding a harp, and with golden bowls full of incense, which are the prayers of the saints" (Rev. 9:8). This must be an indication of the then-prevalent manner of Christian worship, featuring the use of censers and incense.

In describing the plight of the church in latter days, the ecclesiastical writer Hippolytus (c. 170–c. 236) employed the following words: "And the churches, too, will wail with a mighty lamentation, because neither oblation nor incense is attended to, nor a service acceptable to God" (1951, pp. 250–51).

The Didascalia (Ḥāfiẓ Dawūd, 1967) provides an indication as to the necessity of using the censer, instructing that the bishop shall carry the incense and make three circuits round the altar in glorification of the Holy Trinity and then hand the censer to the priest who shall go round the whole congregation carrying it.

In the writings attributed to DIONYSIUS THE PSEUDO-AREOPAGITE is the following statement: "The bishop having made an end of sacred prayer at the divine altar, begins the censing with it, and goes over the whole circuit of the sacred place."

A good many of the early fathers who chose to minimize the importance of using incense in worship, including Athenagoras, Tertullian, CLEMENT OF ALEXANDRIA, Arnobius, Lactantius, and Augustine, were converted to Christianity from cults that relied heavily on the use of incense. They were understandably anxious to divest Christian worship of any apparently heathen customs and to render it strictly spiritual. Thus, Clement of Alexandria preached that "the righteous soul is the truly sacred altar, and that incense arising from it is holy prayer."

Speaking of the efficacy of Christian worship, Saint Ephraem Syrus (c. 306–373) wrote, "Your fasts are a defense for our land; your prayers are a shield for our city; the burning of incense is our propitiation. Praise to God Who has hallowed your offering" (1866). He stressed the point in another context: "I exhort you not to bury me with sweet spices . . . but to give the fumigation of sweet-smelling smoke in the house of God. . . . Burn your incense in the house of the Lord to His praise and honor" (1732–1746).

The use of incense is mentioned in the course of a description given by Saint BASIL THE GREAT of the desolation suffered by the churches during the persecution: "The houses of prayer were cast down by unholy hands, the altars were overthrown, and there was no oblation nor incense, no place of sacrifice, but fearful sorrow, as a cloud, was over all" (1885, col. 496).

According to the witness of Etheria (Egeria), the nun who made a tour of Egypt, the Holy Land, Edessa, Asia Minor, and Constantinople toward the end of the fourth century, incense and censers were used at Jerusalem in the Easter service (1919).

The third of the APOSTOLICAL CANONS offers explicit evidence of the necessity of using incense: "If any bishop or presbyter offer any other things at the altar, besides that which the Lord ordained for the sacrifice . . . let him be deposed . . . excepting oil for the lamps, and incense" (1956, p. 594). Commenting on this law, *The Rudder* adds, "No one is permitted to offer anything else on the altar except oil for the purpose of illumination, and incense, at the time when divine liturgy is being celebrated" (Cummings, 1957, p. 5).

Cross, Manual

In the course of performing any ecclesiastical function, whether inside or outside the church, the patriarch, bishop, or priest must hold in his right hand a cross called *ṣalīb yadd*. With it he makes the sign of the cross over the oblations on the altar, the baptismal water, the heads of the betrothed during the wedding ceremony, or those to be given absolution. He holds it during the reading of the Gospel, while delivering a sermon, and when blessing members of the congregation or their homes.

When a patriarch or bishop is consecrated or a priest is ordained, he is given a manual cross as a token of the authority he receives in the name of Jesus Christ. Its use during the liturgy signifies that he is the minister of Jesus Christ who is the Shepherd and Guardian of souls (1 Pt. 2:25). It also stands for the power Christians can derive through prayer, for just as Christ conquered death and opened the gates of His Kingdom for believers, they can resort to the cross as a weapon with which to fight evil.

Cruet

A cruet is a small vessel with a secure lid, now usually made of glass but in olden times sometimes made of gold or silver, and ornamented with crosses or verses from the Gospel. Two cruets are used during the Divine Liturgy, one for wine and the other for water. In some churches one cruet may be used, from which first the wine and then the water is poured into the chalice (see EUCHARISTIC VESSELS). Larger cruets may also be used on festive occasions where a particularly large congregation is expected to partake of Holy Communion.

Before the celebration of Divine Liturgy, and in keeping with church law, the EUCHARISTIC WINE is first poured into a cup, and the priest looks very carefully to make sure it is free from defect before it is offered for the SACRAMENT OF HOLY COMMUNION (al-Safī al-Dīn Ibn al-'Assāl, 1927, p. 126).

Following the offertory prayers, the priest places the EUCHARISTIC BREAD (in Arabic called *ḥamal*, the Lamb [of God]) inside a silk-mat *lifāfah* (see EUCHARISTIC VEIL) and holds it to the top of his forehead; the deacon does the same with the cruet of wine. Both then make a circuit once around the altar, the priest saying, "Glory and honor, honor and glory unto the All-Holy Trinity; the Father, the Son and the Holy Spirit," and so on. The deacon says, "Pray for these sacred, precious oblations, for our sacrifices and for those who have offered them." Then the priest makes the sign of the cross over both the bread and the wine, places the bread on the paten, takes the cruet from the deacon, and pours the wine into the chalice, completely emptying the cruet. He returns it to the deacon, who wipes it and takes it back to its proper place.

Cruets are also used to hold the following sacramental oils: (1) the holy chrism, the cruet of which may only be handled by the priest, who ensures that it is stored in a securely locked place near the baptismal font, keeping its key in his possession; (2) the kallielaion (or galileon), the oil of the CATECHUMENS, used in the baptismal service (this cruet must also be kept beside the chrism cruet); and (3) the oil for the sick, over which prayers are said on the Friday preceding the Holy Week. These three kinds of chrismal oil must be carefully preserved in cruets with the name clearly indicated outside. Among the contents of some ancient Coptic churches are found curious forms of cruets or CHRISMATORIES, such as the one in the Church of ABŪ SAYFAYN in Old Cairo, described by A. J. Butler (1884, Vol. 2, p. 56) as being "a curious round wooden box with a revolving lid. The box is solid throughout, but has three holes scooped out inside, in each of which is deposited a small phial of oil."

Eucharistic Bread Basket

The eucharistic bread basket is a large wicker basket, with a cross-embroidered lining, to hold the loaves baked for the Eucharist. Only one of the loaves, the most perfect of three or five, is chosen for consecration as the "Lamb" (*ḥamal*), and the remaining loaves are kept for distribution as blessed bread among the congregation at the end of the service.

Fan

A fan made of ostrich or peacock feathers, linen cloth, thin sheets, or fine threads of metal is sometimes used in the church during the Divine Liturgy to drive away flies and other insects from the chalice. It usually carries a drawing of the six-winged cherubim or is made in the shape of the cherubim, but is rarely used in modern churches.

According to the APOSTOLIC CONSTITUTIONS, "Two deacons on each side of the altar hold a fan made of thin vellum, or peacock's feathers, to drive away flies or gnats, lest they fall into the chalice" (*Constitutions of the Holy Apostles*, 1951, p. 486). These deacons represent the cherubim whose wings flap in reverence at the sanctity of the divine mysteries. The DIDASCALIA lays down similar rules to be observed during the celebration of the Holy Eucharist.

Metal fan for liturgy. *Courtesy Coptic Museum, Cairo.*

Metal fans are still in use in Syrian and Armenian Orthodox churches. In the Roman Catholic church, however, where fans had been used since the sixth century, they have been out of use since the fourteenth century (Venables, 1908, Vol. 1, p. 677). In the Greek Orthodox church, fans were in common use in the sixth century but are no longer used. Cyril of Scythopolis, a contemporary ecclesiastical historian, related how "Domitian [stood] at the right side of the holy table, while St. Euthymius was celebrating, with the mystical fan just before the Trisagion" (1939).

In ceremonial processions during the consecration of bishops and ordination of priests, large metal fans with long handles are carried, together with crosses, Gospel books, and candles. Likewise, in the procession held during the preparation and consecration of the chrism, fans are carried in the circuit. Manuscript 44 at the Vatican Library includes a detailed description of the myron procession. Two subdeacons would carry candles, twelve deacons would carry fans, and twelve priests would carry censers; then the high priest would follow carrying the chrism, surrounded by other bishops holding fans and crosses.

Metal box for holding the Gospel (Textus case). Seventh century. *Courtesy Coptic Museum, Cairo.*

Gospel

This is a book bound in metal in which is enclosed a copy of the four Gospels or the complete New Testament, in Coptic or Arabic (sometimes both), and which is placed on the altar during the church services. It may be made of silver or gold and usually measures about 6 inches (15 cm) by about 4.5 inches (11 cm). On one side it has the embossed representation of the Virgin Mary carrying the infant Jesus, with one of the Evangelists in each corner, and on the other side, the saint to whom the church is dedicated.

In the early centuries, because copies of the New Testament were rare and costly, they had to be protected and venerated in such ornate cases, and craftsmen vied in producing highly artistic ones, decorated with crosses and sometimes studded with gems, together with verses chosen from the Gospels and Coptic inscriptions meaning "The Gospel of our Lord, God, and Savior Jesus Christ" (see GOSPEL CASKET).

During the celebration of the Divine Liturgy, the deacon holds the Gospel and a cross while making a circuit around the altar. The book is held by the priest during the reading from the Gospel and during the blessing at the evening and the morning offerings of incense; it is kissed by members of the congregation before they leave.

The Gospel book is also carried during processions. The Coptic church in Jerusalem uses two large gilt books, each embossed with a representation of the Crucifixion on one side and the Resurrection on the other side. These are carried by two priests or deacons.

The custom of placing the Gospel book on the altar follows an old tradition. According to E. Bishop, "it was regarded as representing our Lord Himself, just as the Altar came to be conceived as the Throne of the Great King" (1962, p. 21).

Incense Box

The box or case for incense is usually of silver or carved wood. It is placed at the right hand of the officiating priest. A small spoon is usually placed in the incense box and used for putting the incense in the censer.

BIBLIOGRAPHY

'Abd al-Masīḥ Ṣalīb al-Mas'ūdī. *Kitāb al-Khūlājī al-Muqaddas.* Cairo, 1902.

______. *Al-Kanīsah Bayt Allāh.* Alexandria, 1979.

Atchley, E. G. *A History of the Use of Incense in Divine Worship.* London and New York, 1909.

Athanasius, Bishop. *Kitāb Tartīb Qismat Rutab al-Kahanūt wa-Takrīs Jamī' Awānī al-Madhbaḥ.* Cairo, 1959.

Bishop, E. *Liturgica historica.* Oxford, 1962.

Burmester, O. H. E. *The Egyptian or Coptic Church,* p. 26. Cairo, 1967.

Cummings, D. *The Rudder.* Chicago, 1957.

Cyril of Scythopolis. *Kyrillos von Skythopolis,* ed. Edward Schwartz. Leipzig, 1939.

Etheria. *Peregrinatio Aetheriae: The Pilgrimage of Etheria,* trans. M. L. McClure and C. L. Feltoe. London and New York, 1919.

Ḥāfiẓ Dawūd. *Al-Disqūliyyah aw Ta'ālīm al-Rusul* (The Didascalia). 2nd ed. Cairo, 1967.

Ibn al-'Assāl, al-Ṣafī. *Kitāb al-Qawānīn.* Cairo, 1927.

Ibn Sibā' Yūḥannā ibn Abī Zakarīyā. *Kitāb al-Jawharah al-Nafīsah fī 'Ulūm al-Kanīsah,* ed. Viktūr Manṣūr. Cairo, 1902. Latin version *Pretiosa Margarita de scientiis ecclesiasticis,* trans. Vincent Mistrīḥ. Cairo, 1966.

Isidhurus, Bishop. *Al-Kharīdah al-Nafīsah fī Tārīkh al-Kanīsah,* 2 vols. Repr. Cairo, 1964.

Kassāb, H. E. *Majmū'at al-Shar' al-Kanasī.* Beirut, 1975.

Manassā Yuḥannā. *Tarīkh al-Kanīsah al-Qibṭiyyah.* Cairo, 1983.

Manqaryūs 'Awadallah. *Manārat al-Aqdās fī Sharḥ Ṭuqūs al-Kanīsah al-Qibṭiyyah wa-al-Quddās.* Cairo, 1947.

Neale, J. M. *The History of the Holy Eastern Church,* Vol. 1, p. 396. London, 1847.

Rock, D. *The Church of Our Fathers,* Vol. 3. London, 1849–1853.

Tadrus Ya'qūb Malaṭī. *Al-Qiddīsah Maryam fī al-Mafhūm al-Urthūdhuksī.* Alexandria, 1978.

Venables, E. "Flabellum." In *Dictionary of Christian Antiquities,* pp. 675–78. London, 1908.

William Sulaymān Qilādah. *Kitāb al-Disqūliyyah aw Ta'ālīm al-Rusul.* Cairo, 1979.

ARCHBISHOP BASILIOS

LITURGICAL VESTMENTS. The concept of devoting special apparel for use at worship services has its origin in the Old Testament where God commanded Moses to prepare sacred garments that would impart dignity and grandeur to his brother, Aaron, and his sons (Ex. 6:3; Nm. 3:2). Vestments for the high priest included a breast piece, an ephod, a mantle, a checkered tunic, a turban, and a sash. They were made of finely woven linen, studded with precious stones, and adorned with gold, violet, purple, and scarlet yarn. Ordinary priests had to wear simpler and less colorful vestments consisting of tunics, sashes, and headdresses (Ex. 28:40).

In contrast to vestments of other churches, where shape and style varied from time to time, those in use by the Coptic church underwent little modification across the ages. This fact is attested by the writings of such ecclesiastical historians as Abū Daqn (1963), Vansleb (1677, p. 60), Renaudot (1847, Vol. 1, pp. 161–63), and Denzinger (1863, Vol. 1, p. 130).

White is the predominant color in Coptic liturgical garments, this color being the symbol of purity (Ps. 101:7; Is. 1:18; Rev. 3:4–5; etc.). It is also the color in which the angels are always robed (Mt. 28:2–3; Mk. 16:5; Acts 1:10; etc.). The twenty-four heavenly priests are also dressed in white (Rev. 4:4).

Consecration of Liturgical Vestments

Before they are first used, liturgical vestments must be consecrated by a BISHOP, who says the following prayer over them:

> Master, Lord God Almighty, Father of our Lord, God and Savior Jesus Christ, we beseech and entreat Thy goodness, O Lover of man, to accept unto Thee the offerings of Thy servants, which they have dedicated to Thee. Reward them with eternal gifts in return for their ephemeral ones; heavenly for earthly things; and everlasting in lieu of passing ones. Graciously, O Lord, sanctify this vestment, purify it through the grace of Thy Holy Spirit. Purify our souls, our bodies, and our spirits. Grant unto us Thy Heavenly Gift, through Thy Only Son, our Lord, our God, and our Savior Jesus Christ.

Here the bishop makes the sign of the cross over the vestment, consecrating it in the name of the Father, the Son, and the Holy Spirit.

Before the celebration of the Divine Liturgy, a priest's or deacon's vestments have to be signed by the officiating priest in the name of the Trinity, but when a bishop is present, it is he who signs them. While the vestments are being put on, the priest should recite Psalm 30 ("I will extol Thee, O Lord") and Psalm 93 ("The Lord reigneth, He is clothed with majesty"), in addition to Isaiah 61:10: "I will greatly rejoice in the Lord, my soul shall exult in my God, for he has clothed me with the garments of salvation, he has covered me with the robe of righteousness, as a bridegroom decks himself with a garland, and as a bride adorns herself with her jewels."

Each of the three grades of the ecclesiastical hierarchy has its own liturgical vestments. Those of the episcopate can be more elaborate and decorative than the others. Bishops normally wear large bulbous crowns, except in the presence of the patriarch, in which case they wear a special hood known as a *koukoullion*. The bishop of Jerusalem alone may keep his crown on, as he occupies an apostolic metropolitan see.

Cap

The cap is used by bishops as a close-fitting head cover worn under the hood of the *burnus* (cape) and is usually embroidered with golden or silver crosses. It was also worn by deacons during services as a headdress of white silk or linen material with four embroidered crosses around it and an additional small upright cross on top, but this custom has been dropped in many churches where deacons serve bareheaded.

Cape

The cape (Arabic, *burnus*) is a liturgical outer vestment in the form of a loose sleeveless cloak made of linen or silk and embroidered with crosses or other religious inscriptions. It is worn by priests and bishops, the latter having a shield-shaped section attached at the back, studded with precious stones.

Epitrachelion

The epitrachelion is a liturgical vestment worn by priests and bishops over the sticharion (see below). It is a rectangular band of silk or cotton that measures about six feet by nine inches and is embroidered with crosses or, if worn by a patriarch or bishop, with the figures of the twelve apostles. It has an opening for the head, allowing a small section of it to hang down the back while the remainder reaches down in front to the feet.

The wearing of the epitrachelion is a symbolic allusion to the words of the Psalmist that form part of a hymn chanted by the deacons in the presence of the patriarch when he is thus robed: "Praised be God who has poured His grace upon His priests, like the precious oil upon the head, running down upon the beard, upon the beard of Aaron, running down on the collar of his robes" (Ps. 133:2–3). It also signified the act of carrying the cross and assuming the yoke of responsibility on behalf of the congregation.

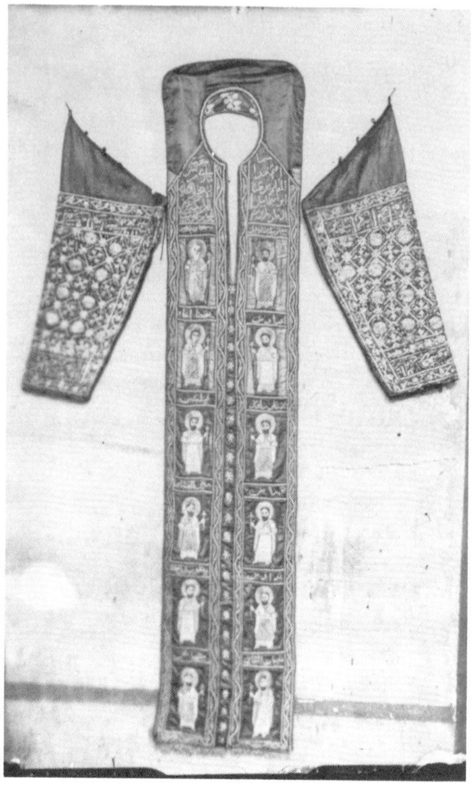

Epitrachelion and two sleeves from the Saint Mark Ezbekieh Cathedral (c. 816). *Courtesy Coptic Museum, Cairo.*

Girdle

The girdle is a band of silk or linen embroidered with golden or silver crosses. Its use is nowadays restricted to bishops on certain ceremonial occasions, though in the past, it formed part of the liturgical vestments of priests and bishop alike. It is worn over the epitrachelion around the waist, with its two ends held together by means of a silver clasp.

The girdle stands for the concept of virtue and piety: "Righteousness shall be the girdle of his waist and faithfulness the girdle of his loins" (Is. 11:5). It also symbolizes vigilance and watchfulness: "Let your loins be girded and your lamps burning" (Lk. 12:35). It is associated with the leather girdle that John the Baptist wore round the waist (Mt. 3:4) and with Saint John's vision of Christ "clothed with a long robe and with a golden girdle round his breast" (Rev. 1:13).

As a liturgical vestment, the girdle was first introduced by the Coptic church. "The use of the girdle in the Coptic Church is more ancient than in the churches of western Christendom," wrote A. J. Butler (1884, Vol. 2, p. 126), who in some churches in Old Cairo had seen fine examples that date back to the eighth century.

As a monastic vestment, the girdle is still an essential part of a monk's garments, made of leather to follow the example of the Baptist and of Saint Antony the Great, the Father of Monks.

Miter

Known in Arabic as *tāj*, the miter, or crown, is a bulbous headdress ornamented with silver or gold and surmounted by a cross. It may also be studded with gems and decorated with the figures of Christ, the Virgin Mary, and the apostles.

The miter is worn by the patriarch and the bishops during the liturgy and in ceremonial processions. It is one of the insignia that, according to the Rite of Consecration of the Patriarch of Alexandria, is bestowed upon the selected patriarch by the senior bishop, the metropolitan of Jerusalem and the Near East, while the deacons sing, "The Lord reigns; he is robed in majesty" (Ps. 93:1) and "Thou settest a crown of pure gold on his head. He asked life of Thee, and Thou givest it him" (Ps. 21:3–4). Here the bishops, with the exception of the metropolitan of Jerusalem, remove their own miters and cover their heads with the omophorion (see below).

Omophorion

This vestment, referred to as the "white *ballin*" in the ordination service of bishops, is a silk scarf about 13 feet (4 m) long and 4 feet (1.25 m) wide, embroidered with large golden or silver crosses, and sometimes ornamented with precious stones.

It may also be worn at the liturgy, on top of the turban, instead of the *burnus*-hood, and folded crosswise on the chest and the back. As a garment, the omophorion symbolizes the breastplate of faith (1 Thes. 5:8), the crown of thorns placed on Christ's head, and the napkin brought by Nicodemus to the burial of Christ.

Orarion

The orarion is a strip of silk or cotton material measuring about 10 feet (3 m) by 6 inches (15 cm) and embroidered with crosses or IC (the first two letters of the name of Jesus Christ). It is worn by deacons over the sticharion (see below). The center section of the strip is held under the right arm and passed upward to the left shoulder across the breast and then allowed to hang down loosely to the feet in front and the back.

Though now commonly used by all ranks of the diaconate (i.e., readers, subdeacons, and deacons), the orarion was originally restricted to deacons alone. According to canon 22 of the Synod of Laodicea (343–381), "the subdeacon has no right to wear an orarion"; similarly, canon 23 says that "the anagnosts [readers or lectors] and psalts [cantors] have no right to wear oraria and thus read or chant." The Coptic church, however, rarely enforced this prohibition, and the orarion forms an essential part of all deacons' vestments, the only difference being that now the lower ranks of the diaconate, among them teenagers, wear it with a horizontal section in the front (in the form of an H) and crossed on the back (in the form of an X).

In the ordination service of a deacon, the officiating bishop, having read the prayers at the altar on behalf of the candidate, turns to the west and places the orarion on the candidate's left shoulder, saying, "Glory and honor to the Holy Consubstantial Trinity."

Sleeves

Sleeves are made of the same material as the epitrachelion and are worn over the sleeves of the sticharion (see below) and fastened with loops and buttons. Although they form part of the liturgical vestments of patriarchs, bishops, and priests, sleeves are now reserved for ceremonial occasions. They are embroidered with braid crosses or studded with gems, and may also have embroidered biblical inscriptions, such as "The right hand of the Lord is exalted: the right hand of the Lord does valiantly" (Ps. 118:16) on the right sleeve and "Thy hands have made me and fashioned me; give me understanding that I may learn thy commandments" (Ps. 119:73) on the left.

The use of sleeves as part of sacerdotal dress may have originated in the Coptic church, from which it later spread to other Eastern and Western churches—a fact for which there is the testimony of A. J. Butler: "Unless we take refuge in the theory of a quite independent origin for this peculiar priestly ornament in the eastern churches and in the Church of Gaul, we are driven to the conclusion that epimanikia [sleeves] were brought from the East—perhaps by some colony of Egyptian monks, such as we know came over to Gaul and to Ireland in the earliest Christian times—and were deliberately adopted by the Gallic clergy. If this idea of eastern influence be correct, it is not merely curious when taken in connection with other tokens of the same influence in the early British and Irish Churches; but it furnishes also an argument for the extreme antiquity of the Coptic sleeves as a sacred vestment" (1884, Vol. 2, pp. 171–72).

The same author expressed particular admiration for a pair of sleeves at the Church of Abū Kīr wa Yūḥannā "made of crimson velvet and richly embroidered with stars and crosses wrought in massive thread of silver. . . . Round either end runs a double border enclosing designs, and while one sleeve is ornamented with a representation of the Virgin Mary and her Son, the other has a figure of an angel with outspread wings. Nothing can exceed the fineness of the needlework and the delicacy of the colours in which these figures are embroidered" (1884, Vol. 2, pp. 166–67).

Slippers

According to Ibn al-'Assal's *Kitāb al-Qawānīn* (1927, p. 121), which sets down the provisions of Coptic ritual, shoes are not allowed inside the sanctuary as a sign of respect for its sanctity and as an implied expression of an inner feeling of security and absence of danger in the house of God; thus, the footwear used by bishops, priests, and deacons is a pair of slippers, made of cotton, wool, or knitted material. The custom of removing the shoes upon entering the church building itself, not merely the sanctuary, was a common practice down to the end of the nineteenth century and may still be observed in the villages of Upper Egypt and, of course, in monasteries. This is done in obedience to God's commandment to Moses (Ex. 3:5) and to Joshua, the son of Nun (Jos. 5:15).

Sticharion. *Courtesy Coptic Museum, Cairo.*

Sticharion

The sticharion is a long-sleeved linen vestment. In his compendium of church ordinance, Ibn al-'Assāl enjoined that the sticharion must be white, not colored, and must reach down to the ankles (1927, chap. 12). It has an opening on one or both shoulders, with buttons and loops. It is worn by various orders of the clergy from bishops down to subdeacons (the higher the rank, the more ornate the embroidery) and is usually adorned with crosses on the front, back, and sleeves. In the past, some sticharia were ornamented with the figure of the Virgin Mary holding the infant Jesus on her left arm, and, below, the figure of Saint George slaying the dragon. Other sticharia had embroidered crosses surrounded with the name of Jesus Christ and some verses from the Gospels and, on each sleeve, an angel with outspread wings. As an expression of the majesty of the Blessed Sacrament, some bishops wear sticharia set with gems or, following an Old Testament tradition, have small bells attached to the sleeves.

It is probable that the term sticharion originally meant a dress used in everyday life. SOZOMEN, who mentioned in his writings that one of the charges brought against ATHANASIUS I by the Arians was that he had required the Egyptians to furnish contributions of linen sticharia, described them as *chitōnion linōn phoron:* "Accordingly, came the first indictment that he had imposed upon the Egyptian a tax on linen tunics" (1864, 2.22; Socrates, 1864, 1.27; *Dictionary of Christian Antiquities,* 1880, Vol. 2, pp. 1933–34).

When a priest or deacon puts on the sticharion to celebrate the liturgy, he is to recite Psalm 30 ("I will extol thee, O Lord, for thou hast drawn me up, and hast not let my foes rejoice over me") and

Psalm 93 ("The Lord reigns; he is robed in majesty").

Ṭaylasān

The *ṭaylasān,* or *shamlah,* is a shawllike strip of white linen or silk, usually embroidered with crosses, worn by priests over the head and shoulders.

BIBLIOGRAPHY

'Abd al-Masīh Ṣalīb al-Mas'ūdī. *Al-Khūlājī al-Muqaddas,* 195–96. Cairo, 1902.

Abū al-Barakāt ibn Kabar. *Miṣbaḥ al-Ẓulmah fī Iḍāḥ al-Khidmah.* Cairo, 1971.

Abū Daqn. *History of the Jacobites,* trans. E. Sadleir. London, 1693.

Butler, A. J. *The Ancient Coptic Churches of Egypt,* Vol. 2, pp. 118–19, 124–27, 134–42, 163–72; Vol. 14, pp. 127–35. Oxford, 1884.

Canons of the Synod Held in the City of Laodicea, In *A Select Library of the Nicene and Post Nicene Fathers of the Christian Church,* 2nd ser. Vol. 14. Grand Rapids, Mich., 1956.

Denzinger, H. *Ritus Orientalium.* Würzburg, 1863.

Duchesne, L. *Origines du culte chrétien,* p. 376. Paris, 1889.

Ibn al-'Assāl, al-Ṣafī. *Kitāb al-Qawānīn,* p. 121. Repr. Cairo, 1927.

Ibn Sibā' Yūḥannā ibn Abī Zakariyyā. *Kitāb al-Jawharah al-Nafīsah fī 'Ulūm al-Kanīsah,* ed. Viktūr Manṣūr. Cairo, 1902. Latin version *Pretiosa Margarita de scientiis ecclesiasticis,* trans. Vincent Mistrīḥ. Cairo, 1966.

Ibrāhim Jabrah. *Ṭuqūs al-Kanīsah,* Vol. 1, pp. 62–64. Cairo, 1947.

Malaṭi, T. Y. *Christ in the Eucharist,* Vol. 5, pp. 288–92. Alexandria, 1973.

Manqariyūs 'Awaḍallah. *Manārat al-Aqdās fī Sharḥ Ṭuqūs al-Kanīsah al-Qibṭiyyah wa-al-Quddās,* 3rd ed., Vol. 2, pp. 40–42. Cairo, 1981.

Norris, H. *Church Vestments: Their Origin and Development.* London, 1949.

Percival, H. R. "Excursus on the Vestments of the Early Church." In *A Select Library of the Nicene and Post-Nicene Fathers of the Christian Church,* ser. 2, Vol. 14, ed. P. Schaff and H. Wace. Grand Rapids, Mich., 1971.

Renaudot, E. *Liturgiarum Orientalium Collectio,* 2nd ed., Vol. 1, 2. Frankfurt, 1847.

Vansleb, J. M. *Histoire de l'église d'Alexandrie.* Paris, 1677.

Yūḥannā Salāmah. *Kitāb al-La'ālī' al-Nafīsah fī Sharḥ Ṭuqūs wa-Mu'taqadāt al-Kanīsah,* Vol. 1. Cairo, 1909.

ARCHBISHOP BASILIOS

LITURGIES, MELODIES OF COPTIC. *See* Music, Coptic: Description.

LOANS. *See* Law, Coptic: Private Law.

LŌBSH, Arabic term [from Coptic ⲗⲱⲃϣ (lōbsh), crown, consummation] used for the title of the final stanza in certain hymns. A *lōbsh* serves as a conclusion for THEOTOKIA except on Sunday. The *lōbsh* of the theotokia of Saturday has two sections known as the first and second SHĀRAH. The many *lōbsh* of the theotokia for Monday and Tuesday are sung to an ADĀM melody. Those for Wednesday through Saturday are sung to a WĀṬUS melody. A *Lōbsh Adām* (sometimes called *psali*) follows the first and second odes (see HŌS), but the second *psali,* which follows the third ode, is properly a *Lōbsh Wāṭus.*

It should be noted that the *Lōbsh Wāṭus* varies according to the season. Thus, there is one for the feasts of the Lord and the days of rejoicing, another for the month of Kiyahk, and so on. These are in addition to the one used for the remainder of the year (*al-Laḥn al-Sanawī*) and sometimes called *Bikawarnidās.*

In *Al-Abṣalmūdiyyah al-Muqaddasah al-Kiyahkiyyah* (1911), additional sections, each called a *lōbsh,* are written after each *lōbsh* of the odes and theotokia, and are concluded by a ṬARḤ.

Those additional *lōbsh* sections given after the original *lōbsh* of each theotokia are in fact selections of the various explanations, interpretations, or paraphrases given in detail in the manuscripts published by De Lacy O'Leary. Their use is optional.

[*See also* Music, Coptic: Description.]

BIBLIOGRAPHY

Al-Abṣalmūdiyyah al-Muqaddasāh al-Kiyahkiyyah (Psalmodia for the Month of Kiyahk). Cairo, 1911. Reprinted Cairo, 1982.

Kitāb al-Abṣalmūdiyyah al-Sanawiyyah al-Muqaddasah (Psalmodia for the Whole Year). Cairo, 1986.

O'Leary, De L. *The Coptic Theotokia.* London, 1923.

EMILE MAHER ISHAQ

LONGINUS, a sixth-century missionary, who, according to ecclesiastical historians, played an important role in bringing Christianity to the Nubian kingdoms both of NOBATIA and of 'ALWA. Information about his life and activities is found in the work of his contemporary, John of Ephesus, and in the later writers Eutychius and AL-MAQRĪZĪ. According to John of Ephesus, he was an Alexandrine who became a member of the Monophysite church of Antioch, and was subsequently dispatched to Constantinople as an envoy of Patriarch Paul of Antioch. He was apparently detained in Constantinople throughout the reign of JUSTINIAN, and subsequently under Justin was imprisoned for a time for his Monophysite sympathies. Escaping from prison, he returned to Egypt in the year 567 and was thereupon ordered by the Patriarch THEODOSIUS I to undertake missionary work in the northern Nubian kingdom of Nobatia. His labors here had been preceded by those of JULIAN the Evangelist and of Theodore, who began the conversion of the Nobatians in 543, but there had been an interruption of missionary activity after 551. Longinus evidently found a great deal still to do, for he remained in Nobatia for six years.

In 575 Longinus returned to Alexandria to assist in the election of a new Monophysite patriarch. He became embroiled in a dispute between Syrian and Egyptian claimants and, having backed the wrong party, was forced into exile for several years on the Arabian Peninsula. In 580 he returned once more to Nobatia, and shortly afterward proceeded onward to the southern Nubian kingdom of ʿAlwā, whose king had previously sent him an invitation. Longinus was not able to travel directly up the Nile from Nobatia to ʿAlwā because of the opposition of the intervening kingdom of MAKOURIA, which had apparently adopted the Melchite Christian confession. As a result the missionary was forced to travel through the Eastern Desert, in the company of a Beja camel caravan. After considerable hardships he arrived in ʿAlwā, where he was met by a royal deputation and conducted directly to the king. According to John of Ephesus the mission was a complete success, and the conversion of the whole kingdom was soon accomplished. Longinus then sent a report of his success to the king of Nobatia, with instructions that it should be forwarded to Alexandria. The recorded biography of Longinus closes on this triumphal note, and no information is given as to his subsequent career.

[*See also:* Nubia, Evangelization of.]

BIBLIOGRAPHY

Adams, W. Y. *Nubia, Corridor to Africa*, pp. 441–43. Princeton, N.J., 1977.

Gadallah, F. A. "The Egyptian Contribution to Nubian Christianity." *Sudan Notes and Records* 40 (1959):38–43.

Monneret de Villard, U. *Storia della Nubia cristiana*, pp. 65–70. Orientalia Christiana Analecta 118. Rome, 1938.

Vantini, G. *Christianity in the Sudan*, pp. 44–50. Bologna, 1981.

WILLIAM Y. ADAMS

LONGINUS OF ENATON, SAINT. *See* Enaton.

LOOMS. *See* Textiles, Coptic: Manufacturing Techniques.

LORD'S DAY. *See* Sunday.

LORD'S PRAYER, the model prayer taught by Jesus Christ to His disciples in Matthew 6:9–13 and in Luke 11:2–4, but in different contexts and in slightly differing words. In Matthew it follows an instruction on prayer in the Sermon on the Mount, and in Luke it is given by Christ to His disciples in answer to their request "Lord, teach us to pray." The form in Matthew is the one used universally by Christians; that in Luke is shorter.

Many Greek Gospel manuscripts, but not the oldest, add the following phrase or a variation of it: "For thine is the Kingdom and the power and the glory forever. Amen." This doxology was used by the Jews at the time of Christ and was probably added to the Lord's Prayer in early times, for it appears in the DIDACHE version of the prayer (c. first century) and is used by Christians in the East. It is found in all the Syriac versions, in the Sahidic version, and in some Bohairic manuscripts. On the other hand, it is wanting in the Old Latin version and in the Vulgate.

In the Coptic church, the regular ending of the Lord's Prayer is not the doxology but the words "through Jesus Christ our Lord," which are added in accordance with John 14:13 and 16:23, 26. Although the doxology does not appear in the Coptic liturgical books at the end of the Our Father, virtually all Copts say it after the phrase "through Jesus Christ our Lord."

From early times the Lord's Prayer was adopted for liturgical purposes. It has regularly found a place in the celebration of the EUCHARIST and was taught to CATECHUMENS at baptism. Its suitability for the Eucharist is stressed by early commentators, who lay emphasis on petitions for the forgiveness of sins and, above all, for the daily, or rather heavenly, bread.

From Saint JOHN CHRYSOSTOM onward, liturgical commentators in the East have witnessed to its use after the eucharistic prayer as a preparation for Communion. In the West, Saint Ambrose and Saint Augustine presuppose its use after the fraction for the same purpose.

In short, all the historic non-Byzantine Eastern rites and all non-Roman Western rites place the Lord's Prayer after the breaking of the bread, which follows the eucharistic prayer. In the Roman rite, since Gregory the Great (d. 604), it precedes the fraction, as in the Byzantine rite.

It is to be noted that while at Jerusalem the bishop and people recited the prayer together, in the West it appears to have been treated as a part of the eucharistic prayer and therefore recited by the celebrant only. This was the case in Africa in Saint Augustine's time.

In the three liturgies now used in Egypt (namely, those of Saint BASIL, Saint Gregory, and Saint CYRIL, otherwise known as that of Saint Mark), the Lord's Prayer is said aloud by the people at the end of the Prayer of the FRACTION (before the embolism). Then the celebrant priest recites the Lord's Prayer inaudibly before the communion, after saying, "Release, forgive, and pardon us our transgression, God. . . ."

The Lord's Prayer also forms a part of the introductory prayers of the Coptic church, said at the beginning of every service with the exception of that of the Divine Liturgy, where only the Prayer of Thanksgiving is recited. The people recite the Our Father together aloud or inaudibly with uplifted hands. Then they sing together with the choir its ending "through Christ Jesus our Lord."

The Lord's Prayer is now recited at the end of each service, even if it is not required by the liturgical books.

In the Book of CANONICAL HOURS the Lord's Prayer is said thrice, i.e., at the beginning, after the Trisagion with its additions, and after "Holy, Holy, Holy, Lord of Sabaoth. . . ."

In the PSALMODIA at the office of midnight prayer, the Lord's Prayer is said at the beginning and at the end after "Holy, Holy, Holy."

In the evening and the morning offerings of INCENSE, it is said thrice—at the beginning, after the Trisagion (see MUSIC) with its additions, and before the Prayer of the Three Absolutions.

During Holy Week, the Lord's Prayer is said after the Old Testament lessons of each hour. Again it is said twelve times each hour following the hymn "Thine is the power and the glory," which is sung twelve times, with a recital of the Lord's Prayer following each.

In the Service of Engagement, and similarly in the Service of Betrothal, an engagement or the betrothal is proclaimed thrice "in the name of our Lord . . . Jesus Christ," followed each time by the Lord's Prayer (see MATRIMONY).

It is also said by the congregation before the Prayer of Absolution, not only at the morning and evening offerings of incense but also at many other services.

BIBLIOGRAPHY

Burmester, O. H. E. *The Egyptian or Coptic Church,* pp. 128, 320. Cairo, 1967.

Chase, F. H. *The Lord's Prayer in the Early Church.* Texts and Studies 1, no. 3. Cambridge, 1891.

Dix, D. G. *The Shape of the Liturgy,* p. 130. Glasgow, 1945.

Drower, E. S. *Water into Wine,* p. 184. London, 1956.

Lowe, J. *The Interpretation of the Lord's Prayer.* Evanston, Ill., 1955. Rev. ed., ed. C. S. C. Williams. Oxford, 1962.

EMILE MAHER ISHAQ

LOUVRE MUSEUM. The oldest evidence of Coptic objects entered at the Louvre Museum appears in the inventory of the Department of Egyptian Antiquities, drawn up under Napoleon III and finished in 1857. Nevertheless, it is difficult to prepare an assessment of them, given that the inventory of the collections was not so precise as at present.

Between 1870 and 1895, under the curatorship of Eugène RÉVILLOUT, the museum gave special consideration to Coptic and demotic documents. During this period, numerous purchases of Coptic manuscripts, papyri, and ostraca took place. George Bénédite, curator of the Department of Egyptian Antiquities from 1895 to 1926, undertook a policy of fairly massive purchases in Egypt itself. From his missions he brought back to the Louvre objects of the Coptic period, purchased for the most part from antiquities dealers in Cairo. But it was the great excavations of the end of the nineteenth century and the first half of the twentieth that truly provided the nucleus of the Coptic section of the Louvre Museum.

Beginning in 1897, Emile Guimet, a manufacturer in Lyons, charged Albert-Jean Gayet to ensure the direction of excavations on the site of ANTINOOPOLIS in Middle Egypt, which continued to 1910. They were subsidized in turn by the Guimet Muse-

Louvre Museum, Coptic Collection. *Courtesy Louvre Museum, Paris.*

um, the Chamber of Commerce in Lyons, the Société du Palais du Costume, the Ministry of Public Education and Fine Arts, and finally the Société française des Fouilles archéologiques. Quantities of objects were then directly given to the Louvre, such as the "Antinoë veil" in 1906, but the largest part of the fruit of the excavations belonged to the Guimet Museum, founded in Lyons in 1879 and transferred to Paris in 1888. It was only in 1948 that the whole of the Egyptian collection, containing very important Roman and Coptic series, was made over to the Department of Egyptian Antiquities.

The ceding of half the product of the excavations of the monastery of BĀWĪṬ (Middle Egypt), which were undertaken from 1901 to 1905 under the direction of Jean CLÉDAT and which were followed by a campaign directed by Jean MASPERO in 1913, endowed the Louvre with architectural pieces in stone and wood of the first importance. Moreover, it is thanks to this donation that it was possible in 1972 to effect a partial reconstruction of the south church of Bāwīṭ (sixth century) in a room in the Louvre.

Other sites yielded series of objects, always interesting although less numerous: Idfū, Elephantine, Medamud, Ṭūd, Kellia. The resumption of the museum's excavations at Ṭūd (Upper Egypt) in 1982 added a quantity of Coptic ceramics in a very good state of preservation. Gifts, of course, and, above all, purchases continue to be the most common method of acquisition.

It was in 1929 that a room called the Bāwīṭ Room was installed in the Flora Pavilion, bringing together objects from the Greco-Roman and Coptic periods. These collections were later accommodated in two rooms on the ground floor of the Department of Egyptian Antiquities, while the small objects were presented in display cases on the first floor of the Egyptian gallery.

The transfer to the Coptic section of the room called the Serapeum made it possible in 1972 to offer the visitor a homogeneous complex of three rooms, illustrating the evolution and the characteristics of Coptic art from the fourth to the twelfth centuries through all the techniques (stone, wood, tapestry, bronzes, glassware, paintings, ceramics, manuscripts).

The major works were naturally displayed in these rooms; the Antinoë veil (fourth century), the horseman Horus (sandstone, fourth century), the shawl of Sabina (sixth century), the Dionysus conch (limestone, fourth century), Daphne (limestone, sixth century), Aphrodite Anadyomene (limestone, sixth century), the Virgin of the Annunciation (wood, fifth century), the paintings from Kellia (eighth century), the censer with the eagle (bronze, ninth century), the tapestry with the "Triumph of the Cross" (ninth century), Christ and the abbot Menas of Bāwīṭ (painting, sixth-seventh century), and all the architectural elements deriving from Bāwīṭ, placed, where possible in their proper context.

Nevertheless, the objects on display are only a small part of a very much larger whole, preserved in the stores. The sculptures in stone, architectural or funerary (stelae), form a series of about 450 objects; a large number of them come from Bāwīṭ. The objects in wood, whether architectural or movable, number 564.

The most important part of the collection is formed by the fabrics and tapestries (between 3,000 and 4,000 pieces), which allow one to follow the evolution of this technique without a break from the fourth century to the twelfth.

There is a small series of about 200 pieces in ivory and bone.

The series of ceramics is far from negligible—about 250 pieces, to which are to be added 45 stamps in unbaked clay and an important collection of ostraca, impossible to evaluate at the present time.

A collection of objects in leather (footwear and sandals, a pannier adorned with an inscription in incised leather, a fragment of the cover of a codex, several pen cases) may be reckoned at about 200 pieces.

The objects in bronze and other metals (copper, silver) offer an interesting sampling of this technique, both through the quality of some objects (polycandilon, crosses, lamps, censers) and through the variety of the forms of vases (about 300 objects).

There is a small collection of about 120 pieces of glassware, the majority of which are small phials that probably served to contain unguents and perfumes.

An important collection of manuscripts (about 300 papyri, 420 parchments, and 10 wooden tablets) is composed, among other things, of fragments of Gospel books, works of Shenute, and magic texts.

Finally, the section possesses some mural paintings, of which 2 derive from Bāwīṭ and 4 from Kellia (Lower Egypt).

Holdings in the Louvre are inventoried below.

Sculptures on stone. 400 objects, including architectural pieces: friezes (172); capitals (3); broken pediments (2), (fragments: 8); statuary (20), (fr: 5). Other items such as vases (3); stelae (16).

Sculptures on wood. Architectural: friezes (18), (not complete: 7), (fr: 91); statuary (10), (nc: 5), (fr: 13); figurative reliefs (8), (nc: 5), (fr: 13); figurative reliefs (8), (nc: 8), (fr: 22); decorative reliefs (18), (nc: 8), (fr: 46). Other items: vases, pots, ornamental boxes, flasks, keys, combs, incised stamps (139), (nc: 108), (fr: 97).

Ivories and bone. Statuary (8); figurative reliefs (25); decorative reliefs (25); other items such as vases, pots, small boxes with and without decoration, weaving implements (220).

Paintings. Murals (2), (nc: 2); portraits (3), (nc: 1), (fr: 1); figures on wood (nc: 1), (fr: 5); decorative friezes (3), (nc: 2) (fr: 30).

Decorated fabrics. 3,000 objects, including outer garments (10), (nc: 2); bonnets and bags (10), (nc: 4), (fr: 4); undergarments (25), (nc: 20), (fr: 190); hangings (2), (nc: 8); cushion pillow covers (20), (nc: 15), (fr: 15); shawls (6), (nc: 3), (fr: 30).

Ceramics. 200 objects, including decorative vases (31), (nc: 9), (fr: 100); goblets (22), (nc: 5), (fr: 45); lamps (18), (fr: 2); Saint Menas phials (20); various items such as figurines, crosses, stamps, corks (7), (nc: 3), (fr: 1).

Bronzes. Crosses (10); inscribed crosses (2), censers (12), (nc: 3); braziers (2); candelabra (6); lamps (40), (nc: 12); lamp bases (7); plain vases (13), (nc: 2); decorated vases (4); ornamental finery (8).

Leathers. Shoes and sandals (15), (nc: 38), (fr: 95); boots (nc: 4), (fr: 3).

Metals. Silver (2), plus one censer; iron (12, including one lead ring [?]).

Glass. 120 objects, including vases (67), (nc: 27), (fr: 21); mirrors (4), (nc: 1), (fr: 4).

BIBLIOGRAPHY

Boreux, C. "Antiquités égyptiennes: La Salle de Baouit." *Bulletin des musées de France* 10 (1929):233–40.

______. *Antiquités égyptiennes: Catalogue-guide*, Vol. 1. Paris, 1932.

Bourguet, P. du. *Musée national du Louvre: Catalogue des étoffes coptes*, Vol. 1. Paris, 1964.

______. "L'Aménagement des nouvelles salles coptes du musée du Louvre." *Musées et collections publiques de France* 124 (1973):165–74.

______. "Les Nouvelles Salles coptes du Louvre." *Bulletin de la Société d'archéologie copte* 21 (1975):153–61.

Graviers, J. des. "Inventaire des objets coptes de la Salle de Baouît au Louvre." *Rivista di archeologia cristiana* 9, nos. 1–2 (1932):51–102.

Rutschowscaya, M. H. *Musée du Louvre, Bois de l'Egypte copte: Réunion des musées nationaux.* Paris, 1986.

MARIE-HÉLÈNE RUTSCHOWSCAYA

LUCIAN OF ANTIOCH (c. 250–312), Anatolian biblical scholar and theologian who was martyred. Lucian was born in Samosata and educated at the school of Edessa (both cities in modern Turkey). He became a follower of Paul of Samosata, excommunicated bishop of Antioch (although this has been disputed by F. Loofs [1924] and G. Bardy [1936]). Lucian founded his own school in Antioch, which taught both theology and scriptural exegesis.

A presbyter in the Antiochene diocese, and known for both pious asceticism and scholarly diligence, Lucian produced a recension of the Greek Bible that not only was important in his time but also has continued to be an influence (especially the New Testament) in the Orthodox church to the present time. His version of the Septuagint, based on a knowledge of Hebrew as well as of Greek, circulated with other versions of the Old Testament, and portions of the Lucianic text are still found in current texts of the Bible. While he was not so prolific an author as ORIGEN or Saint JEROME, Lucian may have written one of the creeds presented at the Council of Antioch in 341, and his students published numerous commentaries on biblical books. His school was dedicated to a literal interpretation of the scriptures, as opposed to the allegorical interpretations of the Alexandrian school.

Lucian is best known, perhaps, for being the perpetrator of SUBORDINATIONISM, a teaching about the nature of Christ that later developed into the Arian heresy (see ARIANISM). In fact, ARIUS and others tainted with the heresy claimed to be students of Lucian. Among the more famous "Collucianists" were Arius, Bishop Eusebius of Nicomedia, Menophantus of Ephesus, Theognis of Nicaea, Maris of Chalcedon, Athanasius of Anazarbus, the sophist Asterius, and Bishop Leontius of Antioch. Because of his beliefs, for most of his life Lucian and his school were not in communion with the orthodox church. Toward the end of his life he made peace with the church for both himself and his school. He was tortured and put to death on 7 January 312 in Nicomedia (in modern Turkey), during the persecutions under Emperor Maximinus. Lucian is regarded as a saint in the Roman Catholic church (feast day 7 Jan.) and the Orthodox church (feast day 15 Oct.).

BIBLIOGRAPHY

Bardy, G. *Recherches sur saint Lucien d'Antioche et son école.* Paris, 1936.
Loofs, F. *Paulus von Samosata.* Texte und Untersuchungen 44.5. Leipzig, 1924.
Metzger, B. M. *Chapters in the History of New Testament Textual Criticism,* pp. 1–41. Grand Rapids, Mich., 1963.
Quasten, J. *Patrology,* Vol. 2, pp. 142–44. Utrecht, 1964.

C. WILFRED GRIGGS

LUCIUS OF ENATON. *See* Enaton, The.

LUXOR (al-Uqṣur), a city located in Upper Egypt on the east bank of the Nile about nine miles northeast of Armant. The city occupies part of the area of the ancient city of Thebes, once the prosperous capital of ancient Egypt, which the Greeks called Diospolis Magna. Arab geographers in the Middle Ages called it al-Uqsurayn (the Two Castles) after the two major temples of Luxor, and from this name the modern al-Uqṣur (Luxor) is derived.

Luxor was a bishopric by the eleventh century, as evidenced by the attendance of Bishop Marqūrah of al-Uqsurayn at a synod in 1078 (Munier, 1943, p. 29). Archaeological remains, however, show the imprint of Christianity in the area at a much earlier date. Copts occupied the Temple of Karnak as early as the fourth century. They built churches and monasteries in it, mutilated statues to make crosses from them, and plastered walls in order to paint murals with apostles, saints, and Christian symbols. Climatic changes brought about by the Aswan Dam have virtually destroyed these remains.

BIBLIOGRAPHY

Munier, H. *Recueil des listes épiscopales de l'église copte.* Cairo, 1943.

RANDALL STEWART

LUXOR TEMPLES. The temple of Amun in the middle of the modern town is one of the best preserved temples of the New Kingdom. It was erected by Amenophis III (1408–1372 B.C.) in the place of a smaller older sanctuary. About a century later Ramses II, with a somewhat different building-axis, added in front the present first peristyle and a pylon. All the walls are decorated with numerous finely worked reliefs of the history and the gods of pharaonic times. In the late period the importance of the temple declined. From the time of Nectanebos (378–360) came an outer walled forecourt, from the north gate of which an avenue of sphinxes started. This linked the Luxor temple with the temple of Amun at Karnak.

In the time of Alexander the Great, a chapel was erected in front of the inner sanctuary of this temple for the keeping of the bark of Amun. The walls carry portrayals of the king before the god Amun and his fellow gods.

In the Ptolemaic and Roman periods dilapidation set in. The last repair measures mentioned in the texts took place in the time of the emperor Tiberius (Daressy, 1920, pp. 163–66).

A new phase in the history of Luxor began when the emperor DIOCLETIAN, on the occasion of the suppression of the Upper Egyptian revolt under L. Domitianus (A.D. 297), set up a large legionary camp in the domain of the Amun temple. The area of the temple was converted into a rectangle, the surrounding walls of which were provided with several gates and projecting semicircular towers. Large parts of these fortifications can still be clearly recognized on the ground. The main axis of the temple became the main street of the camp (*via praetoria*), with the *porta praetoria* at the passage way of the pylon. Some internal structures have also survived, such as several colonnades and two tetrastyla at the intersections of the pillared side streets. The *principia*, which in the time of the tetrarchs served the imperial cult, was set up in the chamber at the end of the hypostyle hall. It contained an apse flanked by columns, and on its walls Diocletian and his coregents were portrayed (Deckers, 1979, pp. 640–47; formerly often mistaken for the apse of a Christian church).

Outside the camp there was a civilian settlement, which was never lacking at any Roman base camp, and in the present case continued right into the Arabic period. It is from this civilian settlement that present-day Luxor developed. The camp itself was very probably in operation down to the time of the Persian conquest (619). Whether it was garrisoned again after the retreat of the Persian occupation army is not evident from the sources presently available.

During excavations by the Egyptian Antiquities Service in the region of the Luxor temple, no fewer than five early Christian churches were brought to light in and around the area of the late Roman camp, all of them erected on the BASILICA pattern. The oldest is in front of the temple pylon, and is to be dated to the turn from the sixth to the seventh century. However, only its sanctuary survived. The rest was pulled down when the site was cleared by the Antiquities Service (Abdul Qader, 1968, p. 253). The apse in the east wall of the church was once adorned with an inner circle of applied columns. The northern side chamber had columns in all four corners and was covered with a dome. In front of the apse opening there was a second triumphal arch raised upon lofty columns. The narthex porch with a stair to the roof, a room with recesses, and a large baptistery adjoining on the north side were, according to the survey report (Abdul Qader, 1968, p. 251), added only later.

All the remaining churches are no earlier than the period after the Arab conquest, when the Roman camp was certainly no longer garrisoned. The church in the northeast corner of the pillared court of Ramses II, underneath the mosque of Abū al-Hajjāj later built over it, is today accessible only in the area of the narthex. It is one of the few churches from the early Christian period still standing to the height of the side windows.

Two more churches are on the west side of the temple. The northern one, close to the court of Ramses II, has a very long and narrow ground plan with a narthex extending to the south beyond the width of the church; to this, further rooms whose purpose is not known are attached on the west side. The sanctuary, probably three-part, has been destroyed. In the northeast corner there is an annex with a circular piscina, probably to be identified as a baptismal font.

Of the southwest church, lying a few paces away, only a few pillars have survived. These have been raised again into position, as well as some quite short sections of wall. This church was also provided with a second triumphal arch in front of the apse opening. The western end is covered by the modern road along the river bank.

The fifth church lies again to the north on the east side of the avenue of sphinxes. Besides the usual western return aisle and the narthex in front of it, it has an additional antechamber in the southwest corner and a long narrow hall on the south side. This building is also equipped with a second triumphal arch raised upon columns. The building of this church is to be dated to the seventh century.

BIBLIOGRAPHY

Abdul Qader, M. "Preliminary Report on the Excavations Carried out in the Temple of Luxor, Seasons 1958–1959, 1959–1960." *Annales du Service des Antiquités de l'Egypte* 60 (1968):227–79.

Daressy, G. "Notes sur Louxor à la période romaine et copte." *Annales du Service des Antiquités de l'Egypte* 19 (1920):159–75.

Deckers, J. G. "Die Wandmalereien im Kaiserkultraum von Luxor." *Jahrbuch des deutschen archäologischen Instituts* 94 (1979):600–52.

Grossmann, P. "Eine vergessene frühchristliche Kirche beim Luxor-Tempel." *Mitteilungen des deutschen archäologischen Instituts—Abteilung Kairo* 29 (1973):167–81.

PETER GROSSMANN

LYCOPOLIS. *See* Asyūṭ.

LYCOPOLITAN. *See Appendix.*

M

MAʿADI. *See* Pilgrimages.

MACARIUS I, fifty-ninth patriarch of the See of Saint Mark (932–952) (feast day: 24 Baramhāt). Macarius, who is cited in the HISTORY OF THE PATRIARCHS as Anbā Maqārah, was a native of a village called Shubra near Alexandria. He became a monk of Dayr Anbā Maqār. Nothing is known about his life beyond his selection and his passage through his native village on the way to Alexandria, which had not been the seat of patriarchs since KHĀ'ĪL III. Macarius wished to visit his old mother and show her the glory of his office. But his mother was unhappy and received him with tears and told him that she would rather have seen him in his grave, for as patriarch he must bear the responsibility for a whole nation, something beyond human forbearance. Macarius departed from his mother in profound grief, but nevertheless remained on the throne of Saint Mark for twenty years.

SUBHI Y. LABIB

MACARIUS II, sixty-ninth patriarch of the See of Saint Mark (1102–1128) (feast day: 4 Ṭūt). Macarius, or Abba Maqārah according to the HISTORY OF THE PATRIARCHS, was a monk of Dayr Anbā Maqār when his selection for the the patriarchate was decided by the Cairene delegation of bishops and the clergy together with the Coptic ARCHONS. He was subsequently confirmed by the Alexandrians. He was a middle-aged man of sufficient vigor, knowledge of monastic rules and traditions, and logic to undertake the heavy burdens of the patriarchate, according to the *History of the Patriarchs*.

At first, he was unwilling to accept the nomination and tried to convince the delegates that he was unsuitable because he was the son of a second wife and because he was ignorant of the meticulous details of the priesthood. But the delegation overlooked his arguments and led him to Cairo, where the vizier, al-Afḍal, permitted his passage to Alexandria. Its inhabitants wished to extract from him the promise of patriarchal contributions toward the maintenance of their churches, but he declined and told them that he was an impecunious monk and implored them to relieve him of their requests and let him return to his cell in the wilderness of Wādī Habīb. At this, the Alexandrians were silenced, and he was forced to go to Saint Mark's Cathedral, where he was formally invested with the patriarchal dignity. Afterward, he was led to Cairo, where another consecration was performed in Greek, Coptic, and Arabic in the Church of the Virgin in Old Cairo.

One of the first historic acts of his reign was the acceptance of a decree transferring all financial transactions connected with the land tax (KHARĀJ) from the Coptic calendar year to the Hegira (A.H.) year. Consequently, all state accounts were computed under Islamic rather than Coptic chronology, and the books were now kept only in Arabic.

The eighth year of the reign of Macarius witnessed two significant natural phenomena that disturbed the population of the whole country. First, there came to pass a tempestuous wind that filled the air with desert sand to the extent that the whole sky was darkened, and people thought that the end of the world was coming. Ultimately, however, the wind subsided and the sun broke out to appease the frightened populace. The second was a series of earthquakes, in which some buildings fell, including the church of Saint Michael on Rodah, later restored by Yūsuf ibn Marqūrah.

The writer of the biography quoted in the *History of the Patriarchs,* Yūḥanna ibn Ṣā'id, devotes a lengthy discussion to the vacancy of the bishopric of Miṣr after the death of its bishop, Anbā Sinhāt, which is indicative of the seriousness with which the population regarded the problem of succession. An interesting series of letters is reproduced by the biographer regarding the search for the right candidate to fill that vacancy. Even extraneous dignities like the Armenian patriarch, who was in Cairo at the time, were consulted before a list of twelve candidates was made. The names were deposited at the sanctuary and a young deacon was to draw the name after a period of prayer. He chose John, the spiritual son and former assistant of the deceased bishop. The selection was communicated to the governor for his sanction. He was then consecrated in a formal service conducted by Anbā Mīnā, bishop of Malīj, Anbā Mīkhā'īl, bishop of Aṭfīḥ, Anbā Yuḥannā, bishop of al-Khandaq, and a priest by the name of Basṭah. The consecration took place in the ancient church of Our Lady at Ḥārit Zuwaylah amid tremendous celebrations. The investiture was, of course, sanctioned by the patriarch, and no mention of a CHEIROTONIA was made.

A very interesting event is recorded by the biographer in the *History of the Patriarchs* from the fifth year of the patriarchate of Macarius II that had a direct bearing on the history of the Crusades. The Crusaders, after the capture of Jerusalem in 1099, continued their conquest in southern Palestine and seem to have reached al-Faramā, on the eastern frontier of Fatimid Egypt, around 1106, under the leadership of Baldwin, the Bardawīl of the *History of the Patriarchs.* The soldiers pillaged al-Faramā and set the city ablaze, but they had to withdraw afterward owing to the death of their leader. They were pursued by the Fatimid armies deep into Palestine. But this information cannot be entirely correct. Western sources do not mention anything about Baldwin's death at that time; in fact, he is known to have returned safely to Jerusalem to rule his kingdom.

What is significant about this is the evidence of the feeling of the Copts toward the crusading movement, and specifically Baldwin's expedition: "God protected us from his deeds. We asked Him, whose name is great, to perpetuate his mercy and his grace; and to inspire us to give thanks to Him and to cause us not to forget the remembrance of Him through His goodness and glory." Indeed, no more eloquent a statement on the Coptic view of the Crusades could be found in a purely Coptic source.

The reign of Macarius was almost identical to that of the Fatimid caliph al-'Āmir (1101–1130). The last important event of his caliphate to be cited by the *History of the Patriarchs* is an attempt by three youths from the east to assassinate the caliph and his minister, al-Afḍal ibn Shāhinshāh. Two of them were cut down by the swords of bodyguards, but the third struck al-Afḍal with a sharp knife, and he was carried home to die of his wound. The caliph, who participated in his funeral, returned to seize the immense wealth he left behind, which included jewels, gold and silver objects, precious textiles and robes, the furniture that filled his palace, and bags filled with 4 million gold dinars.

Little is mentioned about the financial treatment of the patriarch, but it must be assumed that he rendered his *kharāj* land tax. He was left by the Islamic administration to live in peace and security with his congregation throughout his patriarchate of twenty-six years.

BIBLIOGRAPHY

Lane-Poole, S. *The Mohammadan Dynasties.* London, 1894.

______. *History of Egypt in the Middle Ages.* London, 1901.

Runciman, S. *History of the Crusades,* 3 vols. Cambridge, 1953–1954.

SUBHI Y. LABIB

MACARIUS III, 114th patriarch of the See of Saint Mark (1944–1945). He was born on 18 February 1872, at the town of al-Maḥallah al-Kubrā in the Gharbiyyah Province. He was named 'Abd-al-Masīḥ. Later, at the early age of seventeen, he entered the monastery of DAYR ANBĀ BISHOI and was ordained priest. In 1895 CYRIL V appointed him private assistant and raised him to the rank of HEGUMENOS.

On 12 July 1897 he was consecrated metropolitan of Asyūṭ, a position that he occupied for about forty-seven years, when he was elected to the throne of Saint Mark on 13 February 1944.

In Asyūṭ he found that foreign missionaries had made strong inroads into the Coptic church. With remarkable zeal he set about revitalizing the debilitated community: building new churches, restoring old ones, and implementing a daring program of education. In 1900 he established the first Coptic school for boys, followed in 1904 by the first Coptic school for girls, run by a highly qualified English schoolmistress with an Egyptian, English, and French staff. He also set up more than thirty elementary schools for the poor throughout the province, as well as three charitable institutions and scores of benevolent societies and religious groups that were subsidized by the community council.

He put the council in charge of financial matters related to the day-to-day running and upkeep of the church and the other institutions, while he devoted his energies to the spiritual welfare of his people.

In 1920 Macarius drew up an ambitious plan of reform incorporating the following points:

1. setting up a theological college in one of the monasteries to provide the church with properly qualified clergy
2. establishing a Supreme Council to run all the Coptic property given to the church
3. organizing ecclesiastical affairs under the direction of the pope and in collaboration with a group of bishops and spiritual leaders
4. forming an education committee at the patriarchate to supervise the teaching of the Coptic language and religious instruction
5. keeping an up-to-date register of poor families.

Such a program won the hearts of all the Copts in his parish. It also prompted the members of the community council of Asyūṭ, some of whom were also members of the general council in the capital, to nominate Metropolitan Macarius as candidate for the patriarchate. This was in open defiance of the prohibition imposed by the church against the candidature of metropolitans to the papal seat.

The other bishops and abbots, however, who were opposed to the idea of any supervision exercised upon their finances by the community council, declared their unwillingness to cede any of their "sacred" rights. The Holy Synod issued a statement to the effect that the pope's relegation of his powers to the community council was an act that broke church laws.

Unable to reconcile these two warring camps, the embittered patriarch withdrew to the monastery of Saint Antony (DAYR ANBĀ ANṬŪNIYŪS) in the Eastern Desert. A few months later, at the request of some bishops and men of goodwill, he agreed to return to his seat, but not long afterward he died. Of the eighteen months that formed his patriarchate, Macarius III spent six months in retreat in the desert monastery as a result of this schism that prevented him from undertaking his long-hoped-for reform.

MOUNIR SHOUCRI

MACARIUS, HOMILIES OF PSEUDO-.

See Pseudo-Macarius, Homilies of.

MACARIUS, SAINT,

Syrian martyr in fourth-century Egypt (feast day: 22 Abīb). Macarius was the son of Basilides, an Antiochene general under the emperor DIOCLETIAN. His Passion is part of the late Basilidian CYCLE, which emerged in Coptic in a Bohairic codex of the ninth century. The first part of the codex is incomplete, but it can be reconstructed from the Copto-Arabic SYNAXARION.

When Diocletian began to persecute Christians, Macarius refused to give up his faith and was denounced. Since Diocletian did not want to upset the city of Antioch by punishing a prominent citizen, he sent Macarius to the prefect Armenius in Alexandria with instructions that he be tortured and put to death.

Actually, Macarius suffers three martyrdoms in Egypt. The first takes place at Alexandria, the second at Pshati (under a Eutychian prefect), and the third at Shetnufe (Shatānūf, another spot in the Delta). After each of the first two, he is miraculously resurrected, according to a well-known device in this kind of Passion (see HAGIOGRAPHY); the third is final. John of Aqfahṣ, a fictitious personage who generated another cycle and to whom the authorship of the text is ascribed, is present at the third martyrdom. The Passion is followed by a passage narrating the following events: Diocletian is punished by heaven and becomes blind. The emperor Constantine restores Christianity and sends the prefect Eulogius to substitute for the recalcitrant Armenius. Eulogius wants to remove the relics of Macarius, but the latter appears in a vision and orders them to be left at Shetnufe, where a large sanctuary is built. For these supplements, the Passions of EPIMA, ISIDORUS, and EUSEBIUS can be consulted.

BIBLIOGRAPHY

Hyvernat, H. *Les Actes des martyrs de l'Egypte tirés des manuscrits coptes de la Bibliothèque Vaticane et du Musée Borgia.* Paris, 1886–1887.

TITO ORLANDI

MACARIUS ALEXANDRINUS, SAINT,

fourth-century monk at Kellia (feast day: 6 Bashans). He is surnamed the Alexandrian or the Citizen to distinguish him from his contemporary, the celebrated Saint MACARIUS THE EGYPTIAN. He was born at the end of the third century in Alexandria, where, before becoming a monk in circumstances not known, he practiced the profession of a mime, or according to other sources, a merchant of preserved fruits. He died in 394 in the desert of the Kellia at almost 100 years of age. PALLADIUS, who arrived in the desert in 391 and devoted to him chapter 18 of his *Lausiac History*, knew him there over three years. He was then the priest of the monastic community of the Kellia, where the "Origenist" monks grouped around EVAGRIUS PONTICUS and AMMONIUS OF KELLIA were numerous. He was probably in sympathy with their ideas. Evagrius mentions him several times in his books and consulted him as a master (cf. Guillaumont, 1971, pp. 698–99). Although resident in the Kellia, according to Palladius, he had small cells in various places, such as in NITRIA and in SCETIS, where he is found in company with Macarius the Egyptian, with whom he suffered exile in 374 at the time of the Arian persecution.

Comparison has often been made between the two Macarii, equals not only in age but also in ascetic virtues, spiritual gifts, and authority. The historian Socrates (*Historia ecclesiastica* 4.23) says that the Alexandrian was very similar to the Egyptian, but that while the latter was austere and reserved, the Alexandrian was smiling and loved to banter with the young monks. We can, in fact, see him bring some humor even into his numerous ascetic exploits. Quite early there was confusion of the two in the stories, especially in the reporting of miracles, of cures, of resurrections of the dead, and even of fantastic tales like the visit far into the desert paid to the mythical paradise of Jannes and Jambres, pharaoh's magicians in the far-off times of Moses. This story is told of the Alexandrian by Palladius (chap. 18) and by the Latin recension of the HISTORIA MONACHORUM IN AEGYPTO (chap. 29), but also of Macarius the Egyptian in the Greek recension of the same work (Festugière, 1971, chap. 21). The same confusion appears in the APOPHTHEGMATA PATRUM. The alphabetical collection places only three apothegms under the name of the Alexandrian (304–305), but among the forty-one placed under the name of the Egyptian (257–282) several probably belong to the Alexandrian.

Macarius the Alexandrian left no writings. The monastic rules put into Latin under his name, whether alone or in association with others (PG 34, pp. 967–982), certainly do not come from him, for there was no written rule at the Kellia in his time, any more than in Nitria or in Scetis. The same is true of a discourse on the fate of souls after death, transmitted in Greek under his name (385–392) and attributed by the Syriac tradition, equally wrongly, to the Egyptian (Lantschoot, 1950, pp. 159–89).

BIBLIOGRAPHY

Cotelier, J. B., ed. *Apophthegmata Patrum.* PG 65, pp. 71–440. Paris, 1864.

Evelyn-White, H. G. *The Monasteries of the Wadi'n Natrūn*, pt. 2; *The History of the Monasteries of Nitria and Scetis.* New York, 1932.

Festugière, A.-J. *Historia Monachorum in Aegypto. Edition critique du texte grec et traduction annotée*, chap. 21. Brussels, 1971.

Guillaumont, A. "Le Problème des deux Macaire dans les Apophthegmata Patrum." *Irenikon* 48 (1975):41–59.

Guillaumont, A., and C. Guillaumont, eds. *Tractatus practicus* by Evagrius Ponticus, 94. Paris, 1971.

Lantschoot, A. van. "Révélations de Macaire et de Marc de Tarmaqā sur le sort de l'âme après la mort." *Le Muséon* 63 (1950):159–89.

ANTOINE GUILLAUMONT

MACARIUS THE CANONIST, monk-priest of the Monastery of Saint JOHN COLOBOS in Wādī al-Naṭrūn (first half of the fourteenth century). Macarius is known only through his great juridical compilation. There are eleven manuscripts in this collection, but three are only eighteenth-century copies of older manuscripts, most of which are either incomplete or lost. Since Abū al-Barakāt (d. 1325), author of an encyclopedia entitled *Misbāḥ al-Ẓulmah* (Lamp of Darkness), does not speak of Macarius' work, it is supposed that Macarius was his contemporary or perhaps was a little younger. It is known that he lived after the patriarch CYRIL III IBN LAQLAQ (1235–1243), whose canons he cites, and that the two oldest manuscripts that contain his compilation are from the years 1350 and 1352.

An enumeration of the texts that contain his canonical collection, or at least an analysis of the two principal manuscripts, will be found in German in the work of W. Riedel (1900, pp. 121–29). There is also an analysis of one of the most complete manuscripts (National Library; Paris, arabe 251) in G. Troupeau's catalogue; the text is published in R.-G. Coquin's edition of the Canons of Hippolytus (PO 31, fasc. 2, pp. 278–79 and 285–95).

Macarius' juridical compilation has preserved

several documents, among them the Arabic *Didascalia*, the *Letter of Peter to Clement*, the canons of Hippolytus, the canons of pseudo-Basil, the canons of pseudo-Gregory of Nyssa, and the canons attributed to Epiphanius.

BIBLIOGRAPHY

Coquin, R.-G. *Les Canons d'Hippolyte*. In PO 31, fasc. 2, pp. 272–444. Paris, 1966.

Riedel, W. *Die Kirchenrechtsquellen des Patriarchats Alexandrien*. Leipzig, 1900; repr. Aalen, 1968.

Troupeau, G. *Catalogue des manuscrits arabes*, Vol. 1; *Manuscrits chrétiens*, fasc. 1. Paris, 1972.

RENÉ-GEORGES COQUIN

MACARIUS THE EGYPTIAN, SAINT, or

Macarius the Great, illustrious fourth-century anchorite in the desert of SCETIS (feast day: 27 Baramhāt). He was called the Great, or the Egyptian, to distinguish him from his contemporary, MACARIUS ALEXANDRINUS. A monastery in Scetis is still called by his name, DAYR ANBĀ MAQĀR.

Macarius the Egyptian was born about 300 in the village of Jijber, situated in the southwest part of the Delta. After living for some time as a hermit near a village, he withdrew about 330 into the Wādī al-Naṭrūn. He first established himself near the lakes that occupy the bottom of the wadi, then penetrated farther south into the desert region where DAYR AL-BARAMŪS is today. He there prepared for himself a cave comprising two rooms, one of which served as an oratory. He then received his first two disciples, to whom tradition has given the names of MAXIMUS AND DOMITIUS, called the Romans. Later he reached the western part of the wadi and installed himself in a cave not far from the place where the monastery that bears his name stands today. It appears that there quickly gathered around him a numerous community of monks who desired to live following his example and his directions. According to RUFINUS (*Historia ecclesiastica* 2.4) and the SYNAXARION (13 Baramhāt), he was deported with Macarius Alexandrinus during the Arian persecution in 374 to an island in the Delta. He returned shortly afterward to Scetis, where he died about 390.

The Coptic sources—the Life of Saint Macarius (falsely attributed to SERAPION OF TMUIS), the collection of the *Virtues of Saint Macarius*, and the Arabic-Jacobite Synaxarion—have a tendency to exaggerate Macarius' relations with Saint ANTONY. Saint Antony is said to have given him the monastic habit, then advised him to accept priesthood. Furthermore, confusing him with another Macarius, superior of the monastery of Pispir, they have him present at the saint's death and burying his corpse. However, Macarius' relations with Antony are well attested by the APOPHTHEGMATA PATRUM, which reports two visits made by Macarius to Antony. He can be considered a disciple of Saint Antony.

The prestige and authority of Macarius were great even during his lifetime, not only among the monks of Scetis but also among those of the deserts of Nitria and the KELLIA. EVAGRIUS PONTICUS, a resident in the Kellia, traveled about 25 miles (40 km) to Scetis to consult Macarius, who was considered by Evagrius to be a master. It was said of Macarius that he was "a god on earth." Immediately after his death, perhaps even in his lifetime, marvelous stories were spread about him, attributing to him many cures and miracles, sometimes confused with those attributed to Macarius Alexandrinus.

According to a narrative preserved in Coptic about the translation of the relics of Saint Macarius, and according to the Arabic-Jacobite Synaxarion, the people of Jijber, learning of the miracles wrought around his tomb after his death, stole the body of Macarius and carried it to their village to a church specially built to receive it. After the ARAB CONQUEST OF EGYPT, since Jijber was in ruins, the body was transferred to another town, Elmi, and in the time of the Patriarch JOHN IV (775–799) brought back to Scetis, where it was deposited in the church of Dayr Anbā Maqār, where it is venerated today.

Various writings have come down under the name of Macarius. The only one that has some chance of being authentic is a letter known in Latin under the title *Ad filios Dei*, extant also in Syriac and Armenian and in the original Greek text, recently edited by W. Strothmann. A rich collection of treatises, letters, and homilies has been handed down in Greek under his name (and sometimes under that of Macarius Alexandrinus), among them the famous fifty *Spiritual Homilies*, some passages of which are found again in the collection of the *Virtues of Saint Macarius*, a late compilation of Greek origin. But since L. Villecourt showed the close relation of these homilies with the Messalian movement, it is generally admitted that these pseudo-Macarian writings are in reality of Syrian origin.

BIBLIOGRAPHY

Amélineau, E. *Histoire des monastères de la Basse-Egypte*. Annales du Musée Guimet 25, pp. 46–234. Paris, 1894.

Cotelier, J. B., ed. *Apophthegmata Patrum*. In PG 65, cols. 257–81. Paris, 1864.
Dörries, H.; E. Klostermann; and M. Kroeger. *Die 50 geistlichen Homilien des Makarios*. Berlin, 1964.
Evelyn-White, H. G. *The Monasteries of the Wadī'n Natrūn*, pt. 1; *New Coptic Texts from the Monastery of Saint Macarius*, pp. 120–35. New York, 1926. Pt. 2. *The History of the Monasteries of Nitria and Scetis*, pp. 60–72. New York, 1932.
Festugière, A.-J. *Historia Monachorum in Aegypto. Edition critique du texte grec et traduction annotée*, pp. 123–28. Brussels, 1971.
Guillaumont, A. "Le Problème des deux Macaire dans les Apophthegmata Patrum." *Irenikon* 48 (1975):41–59.
Strothmann, W. *Die syrische Überlieferung der Schriften des Makarios*, pt. 1, pp. 74–84 (Syriac text); pt. 2, pp. 16–22 (Greek text); pp. 50–55 (German translation). Wiesbaden, 1981.
Villecourt, L. "La Date et l'origine des 'Homélies spirituelles' attribuées à Macaire." Comptes rendus de l'Académie des inscriptions et belles-lettres, pp. 250–58. Paris, 1920.
Wilmart, A. "La Lettre spirituelle de l'abbé Macaire." *Revue d'ascétique et de mystique* 1 (1920):58–83.

ANTOINE GUILLAUMONT

MACARIUS THE GREAT, SAINT. *See* Macarius the Egyptian, Saint.

MACARIUS OF SCETIS, SAINT. *See* Macarius the Egyptian, Saint.

MACARIUS OF TKOW, SAINT (d. 451/452), bishop of Tkow noted for poverty, sanctity, and healing powers who was martyred for opposing the Council of CHALCEDON (feast day: 27 Bābah). The chief source for his life is the *Panegyric on Macarius, Bishop of Tkow* by Pseudo-Dioscorus of Alexandria. This work cannot have been composed earlier than the second quarter of the sixth century. It appears to be based on episodes dealing with Macarius drawn from the Life of Dioscorus by Pseudo-Theopistus of Alexandria, which the author of the *Panegyric* amplified and to which he added other traditional stories. Internal evidence indicates that the *Panegyric* was composed in Greek in or around Alexandria. It survives in Sahidic and Bohairic translations, and several unedited manuscripts of Arabic versions are extant.

The *Panegyric* tells nothing about Macarius' early life or how he came to be a bishop. His diocese of Tkow (Antaiopolis; Qāw al-Kabīr) is located in Upper Egypt roughly halfway between ASYŪṬ and AKHMĪM. The *Panegyric* is meant to be a discourse delivered by DIOSCORUS I, patriarch of Alexandria, to a group of monks who have come to visit him in exile at Gangra in Paphlagonia on the Black Sea. While still in Alexandria, Dioscorus is brought news by the abbot Paphnutius of the brutal death of Macarius for refusing to subscribe to the decrees of the Council of CHALCEDON and the *Tome* of Pope LEO I, which the emperor had submitted to the bishops of Egypt to sign. Dioscorus then begins a long reminiscence about Macarius, beginning with their meeting on the docks of Alexandria, as he and the Egyptian bishops prepare to embark for Constantinople at the command of the emperor Marcian. Macarius is portrayed as a self-effacing man who is poor, who is accompanied by a single companion, and who speaks and understands only Coptic. Dioscorus must converse with him through an interpreter. When Dioscorus' companion, Theopistus, makes a disparaging remark about the inability of Macarius to speak Greek and calls him "this mouthless one," Dioscorus reprimands him and threatens to censure him unless he begs Macarius' pardon. Then in a speech using Old Testament holy war imagery, Dioscorus predicts that Macarius will play a preeminent role in the defense of Egyptian orthodoxy.

Because all the other bishops are able to escape the trip to Constantinople by bribing the imperial messenger, Dioscorus and Macarius embark without them. During the journey, Macarius heals a blind man and miraculously produces evidence that clears an Egyptian sailor who is falsely accused by his non-Egyptian shipmates. During the journey, Dioscorus compels the companion of Macarius, Pinoution, to recount for him some of the bishop's outstanding virtues and miracles, including his victory over demons who inhabited a pagan temple in his diocese. Pinoution also recounts the vision of Abbot SHENUTE, in which the abbot saw Macarius as a champion of orthodoxy, who, because of Shenute's advanced age (he is 109), will fight in his stead at the coming council.

Upon their arrival in Constantinople, Dioscorus has a vision, in which he learns that Macarius will be buried beside the bodies of Saint JOHN THE BAPTIST and the prophet Elisha. When Dioscorus is summoned to the imperial presence, Macarius is denied entrance by a chamberlain because of his shabby attire, which he refuses to change for an earthly ruler. When he is finally admitted through the intervention of Dioscorus, he is unable to participate in the ensuing debate about doctrine because he can find no one to interpret for him. Meanwhile, Dioscorus presents a rousing defense of Egyptian orthodoxy before Marcian and the empress PULCHERIA, convincing the assembled bishops of the correctness of his position.

After this session, an informant tells Dioscorus that there is a plot to murder Macarius, and he reluctantly sends the bishop back to Egypt. Thus, it would seem that Macarius really never gets to attend the Council of Chalcedon but only some sort of preliminary meeting in Constantinople.

Time passes, during which Dioscorus is removed from his see by the Council of Chalcedon and sent into exile by the emperor. An imperial courier arrives at Alexandria and summons the bishops of Egypt to subscribe to the decrees of the council and to the *Tome* of Leo. When Macarius refuses to accept these documents because he does not judge them to be in conformity with the Council of NICAEA, the courier kicks him so savagely that he dies on the spot. His body is prepared for burial amidst a great outpouring of devotion on the part of the Alexandrian populace, and he is laid to rest next to the bodies of John the Baptist and Elisha, as had been prophesied. A cripple who touches his bier is healed, as is a deaf-mute child, who then recounts that he has seen a vision of John the Baptist and Elisha receiving the soul of Macarius. This, in synopsis, is what we are told of the life of Saint Macarius.

Very little of the life of Macarius as set out in the Egyptian sources can be called historical in the modern sense. Like his contemporary, Shenute, he seems to have made no impression outside the anti-Chalcedonian circles of Egypt and Syria. That he existed at all and was bishop of Tkow, fought against paganism in his diocese, supported Dioscorus' stand against the Council of Chalcedon, and, perhaps, met a violent end because of his beliefs, are all possibilities, but they cannot be corroborated from sources outside the pool of Egyptian orthodox tradition. The relics of Saint Macarius the bishop, still venerated at DAYR ANBĀ MAQĀR together with those of MACARIUS THE EGYPTIAN and MACARIUS ALEXANDRINUS, are probably meant to be those of Macarius of Tkow, but this is uncertain. Their proximity to the recently discovered reliquaries of John the Baptist and Elisha at the same monastery may tie in with the tradition that is found in the *Panegyric* about the burial of Macarius next to these two holy men. The presence of the relics of the three Macarii at Dayr Anbā Maqār is first attested in a list made by Mawhūb ibn Manṣūr near the end of the eleventh century.

More significant, however, for Egyptian church history than the details of his life is the role created for Macarius by the pseudonymous author of the *Panegyric*. This work is characteristic of most early Christian hagiography in that it is less interested in historical accuracy and more intent on exhorting its audience to virtuous behavior through the example of the saint. The *Panegyric* can be best characterized as a hagiographical romance situated in a context of anti-Chalcedonian polemics. The author, in spite of an undercurrent of prejudice against the Coptic language and culture, sets out to make Macarius a model Egyptian orthodox hero for the period immediately following the Council of Chalcedon.

First of all, he establishes his saintliness. Macarius is portrayed as someone who practices evangelical poverty, reminiscent of that practiced by the early monks of the desert. He is poorly dressed by choice and carries almost no money when about to sail for Constantinople. When in trouble, he places his trust in God, who delivers him. He has the ability to read men's hearts and to guide them effectively toward repentence and virtue. He has the power to heal the sick, even after he is dead, and is able to drive out demons. He is devoted to orthodoxy and willing to risk his life for the faith in contrast to other bishops who put personal gain and bodily comfort before orthodoxy. In short, he is a Christ-like figure, suitable for imitation.

Second, his credentials as a spokesman for the Coptic-speaking church are established by the vision of Abbot Shenute, the premier Coptic-speaking religious leader of the period. Macarius is also associated with Paphnutius, a Pachomian abbot who himself has ties to Shenute. Thus Macarius is linked to the sources of the two most important traditions of Coptic-speaking Egypt, men who themselves can look back to their close ties with Saint CYRIL I and the Council of EPHESUS. Finally, the author links Macarius to the Greek-speaking patriarch of Alexandria, Dioscorus, Cyril's successor and the defender of his teachings.

Thus, the work welds these two elements, Coptic and Greek-speaking Egyptian Christianity, into a united front against the perceived heterodoxy of the followers of Chalcedon. Whether the work was composed to foster such ethnic unity, or whether it merely reflects and fortifies what was already the case in sixth-century Egypt, is uncertain and must await the further study of Egyptian church history in the period after 451.

A Saint Macarius the bishop (not otherwise specified) is commemorated in various liturgical texts of the Coptic church. It is not possible to confirm that this is Macarius of Tkow, but the identification seems probable. The *Exegesis on the Feast Day of Michael the Archangel* (Pierpont Morgan Library, Codex 592) is attributed to Macarius of Tkow.

BIBLIOGRAPHY

Nau, F. "Histoire de Dioscore." *Journal asiatique*, ser. 10, no. 1 (1903):5–108, 241–310.

DAVID W. JOHNSON, S.J.

MACROBIUS, SAINT, or Makrāwī, fourth-century bishop of Nikiou, who was martyred under DIOCLETIAN (feast day: 2 Baramhāt). Only one very brief fragment of his Passion survives in Bohairic (National Library, Paris, Copte, 151, 1; ed. Devos, 1949), but the "original" text can be reconstructed through an encomium in his honor written by Mena of Pshati (ed. Hyvernat, 1886–1887, pp. 225–46) and through the summary in the Copto-Arabic SYNAXARION.

This text begins with the ecclesiastical career of the martyr, who becomes bishop and is noted for his zeal. Two emissaries of Diocletian have him arrested. There are then the usual scenes of courtroom questioning and of torture. Macrobius is then sent to Alexandria, where Armenius places him in prison. Here he has a vision of Christ and performs many miracles. He is taken into court again and tortured, but is healed by an angel. Armenius tries to have him drowned, casting him adrift in a boat, but without success; he then tortures him anew. Finally Macrobius is beheaded and his body is taken to his home town of Shmūm.

This Passion was constructed in connection with the Cycle of Julius of Aqfahṣ and its structure reveals late features that can be dated to between the seventh and eighth centuries.

BIBLIOGRAPHY

Baumeister, T. *Martyr Invictus. Der Märtyrer als Sinnbild der Erlösung in der Legende und im Kult der frühen koptischen Kirche,* p. 121. Münster, 1972.

Devos, P. "Le Fragment survivant de la Passion Copte de S. Macrobe (MS Paris Copt. 151)." *Analecta Bollandiana* 67 (1949):153–64.

Hyvernat, H. *Les Actes des martyrs de l'Egypte tirés des manuscrits coptes de la Bibliothèque Vaticane et du Musèe Borgia.* Paris, 1886–1887.

TITO ORLANDI

MADAMŪD, town on the east bank of the Nile, about 5 miles (8 km) northeast of Luxor, and from the pharaonic down to the Roman period an important cultic center of the Theban district-god Month, which still emerges from the place-name today. The temple of Month and of the bull Buchis sacred to him derives essentially from the Ptolemaic period, with some extensions from Roman times. As at many pharaonic sites, after its profanation it was taken over by the neighboring settlement, where the inhabitants at the same time used it as a quarry. Excavations by the French mission were carried only so far as to allow a clarification of the layout of the temple. The remains of the late antique settlement brought to light in the process therefore comprise only a small section, which is not enough to afford any idea of its entire arrangement. However, two early Christian churches were discovered. The older is in the area of the temple itself, in the so-called south court, which was provided along its outer wall with a portico supported by columns. By the addition of a second row of columns, this court was converted into a three-aisled basilican chamber. In addition, various partition walls have survived, and in the east, the remains of an apse including a northern side room. The structures as a whole were carried out in mud brick. In reconstruction of the full rounding of the apse, the fact had to be considered that the Ptolemaic portico column at the right front corner still stood upright. That made the strength of the walls greater, and there was no need for the recesses assumed by the excavators at the entrance to the apse (Vincent, 1928, p. 156). In front of the apse there was a bema, raised one step, with the remains of a screen wall. Further, a part of the neighboring room adjoining to the north seems also to have been incorporated into the spatial plan of the church. The walled-up front area of the former south court took on the function of an atrium. Whether the structures at the west wall with a well and various troughs are to be regarded as a baptistery seems doubtful. Other churches also (as several churches in Old Cairo) are provided with wells or cisterns of a similar kind. Chronologically, the erection of this

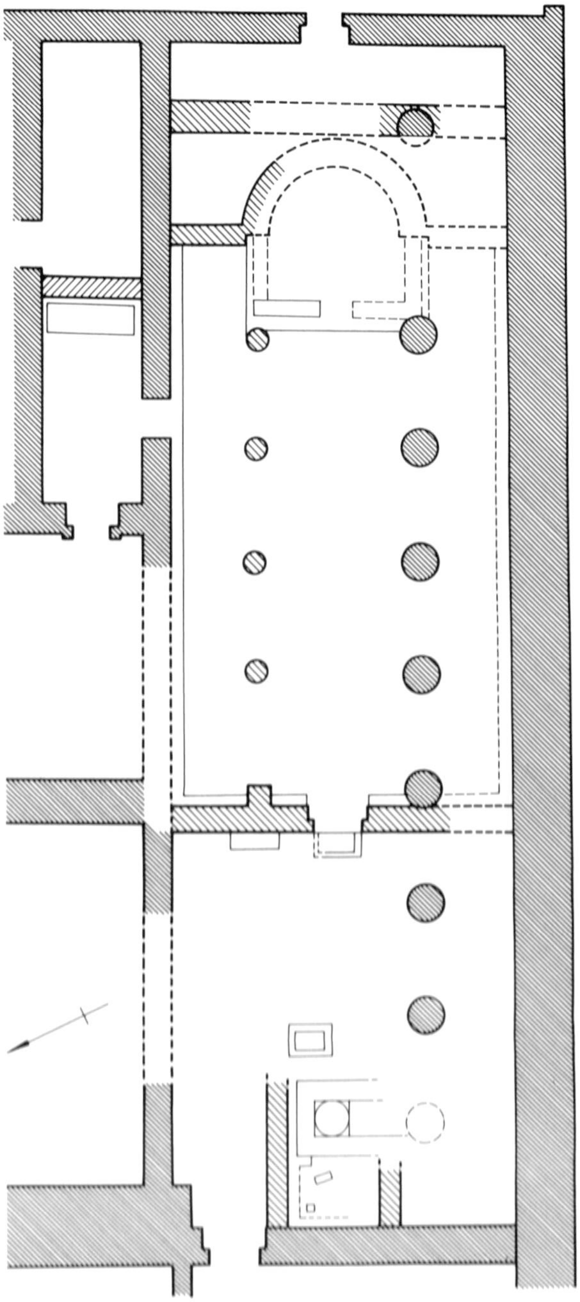

Plan of the three-aisled basilican chamber in the south court at Madamūd. *Courtesy Peter Grossmann.*

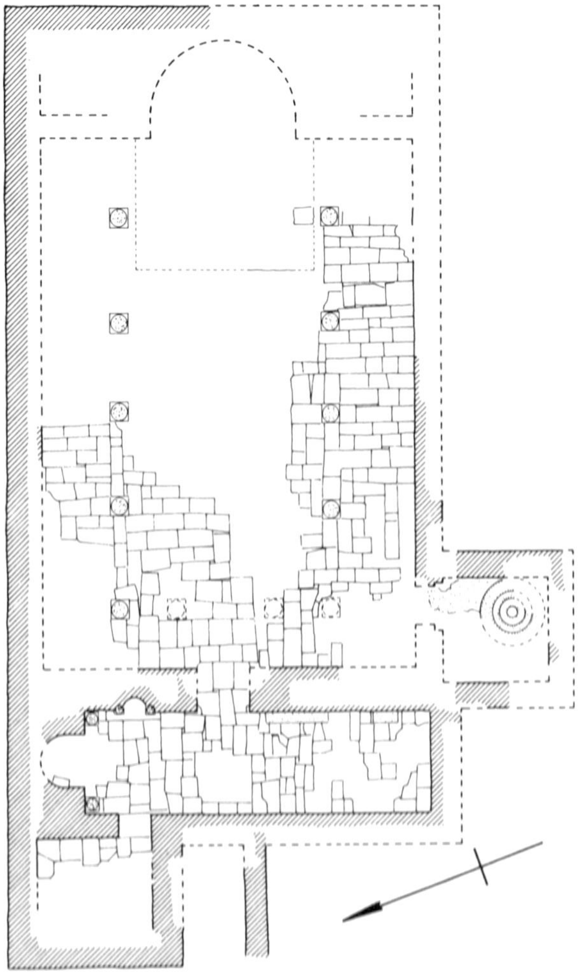

Plan of the church located amid the remains of houses at Madamūd. *Courtesy Peter Grossmann.*

church in the temple may have taken place at the earliest in the course of the sixth century.

The second, somewhat later church lies in the middle of the remains of numerous late antique houses on the south side of the former processional way leading to the temple, a few paces away from the Ptolemaic gate of the temple circuit wall. Of this in particular several bases of columns have survived in situ, but the sanctuary has been razed, apart from the foundation of the outer, northeast corner. The church had a narthex and on the south side a baptistery with a circular pool. It is no longer possible to determine where the entrance to the church lay. The building is dated by the excavators to the seventh century.

The remains of houses in the neighborhood of the church are too incomplete to convey any idea of their significance. The only one worth mentioning is a small house on the south side of the front temple tribune, which contains an oil press. North of the tribune numerous decorative pieces from late antiquity were found, wrought from limestone blocks from the Eighteenth Dynasty.

BIBLIOGRAPHY

Bisson de la Roque, F. *Rapport sur les fouilles de Médamoud (1925).* Fouilles de l'Institut français d'Archéologie orientale 3, 1, pp. 17–20, pl. 3. Cairo, 1926.

———. *Rapport sur les fouilles de Médamoud (1927).* Fouilles de l'Institut français d'Archéologie orientale 5, 1. Cairo, 1928.

PETER GROSSMANN

MADARIS AL-AQBAT AL-KUBRA. *See* Education.

MADĪNAT HĀBŪ, great fortified mortuary temple of Ramses III. The Coptic settlement in the temple area of Madīnat Hābū is the simple continuation and the final stage of a civilian migration into the temple precincts that began as early as the Twenty-first Dynasty (from 1090 B.C.). At first, it was significantly limited only to the area within the girdle wall and went on parallel with some isolated alterations and reconstruction work in the temple buildings themselves. Larger groups of house foundations in the outer areas, for example, the group of houses on the southeast side beside the so-called fortified gate of Ramses III, can only be attested in the Roman period (Hölscher, 1934, pl. 10). After the final extinction of the temple cult in Christian times, rebuilding around the temple was naturally intensified to a considerable degree and took possession of the temple itself, which in the preceding periods had always been left untouched. Numerous remains of house foundations have been identified in the first courtyard. In the second court a church was built. In this way, the Coptic inhabitants pressed forward into the inner part of the actual temple building. Even the roof of the temple was overrun with houses.

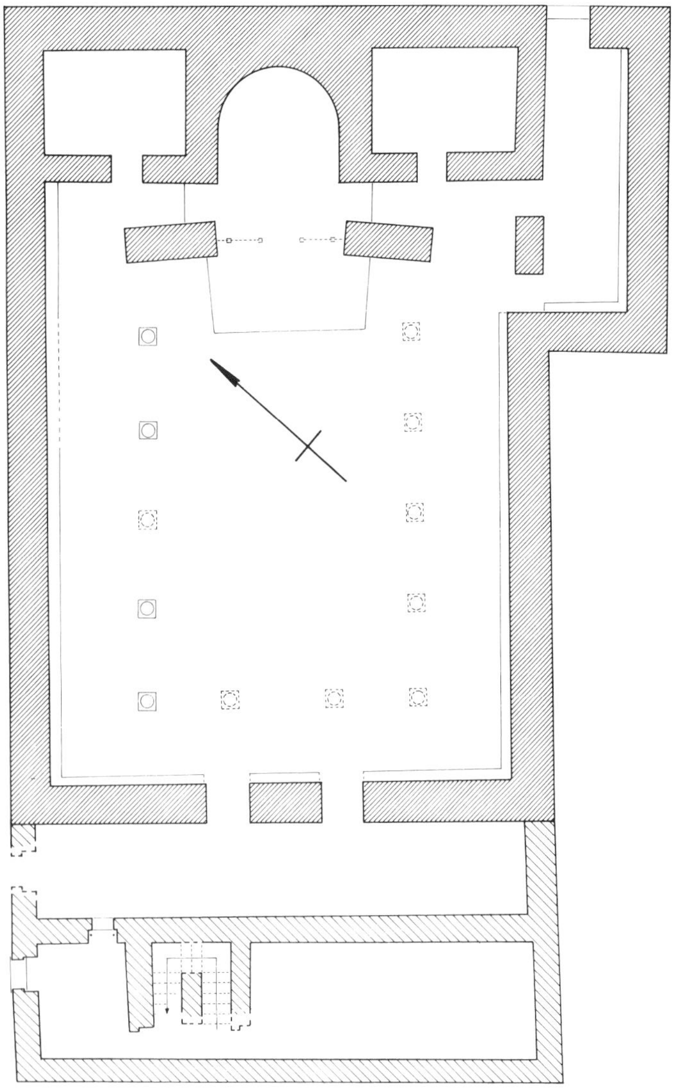

Plan of the church in front of the east gate at Madīnat Hābū. *Courtesy Peter Grossmann.*

Remains of this Coptic occupation of the temple area were identified in large numbers, especially on the north side of the temple (Hölscher, 1934, pl. 32). They have today been razed, but during the period of excavation were sufficiently abundant to give a good idea of the appearance and the forms of life of the settlement at that time. In several houses were found, among other things, many more or less richly developed jar stands (Hölscher, 1954, p. 47), which evidently belonged to the normal equipment of every house. What is striking is the small size of the rooms in most houses. The houses were almost all provided with staircases, and were often several stories high. They were built closely together, but almost all the houses have their own outer walls so that where they adjoin neighboring houses two thick walls sometimes run side by side. The recognizable streets take an approximately straight-line course, but there are many blind alleys.

In general, there are no ground plans of particular houses worthy of notice unless we count the large house 76 at the rear wall of the temple building or the storehouse above the temple of Eye and Horemheb (Hölscher, 1934, pl. 34) to the north, outside the temple precinct. Remarkably, the staircases are never situated beside the entrance, but always in the back part of the house. They thus gave access to the private part of the house, while the front entrance room served as a guest room or reception room (Hölscher, 1954, p. 46).

In the eighth or ninth century A.D. the settlement was abandoned. The reason for this is not known.

In addition to the houses, there were several churches in the area of the temple.

The great five-aisled basilica that once occupied the second temple court is undoubtedly the most important. It was oriented to the east, and therefore across the original axis of the temple. To accommodate the apse, one of the pharaonic columns on the east side was sacrificed. Otherwise only the Osiris pillars were leveled and the space between these pillars walled up, so as to obtain a closed wall surface on the inside. The church was provided with a gallery, but where the staircase for it lay can no longer be recognized. Chronologically, the church probably belongs to the middle or second half of the sixth century. Monneret de Villard (1954, p. 54) dates the building between the fifth and seventh centuries, for at an earlier period so massive an intrusion into the structure of a completely intact temple seems scarcely probable.

The basilica in front of the fortified east gate of the enclosure wall is substantially more modest and clearly of later date. For the understanding of Christian church architecture in Egypt, however, it forms an important stage in the development of the *khūrus* (room between sanctuary and nave) and of the front triumphal arch placed before the opening of the apse. It is the only example in which the eastern row of columns, such as is found especially in Egyptian churches with a triconch sanctuary, has been fused into a massive cross wall, broken only by a large arch opening. The rest of the church conforms to the usual pattern; in the southeast there is an additional side room. The narthex with an outer door and staircase were added later. The adjoining building on the west could be the dwelling of the priest.

The small church in the temple precinct of Eye and Horemheb lies to the north outside the actual temple area of Madīnat Hābū and is the result of the reconstruction of an older Roman building. The church itself is a single-roomed chapel with a single-room sanctuary. In this reconstruction a southern narthex and a larger west room whose purpose is still unexplained were added at the same time.

BIBLIOGRAPHY

Grossmann, P. *Mittelalterliche Langhauskuppelkirchen und verwandte Typen in Oberägypten.* Glückstadt, 1982.

Hölscher, U. *The Excavation of Madinat Habu,* Vol. 1, *General Plans and Views.* Chicago, 1934.

———. *The Excavation of Madinat Habu,* Vol. 5, *Post Ramessid Remains.* Chicago, 1954.

PETER GROSSMANN

MADĪNAT MĀḌĪ, an abandoned site on the southwest edge of the Fayyūm (perhaps identical with the ancient Narmuthis), which grew out of an older temple settlement the beginnings of which reach back into the Middle Kingdom. The temple itself was built by Amenemhet III (Twelfth Dynasty) and contains numerous additions from the Ptolemaic and Roman periods. A long processional way (*dromos*) extends in a southerly direction, and this cuts through the settlement, which spreads especially south and east of the temple.

The remains of buildings that can still be recognized today derive from the late Roman and early Arabic periods (down to the ninth century). Ptolemaic houses are found in the neighborhood of the temple. Mud bricks were used as building materials in all periods, as was the cheap quarry stone. Horizontal wooden inserts (often even palm wood) were

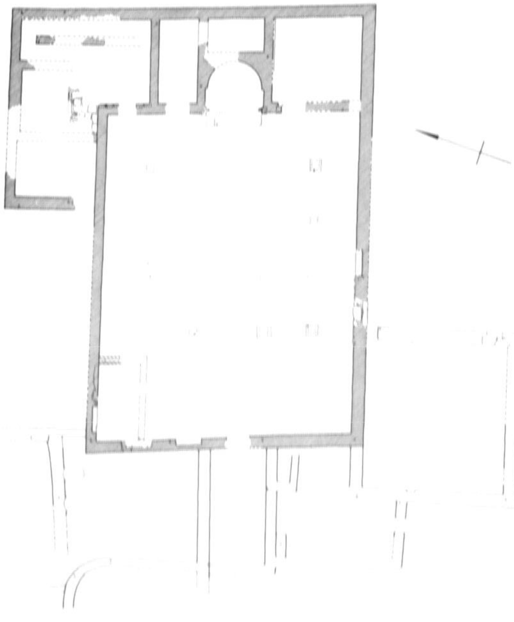

Plan of church CH 87 D at Madīnat Māḍī. *Courtesy Peter Grossmann.*

introduced into many walls as reinforcement.

No public buildings have so far come to light in Madīnat Māḍī. On the other hand, a considerable number of churches have been identified, and some of these have been cleared. In most cases they are modest constructions. However, they deserve attention insofar as similar churches were probably contained in very many places in Egypt in late antiquity, but today are almost everywhere lost.

A characteristic example is the small church CH 84 A. It is entirely built of mud bricks. Only the columns and the door sills are of limestone. The ground plan consists of the three-aisle naos with no return aisle, but with the usual three-part sanctuary and a succession of rooms attached on the outer south side, of which only the somewhat larger east room can be entered from the interior of the church itself. The remaining rooms have their entrances on the outside. Symmetrically in front of this complex there is on the west side a somewhat smaller entrance hall with an antechamber and staircase. Farther to the west is an evidently later court. Chronologically the church may belong to the sixth century. The columns used in it consist exclusively of spolia. In terms of style, these are like the pieces from Ahnas (Herakleopolis Magna), and may have been produced in workshops there.

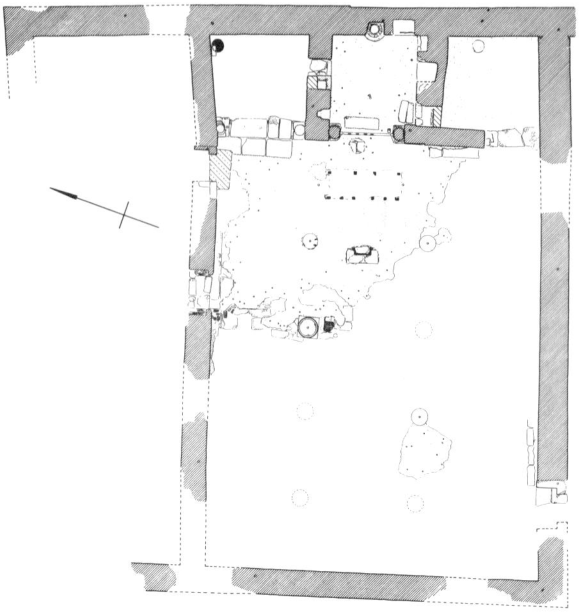

Plan of church CH 87 E Madīnat Māḍī. *Courtesy Peter Grossmann.*

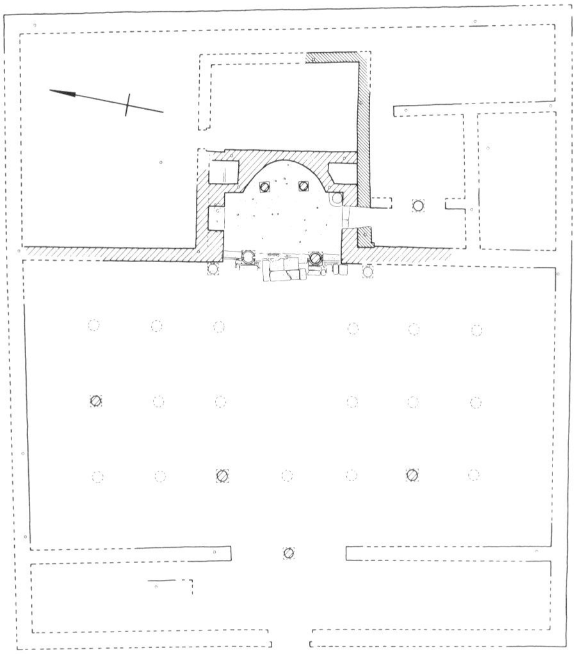

Plan of church CH 88 G at Madīnat Māḍī. *Courtesy Peter Grossmann.*

The church CH 84 B is substantially smaller. The area for the laity is broader than it is long, and has in its interior only four columns, which are moreover very irregularly distributed. Presumably this church was inserted into a building already in existence. When it was cleared, numerous fragments of woodwork (timbers and panels) were discovered. A third church, CH 85 C, is the result of the reconstruction of a secular Roman building. This, too, is nearly square. It has in the interior four columns, with an apse in the east and on the west a small narthex. Once again all the columns consist of spolia. In its final phase this church was used as a dwelling.

Other churches still await excavation. Two of them (CH 87 D and CH 88 H) have a five-aisle naos, one (CH 88 G) even a naos of seven aisles. Nevertheless, none of these churches is particularly large, and the length is even less impressive. CH 88 G is only four bays long, CH 88 H only three. The apse of the latter has an horseshoe-shaped ground plan with an inner circuit of engaged pilasters and two engaged columns at the opening to the nave. The single example of a narthex in these multi-aisled churches is extant in CH 88 G.

The still relatively well-preserved church CH 87 E excavated in spring 1987 has several doors on its two long sides. The sanctuary is as usual tripartite.

The openings into the central and northern rooms are flanked on both sides with columns. The third room to the south is simpler in design and served probably as a *diaconicon*. Farther on a fairly well-preserved little chapel with a narthex and four inner columns is situated in the southernmost region of the town. It has a multiroom sanctuary with several different units around the central altar chamber.

BIBLIOGRAPHY

Bresciani, E. *Rapporto preliminare delle campagne di scavo 1966 e 1967*. Milan, 1968.

———. *Rapporto preliminare delle campagne di scavo 1968 e 1969*. Milan, 1976.

———. "L'attività archeologica dell'Università di Pisa in Egitto (1984): Madinat Madi nel Fayum. Le chiese." *Egitto e Vicino Oriente* 7 (1984):1–7.

Jouguet, P. "Fouilles du Fayoum." *Bulletin de la correspondance hellénique* 25 (1905):380–411.

Vogliano, A. "Rapporto preliminare della campagna di scavo a Madinet Madi." *Annales du service des antiquités de l'Egypte* 38 (1938):533–49.

Zucker, F. "Archäologische Funde im Jahre 1909." *Archäologischer Anzeiger* (1910):247–50.

EDDA BRESCIANI
PETER GROSSMANN

MAGHTIS. *See* Epiphany Tank.

MAGIC, the art of pretending to accomplish actions with the help of supernatural forces contrary to the laws of nature. Coptic magic is a particularly rich field for studying the relationships of the ancient Copts with the invisible forces of heaven and hell that were part of the old Egyptian heritage (Lexa, 1925; Brier, 1980).

Angelicus Kropp (1930–1931) gives information on almost all aspects of Coptic magic. His work contains fourteen magical texts in Coptic (Vol. 1), the German translation of seventy-six texts with corrections and notes (Vol. 2), and a general study on Coptic magic. Viaux (1978) studied modern Coptic magic with spells and amulets in Arabic, sometimes influenced by Islamic features (Winkler, 1930, 1931).

As with other countries, one must distinguish between modest amulets and spells recited by a magician in the presence of his customer at certain hours of the day or the night that are almost like a religious ceremony with burning incense. Amulets were worn even by babies and are seen even today protecting their bearer with the help of God, the angels, and the saints.

With both spells and amulets there were examples showing the names of the persons as ⲁⲁ, dd (*deina deinos*), "N.N." or "So-and-so" and magical texts that effectively worked with the names of the persons mentioned. These texts were followed, as in Egyptian and even in Islamic magic, not by the father's name but by that of the mother, such as Maria, the daughter of Tsibel; Tatōre, the daughter of Tsahai; and Andreas, the son of Marthe (Crum, 1896).

The value of a spell or an amulet is more appreciated if it emanates from a well-known source. In the demotic story of Sethorn Khamois, the hero gets hold of a magical book written by the god Thoth, and the magician reciting a spell asserts that "the books of Thoth" were in his hands (Worrell, 1935). Another spell "to bind a dog," probably a watchdog, mentions that it was written by Isis (Erman, 1895a). In a reply to King Abgar of Edessa, one author asserts, "I am Jesus Christ, I have written this letter with my own hand" (Krall, 1892).

There is great freedom in the layout of magical texts. Old Coptic and even Christian texts contain passages on how a peculiar problem was solved by divine help. It is, in fact, a kind of mystery in miniature, in the sense of Greek or Egyptian mysteries, where a particularly important scene of a god's life is reproduced: as he has helped in the past, he will help in the present case.

Though magical texts present, on the whole, a coherent picture of the existing world, there are so many conflicting features in the details that they do not fit into a comprehensible universe. The following, however, may be considered generally accepted: The seat of God the Father, a combination of throne and chariot, is carried by four cherubim. Under him there are seven heavens and fourteen firmaments supported by four columns apparently placed on the earth. Noun (ⲚⲞⲨⲚ) is both the abyss of the sea and the hell, but Amente (ⲀⲘⲚ̄ⲦⲈ) is only the hell. The Acheronian Sea, borrowed from Greek mythology, is in the netherworld and must be crossed by the deceased. There is a river of fire for punishment and a sea of fire under the throne of the Father. In Upper Egypt (Luxor, Farshūṭ, etc.) the dead have to cross a river of fire to get into paradise (Vycichl, 1938). One spell even speaks of seven rivers of fire (Worrell, 1935, p. 13).

Magical text. Papyrus fragment. Sixth century. *Courtesy Coptic Museum, Cairo.*

In some cases, spells contain indications about the magician. They show the magician as the successor of the Egyptian priest. He not only invokes the old divinities under Christian and even under Islamic rule but he must also be "pure" like an Egyptian priest and wear a white linen garment. In one instance, he even wears a wreath of roses; in another one, a wreath of *shapshap,* an unidentified plant. Another magician holds a myrrh twig in the right hand and a staff, probably a magic wand, in the left hand.

The recitation of a spell is performed like a religious service. In rare cases, offerings of animals are mentioned (chickens, ducks, geese, sheep); the blood is drained from the animal, and the magician and his customer share the meat out between them (Viaux, 1978, p. 41).

In one case, Psalms 39 and 124 are written with the blood of a white pigeon. Hoopoe blood is used to write a particular love charm. The head of a dog or a cat is used to sow discord in a family and to bring bad luck.

The spells mention balsam, benzoin, dates, grapes, lemon and quince juices, laurel leaves, musk, saffron, wine, and such. They call for several kinds of unguents, made from almonds, roses, and radish oil; also different oils of cotton, lettuce, linseed, radishes, olive (especially the green olive of Palestine), and the "oil of the Apocalypse," consecrated on Holy Saturday.

Sometimes the kind of water to be used is indicated in the spells. There is fresh water, Nile water, water of a well that has never seen the sun, bath water, and water from dry places. One special water is Ṭūbah water, consecrated in the church on the night of Epiphany in the month of Ṭūbah.

Each spell must be accompanied by a special incense or mixture of incense. The texts mention incense of aloe, acacia grains, bean straw, benzoin, cloves, cardamom, coriander, mastic, olibanum (frankincense), pepper, sandarac, and storax, among others.

Names and Magical Words

A name is not only a simple means of identification but a part of personality. He who knows the name, the "true name," of a god or a demon has a better chance of coming in contact with him. Some of these names are secret. Thus, Jesus Christ possesses a written name that nobody knows except himself. A spell speaks of the "great, true name of the Father," another of the "great name," and there are also his "true name" and his "hidden names."

A frequent palindrome is Ablanathanalba, probably of Semitic origin, often misspelled, a sign that its palindromic character was not always apparent to the Coptic scribe. Agramma Chamari is often used with the preceding name as well as with Iaō Sabaōth. It is used frequently and has been explained as the name of an angel. Abraxas is not only the Gnostic name of the highest god but occurs also in the combinations Iaō Sabaōth Abraxas and Jesus Abraxas. The name of the Phoenician sun-god, Baalsemes (literally "the Lord of the Sun," Hebrew *ba'al shemesh*), appears among other sun-gods and once in a list of angelic aeons. Bainchōōch, with graphic variants, once written with seven omegas, is Egyptian and means "Spirit of Darkness." Marmaraōth (Syriac, "lord of lords") designates in the Coptic Magical Papyrus of Paris the sun-god Iaō. A similar form, Barbaraōth, the name of the highest god in the same papyrus, remains unexplained. Semesilam is from *semes*, "sun" (Hebrew *shemesh*); the second part of the name has been compared with Hebrew *'ōlam*, "world." Maskelli Maskellō is a strange formation, once used to designate the goddess of fate. The name Zagourē is once written over the design of Typhon or Seth.

Four bodiless creatures with four faces and six wings in the book of Revelation are called Alpha, Leōn, Phōnē, Anēr. Alpha is the bull; Leōn, the lion; Anēr, the man; and Phōnē, the eagle. They represent the four evangelists. The seven archangels are called Michaēl, Gabriēl, Raphaēl, Suriēl, Zetekiēl (Zedekiēl), Salathiēl, and Anaēl. The three men of the burning furnace (Dn. 3:19–23) occur in many texts: Shadrach, Meshach, and Abednego. The twenty-four elders of Revelation 4:4 have names beginning with the twenty-four letters of the Greek alphabet and ending in *-ēl* (Hebrew for "God"): Achaēl, Banaēl, Ganaēl, Dathiēl, and so on.

Coptic magical spells are full of senseless names and deformations. Bēth, apparently the name of a spirit and not the Semitic word for "house," is followed in a spell by Bēthai, Bētha, Bēthari and then by Larouēl, Marmarouēl, Meteтiēl, Sriēl, Ermiēl, and others (Crum, 1905, p. 253).

A love charm begins with the names of demons: Shourin, Shouran, Shoutaban, Shoutaben, Eibonese, Sharsabaner. It is Satanas, the devil, who hits the earth with his stick against the Living God saying, "I, too, I am a god! I implore and call all of you today to descend to me on these [gifts?] that are today in my hands. At the hours when I shall give therefrom to N.N. that she eat or drink of them, you shall bind her heart and her flesh on me forever (. . .)!—Male wheat, blood of the finger." This spell seems to belong to the Christian period, for Satanas is invoked, and the "Living God," and there is no trace of Jewish influences.

In Coptic spells and amulets the seven vowels of the Greek alphabet are widely used, either singly (as in **ⲁⲉⲏⲓⲟⲩⲱ**) or written seven times (**ⲁⲁⲁⲁⲁⲁⲁ**, **ⲉⲉⲉⲉⲉⲉⲉ**, etc.). They are said to have a magical power and some relation to the seven planets. They are found also in other combinations.

Most magical texts are written in Sahidic, and some are Fayyumic, but there is no doubt that there

Magical text. Papyrus fragment. Sixth–eighth century. *Courtesy Coptic Museum, Cairo.*

were texts in other dialects as well. The orthography is as a rule irregular. Texts in Old Coptic frequently use special letters derived from demotic. They have not lost their contact with the pagan terminology and still present other archaic features.

A picture of such an Old Coptic text can be gotten from some passages of the magical papyrus of Paris (no. 574 of the National Library in Paris; cf. Erman, 1883, p. 94). One here finds invoked the god Osiris, "the King of the Netherworld," "the Lord of the Burial," who is "in the South of This," probably in Abydos. His two titles, King of the Netherworld and Lord of the Burial, correspond to the Egyptian titles *ḥk' dw'.t* and *nb ḳrs.t*. After **ⲧⲓⲛ** (Egyptian, Tny) still other sacred places are mentioned: Ebōt (**ⲉⲃⲱⲧ**), or Abydos, and Pnoubs (**ⲡⲛⲟⲩⲃⲥ**), or Pnubs, in Nubia. Then Althōnai ap-

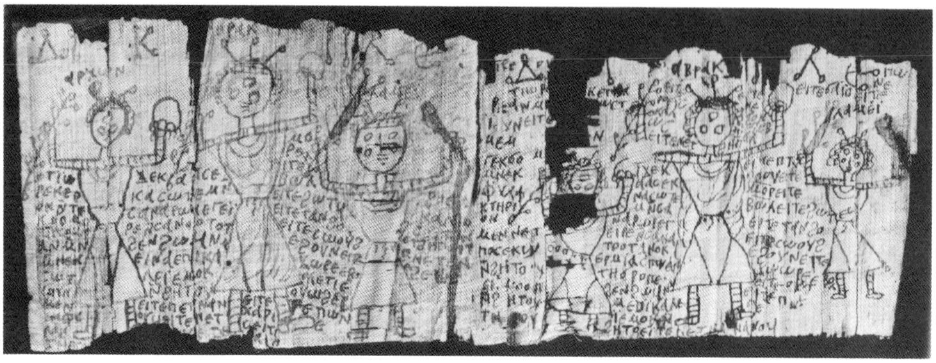

Magical text. Papyrus fragment. Sixth–eighth century. *Courtesy Coptic Museum, Cairo.*

pears, certainly Adōnai (Hebrew for "My Lord"; ⲁⲇⲱⲛⲁⲓ, here written ⲁⲇⲑⲱⲛⲁⲓ) and Michaēl (ⲙⲓⲭⲁⲏⲗ) the angel (Greek, *angelos*) "who is with God" (ⲛ̄ⲧⲉⲡⲛⲟⲩⲧⲉ, n̄tepnoute). Sabaōth (ⲥⲁⲃⲁⲱⲑ) is mentioned, so the Jewish influence is certain. In this context, one finds such pagan gods as "Anubis on the Mountain" (ⲁⲛⲟⲩⲡ . . . ⲧⲃⲁⲓⲧⲱⲩ, anoup . . . tbaitōu; Egyptian, *'Inpw tpy dw*) and "Thoth the twice Great" (ⲑⲟⲟⲩⲧ ⲡⲓⲟ ⲡⲓⲟ, thoout pio pio), with the expression "great of force" (ⲁⲡⲁϩⲧⲉ, apahte). Then there are "goddesses" (ⲛⲧⲉⲣϩⲥⲓⲙⲉ, nterhsime) and "gods" (ⲛⲧⲉⲣϩⲟⲟⲩⲛⲧ, nterhoount), literally "female gods" and "male gods," the first part of which corresponds to the Egyptian plural *ntrw*, gods (Erman, 1895b).

Thoth, the god of wisdom venerated in the form of a baboon, is called Panathoout, the Ape Thoth (ⲡⲁⲛⲁⲑⲟⲟⲩⲧ, panathoout), just as Sēth is called the Ass Sēth (ⲓⲱ ⲥⲏⲑ, iō sēth; Erman, 1883, pl. 101). Another papyrus has retained two Egyptian words not found elsewhere in Coptic, ⲧⲕⲓⲧⲉ (tkite), "the sleep" (Egyptian, *qd.t*), and ϩⲱⲃ (hōb), "to send" (*h'b*) (Erman, 1895b, p. 50). In this context the verb ⲡⲱⲱⲣⲉ (pōōre) still means "to see," like its Egyptian prototype *ptr*, and not "to dream," as in Coptic (Erman, 1883, p. 106).

Two interesting verbal forms are found in the Old Coptic Schmidt Papyrus: ⲛⲉⲣⲁⲉⲓ ⲛⲁϥ (neraei naf), "what I have done to him," and ⲛⲉⲣⲁϥ ⲛⲁⲓ (neraf nai), "what he has done to me" (Satzinger, 1975, pp. 40, 43). This spell also mentions "Hathor, the nurse of Anubis" ([ϩ]ⲁⲑⲱⲣ ⲧⲙⲟⲛ[ⲉ ⲛ]ⲁⲛⲟⲩⲡ, [h]athōr tmon[e n]anoup) and the "son of Osiris, the cowherd" (ⲥⲓⲟⲩⲥⲓⲣⲉ ⲡⲉⲗⲟⲓϩ, siousire peloih).

The Spell

There is no general rule for the disposition of the elements of a spell, but in most cases one can distinguish the following order: (a) invocation of God, gods or goddesses, angels or other spirits, or even objects, such as the nails of the cross or the holy oil; (b) in some cases, a passage about how the invoked person had helped in a similar case; (c) the demand; (d) a final exhortation, such as "Yea, yea, quickly, quickly, straightaway, straightaway."

As a rule the persons or objects invoked give some indication of the period when the spell was written. There are several phases, beginning with the gods and goddesses of ancient Egypt and moving to the invocation of God and the saints of the Christian church.

Foremost in the pagan pantheon is the Osirian family: Osiris, Isis, Horus, Seth, Nephthys. The "great magician" Isis occupies the first place, followed by her son, Horus. Their names are Coptic: ⲟⲩⲥⲓⲣⲉ, ⲏⲥⲉ, ϩⲱⲣ, ⲥⲏⲑ (ousire, ēse, hōr, sēth); only Nephthys is called with her Greek name, ⲛⲉⲫⲑⲩⲥ (nephthys). In the Great Magical Papyrus of Paris one also finds the Old Coptic form ⲛⲉⲃⲑⲱ (nebthō), corrected to ⲛⲉⲫⲑⲱ (nephthō) (Erman, 1883, p. 100, l. 40). Osiris is invoked in the Old Coptic Schmidt Papyrus (Satzinger, 1975). Amon is mentioned as ⲁⲙⲟⲛ (amon), not as Coptic ⲁⲙⲟⲩⲛ (amoun), with the addition "the three gods," meaning the Theban triad (Worrell, 1935, p. 30): Amon, Muth, and Khons. Petbe (ⲡⲉⲧⲃⲉ) is certainly an Egyptian god (Erman, 1895b). Shenoute identifies him with Kronos, just as Hephaistos (ⲏⲫⲁⲓⲥⲧⲟⲥ) is identified with Ptah (ⲡⲧⲁϩ).

While the Egyptian gods are frequently met with in magical spells, Greek gods are encountered only rarely. An exception is Lange's Fayyumic spell, wherein the magician finishes his incantation with the words, "If thou dost not obey the (words) of my mouth and dost not come at once, I shall invoke Salpiax, Pechiēl, Sasmiasus, Mesemaasim and the 70 gods and Artemis, the mother of all gods, and Apollon and Athena and Kronos and Moira, Pallas and Aphrodite, the Dawn (Eos), Serapis, Uranos:

seize him, bring him to my feet" (Lange, 1932, p. 165). Astarte (Greek name of a Phoenician goddess) is misspelled Asparte̅ (ⲁⲥⲡⲁⲣⲧⲏ), "the daughter of the devil" (Worrell, 1935, p. 12).

Moira is Greek for "part" or "portion" and is the personification of destiny. In Coptic, the *moira* is mentioned as a divine power: ⲙⲏⲣⲁ ⲛⲓⲃⲓ ⲉⲛⲑⲏⲣ ⲛⲓⲃⲓ (mēra nibi enthēr nibi), "every *moira*, every god" (Crum, 1905, p. 253). Here *mēra (moira)* replaces the Egyptian god Shai or Agathodaemon. The etymology of *moira* is the same as that of Turkish *kismet*, part, portion, destiny.

Many spells invoke Iaō Sabaōth Adōnai Eloi, where Iaō corresponds to the Hebrew Yahwe. Names of angels like Michaēl and Gabriēl are Jewish, but are also used in Christian texts. A Jewish passage is certainly the invocation of "the God of Abraham, the God of Isak, the God of Iakōb" (Hopfner, 1921, Vol. p. 436). This passage is followed by "Jesus Christ, Holy Spirit, Son of God [in that order] who destroys the realm of the Snake (. . .)" (cf. Gn. 1:14). These forces are invoked to expel "the impure daemon Sadanas [Satanas] who is on him" (Hopfner, 1921, Vol. 1, pp. 435–36). This spell is written in Greek letters.

Christian spells are easily recognizable as they mention the Trinity, the Father, the Son, and the Holy Spirit. The name of Jesus Christ (ⲓⲏⲥⲟⲩⲥ ⲡⲭⲣⲓⲥⲧⲟⲥ) is frequently abridged (ⲓ̅ⲥ̅ ⲡ̅ⲭ̅). Mary (ⲙⲁⲣⲓⲁ) is sometimes called Mariham (ⲙⲁⲣⲓϩⲁⲙ). Here one finds the three men of the burning furnace, the seven archangels, the nails of the cross, the twenty-four elders standing in front of the throne of the Father and the forty martyrs of Sebaste. All these forces appear in the spells with their names (Kropp, 1930, Vol. 3, pp. 40–103).

The appearance of Gnostic ideas corresponds to a completely new conception of the world in which previously existing elements are inserted with a different meaning. To take just one example, aeon is from the Greek *aiōn*, "time, duration, eternity, generation," but in Gnostic texts *aiōn* is applied to powerful spirits corresponding to the seven planets. In an exorcism they are called Iaō, Sabaōth, Adōnai, Elōi, Elemas, Mixanthēr, and Abrasax, and the seven archangels are here Michaēl, Gabriēl, Raphaēl, Suriēl, Ragouēl, Asouēl, and Saraphouēl (Kropp, Vol. 2, p. 201). The name Mixanthēr contains ⲉⲛⲑⲏⲣ (enthēr), gods, here used as a singular, an early Bohairic form corresponding to ⲉⲛⲧⲏⲣ (entēr) in other Old Coptic texts. The first part, Mix-, is derived according to Kropp from the Greek for "mixed" or a similar form. Abrasax is apparently but a scribal variant of Abraxas. Another aeon is Ialdabaōth, the creator of the world, and Bathouriēl, the Great Father, the Father of the heavenly and earthly beings (Kropp, Vol. 3, pp. 31–32).

There is no rigid system in gnosticism. Names and functions change from one text to another. So the seven aeons are called in an exorcism Arimiēl, Davithe, Elelēth, Ermoukratos, Adonai (*sic*), Ermousr, pi-Aoraton (the Invisible), and Bainchōōch (Crum, 1905, no. 1008; Kropp, 1931, Vol. 1, p. 22). The epithets "Unseizable, Incomprehensible, Invisible, Unpronounceable" as well as "God of the gods" are equally found in the Gnostic *Tripartite Tractate* (Kühner, 1980, pp. 61–64).

Elements of different creeds—Egyptian, Greek, Jewish, Christian, Gnostic—may be found together in the same text. In a purely pagan text where Isis appears, the end reads, "It is me who speaks, the Lord Jesus who gives recovery." This spell is from the seventh or eighth century, to judge from the handwriting. Two pieces of the same collection are written on Arabic papyri. In one case, one can still distinguish an Arabic word, *al-amīr*, the prince. This proves that Egyptian gods were invoked even after the ARAB CONQUEST OF EGYPT (Erman, 1895c).

In a spell in which the Christian God is invoked "with his true name Raphaēl, Adōnai, Sabaōth," this last is adjured in the name of his unique Son "whose true name is Sēth, Sēth, the living Christ" (Kropp, 1931, Vol. 2, p. 238). It is true that Sēth, the son of Adam (Gn. 5:3), is written in exactly the same way as the Egyptian god Sēth, but there is no doubt that here the Egyptian god is meant.

The Jewish demon Ashmeday, who had killed seven men who were betrothed to Sarah, one after the other, appears in a Coptic spell with his Greek name, Asmodaios (Kropp, Vol. 1, p. 32). The form Asmodaios certainly proceeds from the Greek translation of the Book of Tobit.

A half-pagan, half-Christian spell tells how Horus had caught a bird in his net, how "he cut it up without a knife, cooked it without fire and (ate) it without salt." Then his belly began to ache. He wanted to send a demon to his mother, Isis, who could help him. Three demons of Agrippa were ready to go to her. The first could do it in four hours, and the second in two, but the third was the quickest: "I go there with the breath of thy mouth and come back in the breath of thy nose!" In fact, he went to Isis and brought her back at once, and she healed Horus with a spell. At the end of the text, the scribe added, "It is me who calls, the Lord Jesus who gives healing!" (Kropp, Vol. 2, pp. 9–12). Here one sees that the pagan spell was adopted in Christian times. The passage of the three demons is found with a slight modification in an old German story (Erman, 1916).

Coptic Magic in the Islamic Period

After the Arabic conquest (641) Coptic magic gradually lost a bit of its originality. The most striking feature was the adoption of the Arabic language and script. Original creations were replaced by copies of Psalms with magical squares in which letters and figures were inserted, each letter representing a figure according to the Arabic system (*abgad, hawwaz, ḥuṭṭī, kalamun, saʿafaṣ, qaraṣhat, thakhadha, ḍaẓagha*). Seals and squares were taken over from Arabic models (Winkler, 1930). They had to be written with a special ink, such as rose water, musk, or saffron essence (Viaux, 1978, p. 46). Special incense was to be burnt: *qāqūlī*, a kind of cardamom; Turkish mastic; *gāwī tanāsirī* (benzoin); and red sandalwood. When writing, the scribe had to sit on the earth to keep in constant touch with the underworld forces.

Several prayers were often copied for amulets: the prayer of Apa Nūb the Confessor, Anbā Samuel the Recluse, and Saint Cyprian. The prayer of the *qarīnah* was written for a woman who gave birth. It also protected children under seven years of age. The prayer was written after a dream of King Solomon. The *qarīnah* corresponds to *aberselia* in Coptic texts, today *warzāliyyah,* a female demon who threatens women in child-bed and their babies (Winkler, 1931). In Arabic she was also called *Umm al-Ṣubyān,* not "Mother of the Children," as one might think, but "the (Witch) of the Children," who kills them. Modern Coptic magic frequently uses Psalms. Every Psalm is used for a special purpose.

The objectives of spells may be the same as in old times, perhaps with the addition of a spell to find hidden treasures or attract a customer into a shop, or an amulet against flies. Four of the latter amulets must be hung upside down on the four walls of a room, and this must be done on Easter, because the flies disappear at that time of the year, the so-called *khamsīn,* or the fifty days between Easter and Whitsun.

A Christian text beginning with the palindrome *Sator Areto Tenet Otera Rotas,* which means nothing but is a widespread magical formula, addresses Iaō Sabaōth, but mentions the Crucified One, and asks for health for Hew, daughter of Maria (Krall, 1892, p. 119). There are texts against an eye disease, fever, and against sickness and demons (Kropp, 1930, Vol. 2).

A spell to heal a sick eye first tells the story of Jesus and a hind. Jesus coming out of the door of paradise saw a hind weeping and shedding tears, because her eye had been hurt.

Jesus: Why, hind, dost thou weep
and shed tears?

The hind: I raised my eyes to the heaven and said:
Sun do not become red,
Moon do not rise,
Henoch, the scribe,
do not dip thy reed into thy ink
until Michael descends
and heals my eye!

Jesus sends Michael, who comes from the sky, and says:

The wound [?] will be healed,
the darkness will be dissolved!
In the name of the Father,
the Son and the Holy Spirit!
(Kropp, Vol. 2, pp. 66–67)

A spell against an aching molar and one against fever for the protection of the mother's bosom and the uterus end with "the seven names" of Mary and of the archangels (without mentioning them). There are, in fact, several spells for the protection of a pregnant woman, for a mother and her child against all powers of darkness.

The "nine Guardians of the Paradise" are invoked "to grant force to Damiane, the son of Kyra Kale" and "to protect him from every evil." Another spell is recited "to get a good voice."

To become strong, a man appeals to Michael, who says, "What dost thou want? I shall do it to thee. If thou wantest the stone, I break it, the iron, I make it water!" But the man answers, "I do not want this or that, but I want the whole force of thy arm for my force and my right arm." Michael directs him to a place where he finds Echouch, Belouch, and Barbarouch, who fulfill his wish (Erman, 1895c, p. 44).

A. Erman thinks the dog is "bound" by the spell that enables a thief to go into a house to steal (Erman, 1895a) but the reciter may be simply afraid of the animal. A long, important spell is directed against a dog. The object is not clear. The dog may be "bound" to hinder it from warning of thieves breaking into a house, or the reciter may simply be afraid of an animal that attacked him when he passed by.

Love charms have appeared frequently at all times. As far as one can tell, it is always the man who makes wishes "to fulfill his heart's desire," never the woman. The oldest pagan spells are almost poetical. There are parallelisms, repetitions, and questions and answers that excite the listener's interest. In the pagan manuscript Schmidt 1, Horus is in love with seven virgins, and his mother Isis helps him:

> Listen to Horus who is weeping,
> listen to Horus who is sighing!
>
> Horus: I have suffered while I was longing (?)
> for seven virgins,
> from the third hour of the day,
> to the fourth hour of the night.
> None of them slept,
> None of them slumbered.

His mother, Isis, answers him from the temple of Habin, her face being turned toward the seven virgins, who have turned toward her:

> What hast thou, Horus, that thou weepest,
> What hast thou, Horus, that thou sighest?
>
> Horus: Thou wilt not that I weep,
> thou wilt not that I sigh,
> from the third hour of the day,
> to the fourth hour of the night,
> as I am longing (?) for seven virgins,
> none of them slept,
> none of them slumbered?

Then Isis answers him: "Though thou hast not found me, though thou hast not found my name, take a cup with a little water. With a little breath, a breath of thy mouth, a breath of thy nose speak the magic word: Pkechp (. . .)!"

Another spell invokes "Oil, Oil, Oil, Holy Oil! Oil that flows from under the throne of Iaō Sabaōth! Oil with which Isis anointed the bones of Osiris!"

> I cry to thee, Oil!
> The sun and the moon cry to thee
> the stars of the heaven cry to thee,
> the consecrators of the sun cry to thee!

He explains his wish: "Mayest thou bring So-and-So to me (. . .) and make love arise in her heart and hers in mine, in the manner of a brother and a sister (. . .). I desire to beget her children (. . .)!" (Worrell, 1935, pp. 184–86). "Brother" and "sister" here mean "companions." In this case, the object of the charm is honest love and matrimony. The manuscript Schmidt 2 (Satzinger, 1975) begins with an introduction. Horus speaks:

> I went in through a stone door,
> I went out through an iron door,
> I went in with the head downwards,
> I went in with the feet downwards,
> I have found seven virgins,
> sitting on a water well,
> I wished, but they did not wish,
> I persuaded [or sim.], but they were not persuaded,
> I wanted to love N.N., the daughter of N.N.
> But she did not want to accept my kiss (. . .).

After a long dialogue with his mother, Isis, Horus gets to know of the magic spell and adds:

> Thou Great one amongst the Spirits,
> I wish N.N., the daughter of N.N.,
> to spend forty days and forty nights,
> hanging on me, like a bitch on a dog,
> like a sow on a boar (. . .)!

A spell invoking King Solomon expresses the lover's wishes as follows (Crum, 1934, pp. 195–200):

> (. . .) that I may become honey in her belly, manna on her tongue, and that she desire me as it were the sun and love me as it were the moon and hang upon me like a drop of water upon a jar and that she be like a honey (bee) seeking (honey), a bitch prowling, a cat going from house to house, like unto a mare going beneath horses in heat!

A love charm to recover an unfaithful husband's affection reproduces a passage from Plutarch's "De Iside et de Osiride." The Great Magical Papyrus of Paris describes the situation as follows: "Isis comes from the mountain, at noon, in summer, her face covered with dust, her eyes full of tears, her heart full of sighs. Her father, Thoth the Great came to her and asked her, 'Why my daughter Isis, covered with dust, are thy eyes full of tears, is thy heart full of sighs, the (. . .) of thy garment soiled? Wipe thy tears!'"

Then Isis explains her case: "It is not my fault, my father, I have found a fault my father, Ape Thoth, Ape Thoth, my father, I have been supplanted by my companion, I have found a fault [or sim.], yes, Nephthys sleeps with Osiris."

Here Thoth is her father, not Kronos. There were four children, two brothers, Osiris and Seth, and two sisters, Isis and Nephthys. Then Osiris, the husband of Isis, slept inadvertently with her sister, Nephthys, whose husband was Seth. The love charm advises Isis how to punish Osiris and to recover his affection (Preisendanz, 1928, Vol. 1, p. 71). In a similar way the magician's "customer" will punish her unfaithful husband and recover his affection.

This charm for women has an addendum for men

against an unfaithful wife: "When she drinks, when she eats, when she sleeps with another man, I shall bewitch her heart (. . .) until she comes to me, who knows what is in her heart, what she does and what she thinks (. . .)." This short addition replaces the mythological introduction on Osiris and Nephthys and was certainly followed by a long incantation (not reproduced here) and a detailed description of the cruel punishment for the adulteress.

By the force of his spell the Coptic magician is able to treat the invoked god or spirit as his subaltern and to menace him if he does not obey (Hopfner, 1921, pp. 139–143).

In one love charm an unnamed god is menaced: "If thou dost not obey according to the utterings of my mouth and the works of my hand, I shall descend into the Netherworld, bring up the *Tartarouchos* [Chief of the Hell] and say to him: 'Thou too, thou art a god. Be complaisant and fulfil my desire for N.N., the daughter of N.N.!' Then the god answers: 'If thou wishest, I split the stone, I transform iron into water, I quickly destroy the iron doors until I bind the heart of N.N., the daughter of N.N. (. . .). If then she does not come, I shall hold back the sun in his cart and the moon on her way, the star crown on Jesus' head, until I quickly accomplish thy desire.'" It is possible that the threat is directed against God the Father, as Jesus Christ is mentioned in the spell.

In another spell, a man invokes Ouriel and Michael to get a "good voice" without hoarseness, without splitting (?), without roughness, "but tender, with a musical sound and diffusing sweetness between the people." But if the angels do not obey, he will "hold back the sun in the east and the moon in the west and fight with the creatures of the sky," and he will tell the sky, "Become copper and give no dew to the earth," and the earth, "Become iron and give no fruit until the Father will send Davithea, who will accomplish my desire."

Coptic magicians of the Christian period never invoke Satan and the forces of evil. They remain within the sphere of the good, invoking God, the angels, holy martyrs, the holy oil, and the like:

> The poor Jacob adjures God the Almighty, Sabaōth, Father, Son and the Holy Spirit, the God of the Cherubim and the Seraphim, the creator of the sun, the moon and the stars, also the seven Archangels, the other Angels, the three holy men of the burning furnace, the four animals, the blood of Jesus Christ and the 24 presbyters to do every evil to Maria, the daughter of Tsibel. He wishes her illness and to her family too. "Put her in the hand of an evil daemon who tortures her, day and night!"
> (Crum, 1896)

The "holy martyrs" are invoked by "Theodora, this wronged woman" against Jōr and his wife:

> I cast myself down before your good selves that you may do my will with Jōr and his wife and smite them and scatter them abroad and that the curse and the worm and the scattering abroad may overtake them and the wrath of God may overtake Jōr (. . .). Holy Martyrs, may you hasten and execute my judgement upon them.
> (Worrell, 1935, pp. 3–4)

The association of God and biblical matters, such as the nails of the cross, with evil human intent is a particularly repugnant feature of some spells (Polotsky, 1935, pp. 421–23).

People in Magical Texts

There were several kings of the town of Edessa (now Urfa, Turkey) named Abgar (132 B.C.–A.D. 216). One of them was a contemporary of Jesus Christ, who invited him to live in Edessa and to share the kingship. This letter is widely used for amulets as well as Jesus Christ's answer, not only in Coptic but also in Greek, Aramaic, Ethiopian, and other languages. The letter begins, "Abgar, the king of the town of Edessa, writes to the Great King, the son of the Living God, Jesus Christ." Christ's answer begins, "Copy of the letter of Jesus Christ, the son of the Living God. He writes to Abgar, the king of Edessa." One passage of the answer gives the following promises: "Thy sickness will be healed, if thou, as a human being, hast committed many sins, they will be forgiven to thee, and Edessa will be blessed for ever!" This passage was undoubtedly the reason that both letters were so widely used for amulets in Oriental countries.

The spells of Kyprianos fill pages 1–325 in Bilabel's (1934) collection, in both Coptic and Arabic. Kyprianos was initially a pagan. Then he was converted to Christianity by his love for the virgin Justina. Martyred under DIOCLETIAN, he is celebrated on 20 Bābah.

Before his conversion he was a magician, and it may be interesting to see how the Copts perceived the apprenticeship of this profession. As a boy he went to Olympus, the mountain of the gods, and learned there the secrets of the divine statues (*eikon*) and how they used to speak. He saw choruses of demons there. Some of them sang hymns; others were waylaying, cheating, and making disturbances. There were armies of each god and each goddess. He spent forty days and forty nights there. At the age of fifteen he was instructed by priests, especially the seven priests of the devil and his prophetess. He learned how the earth was fixed on its foundation and the laws of the air and the ether. He invaded the sea and went down to the underworld (Tartarus).

At Argos he took part in the feast of Hera and was taught how to separate women from their husbands and how to sow hatred between brothers and friends. In Lacedaemon (Sparta) he learned the mysteries of Helios and Artemis, the laws of light and darkness and the celestial appearances. Among the Phrygians, whose language he understood, he was initiated into the seer's art, learning the language of the ravens and other birds and interpreting predictions.

Lecanoscopy

The art of seeing hidden or future things by looking into a cup filled with oil is called *mandal* in Arabic. In Coptic it is *shen-hīn* (ϣⲉⲛ-ϩⲓⲛ), asking the cup, corresponding to *šn-hn* in demotic, attested in the Demotic Magical Papyrus of London and Leiden (Erichsen, 1954, p. 514). The earliest attestation of lecanoscopy in Egypt is found in the Bible (Gn. 44:5), which says that Joseph in Egypt had a silver cup from which he drank and which he used to augur.

In modern times Copts and Muslims use a cup without handles filled with oil (Viaux, 1978, p. 55). The magician who reads the spell burns a mixture of incenses and places a boy who has not yet arrived at puberty in a circle drawn on the earth. The boy sees in the cup future events or hidden things, such as the identity of a thief. The circle is to protect the child from demons.

Coptic magic employs the "Prayer of Abū Tarbū (or Anbā Tarbū)," named after a holy man who had saved the only son of a woman bitten by a mad dog. The ceremony is performed exactly as it was by Abū Tarbū, with seven loaves of bread, seven cheeses, a little wine, a little good oil, seven dates, and a small cup of water (Galtier, 1905, pp. 124–27; Viaux, 1978, pp. 87–89). Seven boys who have not yet reached the age of puberty are present. The priest reads several prayers and "the life of Abū Tarbū," who is unknown to the Coptic Synaxarion, and Psalms 19, 22, 118, and 120. Then he recites a prayer for the person bitten by the dog and groups the seven boys around the victim, and the children begin to circle him seven times. In the meantime, the priest reads an incomprehensible text: *Pesthe napas eshsherperikas, sharrasonthas kershn, pershn, soupenin soukenin pistherpou!*

When the children have circled the bitten one seven times, the cantor or the archdeacon greets the priest, "Peace to thee, Master!" The priest replies, "Peace to thee my child. What dost thou wish?" The reply is, "I have come to ask for the recovery and the health on the part of God and the Saint Abū Tarbū!" Then the priest puts a mouthful of bread, cheese, and dates into the cantor's or archdeacon's mouth, retrieves it, and throws it into the lap of the person who was bitten by the dog. Each of the seven boys says, "I have come to ask for the recovery and the health on the part of God and the Saint Abū Tarbū!" Then each of them takes pieces of bread, cheese, and dates and gives them to the victim. He will eat such a piece every morning and drink a bit of wine and water from the church. At the end, the priest anoints the bitten one with the oil he had brought and leaves him with the blessing of God and Saint Abū Tarbū.

This is the ceremony according to Viaux, but there are some local differences in the various parts of the country. At al-Zīniyyah Qiblī, north of Luxor, the boys mime dogs and menace the victim as if to bite him.

The seal (Arabic, *khātm*) of the *mandal* is written on white unlined paper. At the four sides of the square are the names of the four angels: Mīkā'īl, Gabrā'īl, 'Azra'īl, Isrāfīl. The four strokes that form the square read *Qulluh (qul lahu) al-ḥaqq wa lahu al-mulk* ("tell him the truth and he has the power"). The square in the middle bears the inscription, *Qaddūs rabb al-malā'ikah* (Holy is the Lord of the Angels). Above are written the alphabetic letters sīn and nūn and between them *ya-Nūḥ* (O Noah) and beneath *wa-al-rūḥ* ("and the spirit") with two letters, qāf and hā, upside down.

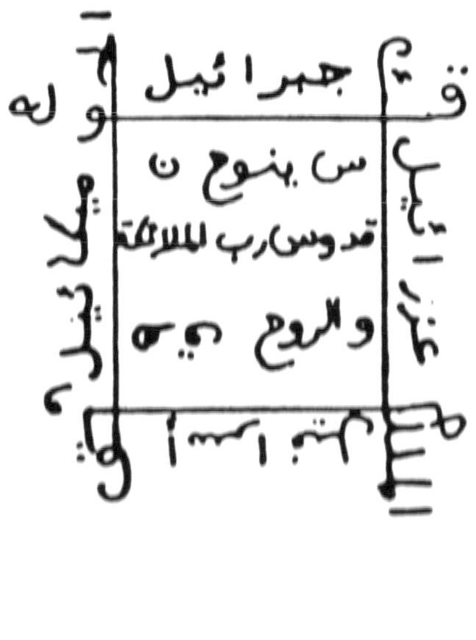

The young boy holds this seal in his right hand during the whole ceremony (Viaux, 1978, p. 103).

An invocation to the angel Hrouphos (apparently Rufus) is written in a spiral form, beginning from a center marked with a big black dot. The beginning reads, "I adjure thee today, O angel Hrouphos!" (Kosack, 1974, p. 297).

The form of this amulet (ghost trap) is certainly of Jewish origin. The Hebrews who lived in the quarters of the eastern half of Babylon and in the western suburbs of the city used to invert terracotta bowls inscribed with magical texts to protect their houses from the attacks of all kinds of evil spirits. The disposition of these spells is exactly the same as that of the Coptic ghost trap.

The British Museum possesses a very large collection of these bowls inscribed with the square Hebrew characters or with Syriac or Mandaic letters. Budge calls these texts in circular form "devil traps" and has published about four of them (1961, pp. 284–89). There is but one difference: the Jewish texts are written on terra-cotta bowls, but the Coptic ghost trap is written on paper.

Similar additions are found in cabalistic amulets where the extremities of Hebrew letters bear a small circle (Budge, p. 404). The circles on the edges of the letters seem to imitate cuneiform writing, but with circles instead of triangles. The following amulet (Bilabel, 1934, p. 380) consists of a short prayer and two lines of letters with small circles:

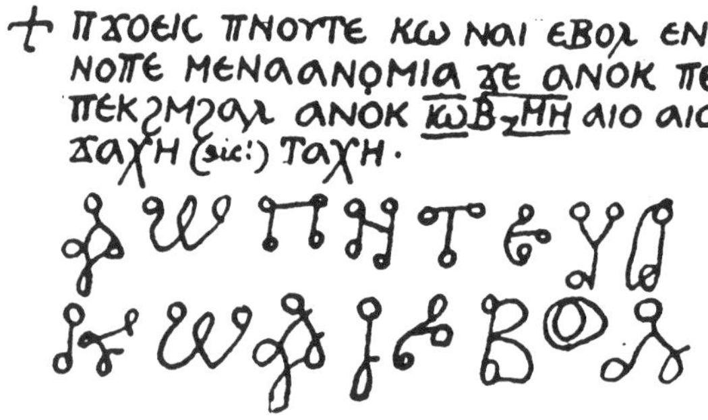

The prayer reads, "ti pjoeis pnoute kō nai ebol ena nope menaanomia je anok pe pekhmhal anok iōb-mē aio aio . . . jakhē takhē," "O Lord God, forgive me my sins and my iniquities, for I am thy servant. I am Iōb, son of Mē. . . . Yea, yea, quickly, quickly!" The two lines below the prayer read, ⲁ ⲱ ⲡⲛⲧⲉⲩⲟ (= ⲱ ⲡⲛⲟⲩⲧⲉ), a ō pnteuo (= ō pnoute), and ⲕⲱ ⲁⲓ ⲉⲃⲟⲗ (= ⲕⲱ ⲛⲁⲓ ⲉⲃⲟⲗ), kō ai ebol (= kō nai ebol), meaning "O God, forgive me!" The scribe was not familiar with this writing, so he wrote ⲡⲛⲧⲉⲩⲟ (pnteuo) instead of ⲡⲛⲟⲩⲧⲉ (pnoute) and ⲁⲓ (ai) instead of ⲛⲁⲓ (nai). Also, stars and other ornaments bear these small circles.

The Coptic amulet in Arabic script shown here was written in 1974 for a student who had to undergo examinations at the university. There are seven pentagrams and a text. The letters are separated and use no diacritical points, and there is no space between the words, so that the contents of the amulet are incomprehensible (Viaux, 1978, p. 47).

In the last line appears the Arabic *Allāh*, God, to the left, nearly at the end of the Arabic line.

BIBLIOGRAPHY

Betz, H. D. *The Greek Magical Papyri in Translation, Including the Demotic Spells.* Vol. 1. Chicago and London, 1985.

Bilabel, F., and A. Grohmann. *Griechische, koptische und arabische Texte zur Religion und religiösen Literatur in Ägyptens Spätzeit.* Heidelberg, 1934.

Brier, B. *Ancient Egyptian Magic.* New York, 1980.

Budge, E. A. W. *Amulets and Talismans.* New York, 1930. Repr. 1961.

Crum, W. E. *Eine Verfluchung.* Berlin, 1896.

———. *Catalogue of the Coptic Manuscripts in the British Museum.* London, 1905.

———. "Magical Texts in Coptic." *Journal of Egyptian Archaeology* 20 (1934):51–53, 195–200.

Erichsen, W. *Demotisches Glossar.* Copenhagen, 1954.

Erman, A. "Die ägyptischen Beschwörungen des grossen Pariser Zauberpapyrus." *Zeitschrift für ägyptische Sprache und Altertumskunde* 21 (1883):89–109.

———. "Zauberspruch für einen Hund." *Zeitschrift für ägyptische Sprache und Altertumskunde* 35 (1895a):132–35.

______. "Heidnisches bei den Kopten." *Zeitschrift für ägyptische Sprache und Altertumskunde* 33 (1895b):47–51.

______. "Ein koptischer Zauberer." *Zeitschrift für ägyptische Sprache und Altertumskunde* 33 (1895c):43–46.

______. "Drei Geister als Boten des Zauberers." *Mitteilungen der vorderasiatischen Gesellschaft* 21 (1916):301–304.

Galtier, E. "Contribution à l'étude de la littérature arabe-copte." *Bulletin de l'Institut français d'archéologie orientale* 4 (1905):123–27.

Griffith, F. L. "The Old Coptic Magical Texts of Paris." *Zeitschrift für ägyptische Sprache und Altertumskunde* 38 (1900):85–95.

Hopfner, T. *Griechisch-ägyptischer Offenbarungszauber,* Vol. 1, Leipzig, 1921; repr., Amsterdam, 1983. Vol. 2, Leipzig, 1924; repr., Amsterdam, 1984.

Kosack, W. *Lehrbuch des Koptischen.* Graz, 1974.

Krall, J. "Koptische Amulette." *Mitteilungen der Papyrussammlung Erzherzog Rainer* 5 (1892):115–22.

Kropp, A. *Ausgewählte koptische Zaubertexte.* 3 vols. Vol. 1, Louvain, 1931; Vol. 2, 1931; Vol. 3, 1930.

Kühner, R. "Gnostische Aspekte in den koptischen Zaubertexten. *Bulletin de la Société d'égyptologie* 4 (1980):61–64.

Lange, H. O. "Ein altfaijumischer Beschwörungstext." In *Studies Presented to F. Ll. Griffith.* London, 1932.

Lexa, F. *La Magie dans l'Egypte antique, de l'Ancien Empire jusqu'à l'époque copte.* 2 vols. Paris, 1925.

Polotsky, H. J. "Zu einigen Heidelberger Zaubertexten" (corrections to Bilabel, 1934). *Orientalia* 4 (1935):416–26.

______. "Suriel der Trompeter." *Le Muséon* 49 (1936):231–43.

Preisendanz, K. *Papyri Graecae Magicae.* 2 vols. Berlin and Leipzig, 1928, 1931.

Rossi, F. "Di alcuni manuscritti copti che si conservano nella Biblioteca Nazionale di Torino." *Memorie della Reale Accademia delle Scienze di Torino* ser. 2, 44 (1894):21–52 (corrections in Kropp, 1930).

Satzinger, H. "The Old Coptic Schmidt Papyrus." *Journal of the American Research Center in Egypt* 12 (1975):37–50.

Viaux, G. *Magie et coutumes populaires chez les Coptes d'Egypte.* Sisteron, 1978.

Vycichl, W. "Der Feuerstrom im Jenseits." *Archiv für ägyptische Archäologie* (1938):263–4.

______. "Die sogenannte Aleph-Bethregel im Armenischen und anderen orientalischen Sprachen." *Handes Amsorya* 75 (1961):21–30.

Winkler, H. A. *Siegel und Charaktere in der muhammedanischen Zauberei.* Berlin and Leipzig, 1930.

______. *Salomon und die Karina.* Stuttgart, 1931.

Worrell, W. H. "Coptic Magical and Medical Texts." *Orientalia* 4 (1935):1–37, 184–94.

WERNER VYCICHL

MAGICAL OBJECTS. In its preventive form, magic was considered in pharaonic Egypt as one of the normal elements of religion. It was a prerogative of divine power and of all who had a share in it. The progressive weakening of the concept of the authentically sacred in the Late Period led also to a degeneration of this view of magic. Oriental and, later, Greek influence hastened the movement toward an idea of magic imposing the will of the user upon the gods, for ends that were sometimes not very reputable. Christianity was unable to eradicate it completely. It is therefore difficult to make any distinction between magical objects used by pagans or by Christians, especially in the first millennium A.D. Nevertheless, it does not appear that the magical role attributed to images during the pharaonic period was passed on to Coptic Christians.

Amulets had always been held in honor under the pharaohs, in particular those used in burials between the bands of linen wrapping mummies, and they persisted into the Coptic period. They consisted of written formulas on papyrus and later on parchment, or figurative forms, drawn, painted, or sculpted, notably in intaglios. In this last technique, Gnostic motifs are mingled with Egyptian, Oriental, or Greek gods (such as the intermediary beings Iao and Sabaoth), or even with Christian symbols.

Mirrors, in ivory or hollow bone, square or round, bearing incised geometric motifs, were fairly numerous among the magic objects. The image of the holder, reflected by the polished metal and seeming to be introducing another world, must have been at the origin of this style of decoration.

Dolls in human likeness stiffly carved or incised with geometric motifs have subsisted until recent times in both Christian and Islamic Egypt. Clay or wax dolls in the likeness of the victim of a magic spell and covered with inscriptions go back to the Egypt of the Middle Kingdom. Under Roman domination such dolls were combined, in a kind of adoption of the Hellenistic *tabulae defixionum* ("formulae of imprecation"), with a bristling of needles piercing thirteen vital places of the body, according to the directions given in the magical instructions of the second century A.D. The only figure that has come down to us intact is a daintily modeled doll from the third century in the Louvre.

A fresco from a chapel in BĀWĪṬ carries evocations of male or female demons that are connected

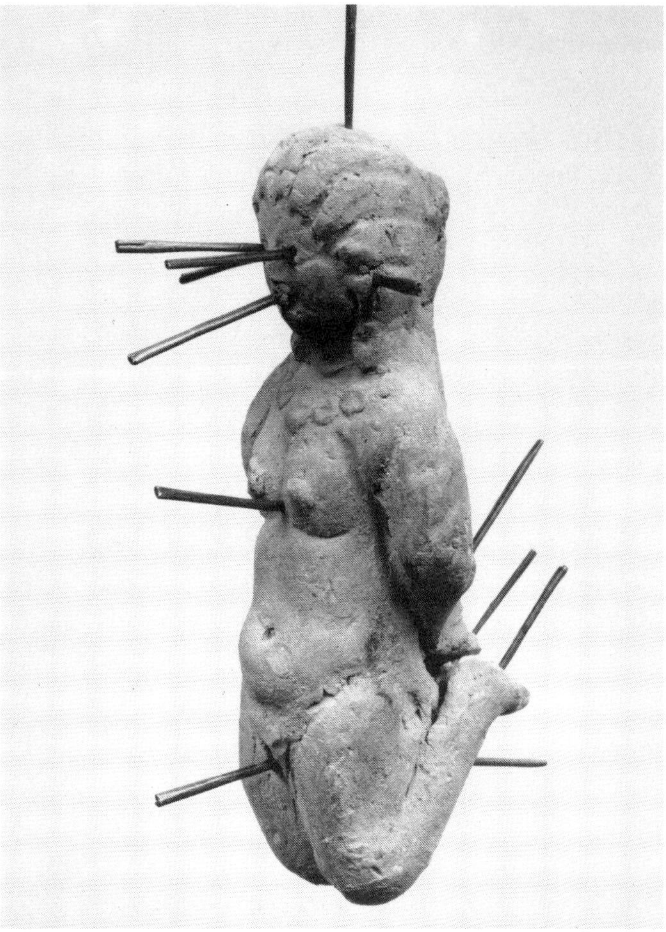

Magic doll for casting spells, pierced with needles. Painted terra cotta. Middle Egypt. Third–fourth century. Height: 9 cm; width: 4 cm; thickness: 4 cm; apparent length of needles: 2 cm. *Courtesy Louvre Museum, Paris.*

with magic. Above the demon Alabastria, pierced with a lance by Saint Sisinnios, are presented baneful animals—a hyena, an owl, a crocodile, an ibis, two serpents, and a scorpion. It also includes an eye pierced with a dagger between two swords. This eye is evidently not that of the Egyptian god Horus, which has beneficial power; it must be an intrusion from late Greek or Latin sources.

BIBLIOGRAPHY

Bonner, Campbell. *Studies in Magical Amulets, Chiefly Graeco-Egyptian.* London, 1950.

Bourguet, P. du. *Un ancêtre des figurines d'envoutement percées d'aiguilles, avec ses compléments magiques, au Musée du Louvre.* Mémoires publiés par les membres de l'Institut français d'archéologie orientale 104. Cairo, 1980.

———. "Magie égyptienne." In *Dictionnaire des religions.* Paris, 1984.

PIERRE DU BOURGUET, S.J.

MAḤALLAH AL-KUBRĀ, AL-, a city located in the middle of the Delta in the Gharbiyyah province. In earlier Arabic sources it was known simply as al-Maḥallah and in Coptic as ϯϣⲁⲓⲣⲓ.

The early history of Christianity in al-Maḥallah al-Kubrā is obscure because the city is seldom mentioned in sources before the Arabic period. However, by the year 1257 al-Maḥallah al-Kubrā was a bishopric, as evidenced by the attendance of Bishop Gregory of al-Maḥallah at the consecration of the chrism in Cairo in that year (Munier, 1943, p. 34).

BIBLIOGRAPHY

Amélineau, E. *La Géographie de l'Egypte à l'époque copte,* pp. 262–63. Paris, 1893.

Munier, H. *Recueil des listes épiscopales de l'église copte.* Cairo, 1943.

Timm, S. *Das christlich-koptische Ägypten in arabischer Zeit,* pt. 4, pp. 1527–30. Wiesbaden, 1988.

RANDALL STEWART

MAḤALLAT ABŪ ʿALĪ, town mentioned in the HISTORY OF THE PATRIARCHS as the home of a dumb, lame man who was brought to Saint Bessus in DAYR YUḤANNIS KĀMĀ where he was healed. This account, which indicates that Maḥallat Abū ʿAlī had a Christian community in the latter half of the eleventh century, does not specify the location of the town. Muslim authors know four places with the name: (1) Maḥallat Abū ʿAlī, now known as Kom ʿAlī, in the district of Ṭanṭā; (2) Maḥallat Abū ʿAlī al-Gharbiyyah, in the district of Disūq; (3) Maḥallat Abū ʿAlī al-Qanṭarah, in the district of al-Maḥallah al-Kubrā; and (4) Maḥallat Abū ʿAlī al-Mujāwirah, in the district of Ṭanṭā. The fact that the account in the *History of the Patriarchs* does not add a specifier such as al-Gharbiyyah or al-Qanṭarah to the name of the town may suggest that it refers to the place known as Kom ʿAlī, which is located in the middle of the Delta about 8 miles (12 km) north of Ṭanṭā in the province of Gharbiyyah.

BIBLIOGRAPHY

Timm, S. *Das christlich-koptische Ägypten in arabischer Zeit,* pt. 4, p. 1530. Wiesbaden, 1988.

RANDALL STEWART

MAḤALLAT AL-AMĪR, town located in the Delta province of Beheira some 5 miles (8 km) southeast of Rashīd.

The HISTORY OF THE PATRIARCHS relates that during the patriarchate of CHRISTODOULUS (1047–1077) the Muslim authorities ordered that Christian churches and monasteries were to be closed and a special tax for Christians was to be assessed. However, al-Mu'ayyad, the amir of Alexandria, was favorably inclined toward the Christians. He warned them in advance of the impending order and admonished them to take all the valuables from their churches before they could be confiscated. In addition he returned 200 dinars that had been collected from the Christians in Rashīd, Idkū, al-Jadīdiyyah, and Maḥallat al-Amīr. This story suggests that Maḥallat al-Amīr was the home of a well-to-do Christian community in the eleventh century.

BIBLIOGRAPHY

Timm, S. *Das christlich-koptische Ägypten in arabischer Zeit*, pt. 4, pp. 1530–31. Wiesbaden, 1988.

RANDALL STEWART

MAḤALLAT MINŪF, a town in the Egyptian Delta about 7 miles (11 km) north of Ṭanṭā, in the Gharbiyyah province. The town was previously known in Arabic as Minūf al-Suflā, in Greek as Onouphis kato, and in Coptic as ⲡⲁⲛⲟⲩϥ ϧⲁⲧ (Panouf khat). Though ancient and medieval sources preserve no descriptions or accounts of Christians, churches, or bishops in Maḥallat Minūf, the fact that the town is listed in the medieval Coptic-Arabic scalae and in the roster of Egyptian bishoprics suggests that it had a significant Coptic community by the early Middle Ages (Munier, 1943, pp. 46, 53).

BIBLIOGRAPHY

Amélineau, E. *La Géographie de l'Egypte à l'époque copte*, pp. 250–51. Paris, 1893.
Maspero, J., and G. Wiet. *Matériaux pour servir à la géographie de l'Egypte*, pp. 202–204. Cairo, 1919.
Muḥammad Ramzī. *Al-Qāmūs al-Jughrāfī lil-Bilād al Miṣriyyah*, Vol. 2, pt. 2, pp. 107–108. Cairo, 1958.
Munier, H. *Recueil des listes épiscopales de l'église copte*. Cairo, 1943.
Timm, S. *Das christlich-koptische Ägypten in arabischer Zeit*, pt. 4, pp. 1573–75. Wiesbaden, 1988.

RANDALL STEWART

MA'IDAH. *See* Refectory.

MAJLIS MILLI, AL-. *See* Community Council, Coptic.

MAJMU' AL-SAFAWI, AL-. *See* Safī Ibn al-'Assāl, al-.

MAJMŪ' UṢŪL AL-DĪN (Compendium of the Fundamentals of Religion), a Coptic *summa theologica* in five parts and seventy chapters, written by al-MU'TAMAN ABŪ ISHĀQ IBRĀHĪM IBN AL-'ASSĀL somewhat before 1260. According to G. Graf (1947) it has a compact, systematic structure and omits church historical material. The introduction has an exposition of the aim and arrangement of the work and a citation of the sources used, along with a list of thirty Christian Oriental writers, past and present. There is a preparatory sketch of elementary logic and tutorial material on concepts, judgments, and argumentation. The main parts include these subjects: Part 1, dogmatics of general subjects, creator and creation, man, divine revelation, and its intelligibility and credibility; Part 2, the Trinity; Part 3, Christology; Part 4, church service and customs, treated uncritically and relying on miracle stories from apocryphal literature; Part 5, eschatology. Al-Mu'taman cites the authors he uses by name and repeats the source material completely or in abstracts.

VINCENT FREDERICK

MAKARIUS SALIB. *See* Salippe Mikarius.

MAKĀRYUS ḤUNAYN (1773–1805), a Copt who became a colonel in the French army during the Napoleonic Wars. Makāryus was born in the district of Būlāq in Cairo on 17 February 1773. He spent his early years training as a goldsmith with his father, Mu'allim Ḥunayn Abū Ḍabb. At the age of twenty, he decided to study with Anṭūn Abū Ṭaqiyyah. Through diligence and determination, he learned to read and write Arabic as well as French—which proved to be useful after the French invasion of Egypt in 1798 under Napoleon Bonaparte. After the triumph of the French, he entered their service as an interpreter. In appreciation of his service, Napoleon appointed him assistant to the leader of the French expedition to Syria. At the age of thirty, Ḥunayn decided to join General YA'QŪB'S

Coptic Legion in the French army as a regular soldier. On the strength of his performance in the military, he was made an officer.

With the departure of the French from Egypt in 1801, General Yaʿqūb also left, and with him went the leading figures in his Coptic Legion, including Makāryus Ḥunayn. In France he became associated with the restructured Coptic Legion. Owing to his bravery and military skills, his general nominated him as a close military escort, with the rank of captain. After that he is known to have participated in the Napoleonic Wars in 1805 against the Russians and the Austrians. He played a prominent part in the Italian battles and was granted the rank of colonel as a reward for valor. Later he fought at Austerlitz, where he was mortally wounded. He died on 18 December 1805.

BIBLIOGRAPHY

Ramzī Tadrus. *Al-Aqbāṭ fī al-Qarn al-Ishrīn,* 3 vols. Cairo, 1911.

A. LOUCA

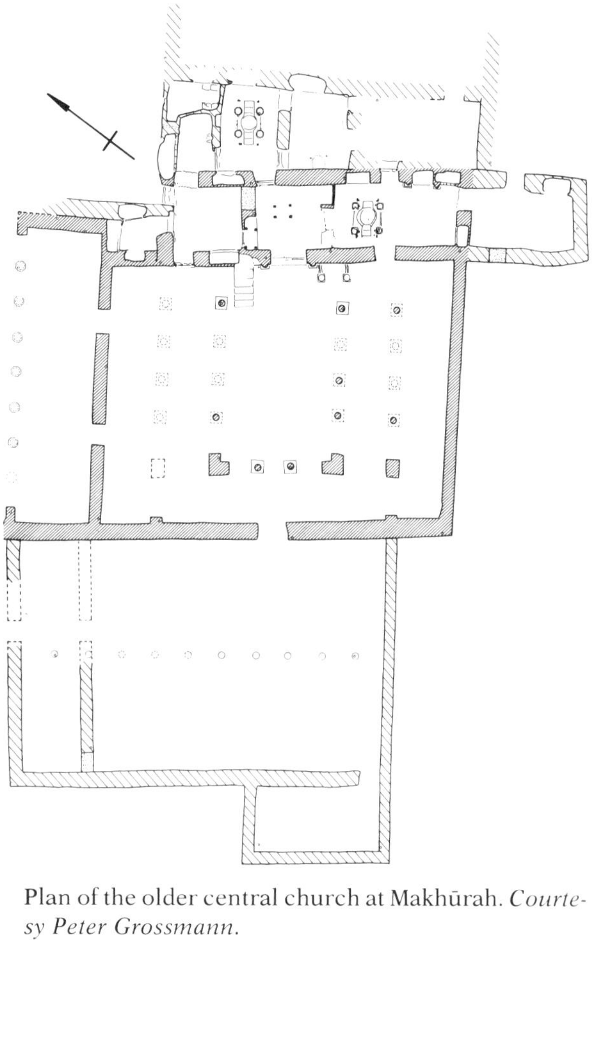

Plan of the older central church at Makhūrah. *Courtesy Peter Grossmann.*

MAKHŪRAH (Mareotis), small late Roman settlement on the Mediterranean coast about 10 miles (16 km) west of ABŪSĪR (Taposiris Magna). Up to now the significance of the place has not been ascertained. Apart from two large churches, there are only a few domestic buildings within the surrounding wall, and the people that lived in them would have been far too few in number to fill these churches. On the other hand, the site is too exposed for a monastery.

Of the two churches only the older central church, which has a higher elevation, has been partially uncovered. It comprises a very short five-

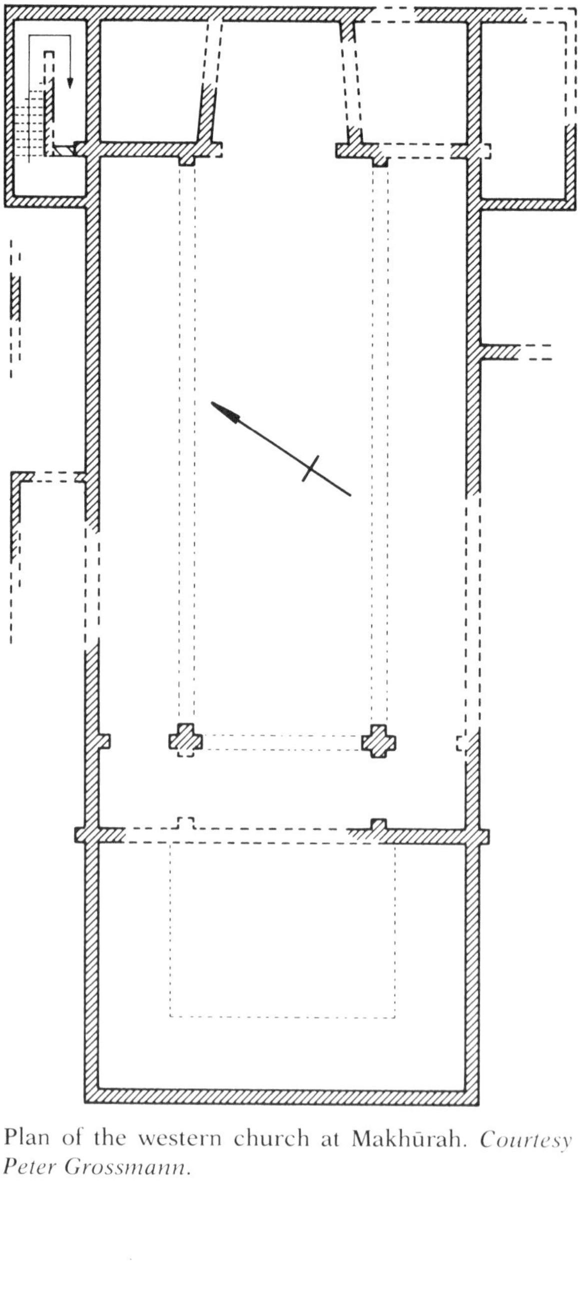

Plan of the western church at Makhūrah. *Courtesy Peter Grossmann.*

aisled basilica with a sanctuary that boasts a remarkable number of rooms including two baptisteries. The majority of them would have been added later. In the walls of the church, which were all constructed badly and with poor material, a number of shapeless dungeons were let in, possibly at a later date.

The western church situated on a lower plateau is a more substantial and carefully built structure and comprises a long three-aisled basilica with narthex and atrium. The east end is made up of five rooms of which the two outer ones extend beyond the side walls. The altar room is narrower at the back than at the front. It cannot be seen whether an apse was installed.

BIBLIOGRAPHY

Grossmann, P. "Zwei frühchristliche Kirchen in 'Ain Mahūra." In *Festschrift Elmar Edel.* Bamberg, 1979.

______. "Arbeiten in Mahūra al-qiblī." *Mitteilungen des deutschen archäologischen Instituts—Abteilung Kairo* 36 (1980):225–27.

PETER GROSSMANN

MAKĪN, IBN AL-'AMĪD AL- (Jirjis ibn Abī Yāsir ibn Abū al-Makārim ibn al-'Amīd al-Makīn), Coptic historian (1205–1273). He wrote a universal history, *al-Majmū' al-Mubārak*, consisting of two distinct sections. The first started with the creation and covered pre-Islamic times; the second dealt with the Islamic period down to his own times in 1260. For the pre-Islamic period, he used the Bible as a principal source for his history. For the Islamic period, he followed the example of the famous Islamic chronicler al-Ṭabarī. Apparently he used the work of his predecessor Eutychius as well as that of his contemporary Ibn al-Rāhib. His chronicle includes a succinct history of the patriarchs of Alexandria (summarized by A. Gutschmidt, 1890, pp. 395–525). It is here that the works of al-Makīn and Ibn al-Rāhib overlap, and it is difficult to distinguish who copied whom.

Al-Makīn was born in Cairo, though his ancestors must have come from Takrit in Mesopotamia. He also lived in Damascus and occupied the office of scribe in the military office in Cairo, where he was later deposed and incarcerated, and then freed. He retired to Damascus, where he died. His world chronicle has been translated into Latin, French, and English.

BIBLIOGRAPHY

Encyclopedia of Islam, ed. H. A. R. Gibb et al. Leiden, London, and Luzac, 1960–.

Gutschmidt, A. von. *Kleine Schriften*, Vol. 2. Leipzig, 1890.

Khayr-al-Din al-Ziriklī. *Al-A'lām*, 10 vols. Cairo, 1954.

'Umar Riḍā Kaḥḥālah. *Mu'jam al-Mu'allifīn*, 15 vols. Damascus, 1954–1961.

AZIZ S. ATIYA

MAKĪN JIRJIS, AL-, *hegumenos* of Alexandria, not to be confused with two famous Coptic authors of the same name—the twelfth-century historian and the fourteenth-century theologian.

Al-Makīn Jirjis was a *hegumenos* who in 1609 bore the title of head of the priests in the three churches of Alexandria. This may correspond to what is now called the "patriarchal vicar" for the city of Alexandria.

At this date he had an illuminated manuscript of 178 sheets copied. It contained the four Gospels in Arabic, with the Canons of Eusebius and introductions. In 1631 this manuscript was given to the library of the Coptic church of Jerusalem. It is now at the Coptic Patriarchate, Cairo.

KHALIL SAMIR, S.J.

MAKOURIA (Arabic, al-Muqurrah), the most important of the Christian kingdoms of medieval Nubia. Its territory probably extended from about the Third to the Fifth Cataract of the Nile, although there is some uncertainty about the locations of both the northern and the southern frontiers. The kingdom presumably took its name from the Makkourai, a Nubian tribal people who are first mentioned by Ptolemy (Geographia, IV, ii, 19).

Nothing is known of the history of Makouria prior to the time its ruler was converted to the Christian faith. According to John of Biclarum, this took place in 569 or 570. The account of John of Biclarum has been taken to imply that Makouria was converted initially by Melchite missionaries, but this has been questioned by recent scholars. After the seventh century, the evidence is very clear that the kingdom, like the neighboring lands of NOBATIA and 'ALWĀ, was firmly in the Monophysite camp, and it so remained until the end of the Middle Ages.

The capital and principal royal residence of

Makouria were at the city of DONGOLA, situated on the east bank of the Nile about halfway between the Third and Fourth Cataracts. The medieval city, now entirely in ruins, should not be confused with the modern provincial capital of the same name. Modern Dongola, or Dongola al-Urdi, is situated about 60 miles (100 km) north of the original Dongola, and on the opposite bank of the Nile.

In the years following their conquest of Egypt, the Arabs tried twice to annex the kingdom of Makouria as well. Their first attack, in 642, resulted in a resounding defeat of the invaders. A second attack ten years later was militarily inconclusive and was followed by the conclusion of a negotiated truce, called the BAQṬ. Under its terms the political and religious independence of the Nubians was guaranteed, in exchange for an annual tribute of slaves. The obligations of the *Baqṭ* were not consistently met, but the agreement remained at least nominally in force for more than 600 years. As a result, the development of Nubia's medieval civilization was little hindered by the Egyptians or other Arab powers.

Late in the tenth century Makouria was visited by the Fatimid envoy IBN SALĪM AL-ASWĀNĪ. The excerpted account of his mission that is preserved in AL-MAQRĪZĪ's *Kitāb al-Muqaffā'* is the most detailed firsthand description of medieval Nubia that we possess. Ibn Salīm describes a peaceful and prosperous realm with many towns and with broad, fertile fields. The kingdom of Makouria proper (i.e., excluding the northern territory of Nobatia, which was under Makourian rule but was separately designated) was under close direct supervision of the king. Muslim traders were not permitted to enter the territory of Makouria, where all foreign commerce was a royal monopoly. As a result, no money was in circulation.

The principal royal seat of Makouria was at Dongola, but according to Ibn Salīm, the king had residences in other places as well. The court retinue consisted of officials called the *domestikos, protodomestikos, meizon, protomeizoteros,* and *primikerius.* These are familiar Byzantine titles, but we know nothing of their specific functions in the Nubian kingdom. Some Arab sources assert that, in addition to the "great king," there were a number of vassal kings in the territory of Makouria. The dependent northern territory of Nobatia was separately governed by the eparch, who was a royal appointee.

It is clear from a number of references that in early medieval Nubia the royal succession passed from father to son. After the eleventh century, however, we can observe a curious reversion to the older Nubian practice of matrilineal succession. According to ABŪ ṢĀLIḤ, "It is said to be the custom among the Nubians, when a king dies and leaves a son and also a nephew, the son of his sister, that the latter reigns after his uncle instead of the son; but if there is no sister's son, then the king's own son succeeds" (Abū Ṣāliḥ, pp. 271–72). This rule of succession apparently was not consistently followed, with the result that there was a great deal of dynastic strife in Makouria in the late Middle Ages.

After the eleventh century both Nubia and Egypt began to be affected by the spirit of military feudalism that was also engulfing Europe and the Levant. The result was a period of economic decline and of growing political instability. The feudalistic Mamluks seized the Egyptian throne in 1250, and they soon began intervening in the dynastic affairs of Nubia as well. A number of military expeditions were sent into Makouria to support the cause of one dynastic claimant or another, and in 1276 the Nubian king Shekenda was forced to accept the Mamluk sultan Baybars as his suzerain. Although the king himself remained a Christian, he and his subjects were now obliged to pay the JIZYAH (poll tax) like any other Christian subjects of the sultan. Under these circumstances many ordinary citizens as well as some members of the royal family converted to Islam, and in 1323 a Muslim claimant succeeded to the royal throne. The great bulk of his subjects, nevertheless, continued to practice Christianity until at least a century later.

The accession of a Muslim ruler ended the Mamluk incursions into Nubia, but it did nothing to restore political stability. Dynastic intrigues continued, and in addition the country was now overrun by various nomad tribal groups that had been driven out of Egypt. Under their influence the kingdom finally broke up into warring principalities, and Makouria ceased to exist as a political entity. The date and circumstances of its final dissolution have not been recorded, but it was evidently before the time of Ibn Khaldūn (d. 1406), who wrote in the *Kitāb al-'ibar* (The Book of Examples):

> The clans of the Juhaynah Arabs spread over their country, settled there, occupied the country and made it a place of pillage and disorder.
>
> At first, the Nubian kings tried to check them, but failed; then they tried to find favor with them by giving them their daughters in marriage. The result was that their kingdom broke up and passed by inheritance to certain sons of the Ju-

haynah on account of their mothers, according to the custom of the infidels which establishes the succession of the sister or the sister's son. In this way their kingdom disintegrated and Arab nomads of the Juhaynah tribe took possession of it. But their rule retained no semblance of the monarchic rule of the kings, because of the evil which makes discipline impossible among them. Consequently, the Nubians divided themselves into many parties, and have remained thus up to the present time. No trace of efficient authority has survived in their country.

(V, 922–23; translated in Hassan, 1967, p. 127)

BIBLIOGRAPHY

Adams, W. Y. *Nubia, Corridor to Africa*, pp. 438–531. Princeton, N.J., 1977.

Hassan, Y. F. *The Arabs and the Sudan: From the Seventh to the Early Sixteenth Century*, p. 127. Edinburgh, 1967.

Ibn Khaldūn. *Al-'ibar wa-diwan al-mubtada' wa-al-khabar*. Beirut, 1879.

Kirwan, L. P. "Notes on the Topography of the Christian Nubian Kingdoms." *Journal of Egyptian Archaeology* 21 (1935):61–62.

Monneret de Villard, U. *Storia della Nubia cristiana*, pp. 61–221. Orientalia Christiana Analecta 118. Rome, 1938.

Ptolemy. *Geographia*, ed. S. Munster. Amsterdam, 1966. Reprint of Basel, 1540.

Vantini, G. *Christianity in the Sudan*, pp. 33–198. Bologna, 1981.

WILLIAM Y. ADAMS

MAKRAMALLĀH THE HEGUMENOS, eighteenth-century priest known from two manuscripts in the library of the Coptic Patriarchate, Cairo.

In 1724 Makramallāh was probably pastor of the Church of Saint Menas of Fumm al-Khalij in Cairo. He copied a small-sized manuscript of 183 sheets containing the Ordo of the Holy Week in Coptic and Arabic; he bore the costs himself, as he informs the reader. He then bequeathed it to the Church of Saint Menas.

In 1737 he was a *hegumenos* serving the Church of the Virgin of Ḥārit al-Rūm in Cairo. In 1740 Makramallāh had a very fine manuscript with gold miniatures copied by Ibrāhīm ibn Sim'ān, the brother of the abbess of the Monastery of al-Amir Tādrus in Cairo. This is a small-sized Arabic manuscript of 133 sheets containing the Gospel of John.

He may have been the father of the deacon and copyist JIRJIS MAKRAMALLĀH AL-BAHNASĀWĪ.

BIBLIOGRAPHY

Graf, G. *Catalogue de manuscrits arabes chrétiens conservés au Caire*. Vatican City, 1934.

KHALIL SAMIR, S.J.

MAKRAM EBEID (1889–1961), Egyptian politician born in Qinā. His family originated from Asyūṭ where his grandfather married a daughter of the famous Mu'allim JIRJIS AL-JAWHARĪ. Makram's father undertook construction work on the railway line from Nag Hammadi to Luxor, on the completion of which he was granted the title bey by the khedive. He was able to buy extensive property from the Royal Domains before his death in December 1925. Of the eleven children in the family, William (this was indeed Makram's given name until he rejected it during the struggle with the British) was the brightest, and his education took place in Qinā, Cairo, and then Asyūṭ, at the American College. Later, at the suggestion of Akhnūkh Fānūs, William was sent to Oxford in 1905. The dean of New College, who admired him, once said that Makram was the youngest of all students ever admitted in his college, except William Pitt. After graduating with a degree in law in 1908, Makram moved to France, where he spent two years studying Egyptology; he also fell under the influence of French socialism.

On his return to Egypt, Makram displayed his nationalistic tendencies, first by adhering to the Orthodox Coptic Church, refusing to duplicate his father's conversion to Protestantism, and then by following the Wafd party in its struggle for the total independence of Egypt under the leadership of Sa'd Zaghlūl. Attracted by his intelligence, eloquence, and loyalty, Sa'd adopted him as his political son and supporter. Gradually Makram became a strong participant in the history of Zaghlūl's nationalistic movement, where he was associated with all the events of the era and was probably the power behind the throne.

It was not until Sa'd's death in 1927 and the succession of MUSṬAFĀ AL-NAḤḤĀS that a change in the political climate became imminent. Alarmed by the spread of corruption and favoritism under the new regime and probably encouraged by the palace, Makram wrote his *Black Book*, in which he unveiled the moral decline and pitfalls of the years under Naḥḥās. He ended up by breaking away from the Wafd in its new form to establish in 1952 a separate Wafdist block (Ḥizb al-Kutlah al-Wafdiyyah).

The rising disunity in the ranks of the majority party heralded the weakening of Naḥḥās's leadership and the decline of Makram's position on the political scene. He died on 5 June 1961 and was eloquently eulogized at his funeral in the Cathedral of Saint Mark in Cairo by Anwar al-Sadat, then Speaker of the National Assembly, who recounted Makram's formidable role and his immortal heroism in the 1919 struggle for independence.

[*See also:* Political Parties: Wafd and New Wafd.]

MUSṬAFĀ AL-FIQĪ

MALAṬĪ YŪSUF, originally the administrative assistant of the bey Ayyūb the *Defterdar* (accountant general), one of the later Mamluk amirs of the powerful party of the bey Muḥammad Abū al-Dhahab, prior to the French Expedition. Malaṭī Yūsuf became better known under French rule. When the French were established in the country, they organized the administration of justice by the creation of a special *diwan* or commission of twelve members, half of whom were Copts and half were Muslim, under the chairmanship of Malaṭī Yūsuf. Little is known of Malaṭī's life and work beyond this commission, though we must assume his relative knowledge of French and of legal studies to have been entrusted with such an important function. In this capacity his name appeared with three Frenchmen, Magallon, Pagliano, and Tallian, together with a Muslim called the effendi Musṭafā, who fixed lawful taxes instead of the confusion of unprescribed imposts under the Mamluks. However, with the termination of French rule of Egypt, Malaṭī was executed by the Ottomans for his active participation with their enemy.

BIBLIOGRAPHY

Jabartī, al-. *'Ajā'ib al-Āthār,* 7 vols., ed. Ḥasan Jawhar et al. Cairo, 1958–1967.

Tawfīq Iskarūs. *Nawābigh al-Aqbāt fī al-Qarn al-Tāsi' 'Ashar.* Cairo, 1910.

Ya'qūb Nakhlah Rufaylah. *Tārīkh al-Ummah al-Qibṭiyyah.* Cairo, 1899.

MOUNIR SHOUCRI

MALĪJ, a town in the Egyptian Delta, the exact location of which is now uncertain, though it may be identical with modern Milīj (province of Minūfiyyah), located about 12 miles (20 km) northwest of Atrīb. The town was a bishopric at least as early as the middle of the eighth century when Bishop Victor of Malīj attended a council in Cairo. Malīj still had a bishop as late as 1349 when Bishop Peter was present at the consecration of the chrism in Cairo (Munier, 1943, p. 41).

BIBLIOGRAPHY

Amélineau, E. *La Géographie de l'Egypte à l'époque copte,* pp. 243–46. Paris, 1893.

Munier, H. *Recueil des listes épiscopales de l'église copte.* Cairo, 1943.

Timm, S. *Das christlich-koptische Ägypten in arabischer Zeit,* pt. 4, pp. 1538–41. Wiesbaden, 1988.

RANDALL STEWART

MALININE, MICHEL (1900–1977), French demoticist and Coptologist. He was a member of the Institut français d'Archéologie orientale du Caire (1930–1935); professor of Coptic at the Institut catholique of Paris (1936–1944); lecturer on Coptic literature at the fifth section of the Ecole pratique des Hautes Etudes (1943–1947); and director of demotic and Coptic studies at the fourth section of the Ecole pratique des Hautes Etudes (1951–1971).

BIBLIOGRAPHY

Cénival, F., and G. Posener. "Michel Malinine (1900–1977)." *Bulletin de l'Institut français d'Archéologie orientale* 83 (1983):v–ix.

Corsu, F. le. "Bibliographie de Michel Malinine (1900–1977)." *Revue d'Egyptologie* 30 (1971):7–9.

RENÉ-GEORGES COQUIN

MALLON, MARIE ALEXIS (1875–1934), French Egyptologist, Coptologist, and archaeologist. He was born at La Chapelle-Bertrin, Haute-Loire. He entered the Jesuit order in 1895. From 1902 he taught Coptic at the Saint Joseph University at Beirut and from 1913 at the Pontifical Biblical Institute in Rome, although living at Jerusalem. He died at Bethlehem.

BIBLIOGRAPHY

Dawson, W. R., and E. P. Uphill. *Who Was Who in Egyptology,* p. 193. London, 1972.

Kammerer, W., comp. *A Coptic Bibliography*. Ann Arbor, Mich., 1950; repr. New York, 1969.

AZIZ S. ATIYA

MAMLUKS AND THE COPTS. Under the rule of the Mamluk dynasty (1250–1517), the Copts were protected by their skill in handling taxation and state finances. Occasionally, as a political subterfuge, the Mamluk sultans dismissed them from office for their refusal to convert to Islam, but Copts were soon again employed to save the state from the resulting confusion in tax operations and civil administration. Another factor in the survival of the Copts and their churches was the relationship with Ethiopia: the emperors, who were of Coptic profession, interceded on behalf of the Copts at the sultan's court, promising to protect the Muslim mosques in Abyssinia.

In fact, after the discomfiture of the Crusade of Louis IX of France at al-Manṣūrah and the accession of the Mamluk sultan Aybak (1250) to the vacant Ayyubid throne, the new potentate employed a Copt by the name of Sharaf al-Dīn Hibat-Allāh ibn Sā'id al-Fā'izī as his vizier. He had powers in the administration of the country and could concentrate on the regulation of the taxation system at a time when the sultan's treasury was in need of funds. The new vizier, according to al-MAQRĪZĪ, devised a new supplementary tax as "the right of the Sultanate" over and above the normal tax imposed by his predecessors. Its results, though detrimental to Muslims and Copts alike, filled the sultan's treasury with the sorely needed funds.

One of Aybak's successors, Qutruz (1259–1260), continued to levy additional taxes for his campaign in Syria. Qutruz was assassinated, and when Baybars (1260–1277) took over, he revoked all taxes. Peace returned to Egypt.

Later, according to the Christian chronicler al-Mufaḍḍal ibn Abī al-Faḍā'il, on Baybars's return from an expensive campaign in Syria, the sultan aimed at extorting additional funds from all DHIMMIS, as non-Muslims were called. He threatened them with burning, and he ordered a large ditch to be dug below the citadel in Cairo and filled it with flammable material in readiness for punishment. (The reason for menacing the Dhimmis with burning was that they had been accused of starting fires in several districts of Cairo as an act of vengeance for the role of the Muslim mob in the destruction of Christian churches [Glubb, 1973, p. 211].) At this juncture, they were saved only by the emergence of a solitary Coptic monk named Būlus al-Ḥabīs, who had reputedly discovered the hidden treasure of the Fatimid caliph al-Ḥākim in a cave and used the money for the relief of the poor and the needy, irrespective of their religion. He ransomed the menaced Dhimmis with 500,000 dinars, to be paid in annual installments of 50,000 dinars, of which the first was paid on the spot (Tājir, 1951, pp. 174–76).

In the meantime, all the Coptic employees in the offices of war and taxation were dismissed and replaced by Muslims, who were not equipped with the requisite skills. In addition, the prosperous DAYR AL-KHANDAQ, outside Cairo in the neighborhood of the gate of Bāb al-Futūḥ, was ordered to be destroyed. But soon Sultan Qalawūn and his son al-Ashraf Khalīl found that their administration was in a shambles, and both were constrained to reappoint the Copts, to set things aright. Al-Maqrīzī said that the returned Copts abused Muslim subjects, and he gave a case in point, about a Copt by the name of 'Ayn al-Ghazāl, whose treatment of a Muslim broker precipitated the wrath of the public and the Mamluk amirs Baydarah and Sinjar al-Shujā'ī. Ultimately both amirs dismissed the Copts from their service and requested other amirs to do the same, while Coptic residences were stormed and pillaged by the angry populace. Alarmed by this outbreak of lawlessness, the sultan was constrained to use military force to end the havoc. Nevertheless, a decree was issued for the retention of Copts in office only if they converted to Islam; otherwise, they would risk decapitation (Glubb, 1973, pp. 189–90).

According to one story, a Maghribī vizier who was on a pilgrimage was passing through Cairo in the year 1301 and happened to observe a richly dressed horseman surrounded by natives who were pleading with him for something and kissing his boots while he ignored them. He was told that the man was a Copt. Consequently the Maghribī vizier approached Sultan al-Nāṣir Muḥammad ibn Qalawūn to protest against Muslim humiliation by Christians. Consequently, the Mamluk amirs who were present, among them the powerful Baybars al-Jashankīr, ordered the Copts to wear the blue turban instead of the white, and the Jews the yellow, to distinguish them from Muslims (Glubb, 1973, pp. 189–90). The Copts also had to wear a certain belt. Moreover, the churches in Cairo were closed for a short period, and those in Alexandria, together with Coptic residences, were attacked by mobs.

In 1303, Sultan al-Nāsir Muḥammad ibn Qalawūn and the amir Baybars al-Jashankīr suppressed the annual celebration of the FEAST OF THE MARTYR, which was a holy day among the Copts. The authorities even went to the Martyr's Church in Shubra and seized the box containing the famous relic of the martyr's finger, which the Copts used to dip in the Nile to ensure the river's annual flooding. They burned it and cast the ashes in the Nile.

But the most calamitous and destructive movement against the Christian churches came to pass in 1320 and subsequent years. This time, the storming of churches was general and could have been carried out only with careful maneuvering and conspiratorial preparation. The destruction of churches was apparently carried out at the same time, after the Friday prayers, from Cairo, Alexandria, and Damietta in Lower Egypt to QŪṢ in Upper Egypt. It seems that the authorities were taken by surprise by this movement and could not do much to stop it. While the sultan was alarmed at the extent of what happened, apparently some monks wanted to avenge this calamity with another—the burning of Cairo. Naphtha and sulfur were used to start fires in a number of Cairene districts, and a wind spread the flames far and wide, leaving hundreds of houses ruined. All attempts to stop the creeping destruction failed.

As the fire subsided, the authorities summoned the leaders of the various religious communities, including the Coptic and Melchite patriarchs, the Karaite rabbis, and numerous others to review these tragic events and to renew the COVENANT OF 'UMAR, to reaffirm the rightful position of minorities. However, under the year A.H. 852/1448, the annalist al-Sakhāwī stated that no church in Egypt escaped some destruction (al-Sakhāwī, 1897, p. 36; Tajir, 1951, pp. 184–94). In sum, these events left an indelible mark on Cairo and Coptic religious foundations throughout the country.

BIBLIOGRAPHY

Glubb, J. *Soldiers of Fortune: The Story of the Mamlukes.* New York, 1973.

Heyd, W. *Histoire du commerce du Levant au moyen âge,* 2 vols. Amsterdam, 1959.

Lane-Poole. S. *A History of Egypt in the Middle Ages.* London, 1901.

Sakhāwī, al-. *Al-Tibr al-Masbūk fī Dhayl al-Sulūk.* Bulāq Edition. Cairo, 1897.

Tājir, Jāk. *Aqbāṭ wa-Muslimūn Mundhu al-Fatḥ al-Arabi ilā 'ām.* Cairo, 1951.

Weit, G. "L'Egypte arabe." In *Histoire de la nation égyptienne,* 7 vols., ed. G. Hanotaux. Paris, 1931–1940.

Zellersteen, A. *Beiträge zur Geschichte der Mamluken-sultanen in den Jahren 690–741.* Leiden, 1919.

AZIZ S. ATIYA

MANASSĀ YŪḤANNĀ (1899–1930), Coptic church historian. He was born at Hūr, near Mallawī in Upper Egypt. He joined the Coptic Clerical College, Cairo, and became a lay preacher before he was ordained priest of Mallawī Church at the age of twenty. He wrote many books on church history and doctrine. His most important work is *Tārīkh al-Kanīsah al-Qibṭiyyah* (History of the Coptic Church; repr. Cairo, 1983).

FUAD MEGALLY

MANASSEH, SAINT, sixth-century archimandrite. The SYNAXARION is silent about Manasseh, who was a relative of ABRAHAM OF FARSHŪṬ. We possess the remnants (about forty pages) of a Coptic Encomium of this saint (Campagnano, 1978, pp. 230, 238).

It seems that Manasseh was an Alexandrian. He was first of all a monk in the community of Saint PACHOMIUS. He founded a monastery to the south of Farshūṭ, "opposite a village called ⲡⲉⲣⲡⲉ (Perpe), a village burnt by Cambyses." We do not know at what age Manasseh became a monk, but he had lost his mother six years before. The text relates that he often went north to see his kinsman Abraham. The bishop of Diospolis Parva (Hiw) came to consecrate the church, and delivered a sermon on this occasion.

Manasseh received some nuns from a convent of Pachomius, that they might place themselves under the protection of his prayer. He built for them a convent equipped with a tower.

We do not know at what date Manasseh died, but the Coptic encomium is important for knowing what Egyptian monasticism was like at the beginning of the sixth century.

BIBLIOGRAPHY

Campagnano, A. "Monaci egiziani fra V e VI secolo." *Vetera Christianorum* 15 (1978):223–46.

RENÉ-GEORGES COQUIN

MANDORLA. *See* Symbols in Coptic Art.

MANICHAEISM. Among the heresies that were spread in Egypt, Manichaeism played a prominent role. This is shown by the discovery of a library of seven volumes in the Asyūṭ dialect of Coptic and of a historical work on Mani written in Greek. This religion spread, in the form of a church, over the entire Mediterranean basin and as far as central and eastern Asia. In the kingdom of the Uigurs it even became a state religion, and after the decline of that kingdom it left traces in the remnant states of Kansu and Chotsko (Chotscho) down to the thirteenth century. In the Roman Empire it suffered severe persecution soon after its emergence and, indeed, was regarded as a concentration of all heresy. Reflecting the number of cultures and peoples among whom it was proclaimed, the tradition has come down to us in many languages: Latin, Greek, Syriac, Coptic, Arabic, Middle Persian, Parthian, Sogdian, Uigur, Tocharian, Chinese. Since the tradition is largely indirect, and in the original sources due attention must be paid to the peculiarity of literary forms often preserved by accident, in reconstructing the Manichaean system we must not be content with the knowledge derived from any one group of texts, not even from a group as comprehensive as the Coptic sources.

Mani (Manichaios, from *Mānī ḥajjā*, the living Mani) came from the Babylonian part of the Iranian empire. He was born on 14 April 216. His father, Pattek, had become a member of the Jewish-Christian Gnostic sect of the ELKASITES. Mani received two revelations, the first at the age of twelve, the second at twenty-four. His "twin" appeared to him and revealed to him the mystery in which the content of the faith was made known to him. He thereupon turned away from the Elkasites and began to proclaim his own teaching. When the Sassanid Ardashir I overthrew the Arsacids in Iran, Mani went to India. He returned under King Shapur I and won his favor, since the king wished to restore the Achaemenian empire and saw in Mani's syncretistic religion a common religion that could bind to his empire the regions of the eastern Mediterranean that he wanted to wrest from Rome. Mani prospered under Shapur's successor Hormizd I (273–274); but when Bahram I (274–276/277) came to the throne in 274, Mani was thrown into prison at the instigation of the Magi, and died after twenty-six days in custody. The year of his death is disputed (276/277). The period of his imprisonment gave him opportunity to prepare his disciples for their task after his death.

The mystery revealed to Mani answered the question of the way to man's redemption. For this, in accordance with Gnostic theology, a knowledge of cosmology was necessary, and this again had to be traced back to its metaphysical roots (*Kephalaia* 15.3–24). As was usual in GNOSTICISM generally, Mani, on the Platonic model, made use of myth for his presentation.

The dualism of good and evil, light and darkness, is original in Mani. Over against the Father of Greatness, consisting of five members of light and surrounded by twelve aeons who dwell in the kingdom of light, stands the king of darkness, Hyle. While peace and joy prevail in the realm of light, the kingdom of darkness is full of unrest and mutual conflict. Hence Mani can apply to it the word of Jesus in Matthew 12:25ff. It is only with a view to winning the kingdom of light that any unity of purpose comes about. This brings the Father of Greatness into difficulty, since his kingdom is ordered for peace and not for war. He therefore decides to take the field himself, in the person of his son the primal man, whom he has begotten of the Mother of Life (also called "of the living"). He puts on the five elements of light—air, wind, light, water, and fire—as souls of light. There is a battle in which the five elements of darkness—smoke, wind, darkness, water, and fire—bind the elements of light by uniting with them, and take the primal man captive. This defeat is, however, only apparent, for the mingling means the binding of darkness, depriving it of its power. The primal man turns for help to the Father of Greatness, who calls forth a new triad, the Friend of the Lights, the Great Architect, and the Living Spirit. The Living Spirit sends a call to the primal man, who gives an answer. Call and answer ascend and, clothed with them, the Living Spirit and the Mother of Life come down to deliver the primal man.

In order that the elements of light, too, may be delivered, the cosmos is created by the Living Spirit. Ten heavens and five earths are formed from the skins of the archons and their bodies. Sun and moon are produced from the best mixture of light. The archons are fixed as stars in the firmament in a wheel of the sphere. The dregs of darkness are swept down from heaven into three trenches. The order of the cosmos is maintained by five sons of the Living Spirit. The Splenditenens (Greek: *Phengokatochos*) oversees the tenth, ninth, and eighth heavens, and holds the world from above. The great King of Honor oversees the remaining heavens. The King of Glory is in charge of the paths on which the elements of light, wind, water, and fire ascend. Atlas (Greek: *Omophoros*) bears the cosmos on his shoulders. The Adam of Light casts down the sea monsters. If in the creation of the world the Living Spirit effected a rough separation of light and darkness, and thereby set up a mechanism for the redemption of the elements of light, it is the task of the Third Emissary, who resides in the sun while the Jesus Splendor has his place in the moon, to set the machinery of purification into motion. In male or female form, by his beauty he provokes the archons of the opposite sex to emit secretions that lead to the formation of the sea monster, the plants, and the archons who move on Earth. In this way a part of the light is refined away. The way of purification leads via the Milky Way, "the pillar of glory, the perfect man," to the moon, from which the light is handed on to the sun.

The archons now, in an obscene fashion, create a man and a woman after the likeness of the Third Emissary. They believe that God will do nothing against His image, and that they will be able to hide behind it. Moreover, the purification of the light is again and again delayed, and practically made impossible, by the multiplication of the human race, unless there is a counterattack on the part of the light. This occurs first of all through the coming of Jesus, who awakens the sleeping Adam and explains his existence to him. By eating from the tree of life Adam becomes able to see, but falls into great affliction. This leads him to a search for deliverance, for which ways are repeatedly offered to him from the primeval age on. Ever new apostles, from Seth to Shem, are sent to mankind. Then appear the three founders of the world religions of the time: Buddha, Zoroaster, and Jesus. Their teachings are falsified soon after their deaths, but in accordance with John 16:7f. the Paraclete, the Spirit of Truth, comes, to appear as the seal of the prophets. The Paraclete, Mani's "twin," unites with him, so that Mani himself is regarded by the believing community as the Paraclete promised by Jesus Christ. In contrast with the majority of the Gnostic heresies, Manichaeism formed a church like those of the Marcionites or the Elkasites, from whom Mani derived much.

The anthropology of Manichaeism affirms that man in his present condition is the ancient man, who through the struggle of the light-*nous* with sin is purified into the new man. This light-*nous* is identical with the first soul-member of the Father of Greatness, so that through Jesus and Mani the illuminator God intervenes among men as an active participant. The purification of the community takes place through a division into two groups of believers, the elect and the catechumens. The designation *auditores* for the latter goes back to an expression used for them in the Syrian church. The way of sanctification can be recognized from the relation between the two. Since the object of all that happens in the world is the final purification of the light out of the world, the propagation of the human race must be ever more restricted. Hence the elect must be unmarried. In order not to harm the light, they may not work, but are supported by the catechumens. The elements of light that pass into their bodies with the food are thereby purified. This is the Manichaean Eucharist. In fasting, also, the elect have more to perform than the catechumens. The latter are under the obligation of prayer, fasting, and almsgiving. Here the catechumen may so enhance his performance, especially by additional sexual abstinence, that he is delivered in a single body. Otherwise the way leads through the transmigration of souls, and one must enter into the body of an elect in order to obtain salvation.

When finally the purification of the cosmos as a whole is almost complete, what is left is gathered into the last "statue" (*andrias*). Then the Splenditenens and Atlas cease their labors, so that the world collapses and passes into a universal conflagration lasting 1,468 years. There is, however, no *apocatastasis* of the original situation; darkness is forever chained in a prison erected by the Great Architect, so that it can never again be dangerous. Some souls, which have not fulfilled their task, are utterly lost. Here we can see the conflict between Fate and freedom of the will, which can also be recognized elsewhere in *gnosis*.

To bring the purification to its completion, mankind must be gripped by Mani's teaching, and the Manichaean church must sanctify all people more and more. Mani sent missionaries to every corner of the earth. Egypt was early in his mind. Because of the uncertainties that the missionaries, like Mani himself, recognized in the traditions of the great religions, Mani believed that the situation could best be remedied by the creation of a canon of sacred writings that he had composed and authorized: (1) the Living Gospel; (2) the Treasure of Life; (3) the Pragmateia; (4) the Book of the Mysteries; (5) the Book of the Giants; (6) the Letters; (7) psalms and prayers. To these Mani added a further volume in which he presented the mythological events in pictorial form, which earned him the name "the painter." For this he also composed an explanation, the Book of the Foundation (perhaps identical with the *Epistula fundamenti* assailed by Augustine). Alongside the canon composed in Syriac there is a work in Middle Persian, the *Shapurakan* (Book dedicated to Shapur). Since, however, Manichaeism was a living religious community, it did not rest content with the canon, but created additional new literature. From the Coptic Manichaean Psalm book we can see how a series of hymn collections was assembled, and beside it there is abundant Iranian, Turkish, and Chinese material. Historical texts in which mention is made of the life and sufferings of Mani served for the edification of the community (the Cologne codex in Greek, the passion of Mani in Coptic, Iranian fragments). In Coptic there is also a sermon on the great war, which begins from an Iranian mythological theme and deals with the last things, with considerable borrowing from the synoptic apocalypse. The *Kephalaia* literature is of extraordinary scope, harking back to the Master's didactic discourses or expanding them, or answering new questions according to the same model.

Mani's mission was concerned with making the message clear and comprehensible by adapting to the forms of expressing religious ideas that were in current use in the several mission fields. In the *Shapurakan* especially, these were Iranian ideas; farther east, other Iranian ideas, but especially Buddhist terms, are to be found above all in the Chinese texts. Rivalry with Christianity in central Asia gave a special prominence to the person of Jesus. The same holds for the West, where Christ assumes the place of the Third Emissary and the figure of the Jesus *patibilis* is identical with the suffering Living Soul, the Cross of Light. This conception of Jesus is particularly strongly manifested in the West, but it is among the essential ingredients of Mani's theology. This is shown by a passage in the Cologne codex and by the interpretation of the words of judgment in Matthew 25:34–46.

Manichaeism is a markedly syncretistic religion that claims to have taken into itself all that was good in earlier religions. It is not an Iranian religion, although Iranian elements—such as the great war, the ascent of the soul after death, and the motif of the fourfold God (God, Light, Power, Wisdom)—are used as vehicles for its expression. Also, one can hardly speak of any fundamental Buddhist constituent. The transmigration of souls derives from the Hellenic heritage, and the rejection of work for the elect is a logical consequence of Mani's idea of the dispersion of the particles of light, which he found confirmed among the Buddhist monks on his journeys to India and eastern Iran. The central motive for the overcoming of dualism, however, derives from Christianity—redemption through Jesus Christ—save that Jesus' various functions are split into various mythological incidents. God appears in His son, the primal man, and suffers in Him and in His children, the elements of light. He is at the same time victorious in Him. The creative activity of God and of His son comes to the fore in the Living Spirit.

The description of the Pillar of Glory as a perfect man goes back to the ecclesiology and Christology of Ephesians 4:11ff., since the totality of souls aspires upward to the moon, where Jesus resides. The Milky Way is seen as the place where Jesus undertakes the purification; indeed, he is sometimes even identified with it. In addition to the Jesus Splendor, the primal man also has his place in the moon. After his return to the Kingdom of Light he is concerned, like the risen and exalted Christ of the Christians, for those who are to be redeemed. But alongside the cosmogonical and cosmological activity, we see Jesus also as a teacher of the first earthly man and in the form of *nous* in every man who is redeemed. Likewise, Jesus comes at the end of the world as its judge. As the means for its presentation Manichaeism makes use, particularly in speculative descriptions, of the astrological view of the world.

The mission probably gained a foothold between 244 and 260. While Manichaeism was being proclaimed in the Roman Empire, Addas came to Alexandria. Mani sent him the Gospel and two other writings, and at the same time gave him scribes. This shows the character of Manichaeism as a book religion. Papos and Thomas worked in Upper Egypt. The latter is probably identical with the author of the Psalms of Thomas; the former appears in Mani's letter book (unpublished). The main center in Upper Egypt was Lycopolis (Asyūṭ). Its dialect, in addition to Greek, became the language of the Egyptian Manichaeans. A few Syriac fragments have also been found in Upper Egypt (Burkitt, 1925, p. 111). However, translation of the literature appears to have been through the medium of Greek. Soon after its appearance, Manichaeism was attacked by the state. The edict of DIOCLETIAN in 297 prohibited it under severe penalties (death, penal servitude, expropriation). People saw in it a Persian superstition; perhaps Iranian agitation was suspected behind some revolts. The Neoplatonic philosophy also, in the person of ALEXANDER OF LYCOPOLIS about 300, turned against Mani's doctrine. It was, however, the church especially that saw in Manichaeism an opponent so dangerous as to have it extirpated until the Arab period. There is a pastoral letter against it as early as the third century (Böhlig, 1980, pp. 194ff.). There are writings from the hands of Egyptian theologians, SARAPION OF TMUIS (d. 362) and DIDYMUS THE BLIND (313–398). ATHANASIUS also may have had a hand in this conflict, as he enrolled ANTONY in such a struggle (*Vita Antonii,* chap. 68). Use was also made of writings against Mani from outside, as Coptic translations prove (CYRIL OF JERUSALEM, 6th Catechesis, 21–24; *Acta Archelai,* cf. Polotsky, 1932). In the fourth century the activity of Aphthonius as leader of the Manichaean community made it necessary for Aetius of Antioch to come to Alexandria for a debate with him. The widespread impact of Manichaeism emerges also from the fact that both the Coptic Manichaean library—consisting of a work on the Living Gospel, letters of Mani, a psalm book, two volumes of *Kephalaia,* various *logoi,* and a historical book—and the Cologne Greek codex were intended for the laity.

BIBLIOGRAPHY

Adam, A. *Texte zum Manichäismus.* Berlin, 1969.

Alexander of Lycopolis. *De placitis Manichaeorum.* In PG 18, cols. 411–48. Turnhout, n.d.

Alfaric, P. *Les Ecritures manichéennes,* 2 vols. Paris, 1918–1919.

Asmussen, J. P. *Xuāstvānīft. Studies in Manichaeism.* Acta Theologica Danica 7. Copenhagen, 1965.

______. *Manichaean Literature. Representative Texts Chiefly from Middle Persian and Parthian Writings.* Persian Heritage Series 22. Delmar, N.Y., 1975.

Baur, F. C. *Das manichäische Religionssystem nach den Quellen neu untersucht und entwickelt.* Hildesheim, 1973. Reprint of 1831 edition.

Böhlig, A. "Die Bibel bei den Manichäern." Theological dissertation, University of Münster, 1947.

______. "Die Arbeit an den koptischen Manichaica." In *Actes du XXVe Congrès international des orientalistes. Moscou 9–16 août 1960,* Vol. 1. Moscow, 1962. Reprinted in Böhlig, *Mysterion und Wahrheit,* pp. 177–87.

______. *Mysterion und Wahrheit,* pp. 175–266. Arbeiten zur Geschichte des späteren Judentums und des Urchristentums 6. Leiden, 1968.

______. "Der Synkretismus des Mani." In *Synkretismus im syrisch-persischen Kulturgebiet,* ed. A. Dietrich, pp. 144–69. Abhandlungen der Göttinger Akademie der Wissenschaften, Philologisch-historische Klasse 96. Göttingen, 1975.

______. *Die Gnosis, III. Der Manichäismus.* With the assistance of J. P. Asmussen; introduction, translation, and commentary by A. Böhlig. Zurich, 1980.

Böhlig, A., and H. J. Polotsky. *Manichäische Handschriften der Staatlichen Museum Berlin I: Kephalaia.* Stuttgart, 1934–1966.

Boyce, M. *The Manichaean Hymn-Cycles in Parthian.* London and New York, 1954.

______. "The Manichaean Literature in Middle Iranian." In *Handbuch der Orientalistik,* Vol. 4.2. Leiden, 1968.

______. *A Reader in Manichaean Middle Persian and Parthian.* Acta Iranica 9. Leiden, 1975.

Brière, M., ed. and trans. *Les Homiliae cathédrales de Sévère d'Antioche.* PO 29, 1.

Brinkmann, A., ed. *Alexandri Lycopolitani contra Manichaei opiniones disputatio.* Leipzig, 1895.

Burkitt, F. C. *The Religion of the Manichees.* Cambridge, 1925.

Casey, R. P., ed. *Serapion of Thmuis Against the Manichees.* Cambridge, Mass., 1931.

Chavannes, E., and P. Pelliot. *Un traité manichéen retrouvé en Chine.* Extract from *Journal asiatique* (Nov.-Dec. 1911). Paris, 1912.

Cumont, F. V. M. *La cosmogonie manichéenne d'après Théodore bar Khoni.* Recherches sur le Manichéisme 1. Brussels, 1908.

Decret, F., *Mani et la tradition manichéenne.* Maîtres spirituels 40. Paris, 1974.

Flügel, G. *Mani, seine Lehre und seine Schriften.* Osnabrück, 1969. Reprint of 1862 edition.

Haloun, G. and W. B. Henning. "The Compendium of the Doctrines and Styles of the Teaching of Mani, the Buddha of Light." *Asia Major* (1952):188–212.

______. "Mani's Last Journey." *Bulletin of the School of Oriental and African Studies* 10 (1940–1942):941–53. Reprinted in Henning's *Selected Papers,* Vol. 2, pp. 81–93. Leiden, 1977.

Nagel, P. *Die Thomaspsalmen des koptisch-manichäischen Psalmenbuches.* Ausgewählte Texte aus der Geschichte der christlichen Kirche, n.s. 1. Berlin, 1980.

Polotsky, H. J. "Manichäismus." In *Pauly-Wissowa Realencyclopädie,* Suppl. VI. pp. 241–72. Stuttgart, 1934.

Puech, H.-Ch. *Le Manichéisme: Son fondateur, sa doctrine.* Paris, 1949.

Rose, E. *Die manichäische Christologie.* Studies in Oriental Religions 5. Wiesbaden, 1979.

Rudolph, K. *Die Gnosis, Wesen und Geschichte einer spätantiken Religion.* Leipzig, 1977; Göttingen, 1978; 2nd ed., 1980.

Säve-Söderbergh, T. *Studies in the Coptic Manichaean Psalm-Book.* Uppsala, 1949.

Schaeder, H. H. *Urform und Fortbildungen des manichäischen Systems.* Leipzig, 1927.

Schmidt, C., and H. J. Polotsky. *Ein Mani-Fund in Ägypten. Originalschriften des Mani und seiner Schüler.* Berlin, 1933.

Taqizadeh, S. H., and W. B. Henning. "The Dates of Mani's Life." *Asia Major* (1957):106–121. Reprinted in Henning's *Selected Papers,* Vol. 2, pp. 505–20. Leiden, 1977.

Tsui Chi. "Mo ni chiao hsia pu tsan" (The lower section of the Manichaean Hymns). *Bulletin of the School of Oriental and African Studies* 11 (1943):174–215, with observations by W. B. Henning.

Widengren, G. *Mani und der Manichäismus.* Stuttgart, 1961.

———, ed. *Der Manichäismus.* Wege der Forschung 168. Darmstadt, 1977.

ALEXANDER BÖHLIG

MANQABĀD (ancient Mallidis), site of a complex of ruins dating from the late Roman period, the classification of which has not yet been ascertained with certainty. The building remains have definite Christian characteristics, so that the foundation of the buildings may be ascribed to the sixth century A.D. It remained in use until the eighth century.

The buildings are laid out in an extensive and more or less rectangular, walled precinct. Close to the middle of the western circular wall a finely constructed gate decorated with corner pilasters and niches was found. The thickness of the wall, however, is not very great, and it lacks towers.

Within the walls several small churches and chapels were found, all of which, however, belong to a later period. Evidently the oldest ecclesiastical building is a small chapel (A) on the south wall that once had a cupola. Inside, it is furnished with a number of niches and windows. On the west side two more rooms are attached, which may be entered only from within the chapel.

Church B, which follows immediately to the east, is appreciably larger and already presupposes chapel A. Two different states of development may be noted in it. The sanctuary in the east originally consisted of a simple three-room group. This was later abandoned and a new apse attached with two lateral side rooms. The facing wall of the original sanctuary was preserved and reused for the *khūrus* (choir) partition wall. The new apse contains several rectangular wall niches as well as a curious round niche in the vertex which is markedly out of alignment.

The third church, which was found on the south side of the street leading out from the west gate of the settlement, was from the beginning provided with a *khūrus* situated in front of the three-room group of the sanctuary. Also it has a single nave and is entered from the north. The apse also contains a niche rising up from the floor and in this particular instance a rectangular one. A small courtyard situated on the west side was added later.

The churches described all come from the period following the ARAB CONQUEST OF EGYPT. In any case, the two churches equipped with a *khūrus* could have been built only at the turn of the seventh to the eighth century.

More to the center of the area, a complex of buildings was exposed consisting of different, and in some cases modified, structures, which contained several rooms with round benches and wall seats. One of the rooms exhibits numerous graffiti in Coptic and Arabic. Buildings of a similar kind were discovered at BĀWĪṬ. It is, therefore, conceivable that here, too, the buildings had a monastic function. Not very far away the most recent excavations (spring 1985) unearthed a large, multiroomed building, in which two consecutive phases lying one on top of the other could clearly be distinguished. The latest structure was presumably an ecclesiastical building, the arrangement of which had completely destroyed the older, substantially smaller-roomed building.

The crypt of the later phase lay well below the floor of the earlier phase.

BIBLIOGRAPHY

Grossmann, P. "Neue frühchristliche Funde aus Ägypten." In *Actes XIe Congrès international d'archéologie chrétienne,* Vol. 2, pp. 1876–79. Paris, 1989.

PETER GROSSMANN

MANSI, GIOVANNI DOMENICO (1692–1769), Italian churchman and prolific author and editor of religious texts. One of his major projects was the issuance of a new edition of Baronius' *Annales ecclesiastici* (1738–1756) supplemented by his own notes and addenda.

However, the main object of his life remained the compilation of the church councils, *Sacrorum Conciliorum Nova et Amplissima Collectio* (31 vols., Lucca, 1758–1798), more widely known as the *Amplissima,* which covered the subject down to the COUNCIL OF FLORENCE in 1439. As far as the Coptic church is concerned, the first six volumes, down to the Council of Chalcedon in 451, are of paramount importance, since the ecumenical movement was recognized by the Copts until that date. Volumes 31 and 31-bis should also be taken into account because of the presence of Coptic and Ethiopian delegations for church unity at the Council of Ferrara-Florence. Since then, continuations of Mansi's work have been conducted by others to Volume 50, reaching the year 1870.

BIBLIOGRAPHY

Leclercq, H. "Mansi, Jean-Dominique." In *Dictionnaire d'archéologie chretiénne et de liturgie*, Vol. 10, pt. 2, cols. 1565–82. Paris, 1932.

Quentin, H. J. *Jean-Dominique Mansi et les grandes collections conciliaires.* Paris, 1900.

AZIZ S. ATIYA

MANṢŪR, ʿABDALLAH (1772–1831), a Copt who fought in the Coptic Legion and became an officer in the French army. He was born in the district of Bāb al Baḥr, Cairo, on 18 July 1772. He received his early education from his father, Muʿallim Mansūr Ḥunayn, who held an administrative position on the estates of the Mamluk amir Ibrāhīm Bey the Great. Owing to his interest in military maneuvers, Mansūr accompanied the soldiers of Ibrāhīm on most of their military exploits and learned horsemanship from them while he quietly studied the French language on his own. Later he joined the Coptic Legion, founded by General YAʿQŪB under the auspices of the French army in Egypt. He attained the rank of commander for his valor in fighting insurgents in Cairo, who rose against the French in 1801. When the French troops left Egypt, he, along with General Yaʿqūb and other Copts, went too. Manṣūr fought in the ranks of the Coptic Legion when it was restructured in France. He was granted the rank of commandant in 1807 and then placed on reserve. He lived in Paris until his death on 15 October 1831. His son, Boktor Manṣūr, visited Cairo in 1877 together with a daughter, who was a member of a French theatrical company that played at the opera house.

BIBLIOGRAPHY

Ramzī Tadrus. *Al-Aqbāṭ fī al-Qarn al ʿIshrīn,* 3 vols. Cairo, 1911.

AZIZ S. ATIYA

MANṢŪRAH, AL-, city located in the Egyptian Delta about 15 miles (24 km) northeast of al-Maḥallah al-Kubrā in the Daqahliyyah province. Al-Malik al-Kāmil founded al-Manṣūrah in 1218/1219 when he was fighting the Crusaders in Dumyāṭ (Maspero and Wiet, 1919, p. 198). Though Christianity is not attested in the city until the seventeenth century, al-Manṣūrah takes a prominent place in the annals of Christian history as the place where Louis IX suffered the defeat in 1249 that effectively spelled the end of the Crusades.

BIBLIOGRAPHY

Maspero, J., and G. Wiet. *Matériaux pour servir à la géographie de l'Egypte.* Cairo, 1919.

Timm, S. *Das christlich-koptische Ägypten in arabischer Zeit*, pt. 4, pp. 1571–72. Wiesbaden, 1988.

RANDALL STEWART

MANṢŪR IBN SAHLĀN IBN MUQASHSHIR, famous Christian physician—probably a Copt—who was attached to the court of the Fatimid caliphs. His scientific knowledge and experience became authoritative for many decades. In particular, al-ʿAzīz (975–996) and al-ḤĀKIM BI-AMR ALLĀH (996–1021) honored him. In 995, he fell ill and was unable to appear at the palace. When he recovered, al-ʿAziz wrote him a letter in his own hand, filled with expressions of kindness and good wishes for a long life. This letter was reproduced by al-Qifṭī.

The Melchite historian Yaḥyā ibn Saʿīd al-Anṭākī in his *Appendix* to the *Annals* of Saʿīd ibn al-Biṭrīq, composed before 1015 and then revised and completed as far as 1028, gave firsthand information, as he was himself a contemporary of these events. His account reads:

> Al-Ḥākim [bi-Amr Allāh] had the Christian staff of the government offices arrested, and they were thrown into prison on Monday the fourteenth day of the month of Jumādā II of this same year (A.H. 393). They were subsequently freed, one week later, at the request of his physician Abū al-Fatḥ [ibn] Sahlān ibn Muqashshir al-Naṣrānī. This physician was one of al-Ḥākim's confidants, who had already received from al-ʿAzīz a great fortune, an important position, and also particular favor and esteem. And al-Ḥākim restored them all to their former employ. (Kratchkovsky, 1976, p. 464)

This date corresponds to Monday 20 March A.D. 1003. The text quoted shows the positive influence exercised by Abū al-Fatḥ at the caliph's court, and indicates he was still alive in the year 1003. Later in the text (pp. 480–81), the same historian records that when Abū al-Fatḥ Manṣur ibn Sahlān died, he was replaced by another Christian physician, ISḤĀQ IBN IBRĀHĪM IBN NASṬĀS, who advised al-Ḥākim to drink a little wine for his health. After some time

Abū Ya'qūb also died, and al-Ḥākim once more banned wine. The historian then recounts an event which can be dated during Lent 1007.

Ibn Abī Uṣaybi'ah also confirmed that Manṣūr ibn Sahlān died during the reign of al-Ḥākim. The date must have been between March 1003 and March 1007, probably around the year 1004.

BIBLIOGRAPHY

Ibn Abī Uṣaybi'ah. *'Uyūn al-Anbā' fī Ṭabaqāt al-Aṭibbā'*, Vol. 2, ed. A. Müller. Königsberg, 1884. New ed., ed. N. Riḍa. Beirut, 1965.

Ibn al-'Ibrī. *Mukhtaṣar Tārīkh al-Duwal,* ed. A. Ṣaliḥāni, S.J., pp. 181–82. 2nd ed., Beirut, 1958.

Ibn al-Qifṭi. *Tārīkh al-Ḥukamā'*, ed. J. Lippert, pp. 334/14–335/8. Leipzig, 1903.

Kratchkovsky, I., and V. Alexandre. *Histoire de Yahya-Ibn-Sa'id d'Antioche, continuateur de Sa'id-Ibn-Bitriq.* PO 23, pt. 3, no. 114, pp. 347–520, pp. 464 and 480–81. Paris, 1932; repr. 1976.

Steinschneider, M. *Polemische und apologetische Literatur in arabischer Sprache,* pp. 115f. Leipzig, 1877; repr. Hildesheim, 1966.

KHALIL SAMIR, S.J.

MANYAL SHIHA. *See* Pilgrimages.

MANZALAH, AL-. *See* Monasteries of the Province of Daqahliyyah.

MAQARAH OF SCETIS. *See* Macarius the Egyptian, Saint.

MAQRĪZĪ, TAQĪY AL-DĪN AL- (A.D. 1364–1442), Arab historian and topographer. Al-Maqrīzī composed two major works, a monumental topographical study, *al-Mawā'iẓ wa-al I'tibār fī Dhikr al-Khiṭaṭ wa-al-Athār* (4 vols.), and a universal history, *Kitāb al-Sulūk li-Ma'rifat Duwal al-Mulūk* (4 vols.).

Though at first concentrating his literary activity on local history and topography, he later extended his labors to include social history and such specific subjects as weights and measures. In the field of general history, however, he was led to deal with countries neighboring Egypt such as Nubia, the Sudan, and Abyssinia. In particular, he became involved in Coptic history, where he produced what is probably the only detailed study on the subject by a Muslim writer. This work proved to be a major accomplishment and an original document of the highest importance in medieval Coptic annals. It was also incorporated within his wider *Khiṭaṭ* under the title *Akhbār Qibṭ Miṣr* (news of the Copts of Egypt), which attracted Western scholarship and was published and translated into some European languages by eminent scholars. In Latin, it first appeared under the title *Makrizii Historia Coptorum . . . ,* edited by H. J. Wetzer (1828). It was edited by the well-known German Orientalist F. Wüstenfeld under the title *Geschichte der Copten* (Göttingen, 1845). An English translation was produced by S. C. Malan, entitled *A Short History of the Copts and their Church* (London, 1873).

Maqrīzī begins his work with two short introductions on the prehistory of the Copts as well as their mythology before they were converted to Christianity. The rest of the book, comprising historic materials concerning the Copts, is divided into a number of sections, each treating a phase of Coptic history. The first section offers details of the Christianization of the Copts. Here he includes the age of persecutions, the conversion of Constantine, and the establishment of Christianity as the state religion, in addition to the early story of the Coptic patriarchs to the end of Byzantine rule.

The following section deals with the ARAB CONQUEST OF EGYPT and the age of Islamic rule in Egypt. The patriarchs of the Copts, including the Melchite patriarchs, are enumerated with interesting episodes of the reign of each of them. A special chapter is devoted to explanatory notices on the Christian sects including the Melchites, the Nestorians, the Jacobites, and "the Barda'aniyyah and the Marqūliyyah," otherwise those of the district of al-Ruhā, thus meaning the Antiochene church. Another brief chapter deals with baptism and the organization of the Coptic church.

The next section enumerates the monasteries, with short notices on each. This is a very interesting section, since it includes the fifteenth-century houses, some of which have disappeared.

The final section is equally interesting as it is devoted to the enumeration of churches throughout Lower and Upper Egypt, including Cairo and Alexandria.

BIBLIOGRAPHY

Encyclopedia of Islam, Vol. 5, pp. 175–76. Leiden, 1987.

Wüstenfeld, F. *Geschichte der Copten.* Göttingen, 1845.

AZIZ S. ATIYA

MAQṢŪRAH. *See* Architectural Elements of Churches.

MAQTA'. *See* Altar-board.

MARCEL, JEAN-JOSEPH (1776–1854), French Orientalist. He studied under Silvestre de Sacy and wrote studies on Arabic and on Arab history. He was a member of Napoleon's commission in Egypt, of which he wrote a history, and was in charge of the printing press of the French expedition. The Copts remained on the periphery of his work. His occasional statements on them were confined to the modern period.

BIBLIOGRAPHY

Carré, J. M. *Voyageurs et écrivains français en Egypte,* 2 vols. Cairo, 1932.
Michaud, J. F. *Biographie universelle,* Vol. 26, pp. 961–63. Paris, 1840.

M. L. BIERBRIER

MARCELLUS, bishop of Ancyra (d. c. 374), a supporter of the HOMOOUSION concept and contender against the Arians at the Council of NICAEA in 325. Nonetheless, he was deposed for heterodoxy in his refutation of the Arian Asterius, probably in 336. He taught that the Son was merely a manifestation of the Father, with no independent personality. When the works of creation and redemption were completed, the Son would be subsumed again in the Father. This doctrine, for which Marcellus incurred the enduring wrath of the Eusebians, combined elements of the teachings of both Paul of Samosata and Sabellius.

Marcellus was restored to his see in 337 at the death of CONSTANTINE, but removed again in 339. The evidence suggests that he did not regain the see thereafter, despite the fact that in a council of Western bishops held in Rome in late 340 or in 341, Marcellus was accepted as lawful bishop of Ancyra; and again at another council in 342 or 343 in Sardica, the Western bishops asserted the orthodoxy of Marcellus. However, the Eastern bishops, who had walked out of the council, convened in nearby Philippopolis and renewed their anathema against Marcellus and his supporters.

BIBLIOGRAPHY

Cross, F. L., ed. "Marcellus." In ODCC. London, 1957.
Foulkes, E. S. "Marcellus (4)." In DCB, Vol. 3, pp. 808–813. New York, 1974.
Frend, W. H. C. *The Rise of Christianity.* Philadelphia, 1984.

RANDALL STEWART

MARCIANUS, eighth patriarch of the See of Saint Mark (143–154). He held the office for ten years and two months during the reign of Emperor Antoninus Pius. He was laid to rest on 6 Ṭūbah near the remains of Saint Mark in the Church of Bucalis at Alexandria.

BIBLIOGRAPHY

Atiya, A. S. *History of Eastern Christianity.* Millwood, N.Y., 1980.

AZIZ S. ATIYA

MARCUS. *See* Mark I, Saint.

MAREA. *See* Hawāriyyah.

MAREOTIS, the Greek name of an ancient city, a district, and a lake in Egypt. The ruins of the ancient city lie in Kom al-Idrīs about 2.5 miles (4 km) north of al-Hawwāriyyah and some 20 miles (32 km) southwest of Alexandria. The name of the modern town and its lake, just below Alexandria, is Maryūṭ.

The district of Mareotis was remote and generally inhospitable. When the patriarch DIONYSIUS (247–264) was exiled to the area by Aemilianus, the prefect of Egypt, he complained because he had heard that Mareotis was not only devoid of Christians and men of character, but was hazardous because of the incursions of robbers (Eusebius *Historia ecclesiastica* 7.11.14–17).

The martyrdom of SHENUFE, which speaks of a number of Christians from Empaiat (Mareotis) including Shenufe himself (Reymond and Barns, 1973, p. 86 [Coptic text]; p. 189 [English translation]), is one of several indications that Christianity was firmly established in the area by the early fourth century. Mareotis also figures prominently in the accounts of Abū Mīnā. Although the different stories about Abū Mīnā do not agree on his homeland, the Coptic version of his martyrdom states that Mīnā's parents were from the area of Mareotis, and the account of his miracles says that Mīnā himself was resident in Empaiat (Drescher, 1946, pp. 2, 10). Mīnā's burial place was in the desert in the district of Mareotis, but the SYNAXARION, under 15 Ba'ūnah, commemorates the dedication of the church of Mīnā in the city of Mareotis and claims that the church, along with the city itself, was built at the place where Mīnā was buried. Apparently the city of Mareotis became associated with Mīnā's burial place, even though this equation was not precise. Abū Ṣāliḥ, for example, identified Dayr Abū Mīnā in the western desert with the city Mareotis and al-MAQRĪZĪ, who wrote in the early to mid-fifteenth century, said the city of Mareotis was still in existence in his day, though he evidently meant the burial place of Mīnā with its accompanying church (Maspero and Wiet, 1919, p. 167).

The HISTORY OF THE PATRIARCHS records that Patriarch SHENUTE I (858–880) went into the church of Mīnā and prayed for divine intervention at a time when the area had not seen rain for three years. A short time later in the patriarchate of Shenute, the church was seized and plundered by members of the Muslim tribe known as the Madaljah.

While PHILO wrote that the Therapeutae, an ascetic sect that he described, lived just south of Lake Mareotis *(De vita contemplativa* 3.22), Christian monasticism in the district of Mareotis appears to have had its beginnings in the fourth century. SOZOMEN reports that some 2,000 monks were preaching philosophy in the neighborhood of Alexandria, some in the district called the Hermitage, and others in the outlying areas of Mareotis and in Libya (*Historia ecclesiastica* 6.29.3). He speaks at some length of Ammon, a man who pursued his dream of living the monastic life by retiring to a desert place south of Lake Mareotis (1.14.3), and of the monk Stephen who lived at Mareotis near Marmarica (6.29.13). Both of these men were contemporary with ANTONY, who died in 356.

ATHANASIUS wrote in the fourth century that the churches in the district of Mareotis had no bishop. Instead they were overseen by presbyters who were directly subject to the patriarchate in Alexandria (*Apologia Secunda* 85.3ff.). However, since Athanasius made this statement when he was involved in a dispute with Ischyras, a church leader in the district of Mareotis who was eventually made bishop of the area by Athanasius' opponents, it is apparent that the assertion is polemical in nature. In 343 Ischyras, who may have been ordained by the schismatic MELITIUS, attended the synod in Sardica as the bishop of Mareotis (Munier, 1943, pp. 6–7). Whether or not Ischyras had a successor as bishop is not known.

The *History of the Patriarchs* relates that Patriarch AGATHON (661–677) was from Mareotis, but there is no indication whether he hailed from the city itself or simply from the district of Mareotis.

BIBLIOGRAPHY

Drescher, J. *Apa Mena: A Selection of Coptic Texts Relating to St. Menas.* Cairo, 1946.

Maspero, J., and G. Wiet. *Matériaux pour servir à la géographie de l'Egypte.* Cairo, 1919.

Munier, H. *Recueil des listes épiscopales de l'église copte.* Cairo, 1943.

Reymond, E. A. E., and J. W. B. Barns, eds. *Four Martyrdoms from the Pierpont Morgan Coptic Codices.* Oxford, 1973.

Timm, S. *Das christlich-koptische Ägypten in arabischer Zeit.* Wiesbaden, 1988.

RANDALL STEWART

MAREOTIS, COPTIC PAINTINGS AT,

painted walls and ceilings in monastic structures of the sixth to seventh centuries in the Mareotis region at the edge of the Western Desert. They were discovered in 1911 by Evaristo Breccia, who was excavating Dayr Abū Jirjā, a series of hillocks not far from the Nybāriyyah Canal, about 22 miles (35 km) southwest of Alexandria. Some of the paintings are now in the Greco-Roman Museum in Alexandria.

Two groups of structures superimposed one above the other have been uncovered; their purpose is unknown. From the higher building, which is the more recent, only the walls have survived, from 3 to 5 feet (1 to 1½ m) high. A few fragments of paintings show a face, the prophet Abraham, and a haloed person praying, standing in the center of a niche. The lower building, which Breccia identified as a crypt, is composed of two rooms connected by a vast bay. The ceilings are covered with paintings in imitation of wooden coffers. The iconographical plan displayed along the walls of these two rooms must have been rather elaborate, involving different scenes with figures. On the lower register large panels are painted in imitation of slabs of marble and porphyry. Above is a procession of figures among whom are an unidentified warrior-saint, Saint Abū Mīnā standing between his camels, a monk, and an Annunciation. This last theme, which is rather rare in the most ancient Coptic painting, was accompanied by the first words of the angel's salutation. Above the door, there is a bust of Christ in Glory in a mandorla. Heavy draperies guide the spectator's eye toward the principal niche, which has complex decoration. In the center, a person praying stands out against a Nilotic landscape of plants and flowers, in the midst of which appear two domed roofs, one accompanied by a fish and the other by a child. The interpretation of this scene is an enigma. Was it perhaps a vision of Paradise or a baptism of Christ in a very particular iconography or an evocation of the Eucharist? The question remains unanswered.

BIBLIOGRAPHY

Rassart-Debergh, M. "Peintures coptes de la région maréotique: Abou Girgeh et Alam Shaltout." *Annuaire de l'Institut de philologie et d'histoire orientales et slaves.* Brussels, 1983.

MARGUERITE RASSART-DEBERGH

MARI JIRJIS. *See* George the Great of Cappadocia, Saint.

MARIYYAH THE COPT, Coptic consort of the Prophet Muḥammad. Her story begins in A.D. 627 with the dispatch of letters from Muḥammad to the rulers of the world, calling them to allegiance to Islam and its prophet as the messenger of Allāh. Those letters included a special message addressed to al-Muqawqas, viceroy of Egypt, who wrote back a considerate and friendly but inconclusive response. He also sent the Prophet gifts of honey and fabrics produced by Egyptian looms, together with two Coptic female serfs who were sisters, Mariyyah and Shirīn (or Sirīn). Apparently both were daughters of a mixed marriage with a Greek mother. According to Yāqūt's geographical dictionary, those two girls were from a village by the name of Ḥafn, situated on part of the ruins of ANTINOOPOLIS, the ancient capital of the Thebaid between the Nile to the west and the mountains to the east.

Of the two girls, the Prophet retained Mariyyah for himself and gave her sister to Hassān ibn Thābit, the famous poet and companion of Muḥammad. Later, Mariyyah bore him an only son named Ibrāhīm, in whose birth the Prophet rejoiced. Her newborn earned her liberation from serfdom, which changed her marital status from concubinage to that of a legal wife. However, her child did not survive long. It is known to have died, probably at the age of less than two years, in the lap of his father, who mourned his death deeply. She survived the Prophet and died in Medina in A.H. 16/A.D. 637.

Mariyyah's native village gained prominence in Islamic records as a pilgrimage site. When it was visited after the ARAB CONQUEST OF EGYPT by ʿAbādah ibn al-Ṣāmit, a companion of the Prophet and a former soldier in the army of ʿAmr ibn al-ʿĀṣ, he built there a mosque that bore his name, Masjid al-Shaykh ʿAbādah. It still stands in Ḥafn, the name of which was consequently changed to its present one, Shaykh ʿAbādah. The natives have managed to preserve the adobe room that was the birthplace of Mariyyah, from a larger building where she had lived before her departure to Arabia. That room is decorated, and the villagers have built a red brick wall around it for protection. The village has an ancient well from which Mariyyah presumably drew water. The well being still in use, sterile women come to drink from its healing water in the hope of conceiving. The actual population of the village today is in the neighborhood of four thousand souls, and its cultivable soil amounts to five hundred acres. Its inhabitants pride themselves on a peaceful life, free from crime.

The administration of Minyā Province, in conjunction with the central Ministry of Tourism, has acknowledged the historic importance of the village of Shaykh ʿAbādah and its potential as a pilgrimage site to be frequented by Muslim tourists.

BIBLIOGRAPHY

Abū Jaʿfar Muḥammad ibn Jarīr al-Ṭabarī. *Tārīkh al-Umam wa-al-Mulūk*, 13 vols. Cairo, 1917.

______. *Chronique*, 4 vols., trans. M. H. Zotenberg. Paris, 1867–1874 (trans. of above).

Amélineau, E. *La Géographie de l'Egypte à l'époque copte.* Paris, 1893.

Butler, A. J. *The Arab Conquest of Egypt,* rev. ed., ed. P. M. Fraser. Oxford, 1978.

Ḥamdī Luṭfī. "Qaryat al-Shaykh." *Al-Hilāl Monthly Review* 90 (July 1982):78–101. See especially p. 92.

Ḥifnī Nāṣif. "Mariyyah al-Qibṭiyyah." *Al-Hilāl Monthly Review* 90 (July 1982):78–101, with ills. See especially p. 80.

Lamīs al-Ṭaḥḥāwī. "ʿAbādah, al-Qaryah al-Miṣriyyah . . ." *Al-Ahram*, 25 June 1981.

Yāqūt ibn ʿAbd Allāh al-Ḥamawī. *Kitāb Muʿjam al-Buldān,* 10 vols. Cairo, 1956–1957.

______. *Jacūt's Geographisches Wörterbuch,* 6 vols., ed. F. Wüstenfeld. Leipzig, 1866–1873; repr. Tehran, 1965. Beirut ed., 4 vols., 1955–1957 (trans. of above).

AZIZ S. ATIYA

MARK, SAINT, one of the Twelve Apostles of Christ, traditionally regarded as author of the Gospel of Mark and first patriarch of the Coptic church (feast day: 30 Baramūdah).

The meager historical sources on Saint Mark's life have given rise to conflicting accounts about his personality and even about his Gospel. Whereas liberal Protestant scholars have woven legendary conjectures about Mark, the Roman Catholic scholarly community tends to portray him as a mere satellite to Saint Peter, as his secretary and his interpreter, and regards his Gospel only as a dictation from the older saint. Attempts at an objective outlook, however, are not lacking. *The New Schaff-Herzog Encyclopedia of Religious Knowledge* is a moderate example. In a Coptic encyclopedia, however, the reader is entitled to learn the traditional view from within the Coptic church of its founder. Consequently, we have tried in these pages to summarize the work written ex cathedra by Anbā SHENOUDA III, pope of Alexandria and 117th patriarch of the See of Saint Mark.

Early Life

Mark, also known in scripture as John Mark, was born in Cyrene, capital of Cyrenaica, in North Africa, some time after the dawn of the first century into a comfortable Jewish family engaged in agriculture. The country was predominantly Greek, partly Jewish, and partly Roman with a hostile Berber community on its periphery. Owing to Berber inroads, the family decided to emigrate to Palestine, where they settled at a new home in Jerusalem just about the time when Jesus began to emerge into prominence. Mark's father died shortly afterward, and his mother, Mary, devoted her fortune to obtaining a thorough education for her son. Mark ultimately became very proficient not only in Hebrew but also in Greek and Latin, then the languages of civilization, which he fully utilized later in his mission. As a young man, he became captivated by the teaching of Jesus and was baptized by Peter, to whom he was related through Peter's wife.

Mark's mother received Jesus, who feasted in her house, and later she opened her residence to his faithful followers, who congregated there for daily prayers. In this way, Mark's house became the first Christian church in history, and it was there that the Holy Spirit descended on the disciples after the Ascension of Jesus. Thus young Mark occupied a place among the disciples, and the Coptic church recognizes him as one of the seventy appointed by Jesus during his life on earth to go and spread the news of the Kingdom of God (Lk. 10:1–12).

Because of his youth, Mark chose to start his mission in Asia in the company of the older missionaries Saint PAUL and Saint Barnabas. With them he went to Antioch, then to Seleucia, sailing afterward to Cyprus, where they proclaimed God's message in the Jewish synagogue at Salamis. They crossed the island to Paphos, where Paul struck a Jewish magician named Bar-Jesus with blindness, in the presence of the governor, Sergius Paulus, who "believed . . . for he was astonished at the teaching of the Lord" (Acts 13:1–12). From Paphos, the missionaries sailed to Perga in Pamphylia, Asia Minor, where Mark left them and returned to Jerusalem. At a later date, possibly after laboring in what is now Lebanon, Mark joined Paul in Rome, where he assisted him in the inauguration of its church. Writing to the Colossians, Paul sent his greetings, and added, "Aristarchus my fellow prisoner greets you, and Mark the cousin of Barnabas (concerning whom you have received instructions—if he comes to you, receive him)" (Col. 4:10). It is possible that at this juncture John Mark extended his preaching in Italy to Aquileia and the area of Venice, the future republic of Saint Mark, and from there proceeded to his birthplace in Cyrenaica.

Mark's Journeys to Alexandria

Mark returned at an unknown date to the country of his birth. Despite the scarcity of materials on his mission there, Mark is known to have planted the seeds of Christianity among his former countrymen (Acts 2:10). Coptic tradition teaches that Mark, after performing miracles of healing in Cyrenaica, followed the road to Alexandria, through inspiration by the Holy Spirit and not by instruction from Peter, whom he had not yet joined in Rome.

There is a divergence of opinion on the route followed by Mark to the great city of Alexandria. According to one view, he walked from Cyrene to the oases in the Western Desert, then crossed the immense sandy wastes until he descended into the valley of the Nile somewhere in Upper Egypt, and moved north along the river until he entered Alexandria. This appears to be fantasy to those familiar with the geography of this forbidding terrain. The other route, which seems humanly possible and direct, was walking along the Mediterranean littoral. It is almost certain that Mark followed this route, known from antiquity, to reach Alexandria, which contained a medley of pagan religions, both ancient Egyptian and Greco-Roman, with a sprinkling of Judaic beliefs and Neoplatonist philosophy. Apparently in the midst of this confusion, there was an occasional Jew, such as Apollos, who had known the Way of God according to Jesus (Acts 18:24).

Arriving at Alexandria totally exhausted, Mark found a cobbler named ANIANUS and asked him to mend a broken strap of his tattered sandal. When the cobbler took an awl to work on it, he accidentally pierced his finger and cried aloud in Greek, "*Heis ho Theos,*" that is, "God is One." Mark's heart fluttered with joy at this utterance, which betrayed the possibility of his companion's monotheism, thus opening the door for the preaching of the New Kingdom. After miraculously healing the man's wound, Mark took courage and delivered the good tidings to the hungry ears of his first convert. In this manner, the initial spark was struck, and the first stone in the foundation of the Coptic church was laid. The cobbler invited the apostle to his home, and he and his family were baptized. There followed other baptisms, and the faithful multiplied. So successful was the movement that the word spread around that a Galilean was in the city preparing to overthrow the idols. Popular feelings began to rise, and people sought out the stranger. Scenting danger in the air, Mark ordained Anianus bishop, with three presbyters (Mylios, Sabinos, and Sardinos) and seven deacons to watch over the growing congregation in case anything befell him. Afterward, he seems to have undertaken a journey to Rome in response to a call for assistance from Paul. Writing to Timothy, Paul said, "Get Mark and bring him with you; for he is very useful in serving me" (2 Tm. 4:11).

Here we face a problem of chronology. The oldest chronicle on record dealing with the story of events in this period is the highly reputed *Historia ecclesiastica* written by EUSEBIUS OF CAESAREA in the fourth century. He devotes chapters to the introduction of Christianity in Alexandria and to the composition and emergence of the Gospel according to Mark. He cites no specific date for either event, but he definitely places them during the reign of the Roman emperor Claudius, who died in 54, and we must therefore place these events prior to that date.

To pinpoint a more definite date, we do not have to look very far in the work of Eusebius, who wrote two more chapters on the works of PHILO OF ALEXANDRIA, a well-known philosopher and a contemporary of Claudius. Philo's dates can be easily coordinated with those of the reign of Claudius, whom he visited in Rome together with a Jewish delegation from Alexandria in the year 42 to solicit permission for his Jewish community, and ostensibly the Judaic Christian communities, to be excused from the obligation of adoration of the imperial statue (Philo of Alexandria *De vita contemplativa*). According to Eusebius, Philo also wrote an account of the religious character of the Christian hermits and ascetics in Egypt as well as of the doctrines of an already established Christian church in that country during the reign of Claudius. This appears to be one of Eusebius' most elaborate chapters, thus indicating the considerable spread of Christianity and the development of the church in the metropolis. A shorter, but nonetheless interesting chapter treats Philo's further writings on biblical books. From a study of Philo's works, it is easy to place Mark's journey to Alexandria as occurring around the same date as that of Philo's embassy to Rome. At any rate, Mark's preaching in Alexandria must have struck roots deep enough in the city years before Philo's death, around the year 50, that we may well be justified in putting the foundation of the Coptic church by Mark in the forties of the first century.

Doubts about the veracity of that date are raised by the argument that Mark was still too young and that he could not have embarked on his Egyptian venture before the Jerusalem synod of 50, but this is too flimsy an argument to outweigh the respected authority of Eusebius, the master historian of Christian antiquity. Mark returned to Alexandria after visiting Rome, possibly several years after the synod and in all probability after the martyrdom of both Peter and Paul possibly in the year 64, which was also the year of the burning of Rome. Whether Mark made this second trip before or immediately after Peter's and Paul's martyrdom is hard to define with certainty. At any rate, he returned via Cyrene to visit and strengthen the faithful there. In Alexandria, he rejoiced at finding that the Christian community was multiplying and had built their first church at Bucalis, an area where cattle grazed by the seashore.

The Gospel According to Mark

The term "Gospel" is an interesting derivative from the Old English word *godspel,* meaning "good news," which is equivalent to the Greek *euangelion.* Most probably he wrote his Gospel some time during his absence from Alexandria, between his two sojourns there. It is sometimes suggested that Peter dictated it to him. It is true that Mark, the enlightened and able scholar, interpreted for Peter, the simple fisherman, in Rome. But this does not imply that Mark only recorded for Peter, his senior in years, though it is quite conceivable that all the disciples pooled details of oral information about the Lord's sayings and acts, which Mark may have legitimately incorporated into his work. Consequently, this Gospel, like the other Gospels, must have contained eyewitness source material of Petrine origin.

The idea has been advanced that the Gospel was written in Latin at the time of the martyrdom of Peter and Paul or shortly thereafter, but this is a very questionable hypothesis, because the Gospel is said to have been known some twelve years after the Crucifixion, which fixes its composition around the year 45, whereas the martyrdom of the two saints occurred in 64. Apparently Mark must have written his Gospel in the popular *koine* Greek without relying on literary brilliance. All he wanted to produce was a forceful text marked by simple directness, vivid scenes, and a depth of feeling to captivate public attention with its unique fascination. According to Papias, bishop of Hierapolis, who wrote before the middle of the second century, there had existed an early Aramaic collection of the sayings of Christ known as the *Logia*, which must have furnished the evangelists and the apostles with a common source. The third-century papyri discovered at Oxyrhynchus in Middle Egypt (see OXYRHYNCHUS PAPYRI) have been found to contain fragments from the *Logia* that are identical with passages from the Gospels. It is possible that the Gospels in turn were copies of more ancient originals. According to modern scholars, however, dating the Gospel of Mark from the sixties of the first century is given priority; it must have been circulated while some apostles were still living, and it could not have differed from their own recollection of Jesus. The consensus among New Testament commentators is that the Gospel of Mark must be regarded as authentic history. Whatever the truth may be, it is certain that Mark brought his Gospel with him to Alexandria, and though his Greek version must have fulfilled its purpose in a city that was preponderantly Greek, the suggestion is made that another version in the Egyptian language could have been prepared outside the metropolis for the benefit of native converts who may not have been conversant with the Greek tongue.

Mark's Martyrdom

At any rate, the Christian population of Alexandria was multiplying at a considerable rate, and rumors ran through the city, as on Mark's first visit, that under the leadership of Mark the Christians were threatening to overthrow the ancient pagan deities. This possibility inflamed the fury of the idolatrous populace. A hostile mob unremittingly hunted the evangelist. In 68, Easter fell on the same day as the festival of the popular pagan god Serapis. A large group congregated in the temple to Serapis on the occasion and decided to move against the Christians, who, with Mark leading their prayers, were celebrating Easter at their Bucalis church. The mob forced its way into the church and seized the saint, put a rope around his neck, and dragged him about the streets. With the connivance of the authorities, Mark was incarcerated for the night. It is said that the angel of the Lord appeared to him during the night and fortified him to bear the approaching martyr's crown. On the following day, he was again dragged over the cobbled roads of Alexandria, his body becoming lacerated and his blood covering the ground, until he finally died. But the mob would not stop at that; they wanted to cremate his mutilated body so that there would be no remains for his followers to honor. Though the sources are silent on the matter, it appears that Mark was decapitated after his martyrdom. At this point, however, a violent wind began to blow, and torrential rains poured down on the populace, which dispersed. The Christians stealthily removed the body of the saint and secretly buried him in a grave that they speedily carved in the rock under the altar of the Bucalis church, which has carried his name ever since.

Mark's Relics

The body of the saint remained intact in the Bucalis church under the jurisdiction of the united Coptic church until 451, when the Melchite Chalcedonians seized that church, which they held until the Arab invasion in 641. In 644, before the withdrawal of the Greek fleet from Alexandria, a sailor entered the church and took the head of the saint to his ship. Tradition says that all other seacraft set sail, save the one containing the head, which remained stationary. As soon as the head was removed, however, the ship began to move. It is said that 'Amr ibn al-'Āṣ summoned the Coptic patriarch BENJAMIN I, who was a fugitive in a Nitrian monastery, returned the head to him, and gave him ten thousand dinars to build a special church for housing it. Benjamin started the construction of Saint Mark's Cathedral in Alexandria to house the head.

The building was completed by his successor, AGATHON, and there the head remained until the persecution by the tenth-century Fatamid caliph al-ḤĀKIM, when it was carried temporarily for security and safekeeping to DAYR ANBĀ MAQĀR in the Nitrian valley.

The body of Saint Mark had been left at Bucalis, but it was stolen by Venetian pirates in 828 and carried to their city. There it was honored, and henceforth the Venetian commune was named the Republic of Saint Mark. The Venetians built a great cathedral, where they deposited the newly acquired sacred relics.

In 1077, during the patriarchate of CHRISTODOULUS, the head was returned to the Alexandria cathedral. From the eleventh to the fourteenth centuries, the head, which was coveted by Muslim governors in order to use for extorting ransom from the Coptic community, was removed from its sanctuary and kept moving from one Coptic family to another in order to delude the authorities. With the return of calm, the head was placed back in its original sanctuary. But in the eighteenth century, new rumors began to circulate that the Venetians were determined to steal the head. It was decided to collect the heads of other saints and place them in a casket together with that of Saint Mark to be kept in the shrine of Saint Mark's Cathedral in Alexandria, where the sacred relics could not be distinguished by thieves and pirates. This is supposed to have taken place in the patriarchate of PETER VI (1718–1726).

In 1968, with the progress of rapprochement between the churches of Rome and Alexandria, the Catholic papacy decided to return the relics of Saint Mark in Venice to the Coptic church. These were ceded to CYRIL VI, who deposited them in a formidable granite casket inside the crypt of the new Cathedral of Saint Mark on the grounds of DAYR ANBĀ RUWAYS, where they now form the object of pilgrimage for pious Copts.

The Iconography of Saint Mark

Saint Mark has been a favorite subject for iconographers of many countries since the Middle Ages. He has usually been depicted with his emblem, the winged lion. This emblem was probably inspired by the opening verses of his Gospel, where John the Baptist roared like a lion in the wilderness saying, "Prepare the way of the Lord, make his paths straight" (Mk. 1:3). His image appears in numerous old manuscripts preserved in the Coptic Museum and monastic libraries. Two thirteenth-century paintings may be traced in a couple of codices, one dated 1220 at DAYR AL-SURYĀN in Wādī al-Naṭrūn (MS no. 21), and another dated A.D. 1291 in the Patriarchal Library in Alexandria (MS no. 5/196). Of his older icons, two may be found on the iconostases of the cathedral church of Dayr al-Suryān, dated 912 and 928. A third from the tenth century exists in the Muʻallaqah Church of the Virgin in Cairo. A thirteenth-century icon was discovered by the American Byzantine Institute Expedition in 1931 at the chapel of Saint Antony in DAYR ANBĀ ANṬŪNIYŪS in the Eastern Desert. This is dated 1233. Modern representations are innumerable in Coptic churches throughout the country.

Paintings of high quality by famous Renaissance artists can be found in numerous churches in Europe. One, dated 1507, by Fra Bartolomeo is in the Dominican Monastery of Saint Mark in Florence. An attractive painting of the saint with the apostles Peter, Paul, and John by Albrecht Dürer, dated 1526, is in Munich. A whole range of paintings, including one of Mark's martyrdom, are preserved in the Cathedral of Saint Mark in Venice. It is impossible to present a complete record of the paintings of Saint Mark in the art museums of Europe and America.

Saint Mark and the Coptic Church

Throughout Egypt there is hardly a church in which the name of Saint Mark is not mentioned with the utmost reverence. In the SYNAXARION, his memory is celebrated annually on 30 Baramūdah, the date of his martyrdom. In Roman Catholic and Orthodox churches his feast day is 25 April.

Churches dedicated to Saint Mark appeared in many countries. In Egypt alone, the Copts had thirty-one such churches in 1975. The thirteenth-century Coptic historian Abū al-Makārim and the fifteenth-century Muslim historian of the Copts, al-Maqrīzī, cite seven other churches, which have disappeared. It would be difficult to cite in detail the impact of Saint Mark on Coptic civilization and culture. However, two items stand out.

First, according to tradition, it is said that Saint Mark composed the first Sunday mass to be recited by the faithful in church, and that he delivered its text to his successor, Anianus. This mass must have constituted the church offices until the days of CYRIL I the Great in the fifth century, when this patriarch took that inherited text and edited it in the form that has reached us as the Cyrillian mass. Because it is several hours long, it is celebrated today almost solely in monastic chapels. Portions of this mass have been discovered on papyrus fragments from the fifth century, scattered in world libraries, identified and unidentified. Sections of the document have been preserved by the Ethiopians in their old Ge'ez liturgy. The Vatican Library contains copies of it in three thirteenth-century codices: the Codex Rossanensis (Vatican Gr. 1970), the Rotulus Vaticanus (Vatican Gr. 2281), and the Rotulus Messanensis (Codex Messanensis Graeca 177).

Saint Mark's second monumental contribution to the church is said to be the foundation of the CATECHETICAL SCHOOL OF ALEXANDRIA, which developed from humble origins to become the most authoritative theological institution of the ancient Christian world. It is conceivable that Mark started a catechetical system for the edification of the newly converted catechumens, who hungered for acquaintance with the scriptures as well as church doctrines. It would, of course, be a mistake to see the highly elaborate institution of Christian learning of the third through fifth centuries as deriving directly from the nucleus established by Mark.

Among the 116 successors to Saint Mark, 8 took his name at their enthronement, in addition to 19 who were called John after his given name. In fact, both John and Mark proved to be popular names, not only with the church hierarchy but also with the Coptic community in general, which indicates the esteem in which the saint is held among all classes of all ages in Egypt.

BIBLIOGRAPHY

Anbā Shenouda III. *Murqus al-Rasūl* (Mark the Apostle), 2nd ed. Cairo, 1975.

Atiya, A. S. *History of Eastern Christianity*. London, 1968.

Butcher, E. L. *The Story of the Church of Egypt*, 2 vols. London, 1897.

Cabrol, F., and H. Leclerq, eds. *Dictionnaire d'archéologie chrétienne et de liturgie*, 15 vols. Paris, 1912–1962.

Cheneau, P. *Les Saints d'Egypte*. Jerusalem, 1923.

Jackson, S. M., ed. *The New Schaff-Herzog Encyclopedia of Religious Knowledge*, 12 vols. New York, 1963.

Kāmil Ṣāliḥ Nakhlah. *Silsilat Tārīkh Bābāwāt al-Kursī al-Iskandarī*. Dayr al-Suryān, 1951.

Lightfoot, R. H. *The Gospel Message of St. Mark*. Oxford, 1950.

Lockyer, W. *All Men of the Bible*. Grand Rapids, Mich., 1964.

Robinson, J. M. *The Problems of History in Mark*. Naperville, Ill., 1957.

Smith, M. *The Secret Gospel [of Mark]*. New York, 1973.

Swete, H. B. *New Testament Commentary*. London, 1902.

Weeden, T. J. *Mark-Traditions in Conflict*. Philadelphia, 1971.

AZIZ S. ATIYA

MARK II, SAINT, forty-ninth patriarch of the See of Saint Mark (799–819) (feast day: 22 Baramūdah). He was an important patriarch, a fascinating individual, a master preacher, and an eminent Coptic writer. Mark's life was closely associated with that of his predecessor, JOHN IV. As a deacon in Alexandria, he became John's disciple and helped his mentor in his church building program as well as in his days of need, when the country was stricken by famine. Then he became a monk of Dayr Anbā Maqār in Wādī al-Naṭrūn. Mark must have been acquainted with the Hellenistic world, since he came from Alexandria. No doubt he knew Greek, Arabic, possibly Syriac, and, of course, Coptic.

His election to the patriarchate was unanimously approved by the clergy and the bishops assembled at Alexandria, partly on account of his predecessor's deathbed reference to him as a worthy successor. Mark fled deep into the desert because, in his humility, he considered himself unworthy of this dignity. After the governor's approval was granted, however, Bishop Mīkhā'īl of Miṣr (al-Fusṭāṭ) returned to take Mark to Alexandria by force; according to the HISTORY OF THE PATRIARCHS, in iron chains.

Beginning with his inauguration homily after his enthronement at Alexandria, Mark demonstrated his preaching ability and his knowledge of Coptic orthodoxy in opposition to the Council of CHALCEDON. Conditions in al-Fusṭāṭ and Alexandria improved for the Christians, as Mark was able to obtain permits to rebuild churches since he maintained a friendly relationship with the governor. The situation in the rest of Egypt is reported to have been secure, and there is evidence that people could resume renewed church building activity elsewhere.

Mark cultivated friendly connections with Syria by writing a synodical epistle to Patriarch Cyriacus of Antioch, defining his Coptic Orthodox faith, and stressing the unity between their churches. More important, he successfully withstood teachings about the Eucharist in Syria by the Abrahamites, a sect so called after their leader. He also convinced the leaderless BARSANUPHIANS, or ACEPHALOI, to affiliate with the Coptic Orthodox Church, although they had been fierce adversaries of PETER III MONGUS (480–488), who had accepted the HENOTIKON (482) of Emperor Zeno. The Barsanuphians had refused to recognize any patriarchs after Peter III, but when their chiefs, George and his son Abraham, were ordained bishops by Mark, their faithful followers returned to the church as well.

Mark overcame many difficulties and jealousies that surrounded him. He helped during a locust plague in the western Delta province of al-Beheira and in Alexandria. He was able to heal the sick and cast away evil spirits, although he himself suffered ill health for twelve years.

But despite his positive accomplishments, problems persisted. After the death of Caliph Abū Jaʿfar Hārūn al-Rashīd ibn al-Mahdī (786–809), Egypt became embroiled in local conflicts within his realm. Traffic was interrupted, especially to Nubia and Ethiopia. Plundering and tax collecting again intensified. Andalusian warriors brought booty to Alexandria from the Roman islands, which dragged the city into the war movement of the eighth and ninth centuries in the Mediterranean, and the Christians participated in the fight between the Lakhmids and Andalusians, many becoming victims. During this period, Mark is said to have bought and freed about six thousand Christian captives intended for the slave market. The Church of the Redeemer, which had been rebuilt by him, was consumed by fire. Together with two companions, the distressed Mark left Alexandria and tried to carry on his duties in absentia.

ʿAbd al-ʿAzīz, governor of the eastern provinces, attempted to help him by decree. And in Syria the new Antiochene patriarch, Dionysius, defended himself against the heretical sect of the Abrahamites, for which Mark expressed pleasure in a letter to his colleague. Mark also saw the Bedouins plunder SCETIS, even taking some of the monks as prisoners.

At Nabarūh, where he resided for five years after leaving Alexandria, Mark died on 17 April 819. His coffin was placed in the village church until it could be moved to Alexandria.

The literary works of Mark consist of twenty Easter epistles (festal letters) and twenty-one books of mystagogy. All were probably written in Greek and accompanied by an authentic Coptic version—at least for the Easter epistles. Undoubtedly, he wrote his synodical letter to Cyriacus of Antioch in Greek.

The homily that was pronounced by Mark at his inauguration exists in Coptic. Not only is it a good example of Coptic rhetoric, but also it shows Mark's knowledge of the Bible and other theological literature. As far as Christology is concerned, the preacher shows Christ as a real man, suffering in the body. Against ARIUS, NESTORIUS, Ibas of Edessa, THEODORUS OF MOPSUESTIA, Theodoret of Cyrrhus, Nectarius, ORIGEN, and the COUNCIL OF CHALCEDON, Mark argues the unity of the divine and human nature in Christ, without any confusion.

L. T. Lefort (1879–1959) discovered that this homily is extant in Arabic under the name of Epiphanius of Salamis (c. 315–403). The Arabic text follows a Greek version of uncertain origin. Another version exists in Old Slavonic. Both of these differ from the Coptic texts, particularly in Christological passages; some parts are missing, and some sections of the Coptic texts are abbreviated.

Obviously some of his Greek texts are revised for Coptic usage. It is possible that Mark made the Coptic revisions himself. Another possibility is that the famous enthronement homily was omitted from Coptic tradition and added to the Greek by an unknown person.

BIBLIOGRAPHY

Orlandi, T. *Elementi di lingua e letteratura copta,* p. 111. Milan, 1970.

Vis, H. de. "Homélie cathédrale de Marc, patriarche d'Alexandrie." *Le Muséon* 34 (1921):179–216; 35 (1922):17–39.

C. DETLEF G. MÜLLER

MARK III, SAINT, seventy-third patriarch of the See of Saint Mark (1167–1189) (feast day: 6 Ṭūbah). Mark's secular name before his investiture in the patriarchate was Abū al-Faraj ibn Abī al-Saʿd ibn Zarʿah. He was a layman of Syrian origin, related to the sixty-second patriarch, Abraham.

He was a bachelor known to all his neighbors, both Coptic and Muslim, for his chastity, his virtue, and his charity. It appears that his predecessor, JOHN V, referred to him in the presence of others as a monastic personality, considered by them as a first step toward his investiture. His selection by the congregation of Miṣr was unanimously approved by the bishops and the clergy in recognition of his religious qualities and his knowledge of Coptic church traditions.

He was a contemporary of the latter years of Fatimid rule under Caliph al-ʿAḍid (1160–1171) and he saw the inauguration of the Ayyubid dynasty. He was a witness to Sālih Sālaḥ al-Dīn's (Saladin's) victories over the crusader kingdom, which were crowned with the reconquest of the city of Jerusalem (1187).

In the early years of Saladin's rule, the Copts suffered heavy calamities, for Saladin decreed that their role in the financial administration of Egypt should be ended by their dismissal and their replacement by Muslims. On the other hand, the establishment of the feudal system under the Ayyubid dynasty and the appropriation of land estates by the leading aristocracy offered the Copts the opportunity to serve in this new field, where their expert knowledge was sorely needed. In other words, the Copts left the government positions to control the growing feudal system established by the Ayyubid sultans.

On the religious scene, the situation of the Copts was worsened by the issuance of new decrees by Saladin, which mandated the removal of all crosses from churches as well as painting the churches black. Bells were also silenced, and the Copts were forbidden to conduct their religious processions in the streets as they were accustomed to do, especially during the holy week, when they moved between churches carrying olive branches and candles. Saladin reinstated previous orders that required Copts to wear distinguishing dark clothing, blue turbans, and girdles (*zunnārs*). He forbade the Copts to ride horses or mules, thus restricting them to the use of donkeys. Wine was forbidden, and this implied interference with their use of sacramental wine on their altars, although it was stated that this restriction was confined to the open use of alcohol. The decrees also prevented prayers from being said loud enough that the public could hear them.

The Islamic sources of this age record the particulars of this fresh wave of persecution, especially the works of the Muslim historian of the Copts, Taqīy al-Dīn al-MAQRĪZĪ. The repression was so intense that Copts feared that the Muslim authorities harbored ideas of exiling them from Egypt and laying hands on the dwellings of all the people of the Covenant (AHL AL-DHIMMAH). This action did not come to pass, because the authorities feared that such a measure might lead to collapse of the economy of the country, which was controlled by the Copts.

The immediate consequence of such trials and tribulations was the enhancement of the process of Islamization, and the patriarch looked upon these developments with alarm, taking solace in prayer.

Nevertheless, the skills of the depressed Copts were directed toward the vocations of commerce and agriculture, where they were able to build up their wealth and recover their economic prosperity. In addition, their active penetration into the Ayyubid feudal system gradually helped them recover what might be considered the equivalent of their lost places in the state administrative system. It is unclear when the humiliating measures imposed by Saladin began to disappear. But with the patience and fortitude of the Copts, their position began to improve even before Saladin's death. It appeared that the forces of nature collaborated with these factors in the amelioration of the situation of the Copts. The Nile flood resumed in its fullness, and that together with the return of rain made the crops produce, and the increasing commodities created a world of plenty in place of former famine and pestilence.

The return to peace and prosperity after a period of hardships and humiliation to the Copts was associated with a curious event, which was regarded as a moral and religious triumph for Mark III. This event was the conversion of a prominent Jew to Christianity at the hands of the patriarch in the eighth year of his reign. His name was Abū al-Fakhr ibn Azhar, and he was made a deacon of the church by Anbā Gabriel, bishop of Miṣr, at the church of Our Lady known as al-'Adawiyyah.

The patriarch also felt free to attend to the restoration of ruined churches and the consecration of new ones with the help and financial assistance of the members of his enriched congregation. Thus the patriarch himself took charge of rebuilding the outer wall of the Monastery of Saint Macarius (DAYR ANBĀ MAQĀR), which was vulnerable to the accumulation of sands from the desert in Wādī al-Naṭrūn. The active work of restoring religious houses spread over the country and was not confined to the major cities of Cairo and Alexandria. The Coptic patriarchate also recovered a number of other churches that had previously been appropriated by the Armenians during the reign of Badr al-Jamālī who, being of Armenian extraction, encouraged the Armenians to settle in Egypt. Badr al-Jamālī was instrumental in the transfer of Coptic churches to his old countrymen, despite his Islamization. These included a noted church in the district of al-Basātīn in the region of Cairo, which was incorporated in the diocese of Miṣr under the direct possession of the patriarchal seat.

Al-Shaykh Abū al-Barakāt ibn Abī Sa'īd, a famous Coptic scribe, used his fortune in the restoration and beautification of the chapel of Saint John the Baptist within the structure of the cathedral church of Abū Sayfayn (Saint Mercurius), which had suffered greatly in the burning of Cairo under the Fatimid minister Shāwār. He personally funded the reconstruction of its timber domes and vaults on four marble columns.

An artistic renaissance was also seen in the iconography in these churches. The names of Coptic painters of sacred icons of the period include Abū Sa'īd ibn al-Zayyāt and Abū al-Fatḥ ibn al-Aqmaṣ, known as Ibn al-Ḥawfī.

It is also noteworthy that Mark III abolished the long-established simoniacal practice known as CHEIROTONIA, by which former patriarchs had offered vacant episcopates to the best bidders. Thus, patriarchal remuneration was left open to the free gifts generously offered by the bishops.

In Mark's time, the Nestorian population became depleted, and the Coptic church was able to recover the Nestorian monastery in Cairo, which became part of the possessions of the patriarchal diocese. The patriarch also acquired the Church of Saint George at Ṭurah, which the Armenians had appropriated from CYRIL II during the vizierate of Badr al-Jamālī.

Perhaps the most significant events on the international scene were those associated with the name of Saladin and the recovery of Jerusalem from the hands of a tottering Frankish kingdom. The reconquest of the Holy Land by the Ayyubid sultan was a major event in Coptic history because it allowed the resumption of the pilgrimages to the holy places, a privilege they had lost under Latin rule.

Issues regarding Ethiopia and Nubia also figure prominently during the patriarchate of Mark III. Al-Maqrīzī makes a special mention of the successive embassies of the Abyssinian sovereigns to the caliphs and sultans of Egypt, beginning with the Fatimid caliph al-'Āḍid, to whom the usual gifts accompanied the Abyssinian missions. This was in order to cement the good relations between the two countries and to request the investiture of a special Coptic archbishop to take care of the religious welfare of a country that was directly under Coptic religious hegemony.

The situation was somewhat different when it came to the southern Christian kingdom of Nubia. Clashes took place between the Jacobite kings of that territory and the neighboring frontier districts of the province of Aswan. It is said that Nubian soldiers took the iniative by raiding a number of villages in the Aswan province. Consequently, Saladin commissioned his brother, Tūrānshāh, to launch a defensive campaign in the south, which resulted in the capture of the region of Qaṣr Ibrīm and its fortifications within the frontiers of Nubia. Tūrānshāh returned with considerable booty, including many prisoners and cattle, and granted the conquered territory as a feudal estate to one of his followers named Ibrāhīm al-Kurdī, who ruled it from Aswan. The vanquished king of Nubia tried to cultivate peace with Egypt by sending a substantial gift to the sultan, but the situation between the two countries remained one of uncertain and shaky peace. The enfeeblement of the Nubian monarchy vis-à-vis the sultanate of Egypt opened the door to the progressive penetration of Islam into that Christian country.

By virtue of his Syrian origin, Mark was interested in strengthening the already existing good relations with the patriarchate of Antioch. Synodical letters were exchanged between the two patriarchates. Missions that were previously interrupted by the crusader kingdom and Saladin's conquest opened the road for communication between Antioch and Cairo.

After a reign of almost twenty-two years, Mark III died in relative peace, a few years before the precarious reign of Saladin came to an end.

BIBLIOGRAPHY

Atiya, A.S. *Crusade, Commerce and Culture*. Bloomington, Ind., 1962.

Hanotaux, G., ed. *Histoire de la nation égyptienne*, 5 vols. Paris, 1926.

Lane-Poole, S. *History of Egypt in the Middle Ages*. London, 1901.

______. *The Mohammadan Dynasties*. Paris, 1925.

Runciman, S. *History of the Crusades*, 3 vols. Cambridge, 1951–1954.

SUBHI Y. LABIB

MARK IV, eighty-fourth patriarch of the See of Saint Mark (1349–1363). Mark's biography in the HISTORY OF THE PATRIARCHS is confined to a few lines stating his dates and the general remark that his days were peaceful. He was a native of Qalyūb in the Delta of Lower Egypt. Little else is known about his early secular life beyond the fact that he was the son of a priest of the CHURCH OF AL-MU'ALLAQAH in Old Cairo and that his name was al-As'ad Faraj. When he became a monk of DAYR SHAHRAN, he changed his name to Gabriel, and he took the name of Mark at his consecration as patriarch. He acceded to the throne of Saint Mark during the early years of the second sultanate of al-Nāsir Ḥasan (1347–1351) and was a contemporary of Ṣāliḥ Ṣalāḥ al-Dīn (1351–1354), al-Nāṣir Ḥasan's third reign (1354–1361) and al-Manṣūr Ṣalāḥ al-Dīn Muḥammad (1361–1363).

Mark's reign was troubled by the calamities that befell the whole country—Egypt was stricken by one of the worst plagues in its history. It is said that at least one-quarter of the population died, and that certain cities such as Bilbays were completely vacated. The plague and the depletion of the population resulted in an economic collapse. Many feudatories lost their labor corps, and agricultural products became scarce. Within the towns, industries also suffered on account of the death of skilled craftsmen. Revenues of the state were depleted, and the church was hardly able to pay the land tax. The Islamic administration had to prey upon individual fortunes, and what made matters even worse was the failure of the Nile floods—the arable lands were desiccated and diminished productivity was the result. The Mamluk amirs became restive and violently deposed one sultan after another. To make matters worse, the bedouin tribes from the desert descended into the valley, especially in the distant and undefended parts of Upper Egypt, and caused further havoc.

In the midst of this confusion, a Copt from the country came to Cairo and took to the streets, crying moralistic dicta and urging people to reform their character. He was arrested by the authorities and brought before the Islamic justice. Here he declared that he warned the Copts who had apostatized to Islam. The judge tried to deflect him from this policy and invited him to become a Muslim, which he adamantly refused preferring martyrdom for Christ. Finally he was decapitated and his body was burned.

The law-abiding Copts, who did not make a noise about religion, did not suffer during those times. And the Islamized Copts, who chose to abide by the new religion, prospered and occupied high positions in the administration. They included 'Alam al-Din 'Abdallāh ibn Zanbūr al-Qibṭī and Fakhr al-Dīn Mājid ibn Qarūnyah al-Qibṭī.

The disastrous crusade of Peter I de Lusignan and his Cypriot hosts took place during Mark IV's patriarchate. In that holocaust, the Coptic community suffered as much as the Muslims in the pillage of the city. There were even Copts among the prisoners carried by the crusaders from the city.

After living in this atmosphere for fourteen years and three months, Mark III died on 6 Amshīr A.M. 1079/A.D. 1363.

BIBLIOGRAPHY

Ibn Ḥajar al-'Asqalānī. *Al-Durar al-Kāminah*, 6 vols. Hyderabad, 1972–1976.

Lane-Poole, S. *History of Egypt in the Middle Ages*. London, 1901.

______. *The Mohammadan Dynasties*. Paris, 1925.

SUBHI Y. LABIB

MARK V, ninety-eighth patriarch of the See of Saint Mark (1602–1618). Mark's biography in the HISTORY OF THE PATRIARCHS is two lines long. The dates of his investiture and his decease are mentioned, as is the length of his tenure. He was the contemporary of three Ottoman sultans, Aḥmad I (1603–1617), Muṣṭafa I (1617–1618), and 'Uthmān II (1618–1620). The *History of the Patriarchs* states that he was a native of the village of Bayāḍiyyah, and O. Meinardus places his monasticism at the Monastery of Saint Macarius (DAYR ANBĀ MAQĀR), where he was elected patriarch. He is said to have died peacefully in 1619, but no further information is available about his burial.

BIBLIOGRAPHY

Hanotaux, G., ed. *Histoire de la nation égyptienne*, 7 vols. Paris, 1931–1940.

Meinardus, O. *Christian Egypt: Ancient and Modern*. Cairo, 1977.

Précis de l'histoire de l'Egypte par divers historiens et archéologues. 4 vols. Cairo, 1933–1940.

SUBHI Y. LABIB

MARK VI, 101st patriarch of the See of Saint Mark (1650–1660). Mark is described as "al-Bahjūrī," which indicates his origin from the city of Bahjūrah. The HISTORY OF THE PATRIARCHS relates his biography in a matter of three lines, which contain the dates of his investiture and his decease. It mentions that he was a monk of DAYR ANBĀ ANṬŪNIYŪS, in the Eastern Desert by the Red Sea. His tenure lasted ten years, and he was a contemporary of two Ottoman sultans, Ibrāhīm I (1640–1648) and Muḥammad IV (1648–1687).

BIBLIOGRAPHY

Hanotaux, G., ed. *Histoire de la nation égyptienne*, 7 vols. Paris, 1931–1940.

Meinardus, O. *Christian Egypt: Ancient and Modern*. Cairo, 1977.

Précis de l'histoire de l'Egypte par divers historiens et archéologues, 4 vols. Cairo, 1933–1940.

SUBHI Y. LABIB

MARK VII, 106th patriarch of the See of Saint Mark (1745–1769). His original name was Sam'ān, and he was a native of the village of Qulūṣanā in the district of Samālūt in Upper Egypt. As a youth, he retired to DAYR ANBĀ BŪLĀ in the Eastern Desert, where he took the monastic vow and therefrom frequented the neighboring DAYR ANBĀ ANṬŪNIYŪS for years until his predecessor, JOHN XVII, died in 1745. At that time the Coptic community began the search for a worthy successor. In the end, it was decided to recruit the monk Sam'ān for the dignity, and a special delegation escorted him to Cairo, where he was consecrated patriarch. He occupied the patriarchate for twenty-four years, three months, and fourteen days until his death.

The first few years of his reign were relatively peaceful. Unsettled times were coming when the Mamluks regained power, owing to the decline of the Ottoman Empire. Mamluk tyranny and intrigues broke out in the ranks of the military forces, involving parties of Mamluk amirs, in which Khalīl Bey, the powerful *amir al-Ḥajj* (prince of the Mecca pilgrimage), 'Alī (Bey) al-Dimyāṭī the *Defterdar* (governor), 'Umar (Bey) Ghaytās, and Muḥammad (Bey) Zadeh were murdered. Others took flight, including Sanjaq 'Umar and his brother, together with Ḥasan, an orderly of Ibrāhīm, as well as 'Umar, governor of Jirjā (al-Jabartī, 1959, Vol. 2, p. 62). They reached Upper Egypt in 1748 and stayed there for eight months. Apparently, these fugitive Mamluks were conciliated with the bedouins whose leader, a certain Hammām, supplied them with corn, butter, and honey in anticipation of bedouin passage to Hijāz from the port of Quṣayr to escape the perils of the Mamluk intrigues at home.

An interesting episode concerning the Copts took place during that period in Egypt. Since the time of the Crusades, the Copts had been forbidden from undertaking pilgrimages to the Holy Land by both the crusaders and the local Muslim rulers of Egypt. The pious Copts resented these restrictions and wanted to resume pilgrimages to the Holy Sepulcher. In 1753 they seized an occasion to secure a *fatwā* (juridical consultation) from Shaykh al-Azhar in return for a bribe of 1,000 gold dinars, which legalized the pilgrimage and prevented interference from the Mamluk amirs or the Muslim population. Consequently, the overjoyed Copts began immediate preparations for the pilgrimage on a grand scale. The rendezvous of the congregating pilgrims was the desert east of Cairo, where daily they arrived in groups, carrying gifts for the Holy Sepulcher. Litters were constructed for women and children, and an escort of bedouins was engaged as guides for the expedition.

However, news soon circulated among the Muslims, who took offense to the Christian project. The *shaykh* al-Azhar 'Abdallāh al-Shabrūhī, who issued the *fatwā*, became the subject of popular ire. To mend his precarious position, it was insufficient for him to deny the Copts the right to make the pilgrimage. Instead, he mustered a body of students in al-Azhar mosque, whom he inflamed against the pilgrimage. Together with the angry mob, they descended upon the camp of the unsuspecting Christians with arms, sticks, and stones. Taken by surprise, the Copts took flight, and their camp was pillaged with no hope of redress from the Mamluk authorities.

Mark VII, like his predecessors, continued to struggle with the foreign missionaries from the Roman See, who thronged the country and attempted to proselytize the Copts by offering them an education that was lacking in the primitive Coptic village schools. In the meantime both Jesuits and Franciscans were active in the establishment of regular schools in a considerable number of districts spread throughout Upper Egypt.

These difficulties, both internal and external, had to be faced by the majority of the Coptic patriarchs of the seventeenth and eighteenth centuries. Mark VII died in 1769, amidst this strife, after a reign of twenty-four years.

BIBLIOGRAPHY

Jabartī, al-. *'Ajā'ib al-Āthār,* ed. Ḥasan Muḥammad Jawhar, 'Abd al-Fattāḥ al-Saranjawī, and al-Sayyid Ibrāhīm Salīm. Cairo, 1959.

Kāmil Ṣālih Nakhlah and Farīd Kāmil. *Khulāṣat Tārīkh al-Ummah al-Qibṭiyyah.* Cairo, 1922.

AZIZ S. ATIYA

MARK VIII, 108th patriarch of the See of Saint Mark (1796–1809). He was able to steer the affairs of the Coptic church and the Coptic community with great wisdom and much diplomacy during the momentous events of the French Expedition (1798) and the French occupation of Egypt. He was still pope of the Coptic church when MUḤAMMAD 'ALĪ (1805–1848) became viceroy of Egypt. Mark VIII made it a habit to issue regular encyclicals to be read in the Coptic churches, urging his people to maintain the traditional Christian doctrines and virtues at a time when many Copts were slipping into vicious customs.

The building of the Cathedral of Saint Mark at al-Azbakiyyah was started toward the end of Mark's reign. The story of obtaining the decree authorizing that building from the Sublime Porte is associated with the name of the notable Copt IBRĀHĪM AL-JAW-

HARĪ, then the head of the scribes of the whole of Egypt. In his official capacity, he was able to organize the pilgrimage to Mecca of one of the sultan's ladies and in the meantime offered to her valuable presents. In recognition of his services, she asked him to submit a wish that she would carry to the sultan. Ibrahim at once requested a decree for building the church, which was immediately granted. The building, however, was carried out in the time of his brother, JIRJIS AL-JAWHARĪ, who succeeded him in the *diwan* after his death. The cathedral was built on land belonging to General YA'QŪB and MALAṬĪ YŪSUF, and that area became the seat of the new patriarchate.

BIBLIOGRAPHY

Tawfīq Iskarūs. *Nawābigh al-Aqbāt wa-Mashāhīruhum fī al-Qarn al-Tāsi' 'Ashar*, 2 vols. Cairo, 1910–1913.

Ya'qūb Nakhlah Rufaylah. *Tārīkh al-Ummah al-Qibṭiyyah*. Cairo, 1899.

MOUNIR SHOUCRI

MARK, GOSPEL OF SAINT. *See* Gospel of Saint Mark.

MARK, LITURGY OF SAINT, a Greek liturgy once used in the Church of Alexandria. A recension of its anaphoric part is found in the EUCHOLOGION of the Coptic church as the Anaphora of Saint CYRIL. Egyptian peculiarities are most evident in its anaphoric part, whose opening eucharistic prayer, after a brief summary of God's saving actions leading to the mystery of the Eucharist as motives for thanksgiving, is interrupted by lengthy intercessory prayers. The people present are explicitly associated with the celestial beings as they sing the triple "Holy," which ends with "Heaven and earth are full of Thy glory." The prayer is then carried forward not by resumption of the word "holy," as in other anaphoras, but by "full," which leads to a first EPICLESIS (peculiarly Egyptian in its position) in which God is asked to fill the sacrifice with His blessing through the descent of the Holy Spirit. The ANAMNESIS after the Narrative of Institution is followed by a second epiclesis in which the Holy Spirit is called down both upon those present and upon the bread and the wine, that He may hallow and perfect them. There are no intercessory prayers between the second epiclesis and the DOXOLOGY that concludes the anaphora proper. Typically Egyptian exclamations by deacon and people are indicated. The same features are found in the anaphora of the fourth-century euchologion attributed to Bishop SARAPION OF TMUIS (except for the place of the intercessions and, perhaps, the second epiclesis) and in a sixth–seventh-century papyrus from DAYR AL-BALAYZAH. There is no doubt that they are proper to Egypt. In the surviving texts of the anaphora, some phrases of the Syrian Liturgy of Saint James appear.

The nonanaphoric parts of the Liturgy of Saint Mark also retain typically Egyptian elements. The prayer to accompany the incensation preceding the readings is a prayer for the forgiveness of sin. The prayer preceding the Lord's Prayer is one of preparation for communion, and a petition for the rising of the river waters is found among the intercessory prayers. Outside the anaphora, however, in the surviving manuscripts a process of assimilation to the Byzantine rite has been carried far. An Egyptian prayer of ABSOLUTION has been converted into a prayer for a lesser entrance, the biblical readings have been reduced to two, there is a greater entrance with the singing of the Cherubicon, the creed follows the KISS OF PEACE instead of preceding it in Egyptian fashion, diaconal litanies in the Byzantine manner have been introduced, and several prayers have been borrowed from the Byzantine rite.

Fragments of the anaphora (one of them from the fourth or fifth century) and the Coptic recension cast light on the evolution of the anaphoric part of the Liturgy of Saint Mark, but little is known of the history of its nonanaphoric part. Its full text, with the anaphora in its Melchite setting, survives in a few late manuscripts, which do not agree in all details. The oldest of those containing the complete text are the thirteenth-century Codex Rossanensis (now Vat. graec. 1970) and the Rotulus Vaticanus (Vat. graec. 2281) of 1207. In the latter, the process of Byzantinization is further advanced. Of the two oldest incomplete witnesses, one, Messina graec. 177, of the twelfth century, has a text similar to that of Vat. graec. 1970, while the other, an unpublished manuscript of the twelfth–thirteenth century in the Monastery of Saint Catherine at Mount Sinai, provides a text similar to that of Vat. graec. 2281. Manuscript 173/36 of the Greek Orthodox patriarchate of Alexandria, a copy of an earlier copy made in 1585–1586, has a text similar to that of Vat. graec. 2281 but with the assimilation to Byzantine usages carried still further. Almost nothing is known of the history of the Greek-Melchite liturgy or the circumstances of its use. The first clear allusion to its use is also the last. Around the year 1203 the Byzantine canonist Theodorus Balsamon, in his responses to questions put by Mark, Melchite patriarch of Alexandria, declared that the use of the Liturgy of Saint Mark (and of the Syrian Liturgy of Saint James), "read in the regions of Alexandria and of Jerusalem," was contrary to the canonical traditions and uses recognized by the See of Constantinople, whose liturgies of Saint JOHN CHRYSOSTOM and Saint Basil alone were to be used by churches in communion with that see.

BIBLIOGRAPHY

The Greek texts of the Codex Rossanensis, the Rotulus Vaticanus, and, for the parts following the Intercessory Prayers, the Rotulus Messanensis (Messina graec. 177) are printed synoptically, with parallel excerpts (in Latin translation) from the Coptic anaphoras of Saint Cyril and Saint Basil and the Ethiopic common order, in C. A. Swainson, *The Greek Liturgies*, pp. 2–73 (London, 1884). Swainson's text of the Codex Rossanensis, supplemented from other sources, is in F. E. Brightman, ed., *Liturgies Eastern and Western*, Vol. 1, pp. 113–43 (Oxford, 1896). The anaphoric part of Brightman's resultant text, edited by A. Raes, is given in A. Hänggi and I. Pahl, eds., *Prex eucharistica*, pp. 101–115 (Spicilegium friburgense 12, Fribourg, 1968). The Greek fragments of the fourth–fifth-century Strasbourg graec. 254 and the sixth-century John Rylands Papyrus 465 are conveniently found on pp. 116–22 of this work. A Sahidic fragment containing a mixture of known and otherwise unknown elements has been published by H. Quecke in *Orientalia Christiana Periodica* 37 (1971):40–54. An Ethiopic version of the anaphoric part of the Liturgy of Saint Mark has been published, with Latin translation by A. T. M. Semharay Selam, in *Ephemerides liturgicae* 42 (1928):507–531.

Translations

English by G. R. Merry in *Liturgies and Other Documents of the Ante-Nicene Period*, pp. 47–71 (Ante-Nicene Christian Library 24, Edinburgh, 1872); German in F. Probst, *Liturgie der drei ersten christlichen Jahrhunderte*, pp. 318–34 (Tübingen, 1870); Latin in E. Renaudot, *Liturgiarum Orientalium Collectio*, Vol. 1, pp. 120–48 (2nd ed., Frankfurt and London, 1847), of which the anaphoric part, adapted by A. Raes to Brightman's Greek text, is reproduced on pp. 103–115 of Hänggi and Pahl, *Prex eucharistica* (see above), to which Raes has added Latin translations of the Strasbourg fragment (by J. Quasten), pp. 117–19, and of the John Rylands fragment (by L. Ligier), pp. 121–23.

Studies

Coquin, R.-G. "L'Anaphore alexandrine de saint Marc." *Le Muséon* 82 (1969):307–356.

Cumming, G. J. "Egyptian Elements in the Jerusalem Liturgy." *Journal of Theological Studies* n.s. 25 (1974):117–24.

Engberding, H. "Neues Licht über die Geschichte des Textes der ägyptischen Markusliturgie." *Oriens Christianus* 40 (1956):40–68.

———. "Das anaphorische Fürbittgebet der griechischen Markusliturgie." *Orientalia Christiana Periodica* 30 (1964):398–446.

AELRED CODY, O.S.B.

MARK, SECRET GOSPEL OF. *See* Secret Gospel of Saint Mark.

MARK THE SIMPLE, SAINT (feast day: 10 Hātūr). The story of Mark who simulated madness is among the perhaps legendary stories of DANIEL OF SCETIS (sixth century). There are versions in several languages of the Christian Near East: in Greek, which seems to be the original (Clugnet, 1900; Clugnet, 1901); in Armenian in the editions of the *Vitae Patrum* (see the different editions of this work in Peeters, *Bibliotheca Hagiographica Orientalia: Subsidia Hagiographia*, Vol. 10, p. 15, and no. 608); and in Arabic (probably made from a Syriac version [if the text was summarized from Greek or Coptic, the name would be Marcos] in the Arabic recension of the SYNAXARION from Upper Egypt, ed. Basset, 1907, pp. 271–73; Forget, Vols. 47–49, pp. 292–93 [text] and 78, pp. 112–14 [trans.]).

The story of Mark is preserved in the stories placed under the name of the HEGUMENOS of Scetis, Daniel (485–570). The text of the Synaxarion from Upper Egypt begins, not like a customary commemoration "In this same day such and such a person died" (or "was martyred"), but like a quotation from a homiletic text: "Know, brethren, that on this same day Saint Anbā Markiya went to his rest" (such a transcription suggests a Syrian provenance). The Arabic text indicates that he was a native of Alexandria, which is not in the Greek. He is said to have undergone the assaults of, or been dominated by, the demon of fornication for fifteen years, then to have returned to himself and become a monk at the monastery of the Pempton (near Alexandria, to the west), where he remained for eight years, which the Arabic omits to say. At the end of the eight years, he decided to go into the town and there simulate madness, which he did. He gained some small change, kept ten small pieces for his own needs and gave the greater part of it to the other "madmen." He lived in the hippodrome, sleeping on its benches, to the point that he was described as "the idiot of the hippodrome." He passed eight years in this way of life. This theme of madness simulated for God is well known both from the example of Mark and from others; it has been studied by Guillaumont (1984, pp. 81–82), who sees in it a supreme form of the eremitic life, and by Vogt (1987, pp. 95–108).

At the end of the eight years, which Mark judged as a penitence, Daniel of Scetis came to Alexandria, for it was the custom that the *hegumenos* of Scetis should pay a visit to the patriarch—this was surely, as H. G. Evelyn-White thinks, TIMOTHY III (d. 535)—for the great feast, beyond any doubt that of Easter. He met Mark, and divined that he was a very holy monk, for Daniel was endowed with a sure discernment. He made him tell him his life and introduced him to the patriarch. He slept in the episcopal residence, near Daniel, but the latter had to confirm in the morning that Mark had died in the night. He held a splendid funeral for Mark, for which he summoned together monks come from Scetis, from Nitria, from the Kellia and, the Greek adds, from all the "lauras" in the neighborhood of Alexandria.

BIBLIOGRAPHY

Clugnet, L., et al. "Vie et récits de l'abbé Daniel de Scété." *Revue de l'Orient chrétien* 5 (1900):49–73; 254–71; 370–91.

______. *Vie et récits de l'abbé Daniel le Scétiote.* Bibliothèque hagiographique orientale 1. Paris, 1901.

Evelyn-White, H. G. *The Monasteries of the Wadi'n Natrûn*, pt. 2; *The History of the Monasteries of Nitria and Scetis.* New York, 1932.

Guillaumont, A. "La Folie simulée, une forme d'anachorèse." *Revue des historiens d'art, des archéologues, des musicologues et des orientalistes de l'Université d'Etat de Liège* 1 (1984):81–82.

Peeters, P. *Bibliotheca Orientalis.* Subsidia Hagiographica 10. Brussels, 1910.

Vogt, K. "La Moniale folle du monastère des Tabennesiotes." *Symbolae Osloenses* 62 (1987):95–108.

RENÉ-GEORGES COQUIN

MĀR MINĀ CULTURAL ASSOCIATION.

This is a Coptic association founded in Alexandria for the purpose of acquainting Copts with their history and cultural heritage. It was inaugurated in 1945 by Bānūb Ḥabachī, the curator of the Greco-Roman Museum and regional inspector of antiquities, who was responsible for the discovery of a marble city in the desert of Mareotis near Alexandria extending over 40,000 square meters. This was dedicated to Saint MENAS THE MIRACLE MAKER, a Coptic saint and martyr of the third century (see ABŪ MĪNĀ). The ruins of an ancient church and monastery were also discovered in that area. The modern recluse by the name of Minā, later consecrated as Patriarch CYRIL VI (1959–1971), the 116th pope of Alexandria, built himself a cell there during his early monastic life. Around that cell arose the reconstruction of a cathedral church and a monastery bearing the name of the saint.

The society organizes lectures and publishes monographs on subjects related to Copts.

BIBLIOGRAPHY

Atiya, A. S., and Mounir Shoucri. *Genius of St. Pachomius* (286–346). Alexandria, 1987.

MOUNIR SHOUCRI

MARQOS I. *See* Ethiopian Prelates.

MARQOS II. *See* Ethiopian Prelates.

MARQOS III. *See* Ethiopian Prelates.

MARQOS IV. *See* Ethiopian Prelates.

MARQUṢ,

fourteenth-century Melchite bishop of Damietta. A manuscript of 206 sheets (*Sinai Arabic 264*) containing an Arabic translation of the *typikon* of Saint Sabas made by Abū al-Fatḥ Qusṭanṭīn ibn Abī al-Ma'ālī ibn Abī al-Fatḥ was completed on 5 December A.D. 1355.

This translator was the father of Bishop Marquṣ, as we learn from a note written by the bishop and added to folio 1, which reads, "This *typikon* was given as an alms by the lord [my] father, during his lifetime, to me, the poor Marquṣ, servant of the see of the port of Damietta, the protected property. This was as a perpetual bequest, in my favor, as long as I live. And after my removal, it shall be a bequest to the Monastery of Mount Sinai, the holy mountain of God . . . . Written on Wednesday 28th Ishbāṭ [*sic*] of the year 6866." The last number is written in Coptic cursive figures. The date corresponds to 28 February 1358.

Another note written in the hand of the Bishop Marquṣ of Mount Sinai anathematizes whosoever should remove this manuscript from the monastery (fol. 1r). The handwriting is more slipshod than the foregoing note, but it is from the end of the fourteenth century. This is probably the Marquṣ mentioned in another manuscript (Sinai Arabic 90, fol. 318v) as being the bishop of the monastery in 1398–1399, when Marquṣ, bishop of Damietta, was already dead, and had bequeathed to Mount Sinai the manuscript of his father.

KHALIL SAMIR, S.J.

MARQUS AL-ANṬŪNĪ. Practically nothing is known of Marqus al-Anṭūnī, save that he died on 28 Abīb, worked many miracles, and must have been a monk at the monastery of Saint Antony, as his name indicates. However, he is not mentioned in the Arabic SYNAXARION.

The account of his life and miracles is found in only one unpublished, little-known manuscript copied at Cairo by the priest ABŪ AL-MUNĀ on 14 July 1679, as commissioned by Buṭrus, disciple of the 103rd patriarch, JOHN XVI (1676–1718). The manuscript is in the Coptic Patriarchate, Cairo Graf, no. 492, Simaykah, no. 627, fols. la–53b [life] and 53b–90a [miracles]).

BIBLIOGRAPHY

Graf, G. *Catalogue de manuscrits arabes chrétiens conservés au Caire,* p. 189 (no. 492). Vatican City, 1934.

KHALIL SAMIR, S.J.

MARRIAGE, the relation between husband and wife. [*Marriage is a sacrament in the Coptic church. The wedding is celebrated in a special church ceremony, and a multitude of customs traditionally surround the occasion. This entry consists of three articles:* The Sacrament of Marriage *and* The Marriage Ceremony *by Bishop Gregorios, and* Marriage Customs *by Cérès Wissa Wassef.*]

The Sacrament of Marriage

Marriage is a spiritual bond between a man and a woman, sanctified by the grace of the Holy Spirit, joining them into an indissoluble unit for the purpose of establishing a caring and harmonious Christian family.

These distinctive characteristics were culled from the Old Testament, the teachings of Christ, the commandments of the apostles, and decrees of various ecumenical councils. God blessed Adam and Eve, and later, Noah, saying, "Be fruitful and multiply, and fill the earth" (Gn. 1:28; 9:1). Likewise, Christ rebuked the Pharisees who importuned Him for a facile justification of divorce by reminding them that "God made them at the beginning male and female, and for this cause a man shall leave father and mother, and shall cleave to his wife, and the twain shall be one flesh" (Mt. 19:5–6).

The presence of Christ at the marriage of Cana was a very significant event. That the Lord accepted an invitation to a wedding and performed His first miracle there reflects the importance He attached to marriage as a sacrosanct institution in the structure of society. On this basis rests the sacramental approach of the Coptic church to matrimony. Consequently, during the sacrament of Holy Matrimony, the priest says this prayer: "O Thou Who wert present at the marriage feast at Cana of Galilee, and blest it, and changed the water into real wine by Thy Divine power, do bless the marriage of Thy servants [names]."

In the early centuries of Christianity, the fathers and theologians of the church strove to establish a permanent solid base for the institution of marriage. CLEMENT OF ALEXANDRIA laid special stress on the recognition of the divine process by which man and woman are unified through marriage. His student and successor at the Catechetical School, Origen, in his commentaries on Matthew wrote, "Certainly it is God who joins two in one, so that when he marries a woman to a man there are no longer two. And since it is God who joins them, there is in this joining a grace for those who are joined by God. Paul knew this, and he said that just as holy celibacy was a grace, so also was marriage, according to the Word of God, a grace." The same attitude was expressed by Ambrose, fourth-century bishop of Milan, in a letter to Pope Siricius: "Neither do we deny that marriage has been sanctified by Christ, since the Divine Word says: 'The two shall become one flesh.'"

In the fifth century Saint CYRIL OF ALEXANDRIA remarked that "when the wedding was celebrated [at Cana] it is clear that it was entirely decorous: for indeed, the Mother of the Saviour was there; and, invited along with His disciples, the Saviour too was there, working miracles more than being entertained in feasting, and especially that He might sanctify the very beginning of human generation, which certainly is a matter concerning the flesh." The fifth-century theologian Saint Augustine maintained that "having been invited, the Lord came to the marriage in order to affirm conjugal chastity and to show that marriage is a Sacrament." Similarly, Epiphanius, fourth-century bishop of Salamis, adduced that "two reasons can be advanced to explain why the marriage was celebrated with external festivities in Cana of Galilee, and why the water was truly changed into wine: so that the tide of bacchanalian frenetics in the world might be turned to chastity and dignity in marriage, and so that the rest might be directed aright to the enjoyment both of wine free of toil and of the favor that presented it; so that in every way it might stop the mouths of those aroused against the Lord, and so that it might show that He is God with the Father and His Holy Spirit."

In contrast to that wave of bacchanalian dissipation and intemperance to which Epiphanius refers, there arose a tendency that veered to the other extreme in advocating strict celibacy and harsh self-restraint. MANICHAEISM and GNOSTICISM frowned upon marriage, and many of their adherents flouted Christian teachings on this subject with derision and contempt. The church, however, continued to affirm the sanctity of marriage. In 345 the Council of Gangra in Asia Minor adopted far-reaching resolutions that were directed against his spirit of false asceticism that condemned marriage and boycotted ordinary services of the church. Among other measures, the council decreed the excommunication of those who inveighed against lawful church marriage, those who refused to receive Holy Communion from the hand of a married priest, and those who remained celibate not because of a genuine pursuit of a state of celibacy but because of contempt for marriage and hatred of married persons. The council also condemned women who deserted their husbands as a result of a similar disdainful outlook on marriage and a false sense of decorum and affected propriety. Likewise, it decreed that members of the clergy who turned away their wives on the grounds of a more pious relationship could be expelled. Clement of Alexandria, in his *Stromateis* (Miscellanies) wrote, "If, however, marriage, though commanded by the Law, were yet sinful—really, I do not see how anyone could say that sin has been commanded by God. If the Law is sacred, then marriage is a holy estate."

In light of these religious sanctions, the marriage ceremony, in harmony with other sacraments, must be conducted in the church. (It is true that in certain cases it can be held in a private house, but this is the exception to the rule, similar to baptizing an invalid at home or administering the HOLY UNCTION of the sick to a dying person in a hospital or at home.) The officiating priest must be in full ecclesiastical vestments, not omitting to take off his shoes. According to Ṣafī ibn al-ʿAssāl, "a wedding may be conducted only in the presence of a priest who shall pray for the bridal couple and administer Holy Communion to them in the *iklīl* ceremony, by which they are united and become one flesh, as God Almighty has ordained. Contrary to this it shall not be deemed a proper marriage, for it is through Church prayer alone that man and woman can become mutually legitimate."

This sanctity of marriage makes it an indissoluble bond that may be broken only on the grounds of adultery (Mt. 5:23, 19:9; Mk. 10:11–12; Jn. 16:18) or death (1 Cor. 7:39; Rom.7:2–3). The church also concedes that certain circumstances may be considered tantamount to death, as when a husband or wife renounces the Christian faith or is absent for a designated number of years, in which cases the partner may be allowed to divorce and remarry.

Marriage is thus a lifelong relationship between man and woman, the purpose of which is the enjoyment of mutual company on the basis of equal partnership, the procreation of children, and the avoidance of sin. The annals of the Coptic church, however, are not devoid of instances in which a couple entered voluntarily into a chaste relationship of spiritual communion, although they were married. According to the SYNAXARION, Saint DEMETRIUS I, third-century patriarch of Alexandria, had been married to his wife for forty-seven years before he was chosen patriarch, but both had lived in strict chastity. Anbā Ammonius, in the fourth century, lived with his wife for seventeen years in complete chastity until her death, when he became a monk. Other examples are Anbā Cyrus of Jawjar in the eighth century and Saint JOHN KAMA, in the ninth century.

The Marriage Ceremony

The marriage ceremony, interspersed with making the sign of the cross, unfolds stage by stage. To solemnize the contract of marriage, the priest, holding a cross in his right hand in the presence of the bridal couple, their relatives, and the church congregation, begins by saying, "In the Name of our Lord, our God and our Saviour Jesus Christ Who has instituted the law of virtuousness and rectitude, we ratify the betrothal of the blessed Orthodox virgin son [name of bridegroom] to his betrothed the blessed Orthodox virgin daughter [name of bride]." Here he makes the sign of the cross and says, "In the Name of the Father, the Son and the Holy Spirit, One God. Blessed be God the Father Almighty, Amen." Thereupon, the deacons chant "Amen" three times, and the congregation recites the Lord's Prayer.

Once again the priest says, "In the Name of our Lord, our God and our Savior Jesus Christ . . .," this time mentioning the name of the bride before that of the bridegroom, and makes the sign of the cross and adds, "Blessed be His Only-begotten Son, Jesus Christ, our Lord, Amen." The deacons again chant "Amen" three times, and the congregation again recites the Lord's Prayer. The priest then repeats the same formula as he said it the first time, making the sign of the cross, and adds, "Blessed be the Holy Spirit, the Paraclete, Amen," and the deacons chant "Amen" three times. Then the priest says, "Glory and honour, honour and glory to the All-holy Trinity, Father, Son and Holy Spirit, now and at all times, world without end, Amen."

After the prayer of thanksgiving and the prayer of incense, the epistle is read, followed by the TRISAGION and the prayer of the Gospel. The reading of the Gospel is taken from Matthew 19:5–6: "For this reason a man shall leave father and mother and be joined to his wife, and the two shall become one. . . . What therefore God has joined together, let no man put asunder." Certain prayers and intercessions follow, then the creed, the prayers of betrothal, and the prayer of absolution. The priest places rings on the ring finger of the left hand of the bridegroom and the bride and ties a girdle (Arabic, *zunnār*) around the man's shoulder.

Next comes the reading of Ephesians 5:22–6:30, wherein Paul speaks of the married life of devout Christians as the relationship between Christ and the church; the key verses are, "For the husband is the head of the wife as Christ is the head of the church," and "Husbands, love your wives, as Christ loved the church and gave himself up for her." There follow some petitions and supplications in which reference is frequently made to the creation of woman from the rib of Adam and to the divine will of Christ to be born of a woman, the Blessed Virgin Mary. Directing his prayers to Christ, "who was present at the marriage feast of Cana of Galilee, and changed the water to wine," the priest requests the Lord to bless the marriage of the bridal couple to assist them in their future life that they may live in peace, piety, and patience without offense.

Then the priest takes in his hand two marriage diadems. A marriage diadem is a coronet of gold or silver called in Arabic *tāj* or *iklīl,* both meaning "crown." (The term *iklīl* also refers to the whole marriage ceremony.) The diadem has a cross in the center surrounded by the words "Glory to God in the highest and on earth peace." Holding the diadems, the priest prays, "God . . . Who dost crown Thy saints with unfading crowns, . . . do Thou also now bless these crowns we have prepared to set upon Thy servants. May they be to them a crown of glory and honour, of blessing and salvation, of rejoicing and good pleasure, of virtue and righteousness, of wisdom and understanding, of comfort and strength." Then he places the diadems, attached by a ribbon, upon the heads of the bridegroom and the bride and says, "Set, Lord, upon Thy servants [names] a crown of invincible grace, of exalted and great glory, of good and unconquerable faith, Amen." At that point he puts a white silk cloth on their heads, saying, "Crown them with glory and honour, O Father, Amen. Bless them, O Only-begotten Son, Amen. Sanctify them, O Holy Spirit, Amen." Then he wraps the diadems and the rings in the cloth. Afterward come the Lord's Prayer and prayers of absolution.

The service concludes with an address by the priest that encapsulates certain commandments and pieces of advice. This address is made up of seven sections, the first six of which are each followed by a short hymn sung by the deacons, while the seventh and last section is followed by the Lord's Prayer. First, he reminds the couple of the wisdom of God's creation of Eve from Adam's rib, so that he may constantly care for her and she may be obedient to him. To the bridegroom the priest says, "It is fitting that you should now receive your wife with a pure heart, upright mind, and guileless intent." The bride is urged to be always prompted by a genuine sense of obedience, duty, love, and respect, so that, like Sarah, who was respectful and dutiful toward Abraham, her husband, she may be blessed with offspring "as plentiful as the stars in the sky and the sand on the seashore."

The service for a second marriage, called digamy (for the widowed and the divorced), is nearly the same, with certain relevant minor modifications. If both parties have been widowed, the crowns are not used, since no one may be crowned twice. Where one has not been married before, he or she will receive the diadem.

The church allows second marriages, in conformity with Paul's words, "I say therefore to the unmarried and widows, 'It is good for them if they abide even as I. But if they cannot contain, let them marry: for it is better to marry than to burn.'" This section is read during the service and is incorporated into the priest's prayers. In *Al-Majmū' al-Ṣafawī* Ṣafī ibn al-'Assāl described the second marriage as inferior to the first; thus the church accords it not the blessing of a crowning but a prayer of forgiveness.

In his "Catechetical Lectures" Saint Cyril of Jerusalem said, "And those who are once married—let them not hold in contempt those who have accommodated themselves to a second marriage. Continence is a good and wonderful thing; but still, it is permissible to enter upon a second marriage."

The church, however, discountenances a third marriage. This was best expressed by Saint Jerome in his letter to Pammachius: "I do not condemn digamists, not even trigamists, and if I may use such a word, not even octogamists. . . . It is one thing not to condemn, another to commend; one thing to grant forgiveness, another to praise as virtuous" (Jerome, 1979, p. 184)

Further subsequent marriages are unequivocally condemned. Ṣafī ibn al-'Assāl wrote, "He who dares to enter upon a fourth marriage . . . let him not call it marriage, nor the children born of it rightful progeny. . . . Such an action merits punishment due to adultery."

Finally, it should be noted that marriages cannot be solemnized during the church fasts preceding Christmas, Easter, the Dormition of the Blessed Virgin Mary, and the Feast of the Apostles Paul and Peter. In very special circumstances, however, dispensation may be granted by the patriarch or bishop.

BIBLIOGRAPHY

Broudehoux, J. P. *Mariage et famille chez Clément d'Alexandrie*. Théologie historique 2. Paris, 1970.

Burmester, O. H. E. *The Egyptian or Coptic Church: A Detailed Description of Her Liturgical Services*. Cairo, 1967.

Butler, A. J. *The Ancient Coptic Churches of Egypt*. Oxford, 1884.

Cummings, D. *The Rudder of the Orthodox Christians; or All the Sacred and Divine Canons*. Chicago, 1957.

Ḥabīb Jirjis. *Asrār al-Kanīsah al-sab'ah* (The Seven Sacraments of the Church). Cairo, 1934.

Hanāniyā Kassāb. *Majmū'at al-Shar' al-Kanasī, aw Qawanīn al-Kanīsah al-Masīḥiyyah al-Jāmi'ah* (Laws of the Christian Universal Church). Beirut, 1975.

Jurgens, William A., ed. *The Faith of the Early Fathers*. 3 vols. Collegeville, Minn., 1970–1979.

Safī ibn al-'Assāl, al-. *Al-Majmū' al-Ṣafawī* (The Ṣafawī Compendium). Cairo. 1908.

Yūḥannā Salāmah. *Kitāb al-La'āli' al-Nafīsah fī Sharḥ Ṭuqūs wa-Mu'taqadāt al-Kanīsah*. Cairo, 1903.

BISHOP GREGORIOS

Marriage Customs

The Coptic wedding ceremony, called "the coronation ceremony," takes place generally on Thursday, Saturday, or Sunday. Some traditions related to this sacrament have gradually disappeared among urban dwellers, but they still persist in the countryside. One such custom is the "Night of the Henna," which takes place on the eve of the wedding day. It is consecrated to the bride, her kinswomen, and her women friends. A trained woman (*mashṭah*) prepares the bride, bathes her, and applies henna to the palms of her hands and soles of her feet and those of the attending guests. The bridegroom is represented at the event by his kinswomen, who arrive loaded with flowers and bearing a candle as tall as the bride, which is supposed to burn all night long in her bedroom. The day ends with a festive dinner for women only.

The bridegroom also spends his day in celebration with his best man (*shibīn*) and male friends. The bride's family presents him with apparel of silk and cotton and with jewelry, according to the means and social standards of the family.

Another popular tradition that has almost disappeared is the procession of the bride on her wedding day. Everyone parades on foot through the streets with musicians leading. For the more affluent, the bride and her female attendants formerly rode in a decorated palanquin on the back of a camel. The camels have now been replaced by carriages and automobiles.

If the wedding is in a hotel, the parade takes place after the ceremony in the hotel and before the lavish banquet dinner. The bride and bridegroom are paraded through the hotel, preceded by musicians and dancers and followed by the guests.

According to a custom rarely observed at present, upon the arrival of everyone at the home of the bridegroom, a lamb or calf was slaughtered, and its blood sprinkled over the threshold, across which the bride had to step. The flesh of the sacrificial animal was distributed among the poor.

The wedding night itself, or "Night of the Bridegroom," begins with a religious ceremony, which is now held in a church but until only a few decades ago took place in the home of the bridegroom. If the home was too small, a large tent was set up made of many colorful pieces of fabric appliquéd in intricate geometric designs. It was adorned with flags and strings of multicolored lamps, and floors were covered with red carpets. Inside, two gilded armchairs were set on a platform and reserved for the couple. These gilded chairs are still used in the church ceremony.

To begin the festivities, the best man goes to the bride's home with bouquets of flowers for the bride and her attendants. The father or the closest male relative will take the bride to her future husband. However, as she is about to step over the threshold to leave her home, custom demands that the household servants close the door and pretend to detain her. They consent to reopen the door only after receiving bids in remuneration for allowing the bride to leave. This latter custom is very rarely seen at present.

For the ceremony itself, the bridegroom, wearing a long cape embroidered in white, waits in the chancel for his bride, who approaches on the arm of her father or a relative. She is preceded by the choir and clergy dressed in festive habits and singing to the accompaniment of cymbals and triangles. She takes her place at the right in one of the chairs on the platform. In front of the couple is a table holding the New Testament, a golden cross, the wedding rings, and incense.

The marriage service begins. At the end, after everyone has recited the Lord's Prayer, the priest, preceded by the choir of deacons singing, leads the newlyweds to the exit.

After the ceremony, every guest is presented with a small box (or other container) of sugar-coated almonds. These boxes, according to the means of the family, may be made of sterling silver, porcelain, cardboard, or other material. A lavish dinner is served, usually in the home of the bridegroom or under a tent especially erected for the occasion. For some decades it has been the custom among the bourgeoisie to host a reception in a large hotel. The amount of pomp and splendor depends on the financial situation of the couple, but even the poorest extend themselves for the occasion. In recent years the festivities have generally ended with the religious ceremony in the church, and dinner has been served only to the close family and friends of the newlyweds.

In the countryside, relatives and close friends help defray the wedding expenses by sending gifts such as sheep, poultry, sugar, rice, coffee, candles, and the like, on the understanding that they receive similar consideration when their turn comes.

On the following morning, friends and relatives call at the bridegroom's house to present their gifts to the newlyweds. Gifts used to consist mainly of cash, which was carefully recorded for reciprocation on later occasions. This custom still exists, although presents of all kinds are also offered.

BIBLIOGRAPHY

Lane, W. E. *An Account of the Manners and Customs of the Modern Egyptians.* London, 1890.

Leeder, S. H. *Modern Sons of the Pharaohs.* London and New York, 1919; repr. New York, 1973.

CÉRÈS WISSA WASSEF

MARRIAGE OF CANA, FEAST OF THE.

See Feasts, Minor.

MARRIAGE CEREMONY. *See* Marriage.

MARRIAGE DIADEM. *See* Marriage.

MARRIAGE IN LAW. *See* Personal Status Law.

MARRIAGE SACRAMENT. *See* Marriage.

MARṢAFĀ, a town in the Delta province of Qalyūbiyyah. Al-MAQRĪZĪ wrote that in the late fourteenth or early fifteenth century there was a restored church of Saint George in Marṣafā.

BIBLIOGRAPHY

Timm, S. *Das christlich-koptische Ägypten in arabischer Zeit*, pt. 4, p. 1593. Wiesbaden, 1988.

RANDALL STEWART

MARSANES, a Gnostic prophet of the second century who was said to have visited heaven while in ecstacy. His name is also the title of a long but very fragmentary Gnostic work that forms Codex X of the NAG HAMMADI LIBRARY. The title is partly preserved at the end of the text. Neither the precise length of the text nor the numeration of the pages can be determined with precision (only folios 1–5 [= pp. 1–10] are numbered in the Codex; in modern editions and commentaries editors place an asterisk by all other page numbers). Even the number of tractates in Codex X has been disputed. The best case however, can be made for a single tractate in the Codex, extending from 1. 1 to 68*. 18. The title suggests that the supposed author of the document is the Gnostic prophet Marsanes, a figure acclaimed in the untitled tractate from the Bruce Codex on Marsanes and Nicotheos (chapter 7) and in Epiphanius *Panarion* 40. 7. 6, on Martiades and Marsianos as experiencing an ecstatic trip to the heavens and receiving glory from the heavenly powers. Such a description of Marsanes fits the present tractate also, since here the author, in the first person, lays claim to visionary revelations and writes a "revelation," or apocalypse, which may resemble not only the apocalypse of Nicotheos alluded to in the Bruce Codex but also the apocalypses of Zoroaster, Zostrianos, Nicotheos, Allogenes, Messos, and others mentioned in Porphyry's *Life of Plotinus* 16.

Marsanes opens predictably with a lacuna but proceeds to relate an exhortation, probably delivered by Marsanes to his Gnostic comrades, on knowledge and "the great Father." It also seems to be Marsanes who describes the thirteen seals, or levels of existence, from the first and lowest "worldly" levels to the last and highest level of the supreme God, "the Silent One who has not been known." The author claims that he—Marsanes—has true knowledge. Through his ascent beyond the limits of this world, he has attained to knowledge of "the entire place" and has reached the conclusion (so striking in a Gnostic context) that "in every way the sense-perceptible cosmos is [worthy] of being completely saved." The topic of salvation leads Marsanes to introduce the descent, work, and ascent of the savior Autogenes, the "Self-begotten One," who "descended from the Unbegotten One" and "saved a multitude." While raising several basic questions about the nature of existence and probing their implications, Marsanes himself rises to an awareness of "the supremacy of the silence of the Silent One" and offers praise. Further revelatory disclosures follow, and it is shown that as "the invisible Spirit" ascends back up to heaven, so also the Gnostics achieve bliss by ascending with him to glory.

After several very fragmentary pages, the tractate preserves portions of a fascinating section on the nature and function of letters, sounds, and numbers, which are linked to the powers and capacities of angels, deities, and souls. Occasionally exhortations to piety interrupt the train of thought, as at 27*. 21–23, where a pronouncement against sin finds its place within the discussion of vowels, consonants, and the shapes of the soul. Reflecting contemporary astrological, magical, and grammatical themes, this long section seeks to instruct the reader in the proper way of calling upon or conjuring the angels, so that the soul might eventually reach the divine. In the words of *Marsanes*, such a knowledge of the alphabet will help Gnostics to "be separated from the angels" and to "seek and find [who] they [themselves] are."

Marsanes is a Gnostic tractate with no clearly Christian elements. It illustrates obvious Platonist traits, and may be seen as representative of Sethian gnosticism.

BIBLIOGRAPHY

Books of Jeu and the Untitled Text in the Bruce Codex, The, ed. C. Schmidt, trans. V. MacDermot. Nag Hammadi Studies 13. Leiden, 1981.

Facsimile Edition of the Nag Hammadi Codices: Codices IX and X. Leiden, 1977.

Pearson, B. A. "Marsanes (X,1)." In *The Nag Hammadi Library in English*, pp. 417–26. Leiden and San Francisco, 1977.

______. "The Tractate Marsanes (NHC X) and the Platonic Tradition," In *Gnosis: Festschrift für Hans Jonas*, ed. B. Aland, pp. 373–84. Göttingen, 1978.

______. "X,1: Marsanes," In *Nag Hammadi Codices IX and X*, ed. B. A. Pearson. Nag Hammadi Studies 15, pp. 229–347. Leiden, 1980.

MARVIN W. MEYER

MARTYR, FEAST OF THE, one of the most popular feasts in Coptic and medieval Egypt, especially for its association with the Nile flood, apparently inherited from remote antiquity, when the Egyptians devoted a period of fifteen days to lavish festivities in honor of the river. The Copts celebrated it just before the occurrence of the annual flood of the Nile on 8 Bashans (16 May). The feast was one of the great national occasions on which both

Copts and Muslims held festivities on the bank of the Nile, drinking, dancing, and singing. The fourteenth-century Arab historian al-MAQRĪZĪ gave a lively account of the feast in his own day at Shūbrā al-Khaymah, a suburb of Cairo bordering the Nile. The Copts began the occasion with a procession, bringing with them a reliquary containing the finger bones of one of their martyrs for the blessing of the river. The legend runs that the flood would begin to rise at that moment.

Al-Maqrīzī told of the immense quantities of wine consumed during that day and mentioned the example of one merchant who sold wine to the enormous amount of 100,000 silver dirhems or the equivalent of 5,000 gold dinars. Debauchery resulted, and the governor of Cairo suspended its celebration from 1303, though it was reinstituted by order of the Bahrite Mamluk sultan al-Nāṣir Ḥasan in the year 1354. It is said that later, al-Mālik al-Ṣāliḥ Ṣālāḥ al-Dīn Ḥajjī (1381–1382) seized the reliquary, burned it, and cast the cinders in the Nile. From that time, the practice stopped, though the commemoration of the flood persisted in a different fashion.

An event known as *Jabr al-Khalīj* (the Opening of the Canal) became the substitute for the older custom by building a dike across the Nile below the Nilometer at Rodah Island. As soon as the flood reached its annual maximum height, the dike was broken in the presence of the chief judge, or *muftī*, who would testify that the flood had reached its legal limit for purposes of taxation, and an official celebration subsequently took place by sailing a gaily decorated ship on the river surrounded by a multitude of other, smaller boats all gaily painted and lighted. In Ottoman times, the celebration was accompanied by fireworks and the firing of canons.

BIBLIOGRAPHY

Bonneau, D. *La Crue du Nil, divinité égyptienne, à travers mille ans d'histoire.* Paris, 1964.

Cérès Wissa Wassef. *Pratiques rituelles et alimentaires des coptes,* pp. 216–17. Cairo, 1971.

Lane, E. W. *Manners and Customs of the Modern Egyptians,* 2 vols. London, 1842.

AZIZ S. ATIYA

MARTYRDOM, the voluntary submission to death for the sake of one's faith. The term "martyr" originally signified one who possessed firsthand knowledge of a matter to which one witnessed in public. In this sense, it was first used to describe the apostles who bore witness for Christ and the Resurrection (Acts 1:8, 22). Later the term came to mean one who professed a certain belief, a confessor. It has now come to stand for one who suffers torture and death in testimony to the truth of the gospel of Jesus Christ rather than recant and live.

The early Christians, in their boundless love for Christ, on the one hand, and their indifference to pain, on the other, made light of physical suffering and did not shrink from martyrdom. This unflinching attitude is best summarized by Tertullian: "Crucify us, torture us, condemn us, destroy us! Your wickedness is the proof of our innocence. . . . The more we are hewn down by you, the more numerous do we become. The blood of martyrs is the seed of Christians" (*Apology* 50.12).

With the rapid spread of Christianity in the various provinces of the Roman empire, Christian values were interpreted as a serious threat to the traditions of a pagan society and to the emperor's authority. Moreover, those who embraced the new religion and refused to sacrifice to the Roman gods or emperors were made scapegoats for any major disasters that occurred. By the time the age of persecution came to an end with the issuance of the Edict of Milan in 313 by Constantine the Great and Licinius, the Christians had suffered ten particularly savage outbursts of massacring under the emperors Nero (54–68), Domitian (81–96), Trajan (98–117), Marcus Aurelius (161–180), Septimius Severus (193–211), Maximinus (235–238), Decius (249–251), Valerian (253–259), Aurelian (270–275), and Diocletian (284–305).

The price that the church in Egypt paid during this dark episode in the history of humanity was very heavy indeed. It has been estimated, though without strict historical substantiation, that the toll reached a million souls, men and women of all walks of life.

It is in the SYNAXARION that the Coptic church zealously preserves the memory of its sons and daughters who gladly laid down their lives for their mother church (see MARTYRS, COPTIC). Their stories are commemorated through the daily readings that give details of their fortitude and their unshakable adherence to their beliefs. These readings occur at a significant point of the celebration of the Divine Liturgy, immediately before the Gospel lections, so that the congregation may benefit from the martyrs' witness, which is held up for imitation.

Eusebius, the fourth-century church historian, kept a record of these persecutions. The following eyewitness account gives an idea of not only the intense pain inflicted upon the victims but also the jubilant spirit in which they earned their crown of martyrdom:

> And we ourselves also beheld, when we were at these places, many all at once in a single day, some of whom suffered decapitation, others the punishment of fire; so that the murderous axe was dulled and, worn out, was broken in pieces, while the executioners themselves grew utterly weary and took it in turns to succeed one another. It was then that we observed a most marvellous eagerness and a truly divine power and zeal in those who had placed their faith in the Christ of God. Thus, as soon as sentence was given against the first, some from one quarter and others from another would leap up to the tribunal before the judge and confess themselves Christians; paying no heed when faced with terrors and the varied forms of tortures, but undismayedly and boldly speaking of the piety towards the God of the universe, and with joy and laughter and gladness receiving the final sentence of death; so that they sang and sent up hymns and thanksgivings to the God of the universe even to the very last breath.
>
> (Eusebius 8.9.4–5)

The memories of the martyrs are held in great veneration and esteem by the Apostolic Constitutions, which prescribe that "concerning the martyrs, we say to you that they are to be had in all honour with you, as we honour the blessed James the Bishop, and the holy Stephen our fellow-servant. For these are reckoned blessed by God, and are honoured by holy men."

They are honored by both the church triumphant and the church militant. Saint John the Divine described the distinguished position accorded to them: "I saw under the altar the souls of those who had been slain for the word of God and for the witness they had borne; . . . Then they were each given a white robe and told to rest a little longer (Rev. 6:9, 11). They are equally honored by being mentioned in every possible occasion in church services: in psalms, doxologies, and benedictions; in prayers of the Morning Offering of Incense; and in various places of the Divine Liturgy. In all these prayers they are mentioned before the saints and are only preceded by the THEOTOKOS, the heavenly host, and the prophets.

Of special significance, however, is the fact that the Copts used the era of persecution and martyrdom as the raison d'être for establishing a calendar of their own. Taking 284, the first year of the reign of Diocletian, as its starting point, the Coptic Anno Martyrii calendar commemorates two things: a glorious episode in the history of the Coptic church and the man who was its archenemy and persecutor.

BIBLIOGRAPHY

Atiya, A. S. *A History of Eastern Christianity*. Repr. Millwood, N.Y., 1980.

Delahaye, H. "Les Martyrs d'Egypte." *Analecta Bollandiana* 40 (1922):5–154.

Frend, W. H. C. *Martyrdom and Persecution in the Early Church*. Oxford, 1965.

Mason, A. J. *The Historic Martyrs of the Primitive Church*. London, 1905.

Scott-Moncrieff, P. D. *Paganism and Christianity in Egypt*. Cambridge, 1913.

ARCHBISHOP BASILIOS

MARTYROLOGY. The *Historia ecclesiastica* of Eusebius contains important information on the persecutions of Christians in Egypt (which here always includes Alexandria) and on Egyptian martyrs. Special importance attaches to those passages in which he quotes from the writings of eyewitnesses or is himself giving a report as an eyewitness. In Book VI.41–42, Eusebius gives an extensive extract from the letter of DIONYSIUS (247–264), bishop of Alexandria, to Bishop Fabius of Antioch, which among other things has a description of the martyrdom of Apollonia in the riots shortly before the Decian persecution. In VIII.10 he quotes from a letter of Phileas of Thmuis, who died a martyr in the persecution under DIOCLETIAN. According to VIII.9, Eusebius witnessed martyrdoms in Egypt. In his *Martyrs of Palestine* he also gives information on the sufferings of Egyptian Christians in Palestine and on deportations to Egypt. Also first-rate sources are papyri from the Age of Persecution, such as the *libelli* of the Decian persecution (Bludau, 1931) and the *Apologia* of Phileas of Thmuis, which contains the conversation between Culcianus, his judge, and the martyr, which was followed, according to the heading, by the latter's death on 4 February 306 (Halkin, 1963, pp. 5–27). A compilation and discussion of all the information about the persecutions, including that found in later authors and in monastic literature, is provided by H. Delehaye (1922, pp. 7–41).

When the Age of Persecution had ended, a flourishing cult of the martyrs grew up in Egypt, with features typical of that country. Despite the opposition of ATHANASIUS, the custom spread of exhibiting mummified martyrs on stands for veneration. Around the year 600, a network of martyrs' sanctuaries covered the country. As the criticism of Shenute of Athribia shows, the feast days of the martyrs were very popular festivals. The sanctuaries of the martyrs Cyrus and John in Menuthis, and especially that of ABŪ MĪNĀ, attracted numerous pilgrims, foreigners among them. (On the cult of martyrs, see Baumeister, 1972, pp. 51–86; also *Römische Quartalschrift* 69 [1974]:1–6 and pl. 1.) In the train of increasing veneration of the martyrs, there was created a whole literature—partly patterned on genuine acts of maryrs—of legends portraying the martyr as a true victor and friend of God to whom one could commit oneself in veneration. In all their variety, the Greek-language legends of the martyrs that came into being in Egypt correspond to the general form of the hagiography of the martyrs. On the other hand, the Coptic passions are more uniform in appearance.

There was a preference for a legend with numerous healings and resuscitations of the martyr before he victoriously passed over to the heavenly world. Variations are provided by frequent changes of location. The link with the martyr's sanctuary is emphasized. It appears that the oldest Greek legend of George, or related literature, was the prototype for this kind of Coptic legend—preference for which may be connected with ancient Egyptian ideas of integrity. In Egypt the trend of translating activities runs from Greek via the Coptic dialects to Arabic. Sahidic initially predominated, then Bohairic. Sometimes texts originating in Egypt were translated into Ethiopic. Greek items may have found their way into all the languages of the ancient church. Thus, for instance, a Sahidic and a Latin version may be witnesses to a Greek original. Consequently, regard must be given to all these languages in undertaking a reconstruction of Egyptian martyr hagiography.

Further literary evidence on the cult of martyrs is constituted by collections of miracle tales, sermons with stories of martyrdom, and calendars showing feast days. There is the Synaxarium Alexandrinum available in the editions of J. Forget (CSCO, *Scriptores Arabici* 3–5, 11–13) and R. M. J. Basset (PO 1–20). Account must also be taken of the Greek synaxaria, the Martyrologium Hieronymianum, and the Ethiopic Calendar of Saints (Delehaye, 1922, pp. 41–113). Archaeology, epigraphy, and travelers' reports provide further testimony.

Modern research on Egypt's traditions about the martyrs began from the moment people took an interest in Coptic manuscripts and began to collect them (eighteenth century). Editing of the texts has not been concluded thus far; much remains to be done. The question of historicity had special priority as a research interest. Delehaye tackled the problem, making use of the hagiographical method developed by the Bollandists. The danger lay in assessing the Coptic legends only in terms of the ideal of historical reporting. Alongside the problem of history there were, early on, interests relating to the history of the language and to grammar and lexicography, which led to involvement with the Coptic texts on the martyrs. E. C. Amélineau obtained important information, from topographical data pertaining to the cult of the martyrs, on the geography of Christian Egypt (1893). There is evidence of efforts to investigate Egyptian martyr hagiography in respect to problems in social history, the history of religion, and church history.

BIBLIOGRAPHY

Amélineau, E. C. *La Géographie de l'Egypte à l'époque copte.* Paris, 1893.

Baumeister, T. *Martyr invictus.* Münster, 1972.

Bludau, A. *Die ägyptischen Libelli und die Christenverfolgung des Kaisers Decius.* Freiburg im Breisgau, 1931.

Delehaye, H. "Les martyrs d'Egypte." *Analecta Bollandiana* 40 (1922):5–154, 299–364.

Godron, G. *Textes coptes relatifs à Saint Claude d'Antioche.* PO 35, 4. Turnhout, 1970.

O'Leary, De L. *The Saints of Egypt.* Amsterdam, 1974. Reprint of 1937 edition.

Orlandi, T., et al. *Testi e documenti per lo studio dell' antichità.* Serie copta. Milan (various dates in progress).

Reymond, E. A. E., and J. W. B. Barns. *Four Martyrdoms from the Pierpont Morgan Coptic Codices.* Oxford, 1973.

THEOFRIED BAUMEISTER

MARTYRS, COPTIC, the souls recognized in Egypt who suffered persecution and died for their faith. The majority of martyrs belong to the period of Roman persecutions from the time of Nero in the mid-first century to the time of Diocletian in the early fourth century. It is, of course, impossible to assemble the names of all the martyrs who were tortured and executed for refusing to offer incense and libations to the ancient gods and emperors, but a fair estimate of their number would be about 1 million.

A new category of martyrs appeared in the Islamic period after the Arab conquest in the seventh century. The "new martyrs" of this period, as they were called, are relatively few. In the main they were Christians who apostatized to Islam but later recanted and returned to their former faith. According to Islamic law, they automatically became subject to the death penalty and were decapitated, thereby earning the crown of martyrdom.

The survival of Christianity in Egypt must be ascribed mainly to the Coptic martyrs in the Roman period. During the Islamic period the church was generally able to resist the temptation to apostasy. Although the significance of the Coptic church and its martyrs was largely forgotten after the advent of Islam, they remain a vital chapter in the rise of Christianity in both the Eastern and Western worlds.

Perhaps the most serious attempt to gather all the names of known martyrs whose historicity has been attested from established documentary sources is that of De Lacy O'Leary, who compiled *The Saints of Egypt in the Coptic Calendar* in 1937. He made a register of all the saints enumerated in the Copto-Arabic SYNAXARION as well as saints derived from other papyrological fragments but not in the Synaxarion. The book registers two categories of saints: martyrs, who died a violent death, and holy men and women, usually monks or anchorites, who ended their lives peacefully. This second category is treated under SAINTS, COPTIC.

The following listing of martyrs is based chiefly on O'Leary's register. The legendary statements in O'Leary's book derived from original sources have been curtailed; only historic material has been given along with the official commemoration date (feast day) of each saint, when available. Many, but not all, appear in the Copto-Arabic Synaxarion. Not all spellings are those used by O'Leary, but alternates, including his, are given. When a saint has a separate biography in the encyclopedia, it is printed in small caps.

Abadion (feast day: 1 Amshīr), bishop of Antinoopolis during the reign of Diocletian. After he was martyred by Arianus, governor of Upper Egypt, a general massacre of Christians in Antinoopolis followed; 5,800 were said to have perished.

Abadir and Erai, see *Ter and Erai*, below.

Abadys, see *Dios*, below.

ABĀMŪN OF TARNŪṬ (feast day: 27 Abīb), a native of Tarnūṭ in Upper Egypt.

ABĀMŪN OF ṬŪKH, or Ammonius (feast day: 13 Abīb), a native of Ṭūkh in the diocese of Banā.

Abīb (or Apip) and Apollo, (feast day: 25 Bābah), close colleagues who entered a monastery. Abīb became a deacon and was martyred. Apollo, distressed, moved deeper into the desert, near Mount Ablūj, followed by a group of ascetics. He too was martyred.

Aesi (feast day: 29 Ba'ūnah), one of the seven ascetics from the village of Tūnah in Upper Egypt executed under Diocletian.

AGATHON (OR AGATHŪN) AND HIS BROTHERS, (feast day: 7 Tūt), fourth-century martyrs with their mother, from Sunbāṭ.

Alexander (feast day: 12 Baramūdah), a student at the Catechetical School in Alexandria under Pantaenus and Saint Clement of Alexandria. Imprisoned under Severus, he died in 251. He is called bishop of Jerusalem in the Synaxarion.

Alexander and Alexander the Egyptian (feast day: 1 Baramhāt), martyred under Decius. They are cited by the historian Eusebius of Caesarea. Alexander is bishop of Cappadocia in the Synaxarion.

Allādyūs (feast day: 3 Ba'ūnah), a soldier in the army of Emperor Constantine the Great, who, presumably, explained the significance of the cross that appeared in the sky before a battle and led to the emperor's conversion. JULIAN THE APOSTATE tried in vain to win him to the pagan gods and then ordered him thrown into a fiery furnace. His emergence unscathed led to the conversion of many spectators. Finally Julian ordered him decapitated (p. 68). He is called a bishop in the Synaxarion.

Ammonius, or Ammon (feast day: 14 Kiyahk), bishop of Latopolis (Isnā), consecrated by Saint Peter I, Patriarch of Alexandria in the early fourth century. Ammonius built a monastery on a hill outside the city, where he spent Tuesday to Friday every week. Arianus, who was touring the country in search of Christians, seized Ammonius, moved him to Antinoopolis, and had him tortured and executed.

Ammonius of Ṭūkh, see Abāmūn of Ṭūkh, above.

Amsah of Qifṭ (feast day: 15 Kiyahk), a native of Qifṭ who was told by an angel in a vision to take a waiting ship on the Nile to Tkow to announce his faith and suffer the consequences. After telling his sister, Theodora, he followed the angel's advice and was tortured by the governor, Arianus, and put to death. His body was thrown into the Nile, but a crocodile pushed it to shore and Theodora buried it with honor.

Ananius and Khūzi (feast day: 16 Kiyahk), natives of Akhmīn who were martyred.

ANASTASIA, *Hilaria, and Aripsima* (feast day: 26 Kiyahk), three women martyrs.

ANATOLIUS (feast day: 9 Ṭūbah), fourth-century martyr in the Basilides Cycle.

Antoninus, or Antonius, or Andūrā (feast day: 25 Abīb), a native of good parentage from Banā, who declared his faith in Antinoopolis. The governor ordered his execution by archers, but Antoninus miraculously remained unscathed. Afterwards he and a companion, Epimachus, went to Alexandria, where they were tortured. Antoninus went on to Pelusium, where he was tortured again and beheaded.

ANUB, or Apā Nob (feast day: 24 Abīb), a martyr under Diocletian.

APAIULE AND TOLEMAEUS (feast day: 21 Ṭūbah), a monk and a soldier martyred under Diocletian.

APOLI (feast day: 1 Misrā), a fourth-century martyr of the Basilides Cycle who was born in Antioch and killed in Egypt.

Apollo (feast day: 10 Amshīr), a martyr under Diocletian.

APOLLONIUS AND PHILEMON (feast day: 7 Baramhāt), musicians who became martyrs under Diocletian.

Aptia and John (feast day: 16 Abīb), martyrs of Sabarou. John is mentioned in the Synaxarion as John of the Golden Gospel.

Archaelaus (feast day: 11 Hātūr), martyr (p. 84).

Archippus, Philemon, and Abfiyyah (feast day: 25 Amshīr).

ARI, or Ūrī (feast day: 9 Misrah), a priest of Shatanūf who was martyred under Diocletian.

ARIANUS (feast day: 8 Baramhāt), a Roman governor of Antinoopolis under Diocletian who persecuted Christians and later became a Christian and was himself martyred.

Arius of Shetnusi, martyr.

Armenius (*or Armanus*) *and His Mother*, (feast day: 8 Ba'ūnah), martyrs.

Arsenius (feast day: 18 Baramūdah), slave of Saint Susinius, an officer in Diocletian's household (p. 87).

Asbah (feast day: 15 Kiyahk), native of Qifṭ (p. 88).

ASCLA (feast day: 20 Ṭūbah), martyr of the Arianus Cycle under Diocletian.

Asra, see *Pihour, Pisouri, and Asra*, below.

Asqalun (feast day: 20 Baramhāt).

Astrolate, a magician whom, according to legend, God released from hell when Astrolate promised to become a martyr.

Athanasia, see *Cyrus, John*, below.

Athanasius and Irene (feast day: 3 Hātūr), brother and sister martyred under Emperor Maximian.

Athanasius, Jerasimus, and Theodotus (feast day: 29 Misrā), a bishop and his two assistants seized, tortured, and killed by Emperor Valerian because Athanasius had baptized the daughter of Antonius, one of Valerian's officers.

Athom, see *Piroou and Athom*, below.

Atrasis and Junia, or Adrūsīs and Yu'annā (feast day: 18 Hātūr), Roman martyrs. Atrasis, daughter of Emperor Hadrian, was converted to Christianity by Junia, daughter of the Christian Filoysofron. When Hadrian returned from a campaign and commanded his daughter to sacrifice to Apollo, she refused. Both women declared their faith and were condemned to death in a trench filled with flames. They marched in voluntarily and were consumed.

Babylas (feast day: 28 Ṭūbah), a bishop who was tried by Emperor Numerianus and beheaded.

Bacchus, see *Sergius and Bacchus*, below.

Badasius (feast day: 23 Ṭūbah), a native of Pbow, who with his brother Yūsāb entered the Monastery of Saint Pachomius and later moved to Qifṭ, where he was warned of his imminent martyrdom by the archangel Raphael.

Bajūj or Kalūj (feast day: 20 Ṭūbah).

Bahnā (feast day: 20 Ṭūbah).

Bahnām and Sarah (feast day: 14 Kiyahk), brother and sister who were martyred.

Bajush, or Pejosh (feast day: 26 Ṭūbah), a rich farmer from Bilad who was charitable and professed his Christianity before the governor Arius. Bajush was sent to Tanā and beheaded in a suburb called Salamūn, where a church was built in his honor.

Balānā (feast day: 8 Abīb), a priest from Barā in Sakhā district who sold his goods and distributed the proceeds to the poor. He professed his faith before the governor Arianus in Antinoopolis and was tortured and beheaded.

Bāninā and Nāou (feast day: 7 Kiyahk), martyrs who were tried before Emperor Maximian near Idfū and beheaded. A church was later built for their remains.

Barbara and Juliana (feast day: 8 Kiyahk). Barbara, daughter of the pagan noble Dioscurus, was converted to Christianity and consequently delivered to the authorities by her father. When they started to torture her, she was joined by Juliana, a woman spectator. Both were beheaded. Later Barbara's remains were transferred to a church in Old Cairo that bears her name.

Barsanuphius, or Ouarshufah, or Warshanūfyus (feast day: 29 Abīb), martyr under Diocletian with Eudemon, his brother Epistemun, and their mother, Sophia.

BARSANUPHIUS (feast day: 13 Kiyahk), a "new martyr" who was a monk in the Church of Abū Mīnā, Cairo.

Basidi, Kutulus, Armada, Musa, Aesi, Barkalas, and another Kutulus (feast day: 29 Ba'ūnah), seven ascetics who declared their faith to the governor and were tortured, burned, and imprisoned but remained unscathed. A group of 130 was converted as a result. Eventually Kutulus the priest was burned and the rest were beheaded (pp. 100–101).

Basil, or Basilios (feast day: 11 Baramhāt), a bishop who was consecrated by Saint Amun, patriarch of Jerusalem. Basil did missionary work in Sharsūnah and revived the governor's dead son but was killed by the Jewish population.

Basil, Theodosius (or Theodore), and Timothy (feast day: 20 Amshīr), martyrs.

Basilidas, or Wāsīlīdas, or Basilides the General (feast day: 11 Tūt), head of a prominent family in Antioch who was sent by order of Diocletian with his family to Egypt. They were separated before being tried, tortured, and put to death. Basilidas is the central figure of the Basilidas Cycle.

Batra, or Mātrā (feast day: 10 Misrah), martyr under Decius, who miraculously survived being thrown into the fire but later had his hands and feet amputated and his head cut off.

Behnam (or Bahnām) and Sarah, (feast day: 14 Kiyahk), children of a pagan king, who were converted by Matthew, a Christian who healed Sarah of leprosy. On their way to join Christian refugees for prayers, they were discovered by the army of Emperor Julian and killed. Matthew cured their father who went insane at the news, and converted him and the queen. The king built a church over the remains of his children and a monastery for Matthew.

Benjamin and Eudoxia (feast day: 28 Misrah), brother and sister who declared their faith to the governor of Shetnufe under Diocletian. They were thrown into a river with stones around their necks, but an angel untied the stones, and they swam ashore at Botra, where they were seized again and beheaded.

BESAMON, son of Basilides the General, martyred under Diocletian.

Bīmīn, or PAMIN (feast day: 9 Kiyahk), a "martyr without bloodshed," who survived Diocletian and lived out his life in a monastery near al-Ashmūnayn.

Bishoi, Hor, and Diodora, or Anbā Bishāy, Apa Hor, and Theodora (feast day: 29 Ba'ūnah), two brothers and their mother who were martyred.

Bishoi Anūb of Naesi or Bishāy Anūb (feast day: 19 Ba'ūnah), a native of Panayus in the diocese of Damietta who was an officer under Cyprian, governor of Atripe. Wishing for martyrdom he declared his faith, was tortured, and was taken to Heliopolis, where he was executed. His story was told by Julian of Aqfahs.

Biuka and Tayaban, or Biyūkhah and Bināyin (feast day: 1 Abīb), two priests of Tūnah who sought the sacrament reserved for the sick. When they found a serpent had devoured it, they killed and ate the serpent to save the holy bread and died as martyrs.

BŪLUS AL-ḤABĪS, or Paul the Solitary, "new martyr" of the thirteenth century.

Callinicus (feast day: 2 Ṭūbah), bishop of Syene (Awsīm) under Diocletian. He professed his faith before the governor Arianus in Antinoopolis, was tortured, and was sent by ship to Ṭūkh. He died en route and his body was cast ashore, where it was buried by the faithful.

CAMOUL, or Chamoul (feast day: 16 Bashans), a native of Kellia who was martyred under Diocletian.

Chanazhum, Sophronius, and Dalasina (feast day: 20 Hātūr), martyrs executed by the governor Arianus at Luxor.

Children, Three (feast day: 14 Hātūr), martyrs who in the book of Daniel were cast into the furnace in Babylon. (See BIBLICAL SUBJECTS IN COPTIC ART: Three Hebrew Children.)

Christopher, or Christophorus (feast day: 2 Baramūdah), martyr under Emperor Decius.

Claudius Stratelates (feast day: 11 Ba'ūnah), son of Ptolemy, brother of Emperor Numerianus who was a general in the Roman army. After fighting in Armenia, he was exiled to Alexandria by Diocletian with the usual letter asking the governor Arianus to win Claudius to the Roman religion. Claudius resisted so Arianus killed him with a javelin.

Colluthus (feast day: 25 Bashans), son of a prominent family of Antinoopolis, he practiced medicine without a fee, then gave up his wealth for a life of asceticism. He was questioned, tortured, and beheaded by a successor of the governor Arianus.

COPRES, late-fourth-century monk who was martyred under the emperor Julian the Apostate.

COSMAS AND DAMIAN (feast day: 22 Hātūr), martyrs with their brothers Anthimus, Leontius, and Eupropious, and their mother, Theodota.

Cyriacus, Anna, and Admon.

CYRIACUS AND JULITTA (feast day: 15 Abīb), a son and his mother who were martyred under Diocletian.

Cyrus, John, and Filya, or Apa Kīr, John, and Philip (feast day: 14 Ba'ūnah), brothers, natives of Damanhūr, who were tortured and beheaded and buried in the Church of Saint Mark, Alexandria.

Cyrus (or Apa Kīr), John, Theodora, Theodosia, Theopista, and Athanasia, (feast day: 6 Amshīr), natives of Alexandria who were killed and thrown to wild beasts. Athanasia was the mother of the three virgins.

Dabamun (feast day: 10 Ba'ūnah), father of a beautiful virgin named Youna, who was sought by the governor Eulogius, who became Christian. All three were taken to Sais and executed by Eulogius' pagan successor.

Daidasa (feast day: 29 Ba'ūnah).

Damnas (feast day: 5 Hātūr).

DANDARAH, Martyrs of (feast day: 15 Bashans), four hundred natives of Dandarah martyred under Diocletian.

Dasyah (feast day: 2 Tūt), an officer of Tanda beheaded by the governor Arianus.

David (feast day: 4 Misrā), martyred with his brother under Diocletian at Sinjār. His body was preserved at the Monastery of Saint Victor in Asyūṭ.

Decius (feast day: 4 Baramūdah), martyr with Victor, Irene, and others.

DIMYĀNAH AND HER FORTY VIRGINS (feast day: 13 Ṭūbah), daughter of the governor of Lower Egypt and her companions.

Diomede, or Dayumīdis (feast day: 8 Tūt), a native of Tarshebi in Dantua diocese who confessed his faith at Atripe and was tortured and killed by Lucianus in Alexandria.

DIOS, or Abadyus (feast day: 25 Ṭūbah), a third-century soldier who was martyred.

Dioscorus and Aesculapius (feast day: 1 Ṭūbah), ascetics on the Mount of Akhmīm who were told by the archangel Michael in a vision to confess their faith to the governor Arianus. According to legend, forty soldiers witnessed the vision and were converted. All were martyred.

Eirene, or Irene (feast day: 21 Misrah), daughter of Governor Lucinius, or King Licinius, who was baptized by a disciple of Saint Paul, tortured by her father, but remained unscathed. She was arrested by Emperor Numerianus and killed by Diocletian but miraculously resuscitated, with the result that her father and 113,000 subjects converted. She died in Ephesus.

Elias the Eunuch (feast day: 28 Ṭūbah), a gardener at Pemdje for the governor Culcianus, whose daughter fell in love with him and tempted him. He therefore castrated himself and sent the organ to her, saying it was what she wanted. The angry woman reported him as a Christian, and he was martyred.

EPIMA, or Bima, or Epiuse, or Anbā Bīmānun (feast day: 8 Abīb), a native of Panokleus in the nome of Pemdje, or al-Bahnasa, who was tortured in Alexandria and crucified up side down in Upper Egypt. Saved by a miracle, he was finally beheaded.

EPIMACHUS OF PELUSIUM (feast day: 14 Bashans), a weaver whose miracles at his death resulted in the conversion of 1,750.

Epimachus and Gordian (*or Azāryanūs*) (feast day: 4 Hātūr), martyrs under Diocletian.

Eudamon (feast day: 18 Misrā), the first martyr from Armant, according to legend informed by an angel of the coming of the Holy Family to al-Ashmūnayn on its flight to Egypt. He hastened there to worship Christ instead of pagan gods and was therefore killed by the people.

Eugenius, see *Eusignius,* below.

Eugenius, Agathodorus, and Elpidius (feast day: 14 Baramhāt), bishops who were murdered by the pagans to whom they preached.

Eulogius and Arsenius (feast day: 16 Kiyahk), Syrian-born ascetics in Dayr al-Ḥadīd at Akhmīm who survived torture but were eventually killed.

Eunapius and Andrew (feast day: 12 Tūt), monks from Kydda who served in Syria. Disciples of Saint Macarius the Egyptian, they were martyred by Emperor Julian the Apostate.

Euphemia (feast day: 17 Abīb), martyr under Diocletian.

EUSEBIUS (feast day: 23 Amshīr), an eminent member of the Basilides family of Antioch under Diocletian.

EUSIGNIUS, or Eusegnius, or Eugenius, or Usaghnīyūs (feast day: 5 Ṭūbah), a soldier or general in the army of Constantine I who was martyred under Julian the Apostate.

EUSTATHIUS AND THEOPISTA (feast day: 27 Tūt), a Roman general and his wife and two sons who were martyred under Trajan or Hadrian.

EXUPERANTIUS (feast day: 1 Tūt), a member of the THEBAN LEGION, martyred in the third century near present-day Zurich.

FEBRONIA, or Afrūnyah (feast day: 1 Abīb), a fourth-century nun who was martyred.

FELIX (feast day: 1 Tūt), a member of the Theban Legion martyred in the third century near present-day Zurich.

Filatis, or Pilate (feast day: 10 Abīb), martyr of African origin.

Fugas, or Phocas (feast day: 10 Ṭūbah), bishop of Bontos who was martyred under Hadrian.

GEORGE (feast day: 23 Baramūdah).

George, see *Jirgis al-Muzāḥim*, below.

George of Alexandria, or Georgius (feast day: 7 Hātūr), son of a rich merchant of Alexandria, begotten through the intercession of Saint George the Great. On his parents' death he was entrusted to the governor Armenius, whose daughter he converted. The angered Armenius seized both and sent George to the governor Arianus at Antinoopolis, where both were ultimately beheaded. Their remains were buried at Manūf (possibly Memphis).

George the Ascetic (feast day: 17 Barahmāt), martyr.

Ginusi, martyr.

GOBIDLAHA, DADO, AND CAXO, a fourth-century Roman governor (Dado) and a Persian prince and princess who were martyred at Persia.

GREGORY THE ILLUMINATOR (*or the Armenian*) (feast days: 15 Kiyahk and 19 Tūt), a fourth-century patriarch of Armenia who was a "martyr without bloodshed."

HAMAI OF KAHYOR (feast day: 11 Amshīr), a fifth-century monk who was martyred in Alexandria.

Harwāj (feast day: 16 Kiyahk), a martyr who was killed with a companion, Mui.

Helias (feast day: 20 Kiyahk), a bishop martyred under Arianus at Antinoopolis.

Heracleas and Philemon (feast day: 18 Kiyahk), martyrs.

HERACLIDES, martyr.

Herai, see *Ter and Erai*, below.

Hilaria (feast day: 25 Abīb), a native of Demeliana near Darirab, she confessed her faith at Tūnah and was sent to Sūsnah, where she was killed.

Hor, martyr.

Hor of Saryāqūs, or Apa Hor of Siryāqūs (feast day: 12 Abīb), martyr tortured at Pelusium and beheaded at Antinoopolis.

Hor, Bishoi, and Daidara, or Apa Hor, Anbā Bishāy, and Theodora (feast day: 29 Ba'ūnah), a soldier, his brother, and their mother, natives of Antioch who were martyred in Alexandria.

IGNATIUS OF ANTIOCH (feast day: 20 December in the East, 17 October in the West), first-century bishop of Antioch who was martyred in Rome.

Ioule and Pteleme (*or Ptolemy*) (feast day: 21 Ṭūbah), martyrs.

Isaac of Shammā (feast day: 25 Abīb), a pious gardener who was tortured and beheaded after declaring his faith.

ISAAC OF TIPHRE (*or of Difrah*) (feast day: 6 Bashans), martyr who miraculously restored sight to the blind and was executed at Pemdje.

ISIDORUS, or Isidore of Antioch (feast day: 19 Bashans), son of the governor Pantaleon of Antioch, who was killed and revived five times before his final martyrdom under Diocletian.

Isidorus (*or Isidore*) *of Takināsh*, (feast day: 18 Baramhāt), a weaver of Pelusium who was seized by Diocletian's soldiers, tortured, and killed.

Isidorus and Bandilaus (feast day: 19 Bashans), men in the service of Diocletian who resigned when he turned against Christians. They became monks at Dayr Anbā Ṣamū'īl. They were arrested, tortured, and executed.

James of Amadjudj, or Jacob the Soldier (feast day: 17 Misrā), martyr under Diocletian who professed his faith to the governor of Antinoopolis and was tortured and killed with Abraham and John of Jamnuti.

JAMES INTERCISUS, or Jacob the Sawn, or al-Muqaṭṭaʿ (feast day: 27 Hātūr), a Persian martyr of the third century.

James (or Jacob) and John (feast day: 4 Hātūr), two bishops who suffered martyrdom under the Persian king Shapur II in the early fourth century.

Jamoul (feast day: 16 Bashans), a native of the Delta, who was martyred.

JIRJS AL-MUZĀḤIM, or George (feast day: 19 Ba'ūnah), a "new martyr" of the ninth century.

John of Ashmūn Ṭanāḥ, or Bīkhībis, or Bikabes (feast day: 10 Misrā), a soldier seized with two bishops, Anbā Kalūj and Anbā Filubbus, and beheaded with ninety-five others at Barāmūn.

John of Heraclia, a Christian general who was martyred.

John of Phanidjoit, a "new martyr," who died in 1209.

John of Psenhowt, a martyr.

John of Sanhūt (or al-Sanhūti) (feast day: 8 Bashans), a shepherd who was beheaded at Atripe.

John the Soldier (feast day: 5 Misrah), a general under Julian the Apostate who was ordered to pursue Christians but secretly helped them. He was found and killed.

JOORE (feast day: 10 Kiyahk), a shepherd who was martyred in the fourth century.

Joshua (or Yashuʿ) and Joseph, (feast day: 13 Baramūdah), ascetics associated with Mount Khorasan.

Julian and His Mother (feast day: 23 Bashans), martyrs in Alexandria.

Juliana (feast day: 26 Kiyahk), martyrs.

Julietta, or Julita (feast day: 6 Misrā), martyr.

Julius of Aqfahs (feast day: 22 Tūt), an army officer who helped martyrs, collected their remains, and recorded their biographies. He was arrested after declaring his faith, tortured, twice killed and miraculously restored, and killed a third time. During the inquest the governor of Samannūd and Atripe and 1,500 people were converted and martyred.

JUSTUS (feast day: 10 Amshīr), the Christian son of Emperor Numerianus, who fought in the Roman army in Persia and was shocked when Diocletian began to persecute Christians. Justus was sent to Alexandria, tried at Antinoopolis, and executed.

Kaou, or Kā'ū (feast day: 28 Ṭūbah), a native of Bimay (Bamwayh) in the Fayyūm who refused to worship pagan gods under Diocletian, was tried by the governor of Antinoopolis, and was killed.

KRAJON AND AMUN (feast day: 25 Abīb), a Roman official at al-Banāwān who was dismissed for bad conduct and became a brigand leader, and his friend. They and the rest of the brigand band overheard the prayers of an ascetic and were converted.

LACARON (feast day: 14 Bābah), native of Tajeli, whose story is considered suspect by some authorities.

LEONTIUS OF TRIPOLI (feast day: 22 Abīb), fourth-century martyr in Syria.

Lucilianus and Four Companions (feast day: 9 Ba'ūnah), a pagan priest who was converted and with his associates arrested under Emperor Aurelianus, tortured, and killed.

MACARIUS (feast day: 22 Abīb), son of Basilides, a minister of Diocletian, who was tortured in Alexandria, executed at Shatānūf, and buried at al-Ashmūnayn.

MACARIUS OF TKOW (feast day: 27 Bābah), a bishop of Tkow and companion of Patriarch Dioscuros I after the Council of Chalcedon in 451. He refused an imperial command to subscribe to the council and was killed.

MACROBIUS, or Makrāwī (feast day: 2 Baramhāt), a native of Ashmūn Jurays, bishop of Nikiou, persecuted and killed under Diocletian.

Maharati (feast day: 14 Ṭūbah), a twelve-year-old girl martyred at Antinoopolis.

Mama (feast day: 6 Tūt), a child from Paphlagonia martyred under Emperor Aurelianus.

MARK I (feast day: 30 Baramūdah and 30 Bābah), one of the four evangelists and the first patriarch of Alexandria.

Matra (feast day: 8 Bābah), martyr under Decius.

Maṭrūnah (feast day: 10 Tūt), martyr.

Maximus, Numitius, Victor, and Philip (feast day: 1 Hātūr), four brothers from Africa who were martyred.

MENAS (feast day: 14 Kiyahk), a foreigner who was martyred in Alexandria. The Greeks commemorate Saint Menas, bishop of Athens, the same day.

Menas the Deacon (feast day: 15 Bashans), martyr.

MENAS OF AL-ASHMŪNAYN, or Menas the Ascetic (feast day: 17 Amshīr), a "new martyr" from Akhmīm, who was killed after the Arab conquest (p. 199).

MENAS THE MIRACLE MAKER, or Abū Mīnā (feast day: 15 Hātūr).

Menas and Hasina (feast day: 7 Bābah), martyrs.

Mercurius (feast day: 18 Tūt), a martyr under Julian the Apostate.

MERCURIUS OF CAESAREA, or Abū Sayfayn, or Marqūrah (feast day: 25 Hātūr), a popular soldier-saint who was martyred under Decius.

Mercurius and Ephraem (feast day: 30 Abīb), natives of Akmīm and monks of the Thebiad, who opposed the Arians and were killed by them.

Michael of Damietta, a "new martyr" in the period 1167–1200. He was a monk of Scetis who apostatized to Islam and then returned to Christianity, for which he was killed.

Milius (feast day: 28 Baramūdah), an ascetic who converted two princes before he was killed under Diocletian.

Moses and Sarah (feast day: 26 Misrā), a brother and sister under Septimius Severus who adopted the monastic life and voluntarily offered themselves for martyrdom.

MOSES THE BLACK (feast day: 24 Ba'ūnah), fourth-to-fifth-century Ethiopian slave who turned brigand, then ascetic. He and six companions were killed in a Berber raid in 407.

MUI, fourth-century martyr in Alexandria.

NABRAHA (feast day: 8 Abīb), a confessor who was tortured under Diocletian but was then exiled and became an ascetic.

Naharua, or Naharūh (feast day: 7 Hātūr), a native of the Fayyūm who went to Alexandria to be martyred under Diocletian.

Nicetas, or Nakīṭā (feast day: 18 Tūt), a martyr.

Nicholas (feast day: 10 Kiyahk), bishop of Myra who was one of the "martyrs without bloodshed" because he was saved from execution by Diocletian's death. He attended the First Council of Nicea in 325.

Nob, Apa, see *Anub*, above.

OLYMPIUS (feast day: 21 Amshīr), a physician of Nicomedia who was martyred under Diocletian.

PAESE AND TECLA (*or Thecla*) (feast day: 8 Kiyahk), brother and sister who were martyred under Diocletian.

Pamin, see *Bimin*, above.

PAMPHILUS (feast day: 16 February in the East, 1 June in the West), third-century philosopher, teacher, and supporter of Origen who was martyred in Palestine.

Pamun and Sarmata (feast day: 27 Abīb).

PANESNEU, a deacon from Pakierkie, martyred under Culcianus.

PANTALEON (feast day: 15 Bābah), a fourth-century physician of Nicomedia who was martyred under Emperor Maximinus.

Paphnutius (feast day: 20 Baramūdah), hermit of Dandarah who was tried before the governor Arianus with Cyril and Cyril's wife, twelve sons, and a daughter, and killed.

Paphnutius (feast day: 11 September in the East), a "martyr without bloodshed," a bishop of the Upper Thebaid who was tortured under Diocletian but liberated after the accession of Constantine. He attended the First Council of Nicea in 325.

Paphnutius of Pbow, a deacon of Pbow.

Papylas (feast day: 16 Bābah).

Patape, or Bidaba (feast day: 19 Abīb), an anchorite who became bishop of Coptos and was martyred under Diocletian.

PAUL OF ṬAMMAH (feast day: 7 Bābah).

Paul the Syrian (feast day: 9 Amshīr), martyr who lived in al-Ashmūnayn, professed his faith in Alexandria, and was tortured and killed in Antinoopolis.

Paul and Salfana (feast day: 24 Kiyahk), martyrs under Diocletian.

Paul, Longinus, and Zeno (feast day: 24 Bābah), martyrs.

PETER I (feast day: 29 Hātūr), early fourth-century patriarch of Alexandria who was beheaded under Diocletian.

PHILEMON, see *Apollonius and Philemon*, above.

PHILOTHEUS OF ANTIOCH (feast day: 16 Ṭūbah), a boy who is martyred under Diocletian.

Phoibammon, or Phoebammon (feast day: 27 Ṭūbah), a native of Awsīm under Emperor Maximian who was called at Ṭāmā, north of Antaepolis (Qaw).

PHOIBAMMON OF PREHT, or Pheobammon, or Bifām, or Epiphanius (feast day: 1 Ba'ūnah), a soldier martyred under Diocletian.

Pihebs, or Bikhībis, or Bikabes (feast day: 10 Misrā), an ascetic of Ashmūn Ṭanāḥ.

Pihur, Pisura, and Asra (feast day: 18 Ṭūbah), natives of Shabas executed at Latopolis.

Piroou and Athom, or Abīruh or Piru and Atom (feast day: 8 Abīb), two brothers, peasants from Tasempoti, under Diocletian, who declared their faith and were beheaded by Armenius, governor of Alexandria.

PISURA (feast day: 9 Tūt), bishop of Maṣīl who was martyred under Diocletian.

Poemen and Eudoxia, see *Benjamin and Eudoxia,* above.

POLYCARP (feast day: 29 Amshīr), second-century bishop of Smyrna who was martyred.

Porphyry, or Porphyrius (feast day: 3 Baramhāt), martyr possibly under Diocletian.

Procopius (feast day: 14 Abīb), pagan governor of Alexandria under Diocletian who was later converted, arrested, and beheaded.

Psote, or Anbā Bisādah the Presbyter, or Ibsadah (feast day: 24 Ṭūbah), martyr who declared his faith in al-Qays and was tortured and beheaded.

PSOTE OF PSOI, or Psate, or Bisādah (feast day: 27 Kiyahk), bishop of Psoi martyred under Diocletian.

Ptolemy, or Pteleme (feast day: 11 Kiyahk), native of Dandarah who confessed his faith and was tortured and killed at Tūkh al-Khayl, near Ṭahā.

Qūnā, or Conon (feast day: 25 Amshīr), a native of Rome who was martyred.

Quzmān (or Cosmos) of Ṭaḥā and His Companions, (feast day: 1 Ba'ūnah).

REGULA (feast day: 1 Tūt), third-century missionary who was a member of the Theban Legion and was martyred in Switzerland.

Repsima (feast day: 29 Tūt), virgin who fled from Rome to Armenia with seventy-eight companions, including her sisters. They were all slain under Diocletian.

Sakhirum of Qallīn, or Abiskhīrūn (feast day: 8 Ba'ūnah), a soldier from Asyūṭ, who with five others confessed his faith and was beheaded.

Ṣalīb (feast day: 3 Kiyahk), a "new martyr."

Sarah and Her Children (or Her Two Sons) (feast day: 25 Baramūdah), martyrs in Alexandria under Diocletian.

SARAPAMON OF SCETIS (feast day: 28 Hātūr), a Jew from Jerusalem who was baptized in Alexandria by Patriarch Theonas, became a monk and bishop of Nikiou, and was beheaded by the governor Arainus under Diocletian.

SARAPION (feast day: 27 Ṭūbah), a native of Bīnūsah in Lower Egypt, who was martyred.

Sebaste, Forty Martyrs of (feast day: 13 Baramhāt), Christians slain by Licinius, a Roman officer, in 320.

Sergius of Atrīb (feast day: 13 Amshīr), martyr, who with his parents was slain by the governor Cyprian. His remains were collected by Julius of Aqfahs.

Sergius and Bacchus, or . . . Wākhus (feast day: 4 Bābah), martyrs slain under Emperor Maximian.

Shamul (feast day: 16 Baramūdah).

Shenube, martyr.

SHENUFE (feast day: 7 Bābah), a martyr under Diocletian.

Shenute, or Sinuti (feast day: 14 Baramhāt), a native of Bahnasā who was slain under Emperor Maximian.

Shenute, or Anbā Shinūdah (feast day: 13 Abīb), a "new martyr" of the seventh century.

Sidhom Bishāy (feast day: 17 Baramhāt), a "new martyr" of the early nineteenth century. A Christian native of Damietta, he was working in a rice factory when a Muslim accused him of blasphemy against Islam and had him taken to court. The judge ordered him flogged and the angry populace tortured him and led him in a procession through the city riding a buffalo. He died five days later.

Simeon (feast day: 14 Kiyahk), a "new martyr" under the Arabs.

Simeon the Armenian (feast day: 19 Baramūdah), an old man of 127 who was slain with 150 other Christians by Shapur, king of Persia.

Sina (feast day: 24 Baramūdah), a high-ranking army officer who was executed with Saint Isidorus. Their remains were preserved at Jamnuti (Samannūd).

Sophia (feast day: 10 Ba'ūnah), mother of Eudamon and Epistamon, with whom she was martyred.

SOPHIA (feast day: 5 Tūt), a holy woman of Egypt or Constantinople, a martyr or an ascetic, whose remains were buried in Santa Sophia, Constantinople.

STEPHEN (feast day: 1 Ṭūbah), archdeacon who was the first martyr under Diocletian.

TER AND ERAI, or Abadīr or Apater and Īrā'ī or Herai (feast day: 28 Tūt), brother and sister from Antioch martyred in Egypt under Diocletian.

Thecla (feast day: 23 Tūt). See CHRISTIAN SUBJECTS IN COPTIC ART: Thecla.

Thecla and Mudji (or Mūjī) (feast day: 25 Abīb),

women from Qurāqas in the Delta who were martyred.

Theoclia (feast day: 11 Bashans), a woman connected with the Basilides family of Antioch who came with them to Alexandria and was tortured and killed in Sais. She converted fellow prisoners, who also were martyred.

Theodorus, or Theodore (feast day: 28 Amshīr), native of Peshotep who was tortured and beheaded (p. 261).

Theodorus (feast day: 10 Abīb), bishop of Pentapolis who was slain under Diocletian.

Theodorus Anatolius, a martyr in the Basilides Cycle.

THEODORUS STRATELATES, or Theodorus the General, or Theodorus of Shotep (feast day: 20 Abīb), a second-century general who battled a dragon and was martyred.

Theodorus and Timothy (feast day: 21 Baramhāt).

Theodosia (feast day: 6 Abīb), martyr slain with twelve other women.

Theodotus (feast day: 29 Misrah), disciple of Saint Athanasius, who was martyred with him and Saint Jerasimus.

Theone, martyr.

Thomas (feast day: 4 Hātūr), a "new martyr," a bishop of Damascus who was beheaded on the charge of reviling Islam.

Thomas (feast day: 24 Misrā), bishop of Mar'ash, Syria, and a "martyr without bloodshed" who was tortured under Diocletian but freed under Constantine.

TIL (died: 7 Amshīr), a soldier who was martyred under Diocletian.

Timolaus, martyr.

Timothy, or Timotheus (feast day: 24 Amshīr), a priest in Gaza who was martyred with the priest Matthias (p. 275).

Timothy (feast day: 13 Hātūr), a "martyr without bloodshed," bishop of Antinoopolis who was seized under Diocletian but freed under Constantine.

Timothy of Memphis, or Timotheus the Egyptian (feast day: 21 Ba'ūnah), Christian soldier under the governor Arianus, who tore up Diocletian's edict ordering worship of pagan gods and was seized, persecuted, and beheaded.

Timothy and Theodorus, see THEODORUS AND TIMOTHY, above.

TOLEMAUS (feast day: 11 Kiyahk), a soldier from Dandarah martyred under Diocletian.

URSUS OF SOLOTHURN (feast day: 30 September), a fourth-century Egyptian who was martyred with the Theban Legion in Switzerland.

Valerianus and Tibarcius (feast day: 26 Hātūr), brothers martyred under Diocletian.

Valesius (feast day: 19 Baramhāt), one of seven martyrs cited by Eusebius.

Victor, a member of Diocletian's court who was martyred.

Victor of Asyūṭ (feast day: 5 Kiyahk), a Roman soldier under Diocletian who refused to worship pagan gods, was seized, tortured, and thrown into a furnace.

VICTOR OF SOLOTHURN, fourth-century soldier of the Theban Legion martyred in Switzerland.

VICTOR STRATELATES, or the General (feast day: 27 Baramūdah), son of Romanus, who, according to legend, was killed and miraculously revived three times before his final death in the persecutions under Diocletian.

Victor, Decius, and Eirene (*or Irene*) (feast day: 4 Baramūdah), martyrs with their companions under Julian the Apostate.

Zadok and His Companions (feast day: 26 Amshīr), Persians who were martyred.

BIBLIOGRAPHY

Amélineau, E. C. *Les Actes des martyrs de l'Eglise copte*. Paris, 1890.

Evelyn-White, H. G. *Monasteries of the Wadi 'n-Naṭrūn*, 3 vols. New York, 1926–1933.

Holweck, F. G. *A Biographical Dictionary of the Saints, with a General Introduction on Hagiography*. St. Louis and London, 1924. Repr. Detroit, 1969.

Hyvernat, H. *Les Actes des martyrs de l'Egypte*, 4 pts. in 1 vol. Hildesheim and New York, 1977.

O'Leary, DeL. *The Saints of Egypt in the Coptic Calendar*. London and New York, 1937. Repr. Amsterdam, 1974.

AZIZ S. ATIYA

MARUCCHI, ORAZIO (1852–1931), Italian Egyptologist and archaeologist. He was director of the Egyptian Museum of the Vatican and the Christian Museum of the Lateran. He published an account of the Egyptian Museum, *Il Museo Egizio Vaticano, descritto ed illustrato da Orazio Marucchi* (1899). He died in Rome.

BIBLIOGRAPHY

Dawson, W. R., and E. P. Uphill. *Who Was Who in Egyptology*, p. 196. London, 1972.

Kammerer, W., comp. *A Coptic Bibliography*. Ann Arbor, Mich., 1950; repr. New York, 1969.

AZIZ S. ATIYA

MARY OF ALEXANDRIA, SAINT. The life of this saint is known only from a summary given by the recension of the SYNAXARION of the Copts from Lower Egypt for 24 Ṭūbah.

There is very little about the childhood of Mary. She was the daughter of Christian parents and was from Alexandria. She refused all the noble matches that were offered to her, which makes one suppose that she was of aristocratic birth. Her parents being dead, she distributed to the poor and the needy all the goods left her by her father and became a nun in one of the monasteries outside Alexandria, which dates this life before the Persian invasion (619–629). (According to the HISTORY OF THE PATRIARCHS, the Persians destroyed 600 monasteries outside of Alexandria, and it is not said that these were later reconstructed.) She there received the monastic habit. She showed herself faithful to the ascetic practices of fasting and prayer for fifteen years (not twelve as the Ethiopic version says). Then she asked and obtained from the superior permission to live the life of a recluse, which she did for twenty-five years. This leads one to think that she took her vows fairly young. On 11 Ṭūbah she asked for a little holy water to be brought to her and washed her face and hands with it, then she received the holy mysteries and drank from the blessed water. She fell sick and was confined to bed until 21 Ṭūbah. On that day she received the holy mysteries for the second time, and invited her sisters to visit her three days later, but when that day came, 24 Ṭūbah, they found her dead. They buried her with the other sisters.

BIBLIOGRAPHY

Budge, E. A. W. *The Book of the Saints of the Ethiopian Church*, 4 vols. Cambridge, 1928.

Crum, W. E. *A Coptic Dictionary*. Oxford, 1939.

RENÉ-GEORGES COQUIN

MARY THE EGYPTIAN, SAINT. The legend of Saint Mary the Egyptian is derived from a Greek Life falsely attributed to Sophronius of Jerusalem (PG 87, cols. 3697–3726). It is there related that a monk-priest named Zosimus from a monastery in Palestine went out during Lent into the desert beyond the Jordan, and there met an old woman who was living as an ascetic in complete solitude. He took her at first for a spirit. Since she was without clothing, she sought to flee. Zosimus threw her his cloak to cover her. She then told him her life story.

A native of Egypt, she left her parents from the age of twelve to go to Alexandria, where she lived for seventeen years in prostitution. One day, near the harbor, she met some men who were going on pilgrimage to Jerusalem. She resolved to go with them, and to pay for her passage continued to ply her trade on the ship. In Jerusalem, on the day of the Exaltation of the Holy Cross, she wished to go into the church with the others. But a mysterious force held her back several times at the door. Realizing that this was because of her sins, she was seized with compunction and supplicated the Virgin. Converted, she decided to go and live as a penitent and solitary in the desert of the Jordan. When Zosimus met her, she had been living there for forty-seven years. She asked him to come back to see her the following year to give her the sacrament. The next year she renewed this request. But when Zosimus returned for the third time, he found her dead. In obedience to a message that she had left for him, he buried her, assisted by a lion, which helped him to dig the grave. This story is also reported, with slight variations, in the SYNAXARION for 6 Baramūdah.

This legend seems to have a historical foundation. In his *Life of Cyriacus*, Cyril of Scythopolis relates how two monks, probably in the first half of the sixth century, met a woman who lived in the desert of the Jordan as an anchorite and who told them her life story before dying and being buried by them in the cave in which she had lived. Named Mary, she had been a cantoress in the church of the Anastasis. Observing that her exceptional beauty invited many men to sin, she resolved to leave Jerusalem to go and live in the desert of the Jordan, where she had been for eighteen years when the two monks met her. The story is also related by John Moschus in his *Pratum Spirituale* (PG 87, col. 3049 A–D). It is probably this text that inspired the story attributed to Sophronius in the seventh century.

BIBLIOGRAPHY

Delehaye, H. "Un Groupe de récits utiles à l'âme." *Studia Hagiographica* 42 (1966):384–93.

Delmas, F. [S. Vailhé] "Remarques sur la vie de Sainte Marie l'Egyptienne." *Echos d'Orient* 4 (1900):35–42; 5 (1901–1902):15–17.
Kunze, K. *Studien zur Legende der heiligen Maria Aegyptiaca im deutschen Sprachgebiet.* Berlin, 1969.
Schwartz, E. *Kyrillos von Skythopolis,* pp. 233–35. Leipzig, 1969.

ANTOINE GUILLAUMONT

MARYŪṬ. *See* 'Abū Mīnā; Amriyyah.

MA'SARAH, AL-. *See* Pilgrimages.

MASHTŪL, town located in the Egyptian Delta approximately 14 miles (22 km) southeast of Banhā in the province of Sharqiyyah. It was known in the sixth century as Mashtūl al-Ṭawāḥīn (mills) because of its many mills and because of the active trade in flour and grains that it carried on with the Ḥijāz (Saudi Arabia). During the Ottoman period in the eighteenth century, Mashtūl held a weekly market and accordingly became known as Mashtūl al-Sūq (Mashtūl the market). The town continues to be known by this name.

BIBLIOGRAPHY

Ibn Mammātī. *Kitāb Qawānīn al-Dawāwīn,* ed. A. S. Atiya, p. 176. Cairo, 1943.
Muḥammad Ramzī. *Al-Qāmūs al-Jughrāfī lil-Bilād al Miṣrīyyah,* Vol. 2. Cairo, 1954–1955.

RANDALL STEWART

MAṢĪL, a town in the northern Delta of Egypt. Though its exact location is uncertain, it appears that Maṣīl lay somewhere within the area defined by Rashīd to the northeast, Fuwwah to the southeast, Lake Idku to the northwest, and Abū Ḥummuṣ to the southwest. In Coptic documents the name of the town was written ⲙⲉⲭⲏⲗ or ⲙⲉⲗⲉⲝ, and in Greek sources as Μελέτης (Melétes) or Μετέλις (Metélis).

The SYNAXARION indicates that Maṣīl was a bishopric at least as early as the end of the third century. Under the date 9 Tūt we read that Bishop Bisura, who presided in the city of Metelis at the time of the emperor DIOCLETIAN (284–305), was martyred during the persecutions of that era. The town was still a bishopric in the Middle Ages (Munier, 1943, p. 14).

BIBLIOGRAPHY

Amélineau, E. *La Géographie de l'Egypt à l'époque copte,* pp. 243–46. Paris, 1893.
Munier, H. *Recueil des listes épiscopales de l'église copte.* Cairo, 1943.
Timm, S. *Das christlich-koptische Ägypten in arabischer Zeit,* pt. 4, pp. 1604–1610. Wiesbaden, 1988.

RANDALL STEWART

MASKS, FUNERARY. *See* Portraiture.

MASPERO, GASTON CAMILLE CHARLES (1846–1916), French Egyptologist. He was born in Paris and was educated at the Ecole normale in Paris. He was appointed professor of Egyptian philology and archaeology in the Collège de France in 1874 and went to Egypt in 1880 as head of the archaeological mission that later became the Institut français d'Archéologie orientale. Then he succeeded A. E. Mariette as director of the Bulāq Museum and Service des Antiquités (1881–1886). He expanded the Service to a regular department with five inspectorates, thus inadvertently helping to reveal the importance of Coptic antiquities.

Of his enormous list of publications only very few touched the field of Coptology. His real contribution to Coptic studies was realized in the person of his son Jean Gaston, whom he had trained in Coptic.

BIBLIOGRAPHY

Dawson, W. R., and E. P. Uphill. *Who Was Who in Egyptology,* pp. 197–98. London, 1972.
Kammerer, W., comp. *A Coptic Bibliography.* Ann Arbor, Mich., 1950; repr. New York, 1969.

AZIZ S. ATIYA

MASPERO, JEAN (JACQUES) GASTON (1885–1915), French papyrologist. He was the son of the celebrated Egyptologist Gaston MASPERO, who early imparted to him a great interest in archaeology and numismatics. Jean became attached to the Institut francaise d'Archéologie orientale as assistant to E. G. CHASSINAT and participated with his father in the cataloguing of the Byzantine papyri of the Cairo Museum for the Catalogue Commission of the Service des Antiquités. He joined the army during World War I and was killed before the publication of his work, which his father saw through the press. His great promise in Coptic studies is testified by some of his contributions: *Histoire des patriarches d'Alexandrie depuis la mort de l'empereur Anastase jusqu'à la réconciliation des églises jacobites* (published posthumously, Paris, 1923); *Fouilles exécutées à Baouit* (Cairo, 1932); *Papyrus grecs d'époque byzantine,* 3 vols., Cairo, 1911–1916. Repr. Osnabrück, 1973.

BIBLIOGRAPHY

Dawson, W. R., and E. P. Uphill. *Who Was Who in Egyptology*. London, 1972.

Kammerer, W., comp. *A Coptic Bibliography*. Ann Arbor, Mich., 1950; repr. New York, 1969.

AZIZ S. ATIYA

MASSACRE OF THE INNOCENTS. *See* Christian Subjects in Coptic Art.

MASS OF THE CATECHUMENS, eucharistic service comprising two distinct, inseparable, and complementary sections: the Mass (or Liturgy) of the Catechumens and the MASS OF THE FAITHFUL, so called because catechumens, who could attend the first part of the service, were not permitted to attend the second until they had satisfactorily completed their course of religious instruction, received the sacrament of baptism, and were accepted into the Christian community of the faithful.

In the early church, the Mass of the Catechumens started with the bishop's greeting, "Peace be with you," to which the response was, "And with your spirit." This was followed by readings from both the Old and New Testaments, after which the bishop or a priest authorized by him delivered a sermon expounding the word of God and the teachings of the church. Finally, a prayer for the catechumens was offered, and the bishop gave them his blessing. At this point, the deacon asked them to leave the church.

According to the Coptic rite, the Liturgy of the Catechumens consists of the three main parts that precede the anaphora: lections, followed by the sermon; intercessional prayers, followed by the creed; and the prayer of reconciliation.

Appointed readings from the scriptures, thematically arranged for each month of the Coptic year, are collected in a four-volume LECTIONARY. The readings fall under the general headings of the Pauline epistle, the Catholic epistle (Catholicon), the Acts (Praxis), the SYNAXARION, the Psalm, and the Gospel. The scripture readings are meticulously chosen to illustrate a certain theme, which runs through all the passages appointed for the day.

During the Mass of the Catechumens, while the appointed passages are being read by various deacons, prayers are said inaudibly by the priest on behalf of the congregation so that it may be endowed with readiness to listen, understand, accept, and act.

Following the Prayer of ABSOLUTION, the officiating priest goes up to the sanctuary, kisses the altar, and puts five spoonfuls of incense into the thurible. Inaudibly he says the Prayer of Pauline Incense to God the Father: "Eternal God, Who art without beginning and without end, great in counsel, and mighty in deeds, Who art in all places and with all beings, be with us, our Master, in this hour, and stand in the midst of us all. Purify our Hearts, sanctify our souls, and cleanse us from all sins which we have done willingly or unwillingly. And grant us to offer before Thee agreeable oblations, and blessed sacrifices, a spiritual incense to enter within the veil, to Thy Holy of Holies."

Meanwhile, the congregation sings the following hymn to the Virgin Mary in Coptic: "This is the censer of pure gold, bearing the sweet spice that was in the hands of Aaron the priest while he offered incense upon the altar." Then it sings the various intercessions in the names of the Mother of God, the seven archangels and the heavenly host, the apostles and disciples, Saint Mark the Evangelist, Saint George, the saints of the day, and the patriarch.

The priest continues with the Three Small Prayers: for the peace of the church, for the patriarch, and for the congregation. He goes round the altar thrice, with the deacon holding the cross and facing him. Coming down from the sanctuary, the priest makes a circuit around the church while offering incense to the people, touching their heads with his hand, and saying, "May the blessing of Paul the Apostle be with you." Then he returns to the sanctuary and says inaudibly the Prayer of Confession of the People, called the Mystery of Return, starting, "God, Who didst receive the confession of the thief on the cross."

The Pauline epistle is read in Coptic and in Arabic while the priest inaudibly says the Prayer of Paul addressed to the Son, beginning with the words, "O God of knowledge and Provider of wisdom, . . . Who of Thy goodness didst call Paul, who was sometimes a persecutor, to be a chosen vessel . . . an apostle and a preacher of the Gospel, . . . bestow on us and on all Thy people a mind without distraction and a purified understanding . . . and make us also worthy to be like him in deed and faith."

The Catholic Epistle (Catholicon) is taken either from the Epistle of James, the two Epistles of Peter, the three Epistles of John, or the Epistle of Jude. In the meantime, the priest says inaudibly the Prayer of the Catholic Epistle, beginning, "O Lord God, Who through Thy holy apostles hath manifested to us the mystery of the Gospel of Christ's glory, . . . make us worthy of their share and heritage." Then, unless it has been already included in the morning offering of incense, the Intercession of the Oblations is also said inaudibly.

The people sing a hymn to the Virgin Mary, "Hail to thee, Mary, the graceful dove who bore for us God the Word," and conclude with, "Blessed art thou, in truth with Thy Good Father and the Holy Spirit, for Thou hast come and saved us."

While the appointed section of the Acts is being read, the priest makes the sign of the cross over the incense box and puts one spoonful of incense into the thurible, and while standing at the door of the sanctuary, he says inaudibly the Prayer of the Acts, beginning, "O God, Who didst accept the sacrifice of Abraham, . . . even so, accept at our hands the sacrifice of this incense." He follows this again with the Three Small Prayers, and he goes around the altar three times and then incenses before the door of the sanctuary. Then he incenses the Gospel and the people in the inner choir only. Standing at the iconostasis, he says the prayer of the Mystery of Return.

Then follows a reading from the Synaxarion, a compendium of the lives of saints and martyrs arranged according to the months of the Coptic calendar. What is being commemorated is not the birth but the death of the saint: "The day of death [is better] than the day of birth" (Eccl. 7:1), and whereas the Pauline epistle, the Catholic epistle, and the Acts are read by deacons, it is usually the priest who reads an account of the life of the martyr(s) of the day or the memorable event attached to it, in order to give further importance to the place of martyrs in the daily practice of the Coptic church. S. H. Leeder is worth quoting here: "Another deeply impressive feature of the Coptic services is the reading of the lives of the saints in Arabic, according to a very ancient custom sanctioned in the fourth century; . . . they keep alive the miraculous traditions which the Coptic people still cherish with undoubted reverence" (1973, p. 194).

Following the Synaxarion reading, the congregation sings the Trisagion, the refrain of which is, in effect, the hymn sung by the Seraphim: "Holy, holy, holy is the Lord of hosts" (Is. 6:3; Rev. 4:8).

Standing at the entrance to the sanctuary, with the deacon behind him holding the Gospel book and the cross, the priest says the Intercession of the Gospel, which begins, "Master Lord Jesus Christ our God, Who said to his saintly disciples and holy apostles, 'Many prophets and righteous men have desired to see the things which you see and have not seen them, and to hear the things which you hear and have not heard them. But you, blessed are your eyes, for they see, and your ears, for they hear.' May we be accounted worthy to hear and act by Thine holy Gospels, through the prayers of Thy saints." Then both priest and deacon enter the sanctuary and go around the altar, while the priest says inaudibly, "Lord now lettest Thou Thy servant depart in peace, according to Thy Word; for mine eyes have seen Thy salvation which Thou hast prepared in the presence of all peoples, a light for revelation to the Gentiles, and for glory to Thy people Israel" (Lk. 2:29–32).

In the meantime, another deacon reads the appointed Psalm in Coptic, followed by the Gospel in Coptic and Arabic, while the priest says inaudibly the prayer of the Mystery of the Gospel, beginning, "O Long-suffering One to whom appertaineth abundance of mercy," and prays, among other things, for the sick, for the safety of men and beasts, for the safety of the country, for the rulers, for the captives, for the fruits of the earth, and for the catechumens.

Then the priest inaudibly says the Prayer of the Iconostasis, which begins, "Maker of all creation, visible and invisible, and Whose providence is over all things, for they are Thine, our Lord, Thou lover of souls, . . . while I approach Thine Holy of Holies and handle this holy rite, grant me, O Lord, Thine Holy Spirit, the fire immaterial and incomprehensible which consumeth all feebleness and which burneth up evil intentions."

The sermon that follows the lections is usually

delivered by the bishop. According to AL-ṢAFĪ IBN AL-'ASSĀL, "following the reading from the Gospel, the bishop shall hold the Gospel-book in hand, and address the congregation, elucidating the contents of the section that has just been read. In the bishop's absence, the priest shall deliver the sermon" (1927, p. 122). It is also normal to allow competent deacons to preach at the invitation of the bishop.

The priest then goes up to the sanctuary and says the following three Great Intercessions, standing at the altar with the deacon facing him on the opposite side:

1. Intercession for Peace: "We pray and beseech Thy goodness, O lover of man, remember, O Lord, the peace of the One Only Holy Catholic and Apostolic Church, which is from one end of the world to the other. Bless all the peoples and all the lands; the peace that is from heaven grant in all our hearts, but also the peace of this life bestow upon us graciously. The king, the armies, the magistrates, the councillors, the multitudes, our neighbors, our goings in and our goings out, order them in all peace."

2. Intercession for the Priesthood: "Remember, O Lord, our Patriarch, honored Father Abba [name]. Preserve him to us in safety many years in peaceful times, fulfilling that holy pontificate, . . . rightly dividing the word of truth, . . . with all the Orthodox bishops, presbyters, and deacons, and all the fullness of Thy One Only Holy Catholic and Apostolic Church."

3. Intercession for the Congregation: "Remember, O Lord, our congregation, bless them; grant that they be to us without hindrance, that they be held without impediment after Thine holy and blessed will, houses of prayer, houses of purity, houses of blessing."

Each intercession is followed by the response "Kyrie Eleison" from the people. Then the creed is recited aloud by the deacons and the congregation. The version in use in the Coptic church is the Nicene-Constantinopolitan Creed, drawn up at the councils of Nicaea and Constantinople (see NICAEA, COUNCIL OF; CONSTANTINOPLE, COUNCIL OF).

While the creed is being recited, the priest washes his hands thrice at the northern side of the altar, then turns to the west and wrings his hands before the congregation as a sign of his own absolution from the guilt incurred by those who dare to partake of the Holy Sacrament unworthily.

He then begins the Prayer of the Aspasmos to the Father (see KISS OF PEACE), at the end of which the deacon exclaims, "Greet one another with a holy kiss."

This brings to an end the Mass of the Catechumens. After the catechumens have left the church, the Liturgy of the Faithful begins. Some church historians, however, hold the view that the departure of the catechumens took place immediately after the bishop gave them his blessing, before the recital of the creed.

The Liturgy of the Catechumens is rich in biblical symbolic associations, including the following instances:

1. During the Prayer of Pauline Incense, the priest, having made a circuit round the altar, leaves the sanctuary and goes all around the church incensing the congregation. This is meant to reflect the comprehensive outward nature of St. Paul's missionary work in bringing the Gospel to the Gentiles. In the Acts Incense, however, the priest does not go beyond the inner choir of the congregation, thus representing the fact that the rest of the apostles concentrated their efforts upon Jerusalem and Judaea.

2. After incensing for the Prayer of the Acts, the priest stands at the iconostasis, without entering into the sanctuary, which is symbolic of the fact that those apostles who departed from Jerusalem in the course of their missionary efforts did not finally return to it, as each of them was martyred in the region where he was chosen to spread the Word of God.

3. The total number of circuits made round the altar during the Liturgy of the Catechumens is seven: three circuits after the Prayer of Pauline Incense, one after the Mystery of the Return, and three following the Prayer of the Acts incensing. These seven circuits reflect the equivalent number of circuits made around Jericho until its walls fell down (Jos. 6:12–20). The analogy expresses the idea of the imminent collapse of the stronghold of evil and iniquity.

4. During the Catholicon, the priest remains inside the sanctuary to represent the idea that Christ commanded the apostles not to leave Jerusalem but to wait for the promises of God the Father (Acts 1:4).

With regard to other ritualistic practices related to consecration or ordination, it is an established tradition in the Coptic church that the consecration of new icons, altar vessels, or instruments take place after reading the Pauline epistle; that ordination to the presbytery take place after the Prayer of

Reconciliation; and that consecration of a new patriarch or bishop take place after reading the Acts and the Synaxarion, to indicate that their task is a continuation of the apostolic mission.

BIBLIOGRAPHY

Carrington, P. *The Early Christian Church,* Vol. 1, p. 269. Cambridge, 1957.

Cummings, D. *The Rudder (Pedalion),* pp. 1, 4, 27, 59, 119, 190, 192, 539, 573, 637, 774. Chicago, 1957.

Ḥabīb Jirjis. *Asrār al-Kanīsah al-Sabʿah,* 2nd ed., pp. 185–236. Cairo, 1950.

Leeder, S. H. *Modern Sons of the Pharoahs.* Repr. New York, 1973.

Mosheim, J. L. von. *Institutes of Ecclesiastical History,* trans. J. Murdoch. London, 1865.

Ṣafī Ibn al-ʿAssāl, al-. *Kitāb al-Qawānīn,* pp. 28–68. Repr. Cairo, 1927.

Shaff, P. *History of the Christian Church,* Vol. 1, pp. 495–96, 500. Grand Rapids, Mich., 1955.

ARCHBISHOP BASILIOS

MASS OF THE FAITHFUL, the major section of the eucharistic service, during which the oblations are consecrated and the bread and wine become the body and blood of Jesus Christ. It is preceded by the MASS OF THE CATECHUMENS, which, in the early church, was the only part of the Divine Liturgy open to those who had not received the sacrament of baptism and, consequently, were not yet fully accepted into the Christian community of the faithful. The mass consists of the eucharistic prayers, the consecration, collective prayers, the FRACTION, and the COMMUNION.

Eucharistic Prayers

These include the following hymns of praise and thanksgiving:

The Heavenly Hymn. The deacon calls upon the congregation to stand in awe and offer to God the sacrifice of praise, which, according to Saint Paul, is a tribute uttered by lips that acknowledge His name (Heb. 13:15). It is a token of gratitude in remembrance of the expression of thanks rendered by Christ when He instituted the sacrament of the Eucharist (Mt. 26:26–27; Mk. 14:22–23; Lk. 22:19; 1 Cor. 2:23–25). The congregation responds, "The mercy of peace, the sacrifice of praise."

Then the priest and the deacon lift the *prosphereín,* the great veil covering the oblations, and shake it gently, a symbolic representation of the rolling of the stone away from the entrance of the tomb and of the Resurrection, which brought about the reconciliation between God and man.

During the mass, the priest takes the mat that is over the host into his right hand and makes the three following signs of the cross: first, to the west, signing the congregation and saying, "The Lord be with you all," to which it responds, "And with your spirit"; second, to the east, signing his fellow servers and saying, "Lift up your hearts," to which the congregation responds, "They are with the Lord"; and, third, he signs himself, saying, "Let us give thanks to the Lord," to which the congregation responds, "It is meet and worthy."

The first of the eucharistic prayers is a thanksoffering to God for His loving kindness.

The Cherubic Hymn. The choir and the congregation then sing the Cherubic Hymn, which Saint Gregory Dialogos called "the triumphal hymn of our salvation," the words of which are derived from Isaiah 6:3. This hymn, which occurs in most ancient liturgies and in the Constitutions of the Holy Apostles, appears to have been first used by the Church of Alexandria. "We have seen that the Sanctus, preceded by an account of the angels' worship, is to be traced to Alexandria in the work of Origen (c. A.D. 230) and probably goes back in the Alexandria use to a period well before that date" (Dix, 1960, p. 237).

The Angelic Worship. The priest places the mat that is in his left hand upon the altar; then he moves the other mat from his right to his left hand and takes the mat that is upon the chalice. Holding it, he makes three signs of the cross, first upon himself, then upon the servers standing at the altar, and lastly upon the congregation, each time saying, "Holy."

He continues praying from Saint Mark's Liturgy, "Truly heaven and earth are full of Thy holy glory, through Thine Only-begotten Son our Lord and God and Savior and King of us all, Jesus Christ. Fill this Thy sacrifice, O Lord, with the blessing which is from Thee, by the descent upon it of the Holy Spirit."

The corresponding prayers from Saint Basil's and Saint Gregory's liturgies are more comprehensive. The former includes memorials of man's fall, of the prophets sent by God to teach man of things to come, of the incarnation of Jesus Christ in the fulness of time, of His Passion, His Resurrection, Ascension, and promised Second Coming. Saint Gregory, in his liturgy, addressed Christ, referring to the indescribable majesty of God's glory and the depth of His love for mankind: "Thou hast formed me and laid Thy hand upon me, and inscribed in me the image of Thy power. Thou has endowed me with the gift of reason, . . . Thou hast bestowed upon me Thy knowledge."

The Consecration Prayers

The Institution Narrative or Crossing the Gifts. Pointing to the bread and the wine, the priest says, "He instituted for us this great Mystery of godliness." Here the deacon brings the censer nearer to the priest for him to incense his hands, after which he continues, "For having resolved to give Himself up unto death for the life of the world." The congregation responds, "We believe." He takes the bread into his left hand and raises the mat that was under the host and places it on the altar, saying, "He took bread on His pure hands, which are blessed, life-giving and without blemish." The congregation says, "We believe this is true, Amen."

With his eyes looking upward, the priest continues, "He looked up towards heaven, to Thee, O God, His Father and Lord of all. He gave thanks. He blessed it. He sanctified it." The last three sentences are each accompanied by the sign of the cross and responded to by the congregation with the word "Amen," and finally, "We believe, we confess, and we glorify."

The priest carefully breaks the oblation into one-third and two-thirds without separating them, and says, "He divided it and gave it to His saintly disciples and pure apostles saying, 'Take, eat of it, all of you, for this is My Body which is to be broken for you and for many, to be given for the remission of sins. Do this in remembrance of me.'"

Then the priest signs the chalice: "Likewise the chalice after supper, He mixed it of wine and water. He gave thanks. He blessed it. He sanctified it. He tasted and gave it to His saintly disciples and pure apostles, saying, 'Take, drink of it, all of you. For this is my Blood of the New Covenant, which shall be shed for you and for many, to be given for the remission of sins. Do this in remembrance of me.'" The people respond here as they have previously done during the consignment of the bread.

The Anamnesis. Pointing first to the Body and then to the Blood, the priest says, "For every time you shall eat of this bread and drink of this cup, you will preach my death and confess my resurrection, and remember me until I come."

The congregation responds, "Amen, Amen, Amen, Thy death, O Lord, we do preach, and Thy holy resurrection and ascension to heaven we do confess. We praise Thee, we bless Thee, we give thanks unto Thee, and we supplicate Thee, O our Lord."

Here one must stress the dynamic aspect of such a memorial, which is not merely a mental exercise of bringing an event to memory. According to Jean Danielou, "the Greek term 'anamnesis' does not mean merely a remembrance or a memorial of a thing regarded as being absent, but it means a recalling or representing the thing in an active sense. It does not mean a remembrance of the sacrifice of Christ as something purely of the past, something that was done, but as a real and present sacrifice which has its effect on us. It is an efficacious commemoration" (1956, pp. 136–37).

The Epiclesis, or the Invocation of the Holy Spirit. This is a petition for the descent of the Holy Spirit on the oblations to change them into Christ's body and blood. Kneeling down, the priest says inaudibly the following prayer: "We pray Thee, O Lord our God, we Thy sinful and unworthy servants. We worship Thee by the pleasure of Thy goodness, that Thy Holy Spirit may descend upon us and upon these offerings placed here, to purify them, transubstantiate them, and manifest them holy unto Thy saints."

Here the deacon exclaims, "Let us attend. Amen," and all raise their heads. The priest crosses the oblation in the paten thrice and says, "And may He make this bread His Holy Body," to which each member of the congregation says, "I believe," and the priest stretches out his hands and bows his head to the Lord, saying, "Our Lord, our God, and our Savior, Jesus Christ, to be given for the remission of sins and unto eternal life for all who partake thereof," and the people say, "Amen."

Signing the chalice three times, the priest continues, "And this cup, also, the Precious Blood of His New Testament," to which the people respond as previously, and then he also continues as before. Finally, they say Amen, followed by a threefold *Kyrie eleison.*

While some theologians believe that the actual consecration of the oblations is effected through the recitation of the very words of Jesus Christ in the institution narrative, others are of opinion that only at the descent of the Holy Spirit can such consecration take place. But rather than attributing the process of the consecration to the Son separate from the Holy Spirit, it would be more appropriate to interpret the act of the consecration of the oblations as the combined sanctification by the Holy Trinity. It is noteworthy that in Saint Gregory's Liturgy the priest supplicates the Son to send His Holy Spirit upon the worshipers and upon the oblations, stressing at the same time the positive role of the Son in the process of transformation: "Thou, O Master, only by Thy own voice, change these gifts which are presented. . . . Send the grace of the Holy Spirit upon us to sanctify and transform these oblations which are presented into the Body and Blood of our salvation."

Collective Prayers

These are of a comprehensive nature, as they embrace the entire community of the church, both militant and triumphant, united in Jesus Christ. They include the smaller intercessions, the commemoration of saints, and the diptychs.

The Seven Smaller Intercessions. Holding a mat in each hand, the priest says these intercessions preceded by the following prayer: "Make us all worthy, O Lord, to partake of Thy Holies unto the sanctification of our souls, our bodies and our spirits, that we may become one body and one spirit, and be given a portion and an inheritance with the saints who have been well-pleasing unto Thee since the beginning." The seven intercessions are as follows:

1. Intercession for Church Peace: "Remember, O Lord, the peace of Thine One, Holy, Universal, and Apostolic Church."

2. Intercession for the Church Fathers: "The Church which Thou hast purchased unto Thyself with the Precious Blood of Thy Christ. Keep her and all her Orthodox bishops in peace. And remember first, O Lord, our blessed Father, Pope, and Patriarch [name]."

3. Intercession for the Church Presbyters: "And those who with him [i.e., the patriarch] rightly divide the word of Thy truth in uprightness. Preserve them unto Thy Church to shepherd Thy flock in peace. Remember, O Lord, the Orthodox priesthood and the diaconate."

4. Intercession for Mercy: "And all ministers, and all who are in virginity, and the purity of Thy faithful people. Remember, O Lord, to have mercy upon us all."

5. Intercession for the Place: "Remember, O Lord, the safety of this holy place, which is Thine, and all other places and monasteries of our Orthodox fathers."

6. Intercession for Nature: Prayers are said for the waters, plants, the weather conditions, and the rising and falling of the river Nile. The wording of this intercession is closely related to the particular season of the year and the cultivation cycle.

7. Intercession for the Oblations: "Remember, O Lord, those who have offered these oblations, those for whom they have been offered, and those through whom they have been offered. Give them all the heavenly recompense."

These seven intercessions pertain to Saint Basil's Liturgy. Saint Gregory's, on the other hand, includes a few more, namely, intercessions for kings and rulers, for rich and poor, for young and old, for celibates and married couples. It is to be noted that here, but not in the Liturgy of Saint Mark, the intercessions follow, not precede, the epiclesis prayers.

The Commemoration of Saints. The recitation of the names of saints is a significant part of the Divine Liturgy. In this section of the Liturgy, the priest says, "For such, O Lord, is the commandment of Thy only-begotton Son, that we share in the commemoration of Thy saints. Graciously, O Lord, remember all the saints who have pleased Thee since the beginning: our holy fathers and patriarchs, the prophets, the preachers, the evangelists, the martyrs, the confessors, and all the spirits of the righteous who were consummate in their faith."

The Diptychs. At the close of the commemoration of saints, the deacon says, "Let the readers say the names of our fathers the holy patriarchs who have fallen asleep; may the Lord repose their souls, and forgive us our sins." Here the priest inaudibly says, "Remember also, O Lord, all those who have fallen asleep and rested, in the priesthood and the laity. Vouchsafe, O Lord, repose their souls in the bosoms of our saintly fathers Abraham, Isaac, and Jacob." The significance of the diptychs—the commemoration of, and prayer for, the departed—was stressed by many of the early fathers.

The Fraction

This is the ceremonial breaking of the consecrated bread in the eucharistic service (see FRACTION).

The Communion

This is the culmination of the eucharistic service, in preparation for which the priest says, "Make us all worthy, O Lord, to partake of Thy Holy Body and Thy Holy Precious Blood, in purification of our souls, our bodies, and our spirits, and forgiveness of our sins and trespasses, that we may become one body and one spirit with Thee. Glory be to Thee, with Thy Good Father and the Holy Spirit, forever. Amen."

The celebrant then partakes of the communion himself, followed by the other priests serving with him, before administering Holy Communion to the deacons and the members of the congregation. Meanwhile, the rest of the congregation sing Psalm 150, standing throughout as a mark of respect until the celebrant has completed the washing of the liturgical vessels and offered thanks to God, saying, "Our mouths are filled with exaltation, and our tongues with joy, having partaken of Thy immortal Sacraments, O Lord."

Taking a little water in his palms, the celebrant sprinkles it on the altar, saying, "O Angel of this oblation, who fliest up to the heights with this our praise, remember us before the Lord, that He may forgive us our sins." After the Lord's Prayer, he dismisses the congregation with the words "Go in peace, may the peace of the Lord be with you."

BIBLIOGRAPHY

Brightman, F. E. *Liturgies Eastern and Western.* Oxford, 1967.

Coquin, R. G. "Anaphore alexandrin de St. Marc." *Le Muséon* 82 (1969):307–356.

Danielou, J. *The Bible and the Liturgy.* London, 1956.

Dix, G. *The Shape of the Liturgy.* London, 1960.

Jungmann, J. A., S. J. *The Early Liturgy to the Time of Gregory the Great,* trans. Francis A. Brunner. London, 1960.

Leitzmann, H. *Mass of the Lord's Supper.* Oxford, 1974.

Malaṭī, T. Y., *Christ in the Eucharist.* Cairo, 1986.

ARCHBISHOP BASILIOS

MATARIYYAH, AL-. *See* Pilgrimages.

MATINS, LITURGY OF, the prayer of the first of the seven CANONICAL HOURS, to be said at daybreak, with reference to the coming of the True Light (i.e., Jesus Christ). It was instituted to offer thanks to God for having brought believers safely to the morning.

Morning prayer was prescribed in the Constitutions of the Holy Apostles (1951, p. 496): "Offer up your prayers in the morning, at the third hour, the sixth, the ninth, the evening, and at the cock-crowing: in the morning, returning thanks that the Lord has sent you light, that He has brought you past the night, and brought on the day."

Reference to morning prayer occurs also in the writings of most of the early fathers. Dwelling upon the special significance of each canonical hour, Saint Cyprian (*The Treatises* 4.34–35) wrote: "But for us, beloved brethren, besides the hours of prayer observed of old, both the times and the sacraments have not increased in number. For we must also pray in the morning, that the Lord's resurrection may be celebrated by morning prayer. . . . Also at the sunsetting and at the decline of day . . . when we pray and ask that light may return to us again, we pray for the advent of Christ."

Historically, morning prayer was originally performed following the Psalmody of Midnight and, in a later development, became a separate office. This is evident from the writings of John CASSIAN (c. 360–435), who, as a young man, joined a monastery at Bethlehem and later studied monasticism in Egypt. He paid tribute to the rigorous practices of Egyptian monks in SCETIS, in contrast with those of their Western counterparts: "But you must know that this Mattins, which is now very generally observed in western countries, was appointed as a canonical office in our own day, and also in our own monastery, where our Lord Jesus Christ was born."

The institution of the Office of Morning Prayer had, however, been mentioned by Saint BASIL THE GREAT (c. 330–379) prior to the time of John Cassian: "Among us the people go at night to the house of prayers, and, in distress, affliction, and continual tears, making confession to God, at last rise from their prayers and begin to sing psalms . . . and so after passing the night in various psalmody, praying at intervals as the day begins to dawn, all together, as with one voice and one heart, raise the psalm of confession to the Lord, each forming for himself his own expression of penitence" (*Letters* 207, 3 [p. 247]).

As in all seven canonical hours, the first hour starts with an introductory section consisting of the Lord's Prayer, a prayer of thanksgiving, and Psalm 50.

The prelude to the morning prayer service is characterized by a tone of earnest request, gradually increasing in fervor: "O come, let us worship! O come, let us request Christ our God! O come, let us worship! O come, let us beg Christ our King! O come, let us worship! O come, let us entreat Christ our Savior!"

The Pauline-epistle reading, which is taken from

Ephesians 4:1–5, incorporates a Christian plan of action for the day, supplied by Saint Paul's words, "I therefore, a prisoner for the Lord, beg you to lead a life worthy of the calling to which you have been called, with all lowliness and meekness, with patience, forbearing one another in love. . . ."

This is followed by the reading of nineteen Psalms, as follows: Psalms 1–6, 8, 12, 13, 15, 16, 19, 25, 27, 63, 67, 70, 113, and 143. The Gospel reading is taken from John 1:1–17 and is followed by a commentary, the Angelic PSALMODY, the TRISAGION, and the creed, preceded by its introduction. "Kyrie Eleison" is then said forty-one times, followed by the absolution and the Lord's Prayer.

ARCHBISHOP BASILIOS

MATTEWOS. *See* Ethiopian Prelates.

MATTHEW I, eighty-seventh patriarch of the See of Saint Mark (1378–1409) (feast day: 7 Kiyakh). Matthew I is better known by the title of Mattā al-Miskīn, or Matthew the Poor. He was a native of a small village called Banī Rūḥ in the district of al-Ashmūnayn in Upper Egypt. His life is better known than that of his immediate predecessors, and the HISTORY OF THE PATRIARCHS contains ample material on his actions and movements. He also appears in the Islamic sources of the fourteenth and fifteenth centuries.

Born in a family of meager means whose vocation was agriculture, he spent his early years as a shepherd looking after his parents' sheep. He had a religious temperament, and as a child, he liked to play the ecclesiastical game of investing other children with the ranks of deacon and presbyter, while laying his hands on them and pronouncing the blessing *axios* (worthy) three times. This story is reminiscent of young ATHANASIUS I, the Apostolic, when he was discovered by ALEXANDER I baptizing other children on the seashore. At the age of fourteen, Matthew left home and went to one of the neighboring monasteries in Upper Egypt, and there he continued to act as a shepherd for their sheep. Those who knew him at the time admired his courage and his spiritual ability to prevent the wild beasts and hyenas from harming his flock. He was sparsely dressed and was girdled with a simple rope. But he was a young man of great charm and was admired by a girl who praised his eyebrows. In order to get rid of her, he shaved his eyebrows and, feigning madness, presented them to her.

It was not long before his bishop discovered his qualities and anointed him in the priesthood at the age of eighteen years. When the bishop was criticized for doing this, his answer was that the young man was fit to become not only a priest but also a patriarch. As priest, Matthew decided to go to the Monastery of Saint Antony (DAYR ANBĀ ANṬŪNIYŪS), where he acted as a deacon, concealing his priesthood. After some time in that wilderness, he moved to Jerusalem, where he spent his time in ardent prayer and fasting as well as in rendering service to others. Returning to Egypt, he headed for Qusqām and the Monastery of Our Lady, better known as DAYR AL-MUḤARRAQ. Although affiliated with that monastery, he lived as a solitary in a neighboring cave, where he was subjected to many trials and exposed to the company of wild beasts that he managed to tame. Despite his seclusion from society, his fame began to spread; and after the death of GABRIEL IV, it was decided by the community of the faithful to recruit him for the patriarchate. Matthew was reticent in accepting this nomination. But when pressed beyond his power, he proposed going back to the old Monastery of Saint Antony and asking for the verdict of its elders, hoping that they might deter the congregation from his recruitment. However, the elders confirmed the proposal and he was forcibly carried to Alexandria for his investiture on 16 Misrā, which happened to be the commemoration day of the Virgin.

As patriarch he served the community in every way imaginable, and he retained his humility by participation with others in the most menial tasks, although this never diminished his respectability in the eyes of others. All his income was spent in helping the needy, the poor, the monks, and the nuns. He helped all who were in need, whether they were Copts, Muslims, or Jews. Individual stories of his generosity are enumerated in detail in the *History of the Patriarchs*.

In 1365 Egypt had sustained a great defeat by the crusaders at Alexandria. Pierre de Lusignan and the hosts of Cyprus had descended on the city and wreaked havoc within its walls; they withdrew carrying with them not only tremendous loot but also many prisoners and captives. Egypt had to pay a heavy price for the liberation of those captives, who were primarily Muslims. Matthew participated with all the means at his disposal in buying the freedom of these prisoners, which must have courted the sympathy of the Islamic administration of the country. In the meantime, he acted as a forceful liaison between the sultans of Egypt as well as the crusading Franks and the sovereigns of the Christian kingdom of Ethiopia. Valuable gifts were exchanged between the two sides, one of the most highly valued presents to the religious kings of Ethiopia being a fragment of the true Cross.

Matthew's contemporary Mamluk sultans included 'Alā' al-Dīn 'Alī (1377–1381), Ṣalāḥ al-Dīn Ḥājjī (1382), Barqūq (1383–1389), al-Nāṣir Faraj (1398–1405), 'Izz al-Dīn 'Abd al 'Azīz (1405), and al-Nāṣir Faraj (second reign 1406–1412). Sultan Barqūq requested Matthew to write to the Ethiopian sovereign on his behalf in order to establish peaceful and friendly relations between their two countries. It is interesting to note that the patriarch's letter was addressed to Dāwūd, brother of the reigning sovereign, and that Dāwūd had deposed his brother and seized the crown by the time the letter reached the Ethiopian capital. Because of this, Matthew was considered to have prophetic qualities.

Matthew's reign was not free from local troubles, not only from the Muslim amirs but also from the members of his own church. In one case, two Coptic monks sought to join the priesthood and were refused by the patriarch because of their unfitness. They decided to vilify the patriarch and poison the minds of the administration against him. When their report was discarded, they attacked the patriarch in person and told him that one of them should replace him as patriarch and that the other should be a bishop. Matthew smiled and asked them to wait forty days, after which they could come and take his seat. He even prayed for them and gave them holy communion. Within thirty days, the dissident monks died, and this was regarded as a miracle of a holy man. Another monk rebelled against the pope and apostatized to Islam, and even enlisted in the Muslim army. The congregation requested the pope to curse him, but instead Matthew prayed for him and his return to the faith. The monk recanted and suffered martyrdom, the fate of those who withdrew from Islam. This was also regarded as a miracle. Cases of those who recanted from Islam and returned to Christianity in Matthew's reign became numerous, and all suffered martyrdom. The Islamic historian al-MAQRĪZĪ mentions a number of specific cases and the *History of the Patriarchs* says that forty-nine martyrs suffered decapitation as the penalty for their withdrawal from Islam after their conversion to it.

Matthew's relationship with the Muslim administration was sometimes precarious. He was in the good graces of Barqūq, who was defeated by a Mamluk amir by the name of Minṭāsh, after which Matthew retired to the Karak. Then a dissident member of the Coptic community fraudulently informed Minṭāsh that Barqūq had left his treasure in the custody of the patriarch. Consequently Minṭāsh summoned the patriarch and demanded the treasure, which he did not possess. The patriarch was subjected to torture, but was freed after the truth became evident. Another Mamluk by the name of Yalbogha al-Sāmirī once threatened the pope with decapitation, but the fearless pope extended his neck to his persecutor, who withdrew his sword upon seeing such unusual courage.

In fact, Matthew displayed this unusual courage on numerous occasions when defending the church and his community. When some dissidents and the Muslim mob wanted to destroy DAYR SHAHRĀN, the pope stood fast against them. The case reached the attention of Barqūq, who sent the judges of the four Muslim sects with an explicit order to find the truth about the allegations that the structure was renewed against the stipulations of the COVENANT OF 'UMAR. When it was found that these reports were fraudulent, the case was dismissed and the monastery saved. The *History of the Patriarchs* mentions another instance where Matthew succeeded in stopping an act of humiliation to Coptic women. The Mamluk amir Sūdūn once decreed that Coptic women dress in dark blue robes. Matthew objected and argued against this innovation and won.

Perhaps the last memorable episode of the patriarch's long reign was the one associated with the strong Mamluk amir Jamāl al-Dīn, detailed in the *History of the Patriarchs*. He accused Matthew of complicity in a scheme with Ethiopia to destroy Mecca and the Muslim holy places. The penalty for such a crime was death. Matthew prayed for a natural end before Jamāl al-Dīn should inflict the punishment on him; his prayers were answered. Matthew died at the age of seventy-two on 22 Ṭūbah. Of these years, he spent forty as a bachelor and a monk, and thirty-two as patriarch. Apparently his funeral was a turbulent occasion in which innumerable people congregated from all walks of life. He was buried in the tomb he had prepared for himself at DAYR AL-KHANDAQ in Cairo.

BIBLIOGRAPHY

Ibn al-Ṣayrafī, 'Ali ibn Dāwūd. *Nuzhat al-Nufūs wa-al-Abdān fī Tawārīkh al-Zamān*. Cairo, 1970.

Lane-Poole, S. *History of Egypt in the Middle Ages*. London, 1901.

______. *The Mohammadan Dynasties*. Paris, 1925.

SUBHI Y. LABIB

MATTHEW II, ninetieth patriarch of the See of Saint Mark (1452–1465). Matthew appears in the HISTORY OF THE PATRIARCHS under the name Mattāwus. Briefly recorded are the dates of his consecration and decease and the fact that he was a monk of the Monastery of Our Lady known as DAYR AL-MUḤARRAQ. Any other information about his life, either before or after his investiture, we must gather from the Islamic sources.

The Muslim historian al-Sakhāwī tells us that his secular name before taking the monastic vow was Sulaymān al-Ṣaʿīdī (the Upper Egyptian), which he changed to Mattā or Mattāwus when joining al-Muḥarraq Monastery. He acceded to the throne of Saint Mark during the later years of the reign of the Mamluk sultan Jaqmaq (1438–1453) and he was a contemporary of Fakhr al-Dīn ʿUthmān (1453), Sayf al-Dīn Īnāl (1453–1460), Shihāb al-Dīn Aḥmad (1460), and Sayf al-Dīn Khushqadam (1460–1467).

Matthew II was consecrated and lived in the historic Church of the Virgin at ḤĀRIT ZUWAYLAH, which was a Coptic quarter. Apparently the situation of the Copts in his times was relatively secure and peaceful, the sultans being too involved in their own troubles with their Mamluk amirs to devote much time to the patriarch and his church. However, shortly after his investiture, probably in the year 1453, an Ethiopian embassy arrived in Cairo with gifts for the sultan. They wanted Matthew to appoint a Coptic archbishop for their country, and they pleaded for peace and security for the Copts and their churches in Egypt. A monk named Gabriel was consecrated as bishop of the Abyssinian diocese.

An event of universal importance took place in 1453 when Constantinople fell to the Turks under Muḥammad the Conqueror, who sent an embassy to the court of Sultan Jaqmaq to announce his triumphant entry into the Byzantine capital.

BIBLIOGRAPHY

Lane-Poole, S. *History of Egypt in the Middle Ages.* London, 1901.

______. *The Mohammadan Dynasties.* Paris, 1925.

SUBHI Y. LABIB

MATTHEW III, one hundredth patriarch of the See of Saint Mark (1634–1649). Matthew is described in the HISTORY OF THE PATRIARCHS as al-Ṭūkhī, which fixes his provenance as the city of Ṭūhk al-Naṣārā in Lower Egypt. His biography is less than three lines in the *History,* where his dates of investiture and death are mentioned. It also mentions the fact that he was an ascetic monk at DAYR AL-BARĀMŪS when he was elected to this high office. O. Meinardus states that he was also a resident of the Monastery of Saint Macarius (DAYR ANBĀ MAQĀR). He was a contemporary of the Ottoman sultans Murād IV (1623–1640) and Ibrāhīm I (1640–1648). Because he lived in one of the darkest periods of Egyptian history, it is impossible to discover further information about his life.

BIBLIOGRAPHY

Hanotaux, G., ed. *Histoire de la nation égyptienne,* 7 vols. Paris, 1931–1940.

Meinardus, O. *Christian Egypt: Ancient and Modern.* Cairo, 1977.

SUBHI Y. LABIB

MATTHEW IV, pope of Alexandria and 102nd patriarch of the See of Saint Mark (1660–1675). Matthew (Mattāwus or Mattā al-Mīrī) of Mīr in Upper Egypt was a monk of DAYR AL-BARĀMŪS when he was selected to the patriarchate. He remained in office for fourteen years and six months. This is all the information supplied by the HISTORY OF THE PATRIARCHS in one of the darkest periods of Egyptian history. He was a contemporary of the Ottoman sultan Muḥammad IV (1648–1687). During Matthew's patriarchate Egypt was governed by a viceroy appointed from Constantinople without ostensible impact on the patriarch or the Coptic church beyond the levy of the annual tax.

BIBLIOGRAPHY

Hanotaux, G., ed. *Histoire de la nation égyptienne,* 7 vols. Paris, 1931–1940.

Meinardus, O. *Christian Egypt: Ancient and Modern.* Cairo, 1977.

SUBHI Y. LABIB

MATTHEW THE POOR, SAINT, early-eighth-century holy man. Matthew is mentioned in the Arabic SYNAXARION of the Copts, at the day of his feast, 7 Kiyahk. The recension from Lower Egypt gives him a rather small place and puts him at Aswan instead of Aṣfūn, but the recension from Upper Egypt accords him a much longer notice.

Numerous Coptic fragments, belonging to three codices, have come down to us (Campagnano, 1978, pp. 223, 229, 233, and 234). He is mentioned also in the Life of ALEXANDER II (705–730; PO 5, pt. 1, p. 79). ABŪ ṢĀLIH THE ARMENIAN speaks of him in several passages. Through confusion of the diacritical marks, he confuses ISNĀ with Anṣinā and Askīt with Aṣfūn.

According to the HISTORY OF THE PATRIARCHS, Apa Matthew was a native of Aṣfūn, but the *Synaxarion* makes him a native of Bīshnāy, a small village in the nome of Qūṣ, now vanished. The *History of the Patriarchs* and Abū Ṣālih say that he was a fisherman. He is also called an ANCHORITE, but Coptic fragments say that he founded a monastery in the name of Saint PACHOMIUS, without specifying the place. It seems that this was the present monastery of Matthew the Poor at Isnā. It is called the Monastery of the Potter, but we cannot explain this name.

The *History of the Patriarchs*, the Synaxarion, and the Coptic fragments recount above all his miracles, but the personality of Matthew shines through them. He seems to have been very severe in making the law of God prevail. The miracles are interesting because they show the Christian mentality at this period.

BIBLIOGRAPHY

Campagnano, A. "Monaci egiziani fra V e VI secolo." *Vetera Christianorum* 15 (1978):223–46.

Winlock, H. E., and W. E. Crum. *The Monastery of Epiphanius at Thebes*, pt. 1. New York, 1926.

RENÉ-GEORGES COQUIN

MAUNDY THURSDAY. *See* Feasts, Minor.

MAURITIUS, SAINT

MAURITIUS, SAINT (feast day, 25 Tūt), the favorite and most widely venerated of the saints of the THEBAN LEGION. During the Middle Ages, he was revered as the guardian of several professions, including soldiers, armorers, and dyers. Several orders were established in his honor, including the Order of the Golden Fleece, founded by Philip the Good of Burgundy (1429), and the Order of Saint Maurice, founded by Amadeus VIII of Savoy (1434). He is recognized as the patron saint of the diocese of Sitten (Sion, capital of the canton of Valais), of the city of Saint Maurice-en-Valais (ancient Agaunum), of Saint Moritz in the upper Engadine, and of the canton of Appenzell I (Rhine), where his feast day is a cantonal holiday. He also became the patron saint of entire communities and kingdoms: the Langobardi, the Merovingians, the Carolingians, the Burgundians, and later the Savoyards.

The Holy Roman Emperors looked to him for protection. In 926, Henry I of Germany (919–936) ceded the present Swiss canton of Aargau in return for the lance of Saint Maurice; henceforth, this lance, along with his sword and spurs, were among the most significant insignia of the imperial throne. Furthermore, certain emperors were anointed before the Altar of Saint Maurice in Saint Peter's Cathedral at Rome.

More than 650 religious foundations dedicated to the saint can be traced in France and other European countries. A large number of churches and altars in Switzerland bear his name; a few of them may be enumerated by canton: *Canton Aargau:* Pfarrkirche in Berikon, Beinwil/Freiamt, Oberrohrdorf, Wölflinswil, as well as in the formerly Catholic churches of Suhr, Umikon, and Zofingen; *Canton Lucerne:* Emmen, Pfeffikon, Ruswil, Schötz, Ohmstal, and Saint Leodegar in the Hofkirche in Lucerne; *Canton Solothurn:* Dornach, Kleinützel, Kriegstetten, and Trimbach; *Appenzell I (Rhine):* the Stosskapelle. Special mention may be made of the Church and Abbey of Saint Maurice-en-Valais, of the Church of Saint Moritz in the Engadine, and of the Monastery Chapel of Einsiedeln, where his name is highly revered.

The Egyptian origin of the saint is attested by etymological considerations. The Coptic Greek name Maurikios (fem., Maurikia) appears in the papyri and is identical with the Roman name Mauritius, according to G. Heuser. P. Müller suggests that the name may have been derived from Moeris, which is associated with the ancient lake in the Fayyūm; indeed, we encounter this name on epitaphs of the Ptolemaic and Coptic periods, and it is identical with the name of this lake, which is still used as a personal name among the Copts.

[*See also:* Felix and Regula; Ursus of Solothurn; Verena of Zurzach.]

BIBLIOGRAPHY

Balthasar, J. A. F. *Schutzschrift für die tebaïsche Legion oder den Heiligen Mauritius und seine Gesellschaft, wider Prof. Sprengen*. Lucerne, 1760.

Berchen, D. van. *Le martyr de la légion Thébaine*. Basel, 1956.

Braun, J. W. J. *Zur Geschichte der thebaischen Legion*. Bonn, 1855.

Dupraz, L. *Les Passions de S. Maurice d'Agaune.* Studia Friburgensia, n.s. 27. Fribourg, 1961.
Grenfell, B. P., and A. S. Hunt. *The Tebtunis Papyri,* Vols. 1–3. London, 1902–1938.
Herzberg, A. J. *Der heilige Mauritius.* Düsseldorf, 1936.
Heuser, G. *Die Personennamen der Kopten.* Leipzig, 1929.
Preisigke, F. *Sammelbuch griechischer Urkunden aus Ägypten.* Strasbourg, 1913.
———. *Namenbuch.* Heidelberg, 1922.
Rettberg, F. W. *Kirchengeschichte Deutschlands.* Göttingen, 1846.
Theurillet, J.-M. "L'abbaye de Saint Maurice d'Agaune dès origines à la réforme canoniale (515–530)." In *Vallesia,* Vol. 9, pp. 1–128. Sion, 1954.

SAMIR F. GIRGIS

MAWHŪB IBN MANṢŪR IBN MUFARRIJ AL-ISKANDARĀNĪ (c. 1025–1100), a redactor and coauthor of the HISTORY OF THE PATRIARCHS, begun by SĀWĪRUS IBN AL-MUQAFFA'. This important historical text actually owes its survival to Mawhūb, who, with the assistance of others, collected the patriarchal lives written by earlier biographers and compiled them into one book, which he completed by adding the biographies of the two patriarchs of his own lifetime. In this contribution of his own, he stresses the unity with the earlier lives by referring to them regularly and sometimes even by completing them.

The many autobiographical notes scattered throughout Mawhūb's text allow one to reconstruct a fairly accurate picture of his life and personality, in contrast to most other contributors to the *History of the Patriarchs,* some of whom remain totally anonymous.

Mawhūb belonged to one of the most prominent Coptic families of Alexandria. Around 1050, his father was entrusted with the preservation of the skull of Saint MARK. At his father's death, Mawhūb himself inherited this honor. He had a brother, Abū al-'Alā' Fahd, who suffered martyrdom in 1086. Mawhūb's wife is mentioned once, and his son Yūḥannā, twice. He also referred to his maternal uncle Ṣadaqah ibn Surūr, who was a nephew of Tādrus, bishop of Rashīd.

Mawhūb's wealth and social prestige appear particularly in episodes in which he acts as an intermediary between the Coptic community and the Muslim authorities. When the governor manages to keep the church of Mār Jirjis in Alexandria open, despite the closing of churches all over Egypt, Mawhūb is among the persons who secretly receive the keys. When the marauding Lawata Berbers take the patriarch CHRISTODOULUS (1047–1077) as a hostage, it is Mawhūb who pays the ransom.

Although the name of Sāwīrus ibn al-Muqaffa' is usually attached to the *History of the Patriarchs,* it has been recognized for some time that his contribution, according to most scholars, consisted of the collection of Coptic source texts and their translation into Arabic, whereas the final redaction was the work of Mawhūb (Graf, 1947, p. 302; Samir, 1975, p. 157; Johnson, 1977, pp. 106–110, 115–16). Among those authors, D. W. Johnson (1977, p. 108) drew attention to the problem of the striking parallels between the redactional notes ascribed to Sāwīrus and those of Mawhūb. J. den Heijer, contending that all those notes must be attributed to Mawhūb, concludes, therefore, that Mawhūb is thus to be considered the collector of the Coptic sources and the main editor of the *History of the Patriarchs.* Den Heijer was assisted in this task by the deacon Abū Ḥabīb Mīkhā'īl ibn Badīr al-Damanhūrī, by the priest Yu'annis, known as Zukayr, superior of the monastery of Nahyā, and by the deacon Baqīrah. Nakhlah (1943, p. 20) ascribed to Sāwīrus the note in which these men are mentioned and therefore regarded them as his contemporaries. (For the text of this note, see Seybold, 1912, p. 132, and 1904–1910, p. 141).

The deacon Abū Ḥabīb also acted as translator of the Coptic texts into Arabic. Mawhūb started his work in March or April 1088. He apparently completed his edition of Lives 1–65 after the death of the caliph al-Mustanṣir in 1094. At this point, he started writing his own two biographies of the patriarchs of his own times (den Heijer, 1984, cols. 339–47).

The two patriarch lives of Mawhūb's hand are those of CHRISTODOULUS (1047–1077) and CYRIL II (1078–1092). G. Graf (1947, p. 302) and most later authors erroneously attribute only the first of these to Mawhūb and the other to his successor, Yūḥannā ibn Ṣā'id (cf. den Heijer, 1983, pp. 107–124). For the lifetimes of these two patriarchs, Mawhūb's text is a unique contemporary source, which as such has not yet been adequately appreciated by students of medieval Egyptian history. Most Arab geographers and historians who dealt with this period (which roughly coincides with the caliphate of al-Mustanṣir Billah) flourished considerably later. Compared to these later authors, Mawhūb's text is, of course, rather limited from the chronological point of view. And, since he dealt with many events with the authority of an eyewitness, he did not always display the same objectivity that they did toward the events described. Rather, he consciously sought to present not only the official history of the Coptic church but also an expression of allegiance to the Fatimid caliphate and to the amir al-Juyūsh, Badr al-Jamālī. As for Mawhūb's methods as a historian, he usually made sure to indicate his sources carefully, and his style can generally be called clear and simple. The difficulties one may nevertheless encounter in perusing Mawhūb's two biographies are caused by their associative rather than strictly chronological or thematical arrangement.

Mawhūb's biographies consist of a series of passages of varying length in which three categories of subjects may be discerned: pure ecclesiastical history; relations between the Coptic community and the Muslim rulers; and various political, economic, and social affairs.

As for internal church matters, the lives of the two patriarchs in question, which constitute a rough chronological framework for all other topics, are dealt with elaborately. Important are the information on the consecration and the residence of the two patriarchs. Under Christodoulus, the patriarchal see was transferred to Cairo. Furthermore, the biography of Christodoulus contains the canons composed by this patriarch. It also provides plenty of information on the bishops and bishoprics of the time, culminating in a historically important list of the bishops in 1086 (presented by Munier, 1943, pp. 27–29; cf. Muyser, 1944, pp. 151–53). Mawhūb's accounts on the monasteries, the monks and their relations with the patriarchs have been studied by H. G. Evelyn-White (1932, pp. 351–70). Particularly noteworthy are the passages on the monk Bisūs.

The episodes concerning the position of the Coptic church under the Fatimid caliphate of al-Mustanṣir and the Armenian ruler Badr al-Jamālī have been exploited to some extent in most studies on the subject (e.g., Butcher, 1897, pp. 39–68; Meinardus, 1970, pp. 354–64). The most important aspects of these episodes are the Coptic secretaries and other officials involved in the Fatimid administration, the role of the Muslim administration, the role of the Muslim authorities in the election of the patriarch and the nomination of bishops, the closing and reopening of churches, and, in one instance, the martyrdom of a young man who, after embracing Islam, returned to his former religion. Mawhūb also deals with the relations between Copts and other Christians in Egypt, such as Melchites, Syrians, and especially Armenians, as well as with foreign countries, particularly Nubia and Ethiopia (used in the analysis by Meinardus, 1970, pp. 376–78, 418–19).

The main themes of nonconfessional history treated by Mawhūb are the political chaos and the strife between the Turkish and African batallions, the subsequent restoration of order by Badr al-Jamālī, the great famine of 1066–1072, the rise of the Nile, agriculture, and natural disasters.

BIBLIOGRAPHY

Burmester, O. H. E. "The Canons of Christodulos, Patriarch of Alexandria." *Muséon* 45 (1932):71–84.

Butcher, E. L. *The Story of the Church of Egypt.* London, 1897.

Evelyn-White, H. G. *The Monasteries of the Wadi 'n Natrun,* Vol. 2, *The History of the Monasteries of Nitria and of Scetis.* New York, 1932.

Heijer, J. den. "Quelques remarques sur la deuxième partie de l'Histoire des Patriarches d'Alexandrie." *Bulletin de la Société d'archéologie copte* 25 (1983):107–24.

______. "Sāwīrus ibn al-Muqaffa' Mawhāb ibn Mufarrij et la genèse de L'Histoire des Patriarches d'Alexandrie." Bibliotheca Orientalis 41 (1984):336–39.

Johnson, D. W. "Further Remarks on the Arabic History of the Patriarchs of Alexandria." *Oriens Christianus* 61 (1977):103–16.

Kāmil Ṣāliḥ Naklah. *Kitāb Tarīkh wa-Jadāwīl Baṭārikat al-Iskandariyyah al-Qibṭ.* Cairo, 1943.

Meinardus, O. E. A. *Christian Egypt, Faith and Life.* Cairo, 1970.

Munier, H. *Recueil des listes épiscopales de l'église copte.* Cairo, 1943.

Muyser, J. "Contribution à l'église copte." *Bulletin de la Société d'archéologie copte* 10 (1944):115–76.

Samir, Khalil. "Un Traité inédit de Sévère ibn al-Muqaffa' (Xe siècle), Flambeau de l'Intelligence." *Orientalia Christiana Periodica* 41 (1975):150–68.

Seybold, C. F. *Alexandrinische Patriarchengeschichte von S. Marcus bis Michael I (61–767) nach der ältesten 1266 geschriebenen Handschrift.* Hamburg, 1912.

______, ed. *Severus Ben al-Moqaffa' Historia Patriarcharum Alexandrinorum.* CSCO 52, 59, *Scriptores arabici* 8, 9, ser. 3, pts. 1–2.

JOHANNES DEN HEIJER

MAXIMUS, fifteenth patriarch of the See of Saint Mark (264–282). Maximus succeeded DIONYSIUS THE

GREAT and remained at the head of the Coptic church for eighteen years. He was a contemporary to six Roman emperors, beginning with the relatively mild reign of Gallienus (260–268), followed by Claudius II (268–270), Aurelianus (270–275), Tacitus (275–276), Florianus (276), and Probus (276–282). He spent his earlier years as presbyter and companion of Dionysius, with whom he shared the agonies of VALERIANUS' persecution and exile to Kefro, a frontier town of the Libyan Desert, and Colluthius in the district of Mareotis by the prefect Aemilianius. He was ultimately permitted to return with his bishop to the metropolis, where they started ministering to the faithful, undisturbed by the stormy years under preceding emperors. In fact, the episcopate of Maximus, compared with that of his predecessor, was relatively peaceful, allowing the patriarch to combat rising heresies in the Middle East.

Most important and most dangerous among these heresies was the one associated with the name of Paul of Samosata, bishop of Antioch. Paul interfered in theological discussions and invented a new doctrine that Christ attained godhead by a gradual development, that the Trinity was a closely knit combination of Father, Wisdom, and Word in a single HYPOSTASIS. His Christology resembled the forthcoming Nestorian doctrine that Jesus the Incarnate Word was one person, different from the Divine. For the first time, the HOMOOUSION controversy was raised. A council was convened at Antioch, attended by more than seventy bishops, where these confused ideas were exposed. The discussions were led by a certain Malchion, head of the theological school of Antioch. Dionysius was invited to participate, but, owing to his advanced age and feeble body, he wrote a special epistle to the synod, which was supported by Maximus after him, and, in the end, Paul was deposed and excommunicated in 268. It is possible, but not certain, that Maximus attended this synod. At any rate, he played a role in the termination of Paul's heretical assumptions by supporting the arguments set forth in the epistle of Dionysius on the subject.

The HISTORY OF THE PATRIARCHS offers pious details about two movements that filled the reign of Maximus. The first concerns the heresy of Paul of Samosata, and the second is the emergence of MANICHAEISM and the life of Mani, whose preaching struck roots in Egypt in the third century and survived in the fourth alongside Gnostic teachings. Mani's life (216–276 or 277) overlapped with Maximus' episcopate. This explains the space given to the development of his syncretistic religion under the biography of Maximus in the *History of the Patriarchs*. We need not enter here into the intricacies of Mani's thought. But it looks as if in the period of his exile from Persia for thirty years by Sapor I, he must have spent some time in Palestine preaching his religion and adapting elements of it to Christian doctrines. The *History of the Patriarchs* gives an account of Mani's encounter in a Palestinian city with a certain Bishop Archelaus, who refuted his arguments. Nevertheless, Mani's teachings seem to have spread to Egypt, where they survived until the complete eradication of Manichaeism from that country in the fourth century.

On the whole, the episcopate of Maximus was preeminently devoted to ministrations to the faithful and to combating heretical movements, in an atmosphere of relative peace from active persecution because the empire was involved in strife between rival claimants to the imperial throne and in fighting pestilence. Local unrest and political separatism in Alexandria kept pagan minds from acting on their traditional hostility toward their Christian neighbors.

Maximus died on 14 Baramūdah, the day of his commemoration in the Coptic SYNAXARION.

BIBLIOGRAPHY

Altaner, B. *Patrology*, Eng. trans. Hilda Graef. London, 1958.

Bardenhewer, O. *Geschichte der altkirchlichen Literatur*, 3 vols. Freiburg, 1902–1912.

Duchesne, L. *Early History of the Christian Church*, Vol. 1, pp. 341ff. London, 1909.

Quasten, J. *Patrology*, 3 vols. Utrecht and Antwerp, 1975.

AZIZ S. ATIYA

MAXIMUS THE CONFESSOR, a Byzantine monk who fought against monothelitism; he died in 662. At least three of his works were translated into Arabic in the high Middle Ages: the 400 *Chapters on Charity* (*Clavis Patrologia Graeca*, 7693), the 200 *Theological and Ecumenical Chapters* (*Clavis Patrologia Graeca*, 7694), and his discussion with Pyrrhus (*Clavis Patrologia Graeca*, 7698), translated by 'Abdallāh ibn al-Faḍl al-Anṭākī in the first half of the eleventh century. Other works of his probably exist in Arabic in the Sinai collection or elsewhere (Graf, 1944, Vol. 1, p. 372, no. 3).

Probably because of his theological attitude, Maximus was not very widely read among the Copts.

Al-Mu'taman ibn al-'Assāl does not mention him in the bibliography he inserted into the first chapter of his *Summa Theologiae,* composed around 1265, nor does Abū al-Barakāt IBN KABAR in Chapter 7 of his *Lamp of Darkness,* completed around 1320.

Nevertheless, a Coptic Arabic manuscript dated 21 Kiyahk A.M. 1008/17 December A.D. 1291 contains the 200 *Theological and Ecumenical Chapters* (PG 90, cols. 1084–1176; *Clavis Patrologia Graeca,* 7694). This is at the Coptic Patriarchate, Cairo (*Theology 245,* Graf, no. 398, Simaykah, no. 451, fols. 76b–98b). However, the manuscript is incomplete, containing only eighty-two chapters according to Graf, or all 100 according to Simaykah, from the first hundred; and forty-three according to Graf, or fifty-two according to Simaykah, from the second hundred. The name of the translator, most probably a Melchite, is not given.

BIBLIOGRAPHY

Graf, G. *Catalogue de manuscrits arabes chrétiens conservés au Caire.* Vatican City, 1934.

KHALIL SAMIR, S.J.

MAXIMUS AND DOMITIUS, SAINTS.

[*The entry on these two brothers consists of two parts: the* Coptic Tradition *and the* Arabic Tradition.]

Coptic Tradition

The Life of the brothers Maximus and Domitius is known through one long document attributed to a certain PSHOI OF SCETIS, who professes to be a native of Constantinople and who ended his days at Scetis as a disciple of the great MACARIUS (d. c. A.D. 390). He claims to have received the personal testimony of Macarius. In fact, the most recent person quoted in this document is Theodosius the Younger, who began to reign in 408.

Pshoi's long account is not the oldest life of Maximus and Domitius. In fact, he quotes—using the formal epithet "it is written that"—an apothegm of Saint Macarius (no. 33 in the Greek nominal collections and in the Old Latin translation). The episode tells anonymously how Saint Macarius received two young "Romans" (i.e., Greeks) in the desert of Scetis, and how that was the occasion of the founding of a monastery. In a shorter form, the episode is also inserted in the Life of Saint Macarius of Scetis (Bibliotheca Hagiographica Orientalis 573, ed. Amélineau, 1894, p. 87) attributed to SERAPION OF TMUIS (d. c. 362). As nothing precise is known about Pshoi, who authored the Life of the two brothers, only internal criteria allow one to estimate the date of composition of the Life. Nobody has cast doubt on the reality of the foundation of the DAYR AL-BARAMŪS (or pa-Rhomaios, that of the Romans) by the two brothers received by Macarius, but their names appear only in Pshoi's Life.

Pshoi's account has come down in two different forms in Coptic. The more important is a Sahidic version translated and published in 1917 by H. Munier (Pierpont Morgan Library, codex 40, tenth or eleventh century). Unfortunately, the text lacks a beginning. About ten leaves dealing with the youthful years of the saints are missing from the beginning of the Life. Details of the beginning can be found only in the second document, a Bohairic *Life* (Vatican Library, Coptic manuscript 67, fols. 34–58, published by E. Amélineau, 1894). Comparison of the second part of the two *Lives* in the two versions shows that the Sahidic redaction is more complete and more precise. Through accident or negligence, many details have been omitted in the Bohairic version, which, when it adds something is specific and modernized. One example is the camel driver of Djebro Menesine, who is mentioned in the Sahidic version; the Bohairic versions adds "from the diocese of Arbat" or 'Arwat.

The legend may be summarized as follows. Under Valentine, son of Jovian (363–364), religious peace reigned. Maximus and Domitius, the sons of Valentine, the new Constantine, receive a perfect education in asceticism and mysticism and seek to become monks. They first go to NICAEA, the place of the 318 fathers, where they meet the holy priest John. The latter cannot receive them, but recommends them to Agabos of Tarsus, a Syrian anchorite. Agabos cannot accept them either, but in a dream he sees Saint Macarius of Scetis, who will receive the two youths. There follows a series of miracles occurring in different towns. In Askalon, Saint Macarius delivers a man possessed, as he approaches the dwelling of the holy brothers; at Iconium a greedy dragon is immobilized and neutralized by the prayer of the miracle workers; at Lystra a leper is cured; at Pisidian Magdala a man with an inverted face is put straight. Pshoi informs us that he has his information from merchants met earlier in Constantinople (no doubt it has to do with the miracle worked by COSMAS AND DAMIAN on the person of Carinus; even the names of these two thaumaturges are not too remote from those of the two brothers). At Gabala, a certain Zachariah performs miracles through the power of the devil. He is exorcised by an order written by Maximus in the name of Macarius. From this point, the Sahidic account allows us to recover the story whose beginning is lost of a Laodicean woman who appears to have killed her illegitimate child; at Seleucia in Isauria a concubinary priest, suffering from cancer of the stomach, is healed in the name of Agabos and Macarius; in Athens Skeptic philosophers, simulating illnesses, are stricken with the very maladies that they had imitated, and are then cured by Domitius (this miracle and that of the dragon are found particularly in the work of Gregory Thaumaturgus).

But after some time, Valentine finds the youths with the help of sailors from Antioch who had called on the protection of the saints by putting their names on their ship's sails. However, the emperor consents to leave them in their own way of life. From this moment, the text speaks of the "Egyptian" origin of Theodosius the Great (379–395), chosen by Valentine before his death. The Sahidic version contains the comment "Let no Arian sit on the throne of our fathers" (p. 125). The generals Sergius and Anastasius are given the responsibility for ensuring the succession against a rival, "a friend of Julian [the Apostate]." Theodosius affirms the doctrine of Nicaea and assures its transmission through Honorius, Arcadius (395–408), and Theodosius the Younger (408–450). The critical moment for the two saints comes when the archbishop of Constantinople dies; only the Bohairic text calls him John. With a delegation of one *magistrianos* escorted by twenty five soldiers, Theodosius seeks out Maximus to establish him in the see of the capital. However, their mother warns them and urges them to flee. The saints then start on a long and exhausting march, incognito and tortured by the heat of the sun and by thirst. They are saved at the moment of death by an angel who leads them to Scetis. They are at once welcomed by Macarius. They heal the camel of a faithful servant, whose eye has been mutilated by wicked men. At the moment of his death Maximus relates particularly that he can see the apostle Paul telling the emperor Constantine to give him the book of Nicaea. Maximus dies on 14 Ṭūbah/9 January and Domitius on 17 Ṭūbah/12 January, both martyrs "without the sword."

This Life almost organizes all the hagiographic stereotypes. It is, however, difficult to imagine its composition after the exile of Nestorius. The character of Valentine was undoubtedly Valentinian I (d. 375), called to succeed Jovian on 25 February 364 at Nicaea. Potentially, what is in the mind and the aim of the hagiographer was that Maximus and Domitius were the half-brothers of Valentinian II, the friend of Ambrosius, a pious and ascetic young man, proclaimed Augustus at the age of four in 375 and assassinated in 392 at the age of twenty-one. His intense religious life is a fact of history. The potential rival of Theodosius was evidently the brother of Valentinian I, Valens (28 March 364 at Constantinople to 9 August 378), whose legitimacy Pshoi absolutely denies. Indeed, already toward 371, there were intrigues aimed at making Theodosius emperor. In 380 there was a Maximus in the see of Constantinople for some months after GREGORY OF NAZIANZUS. Pshoi's thesis is clear: The eastern part of the empire, subject to the Arian Valens, is saved by the thaumaturgical spirit of Macarius acting through the legitimate heirs of Valentinian I. One can scarcely prove that the existence of this Pshoi of Constantinople is pure fiction nor can one discount his appreciation of each miracle and each hagiographic theme.

BIBLIOGRAPHY

Amélineau, E. *Histoire des monastères de Basse-Egypte.* Annales du Musée Guimet 25, pp. 262–313. Paris, 1894.

Munier, H. "Une Relation copte sahidique de la vie des saints Maxime et Domèce." *Bulletin de l'Institut français d'Archéologie orientale* 13 (1917):93–140.

MICHEL VAN ESBROECK

Arabic Tradition

The Arabic synaxarion of Mīkhā'īl of Malīj assigns 17 Ṭūbah as the commemoration of the brothers Maximus and Domitius, sons of the Emperor Lāuntiyūs and disciples of the great Saint Macarius of Scetis. This has nothing to do with the Emperor Leo I as one would be tempted to think since Valentinus has been altered to Lāuntiyūs in Arabic. All the extant texts seem to depend on the Coptic Life by Pshoi. G. Graf (1944) has compiled a list of manuscript witnesses. An Arabic manuscript of 1332 (Sin. Ar. 530, fols. 300r–52r) has also changed Jovian into Būqiyūs (fol. 302r), while a thirteenth-century manuscript (Sin. Ar. 475, fols. 222v–76v), which is mutilated toward the end of the account, alters Jovian to Nūfītus (fol. 227) and begins the evolution of the name Domitius through Dumadā'us toward Timothy, which is found in more recent documents. Another manuscript (Sin. Ar. 530) changes the date of death to 17 Kanūn I, a Syrian date. And, in fact, Baumstark (1922) points to a series of eleventh- and twelfth-century manuscripts that preserve the legend in Syriac (British Museum, Add. 14655, Add. 17262 and 14735, fols. 72–173; a Syriac résumé was published from the Paris manuscript Syr. 234 by F. Nau, 1910, pp. 752–66). This résumé, too, is still dependent on Pshoi's legend. Some details are missing, even in the Sahidic version. Thus the name of Valentine is sometimes correctly Valentianus, closer to Valentinian. The date of the 12 Kanūn I is again Syrian and is also to be found in some Syriac calendars. There is an Arabic Garshūnī translation of this Syriac Life (Saint Mark of Jerusalem manuscript 4; see Graf, 1944). Graf also points to a collection of miracles, interrupted at the 27th (Cambridge Add. manuscript 3214, fols. 94–165). One of the miracles described by Nau is not represented in Coptic: that of a sick and dead calf restored to its mother.

BIBLIOGRAPHY

Baumstark, A. *Geschichte der syrischen Literatur*, p. 293, n. 12. Bonn, 1922.

Nau, F. *Les Légendes syriaques d'Aaron de Saroug, de Maxime et Domèce, d'Abraham maître de Barsoma, et de l'empereur Maurice*, PO 5. Paris, 1910.

MICHEL VAN ESBROECK

MEDICAL INSTRUMENTS AND KIT. *See* Medicine, Coptic.

MEDICINE, COPTIC. The first evidence for Coptic medicine comes from Pachomius in the first half of the fourth century (Lefort, 1933, 87ff.). All other Coptic texts dealing with medicine are preserved in copies that date from the fifth to the twelfth centuries. From the mid-nineteenth century on, Coptic medicine, evidence for which is available in a number of brief works dealing with diseases attested in the Coptic language, has been studied scientifically. The extant material in this area, however, is still so incomplete that a classification corresponding to that of Old Egyptian medicine has not been possible. The Coptic-Arab period is not included in this discussion.

Chronological Table of Ostraca and Papyri Dealing with Medicine

WM (Worrell, 1935): eight leaves of parchment — c. 5/6 cent.

Page No.	Lines	Page No.	Lines
WM 1 19	34–38	16 27	207–210
2 19	38–40	17 27	210–212
3 20	53–55	18 27	212–220
4 20	56–59	19 27	221–240
5 23	133–160	20 188	a 1–10
6 24	161–178	21 188	a 11–b5
7 25	176–182	22 188	b 6–12
8 25	183–186	23 188	b 13–22
9 26	186–193	24 188	b 23–26
10 26	194–195	25 189	a 1–20
11 26	195–198	26 190	a 21–b15
12 26	198–200	27 189	b 16–25
13 26	200–202	28 193	10–14
14 26	203–205	29 193	15–18
15 27	205–207		

KW (Till, 1949): papyrus	c. 7/8 cent.
CO (Crum, 1902): ostraca	c. 7/8 cent.
Ep (*Metropolitan Museum of Art*, 1926): ostraca	c. 7/8 cent.
Hall (Hall, 1905): ostraca	c. 7/8 cent.
Saq (*Excavations at Saqqara*, 1909): leaves of parchment	c. 7/8 cent.
ZB (Zoega, 1903): leaves of parchment	c. 8/9 cent.
BA (Bouriant, 1888): leaf of parchment	c. 9 cent.
Ryl (Crum. 1909): leaves of parchment	c. 9 cent.
Ch (Chassinat, 1921): large papyrus	c. 9/10 cent.
BKU (*Ägyptische Urkunden*, 1904): Coptic documents	c. 996–1020
MK (Munier, 1918): paper	c. 11/12 cent.
TM (Turaev, 1902): paper	c. 11/12 cent.

Primary Literature in Monastic Libraries

In monastic libraries we find evidence of first aid for the brothers, guests, and refugees: "Prescription book, simply named" (Bouriant, 1889), and other prescription books that show a great number of pages (Zoega, 1903, pp. 626–30). Skin diseases are mentioned, together with the prescriptions necessary for them. Impetigo and itching ailments are named and the following treatment recommended: swabbing with warm vinegar, attar of roses and water, or the juice of a sea leek (aloe) mixed with the contents of a melon (ZB 8 [for abbreviations see the chronological table below]). Another prescription called for the use of canine excreta, which was smeared on a bandage and applied to the psora scabs; guarantees were given that no irritation would ensue from such treatment (ZB 18). Leprosy (Kolta, 1982, pp. 58–63), efflorescence, and diseases of the liver (including jaundice) and of the kidneys are also mentioned in this book of prescriptions (ZB 28). Diseases in all parts of the body, including the genitals, are listed. Thus, for example, a prescription for treating pain in the breasts or the penis or the testicles recommends the application of breast milk to the affected part of the body. Fat or attar of roses also could be used (BA 3).

Literature of the Fifth and Sixth Centuries, Upper Egypt

A Coptic text on parchment from the fifth or sixth century was written by or for practicing doctors and dealt with various ailments: for instance, diseases of the spleen (WM 1, WM 29), and constipation, for which purgatives are recommended (WM 15, WM 25). This text also deals with illnesses of women and children, for instance, a painful uterine complaint (WM 6) and a prescription to treat the pain of a teething baby (WM 3). For adult toothache, it was recommended to rinse the mouth with warm asses' milk (WM 13).

A few prescriptions took into consideration the treatment of wounds, for example, stanching of blood and relief of hemorrhages (WM 21, WM 23). Consideration was given to domestic hygiene in connection with elimination of vermin from houses (WM 7). In addition to the medical prescriptions from the Coptic material in the Vienna collection, which contains prescriptions for "palpitations" and sleeplessness (Till, 1949, pp. 43–49), there are references to *podagra* (gout), sleeplessness, palpitations, and also hemoptysis (*Ägyptische Urkunden*, 1904, pp. 24–31).

The Ninth and Tenth Centuries: Chassinat Papyrus

A collection of 237 prescriptions from the ninth–tenth centuries, published in 1921 by Emil Chassinat, contains unsystematically recorded prescriptions for various diseases but predominantly eye diseases, which have been the plague of Egypt for centuries. Among those mentioned are cataracts, shortsightedness, film on the eye (Till, 1951, p. 17, D.17), inflammation, abscesses, trichiasis, and cicatrized eyelids resulting from trachoma (Kolta, 1978,

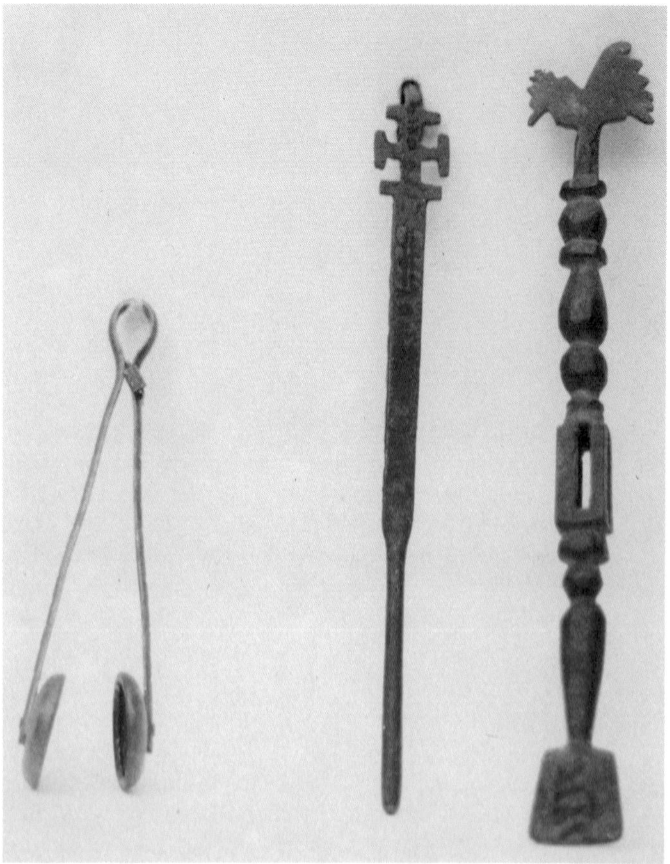

Medical Instruments. Fifth–seventh century. Left to right: forceps, dilator for urethra, chisel for bone surgery. *Courtesy Coptic Museum, Cairo.*

pp. 41–50). A number of prescriptions refer to tooth complaints (e.g., teeth with sore gums (CH 153), various stomach ailments, and even flatulence or attacks of worms, the recommended treatment for which consisted of powdered lettuce seeds in warm water (CH 11) in order to expel the worms. While Old Egyptian medicine (e.g., the Ebers papyrus and the Kahun papyrus) was concerned with medicine for women, the Chassinat papyrus contains only four prescriptions (CH 24, CH 123–25) for women who suffer from a painful or tight uterus (Till, 1951, p. 27). Children's medicine is rarely mentioned (CH 38, CH 230, CH 231).

Although diagnoses and clinical descriptions are not recorded in the Coptic literature, there are allusions to the wider sphere of Coptic medicine that included injuries and diseases of the various organs —head, brain, temples, eyes, ears, mouth, teeth, breasts, stomach, bowels, liver, kidneys, spleen, sexual organs, and skin—as well as pains in the extremities.

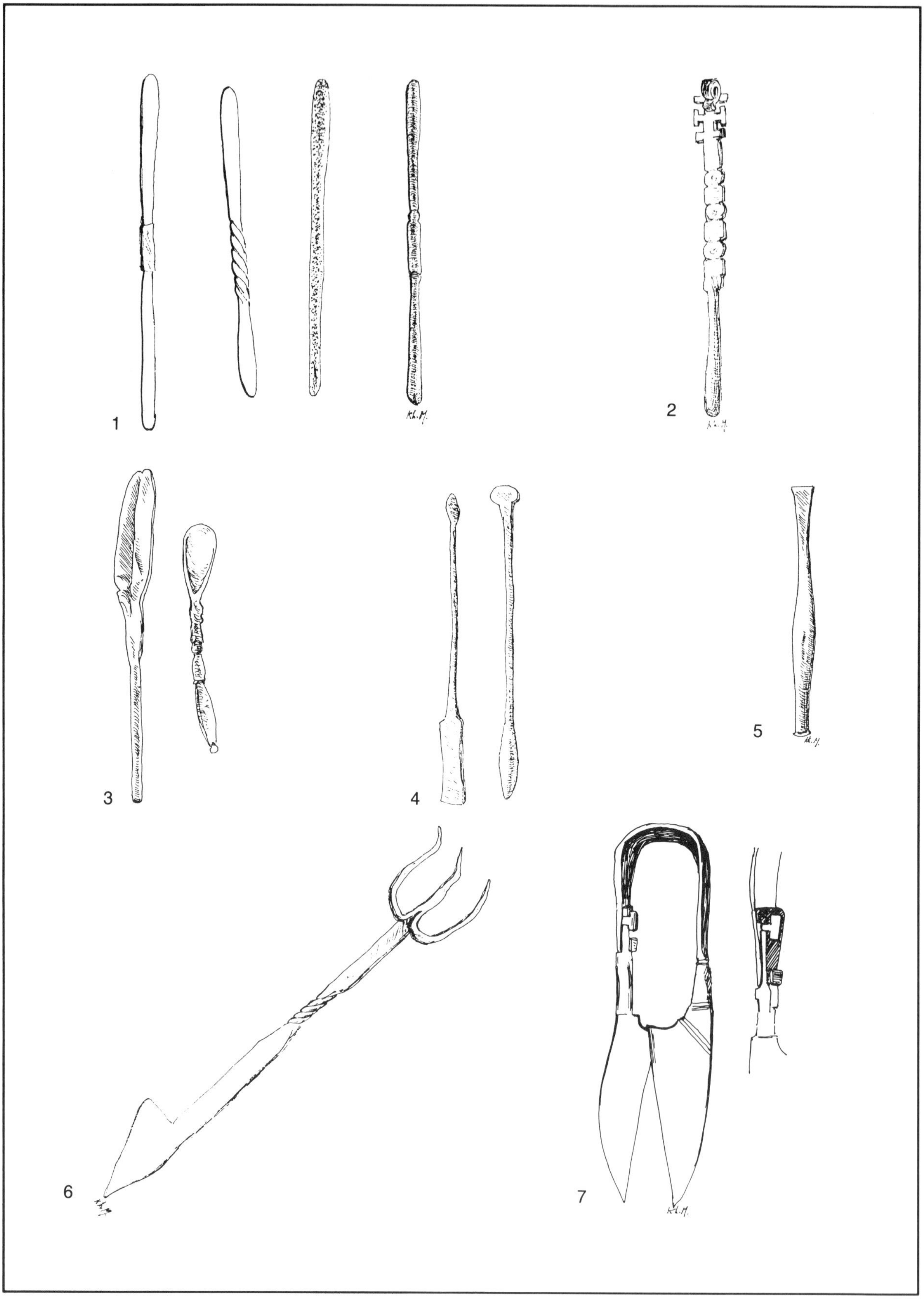
1
2
3
4
5
6
7

One prescription lists all the diseases of the head, the temples, and the brain that cause pain (Crum, 1909, no. 107). Another prescribes opium, milk, and calf's fat, which should be warmed and placed, a drop at a time, into the painful ear (CH 114). A patient with a toothache ought to rinse the mouth with a small amount of warm asses' milk (WM 13). Weak or painful breasts should be smeared with breast milk (BA 3) or rubbed with a mixture of starch, pig fat, and attar of roses (BA 4).

One text records the diseases of the swollen stomach, which emits black bile, leaving it sore (CH 70). Diseases of the sexual organs are also mentioned. The penis and the testicles can be infected with disease (BA 3). Problems with the uterus are described as follows: it can hurt and also can be tight (CH 125).

In addition to descriptions of pains in the extremities—the hand, the foot, or the knee—a number of Coptic medicinal texts found here (as in the finds from the monastic library) deal with skin complaints—for instance, psora scabies of various kinds: the prurient (CH 127 and ZB 13), the wild (ZB 16), and the water psora (ZB 14). The papules are also described in great detail (CH 163), and prurigo is mentioned (ZB 29). There are also prurigo blisters (CH 219, ZB 27). Till thinks these refer to shingles (Till, 1951, p. 32, Q 23).

Leprosy was recognized in the Coptic period. A prescription names a medicine for "all diseases of leprosy" (ZB 28). A mummy dating back to the sixth century has extremities that show signs of *lepra mutilans* (Kolta, 1982, pp. 58–63). In direct contrast with Old Egyptian medicine, surgical operations and surgical instruments are described only to a very limited extent. The sole mention of an instrument is in circumcision or the pulling of a tooth by means of a pair of tongs or an iron instrument (CH 151).

Among psychic disorders only sleeplessness (BKU 2) and possession are referred to (BKU 8 and 12). Therapeutic measures are given for ophthalmological and skin complaints, as well as the treatment of open wounds. Ointments, powders, plasters, baths, eye drops, tablets, and fumigations were prescribed.

Medical Profession and Nursing

The hierarchy of Coptic doctors was not as clearly demarcated as among the ancient Egyptians, and there were no specialists for particular diseases. Occasionally fields of activity are given; for instance, doctor and chiropractor (Coptic MSS in the Bodleian Library, P 32), as well as veterinarian ("doctor for horses"; Crum, 1939, p. 342b). There were "teaching doctors" or "masters" as well as "medical practitioners," and uppermost in the medical hierarchy was the "senior physician." That there were doctors of both sexes is made clear by one text that mentions a woman doctor who performed her rounds in the monastic communities (Leipoldt, 1908–1913, vol. 4, 161, 6). Such descriptions of attendance on patients in the monastery furnish us with the evidence we have for the fourth–fifth centuries, the precursors of hospitals. The monastic rules of Pachomius provide an insight into the nursing duties, especially as they affected the conduct of patients: (1) it was customary for the patient to lie down on a bed; (2) no one was allowed to oil a patient or to bathe him without explicit permission; (3) when a brother suffered an injury and did not go to bed, but wandered about looking for a hospital garment or some oil, the hospital manager had to go to the place of the community (a sort of dispensary) and fetch what was necessary.

A report by Apa Shenute on the siege of the present-day city of QŪṢ in Upper Egypt describes the nursing practice in the White Monastery in the middle of the fifth century (Leipoldt, 1908–1913, Vol. 3, p. 69).

The medical literature of the ancient Egyptians and of the Copts was transmitted anonymously.

Surgical instruments are displayed by the Coptic Museum but their provenance is not known. They are made of bronze. They consist of the following items:
1. *Cauteries.* These are differently shaped. They were used to remove malignant tumors, hemorrhoids, hydrocele hernia, warts, etc. **2.** *Cautery* with crosses on its handles. **3.** *Spoons*, used to put powdered medicines, sometimes caustic, in deep wounds, in fistulas, on the uvula and tonsils, and on inflammed organs such as piles. **4.** *Curettes*, used to clean large, infected wounds in soft tissue or bone, or to prepare it for the application of medicines. **5.** *Chisels or levers*, used in bone surgery, maybe to remove small pieces of fractured bones, or as a lever during the extraction of carious teeth. **6.** *Hook and knife*, an interesting tool with no parallel in ancient Egyptian or modern surgical tools. The knife was to cut the dead fetus, and the hook extracted the cut parts. It dates back to the seventh or eighth century A.D. **7.** *Spring scissors* with lock to trim large wounds before suturing and to cut lint bandages. *Courtesy Khahlil Messiha.*

Medical texts are found on leaves of parchment, on ostraca, and on monastery walls (Thompson in Quibell, *Excavations at Saqqara,* Vol. 3, 1909, p. 57, no. 103). In recent times it has been established that the medical literature of the ancient Egyptians did not come to an abrupt end, but resurfaced in a number of instructions in the collection of prescriptions in the Coptic language. This has been recognized in the work of Sigerist (1963, p. 329) and Grapow (see Deines, Grapow, and Westendorf, Vol. 2, 5, n. 3).

BIBLIOGRAPHY

Ägyptische Urkunden aus den Königlichen Museen zu Berlin. Koptische Urkunden, Vol. 1. Berlin, 1904.

Bouriant, U. "Fragment d'un livre de médecin en copte thébain." *Académie des inscriptions et belles-lettres, Comptes rendus 1887,* ser. 4, 15 (1888):319–20, 374–79.

______. Notes de voyage." *Recueil de travaux 11* (1889):135.

Chassinat, E. *Un papyrus medical copte.* Mémoires Publiés par les Membres de l'Institut français d'Archéologie orientale du Caire 32. Cairo, 1921.

Crum, W. E. *Coptic Ostraca from the Collections of the Egypt Exploration Fund, the Cairo Museum and Others.* Oxford, 1902.

______. *Catalogue of the Coptic Manuscripts in the Collection of the John Rylands Library Manchester.* Manchester, 1909.

______. *A Coptic Dictionary.* Oxford, 1939.

Deines, H. von; H. Grapow; and W. Westendorf, eds. *Grundriss der Medizin der alten Ägypter,* 9 vols. Berlin, 1954–1973.

Excavations at Saqqara (1907–1908), Vol. 3, *The Coptic Inscriptions,* ed. H. Thompson. Cairo, 1909.

Hall, H. R. *Coptic and Greek Texts of the Christian Period from Ostraka, Stelae, etc. in the British Museum.* London, 1905.

Ḥasan Kamāl. *Ap-Ṭibb al-Misrī al-Qadīm,* 4 vols. in 2, 2nd ed., Cairo, 1964.

Kolta, K. S. "Zur Geschichte der Diagnose der altägyptischen Augenkrankheit 'Trachom.'" In *Medizinische Diagnostik in Geschichte und Gegenwart, Festschrift für Heinz Goerke,* ed. C. Habrich, F. Marguth, and J. H. Wolf. Munich, 1978.

______. "Die Lepra im alten Ägypten in der koptischen Zeit." In *Aussatz-Lepra-Hansen-Krankheit. Ein Menschheitsproblem im Wandel. Katalog der Ausstellung im Deutschen Museum,* pp. 58–63. Munich, 1982.

______. "Neue Ergebnisse zur Medizin der Kopten." *Sudhoffs Archiv* 68 (1984):157–72. Discusses recent developments in the investigation of Coptic medicine.

Lefort, L. T. *Pachomii vitae sahidice scriptae.* Paris, 1933.

Leipoldt, J. *Sinuthii Opera,* Vols. 3–4. Paris and Leipzig, 1908–1913.

The Metropolitan Museum of Art Egyptian Expedition. The Monastery of Epiphanius at Thebes, Pt. 2, *Coptic Ostraca and Papyri,* ed. W. E. Crum. New York, 1926.

Munier, H. "Deux recettes médicales coptes." *Annales du Service des antiquités* 18 (1918):284–86. These texts have been reedited in E. Chassinat, "Deux formules pharmaceutiques coptes." *Bulletin de l'Institut français d'archéologie orientale* 49 (1949):9–22.

Quibell, J. E. *Excavations at Saqqara (1905–6), (1906–7), (1907–8), (1908–9, 1909–10).* 4 vols. Cairo, 1907–13. The Coptic inscriptions ed. Sir Herbert Thompson.

Sigerist, H. *Anfänge der Medizin.* Zurich, 1963.

Till, W. C. "Koptische Rezepte." *Bulletin de la Société d'archéologie copte* 12 (1949):43–55.

______. *Die Arzneikunde der Kopten.* Berlin, 1951.

Turaev, B. A. *Materialy po archeologii christianskavo Egipta. Otdel'nyj ottisk iz t. 2. Trudow Kiewskavo Sezda,* no. 9. Moscow, 1902. Reedited by W. Till in *Bulletin de la Société d'archéologie copte* 12 (1949):49–54.

Worrell, W. H. "Coptic Magical and Medical texts." *Orientalia* 4 (1935):1–37, 184–94.

Zoega, G. *Catalogus codicorum manuscriptorum, qui in Museo Borgiano Velitris adservantur.* Leipzig, 1903. Reprint of 1810 edition.

KAMAL SABRI KOLTA

MEIR, village close to Ṣanabū in the Libyan mountains and site of the necropolis of the ancient capital of the nome, Kousit (today the village of al-Quṣiyyah). The tombs of the Sixth Dynasty were fitted up to serve as dwellings by Christian hermits, and in particular those of Senbi and Oukhotep preserve traces of monastic occupation.

On the outside in the façade with portico and columns, the hermits raised a wall of unbaked bricks in such a way as to form chambers. On the inside, the columns were cut away to enlarge the free space. Niches and apses were hollowed into the walls, the sculptures were mutilated, and the paintings were covered with plaster. The Greek and Coptic inscriptions have been published, the former by G. Lefebvre (1911, p. 248), the latter by J. Clédat (1901, pp. 87ff.).

The plans of these tombs are found in Blackman (1915) and in Badawy (1953, pp. 67–89). An up-to-date description of these hypogea is given by Meinardus (1st ed., 1965, p. 271; 2d ed., 1977, p. 377).

BIBLIOGRAPHY

Badawy, A. *Les Premiers établissements chrétiens dans les anciennes tombes d'Egypte.* Tome commémoratif du millénaire de la Bibliothèque patriarchale d'Alexandrie), pp. 69–89. Alexandria, 1953.

Blackman, A. M. *The Rock Tombs of Meir.* London, 1915.

Clédat, J. "Notes archéologiques et philologiques." *Bulletin de l'Institut français d'archéologie orientale* 1 (1901):87–97; 2 (1902):41–70.

Lefebvre, G. "Egypte chrétienne 4." *Annales du Service des Antiquités de l'Egypte* 11 (1911):238–50.

Meinardus, O. *Christian Egypt, Ancient and Modern.* Cairo, 1965; 2nd ed., Cairo, 1977.

René-Georges Coquin
Maurice Martin, S.J.

MELCHITES AND COPTS.

MELCHITES AND COPTS. Melchites (almost all Greeks) and Copts (native Egyptians) lived in relative tolerance until the Council of CHALCEDON (451), when Rome and Constantinople, under the cloak of theological problems, inflicted the first sharp defeat sustained by the Copts in the ecumenical field. The humiliation, deposition, and exile of the native Egyptian DIOSCORUS I (444–458), pope of Alexandria, were immediately followed by the installation of a Greek as successor on the patriarchal throne of Saint Mark. Proterius (452–457) revealed himself as a docile friend of Byzantine imperialism. The Egyptian Christians elected a native rival, TIMOTHY II AELURUS (458–480). Consequently, the hitherto united see of Saint Mark was split between two lines of patriarchal succession: the Coptic and the Greek, later called Melchite (or royalist), which originated from Constantinople while obeying Chalcedon. The split in the patriarchal see of Alexandria was consummated from the juridical point of view but not dogmatically, in spite of the appearances. Even up to the present the normal liturgy of the Coptic church is the Liturgy of Saint Basil. The Copts remained devoted to the national cause of the Egyptian people, while repudiating Byzantine-Melchite hegemony. The Melchites involuntarily developed within the emerging Egyptian nationalism as it became stronger. Thanks to a stubborn fidelity to Cyrillian Christology, the Coptic church stood firmly within the pre-Chalcedonian Christological orthodoxy.

BIBLIOGRAPHY

Atiya, A. S. *A History of Eastern Christianity.* London, 1968.

Heiler, F. *Die Ostkirchen.* Basel, 1971.

Karalevsky, K. P. *Histoire des patriarcats melkites (Alexandrie, Antioche, Jérusalem) depuis le schisme monophysite du sixième siècle jusqu' à nos jours,* Vol. 2, fasc. 1; Vol. 3, fasc. 1–2. Rome, 1909–1911.

Martiniano P. Roncaglia

MELCHIZEDEK,

MELCHIZEDEK, a priest in the Old Testament and various other Jewish, Christian, and Gnostic sources, who is sometimes regarded as a prefigure of Christ. A fragmentary codex in the NAG HAMMADI LIBRARY (IX. 1–27.10) is given the title *Melchizedek,* which suggests that the supposed author is none other than the biblical figure. This tractate may be described as a Gnostic apocalypse, or book of revelation, and in fact its contents are designated as "these revelations" (27. 3–4). In addition to the title itself, the opening words of the tractate refer to "Jesus Christ, the Son [of God]" (1. 2–3) and establish the text as unmistakably Christian.

Typical of apocalyptic literature, revelations predominate in *Melchizedek.* Initially an interpreting angel, probably Gamaliel, informs Melchizedek of Gnostic truths having to do with the salvation of "the congregation of [the children of] Seth" (IX. 5. 19–20). Most remarkable in this revelation is the polemical passage directed against those Docetists who deny the reality of the incarnation, death, and resurrection of Jesus: "They will say of him that he is unbegotten although he has been begotten, he doesn't eat even though he does eat, he doesn't drink even though he does drink, he is uncircumcised although he has been circumcised, he is unfleshly although he did come in flesh, he didn't come into suffering [although] he did come into suffering, he didn't rise from the dead [although] he did rise from the dead" (IX. 5. 2–10). This first revelation comes to a close with the angel warning

Melchizedek not to disclose the secrets to the profane.

In the next section of the tractate Melchizedek in the first person singular responds to the revelation by participating in prayer, baptism, and liturgical praise and confession. Then another major revelation is recounted from approximately folio 19 to the end of the tractate. Unfortunately, little remains of the text of these last pages. Several heavenly messengers seem to communicate knowledge to Melchizedek and exhort him to be strong. Finally after another warning to keep these "unfleshly revelations" from fleshly persons, the text concludes with the angelic "brothers" ascending back to heaven.

The person of Melchizedek is portrayed in the tractate as the ancient hero, "the priest of God Most High" (IX. 12. 10–11; IX. 15. 9–10; IX. 19. 14–15; cf. Gn. 14:18). Furthermore, in Jewish apocalyptic literature (cf. 11 *Q Melch*) this priestly figure has a future eschatological role as well and may function as a holy warrior and heavenly commander. In the Coptic tractate Melchizedek is not only a heavenly warrior but is also identified with Jesus Christ, as he is in the New Testament Letter to the Hebrews. Thus Melchizedek, like Christ, struggles through suffering and death against his enemies and ultimately prevails over them and destroys them (IX. 26. 2ff.).

BIBLIOGRAPHY

Facsimile Edition of the Nag Hammadi Codices: Codices IX and X. Leiden, 1977.

Pearson, B. A. "The Figure of Melchizedek in the First Tractate of the Unpublished Coptic-Gnostic Codex IX from Nag Hammadi." In *Proceedings of the XIIth International Congress of the International Association for the History of Religions,* ed. C. J. Bleeker, et al., pp. 200–208. Leiden, 1975.

———. ed. "IX,1: Melchizedek." In *Nag Hammadi Codices IX and X.* Nag Hammadi Studies 15. Leiden, 1980.

Pearson, B. A., and S. Giversen. "Melchizedek (IX, 1)." In *The Nag Hammadi Library in English.* Leiden and San Francisco, 1977.

MARVIN W. MEYER

MELISMA. *See* Music, Coptic: Description.

MELITIAN SCHISM, begun when MELITIUS (or Meletius), bishop of Lycopolis (modern Asyūṭ) in Upper Egypt, objected to the terms set by PETER I of Alexandria for the readmission of lapsed Christians. Melitius began to ordain supporters of his stricter policy, and they constituted the core of the movement. Persecution continued and Melitius was exiled. Upon his return from exile (after A.D. 311), he began to organize a schismatic church.

ACHILLAS and then ALEXANDER I, successors of Peter as bishop of Alexandria, apparently failed to reach agreement with the Melitian party. A serious attempt to heal the breach was made at the First Council of NICAEA (325). It was decided that clergy ordained by Melitius could retain their status; Melitian bishops, if properly elected, could succeed Catholic bishops when the sees became vacant; and Melitius would retain his title.

These measures of reconciliation were not sufficient, perhaps because ATHANASIUS I, who succeeded Alexander in 328, did not approve of them. From this point on, there are many references in the writings of Athanasius to the continued activity of the Melitians. They joined with the Arians in opposition to Athanasius, though it is unclear to what extent they supported the Arian theological position. In 332 they brought various accusations against Athanasius to the emperor; whatever the truth of specific charges, this action shows that the reconciliation planned at Nicaea was being undermined by both parties. Melitius was succeeded by John Arkaph (date unknown; probably between 325 and 332) as leader of the sect; the names of subsequent leaders are unknown. There is papyrological evidence for a thriving Melitian monasticism in the fourth century. The Melitian monks lived together in groups, but it is unclear whether they had structured cenobia (like the Pachomians) or semi-eremitic communities (like the monks of Nitria and Scetis). Scattered references indicate that the sect survived until the eighth century, but it seems gradually to have changed its character and purpose. It began as a movement in favor of strict discipline, later formed an alliance with the Arians, and, according to a reference in Theodoret (*Compendium* 4.7), still later developed distinctive forms of worship that included hand clapping and music.

The Melitian sect had some success with Coptic-speaking Christians. This is suggested by the Egyptian names of some of the Melitian bishops (see the list in Athanasius *Apologia contra Arianos* 71), by the papyri that mention Melitian issues, and by the references to the sect in the Coptic writings of the Pachomians and SHENUTE of Atrībe.

BIBLIOGRAPHY

Bell, H. I. *Jews and Christians in Egypt.* London, 1924; Westport, Conn., 1972. Contains the Melitian papyri and a brief history of the sect.

Hardy, E. R. *Christian Egypt: Church and People.* Oxford, 1952.

Kettler, F. H. "Der meletanische Streit in Ägypten." *Zeitschrift für die neutestamentliche Wissenschaft* 35 (1936):155–93. A modern work on the subject.

JANET TIMBIE

MELITIUS, fourth-century schismatic bishop of Lycopolis. Little is known about Melitius (also spelled Meletius), bishop of Lycopolis (ASYŪṬ) in Upper Egypt, until he became involved in a dispute with PETER I, bishop of Alexandria. DIOCLETIAN's persecution of Christians (beginning in 303) raised the question of how to treat lapsed Christians who wanted to rejoin the church. Melitius felt that Peter's treatment of the lapsed was too lenient. He began to ordain supporters of his views and was excommunicated in 306. A new outbreak of persecution led to Melitius' banishment to the mines and to the death of Peter I of Alexandria (311). When the persecution ended, Melitius returned from exile and continued to build his schismatic church, with considerable success. The matter was discussed at the First Council of NICAEA (325), where measures were agreed upon to bring the schismatics back into the church. Melitius was to retain his title as bishop. But these measures were ineffective, and at the time of Melitius' death (date unknown, but probably before 332) the Melitian movement was flourishing in Egypt.

BIBLIOGRAPHY

Coptic sources do not contain any information about Melitius. The many references in the works of Athanasius (particularly *Apology Against the Arians*) are the main patristic source. For modern work, see C. Vagaggini, "Melizio di Licopoli," in *Enciclopedia cattolica*, Vol. 8, cols. 640ff. (Vatican City, 1952), and E. R. Hardy, *Christian Egypt: Church and People* (Oxford, 1952).

JANET TIMBIE

MELITO OF SARDIS (d. c. 177). EUSEBIUS OF CAESAREA (*Ecclesiastical History* 5.24.2–6) has preserved for us a letter of about 190 of Polycrates of Ephesus, who praises the important Christians of Asia Minor who clung to the custom of celebrating Easter on the Jewish calendar day of 14 Nisan, rather than on the Sunday after the first spring moon. Among them, Polycrates mentions "Melito, the eunuch whose entire work is in the Holy Spirit, and who rests at Sardis, awaiting the visitor from heaven when he will rise from the dead." Melito composed an apologia intended for Marcus Aurelius between 169 and 177. Eusebius enumerates the titles of about fifteen other works by Melito, of which either only the titles are known or only some fragments exist that are difficult to connect with one of the titles mentioned by Eusebius.

One work has resurfaced. C. Bonner discovered, at the end of a fifth-century Greek papyrus codex in the Chester Beatty collection (partly at Michigan), the text of the *Peri Pascha.* He identified other texts in Greek, Syriac, and even Sahidic Coptic. He perceived, in fact, that homiletic fragment 17, a fifth-century Coptic papyrus leaf coming from the Danish excavations at Wādī Sarjah, corresponded to a passage in the *Peri Pascha.* This leaf still bears the page number 93 on the back. It was published by W. E. Crum and H. I. Bell (1922, p. 47). W. H. Willis announced in 1961 the discovery of a very old Coptic papyrus in the Crosby codex in the University of Mississippi Library, containing the second part of the homily of Melito (Willis, 1961, pp. 381–92). Its period would, however, be the fifth and sixth centuries (Hall, 1979, p. 7). H. Chadwick recognized a résumé of the same homily in Latin, under the names of Leon and Augustine (1960, pp. 76–82). Finally, M. Testuz published the Bodmer Papyrus 13 (1960). This time the codex is indeed from the third century. The homily on Easter thus rediscovered was probably composed about 164–166. J. N. Birdsall published the Georgian version, paragraphs 1–45, identified by M. Richard (1967, pp. 121–38). O. Perler made a synthesis of everything in *Sources chrétiennes* (1966). But there appeared, further, the second half of the Georgian homily, paragraphs 46–105, by M. van Esbroeck (1971, pp. 373–94).

Finally, Stuart G. Hall had access to all the witnesses, having been able to consult reproductions of the papyrus of Mississippi 1, still to be published. Hall, provided with the entire collection, published the Greek edition, taking account of the variants or interesting lessons of each manuscript. Paragraphs 11–16 are represented there by the initial C, which indicates the page from Wādī Sarjah, while the same initial designates the Mississippi text from paragraphs 49–105. Better agreement can quite often be recorded between the Bodmer papyrus and the Coptic version. This fact is calculated to stimulate the appreciation of literature that is restored only in Coptic. The text of the homily itself is on the borderline between theology, with the great figures of the fulfillment of the Old Testament Passover through Christ's passion, and a form of literature that occasionally touches on hymnography. This type of literature belongs to the second Greek Sophist movement. The antitheses and the balance of the members in the enumerations make the text highly concentrated.

BIBLIOGRAPHY

Birdsall, J. N. "Melito of Sardis ΠΕΡΙ ΤΟΥ ΠΑΣΧΑ in a Georgian Version." *Le Muséon* 80 (1967): 121–38.

Bonner, C. "A Coptic Fragment of Melito's Homily on the Passion." *Harvard Theological Review* 32 (1939):141–42.

Chadwick, H. "A Latin Epitome of Melito's Homily on the Pascha." *Journal of Theological Studies*, n.s., 11 (1960):76–82.

Crum, W. E., and H. I. Bell. *Wādī Sarjah*. Copenhagen, 1922.

Esbroeck, M. van. "Le Traité sur la Paque de Méliton de Sardes en Géorgien." *Le Muséon* 84 (1971):373–94.

Hall, S. G. *Melito of Sardis: On Pascha and Fragments*. London, 1979.

Perler, O. *Méliton de Sardes, Sur la Paque*. Sources chrétiennes 127. Paris, 1966.

Richard, M. "Rapport sur une mission d'étude au Grèce et à Chypre." *Bulletin de l'Institut d'histoire et de recherche de textes* 13 (1964–65):49–50.

Testuz, M. *Méliton de Sardes, Homélie sur la Pâque*. Geneva, 1960.

Willis, W. H. "The New Collection of Papyri at the University of Mississippi." *Proceedings of the IXth International Congress of Papyrology*, pp. 381–92. Oslo, 1961.

MICHEL VAN ESBROECK

MEMNONIA, name presumably derived from Memnon, roughly designating the area where, to this day, the majestic statues of Memnon's colossuses stand in the fields on the west bank of the Nile at Thebes. In other words, this is the village that arose from dynastic times around MADĪNAT HĀBŪ or the funerary temple of Ramses III, known to travelers from the seventeenth century who described its Coptic houses as narrow and rather high. These habitations were cleared by the Chicago Institute in its efforts to record the great temple inscriptions between 1927 and 1933.

The village bearing that name is identical with the Coptic Djeme and the Demotic Jama or Jamu. That village grew into numerous subsidiary suburbs strewn over the hills of the west bank from Madīnat Hābū to DAYR AL-MADĪNAH and Dayr al-Baḥrī. In fact, the growth of this village into an extensive township must have taken place after the decline of Thebes in Ptolemaic times during the first century B.C. and the transfer of Theban economic and industrial activity to Memnonia. During the early Christian centuries, its Coptic population grew and transformed the ancient monuments into Christian religious foundations. From the recorded inscriptions on papyri and ostraca found on the site, it transpires that a total of twenty-eight churches and monasteries must have existed within that region. Four of them were established inside the temples and can be identified, while most of the remaining foundations have completely disappeared.

BIBLIOGRAPHY

Bataille, A. *Memnonia*. Cairo, 1952.

Crum, W. E., and G. Steindorff. *Koptische Rechtsurkunden der achten Jahrhunderts von Djeme* (Theben). Leipzig, 1912.

Hölscher, U. *Medinet Habu Excavations*, 5 vols. Chicago, 1934–1954.

HISHMAT MESSIHA

MEMPHIS, the Greek name of the city known in Egyptian as Mennufer and in Coptic as ⲘⲈⲘⲂⲈ or ⲘⲈⲚϤ (variant spellings of the name abound in Coptic documents). The city was one of the most populous places in ancient Egypt and played an important part in the administrative and religious life of the Egyptian people. The remains of Memphis, which include a number of temples, a palace, an embalming house, tombs, and necropolises, are located near the modern village of Mīt Rahīnah on the west side of the Nile about 12 miles (19 km) south of Cairo.

Before A.D. 325 Memphis is mentioned only a few times in Coptic texts. Among the significant occurrences of the name in this literature is the account in the martyrdom of SHENUFE that recounts how Shenufe was taken by ship from Chortasa to Memphis and then to Dalāṣ. The story explains that there were a number of temples and pagans in Memphis for whom Shenufe performed various miracles (Reymond and Barns, 1973, p. 90 [Coptic texts]; p. 192 [English translation]).

Our knowledge of bishops in Memphis begins with the report of ATHANASIUS that around 325 a man named John was the Melitian bishop in the city (Munier, 1943, p. 3). Lists of the bishops who took part in the Council of NICAEA in 325 indicate that Memphis was also an orthodox bishopric at this early period; Bishop Antiochus represented Memphis at the council (Munier, 1943, p. 5). Sometime after Antiochus Perius (the transmitted spelling is perhaps a scribal error for Pestorius) was bishop of Memphis. Contemporary documents indicate that Perius was known as a pillar of orthodoxy (Rossi, 1885, pp. 102–103). A later bishop was Philippus, who compiled a life of Saint Maharati (Graf, 1944, p. 535).

The first bishop of Memphis mentioned in the historical sources for the period after the ARAB CONQUEST OF EGYPT is Mennas, who presided in the middle of the eighth century. The HISTORY OF THE PATRIARCHS records that he once assisted KHA'IL I (744–767) in a prayer service for the rising of the Nile. The successor of Mennas appears to have been Apa George, who accompanied Bishop Michael of Cairo and Patriarch JOHN IV (775–799) to Alexandria sometime around 798. A Coptic text from the Monastery of Jeremiah at Saqqara (see DAYR APA JEREMIAH) names Jacob, bishop of Memphis, as a contemporary of Patriarch YŪSĀB I (830–849). Another text from the same monastery speaks of Bishop Antony of Memphis, but there is no indication whether he preceded or followed Jacob in the office of bishop (Quibell, 1912, no. 331). Memphis was still a bishopric around 1240 when Mark, bishop of Awsīm (Wasīm) and Memphis subscribed to the canons of Patriarch CYRIL III IBN LAQLAQ (1235–1243).

Monasticism was established in the area around Memphis at an early period. At the end of the fourth century the author of the HISTORIA MONACHORUM IN AEGYPTO reported seeing many fathers and a large number of monks around Memphis and the *Apophthegmata Patrum* says that the Monastery of Arsenius was located near Ṭurah, above Babylon, across from Memphis. The most famous of the monasteries in the area was DAYR APA JEREMIAH in Saqqara, the old necropolis of Memphis.

ABŪ ṢĀLIḤ THE ARMENIAN, who wrote at the beginning of the thirteenth century, knew of only two churches in Memphis. One of these churches, which he said was spread with mats, was located next to a house constructed of green granite. The other church, which had been restored in his day, was next to the place where Moses was said to have slain the Egyptian (Ex. 2:11–15).

BIBLIOGRAPHY

Burmester, O. H. E. "The Canons of Cyril III ibn Laklak." *Bulletin de la Société d'archéologie copte* 14 (1950–1957):113–50.

Cotelier, J. B., ed. *Apophthegmata Patrum. PG 65, cols. 71–440. Paris, 1864.*

Festugière, A.-J., ed. Historia Monachorum in Aegypto. Brussels, 1971.

Munier, H. *Recueil des listes épiscopales de l'église copte.* Cairo, 1943.

Quibell, J. E. *Excavations at Saqqara (1908–9, 1909–10): The Monastery of Apa Jeremias.* Cairo, 1912.

Reymond, E. A. E., and J. W. B. Barns, eds. *Four Martyrdoms from the Pierpont Morgan Coptic Codices.* Oxford, 1973.

Rossi, F. "Trascrizione di alcuni testi copti tratti dai papiri del Museo egizio di Torino." *Memorie della Reale Accademia della Scienze di Torino,* ser. 2, 36 (1885):89–182.

Timm, S. *Das christlich-koptische Ägypten in arabischer Zeit,* pt. 4, pp. 1549–58. Wiesbaden, 1988.

RANDALL STEWART

MEMPHITIC. *See Appendix.*

MENARTI, the name given in modern times to a small island situated at the foot of the Second Cataract of the Nile, a few miles south of the town of Wādī Halfā. The name in Nubian means "island of Mei," but some scholars believe this may be a corruption of Mikhailnarti (island of Michael). Near the southern tip of the island was a fairly large village that in medieval times was apparently an important administrative center as well as the home of a monastic community.

Geographical evidence suggests that the village at Menarti may be the Takoa or Bakwa mentioned in the no longer extant, but oft-quoted tenth-century travel account of IBN SALĪM AL-ASWĀNĪ, entitled *Reports on Nubia, Makouria, 'Alwā, Beja, and the Nile.* According to Ibn Salīm, this was the limit of upriver navigation for boats coming from Egypt, and was a customs post on the frontier between Lower and Upper Nubia. At this point all cargoes were delivered into the hands of the eparch of NOBATIA, and no merchant was allowed to pass beyond Takoa except with his permission (Burckhardt, 1819, p. 494). It is possible also that Menarti was the site of the Monastery of Michael and Cosmas, which is described but not located in ABŪ ṢĀLIḤ's *Churches and Monasteries of Egypt and Some Neighbouring Countries*. Archaeological excavations in 1963–1964 revealed unmistakable evidence of a monastery.

There is good evidence for identifying Menarti with the Island of Michael that is mentioned in a number of late medieval Arabic histories. According to AL-NUWAYRĪ (d. 1332), the Island of Michael was "at the head of the cataract of Nubia, a place full of rock outcrops in the middle of the river." This perfectly describes the situation of Menarti prior to its flooding by Lake Nasser. Al-Nuwayrī further recounts that the Island of Michael was three times captured by Mamluk armies between 1276 and 1366. The eparch of Nobatia, or Lord of the Mountain, as he is usually called in Arabic texts, is described as having jurisdiction over the island, with the implication that he had a residence there. Other Arab historians list the Island of Michael among the territories in Nubia that were ceded by the king of MAKOURIA to the Mamluk sultan Baybars, but it is evident from both historical and archaeological evidence that Mamluk control was never more than nominal.

A large part of the archaeological site at Menarti was excavated by the Sudan Antiquities Service between 1963 and 1965. The excavations revealed that the settlement was first established in late Meroitic times, around A.D. 300, and thereafter was occupied until sometime around 1500. Most of the excavated remains proved to be those of ordinary houses, but there was also a church and, in the later medieval period, a small monastery. This latter showed evidence of deliberate vandalism (probably in the course of one of the Mamluk incursions), and subsequently most of it was dismantled and replaced by a sturdy castlelike structure. This building was probably the occasional residence of the eparch. The final abandonment of Menarti apparently coincided with the end of the Christian Nubian period, between 1500 and 1550.

[*See also:* Nubian Archaeology, Medieval; Nubian Monasteries.]

BIBLIOGRAPHY

Adams, W. Y. "Sudan Antiquities Service Excavations in Nubia: Fourth Season, 1962–63." *Kush* 12 (1964):222–41.

______. "Sudan Antiquities Service Excavations at Meinarti, 1963–64." *Kush* 13 (1965):148–76.

______. "Settlement Pattern in Microcosm: The Changing Aspect of a Nubian Village During Twelve Centuries." In *Settlement Archaeology*, ed. K. C. Chang. Palo Alto, Calif., 1968.

______. *Nubia, Corridor to Africa*, pp. 488–93. Princeton, N.J., 1977.

Burckhardt, J. L. *Travels in Nubia*, p. 494. London, 1819.

WILLIAM Y. ADAMS

MENAS, superior of Dayr Apa Apollo at Bāwīṭ. Menas is not known other than from a very fine icon of large dimensions (57 x 57 cm) preserved in the Louvre Museum in Paris and often reproduced, for it is a magnificent example of Coptic art.

We may be confident that he was the superior of a monastery, for this painting describes him as "Menas, *proestos*," a title that is inscribed twice, whereas Christ who protects him with a familiar gesture (passing His right arm over his shoulders) receives the title Savior (*soter*) only once. The gesture, with the nimbus that surrounds Menas's visage, is proof that he was venerated by his contemporaries. The title *proestos*, often given, is applied to the superior of a large monastery, but may also be given to the superior of a simple "house." We may cautiously conclude that this title does not necessarily indicate that this Menas was at the head of a large monastery.

Historians of art, noting that the style of this icon was very close to the paintings from Bāwīṭ, have thought that this painting also had some chance of deriving from there. Thus P. du Bourguet (1968, pp. 39, 132; 1964, no. 164), as in the *Catalogue français de l'Exposition copte*, affirms that this piece derives from Bāwīṭ; K. Wessel (1963, pp. 186–88) calls him abbot and saint. However, examining the case of the icon representing "Abraham, bishop" in the State Museum of Berlin, which is often said to derive from Bāwīṭ, M. Krause takes issue with this assertion and compares the case with that of the icon of Menas, which was given to the Louvre Museum before the excavations by J. Clédat and J. Maspero (1971, pp. 106–11; see in particular p. 108, n. 17). We thus have no proof, direct or indirect, that this icon derives from Bāwīṭ (no inscription published by Clédat or Maspero mentions an abbot Menas, a name very common in Egypt). Besides, it is very possible that one and the same artist, whose talent was well known, could have worked at several places. Much later, certainly, we know from his signature that a single artist was able to execute his work at Akhmīm, at Isnā, and at Aswan (see Coquin, 1975, p. 278): the painter Mercurius, who executed his paintings between 1301 and 1318. It is therefore not impossible that the same artist carried out work at several places, which leaves us uncertain about the provenance of the painting in the Louvre Museum, as about that in the State Museum of Berlin. It seems, as Krause advises, more prudent to confess our ignorance.

BIBLIOGRAPHY

Barison, P. "Ricerche sui monasteri dell'Egitto bizantino ed arabe, secondo i documenti dei papiri greci." *Aegyptus* 18 (1938):29–148.

Bourguet, P. du. *L'art copte.* Catalogue of the exposition of Coptic art in the Musée du Petit Palais, Paris, 17 June–15 September 1964. Paris, 1964.

______. *L'art copte.* Paris, 1968. Translated as *The Art of the Copts* by C. Hay-Shaw. New York, 1967.

Coquin, R.-G. "Les inscriptions pariétales des monastères d'Esna: Dayr al-Suhada'-Dayr al-Fahuri." *Bulletin de l'Institut français d'Archéologie orientale* 75 (1975):241–84.

Kahle, P. *Bala'izah,* 2 vols. London and Oxford, 1954.

Krause, M. "Zur Lokalisierung und Datierung koptischer Denkmäler." *Zeitschrift für ägyptische Sprache und Altertumskunde* 97 (1971):106–111.

Wessel, K. *Koptische Kunst, die Spätantike in Ägypten.* Recklinghausen, 1963. Translated as *Coptic Art* by J. Carroll and S. Hatton. London, 1965.

RENÉ-GEORGES COQUIN

MENAS, SAINT, eighth-century bishop of Tmuis. The life of Anbā Menas is known from the SYNAXARION, the notice of which is read on 7 Hatūr, and the HISTORY OF THE PATRIARCHS, in the notice on KHĀ'ĪL I.

Menas was a native of Samannūd in the Delta. He was an only son, and was married against his will. He kept his virginity with his wife, and they put on haircloth belts under their garments and spent the night in prayer. Menas left his wife and went to DAYR ANBĀ ANṬŪNIYŪS, where he met Khā'īl I, the future patriarch of Alexandria. They went to the monastery of Saint Macarius in Scetis, where at this time ABRAHAM AND GEORGE had made themselves famous. Soon Menas was named bishop of Tmuis by the patriarch SIMON I (689–701). He was the spiritual father of four patriarchs and laid his hands on them at their consecration: ALEXANDER II (705–730); COSMAS I (730–731); THEODORUS (731–743); and Khā'īl I (744–767). He died probably in 768.

RENÉ-GEORGES COQUIN

MENAS OF AL-ASHMŪNAYN, SAINT, or Menas the Ascetic, a "new martyr," who was killed after the Arab conquest (feast day: 17 Amshīr). According to the SYNAXARION, he was born at Akhmīm of Christian parents who were farmers. He received the call to the monastic life quite early and became a monk in a monastery at Akhmīm. Later he went to a monastery near al-Ashmūnayn. Having heard that the Arabs denied that God had a Son, he went off after obtaining the authorization of the superior of the monastery, outside the town of al-Ashmūnayn, to find the leader of the Muslim army, and asked him if he truly denied that God had a Son. When the commander affirmed that he did, Menas quoted the Gospel of John: "He who believes in the Son shall have eternal life, and he who does not believe in the Son shall not see life, but the wrath of God shall descend upon him." The commander flew into a violent rage, and ordered that Menas should be cut in pieces and thrown into the Nile. The faithful gathered him together, and celebrated his feast on the anniversary of his death.

RENÉ-GEORGES COQUIN

MENAS THE MIRACLE MAKER, SAINT. The Coptic church commemorates Saint Menas on 15 Hatūr. On his person, life, and death we have extensive sources in Greek, Coptic, Old Nubian, Ethiopic, Latin, Syriac, and Armenian. Many of these texts have not yet been published. The sources may be subdivided into martyrdom, Synaxarion, Encomium, miracle collections, and other categories (Krause, 1978, pp. 1125–28). Their statements are contradictory. Basically, the Encomium expands the statements of the martyrdom and contradicts other statements. Menas was an Egyptian—according to the Encomium, a well-born Egyptian from Nikiou. Statements that he came from Nepaiat or from south of Mareotis and that he had been a camel driver are refuted. According to the martyrdom and the Encomium, he was a soldier stationed in Phrygia. After he had abandoned his unit and withdrawn into the wilderness, he confessed his Christian faith and on 15 Hatūr 296 suffered a martyr's death. According to the Encomium, Menas's regiment was transferred to Egypt for the protection of Mareotis, and his body taken along as a relic. He effected a peaceful crossing, and by fire drove away sea monsters with long necks. On the march to Mareotis the body was laid upon a camel. When the camel, and also other camels on which the body was laid, refused to stand up, this was interpreted as the wish of the martyr to be laid to rest at Mareotis, and there he was buried.

The beginning of the cult of Menas is variously related. According to the Encomium, the first healing was of a youth, crippled from birth, who slept at the grave of Menas. According to the SYNAXARION, mangy sheep smeared with a mixture of earth from the grave and water were healed, and only thereafter were people cured. According to the Encomium, a small oratory in the form of a tetrapylon was built over the grave. Other churches followed (see ABŪ MĪNĀ).

The contradictions in regard to the person of Menas, his sojourn in Phrygia, and his burial in Egypt; the fact that there were several martyrs by the name of Menas outside of Egypt (O'Leary, 1937, pp. 194ff.) but that no Egyptian martyr named Menas is attested from the time of DIOCLETIAN (Delehaye, 1922, p. 31); and the relationship of the martyrdom of Menas to the eulogy of BASIL THE GREAT on Gordius have raised the question of the historical Menas (Drescher, 1946). Four hypotheses can be advanced: (1) Menas was an Egyptian martyr (Delehaye); (2) Menas was a Phrygian martyr; (3) there were two martyrs by the name of Menas, one in Egypt and one in Phrygia, and the two were confused by the hagiographers (Drescher); (4) Menas is not a historical figure at all but replaces a pagan god (Horus or perhaps a Phrygian god; Ramsay, 1918, p. 166). Advocates of this last thesis have to postulate a Christianized pagan cult, which so far they have been unable to demonstrate archaeologically. A derivation of the iconography of Menas from the representations of Horus is also not tenable (Krause, 1978, col. 1132).

[*See also:* Christian Subjects in Coptic Art.]

BIBLIOGRAPHY

Delehaye, H. "Les martyrs d'Egypte." *Analecta Bollandiana* 40 (1922):5–154, 292–364.

Drescher, J. *Apa Mena. A Selection of Coptic Texts Relating to St. Menas.* Cairo, 1946.

Krause, M. "Karm Abu Mena." In *Reallexikon zur byzantinischen Kunst,* Vol. 3, cols. 1116–58. Stuttgart, 1978.

Miedema, R. *De heilige Menas.* Rotterdam, 1913.

O'Leary, De L. *The Saints of Egypt.* London, 1937.

Ramsay, W. "The Utilization of Epigraphic Copies." *Journal of Hellenic Studies* 38 (1918):124–92.

MARTIN KRAUSE

MENELIK II (1844–1913), emperor of Ethiopia. From 1865 to 1889, he was king of Shewa (Sawā), and from 1889 to 1913, emperor of Ethiopia. He was the last Ethiopian sovereign to expand the empire by conquest and he enlarged it to about three times the original size of the Christian core area. He also set the empire on the course of modernization by establishing an economic infrastructure, constructing means of communication, reorganizing the state administrative institutions, and opening schools in which the Copts played a significant role.

Menelik's parents were the negus Khāyla Malakot of Shewa and a woman of humble origin named Eğğegāyyahu. Upon the death of his father in 1855, he was taken captive by Emperor Tēwodros II (1855–1868) who incorporated Shewa into the empire after over a hundred years of autonomy. He was treated well, as the emperor saw to it that he continued his education. Later he gave him his own daughter in marriage. But as the political instability of the empire increased in the 1860s, the emperor kept him in confinement. Menelik escaped in 1865 and installed himself on the throne of his fathers. In 1867, he threatened the stronghold of Magdalā on behalf of the Coptic metropolitan, Abuna Salāmā IV (c. 1817–1868), with whom he was in secret contact, but he withdrew soon for strategic reasons. The metropolitan died in confinement in October of the same year.

Though he claimed the imperial insignia and title, Menelik was not crowned nor did he have a bishop. The territorial acquisition of Ismaīl Pasha around the Red Sea resulted in a conflict with Emperor Yoḥannes IV, and Menelik tried to exploit the situation by entering into correspondence with the khedive. He sent an educated cleric as an envoy, who returned with an Egyptian force led by Munzinger Pasha, who tried to reach Shewa through the Danakil depression, but the commander and his force were surprised and routed. Yoḥannes IV defeated two other Egyptian contingents in the north in 1875–1876 and then with his newly captured weapons turned southward to Menelik, who submitted to Yoḥannes IV without fighting in 1878. He assured his subjects of his orthodox faith and tried to implement the imperial policy of obliging the Muslim subjects to convert to Christianity. In 1882 Yoḥannes IV assigned to Menelik one of the four bishops he had brought from Alexandria, Abuna Mātēwos.

After the death of the emperor, Menelik became the logical heir to the throne, and the metropolitan, Abuna Ṗetros, submitted to him. But Menelik favored Mātēwos and after consulting with the patriarch in Alexandria, he raised him to the status of a metropolitan, by whose hands he was crowned emperor of Ethiopia in November 1889. Menelik also involved the metropolitan in state affairs. In 1902, he sent him on a diplomatic mission to Russia, and in 1907 he let him take control of education. Traditionally, education was sponsored by the Ethiopian Orthodox Church.

Early in the twentieth century, Menelik initiated the first secular government schools in Addis Ababa and some of the provinces, and staffed them with Coptic Christian recruits. One of their number, Ḥannā Ṣalīb Bey, became the first director of the school opened in the capital, and a year later he became director of education for the whole empire. Menelik suffered a stroke in the same year from which he never fully recovered.

BIBLIOGRAPHY

Guèbrè Sellasié. *Chronique du Règne de Ménélik II roi des rois d'Éthiopie*, ed. M. de Coppet, Vols. 1 and 2. Paris, 1930–1931.

Māhtama Śellāsē Walda Masqal. *Zekra nagar* (Historical memoirs), 2nd edition. Addis Ababa, 1962.

Marcus, H. G. *The Life and Times of Menelik II of Ethiopia, 1844–1913*. Oxford, 1975.

Pankhurst, R. *Economic History of Ethiopia, 1800–1935*. Addis Ababa, 1968.

———. "Menilek and the Utilisation of Foreign Skills in Ethiopia." *Journal of Ethiopian Studies* 5, series 1 (1966):29–86.

BAIRU TAFLA

MENOU, JACQUES FRANÇOIS ʿABDALLAH,

MENOU, JACQUES FRANÇOIS ʿABDALLAH, French general born in 1750 in Boussay de Loches (Touraine) and died in Venice in 1810. He took part in the French Expedition to Egypt in 1798 and was military governor of the province of Rosetta until Kléber gave him the command of Cairo. After the murder of Kléber by a Syrian Muslim, he succeeded him in the supreme command of the French Oriental Army.

From the beginning, Menou had been a burning advocate of Napoleon's religious and colonial policy. Napoleon had tried to win the sympathies of the Muslim population by systematic propaganda and demonstration of his pro-Islamic attitudes. However, Menou's support for Islam soon went beyond mere manifestations of respect. Early in March 1799 he converted to Islam and adopted the first name ʿAbdallah. He also married a *sharīfah*, a woman who traced her line of descent back to the prophet Muḥammad on both her father's and her mother's side. He then acted in accordance with his religious belief when he became the head of the "Egyptian colony." Menou relied upon the Muslim elite and took advice from the *ʿulemas* (Muslim religious leaders). His orders concerning the administration of law and public revenues as well as his proclamations concerning social problems proved his desire to preserve Islamic institutions and even to reform them in accordance with French standards.

Menou's relationship with the non-Muslim groups of the population was decisively influenced by his experiences as governor of the province of Rosetta. There his attitude toward the Copts in the administration of public revenue as well as the leaders of the Syrian Christians had been permanently strained. This resulted in his unfavorable disposition toward the Egyptian Christians. Whereas his sympathy for the Muslims became ostensible, his antipathy toward the Christian minorities was accentuated by political motives. He viewed them as supporters of despotism, who exploited the population by fraudulent dealings and only worked for their own profit. Because of this basic attitude, he was anxious to restrict their newly won rights and the influence of all minorities. After Menou had taken over the supreme command of Egypt, he put the Coptic administration of public revenues especially under pressure. It was his intention to remove the Copts from this and other areas, but he did not succeed in displacing them within a short time. The Syrian Christians lost their customs monopoly, which had been one of the primary pillars of their economic and political power. The Greeks and Jews living in Egypt were able to replace the Copts and Syrians in Menou's favor. The only native non-Muslim who found grace in his eyes was the Copt YAʿQŪB (also called "the General"). Menou publicly praised him and appointed him *général de brigade*. No Egyptians, either Copt or Muslim, won such confidence of Menou as Yaʿqūb did.

Under the command of Menou the French occupation army could not resist a combined British-

Ottoman attack against Egypt in 1801, which forced him to capitulate.

BIBLIOGRAPHY

ʿAbd al-Raḥmān al-Rāfiʿī. *Ta'rīkh al-Ḥarakah al-Qawmiyyah wa-Taṭawwur Niẓām al-Ḥukm fī Miṣr*, vols. 1–2. Cairo, 1948.

La Jonquière, C. E. L. M. de Taffanel. *L'Expédition d'Egypte, 1798–1801*, vols. 1–5. Paris, 1899–1906.

Motzki, H. *Dimma and Egalité. Die nichtmuslimischen Minderheiten Ägyptens in der zweiten Hälfte des 18. Jahrhunderts und die Expedition Bonapartes (1798–1801)*. Bonn, 1979.

Reybaud, M. R. L. *Histoire de l'expédition française en Egypte*, vols. 1–6. Paris, 1830–1836.

Rigault, G. *Le Général Abdallah Menou et la dernière phase de l'expédition d'Egypte (1799–1801)*. Paris, 1911.

Rousseau, François. *Kléber et Menou en Egypte depuis le départ de Bonaparte, août 1799–septembre 1801*. Paris, 1900.

HARALD MOTZKI

MERCURIUS OF CAESAREA, SAINT, a Roman army officer who was martyred in the third century in Caesarea, Cappadocia, and is credited with many subsequent miraculous appearances. Known in Arabic as Abū Sayfayn, he is commemorated by the Coptic church on 25 Hātūr. In addition, two other feast days are observed in memory of this saint: 9 Ba'ūnah, when parts of his sacred relics were brought to Egypt, by Patriarch JOHN XIII (1484–1524); and 25 Abīb, when these relics were preserved in a church in Old Cairo dedicated to his name.

The Christian Tradition

Coptic material on Mercurius is plentiful. (1) *Saint Mercurius' Passion Under Decius*, which is substantially in agreement with the principal Greek text (*Bibliotheca Hagiographica Graeca* 1274), is preserved in five manuscripts. The oldest, from the ninth century, is in the Pierpont Morgan Library, New York (M 588). Others are in the British Museum, London, (Or. 6801); the National Library, Paris (fragment 129.15, 19); and the Morgan Library (M 589), a Fayyumic version from the tenth century. (2) There is a fragment of another Passion in the British Museum (Or. 6802) at the beginning of an anonymous text (Budge, 1915). (3) An abridgment of the Passion is within an incomplete version of a Panegyric of Mercurius attributed to Acacius of Caesarea in the Morgan Library (M. 588, 589). (4) An account of seven miracles performed at the construction of Mercurius' martyrium in Caesarea is in the Morgan Library (M. 588, 589) and in another version of the Panegyric by Acacius in the British Museum (Or. 6802). (5) Fragments of other miracle stories are in a manuscript from Dayr Anbā Shinūdah now in the National Library, Paris (129.15, 20), and fragments in the National Library, Vienna (K9456) and K7655 a–b). (6) The complete Panegyric by Acacius (the only one in existence) is in the British Museum (Or. 6802). (7) A panegyric attributed to Saint Basil the Great (Orlando, "Basilio . . . ," 1976, pp. 56–58) seems to be part of a pseudo-Basilian CYCLE in which the presence of the Sarmates tribe in Lazica regularly occurs.

An account of Mercurius' miraculous execution of the emperor Julian the Apostate is attached to the *Passion under Decius* in the British Museum (Or. 6801) and is also in the panegyric by Acacius in the Morgan Library (588) (Orlandi, "Passione . . . ," 1976, pp. 54–61), where it states that the account is taken from Eusebius' *Ecclesiastical History* (chaps. 10 and 11).

The basic account of Mercurius' life is as follows. Born to a pagan Macedonian family of hunters in the third century, he is named Philopater. Later, Gordianus, his father, is miraculously rescued from the jaws of death through the intervention of an angel, an event that prompts him to seek conversion to Christianity. The local bishop who baptized the family names the child Mercurius. As a twenty-year-old soldier, Mercurius distinguishes himself in the Roman war in Armenia, fighting in the cohort of Martenses under the command of Saturninus (Sardonicus or Bartonikos in Coptic). The vision of a dazzling man, an angel, helps him to victory. Consequently, the emperor Decius makes him a general. But the angel tells him his victory came from the Lord, the God of the Christians, of whom he had heard in his childhood from this father, Gordianus, an officer in the same cohort. When Mercurius refuses to accompany those who sacrifice to Artemis, the moon goddess, Decius summons him. Mercurius throws down his arms at the emperor's feet in order to take up the arms of Christ. Decius then subjects him to a series of tortures. He is nailed by his arms and legs over a fire, but his blood extinguishes the fire and he is healed in prison. Then he is hung upside down with a stone hung around his neck and beaten with four-ply cords and burnt with a red-hot iron. Finally the emperor orders him taken back to Cappadocia to be finished off with a sword. The journey is accomplished in long stages. At the moment of execution, the saint's body turns white and emits heavenly fragrances. The execution is commemorated on 25 Hātūr.

The miracles performed by Mercurius on the occasion of the construction of his martyrium in Caesarea are the chief subject of the panegyric attributed to Acacius. The scenes are very lively and much more Egyptian than Cappadocian in feeling. Through his innumerable appearances, Mercurius punishes the rich who wish to evade cooperation in the erection of the church. One appearance is to a rich pagan who is stealing the bricks brought by the faithful. The man is knocked down by his camel, while Mercurius appears to him with his lance, striking his foot. Then the camel seizes him by the foot, and the plan of the building, according to the word of Mercurius, is drawn on the ground with the wretched man's back. Needless to say, he is converted and is instantly healed of his wounds.

Another appearance is in connection with a little love drama evoked for the making of the martyrium. A young man, broken-hearted to see his sweetheart promised in a more worldly match, interviews a wizard, who inflicts a fatal headache on the girl. Saint Mercurius disentangles the threads of the drama on his feast day, at the foot of the shrine containing his relics. The wizard is converted and goes off to be a monk; the girl is saved and marries the repentant young man. Caesarea, the place itself, is mentioned only once.

The most complicated and famous of the miracles of Saint Mercurius is the death of Julian the Apostate in 363. Julian's contemporaries wondered about his sudden assassination [he died in battle in Persia], without being able to explain it other than as a result of divine reproach for the emperor's attempt to bring the empire back to paganism. This idea is expressed popularly by showing Julian, in the middle of his Persian campaign, to be a direct victim of saints who died in previous persecutions.

According to two Syriac sources, *The Romance of Julian the Apostate* and *The Life of Eusebius of Samosata* (Bibliotheca Hagiographica Orientalis 294), the executioner was none other than Mār Qūrus, one of the forty martyrs of Sebaste. And so St. Binon and P. Peeters have taken the view that this identification explains the name Mercurius itself and makes the saint's history under Decius completely apocryphal. The martyrdom at Sebaste alone would suffice to produce the whole collection of the Mercurius material. In 1968 T. Orlandi completely upset this perspective (Orlandi, 1968, pp. 87–105). Indeed, two Coptic versions of the same story juxtapose the two interpretations—in one the executioner is one of the forty martyrs, and in the other Basil sees Saint Mercurius in a vision executing Julian and the next day finds that the saint's lance in an icon is covered with blood. This account is found in *The Life of Basil* by Amphilochius (Bibliotheca Hagiographica Graeca 247–60), a text placed in the ninth century according to very old criteria. Orlandi shows that the text was already translated into Latin in the ninth century. A readaptation of two miracle stories can be found in a Sinai Georgian manuscript dated 864, and the miracle about Peter of Sebasteia (Bibliotheca Hagiographica Graeca 257) is found in an Arabic manuscript dated 855 (Shanidze, 1959, pp. 70–73; van Esbroeck, 1978, p. 384).

Orlandi therefore distinguishes two separate centers for the blossoming of the legend of Julian: Antioch, where the forty martyrs are the protagonists, and Caesarea, where Saint Mercurius is the executioner of Julian. The explanation in the Syriac tradition would be the result of compiling and harmonizing with word play on Mār Qūrus, Cyrus being the actual name of one of the forty martyrs. This explains the lack of any Passion of Saint Mercurius in Syriac, while in Armenian and Georgian the martyrdom under Decius is well represented.

The Arabic Tradition

Abū Sayfayn means "the father with the two swords"; the weapons that always accompany his image doubtless originate from accounts of Mercurius's execution by Julian the Apostate. Abū Sayfayn is treated in many sources. His martyrdom under Decius is described in a nineteenth-century manuscript in the National Library, Paris (Arabic 4781, fols. 108–117) and in a fourteenth-century manuscript from the Monastery of Saint Catherine, Mount Sinai, in the National Library (Arabic 397, fols. 193–210). The Mount Sinai manuscript follows the Passion with Basil's account of the story of Mercurius and Julian. A collection of eleven miracles is in a manuscript in the National Library (Arabic 4781, fols. 118–51); fifteen miracles are recounted in a seventeenth-century manuscript there (Arabic 4793, fols. 49–122). A panegyric attributed to Acacius has been translated from Coptic into Arabic in an eighteenth-century manuscript in the Coptic Museum, Cairo (Graf 479, fols. 172–91).

Abū Sayfayn appears with his two swords in many icons. In the tenth century Abraham, patriarch of Alexandria, built a church in Cairo in his honor, dedicating it on 25 Abīb. In the eleventh century

Patriarch Christodoulus made the church his residence. The saint's relics were moved there in 1488.

According to Delehaye (1975), the cult of Abū Sayfayn is most widely spread in Egypt. ABŪ ṢALĪḤ THE ARMENIAN states that a monastery and a large number of the churches were dedicated to him in that country.

In Cairo alone, three churches are dedicated to the saint, one in QAṢR AL-SHAM' in Old Cairo (dating from the sixth century), another associated with a convent of women known as DAYR AL-BANĀT, and a third at ḤĀRIT ZUWAYLAH.

BIBLIOGRAPHY

Binon, S. *Essai sur le cycle de saint Mercure*. Paris, 1937.

Budge, E. A. W. *Miscellaneous Coptic Texts in the Dialect of Upper Egypt*. London, 1915.

Delehaye, H. *Les Légendes grecques des saints militaires*, pp. 91–101. Paris, 1909; repr. New York, 1975.

Esbroeck, M. van. "Un feuillet oublié du codex arabe or. 4226 à Strasbourg." *Analecta Bollandiana* 96 (1978):384.

Orlandi, T. *Storia della chiesa di Allessandria*, Vol. 1 Milan, 1967.

______. *Studi copti*. Milan, 1968.

______. *Koptische Papyri theologischen Inhalts*. Vienna, 1974.

______. "Basilio di Cesarea nella litteratura copta." *Rivista degli studi orientali* 49 (1976):56–58.

______. *Passione e miracoli di S. Mercurio*. Testi e documenti per lo studio dell 'antichità, Serie copta 17, 22, and 54. Milan, 1976.

Till, W. *Koptische Heiligen- und Märtyrerlegenden*. Rome, 1935.

MICHEL VAN ESBROECK

MESODIALECT. *See Appendix.*

MESOKEMIC. *See Appendix.*

METADIALECT. *See Appendix.*

METALWORK, COPTIC, objects made of metal in Egypt from the second to the thirteenth century. The study of Coptic metalwork presents serious problems. One is that metal objects recently removed from an environment that has sheltered them for centuries are subject to change and must be carefully preserved. Another is that scientific methods of metallographical analysis, which would give information on their origin, manufacture, and history, have rarely been applied to them. Until they are, scholars can attempt only a limited, empirical study based on general knowledge of ancient metalworking, on documentary evidence such as old texts as iconography, and on the objects themselves.

Often it is not known where metal objects regarded as Coptic were found. Many have been acquired through the art market. Aside from archaeological discoveries, an Egyptian origin is most often suggested for them by reason of their style. But Coptic forms cannot be clearly distinguished from late Roman, Syrian, Byzantine, and, ultimately, Muslim types. It is only those objects found in situ or those with an inscription in Coptic that can with confidence be described as Coptic, and these are few in number. Also, it is idle to try to establish a distinction between Christian and non-Christian objects except where the signs are clear. It is understood that Coptic art is Egyptian art produced during a period that witnessed the end of paganism, the spread of Christianity, and the beginning of the Muslim era. Thus, what was produced was not exclusively the work of Christian craftsmen; nor was it intended just for Christians.

Dating is equally problematic. In the present state of research, it would be premature to allot a date to each object studied. Publications often suggest dates but only too rarely offer adequate evidence for them. The means of dating are stratigraphy for archaeological finds, and comparative studies. Examination of the style of the motifs represented on metal objects or comparison of such motifs with their representation in other techniques may offer clues, but only under the presupposition that the dating of the works used for comparison is accurate.

Economic and Stylistic Aspects

In the Coptic period, Egyptians worked those metals that were traditionally known in the ancient world—gold, silver, copper, and bronze (an alloy of copper with tin or lead), which were most frequently used. Iron and lead were used more rarely.

Extraction. Deposits of metallic ore were located in the Eastern Desert, in Sinai, and in Nubia. Some metals, such as tin or silver, were found in small quantities in other materials or were imported. Gold and some copper and iron were present in a free state; the remainder had to be extracted from ores. The initial operations—crushing and casting of the ore, and shaping of the ingots—were carried out on site. The ingots were then hammered and tempered to yield more resistant products. The metalworkers used rudimentary metal tools and improvised crucibles and furnaces. In this technology they drew on an inheritance that went back to the times of the pharaohs.

Metalworking Techniques. In a second stage the metals were forged or cast to manufacture objects. They could all be hammered hot or cold. The sheets obtained were then cut, shaped by hammer on an anvil, and put together or hammered thin for plating; sometimes the metal was drawn into fine wire. Casting made it possible to create small objects with complex shapes. The traditional lost-wax process (using a wax-coated model, a clay or stone mold, and molten metal) was still in use. Steatite molds used to cast pendants and amulets have survived to the present day in the Egyptian Museum, Berlin, and the Brooklyn Museum. The unmolded metal object was then finished with a chisel and decorated. Decorative techniques included repoussé (hammered) work, engraving (incising) with a graving tool, perforations, inlaying, burning on a lathe, or joining by welding or riveting. Goldsmiths also did filigree work and granulation and set stones.

Organization of the Trade. Much is still unknown about the organization of the metalworking trade. Though workshops of the Early Christian period have been found in Europe and the Middle East, evidence from Egypt is lacking. The existence of such workshops, however, is indicated by marks from engravers' tools and by inscriptions. Alexandria was probably one of the great centers of the goldsmith's trade in the ancient world. Nevertheless, we must not suppose for this period any highly developed specialization either in metalworking technique or in the status of the craftsman. Some smiths worked on their own account, and traveling smiths in the countryside made objects of the lowliest type. But a workshop of considerable dimensions was necessary for some metalworking. Rich men or municipal or religious institutions could lease such shops to craftsmen. E. Wipszycka (1972, pp. 62, 103) mentions churches that had a metallurgical workshop. The founders of such shops were privileged, for the Theodosian code exempted them from personal imposts. Goldsmiths were also merchants and bankers of a kind, and they could employ many craftsmen.

Style. The style of an object is often bound up with its material but not always. Some metal flasks, for instance, might imitate glass or ceramic bottles. Conversely, potters sometimes copied metal containers. Style does not necessarily enable us to give the precise date of a piece. Only certain representation elements in metalwork can be compared to the same elements sculptured in stone or wood, which have been more extensively studied, to give us an indication of chronology. Style may also be affected by fashion and by foreign imports. Trade was brisk in the ancient world, and liturgical objects from Syria and goldwork from Byzantium were probably imported into Egypt. Thus many Coptic objects are comparable to Syrian and Byzantine metalwork. Conversely, objects in the Coptic style found in Nubia, North Africa, and Europe had perhaps been exported from Egypt or had been copied from Egyptian models or exports.

Articles for Liturgical and Everyday Use

Some metal objects such as cups and buckets were for everyday use. Others were for liturgical use, as attested by church inventories and representations of censers, lamps, and crosses in other

Benediction cross. Bronze. Height: 20.3 cm; width: 8.8 cm; thickness: 1.2 cm. *Courtesy Louvre Museum, Paris.*

forms of art. Sculpture, painting, and textiles also show us metalwork used as jewelry, musical instruments, and harness pieces. Almost all the liturgical and everyday objects mentioned below are made of bronze. Except for lamps and censers, whose functions are clear, they will be classified by shape rather than function.

Crosses. The cross is a frequent motif in metalwork, either for its symbolic value or as decoration. Some crosses were formerly attached to other objects as handles or appendages. Some were designed as pendants (see the section "Luxury Objects"). Others, as can be seen in iconography in other materials, were fixed on long handles or staves to be used in giving benedictions. Such benedictional crosses are small and show great variety of ornamentation. Generally their branches are of equal length; sometimes they have flared ends and decorative attachments such as balls or palmettes. The lower branch is extended by a handle, so the cross could be waved about, or by a socket for fixing to a shaft. The cross may be decoratively engraved with circles, inscriptions, the Virgin's face, as in an example in the Louvre Museum, Paris, or Christ's face, as in the Egyptian Museum, Berlin. The point of a silver cross found at Luxor now in the Coptic Museum, Cairo, must have been such a benedictional cross.

Similar crosses, but larger, were perhaps carried in procession. Their horizontal branches have hooks attached, from which hang small crosses and

Patera. Bronze. Height: 7.3 cm; width: 10.1 cm. *Courtesy Louvre Museum, Paris.*

pearls. Examples are in the Metropolitan Museum, New York; and the Egyptian Museum, Berlin. There is also a fine silver votive cross in Berlin. Four holes have been made at the bottom of the transverse branches, but the pendants have disappeared. The front and back are decorated with inscriptions and incised faces: Christ, the Virgin, Saint John, Apa Shenute, Ama Mannou, two angels, and the archangel Gabriel.

Paterae. Paterae are shallow cups or saucers used by pagans for pouring libations on tombs and by Copts in the liturgy. Coptic paterae are bronze cups fitted with a handle. There is some doubt whether to classify the simpler ones of relatively deep proportions and a horizontal handle as paterae or just ordinary pots. Examples are in the Coptic Museum, Cairo, and the Egyptian Museum, Berlin. The decoration of the paterae was placed at the base, around the cup, and on the handle. One of them, in the Dumbarton Oaks Collection, Washington, D.C., shows a raised foot, incised motifs, and an invocation for purification engraved on the handle. The rim may be emphasized by a perforated horizontal festoon, or it may be surrounded by pearls or inscribed. The handle may be decorated by a geometrical or figural motif such as the body of an animal (as in examples in the Benaki Museum, Athens; the Coptic Museum, Cairo; and the Louvre) or a nude woman with crossed legs and raised arms, showing a palm and a crown (as on a fragment from the Benaki Museum), or just a crown containing a cross (as in the Coptic Museum, Cairo; and the Louvre). The two dolphins surrounding the crown suggest a pagan origin from the Aphrodite cycle for this Christianized motif.

Lighting Equipment. Coptic lighting equipment, like that of other peoples in the ancient world, included a variety of oil lamps, candelabra, and chandeliers.

Bronze *lamps* consist of a reservoir for the oil; a mouth, which may be provided with a lid, for receiving the oil; and one or more spouts for the wick. Shapes vary, depending on how the lamps are to be held or arranged: handle, flat bottom, feet, or a hole for slipping it on to a candelabrum, rings for hanging it on chains, or a hook ending in a duck's head, such as an example in the Egyptian Museum, Turin. Some lamps, for example, in the Louvre and the Egyptian Museum, Berlin, have a rectangular body with one rounded side carrying the handle. On the opposite side, two channels extend for the wicks. These box-shaped lamps are closed by a lid with hinges and rest on four feet. The most common lamps are like those made of terra-cotta. They have a flat bottom, and a small lid can close the supply opening. Some examples are more original and include lamps in the shape of a shoe, ball-shaped lamps with two or three spouts, or lamps with a foot and two spouts symmetrically placed. The more elaborate lamps are distinguished by their decoration.

Some lamps have a reflector, a movable leaf connected by a hinge to the rear of the lamp, which increases the light. It is decoratively worked with a leaf, shell, or rosette with perforation. This type of lamp was often placed on a candelabrum.

Lamps decorated with a cross have the general appearance of lamps with a reflector. Between the handle and the filler hole there rises a cross either set in a crown or with widening branches that curve at the ends. This decoration may indicate a liturgical use.

Lamps with scrolled handles are fitted with a lid, have one or two slender spouts, and have a foot that fits, for the most part, on a candelabrum. The handle shows an elegant scroll development, reminiscent of foliated scrolls and sometimes with leaves. Other motifs may be intermingled with them, such as crosses, birds, or a small figurine like the Thorn Extractor in the Egyptian Museum, Turin, which is hellenistic in inspiration.

Some lamps represent human figures. The body of a lamp in the Egyptian Museum, Berlin, consists of a person seated with outstretched legs. Other lamps have a face as a decoration, either on the reservoir section or at the reflector or handle level. Finally, a lamp of great originality in Berlin resembles a boat holding five sailors and a dog.

Elongated lamp with lid. Bronze. Length: 14 cm; Height: 4.5 cm. *Courtesy Louvre Museum, Paris.*

Lamp with scrolled handle. Bronze. Height: 20 cm; length: 26 cm. *Courtesy Louvre Museum, Paris.*

Lamp decorated with cross. *Courtesy Coptic Museum, Cairo.*

Other lamps have animal decoration. The handle may be worked into the shape of a horse's or griffin's head. Lamps shaped like animals are more numerous; and among them we may distinguish beasts, birds, and dolphins.

Some rare samples represent an animal poised on its paws, for example, camels in the Louvre and the Coptic Museum, Cairo, or the two-headed bull and the lion in the Egyptian Museum, Berlin; or upside down with its paws tied together, such as gazelles in the Egyptian Museum, Turin, and in the Louvre. Birds were a great inspiration for Coptic bronze workers. We can distinguish a cock in the Egyptian Museum, Berlin, and the Archaeological Museum, Florence, a duck in the Egyptian Museum, Turin, and numerous doves and peacocks. The body constitutes the oil reservoir, with the lid on the back; the head, sometimes turned backward, forms the handle. The spout of the lamp has its opening in the tail, which may be divided. This tail rests on the bird's feet, but generally this type of lamp could be hung by means of chains, and some also could be fitted on a candelabrum.

The dolphin, which is very popular in Coptic art, lent its shape to some lamps. Some are very rounded; one in the Louvre is straddled by a putto (cupid). Others, more elongated, may or may not rest on a support. The head, sometimes surmounted by a cross, is in the middle of the lamp, and from its open mouth either one or two spouts emerge. The tail is raised and widens out, like a flower, round a supply orifice. Sometimes such a lamp is so tapered and the dolphin so stylized that it is no longer recognizable.

Candelabra are many-branched stands that hold lamps or candles. Stability is ensured by a base consisting of three feet, generally executed in the form of feline paws or even like three lionesses rampant, as on a candelabrum in the Dumbarton Oaks Collection. The three feet are sometimes covered by a light drapery form. Above rises a shaft designed as a little column, a baluster, or a cross. It is surmounted by a disk and the point on which the gallery light was fixed. On a notable example in the Nelson-Atkins Gallery of Art, Kansas City, Missouri, the shaft is a figurine of Aphrodite at her toilet, and the feet are sea centaurs straddled by Nereids. According to M. C. Ross (1942), this unique object would have been a wedding gift.

There are also simple *candlesticks* holding one candle. They have a splayed foot and are decorated with moldings.

Even a lamp with several spouts provided only relatively low lighting. To illuminate large areas such as churches, multiple lighting sources were a necessity. A *chandelier* (*polycandelon*), a hanging lighting fixture with several lights, gave a more intense illumination. Chandeliers occur in two forms. The first is a perforated bronze disk, with sockets around the circumference to take small bowls or cups filled with oil. The one in the Rhenish State Museum, Trier, still has two glass cups. It is decorated with crosses, one of which has a representation of Christ, the Virgin, and Saint John. The cross is a frequent decoration for these chandeliers. It can be set in a circle or repeated on a radiating wrought metal shape.

A second type of chandelier is a cylinder, to which are attached by hinges various items, often dolphins, carrying small cups for oil. The one in the Louvre shows a perforated inscription. Two complete examples are preserved in the Coptic Museum, Cairo, and in the Egyptian Museum, Berlin.

Cruets are small hemispherical cups fitted with a flat handle and a narrow spout, probably used for pouring oil into lamps. The handle, which is elegantly carved, is sometimes decorated. Examples in the Egyptian Museum, Berlin, and the British Museum, London, have a motif of guinea fowl face-to-face on either side of the tree of life. Such oil-pourers were produced in Islamic areas as far away as Iran.

The Louvre has preserved a *snuffer,* something that looks like a pair of scissors that must have been used for snuffing candles.

Polycandelon disk. Bronze. Length: 24.5 cm; width: 23.1 cm. *Courtesy Louvre Museum, Paris.*

Censers. Censers, or incense burners, were important liturgical objects. Most were made of bronze, but two valuable examples of silver, found at Luxor, are in the Coptic Museum, Cairo. Swung with the help of hand-held chains or a handle, they may be divided into three groups according to shape: hollow-dish censers, box censers, and censers with a handle. However, the presence or absence of a lid, the way of holding or suspending the censer, and the extraordinary decorative variety make each one almost unique.

Hollow-dish censers are derived from the open dish or covered chalice. Three rings on the edge of the dish make it possible to hang the censer on chains linked by a holding ring. But the censer can also rest on a base or on three feet similar to those of candelabra, as, for example, in the Coptic Museum, Cairo. Three-footed censers have the dish in the shape of a hemisphere, as in examples from Saqqara (Quibell, 1912) or, more frequently, a polygon. An example of this type in the Walters Art Gallery, Baltimore, has a cross above the terminal ring. The most unusual example, in a private collection, consists of a baluster shaft between the three feet and the dish. It is decorated by a perforated festoon with birds (*Pagan and Christian Egypt*, 1941).

Censer with handle. Height: 21.3 cm; length: 25.5 cm. *Courtesy Louvre Museum, Paris.*

Hollow-dish censers without a lid have bowl-shaped bellies decorated with moldings, flutings, a perforated geometrical motif, for example, one found at Kellia in 1982, or the features of the four apocalyptic figures on an example in the Louvre. Here we must remember the group of so-called Syrian censers, several of which were discovered in

Censer with chain. Silver. Censer—Height: 16.2 cm; diameter: 10.2 cm; Chain—Length: 14 cm. *Courtesy Louvre Museum, Paris.*

Censer without a lid, decorated with the four apocalyptic figures. Bronze. Height: 7.5 cm; width: 13.5 cm. *Courtesy Louvre Museum, Paris.*

Egypt and which would be imports or local copies of a Middle Eastern type. They are decorated with scenes from the life of Christ in relief (Leroy, 1976, pp. 381–90).

Some hollow-dish censers with a lid are shaped like a chalice, the belly of which is a hemisphere, mounted on a slender foot. A hemispherical lid connected by a hinge makes the chalice a complete sphere. It is perforated and surmounted by a cross, as in examples from Madīnat Hābū (Hölscher, 1954), the Coptic Museum, Cairo, and the Egyptian Museum, Berlin, or by a baluster, as in a silver censer from Luxor in the Coptic Museum. Masks perforated at eye and mouth levels are engraved on the lid of another silver example in the Louvre. For some lidded censers it is the belly that has been shaped into a human face. Examples are found in the Louvre, with lids that also show faces, and in the Walters Art Gallery and the Egyptian Museum, Berlin. These last are more squat and have a lid like a cap. Another example in Berlin is reminiscent of a pine cone set on a perforated foot.

Box censers may be cylindrical, rectangular, or polygonal in shape and are set on several feet. Generally such censers have little in the way of decoration, except for two examples in the Egyptian Museum, Berlin. One shows a Bacchic scene and the other, in silver, has animals in relief. They have lost their lids. In other box censers it is the lid that gives them distinction, since it is perforated and linked to the box by a hinge and a fastener or a groove. To this is sometimes added an arrangement for hanging the censer. One example in the Dumbarton Oaks Collection is somewhat reminiscent of a chapel. The most intriguing type, of which eight examples are known, is surmounted by an animal group in relief such as a lioness bringing down a boar. M. C. Ross sees in this a homogeneous group manufactured in the Thebaid and dating from the end of the fifth or the beginning of the sixth century, because of the hard sculptural style (1942, pp. 10–12).

Some censers do not really come into the catego-

Box incense burner with bowl and cover shaped like a human head. Bronze. Sixth century. Height: 20 cm. *Courtesy Louvre Museum, Paris.*

Open box censer ornamented with birds and pigeons. Bronze. *Courtesy Coptic Museum, Cairo.*

Perfuming pan and lid decorated with a wild animal riding a pig and provided with a chain. Height (total): 16.5 cm; length (total): 12.6 cm. Perfuming pan—Height: 6.4 cm; width: 6.3 cm; length: 10.2 cm. *Courtesy Louvre Museum, Paris.*

ry of boxes but are considered part of the above series because of their animal design, for example, a fish censer at the Walters Art Gallery, and horses on censers in the Egyptian Museum, Turin, and the State Hermitage Museum, Leningrad.

Censers with a handle have a slightly rounded dish camouflaged by a cylindrical framework, from which emerges a handle or a ferrule intended to receive a handle. These censers were meant to be held, not swung. The cylindrical part may be perforated in the design of a grid, foliations, or animals. It rests on three feet that represent feline paws, hares, or aediculae (small shrines). These censers have a dome-shaped lid attached by a hinge and sometimes also a fastener. Perforated with an elegant foliated trellis, the lid is crowned by a decorative grip in the shape of a baluster, aedicula, or animal, such as an eagle holding a serpent in its beak on an example in the Louvre. This type of censer had an influence on Muslim productions (Aga-Oglu, 1945, pp. 28–45).

Braziers. It is not easy to classify as censers certain bronze objects that are perforated and are of uncertain purpose but that may well have been related to some kind of combustion. These are, for instance, cups in the Louvre that are almost flat-bottomed and have a highly pierced belly with foliation or letters. One of them has the style of a dish-shaped censer with hanging rings. A support for a censer, the cut-out pattern of which constitutes a series of monograms, is preserved in the Egyptian Museum, Berlin.

Cups, Basins, Cauldrons, and Buckets. Numerous containers may have been used as cult objects or braziers, and some of their shapes are found in censers. But failing proof of their function, it is better to classify them by shape along with secular utensils.

Cups may be, on the one hand, simple bronze bowls without any decoration, such as those found at Madīnat Hābū (Hölscher, 1954); the biggest of them are shallow bowls, or *basins.* On the other hand, cups may be more elaborate in form or decoration. The rim may be flared, flat, or bounded by a carina (ridge). The bowl may be decorated with simple motifs, in relief, incised, or even inlaid with silver, and it may rest on one or more feet. One elegant series has feet and two articulated handles on the rim, which can be festooned. These cups are sometimes adorned with gadroons, as are examples in the Coptic Museum, at Cairo; the Egyptian Museum, Berlin; and the Louvre. Another form has a round belly resting on three feet, a cylindrical neck, and a flat rim. The finest example of this type is in a private collection (*Pagan and Christian Egypt* 1941, no. 82). An inscription and crosses inlaid with sil-

Brazier. Bronze. Height: 16.8 cm; diameter: 6.5 cm. *Courtesy Louvre Museum, Paris.*

Small cauldron. From excavations at Ṭūd, 1980. Height: 13 cm; diameter: 12 cm. *Courtesy Louvre Museum, Paris.*

ver show that it was a liturgical object. Another, with a chain, was found at Ṭūd in 1980. One wonders if it should be regarded as a censer. A cup in the Coptic Museum, Cairo, has a lid pierced by a hole and decorated with animals in high relief.

Small cylindrical dishes fitted with a pouring spout are cruets perhaps intended for filling lamps with oil.

Wider cylindrical containers, with or without a foot, may be regarded as *cauldrons.* One of them, decorated with figures in relief under archways, is in the Coptic Museum, Cairo.

Similar to the cauldrons, but a little higher than they are wide, are *buckets,* which have a flared or slightly convex belly. Their movable handle is attached to two rings at the top. One bucket in the Coptic Museum, Cairo, is accompanied by a tripod support. More elegant examples are in the form of a bowl in Cairo or of a situla (bucket) in the Louvre. Finally, M. C. Ross draws attention to two bucket censers, the bellies of which are worked in the form of a bust, perhaps of Dionysus. Because of their Roman derivation, he places them at the very start of the Coptic period (1970, p. 34).

Goblets, Flasks, and Jugs. *Goblets* with a cylindrical body, fitted with a vertical handle and with small feet, resemble tankards. A brief inscription appears on the one in the Louvre, while the handles of two in the Coptic Museum, Cairo, have a feline shape.

Felines are also found on two *flasks* (narrow-necked containers) preserved in the Louvre. One is in the shape of an amphora (two-handled vase); the second has only one handle and rests on a triangular support. Some flasks of the same kind in the Louvre and the Egyptian Museum, Berlin, lack a handle and have a perforated support. These bronze flasks can be compared with the wooden phials (small bottles) studied by M. H. Rutschowscaya (1976, pp. 1–5).

Other bronze flasks, which may be called phials or bottles depending on their size, exhibit great diversity. Two types stand out. One type has a rounded belly or ribs set on a small base and narrows to a neck that ends in a wider, molded rim. Examples are in the Coptic Museum, Cairo, and the Louvre or were found at Saqqara (Quibell, 1912) or Madīnat Hābū (Hölscher, 1954). A jug in the British Museum has the same shape but with a turned handle decorated with a horse's head. The second type

Situla. Bronze. Height: 17 cm; including the ring: 27 cm; width: 13.6 cm. *Courtesy Louvre Museum, Paris.*

Dish, Ewer, Flask (left to right). Engraved silver. *Courtesy Coptic Museum, Cairo.*

of flask has a cylindrical belly that rests on several feet and is laden with decorations in relief. The decorations may be geometrical, or they may represent plants or figures under archways, like the dancers with *crotala* (castanets) or the musicians on flasks in the Coptic Museum, Cairo. The neck is between two scalloped crowns. Two leaden eulogy AMPULLAE (small, two-handled flasks) are in the Coptic Museum, Cairo; one is an effigy of Saint Menas, of a type generally made of terra-cotta; the other represents Saint Theodorus.

There are two *jugs*, or pitchers, in the Egyptian Museum, Berlin, each equipped with a hinged lid. One is elongated like an ewer; the other has a rounded belly that displays a human face.

Ladles and Spoons. The *simpulum* (small ladle) was used in the Greco-Roman period in either a liturgical or secular context and continued to be used by the Copts. It consists of a small cup at the end of a long, vertical handle, which is often crooked so that it can be hung from the top of the container from which it dips liquid. Several *simpula* have been found in excavations at Idfū in 1938, Madīnat Hābū (Hölscher, 1954), and Ṭūd in 1981. An example in the Coptic Museum, Cairo, has a cylindrical cup and is ornamented with foliated reliefs and with rearing horses where the broken wrought metal handle begins.

Some ladles have handles worked in the shape of a duck's head, a motif inherited from the pharaonic period but also found in Roman silverware. A ladle in the Museum of Art and History, Fribourg, Switzerland, has a duck incised on part of the handle, which has been wrought as a medallion. On some ladles the handle is made of two sliding parts that allow it to be extended.

A curious serving implement in the Coptic Museum, Cairo, has a bowl with a spout worked in the shape of a camel's head and a horizontal handle.

Alongside wooden or bone spoons, there are more luxurious ones made of bronze. A shell spoon-bowl is associated with an iron handle in an example in the Coptic Museum, Cairo.

Weights and Balances. The Copts used two types of instruments for weighing. The first type, the balance scale in use since pharaonic times, consisted of a haft, or fulcrum, connected by a bolt to a beam from which hung two pans. When the object to be weighed in one pan and the weight in the other were in equilibrium, a pointer on the beam aligned with the haft. This extremely precise instrument was designed to weigh small quantities and must

Ewer decorated with a cross. Bronze. *Courtesy Coptic Museum, Cairo.*

Key. Iron. *Courtesy Coptic Museum, Cairo.*

have been used by goldsmiths. It was stored with the weights in a compartmented wooden box (Rutschowscaya 1979, pp. 1–5). Some examples have been preserved at University College, London, and in the Metropolitan Museum, New York. Another example, without a box, is in the Coptic Museum, Cairo.

The second type, the steelyard scale, or Roman balance, was introduced into Egypt by the Romans and is still in use for weighing gross amounts. It consists of a bar or rod of two unequal portions. The quantity to be weighed is hung, in a pan or by itself, from the shorter portion. Three hooks allow the rod to be held in three positions. The longer portion is triangular in cross-section and marked on each face with a scale corresponding to the hanging position. A hanging counterweight slides along the triangular section until the rod is level. The mark where it stops indicates the weight. The metal counterweights are spheres, cubes, or polygons. They are engraved and sometimes inlaid with silver with marks and motifs such as the cross, which may be in a crown or a stylized chapel, or sacred personages. Examples are in the Coptic Museum, Cairo, the Egyptian Museum, Berlin, the British Museum, and the Dumbarton Oaks Collection. A whole balance has been preserved at University College, and another is in a private collection (Engelbach, 1919, p. 46).

Keys. Keys of iron or bronze are preserved in large numbers in the Coptic Museum, Cairo, and the Egyptian Museum, Berlin. A complete set was found at Madīnat Hābū (Hölscher, 1954). Their shapes are extremely diverse. The shaft may be curved, and at the opposite extremity from the steps there is a ring. The finest examples are decorated with capitals and with animal figures and are inlaid with silver, as, for example, are keys of the convents of Suhāj in the Coptic Museum, Cairo.

Musical Instruments. Judging from numerous iconographical evidence, one of the chief Coptic instruments was the *crotala*, or castanets, which consisted of two small bronze cymbals fixed between the limbs of a wooden grip, as in the Museum of Art and History, Fribourg, Switzerland, or a

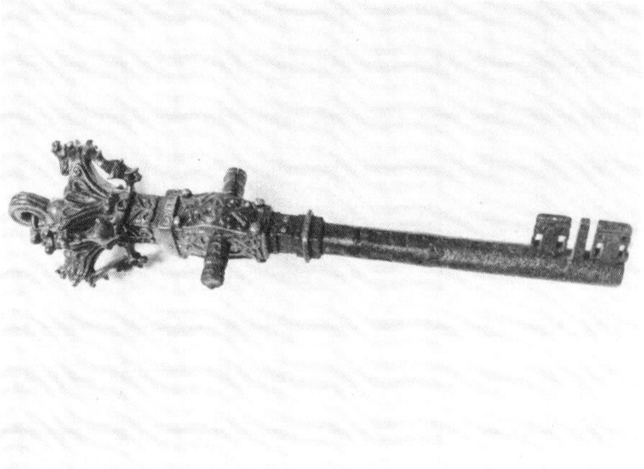

Key from Dayr Anbā Shinūdah. *Courtesy Coptic Museum, Cairo.*

bronze grip, as in the Coptic Museum, Cairo, which also has little bells. Various disks have been found, singly or in pairs. Some were part of *crotala,* and others were small cymbals played horizontally or like castanets (Hickman, 1949, pp. 517 ff.).

Small bronze bells were used more as a signal for gathering people together than as a musical instrument. For example, they were used in monasteries or churches; the stylized representation of a chapel on a bell in the Louvre seems to indicate its religious purpose. Hand bells or small round bells might embellish certain objects, such as the *crotala* referred to above, or pieces of harness. They also served to identify cattle. (See MUSIC, MUSICAL INSTRUMENTS.)

Miscellaneous Objects. *Lance tips* and *arrowheads* were made of metal, but it is hard to distinguish those in museums dating from the Coptic period unless they come from excavations such as Idfū and Madīnat Hābū (Hölscher, 1954).

Metal was used for *harnesses,* such as one found in the ruins of Madīnat Hābū (Hölscher, 1954). M. C. Ross calls attention to certain decorative parts adorned with the cross (1970, p. 37).

Small bell decorated with a chapel façade. Bronze. Eighth century. *Courtesy Louvre Museum, Paris.*

Utensils and instruments such as chisels, knives, hooks, needles, nails, and razors are undecorated functional objects of bronze or iron. Sometimes they are gathered together on a ring, for example, the tongs and needles from Idfū in the Museum of Art and History, Fribourg. An ivory case preserved in the Louvre contains some scalpels that could have belonged to an eye surgeon.

Luxury Objects

Plated Boxes. Some objects may be embellished with decorative metal plates to make them more precious. Thus some boxes were adorned with small plates surrounding the lock or with plate panels covering all their surfaces or simply one of them. The decoration is then incised, as in a weights box in the Louvre, or wrought in repoussé, as on boxes in the Coptic Museum, Cairo, and the Egyptian Museum, Berlin. The subjects are often drawn from pagan mythology: the hunt, centaurs, Gorgon masks, figures from the Aphrodite cycle, or the Isis cycle. A perforated plating on one box in Berlin shows animals in frames, set out in such a way as to form a cross inscribed in a circle.

Jewelry. Two kinds of jewelry have been found in Coptic Egypt. One kind is very luxurious in Byzantine fashion, such as the sumptuous jewelry made of gold and precious stones in the treasure of Antinoë (Dennison and Morey, 1918). The other kind is extremely simple, fashioned out of less splendid materials, clearly because of the poverty of Egypt and the precepts of austerity counseled by the clergy.

Metal-plated box for weighing. Height: 4.2 cm; width: 12 cm. *Courtesy Louvre Museum, Paris.*

Palettes (arm bands). Silver. *Courtesy Coptic Museum, Cairo.*

Bracelets show varied decorations, from the simplest, made of bronze or iron, to the most elaborate of gold, silver, or precious stones. Where the bracelet is an open circle, its extremities are either plain or decorated with flowers or animals' heads. The serpent shape is an inheritance from Greek or Roman jewelry. The closed-circle bracelet often shows a series of medallions with incised decorations, such as inscriptions, geometrical motifs, or figures of saints. The most sophisticated have a fastening and are embellished with torsades (twisted cords), granulation, medallions, and additional insertions.

Earrings are of gold, silver, or bronze, and are sometimes decorated with pearls and semiprecious stones. The decorative element is fixed on the open ring that goes through the lobe of the ear. It is composed of a polyhedral bead of perforated metal, or a crescent, or a disk with networks of scrolls, sometimes delineating the cross. The decorative element may also be a pendant consisting of a single drop, or a row of beads and drops, sometimes in three tiers.

Pair of earrings. Silver. Length: 11.6 cm; width: 3.8 cm. *Courtesy Louvre Museum, Paris.*

Two iron mirrors in the Egyptian Museum, Berlin, consist of a disk, decorated with peacocks facing each other on a floral background, and a worked handle. In University College are a simple mirror of tinned copper stored in a wooden case and a small bronze mirror decorated with interlaced designs and fitted with a small handle. A replica is in the Egyptian Museum, Berlin. The Louvre has a genuine glass mirror set in a bronze frame fitted with a ring.

Some necklaces consist of a circle of bronze or iron, which may be augmented by pendeloques (pear-shaped pendant jewels) and medallions. A cross is attached to the necklace of Serapion found at Antinoë and preserved in the Louvre. Other necklaces are made of gold chains with decorative motifs. The chains are derived from Greco-Roman jewelry. They are embellished with perforated disks, beads, representational elements, such as ducks in the Walters Art Gallery, or pendants, such as a medallion of the Annunciation from Antinoë and a magnificent gold and lapis lazuli shell containing a figure of Aphrodite in the Dumbarton Oaks Collection.

Pendants and amulets have been found in isolation, but they may have been part of jewelry. The most numerous are in the form of a cross. Small crosses were also hung on the arms of the large votive crosses. Those that bear representations in relief of Christ, the Virgin, and archangels are pendants or *encolpia* ("reliquary crosses").

A Christian iconography can also be seen on medals and amulets made of bronze or lead: the life of Christ, angels, and saints on horseback. Inscriptions identify the figure or the owner of the object.

Some bronze pins were perhaps used in hair dressing. As far as we know, no diadems have been

Mirror encased in a bronze disk with a border of small medallions. Bronze and Glass. Diameter: 6 cm. *Courtesy Louvre Museum, Paris.*

found in Egypt despite the numerous representations that testify to their existence. Brooches, fibulae, and belt buckles are in the University College and the British Museum.

Besides some simple rings, open or closed, there are numerous seal rings that are similar to amulets in their iconography or inscriptions. They are generally made of bronze. Sometimes the seals are not mounted in rings. Some were used for stamping the eucharistic bread.

Missoria. *Missoria* are richly decorated dishes used as luxury table service at banquets since Roman times. Only a few examples come from Egypt. The fragmentary bronze dish in the Coptic Museum, Cairo, is decorated with episodes from the life of Achilles. Two others of gilded silver in the Dumbarton Oaks Collection show two persons in a medallion surrounded by palmettes, perhaps the Hippolytus cycle. Three dishes from the Benaki Museum were obtained in Egypt and show mythological and Nile scenes. The luxurious material and style of these *missoria* have nothing Coptic about them. They could have been manufactured in Egypt or imported from Constantinople. In the silver treasure found at Luxor and now in the Coptic Museum, Cairo, are three rectangular trays, which might also be regarded as *missoria*. They are decorated with crosses or *chi-rho* monograms and with religious dedications.

Figurines. Full-size Coptic metal statuary is almost nonexistent. Among the numerous bronze figurines, real statuettes are rare, except for some animals in the Egyptian Museum, Berlin. The others were, or still are, part of the decoration for other objects such as paterae (saucers), vases, lamps, and censers. There is an important group of small animals and birds, some of which may have been amulets. Some of the animals are decorations for handles or spouts. Among persons represented, dancers and musicians are frequent, for example, on the handles of paterae and figurines in the Egyptian Museum, Berlin. An Aphrodite, perhaps at her toilet, constitutes the foot of a candelabrum (see above). The galloping soldiers in the Charles Ratton Collection in Paris and the Egyptian Museum, Turin, are probably saints on horseback, as suggested by a cross on top of the shaft held by the soldier in Turin.

BIBLIOGRAPHY

Aga-Oglu, M. "About a Type of Islamic Incense Burner." *Art Bulletin* 27 (1945):28–45.

Badawy, A. *Coptic Art and Archaeology*. Cambridge, Mass., and London, 1978.

Benazeth, D. "Les encensoirs de la collection copte du Louvre." *Revue du Louvre* (1988):294–300, 464.

Boube-Piccot, C. "Bronzes coptes du Maroc." *Bulletin d'archaéologie marocaine* 6 (1966):329–47.

Dalton, O. M. *Catalogue of Early Christian Antiquities and Objects from the Christian East of the British Museum*. London, 1901.

Dennison, W., and C. R. Morey. *Studies in East Christian and Roman Art*, pt. 2. New York, 1918.

Engelbach, R. *Ancient Egypt*. London and New York, 1919.

Forbes, R. J. *Studies in Ancient Technology*, Vols. 8, 9. Leiden, 1964.

Hickman, H. "Cymbales et crotales dans l'Egypte ancienne." *Annales du Service des antiquités de l'Egypte* 49 (1949):517ff.

Hölscher, U. *The Excavation of Medinet-Habu*, Vol. 5. Chicago, 1954.

Leroy, J. "L'Encensor 'syrien' du couvent de Saint-Antoine dans le desert de la mer rouge." *Bulletin de l'Institut français d'archéologie orientale* 76 (1976):381–90.

Lucas, A. *Ancient Egyptian Materials and Industries*, 4th ed. London, 1962.

Michalowski, K., et al. *Tell Edfou,* 3 vols. Cairo, 1937, 1938, 1950.
Pagan and Christian Egypt. Exhibition catalog. Brooklyn Museum, 1941.
Petrie, F. *Objects of Daily Use.* London, 1929.
Quibell, J. E. *Excavations at Saqqara (1908–1909; 1909–1910).* Cairo, 1912.
Ross, M. C. "A Group of Coptic Incense Burners." *American Journal of Archaeology* 46 (1942):10–12.
______. "Byzantine Bronzes." *Ars in Virginia* 10, no. 2 (1970):34.
Rutschowscaya, M. H. "Objets de toilette d'époque copte." *Revue du Louvre* (1976):1–5.
______. "Boîtes à poids d'époque copte." *Revue du Louvre* (1979):1–5.
Schwartz, J. "A propos d'utensiles 'coptes' trouvés en Europe occidentale." *Bulletin de la Société d'archéologie copte* 14 (1950–1957):51–58.
Strzygowski, J. *Koptische Kunst.* Catalogue général des antiquités égyptiennes du Musée du Caire. Vienna, 1904.
Wipszycka, E. *Les Ressources et les activités économiques des églises d'Egypte du IVe au VIIe siècle.* Brussels, 1972.
Wulff, O. *Beschreibung der Bildwerke der christlichen Epochen.* Königliche Museen zu Berlin, Vol. 3, pt. 1. Berlin, 1909.

DOMINIQUE BENAZETH

METANOIA, MONASTERY OF THE. The Alexandrian Monastery of the Metanoia (Penitence), also called the Monastery of Canopus or of the Tabennesiotes, played a prominent role in the religious history and the administrative life of Byzantine Egypt. One can merely catch a glimpse of this, for sources contain obscurities and contradictions.

Origins

No archaeological traces of the Metanoia remain. It is known only that it was situated twelve miles east of Alexandria, in the coastal suburb of Canopus, the present Abū Qīr. It is mentioned for the first time under the name Metanoia in 404, by Saint JEROME in his preface to a translation of normative Pachomian writings intended in part for its monks (PL 23, pp. 62–63). The original nucleus of this foundation was a colony of Pachomian monks (see PACHOMIAN MONASTICISM), or Tabennesiotes, from Upper Egypt settled at Canopus in 391 by Archbishop THEOPHILUS, on the site of pagan sanctuaries that had just been suppressed. It appears also that Theophilus endowed this colony with the means of existence (Orlandi, 1965–1970, Vol. 2, pp. 61–62, 66–67). This entailed uprooting the traditional cults and eliminating the influence of the philosophical school of Canopus, which, given its proximity to the city, was particularly offensive to the church of Alexandria. On this score, the foundation of the monastery fit very well into the religious policy of Theophilus, who was violently hostile to paganism. The archbishop, whose good relations with the Pachomians are otherwise well known, would have had difficulty in finding more trusty auxiliaries and better moral exemplars than these monks, who were strongly organized and already enjoyed an excellent reputation throughout the Mediterranean world. And it must be said that the Tabennesiotes did what was expected of them, both by their "asceticism and prayer" and, above all by establishing on the site the cult of the relics and of the martyrs, one of the best weapons of Christian propaganda at that time. It seems, incidentally, that part of the celebrity of the Tabennesiotes related to the wealth of relics in their church: a shroud of the Holy Face and the cloth with which Jesus girded himself when he washed the feet of his disciples. There was also a "venerable cross" (John of Nikiou, 1883, pp. 515, 574; cf. Butler, 1978, p. 314, n. 2). On a more militant level, the Tabennesiotes took an active part about 482–489, on the orders of the patriarch PETER MONGUS, in the destruction of a clandestine shrine of Isis at Menouthis, quite close to Canopus (Kugener, 1907, pp. 16–35, esp. 27–32).

It seems that the foundation was at first called simply the Monastery of Canopus and only later, between 391 and 404, adopted the name Metanoia. This change, which Jerome judges happy, betrayed a new objective. Canopus was renowned in antiquity for its ribald relaxations: no doubt it seemed necessary to unite the task of reforming morals with that of converting hearts (on the particular vocation of the institutions called Metanoia at Byzantium, see Du Cange, 1688).

Under Theophilus, the monastery appears to have rapidly acquired great prestige. According to Jerome, it attracted "very numerous Latins" (cf. Rémondon, 1971, p. 781, n. 43). The celebrated anchorite ARSENIUS OF SCETIS AND ṬURAH, of Roman origin, made a stay of three years there before returning to Ṭurah. A woman of senatorial rank came from Rome to visit him. Later on, Archbishop Saint Cyril (PG 77, pp. 1100–101) pronounced two short homilies at the Metanoia in honor of the famous local saints, Cyrus and John.

In the middle of the fifth century the name Metanoia had replaced that of Canopus. It appears that at that time the suburb as a whole benefited, by virtue of an "ancient custom," from the signal privilege of asylum, guaranteed by the monastery itself and by the archiepiscopal church, but was probably a heritage from the pagan regime. Within the immunity perimeter there was a bathing establishment. This information is drawn from the testimony of a priest at the Council of CHALCEDON (451), who declared that he found refuge there against the persecutions of the archbishop DIOSCORUS (Schwartz, 1938, 2.1.217). Hence, the Metanoia was already indirectly involved in the religious quarrels that developed around the council. This is the place to ask about the later Christological choices of the establishment.

The Metanoia after Chalcedon

Some authors see in the Metanoia a "bastion" of Chalcedonianism (cf. Rémondon, 1971, p. 771 and n. 11). Here are the facts that can be adduced for this view. The archbishop Timothy Salofaciolus came originally from the ranks of the house of Canopus, and it was there that he went into hiding upon the arrival of his anti-Chalcedonian rival TIMOTHY AELURUS in 475. On his death, the Tabennesiote John Talaia maintained for three years the line of the Chalcedonian pontiffs. This John had formerly been a member of a delegation sent to the emperor Zeno to bring him a petition. In 482 the Chalcedonians withdrew to Canopus in protest against the HENOTICON of the same emperor. Between 537 and 539 the Tabennesiotes supplied a third "Melchite" archbishop in the person of their superior Paul. Finally, in September 641, on the eve of the peace negotiations with the Arabs, the Chalcedonian archbishop Cyrus secretly deliberated with the general Theodorus behind the closed doors of the church of the Tabennesiotes. It was no doubt from there that he went in procession to the Alexandrian church of the Caesareum bearing the "venerable cross" of his hosts.

All this is impressive. But some of the facts recounted here take on a "Chalcedonian" sense only according to one's perspective. In themselves they are not very conclusive. That some Tabennesiote archbishop adhered to the doctrine of Chalcedon does not mean that his monastery followed suit. It is known that when Paul the Tabennesiote was raised to the episcopate, he found himself at Constantinople threatened with an accusation launched by his monks. His religious views may well have played a part in this conflict.

From time to time, traces of anti-Chalcedonianism have been found at Canopus. According to a Coptic source that is of mediocre historical value but must be taken into account because of the spirit which it embodies, PAPHNUTIUS, archimandrite of the Pachomian house of Tabennēsē in Upper Egypt, a fervent adherent of Dioscorus, stayed for a year at Canopus shortly before the council. He there received another persecuted friend of the archbishop, MACARIUS, BISHOP OF TKOW. On the death of Macarius, the monastery harbored his deacon Pinoution. About 482–489 the monks had no difficulty over obeying the order of Peter Mongus regarding the shrine of Isis at Menouthis. Hence, they recognized his authority. If in the time of Archbishop Timothy III (517–535), and no doubt at his instigation, their church received precious relics of Jesus Christ, it was evidently because the relations were good. Between 556 and 564, in a period when Justinian was trying to unite the separated churches doctrinally, two "ultra-Chalcedonian" bishops were imprisoned at Canopus, one of them Victor of Tunnuna. Finally, toward 620, the monks, spared by the Persians, welcomed the future archbishop BENJAMIN.

From this, one may conclude that the Christological line of the Tabennesiotes of Alexandria was in a state of flux, which may reflect divergences of opinion, opportunism, or even indifference or passivity.

On the organization of this monastery, there survive, by a rare chance, three papyrological dossiers from the sixth and seventh centuries that show it essentially preoccupied with its material and disciplinary affairs, respectful of the civil authority, and even supportive of the administration in its most vital task, the collection and forwarding of the annonary taxes.

The first of these dossiers (P. Fouad, 86–89) is a total of four letters deriving probably from Middle Egypt of the sixth century, as indicated by the handwriting. The letters were addressed with great deference to Abba George, the superior or PROESTOS of the Metanoia, by monks dependent upon the foundation at Canopus. Some were en route to the mother house of the Pachomian order, the Bau (a Greek form of Pbow). This was a case of two monasteries situated in these parts, obviously in some kind of affiliation with the Metanoia. A letter from the monks of one of these monasteries accuses their old superior of maladministration—no more provisions, no more money, nothing but debts, according to the accounts—and says that a lay authority is busy with the affair. Another letter relates to quarrels with a slanderer. There is fear that he may harm the monasteries in the eyes of the duke of the Thebaid at Antinoopolis. It appears that the superior general of the Pachomians and the superior of the nuns, following the example of Archimandrite Paphnutius, were then resident at Canopus, close to Abba George.

The other two dossiers, collected and brilliantly commented on by Rémondon (1971, pp. 769–81), derive from Aphrodito (Middle Egypt) and Hermopolis. The documents in the first date from between 541 and 550, or even 567, and in the second, from the first years of the seventh century. These two dossiers contain essentially fiscal documents. Thus, one learns that the Metanoia, represented by local agents sometimes called diaconites, collected, accounted for, and conveyed in its own boats part of the wheat levied as taxes. Perhaps it even carried it to Constantinople. In this regard, one must recall that there was among the Pachomians an old tradition of boatmanship, going back to the origins of the order (Chitty, 1966, pp. 25, 37); that sea voyages as far as Constantinople held no terrors for "the brothers of Tabennisi" (Johnson, 1980, p. 81), and that the use of their fleet by the state is also very early attested by Rupprecht (1983, 11972).

This is all that is known for certain about the Metanoia. The sources scarcely go beyond the end of the seventh century. (It may be deduced from John of Nikiou that the church of the Tabennesiotes was then still standing.) What happened thereafter to the monastery remains a mystery.

Pachomian Foundations at Alexandria

Alone among the authors who have dealt with the Metanoia, Van Cauwenbergh (1914, pp. 76–77) distinguished a second Tabennesiote establishment (which he located *extra muros*) from the house of Canopus, without, it must be said, very convincing reasons. Given the present state of the documentation, however, one might advance some arguments in favor of the existence of a second foundation, but one situated *intra muros*, although the sources, in view of the confusion, do not allow of any agreement on this issue.

According to Orlandi, the Pachomian colony called to Canopus by Theophilus to drive out the demons of paganism was endowed by him with a garden that had belonged to Saint ATHANASIUS, situated in the south of Alexandria. The monks installed themselves there and built a church on the north flank. Theophilus himself erected close by a martyrium of Saint John the Baptist. Eunapius affirmed that there were in fact two monks' establishments, one at Canopus and the other on the site of a Serapeum, obviously that of Alexandria, located in the southwest of the city. RUFINUS says that in his time the "sepulcher" of Serapis was razed to the ground. On one side there rose a martyrium of John the Baptist and on the other a church (Orlandi 1970, Vol. 2, pp. 61–62; cf. Orlandi, 1968, Vol. 1, pp. 66–67).

These otherwise incoherent data do agree on some points, notably the existence of an establishment of Pachomians at Alexandria concurrent with that at Canopus, toward the south (Orlandi and Eunapius), and of a church and a martyrium of the Baptist (Orlandi and Rufinus). The latter building will later be found associated twice with the Tabennesiotes, in a manner that might lead one to believe that they were not far from it. It was here that the funeral of Macarius of Tkow, the guest and protégé of the monks, took place (Johnson, 1980, p. 96). The building was dedicated to Elisha and John (Nau, 1903, p. 304). The archbishop John Talaia the Tabennesiote is said to have been priest and steward there (PG 147, col. 136). One might also identify the church of which Orlandi and Rufinus spoke with the "church of the Tabennesiotes," the resting place of the relics of Christ, to which Cyrus the Muqawqas retired in September 641 before going to the Alexandrian church of the Caesareum armed with the cross of his hosts. A procession from Canopus to Alexandria takes several hours. In all probability, the point of departure was within the city itself.

The sources are seriously divergent in regard to the site of the foundations, giving a garden (Orlandi) and a Serapeum (Eunapius and Rufinus). Again, the historical tradition varies on the person to whom the building or buildings that replaced the Serapeum were dedicated. Thus, one reads of a church of Arcadius, Theodosius, or Honorius (see Schwartz, 1966, p. 99, n. 3; Orlandi, "Uno scritto . . .," 1968, pp. 295–304; *Storia . . .* , 1968, Vol. 1, pp. 94–98; Vol. 2, 1970, pp. 95–97, 100–02). Nor is there any more unanimity in regard to the functions of John Talaia before his accession to the episcopate: for some he was general steward of the archiepiscopal church and no longer steward of the martyrium. This is puzzling. As to the other facts, the inferences about the funeral of Macarius of Tkow and the withdrawal and return of the Muqawqas have, on the whole, no firm basis.

It is also permissible to think that if there had been a second Pachomian monastery at Alexandria, Jerome would not have failed to mention it in his preface. Finally, other literary allusions to the Tabennesiotes direct one toward Canopus, or at the very least never absolutely prohibit that interpretation.

What may one finally concede? That one or two religious buildings in Alexandria, one of them dedicated to John the Baptist but both hard to place accurately, are rather obscurely placed by an incoherent historical tradition in the tenure of the Pachomians. Perhaps this martyrium and church were served by Tabennesiotes established nearby, attached to the Metanoia at Canopus. This colony, if it ever existed, seems insignificant in comparison with the house of Canopus, whose historicity is at any rate not in doubt.

BIBLIOGRAPHY

Butler, A. J. *The Arab Conquest of Egypt and the Last Thirty Years of the Roman Dominion.* Oxford, 1902; 2nd ed. (ed. P. M. Fraser), Oxford, 1978.

Cauwenbergh, P. van. *Etude sur les moines d'Egypte depuis le Concile de Chalcédoine (451) jusqu'à l'invasion arabe (640)*, pp. 76–78. Paris and Louvain, 1914.

Chitty, D. J. *The Desert a City*, pp. 54–55, 66, 92. Oxford, 1966.

Cotelier, J. B., ed. *Apophthegmata Patrum*, pp. 71–440. PG 65. Paris, 1864.

Crum, W. E. "Review of *S. Pachomii Vita Bohairice Scripta*." *Journal of Theological Studies* 28 (1926):326–28.

Du Cange, C. *Glossarium ad Scriptores Mediae et Infimae Graecitatis.* Lyons, 1687. Reprint in 2 vols. Bologna, 1977.

Hardy, H. R. *The Large Estates of Byzantine Egypt*, pp. 46–47. New York, 1931.

John of Nikiou. *Chronique de Jean, évêque de Nikiou*, ed. and trans. H. Zotenberg, pp. 125–608. Notices et extraits des manuscrits de la Bibliothèque nationale 24. Paris, 1883.

Johnson, D. W., trans. *A Panegyric on Macarius, Bishop of Tkôw, Attributed to Dioscorus of Alexandria.* CSCO 416. Louvain, 1980.

Kugener, M. A., ed. and trans. *Vie de Sévère par Zacharie le Scholastique.* PO 2. Paris, 1907.

Ladeuze, P. *Etudes sur le cénobitisme pakhomien*, pp. 201–202. Paris and Louvain, 1898.

Maspero, J. *Histoire des patriarches d'Alexandrie.* Paris, 1923.

Nau, F., ed. and trans. "Histoire de Dioscore, patriarche d'Alexandrie écrite par son disciple Théopiste." *Journal asiatique* 10 (1903):5–108, 241–310.

Orlandi, T., ed. and trans. *Storia della chiesa di Alessandria.* 2 vols. Milan, 1968–1970.

______. "Uno scritto di Teofilo alessandrino sulla del Serapeum?" *La Parola del Passato* (1968):295–304.

Rémondon, R. "Le Monastère alexandrin de la Metanoia était-il bénéficiaire du fisc ou à son service?" *Studi in onore di Edoardo Volterra*, Vol. 5, pp. 769–81. Milan, 1971.

Rupprecht, H. A., ed. *Sammelbuch griechischer Urkunden aus Ägypten*, Vol. 14. Wiesbaden, 1983.

______. In *Essays in Honor of C. Bradford Welles.* New Haven, Conn. 1966.

JEAN GASCOU

METROLOGY, COPTIC.

In stone and textile workshops, Coptic craftsmen probably used sample books with favorite patterns and wooden stencils in order to reproduce certain patterns many times. Both samples and stencils require a general system of measurements, and stonemasons ordered their quarry blocks according to standard sizes. Some measurements taken from third- to ninth-century reliefs and textiles in the Museum Simeonstift, Trier, and the Coptic Museum, Cairo, give evidence that Coptic craftsmen refused the Roman foot of 11⅔ inches (29.57 cm), but adhered to the royal Egyptian yard of 20⅔ inches (52.5 cm), the smallest unit being one-fifteenth, that is, 1⅓ inches (3.5 cm). To what extent, however, there were minor changes of this system due to local Coptic traditions and centers remains doubtful unless large-scale investigations are carried out.

BIBLIOGRAPHY

Nauerth, C. *Koptische Textilkunst im spätantiken Ägypten.* Trier, 1978.

DIETER AHRENS

METROPOLITAN.

In the early days of the Christian era, the apostles chose metropolitan cities as centers for the dissemination of their evangelistic teaching. Here they established churches, which they put in the charge of bishops. With the gradual spread of Christianity and the increase in the number of churches, the older church came to enjoy a mother-daughter relationship with the more recently established ones. Its bishop was accordingly designated metropolitan, a term first used in 325 by the Council of Nicaea (see NICAEA, COUNCIL OF).

A metropolitan has seniority over other bishops in the province. Apostolic Canon 34 stipulated, "The bishops of every nation must acknowledge him who is first among them and account him as their head, and do nothing of consequence without his consent; but each may do those things only which concern his own parish, and the country places which belong to it."

A metropolitan has the right to convoke provincial synods and preside over their sessions.

A metropolitan has the right to confirm the election of bishops in his province. The First Ecumenical Council of Nicaea decreed, "It is by all means proper that a bishop should be appointed by all the bishops in the province; but should this be difficult, either on account of urgent necessity or because of distance, three at least should meet together, and the suffrages of the absent [bishops] also being given and communicated in writing, then the ordination should take place. But in every province the ratification of what is done should be left to the Metropolitan." Canon 6 of the same council adds, "And this is to be universally understood, that if anyone be made bishop without the consent of the Metropolitan, the Great Synod has declared that such a man might not be a bishop."

In 341 the Synod of Antioch stipulated, "A bishop shall not be ordained without a synod and the presence of the metropolitan of the province. And when he is present, it is by all means better that all his brethren in the ministry of the Province should assemble together with him, and these the metropolitan ought to invite by letter."

In recognition of the preeminent position of the metropolitan, his formal approval was required by members of the priesthood who requested interviews with the head of state: "If any bishop, or presbyter, or anyone whatever of the canon shall presume to betake himself to the Emperor without the consent and letters of the bishop of the province, and particularly of the bishop of the metropolis, such a one shall be publicly deposed and cast out. . . . But if necessary business shall require anyone to go to the Emperor, let him do it with the advice and consent of the metropolitan."

Similar recognition was decreed by the council held in Carthage. "Bishops shall not go beyond seas without consulting the bishop of the primatial see [the metropolitan] of his own province, so that from him they may be able to receive a formal or commendatory letter."

BIBLIOGRAPHY

Cummings, D. *The Rudder (Pedalion)*. Chicago, 1957.

ARCHBISHOP BASILIOS

METROPOLITAN SEES. The ancient privileges of the See of Alexandria, as confirmed by the sixth canon of the Council of NICAEA (325), placed the provinces of Egypt, Libya, and the Pentapolis in Cyrenaica under the jurisdiction of the bishop of Alexandria, although these provinces had their own metropolitans.

Ancient and Medieval Times

The Metropolitan See of Ptolemaïs in the Pentapolis (Cyrenaica) was established by Saint MARK the Evangelist before he visited Alexandria for the first time. After consecrating ANIANUS (68–85) bishop of Alexandria, he returned to the Pentapolis "and remained there two years, preaching and appointing bishops and priests and deacons in all their districts," according to Sāwīrus. The following were among the bishops of this see: Basilides, whose name was recorded by Eusebius as "bishop of the parishes in the Pentapolis," to whom DIONYSIUS, patriarch of Alexandria (d. 264), addressed various epistles. Only one epistle has survived; it contains explanations given as answers to questions proposed by that bishop on various topics, later received as canons of the Council in Trullo.

Siderius, bishop of Palaebisca and Hydrax, was consecrated by one bishop (Philo), not three as was the custom. Saint Athanasius (326–373) condoned that irregularity in view of the Arian troubles. He was later translated to the metropolitan see of Ptolemaïs. Synesius (c. 370–414), though married (contrary to the canons of the church), was consecrated bishop of Ptolemaïs by Pope THEOPHILUS of Alexandria (Smith and Wace, 1974, pp. 756–80).

This see must have continued until the end of the fifteenth century, for Qiryāquṣ, metropolitan of the Pentapolis, was mentioned by Pope JOHN XIII (1484–1524). He was among those bishops who were unable to reach their sees at the beginning of the sixteenth century because of the Ottoman conquest of that region. Consequently the metropolitan was obliged to abandon his see and live in the desert of SCETIS (Kām'īl Ṣaliḥ Nakhlah, 1954, Vol. 4, pp. 59–60). Thereafter, no mention is made of that see except for the inclusion of its name in the honorific titles of the patriarch of Alexandria.

As a first step in formally reestablishing the See of the Pentapolis nowadays, Pope SHENOUDA III added the name of Pentapolis to that of the metropolitan See of Beḥeirah, in the process of consecrating its present bishop.

The Metropolitan See of Ethiopia was established by Pope Athanasius, who consecrated FRUMENTIUS as bishop (c. 340). Frumentius was called ABŪN (our father), and until 1950 the metropolitan or *abūn* of Ethiopia was an Egyptian appointed by the patriarch of Alexandria. The last Egyptian *abūn* of Ethiopia was consecrated in 1929 and died on 22 October 1950. Thereafter, Anbā Basilius, the Ethiopian bishop of Shewa, was chosen the first Ethiopic *abūn* of Ethiopia by Pope YŪSĀB II (1946–1956). On 2 September 1951, five Ethiopian bishops were consecrated by Abuna Basilius, in accordance with the patriarch's approval.

In 1959, after long negotiations, the status of the Ethiopian church was finally recognized by the See of Alexandria as autonomous and autocephalous, and its head was consecrated by the patriarch of Alexandria as "Catholicus," though in Ethiopia itself he bears the title Patriarch.

Pope CYRIL III IBN LAQLAQ (1235–1243) was the first Alexandrian patriarch to consecrate a Coptic metropolitan for Jerusalem, the Littoral, and Syria (see JERUSALEM, COPTIC SEE OF); this caused considerable friction between him and the patriarch of Antioch (Kām'īl Ṣāliḥ Nakhlah, 1954; Vol. 1, pp. 59, 82–90). The patriarchs of Alexandria and Antioch shortly afterward reached a compromise: the latter recognized the jurisdiction of the new metropolitan, and the former agreed to extend it no farther than Gaza.

It is decreed in the fifth canon of Cyril ibn Laqlaq "that the signature of the metropolitan of Gaza and that which ajoins it shall be required for conforming to the aforementioned belief of the Jacobite Church, and for [his] conformity to that which conforms to it, and that he rejects those whom the Councils reject, and that if he does not conform with this, he shall be excommunicated" (Burmester, 1946–1947, p. 108).

Despite this, the see has always been regarded as the metropolitan See of Jerusalem and the Near East. It is now recognized as a patriarchate, although it is superintended by a metropolitan.

The site now known as Old Cairo is mentioned by Strabo, the Greek geographer and historian (24 B.C.), and by Ptolemy (A.D. 121–151) under the name BABYLON. This city was a bishopric by the fifth century or before, since there is mention of a certain Cyrus, bishop of Babylon, among the Egyptian bishops who were present at the Council of Ephesus held in 449 (Munier, 1943, p. 19).

After the ARAB CONQUEST OF EGYPT there arose a new quarter called al-Fusṭāṭ; the city became the capital of Egypt and the seat of government, and was eventually known as Miṣr. Hence, it was sometimes recognized as a metropolitan see. Already in 743 we read of a certain Theodorus the Metropolitan, bishop of Miṣr, who assisted in the election of Pope KHĀ'ĪL I (Munier, 1943, p. 25).

The See of Miṣr replaced the older See of Babylon, and its cathedral church was that of Saint Mercurius (CHURCH OF ABŪ SAYFAYN) until the reign of Pope CHRISTODOULUS (1047–1077), who transferred the seat of the patriarchate from Alexandria to Cairo and made this church a patriarchal one. On the death of Anbā Yu'annis, bishop of Miṣr (1122), Pope GABRIEL II ibn Turayk (1131–1145) did not consecrate anyone after him for Miṣr. But, in 1240, in the patriarchate of Cyril III Ibn Laqlaq, Anbā BŪLUS AL-BŪSHĪ was consecrated bishop of the See of Miṣr (Burmester, 1950–1957, pp. 117–31).

Pope CYRIL IV (1854–1861) reestablished the metropolitan See of Miṣr by consecrating Anbā Buṭrus as bishop and promoting him to the metropolitan rank. This was the last metropolitan of the See of Miṣr.

The date at which the See of Damietta (DUMYĀṬ) was raised to metropolitan status is uncertain. In the twelfth century, there was Mīkhā'īl, bishop of Damietta, who was a contemporary of Pope MICHAEL V and who refuted Murqus ibn Qanbar in the days of Pope MARK III (Burmester, 1936, pp. 101–128).

In the thirteenth century, there was Anbā Christodoulus ibn al-Duhayrī, metropolitan of Damietta, who wrote a Coptic grammar (Graf, 1947, p. 378). He was a contemporary of Pope Cyril ibn Laqlaq III, who spoke of the metropolitan See of Damietta in his canons, indicating "that the rank of the metropolitan of Damietta who is at present [occupying this see] shall remain according to the custom of those who preceded him in the aforementioned frontier city of Damietta and according to that which in contained in the biographies of the patriarchs for those like him [who are] in it" (Burmester, 1946–1947, p. 108).

In the fourteenth century, Gregory, metropolitan of Damietta, attended the consecration of the holy chrism in 1320 and in 1330 (Kāmil Ṣāliḥ Nakhlah, 1954, pp. 34, 52).

Gradually, however, this see lost its distinctive status to become part of a larger adjacent see for long periods. It was reinstated in the twentieth century, but was headed by a bishop, not a metropolitan.

Seventeenth Century

According to A. J. Butler (1884, Vol. 2, p. 313), who quoted the seventeenth-century traveler J. M. Vansleb, there were only three metropolitan sees: Damietta, Jerusalem, and Ethiopia. According to Vatican Coptic manuscript 45 (seventeenth-century, though probably copied from a thirteenth-century one) the metropolitan sees were Damietta, Abyssinia (Ethiopia), and Jerusalem (Munier, 1943, p. 65).

Eighteenth Century

In addition to the three sees just noted, one reads of Anbā Buṭrus, metropolitan of Jirjā and Upper Ṣa'īd, who was consecrated by Pope MARK VII (1745–1769). In a pastoral letter, Anbā Buṭrus mentioned his metropolitan jurisdiction as the See of Jirjā and Upper Ṣaīd, and all the Christian people in the See of Akhmīm, Jirjā, Qifṭ, Qūṣ, Naqādah, Isnā, Armant, and their environs.

Nineteenth Century

Metropolitan Theophilus was consecrated (1808) by Pope MARK VIII (1796–1809) as a general metropolitan and acted as the pope's assistant until his death six months later. Subsequently, Theophilus was elected to the patriarchate under the name of PETER VII, surnamed al-Jāwlī (1809–1852).

Metropolitan Cyril, who was consecrated a general metropolitan in April 1853 following the decease of Peter VII, was installed as patriarch under the name Cyril IV in June 1854.

Four more metropolitans were consecrated by Pope Cyril IV (1854–1861): Anbā BASILIUS, metropolitan of Jerusalem, al-Sharqiyyah, al-Daqahliyyah, al-Gharbiyyah, and al-Qanāl (Suez Canal); Anbā Yu'annis, metropolitan of al-Minūfiyyah; Anbā Murqus, metropolitan of Beḥeira; and Anbā Buṭrus, bishop and, later, metropolitan of Cairo.

Butler (1884, Vol. 2, pp. 312–13) mentioned four metropolitans or archbishops under the jurisdiction of the Coptic patriarch, those of Alexandria, Minūfiyyah, Jerusalem, and Abyssinia.

Twentieth Century

The title metropolitan is now used in purely honorific sense for those with only diocesan, not provincial, powers.

Apart from Ethiopia, which became a patriarchate in 1951 (headed by a catholicus having his own metropolitans and bishops), and Jerusalem, which is a Coptic patriarchate superintended by a Coptic metropolitan, all the dioceses of Egypt and the Sudan are now called metropolitan sees, which, though sometimes headed by metropolitans, are more commonly superintended by bishops liable to promotion in due course.

At present there are eight metropolitan sees: Asyūṭ; Jerusalem and the Middle East; Jirjā; Nubia, Umm Durmān, and 'Aṭbarah; al-Kharṭūm South and Uganda; al-Qalyūbiyyah; Banī Suef and al-Bahnasā; and Giza and Aṭfīḥ.

BIBLIOGRAPHY

Burmester, O. H. E. "The Sayings of Michael, Metropolitan of Damietta." *Orientalis Christiana Periodica* 2 (1936):101–128.

———. "The Canons of Cyril II ibn Laqlaq." *Bulletin de la Société d'archéologie copte* 12 (1946–1947):81–136, and 14 (1950–1957):113–50.

Butler, A. J. *The Ancient Coptic Churches of Egypt.* Oxford, 1884.

Kām'īl Ṣāliḥ Nakhlah. *Silsilat Tārīkh al-Bābāwāt Baṭārikat al-Kursī al-Iskandarī.* Dayr al-Suryān, 1954.

Munier, H. *Recueil des listes episcopales de l'église copte.* Cairo, 1943.

Neale, J. M. *A History of the Holy Eastern Church: The Patriarchate of Alexandria,* 2 vols. London, 1847.

Ṣamū'īl al-Suryānī. *Al-Adyirah al-Miṣriyyah al-'Āmirah.* Cairo, 1968.

EMILE MAHER ISHAQ

MICHAEL. *See also under* Mīkhā'īl or Khā'īl.

MICHAEL IV, saint and sixty-eighth patriarch of the See of Saint Mark (1092–1102). Little is known about Michael's secular life before he took the monastic vow, nor do we know with precision the date of his enrollment in the monastic order. Historical references to him start with the statement that he was a middle-aged monk who, after attaining the priesthood, decided to become a solitary in a secluded cell at SINJĀR. There a deputation of bishops and clergy, together with a number of leading Coptic archons, mainly from Alexandria, offered him the church leadership. The group had first convened in Alexandria, then in Cairo, where they were joined by a number of Upper Egyptian bishops. They were directed to a Syrian solitary monk by the name of Samuel by a deacon of the monastery of Saint Macarius. On interviewing Samuel, however, they had doubts about his orthodoxy and his knowledge of Coptic church traditions. Finally their search led them to Michael at Sinjār, to whom they offered the patriarchate on certain conditions, which he accepted in writing. Michael agreed that he would not use simony (CHEIROTONIA); that he would not claim any share in episcopal income; and that he would return to the bishops all the religious property and churches that his predecessors had confiscated. After signing this document, Michael accompanied the delegation to Alexandria for his consecration, then to DAYR ANBĀ MAQĀR, and finally to the Muʿallaqah church in Old Cairo, where the seat of the patriarchate had been moved from Alexandria during the tenure of Pope CHRISTODOULUS (1047–1077).

There was no reticence on Michael's part in accepting the nomination, as there had been with many previous patriarchs. And it is doubtful that he ever intended to keep his written promises to the delegation. His patriarchate was filled from the outset by problems relating to his signed documents, which he wanted to recover from the bishops after his investiture. After he became patriarch, he denied his promises and refused to return the confiscated churches and monasteries to the bishops. This resulted in a major clash between them—especially with Anbā Sinhūt, bishop of Miṣr. Michael even threatened the possessors of the signed document with excommunication if his will was resisted. Anbā Sinhūt eventually had to flee to Dayr Anbā Samū'īl in Qalamūn in the Fayyūm province, where he found shelter from patriarchal wrath. But Anbā Sinhūt was popular with the congregation, which sent a delegation to the patriarch to seek a solution to the problem. They hinted that they might appeal to the Islamic state as a last resort. Thus, the intimidated patriarch had no choice but to absolve the bishop of Miṣr and allow him to return to his diocese. The root of the problem, which was the common interest of both in the finances and the ecclesiastical organization of a diocese shared between them, remained unsolved. As a solution to the problem, the patriarch started to contemplate the excommunication of Anbā Sinhūt, who again fled, this time to the more distant Monastery of Saint Severus (DAYR ANBĀ SĀWĪRUS) in the region of Asyūṭ. In 1102, Michael was stricken by the plague and died after a few days.

Perhaps the most momentous international event during Michael's reign was the beginning of the Crusade movement in Western Europe and the fall of Jerusalem to the Latins in 1099. For the Copts this was a major event, since the Roman Catholic occupants of the Holy Land regarded the Coptic Monophysites as heretics and consequently barred them from pilgrimage to the holy places. This situation persisted until the recovery of Jerusalem by Saladin in 1187.

BIBLIOGRAPHY

Lane-Poole, S. *History of Egypt in the Middle Ages.* London, 1901.

SUBHI Y. LABIB

MICHAEL V, seventy-first patriarch of the See of Saint Mark (1145–1146). Michael, or Mīkhā'īl ibn Danashtarī as he is listed in the HISTORY OF THE PATRIARCHS, was a monk of the Monastery of Saint Macarius (DAYR ANBĀ MAQĀR). He was a man of fine stature and he was dignified, chaste, and saintly. Nothing is known about his secular life beyond the fact that he was not a highly educated man. Michael concentrated on the art and traditions of monasticism, without aspiring to higher office. When his predecessor, GABRIEL II, died and the bishops and archons began their arduous search for a worthy successor, a monk of Anbā Maqār by the name of Wanas or Yūnus ibn Kadrān came forth and requested the nomination for himself. This automatically rendered him unworthy of consideration in the eyes of the majority of the congregation, despite the support that he secured from a few members of the community. Thus, it was decided in the absence of a clear choice to write three names on three cards and a fourth with the name of Jesus Christ and place them on the altar. After praying for three successive days and nights, they asked an innocent child to pick up the winning name. Michael's name emerged from the lot as the Lord's candidate.

Michael was made a deacon, then a presbyter, and on the third day he became a HEGUMENOS or archpriest. His final nomination was sanctioned by the caliph. He was taken to Alexandria for formal consecration in the Cathedral of Saint Mark, where he was met by the dignitaries of the capital with great honor. The *History of the Patriarchs* states that his days were secure and peaceful and that nothing special occurred in his reign beyond the consecration of five new bishops. Nothing is said about simoniacal imposts (CHEIROTONIA) from any of these bishops, and it must be assumed that his short reign was uneventful because he rendered his taxes without protest.

Michael's patriarchate lasted eight months and four days, the last five months of which he spent severely ill at the Monastery of Saint Macarius, where he died and was buried. Some say that his death was precipitated by poisoning at the hands of the supporters of his old rival Ibn Kadrān, but this view is not authenticated.

SUBHI Y. LABIB

MICHAEL VI, ninety-second patriarch of the See of Saint Mark (1476–1478). Michael (or in Arabic, Mīkhā'īl) is briefly mentioned in the HISTORY OF THE PATRIARCHS; the dates of his investiture and his death are given, but no reference is made to the monastery from which he was chosen to occupy this ecclesiastical high office.

The See of Saint Mark remained vacant for more than a year after the decease of his predecessor GABRIEL VI. The Coptic sources provide no explanation for this long interregnum, so it must be assumed that the clergy, the bishops, and archons could not find a suitable candidate for this important post, so vital to the Coptic community.

Michael was the son of a priest named Yuḥannā ibn Sumay'ah, and his native town was Manfalūṭ in Upper Egypt. He remained in the patriarchate for the rather short period of two years and one month and twenty-two days. The Islamic chronicler Ibn Iyās says that Michael died of the plague during the reign of the Burjī Mamluk sultan Qa'itbāy (1468–1495). Apparently the Copts enjoyed relative security during his short tenure, since Ibn Iyās states that the sultan gave Michael a robe of honor when he went to pay homage to him. Furthermore, Ibn Iyās praises Michael as a patriarch of good character, who was beloved by his coreligionists.

Although the Coptic sources are silent on the significant Coptic personalities of this short reign, the Islamic sources name several eminent Islamized Copts in this period who occupied the most important positions in the government of Egypt. They are listed by the Muslim names to which they changed after their conversion. Their names are found in the obituaries of the annals of the chronicler Ibn Iyās. The following is a list of these names, each of which was followed by the epithet al-Qibṭī (the Copt) in spite of their Islamization. (See PROFESSIONAL ACTIVITIES OF COPTS IN LATE MEDIEVAL EGYPT.)

- Al Ṣāḥib Sharaf al-Dīn Yaḥya ibn Ṣanī'ah al-Qibṭī
- Al-Qāḍi 'Abd al-Karīm ibn Abī al-Faḍl Muḥammad ibn Isḥāq al-Qibṭī
- Al-Qāḍi Zayn al-Dīn 'Abd al-Qādir ibn 'Abd al-Raḥmān ibn al-Jī'ān al-Qibṭī
- Sharaf al-Dīn Mūsa ibn Yūsuf al-Qibṭī
- Al-Qāḍi 'Alam al-Dīn Shākir ibn al-Jī'ān al-Qibṭī al-Dumyāṭī
- Abū al-Baqā' ibn al-Jī'ān al Qibṭī
- Al-Qāḍī Sharaf al-Dīn Yaḥyā ibn al-Jī'ān al-Qibṭī

Apparently most of them attained the ministerial position of vizier in the sultan's administration, and Ibn Iyās makes special mention of 'Alam al-Dīn Shākir for his profound knowledge, his humility, and the high regard in which he was held by the sultans. He was the founder of the mosque in the region of Birkat al-Raṭl, and he lived to be a centenarian (1368–1477).

Michael was buried in Cairo at the Church of Babylon al-Daraj.

BIBLIOGRAPHY

Ibn Iyās, Muḥammad ibn Aḥmad. *Badā'i' al-Zuhūr fī Waqā'i' al-Duhūr.* 5 vols. Cairo, 1960.

Lane-Poole, S. *History of Egypt in the Middle Ages.* London, 1901.

______. *The Mohammadan Dynasties.* Paris, 1925.

SUBHI Y. LABIB

MICHAEL THE ARCHANGEL, FEASTS OF SAINT. *See* Festal Days, Monthly.

MICHAEL THE ARCHANGEL, SAINT. In Coptic Christian tradition, Saint Michael the Archangel holds an important place, comparable to that of the Virgin Mary. Of the Eastern churches only the Copts and the Ethiopians have developed devotion to the archangel to the same degree. Among the archangels, Michael is explicitly named in the Old Testament (Dn. 10:13, 21; 12:1) and in the New Testament (Jude 9 and Rev. 12:7). The cult of angels developed very rapidly in the early church (Barbel, 1941). The most famous (shrine of Michael) was at Khonai, between Colossae and Hierapolis in Asia Minor, but recently a building of the same type was discovered at Apamea in Syria; similar buildings existed from the early fourth century in Constantinople and other towns (Canivet, 1979, pp. 364–65).

The principal functions ascribed to Michael are the presentation of the prayers of the righteous before God, acting as a psychopomp (one who welcomes the souls of the dead to heaven), achieving victory over the devil, and serving in the cosmological role of Angel of the Lord. All these functions are to be found in the rich Coptic documentation concerning Michael.

Two festivals stand out in the SYNAXARION: 12 Ba'ūnah, the festival of the dedication of his church, and 12 Hātūr, the festival of his investiture in heaven. There is also a festival of Saint Michael on the twelfth of each month. This triple liturgical program will be illustrated with the help of some literary texts. Then follows a survey of the principal Coptic texts that speak of Saint Michael.

The Dedication of the Church of Saint Michael

The festival of 12 Ba'ūnah has the following story in the Synaxarion. A pious woman named Euphemia was married to a man who gave alms generously. They celebrated three festivals every month—on the twelfth, Saint Michael; on the twenty-first, the Virgin; and on the twenty-ninth, the Nativity. When the husband was dying, he made the wife promise to continue this practice. In token of this faithfulness, he left her an icon of Saint Michael. Satan, in the form of a monk, tormented the woman, trying to seduce her and make her give up her pious practices. On 12 Ba'ūnah, Satan appeared to her in the guise of Michael himself. But the woman recognized him because he did not make the sign of the cross. When Satan tried to strangle her, the true Michael appeared and vanquished him. He then said to the woman, "Prepare yourself, for today you are going to leave this world!" The woman gave away all that she had to the poor, embraced the icon of Saint Michael, and expired. Euphemia suggests Saint Euphemia, a fourth-century martyr who was claimed by both sides of the dispute at the Council of Chalcedon.

The Synaxarion then explains the date of 12 Ba'ūnah. In Alexandria, there was a great temple built by Queen Cleopatra and dedicated to Saturn. Inside was a horrible bronze statue still honored on 12 Ba'ūnah by human sacrifice. ALEXANDER I, patriarch of Alexandria in the early fourth century, wanted to destroy the statue, but the people of Alexandria opposed him, asserting that eighteen patriarchs had already held the see without coming to this point. Alexander suggested as a compromise that the temple become a church dedicated to Saint Michael. The church is usually called the Caesarion. It was later the site of a fateful scene in which the anti-chalcedonian radical Saint MACARIUS OF TKOW was killed by a kick from the emissary of Constantinople.

The etiological part of this account can be confirmed by the tenth-century chronicle of Sa'īd IBN AL-BITRĪQ, which, however, speaks of the god Hermes; by al-Maqrīzī, who speaks of Saturn (*zuḥal*); and by JOHN OF NIKIOU, who specifies that the Caesarion had been built by Cleopatra in honor of Caesarion, the son she bore to Julius Caesar. According to Athenaeus, the second-century author of the *Deipnosophistes*, there was a temple of Cronos (a Greek agricultural god identified with the Roman Saturn) in Alexandria. A homily attributed to PETER I, patriarch of Alexandria from 300 to 310, says that the cult of Saint Michael dates to the time of his immediate predecesser, THEONAS. A number of manuscripts or fragments of this homily exist (see Hyvernat, 1922; Crum and von Lemm, 1907 and 1908; Simon, 1935).

In fact, the substitution of the cult of Saint Michael for that of Cronus is considered to have occurred in the early second century, a period when astrology and syncretism were popular. Michael was sometimes identified as the successor of Cronus, whose cult was already celebrated in Greece on 12 Hekatombaion, and with Cronus-Aion-Zurvan, an amalgamation of Cronus with two lion-headed Mithraic gods associated with time. The representation of this divinity, a man with a lion's head whose body was tightly encircled by a snake devouring its tail, justifies the adjective "horrible" in the Synaxarion account. Moreover, the name of the idol, Boz or Boh in Coptic, is comparable to that of the Egyptian god Bes, who had a lion head. At other times Michael was identified as the successor of Hermes-Thoth, an amalgam of Greek and Egyptian gods of learning, who was also a psychopomp. At one time the Jews gave the name Michael to Wednesday, the day of Mercury (the Roman version of Hermes). This identification is strongly supported by G. Lanczkowki but corresponds only in a limited way to Michael's functions.

Through Michael's connection with Mithraism, he may be seen as one of seven archangels in a much older syncretism arising from the Zoroastrian reform of the Indo-Iranian pantheon (Dumezil, 1945). This kind of syncretism evolved into the personality of Sol Invictus, or Mithra, the Iranian warrior god of light and trust, the focus of Mithraism, which had much in common with Christianity. These Mithraic features suggest a possible assimilation to Michael even before Patriarch Alexander's official founding of the Church of Saint Michael (Nilsson, 1974, pp. 449–519).

Saint Michael's Investiture in Heaven

The other festival of Saint Michael in the Synaxarion, 12 Hātūr, concerns his investiture in heaven as the replacement for Mastema, or Satan, who had been thrown out of heaven for refusing to worship Adam newly emerged from God's hands. The Synaxarion underlines Michael's cosmological role, notably in his connection with the flooding of the Nile, and describes a miracle illustrating Michael's fidelity to his devotees. The archangel asks Dorotheus and his wife Theopista to spend on the archangel's festival all they possess except their clothes. When they comply, Michael goes to their house and has them open the belly of a fish, where they discover a purse full of gold.

The festival of Michael's investiture in heaven is described in an apocryphal work attributed to Saint John the Apostle, *The Book of the Investiture of Michael,* preserved in its entirety in Sahidic and almost completely in Fayyumic (published by C. D. Müller, 1962). The work was attacked by Saint John, bishop of Parallos, shortly before 600 (published by A. van Lanschoot, 1946) for making Michael chief of the angels only after the devil's fall and for giving the festival a precise date, 12 Hātūr. *The Book of the Investiture* is related at many points to the *Transitus Mariae,* a body of apocryphal works about the death of the Virgin Mary dating from the fifth century. In the *Book of the Investiture* Michael is responsible for transplanting to earth the Tree of Life stolen by Mastema. The Ethiopian text of the *Transitus* (Arras, 1973, pp. 3–6), incomprehensible without the help of the *Book of the Investiture,* explains the origin of evil by the refusal of Saklabaoth, greatest of the angels, to worship man. He becomes chief of the demons, and Michael is enthroned in his place. In heaven he describes a series of souls, among them that of the paralytic healed by Saint Peter (Acts 14:8) on 12 Hātūr. This text, however obscure and incoherent in its details, is a remarkable witness to the cult of Saint Michael.

A homilitic text attributed to Saint John Chrysostom (Vatican Library, Coptic Codex 58, Simon, 1934) is an exemplary demonstration of the monthly celebration of the archangel. His appearances on earth are described as follows: on 12 Ba'ūnah he visits Abraham as one of three angels including Christ and Gabriel; on 26 Ba'ūnah he appears to Lot to save him from Gomorrah and also to Joshua when the walls of Jericho crumble; on 12 Baramhāt, he speaks to Jacob at Bethel; on 24 Bashans, he announces Samson's birth to Manoah; on 24 Baramūdah, he urges Nebuchadnezzar to attack Jerusalem and later speaks to Daniel in prison; on 12 Bashans, he seizes Habakkuk by the hair to feed Daniel in the pit; on 29 Baramhāt (Easter) he sits on the Savior's tombstone; on 23 Amshīr, he blesses the fruits of the earth; on 12 Baramūdah, he delivers Peter from Herod's prison; on 12 Bābah, he appears to the centurion Cornelius; on 10 Baramhāt, he appears to Constantine, giving him victory over the Persians; on 12 Hātūr, he smashes the idol Boz under Saint Eumenius, patriarch of Alexandria. This series of anniversaries is the occasion of the monthly devotion.

There are a great many other homilies on Saint Michael preserved in Coptic. A homily attributed to Saint Eustathius of Antioch, later exiled to Thrace, was delivered in a sanctuary built in honor of Saint Michael by Saint John Chrysostom during his legendary exile in Thrace (actually in Armenia). The Bohairic text was published and translated by E. A. W. Budge (1894), the Sahidic text by A. Campagnano (1977). The homily belongs to a series of works with an anti-Chalcedonian tendency. Thrace (in modern Greece and Bulgaria) was where the archangel Michael helped the emperor Constantine conquer the Persians, according to a later application to Michael of a legend about Mercury, and it was said to be where John Chrysostom took refuge. The homily relates the story of pious Euphemia with a host of detail that the Synaxarion passes over in silence. She is given senatorial rank through her husband, who is called Aristarchus ("excellent general"), a man who was loyal to the emperors Honorius and Arcadius.

A homily attributed to Saint Macarius of Tkow (Lafontaine, 1979) is an anti-Chalcedonian text on Saint Michael in his church on his feast day. It mentions John Chrysostom as persecuted by the Empress Eudoxia, Arcadius' wife. A homily attributed to the patriarch Severus of Antioch preserved in Sahidic and Bohairic (Budge, 1894) tells of the foundation of Saint Michael's Church in Thrace by John Chrysostom.

A homily attributed to the fifth-century patriarch of Alexandria Timothy II Aelurus is the closest to the *Book of the Investiture.* Even if the writers were thinking of Timothy I, the content agrees perfectly with the visions of Saint John the Apostle in the *Book of the Investiture.* Also attributed to Timothy

II Aelurus is a homily on Abbaton, the fallen angel whom Michael replaced (Budge, 1915).

Opposing these strongly anti-Chalcedonian works were homilies that followed the example of John of Parallos' attack. The homily of Saint Theodosius I, sixth-century patriarch of Alexandria (Budge, 1904, in Bohairic; Budge, 1914, in Sahidic) criticizes formulations like those in the *Book of the Investiture*, which it suggests redating to the early sixth century. It tells a highly developed version of the story of Dorotheus and Theopista in the Synaxarion. A homily attributed to Gregory the Theologian, written in response to Eusebius, bishop of Armenia (Lafontaine, 1979), keenly opposes the position taken by the *Book of the Investiture*.

Not all the homilies on Michael necessarily belong to one side or the other of the Chalcedonian dispute. A homily attributed to Saint Athanasius I, fourth-century patriarch of Alexandria (Pierpont Morgan Library, New York, M 602; Orlandi, 1981) describes a visit from Saint Pachomius to Athanasius and, through the intercession of Saint Michael, the detection of a deacon who is a murderer. The same codex contains two homilies attributed to Saint Basil the Great (Orlandi, 1975). There Saint Michael is seen making a fortress against the Persians in Lazique—no doubt a late adjustment for the legendary Thrace. The same manuscript contains two other homilies of Athanasius in which Saint Michael occurs in the title.

Other homilies are preserved more or less complete under the name of Saint Severian of Gabala or Saint John Chrysostom (Pierpont Morgan Library, M 592, fols. 1–7), and there are many fragments. There are, in addition, innumerable appearances of Saint Michael at the end of the martyrs' torments (see the inventory in Müller, 1959, which includes the magic papyri, amulets, and everything written in Coptic that contains the name of Saint Michael). This evidence, less literary, shows clearly the impact of devotion to the archangel in everyday life. The texts in the Pierpont Morgan Library come from the Monastery of Saint Michael at Hamūlī, and therefore, it is not surprising that a great many texts have been saved.

Finally, in the literature of the *Transitus Mariae*, the function of Saint Michael seems to be divided between the role of an angel created from the beginning as chief of the heavenly hosts and the role of the third creature, after the first creature, Mastema, and the second, Adam (or more exactly the body of the Virgin from which Christ would be born). This "Manichaean" notion is explicitly related to the apocryphal *Gospel of the Hebrews* in the Coptic homily attributed to Saint Cyril, fourth-century bishop of Jerusalem (Budge, 1915, p. 59). However disconcerting the Coptic literature on Michael may at first appear, it contains strictly historical information about the movement of ideas among the different parts of the church in Armenia and Egypt.

BIBLIOGRAPHY

Arras, V. *De Transitu Mariae Apocrypha Aethiopice.* CSCO 343. Louvain, 1973.

Barbel, J. *Christos Angelos.* Bonn, 1941.

Budge, E. A. W., ed. *Saint Michael the Archangel: Three Encomiums by Theodosius, Archbishop of Alexandria, Severus Patriarch of Antioch and Eustathius Bishop of Trake.* London, 1894.

______. *Miscellaneous Coptic Texts in the Dialect of Upper Egypt.* London, 1915.

Campagnano, A., A. Maresca, and T. Orlandi. *Quattro omilie copte. Vita di Giovanni Crisostomo, encomio dei 24 vegliardi, encomio di Michele archangelo di Eustazio di Tracia,* pp. 107–72. Testi e Documenti per lo Studio dell'Antichità Serie Copta 60. Milan, 1977.

Canivet, P. "Nouvelles inscriptions grecques chrétiennes à Hūarte d'Apamée (Syrie)." *Travaux et Mémoires* 7 (1979).

Crum, W. E. "Hagiographica from Leipzig Manuscripts." *Proceedings of the Society of Biblical Archaeology* 29 (1907):305.

Devos, P. "De Jean Chrysostome à Jean de Lycopolis; Chrysostome et Chalkèdon." *Analecta Bollandiana* 96 (1978):395–98.

Dumézil, G. *Naissance d'archanges.* Paris, 1945.

Hyvernat, H. *Bibliothecae Pierpont Morgan codices photographice expressi.* Rome, 1922.

Itinerarium Burdigalense, ed. P. Geyer and O. Cuntz. Corpus Christianorum, Series Latina 175. Turnhout, 1965.

Lafontaine, G. "Un éloge copte de Saint Michel, attribué à Macaire de Tkow." *Le Muséon* 92 (1979):301–320.

Lantschoot, A. van. "Fragments coptes d'une homélie du Jean de Parallos contre les livres hérétiques." In *Miscellanea Giovanni Mercati* 1. Studi e Testi 121. Vatican City, 1946.

Müller, C. D. G. *Die Engellehre der koptischen Kirche.* Wiesbaden, 1959. Contains full sources in the footnotes.

______, ed. *Die Bücher der Einsetzung der Erzengel Michael und Gabriel.* CSCO 225, *Scriptores Coptici* 37. Louvain, 1962.

Nilsson, M. P. *Geschichte der griechischen Religion,* Vol. 2. Munich, 1974.

Orlandi, T. "Basilio di Cesarea nella letteratura copta." *Revista degli Studi Orientali* 49 (1975):49–59.

———. *Testi e Documenti per lo Studio Dell'Antichita.* Serie Copta 60. Milan, 1977.

Simon, J. "Homélie copte inédite sur S. Michel et le bon larron." *Orientalia* 3 (1934):217–42; 4 (1935):222–34.

MICHEL VAN ESBROECK

MICHAEL OF DAMIETTA. *See* Mīkhā'īl.

MICHALOWSKI, KAZIMIERZ (1901–1981), Polish archaeologist and Nubiologist. He studied classical archaeology at Lvov and continued his studies in Berlin, Heidelberg, Münster, Paris, Rome, and Athens. In 1934 he collaborated with the Institut français d'Archéologie orientale in Egypt in its excavations at DAYR AL-MADĪNAH, near Luxor.

After World War II he resumed his activities, beginning with the excavation at TALL ATRĪB (1957) and a visiting professorship at Alexandria (1957–1958). In the spring of 1959, he founded the Polish Center for Mediterranean Archaeology at Heliopolis. As president of the Society of Nubian Studies for many years, he distinguished himself in the field of Christian Nubiology.

His major publications include *Palmyra* (Warsaw, 1968); *Faras, centre artistique de la Nubie chrétienne* (Leiden, 1968); *The Art of Ancient Egypt* (London, 1969); and *Karnak* (translated from Polish; London and New York, 1970). His festschrift is *Mélanges offerts à K. M.* (Warsaw, 1966).

AZIZ S. ATIYA

MIDDLE EGYPTIAN DIALECT. *See Appendix.*

MIEDEMA, REIN (1886–1954), Dutch Coptologist, archaeologist, and art historian. He was privatdocent at the universities of Leiden and Utrecht, and was director of the Institute of Religious and Ecclesiastical Art in Utrecht.

BIBLIOGRAPHY

Dawson, W. R., and E. P. Uphill. *Who Was Who in Egyptology,* p. 202. London, 1972.

Kammerer, W., comp. *A Coptic Bibliography.* Ann Arbor, Mich., 1950; repr. New York, 1969.

AZIZ S. ATIYA

MIGNE, JACQUES-PAUL (1800–1875), French priest and editor. He received his ordination in 1824. Seeing that the patristic and ecclesiastical sources were dissipated in a multitude of collections and were often incomplete or unavailable, he conceived the idea of bringing these together in a series or set of series of uniform size for the benefit of scholars. His preliminary plan envisioned 979 quarto-size volumes with two columns to the page. This included Patrologia Latina (221 vols.), Patrologia Graeca (161 vols.), the Encyclopédie théologique (171 vols.), and a number of other series of documentary and ecclesiastical character. He succeeded in publishing his initial volumes at Bailly in Paris, which brought him many subscribers. But his ambition went far beyond his estimate, for he eventually conceived of the publication of about two thousand volumes.

In 1850, with the encouragement and support of the archbishop of Versailles, he found it necessary to establish his own printing press and collaborate with regular technicians in the art of printing. Migne had the vision and ability to recruit highly qualified priestly assistants in various fields, such as Hebrew, Greek, and Latin. In the end, a vast press, with all its divisions, and an army of three hundred workers made it possible for a succession of series to see the light of day. A new volume appeared almost every week. Standing high among his products of enduring value, in spite of the existence of textual errors and misprints, are the two Patrologiae: the Latina comprising as complete as possible a body of ecclesiastical writings in Latin to the reign of Innocent III, in 221 volumes (Paris, 1844–1864), including four volumes of indices; and the *Graeca,* with the Greek original and a parallel Latin translation, in 161 volumes (Paris, 1837–1886), brought down to the year 1439.

In 1868 a fire destroyed the printing establishment, but the printed texts of both works continued to be reproduced with all their imperfections as the only complete record of patristic literature in existence. Naturally these volumes included the fathers of the Coptic church, who wrote mainly in Greek and partly in their native Coptic.

BIBLIOGRAPHY

Leclerq, H. "Migne (Jacques-Paul)." In *Dictionnaire d'archéologie chrétienne et de liturgie,* Vol. 11, pt. 1. Paris, 1933.

AZIZ S. ATIYA

MIGRATION, COPTIC. The Copts as a community were sedentary by nature and upbringing. They loved the land of their birth and were averse to migration to other countries throughout their long history. The idea of moving from their ancestral home to a new milieu in search of better opportunities dawned upon them only recently, after the middle of the twentieth century, when they began under various economic and social influences to seek other opportunities abroad.

In the following sections, information is provided about specific communities in Africa, North America, Australia, and Europe. Even more interesting is the establishment of Coptic churches in the Arab world. A church was founded by Pope CYRIL VI (1959–1971) in Kuwait. In 1972 Pope SHENOUDA III consecrated a church in Beirut, Lebanon. Other churches followed during the 1970s in Amman (Jordan); Baghdad, Basrah, Mosul (Iraq); Dubai, Abū Dhabi (United Arab Emirates); Masqaṭ (Oman), and al-Manāmah (Bahrein). There is a church at Benghazi and another at Tripoli that was presented to the Coptic community by Colonel Qaddafi in 1972.

When the Copts migrated to new countries, they immediately sought a place of worship. Their financial resources as newcomers in a new land being modest, they found a solution by borrowing or buying old churches from other Christian denominations (frequently without payment or for a nominal price). Later, with an increase in members and more affluence, they were able to build their own churches or to adapt the acquired ones to suit their architectural and religious traditions.

Priests and monks from Egypt are assigned to serve abroad. With the exclusion of the Holy Land, where Copts struck roots centuries ago (see JERUSALEM, COPTIC SEE OF), the Coptic church is expanding outside Egyptian borders. Churches, small monasteries, seminaries, and religious and cultural centers are being established in many parts of the world. However, it is difficult to give absolute numbers of Copts abroad, owing to the lack of accurate registration.

POPE SHENOUDA III

Canada

The establishment of the Coptic church in North America began in Canada under the pontificate of Pope Cyril VI (1959–1971). The first priest, Father Murqus, with the help of thirty-six Coptic families already living in Toronto, established a congregation there.

The ground-breaking ceremony of the first Coptic Orthodox Church to be built in North America took place during the visit of Pope Shenouda III to Toronto. The Toronto congregation participating in the event consisted of 700 Coptic families. Canada at the time had 1,300 Coptic families.

Churches in Canada include five in Ontario (Toronto, Mississauga, Kitchner, and Ottawa), one in Alberta (Edmonton), three in Quebec (Montreal), and one in British Columbia (Vancouver).

BIBLIOGRAPHY

Brown, Lawrence G. *The American Immigration Collection: Cultural Conflicts and Social Adjustments.* New York, 1969.

el-Masri, Iris H. *The Story of the Copts.* Cairo, 1956.

FAYEK M. ISHAK

United States of America

The Copts' attraction to the United States was fostered by the American schools established in almost all important cities in Egypt and the missionary movement that had been active in the country for a long time. Migration to America, strictly speaking, was not confined to the Copts. It included Muslims as well. According to the 1970 American Census (U.S. Bureau of the Census, 1970, Table 192), the Egyptian immigrants totaled 31,358, of whom approximately 25,000 were Copts. The census of successive years showed a steady flow of refugees immigrating through Lebanon under the auspices of the World Council of Churches, the Catholic Missionary Services, and other organizations. More immigrants came to join already naturalized American citizens from Egypt. In 1973, thousands of Copts became citizens of the United States and were consequently instrumental in bringing over more members of their families. The increase in the Coptic population is reflected in the number of Coptic churches in the United States. These rose from two churches in 1970 to forty-one churches in 1989. The number of Copts in 1989 was estimated to be around 160,000–180,000.

The first priest appointed to the United States (September 1970) was Father Gabriel Abdelsayed for the first church in the United States, in Jersey City, New Jersey.

Coptic churches in the United States include nine in California (one in San Francisco and eight in Los Angeles; there is also a small monastery in Barstow), one in Colorado (Englewood), four in Florida (Plant City, Orlando, Pompano Beach, and Daytona Beach), one in Georgia (Atlanta), two in

Illinois (Chicago), one in Massachusetts (Nattick), one in Michigan (Detroit), one in Minnesota (St. Paul), one in Missouri (St. Louis), four in New Jersey (two in Jersey City and one each in East Brunswick and East Rutherford), six in New York (Brooklyn, Queens, Staten Island, Long Island, Pearl River, and Rochester), one in North Carolina (Raleigh), three in Pennsylvania (Philadelphia, Lancaster, and Pittsburgh), one in Rhode Island (Providence), three in Texas (San Antonio, Dallas, and Bel Air), one in Virginia (Falls Church), and one in Washington state (Seattle). Some groups are not yet large enough to justify a church. In this case they gather in one place and a Coptic priest from the nearest area holds a mass for them at regular intervals. Examples are Baltimore (Maryland), and Hamden (Connecticut).

BIBLIOGRAPHY

Brown, Lawrence, G. *The American Immigration Collection: Cultural Conflicts and Social Adjustments*. New York, 1969.

Constant, H. J., Jr., *Yearbook of American and Canadian Churches*. New York, 1989.

GABRIEL ABDELSAYYED

Africa

Modern Christianity in Africa owes its inception to the European and American missionaries who came in the train of the white colonialists. With the disappearance of colonial regimes and the rise of independent nation-states, the missionaries began to disappear. The leadership of the churches was assumed by Africans who were educated and trained abroad. However, many Africans separated themselves from the missionary churches and/or formed their own indigenous churches known as African Independent Churches (more than six thousand churches all over Africa). Their leaders led their native constitutents into a tribal and cultural form of worship that mixed native elements with Christian teachings.

Since Christianity in Africa originated through Saint Mark, the Cyrene-born apostle who organized the Coptic church in Egypt in the first century, the Coptic church could fill the vacuum created by the exit of the foreign missionaries. With the background of a long-standing history of an established ETHIOPIAN ORTHODOX CHURCH the Copts were encouraged to enter the African field, with their labors initially concentrated in Kenya.

So it was that the Coptic church was established in the 1970s with the consecration in Cairo of a bishop of African affairs, to reside in Nairobi. On 13 June 1976, Father Antonios al-Baramūsī, a monk of DAYR AL-BARAMŪS and formerly a practicing physician as well as a deacon and layman, was elevated and given the name Bishop Antonius Marcus. At first, his flock consisted of seventy-five Copts of Egyptian origin and 2,000 Ethiopians. Aided by two Coptic monks, Bishop Antonius was able to gain 4,100 converts of Kenyan origin and to serve many newcomers from Ethiopia.

With the steady expansion of Coptic Christianity in East Africa, numerous churches were founded in various areas of that vast country. At present, the Coptic churches number twelve, including a Cathedral of Saint Mark and a Church of Saint Antony in Nairobi. The remaining churches are evenly distributed in the western Nyanza provinces around Lake Victoria and the Ukambani area. Furthermore, the Copts have a church in Harari (Zimbabwe) and one in Lusaka (Zambia).

The services are conducted in the local vernacular and the Coptic liturgies have been translated into five native dialects. In addition to priests from Egypt, native Kenyans are now being ordained as priests.

Two modest beginnings of monastic institutions have been established in the diocese of Africa: the Monastery of Saint Antony in Nairobi and Saint Menas' Monastery in Ebusakami in the Western province.

Each church has its Sunday school. Each of the monasteries includes a cultural center as well as a modest theological college and a modest vocational center for the training of women.

BISHOP ANTONIUS MARCUS

Australia

Coptic migration to Australia was precipitated by circumstances associated with the economic policies of the Nasser regime. It was natural for the Copts to envisage migrating to Europe and America, but with the difficulties that arose in accepting immigrants to the Western European countries as well as to the United States and Canada, Copts began to look to the still-open door in Australia. Emigration of Copts to Australia had started in a small way as early as 1964, and gradually reached its peak in 1969. They concentrated along the populous eastern coast where they numbered approximately

35,000. In 1969, the Copts established their first church in the city of Sydney, which they dedicated to Saint Mark. Other churches followed. In 1989, Australia counted fourteen churches: six in Sydney, four in Melbourne, and one each in Adelaide, Perth, Brisbane, and Canberra. The concentration of Copts in the large city of Melbourne led to the establishment of a Coptic monastery in that area.

GABRIEL ABDELSAYYED

France

For centuries the Christian faith in France had kept close ties with the Holy Land, Egypt, and the desert fathers. Beginning in the fourth century, the maritime connections between Alexandria and Marseilles helped the infiltration of Alexandrian Christian thought in Gaul.

It was at the beginning of the fifth century that John CASSIAN, imbued with Egyptian monastic ideals, arrived in Marseilles. Two of his books, the *Institutes* and the *Conferences*, in which he wrote about the life, customs, and wisdom of the desert fathers, were the result of his stay among them. A testimony of his influence still exists in Saint Victor in Marseilles and the monastery of Lérins on the island of Saint Honorat (opposite Cannes); Pachomian monasticism inspired the rule of these establishments as well as the rules of many others across Europe. This influence continued for centuries.

On Pentecost 1974 (2 June), assisted by seventeen bishops and archbishops of the Holy Synod, Pope Shenouda III canonically established the Eparchy of France by ordaining two European monks who had shared the life of their desert brothers in DAYR ANBĀ BISHOI. The monk Marcos from Amsterdam was made bishop of Marseilles, Toulon, and all of France. The monk Athanasios, a French national, received the title of chorepiscopus of the city of Paris.

Five spiritual centers have been established since. The Coptic Orthodox Hermitage of Saint Mark, with a chapel dedicated to Our Lady of Zaytūn, is the seat of the bishop in Le Revest-les-Eaux near Toulon. In Plessis l'Eveque, near Meaux, the Priory of Saint Mark is the seat of the chorepiscopus; its chapel is dedicated to the Mother of God and Saint Mark. In Paris, the Coptic parish of Saint Mary and Saint Mark holds services in the crypt of the Church of Saint Sulpice. In Marseilles the parish of Saint George and Saint Mark was founded in 1983; mass is held in the Church of Saint Nicholas. A small private chapel is also in use in Tamaris-sur-Mer near Toulon; it is dedicated to Saint Antony and Saint Michael. The largest Coptic congregation is in Paris with over 700 members. Marseilles and Toulon follow with around 400 members each. With the exception of the chapel at Le Revest-les-Eaux, the Copts in France celebrate mass in host churches.

BIBLIOGRAPHY

Chadwick, O. *John Cassian, a Study in Primitive Monasticism.* Cambridge, 1950.

Cristini, L. *Jean Cassien ou la spiritualité du desert,* 2 vols. Paris, 1946.

PIERRE DE BOGDANOFF

Germany

The Coptic church in Germany was inaugurated in March 1975 by Pope Shenouda III, in response to an appeal from the growing Coptic community in the Federal Republic. Father Ṣalīb Suryāl was delegated as its first minister in Frankfurt, where the Copts secured a historic Evangelical church nearby, known as the Bethlehem Church, built in 1799. They named it the Coptic Orthodox Church of Saint Mark. Another church followed at Stuttgart and was dedicated to Saint George. At present, Germany has a total of seven Coptic churches. Besides the above there are churches at Düsseldorf (dedicated to the Virgin Mary), Munich (a gift from the Roman Catholic church, which was dedicated to Saint Menas), Hannover (a gift from the Evangelical Protestants, dedicated to Saint Athanasius the Apostolic), Berlin (dedicated to Saint Antony and Saint Shenute), and Hamburg (dedicated to Saint Peter, Seal of the Martyrs).

The Copts in Germany in the late 1980s consisted of approximately 500 families.

A Coptic center at Kresselbach near Frankfurt became the nucleus of a monastic institution.

ṢALĪB SURYĀL

Great Britain

The modern history of Egypt has fostered closer cultural relations with Britain than with any other Western country. From the early decades of the twentieth century, Egyptian students were sent to pursue higher studies in British universities. A good proportion of those students were Copts who subsequently were able to secure positions in the medical profession and various academic institutions throughout Britain. This proved a great incentive for many to seek permanent residence in Britain. This small community of expatriates grew considerably during the 1970s as a result of the easing of emigration restrictions previously imposed by the Egyptian authorities.

The first recorded Coptic liturgy to be celebrated in Britain took place in London on Friday, 10 August 1954. The celebrant on that occasion was Father Makārī al-Suryānī (later to be ordained Bishop SAMUEL). The liturgy was held at a Greek Orthodox church in London.

Efforts toward more organized religious activities were intensified in the 1960s. But it was not until 1971 that the first Coptic priest in England, Father Anṭūniyūs al-Suryānī (later Bishop Bakhumius of Beheira) celebrated the Divine Liturgy at Saint Andrew's Church, Holborn, London, by special arrangement with its archdeacon.

A Coptic church in London was realized in 1976 when the church council purchased a church in Kensington. In January 1978, after it had been redesigned into a proper Coptic church, the church was formally consecrated and dedicated to Saint Mark. Another church in Croydon, south of London, was acquired in the late 1980s.

With the increase in the number of Coptic residents in England, other churches were later established in Manchester and Birmingham. In addition the clergy take turns visiting smaller communities in other areas such as Cardiff, Glasgow (Scotland), and Dublin (Irish Republic).

FUAD MEGALLY

Switzerland

The number of Copts in Switzerland in 1989 was about 700. They live mainly in Zurich, Geneva, Lausanne, Basel, Lucerne, and Lugano.

In 1981 Pope Shenouda III ordained a monk, Serapion Anbā Bischoy, from the Anbā Bishoi Monastery, as the first priest of the Coptic church in Switzerland. When he later was consecrated bishop and moved to Cairo, others were appointed to replace him. With the exception of Geneva, where the Copts rent a government-owned church, the other congregations use mainly Catholic churches.

BISHOP SERAPION

Other Countries

It is difficult to follow Coptic immigrants to other countries of Europe, since there is no official register to indicate their continuous movements. However, Coptic communities are known to exist in Austria, where congregations meet regularly in Vienna, Linz, Klagenfurt, and Graz. The Copts in Amsterdam purchased a church that they dedicated to Saint Mark. A Coptic church was established in Milan in 1986, while small congregations are found in Athens and Madrid. One Coptic church exists in Stockholm and another in Copenhagen.

GABRIEL ABDELSAYYED

MIKA'EL I. *See* Ethiopian Prelates.

MIKA'EL II. *See* Ethiopian Prelates.

MIKA'EL III. *See* Ethiopian Prelates.

MIKA'EL IV. *See* Ethiopian Prelates.

MĪKHĀ'ĪL I. *See* Jerusalem, Coptic See of.

MĪKHĀ'ĪL I, II, III. *See* Khā'īl I, II, III.

MĪKHĀ'ĪL, twelfth-century bishop of Damietta. The dates of the birth and death of this celebrated Coptic bishop are not known, only that he lived under the patriarchs MARK III (1167–1189) and JOHN VI (1189–1216), that he completed the first edition of his Nomocanon in 1188, as he says himself, and that he was still alive when his adversary Murqus ibn Qanbar died in 1208. He was the first Coptic bishop to receive the honorific title of *muṭrān* (metropolitan), which does not confer any particular jurisdiction in Egypt. The division of the territory into provinces did not exist, but each bishop was directly dependent on the patriarch, so much so that the word *muṭrān* in Egyptian Arabic became synonymous with bishop. Mīkhā'īl handed on this privilege to his successors.

Mīkhā'īl of Damietta's principal work is his Nomocanon, of which a first version was completed in 1188 in Luxor, as was indicated in his manuscript (National Library, Paris, Arab. 7428; cf. Bouriant, 1886, p. 393, n. 1).

He had to combat one of his priests, Murqus ibn Qanbar, against whom he wrote several polemical works, among them *A Justification of the Peculiarities of the Copts*, a work recapitulated later in his *Ten Canons of Michael of Damietta* (Burmester, 1936, pp. 101–128), and "Letter to Mark ibn al-Qanbar" (Graf, 1923, pp. 180–192), written after the latter had joined the Melchites. He also acted as a polemicist against the Muslims in a letter known as "Letter to One of the Learned Muslims," unfortunately still unpublished.

Apart from the *Ten Canons*, which have been preserved in chronological canonical collections as a summary of his controversial work against Murqus ibn Qanbar, he wrote, according to Abū al-Barakāt IBN KABAR, a work in five chapters with the title *Kitāb samā' al-bughyah liman ṭalaba linafsihi al-khalāṣ wa-al-najāt yawn al-qiṣāṣ* (The Desire of Him Who Seeks for Himself Salvation on the Day of Retribution). Two manuscripts are noted by P. Sbath (Cairo, 1938, p. 65), but their present whereabouts are not known.

Another work that appears to be lost is quoted in a liturgical directory (Vat. Arab. 58). The title translated into English means Book of the Demonstration, and Guide in the Safe Way and the Very Practicable Path on the Doctrine of Faith and the Refutation of the Melchites (Graf, 1947, p. 335).

Finally, a short treatise of refutation of the obligation of confession could well be by Michael of Damietta, although it is anonymous.

BIBLIOGRAPHY

Bouriant, U. "Rapport au ministre de l'instruction publique sur une mission dans la Haute-Egypte (1884–1885)." *Mémoires publiés par les membres de la Mission archéologique française au Caire*, 1 (1886):367–408.

Burmester, O. H. E., ed. and trans. "The Sayings of Michael, Metropolitan of Damietta." *Orientalia Christiana Periodica* 2 (1936):101–128.

Graf, G. *Ein Reformversuch innerhalb der koptischen Kirche im zwölften Jahrhundert*. Paderborn, 1923.

Samir, K. "Bibliographie du dialogue islamo-chrétien." *Islamochristiana* 2 (1976):230.

Sbath, P. *Al-Fihrist*, nos. 528–529. Cairo, 1938.

RENÉ-GEORGES COQUIN

MĪKHĀ'ĪL, thirteenth-century bishop of Atrīb and Malīj. The exact dates of his birth and consecration as bishop or of his death are not known. We are certain only about the dates of twelve small theological treatises written between 1243 and 1247 before he became bishop. O. H. E. Burmester believed that he lived in the fourteenth century, on the ground that IBN KABAR (after 1324) does not speak of him in the catalog of the Arabic Christian authors in his encyclopedia the *Lamp of Darkness* (*Miṣbāḥ al-Ẓulmah*)); G. Graf remarks that this silence is not conclusive, for Ibn Kabar also omits to mention the patriarch GABRIEL II ibn al-Turayk (1131–1145), to whom, however, several works are attributed, among them the *Book of Easter*. The silence can be explained, for Mīkhā'īl is considered to be the author or corrector of the recension of the SYNAXARION from Lower Egypt: Ibn Kabar would have had to speak of him in connection with the liturgical books. His silence in his catalog of writers does not prove that Mīkhā'īl lived after him.

Graf thinks that he must have been consecrated bishop after the death of CYRIL III ibn Laqlaq (1235–1243), a patriarchate that was followed by a vacancy of seven years; he places Mīkhā'īl's consecration after 1250. It may be noted that the minutes of the consecrations of the holy chrism at the monastery (DAYR) ANBĀ MAQĀR indicate in 1300 a Butrus (Peter) as bishop of Atrīb and Malīj; he was probably the successor of Mīkhā'īl, who in consequence would have died before 1300 (Muyser, 1944, p. 155). We can thus say only that he was an author of the thirteenth century. If we have no further information, this is due no doubt to the fact that the HISTORY OF THE PATRIARCHS, if it gives a detailed life of the Patriarch Cyril III ibn Laqlaq, has preserved only very brief notices on the later patriarchs.

We have more information about the writings of this bishop. A series of twelve small theological treatises deal with the following themes: (1) a report by Mīkhā'īl of an interview he had with some Muslim jurists, the object of which was the rejection of the Jews by God, because of their constant idolatry; (2) a reply to the question of the compatibility of the human activities of Christ with His divinity, debated by the same interlocutors in an interview dated to 1247; (3) a dissertation on the basic teachings of the Christian religion, and the things common and distinctive in the Christian sects; (4) a reply to the question of the worship of images dated to 1243; (5) a reply to the question whether or not the repentant sinner may receive communion; (6) a reply to the question whether souls receive their recompense for the good or the ill they have done immediately after their separation from the body, or whether their retribution is deferred to the day of judgment; (7) a dissertation on predestination, or reply to the question, does God reward every man in the same manner, or a little more or a little less, or according to the quantity of virtues and vices?; (8) a reply to the question, is the duration of life fixed without any possibility of extension or contraction, or does the death of men come by chance?; (9) a treatise on redemption by the Cross of Christ (this treatise must be identical with the one that he intended for a friend, when he was bishop of Malīj, entitled "to refute those who pretend that Christ redeemed only sinners, or those who say that he redeemed only those to whom the good things are attributed"); (10) a reply to the question, can a part of the body of Christ (that is, a part of the consecrated host) be called the Christ?; (11) a question and answer on the duration of the fast before receiving communion; and (12) a question and answer on the subject of the meaning of the tree from which Adam ate. Graf notes that this series of twelve treatises is preserved in two manuscripts (P. Sbath collection, no. 1040, A.D. 1787; Yūḥannā Balīṭ collection, which Sbath himself does not otherwise call attention to nor does he indicate the date).

At the end of the fifth treatise he cites one of his works entitled *Book of the Exposition of the Union* (in Christ). This is preserved in a manuscript belonging, like that of the preceding texts, to the Yūḥannā Balīṭ Collection (Sbath, *al-Fihris*, no. 525, p. 65).

There is also a treatise entitled *Book on the Christian Religion*. It is preserved only in a single manuscript (Sbath, *al-Fihris*, no. 524, p. 65), belonging to a Catholic Syrian named Bakhkhāsh Salīm. We do not know if this manuscript still exists.

The authorship of the work entitled *Book of Spiritual Medicine*, which had a great vogue and was translated into Ethiopic in 1667 (Cerulli, 1968, p. 176), remains problematic. It is a manual of moral and pastoral theology, a kind of penitential: the European editor of this text, J. Cöln (1906, pp. 70–237; 1907, pp. 1–135; 1908, pp. 110–229; edition in Garshuni with a Latin translation) thought that the author of this work could be Murqus ibn Qanbar, by reason of the passages that reveal the author to be a Melchite. In fact, the manuscripts are now of Coptic origin, now of Melchite provenance; some appear to be of unknown origin. U. Zanetti has thought to have rediscovered the book *Of the Master and the Disciple* by Murqus ibn Qanbar, a book that has some resemblances with the former (1983, pp. 426–33). Despite the title, which its editor gave it, and the fact that it has been plagiarized by Farajallāh al-Akhmīmī in a *Nomocanon*, we cannot, like Graf, give it this name, for it is not a true canonical or chronological collection, nor systematic, but is limited to questions of penitential discipline.

A series of thirty-seven questions and responses attributed to a "Michael, bishop of Malīj" may be from the pen of Mīkhā'īl, or another of the same name. By its content, this compendium resembles the preceding work, although it is not possible to determine the true author. The language, very vulgar, suggests assigning a later date to this compilation, at the decline of the theological literature of the Copts.

The compilation of the recension of the SYNAXARION of the Copts from Lower Egypt is attributed to Michael, bishop of Atrīb and Malīj. Two things must be noted. First, the Synaxarion is, in general, written in two semesters. In the most ancient manuscripts of the first part, the name of Michael, bishop of Atrīb and Malīj, does not appear. Only the beginning of the second part gives his name. We may thus deduce that he worked only on this second part. Second, none of the manuscripts can give us his redaction, for all the manuscripts that have come down to us mention Saint BARSŪM THE NAKED, who died in 1317. This date is given, on the one hand, by the Synaxarion itself, at 5 al-Nasī and by the work of Ibn al-Suqā'ī (ed. Sublet, 1974, p. 210, no. 307). On the other hand, it speaks of the relics of John of Sanhūt as if they were still in the church of Damanhūr-Shubrā. Al-Maqrīzī says expressly that they were burned by the order of the Muslim governor in 1354, and notes that the cult of these relics then disappeared. We must then locate the recension of the Synaxarion of the Copts from Lower Egypt between these two dates, 1317 and 1354. For the rest, the Ethiopic version of this same recension does indeed give Mīkhā'īl, bishop of Atrīb and Malīj, as author of the compilation, which it dates to 1246–1247 (ed. Colin, 1986, p. 326), but it indicates as coauthor JOHN, bishop of Parallos.

We therefore cannot know with any precision what was the work of Mīkhā'īl, bishop of Atrīb and Malīj. If it was he who compiled what was to become the Synaxarion of the Copts along with John, bishop of Parallos, we cannot know in what Mīkhā'īl's "compilation" consisted. Notable stylistic differences (vocabulary, syntax) exist between the two parts, but we do not know whether they are due to the pen of Mīkhā'īl of Atrīb and Malīj or to a later redactor. It would be appropriate to compare this Synaxarion with the twelve small treatises, which have some chance of being from his pen.

BIBLIOGRAPHY

Cerulli, E. *La letteratura etiopica.* Le letterature del mondo 30. Florence and Milan, 1968.

Colin, G. *Le Synaxaire éthiopien. Mois de Maskaram.* PO 43, pt. 3. Turnhout, 1986.

Cöln, Fr. J. "Der Nomokanon Mihāils von Malig." *Oriens Christianus* 6 (1906):70–237; 7 (1907):1–135; 8 (1908):110–229.

Munier, H. *Recueil des listes épiscopales de l'église copte.* Cairo, 1943.

Muyser, J. "Contribution à l'étude des listes épiscopales de l'église copte." *Bulletin de la Société d'Archéologie copte* 10 (1944):115–76.

Sbath, P. *Bibliothèque de manuscrits Paul Sbath, prêtre syrien, d'Alep,* 3 vols. Cairo, 1928–1934.

______. *al-Fihris (catalogue de manuscrits arabes).* Cairo, 1938.

Zanetti, U. "Le Livre de Marc Ibn Qanbar sur la confession retrouvée." *Orientalia Christiana Periodica* 49 (1983):426–33.

RENÉ-GEORGES COQUIN

MIKHAIL, KYRIAKOS (1877–1957), Egyptian journalist and politican. He was born at al-Marāghah, near Suhāj, in Jirjā, and educated at the American College of Asyūṭ and the Coptic College in Cairo (Madrasat al-Aqbāṭ al-Kubrā). His interest in journalism was demonstrated at an early age when he combined his reporting to the *Egyptian Gazette* and the Arabic-language newspapers *Al-Mu'ayyad* and *Al-Waṭan* with his teaching profession. Later he assumed a full-time job as a correspondent and moved to Alexandria in 1908. Here he wrote to the London press a vehement criticism of the High Commissioner Sir Aldon Gorst's Annual Report of 1911, in which Gorst attacked the Coptic Congress for its show of "Coptic grievances" in that year (Mikhail, 1911, pp. 28–29; Kīlānī, 1962, pp. 105–106; Baḥr, 1979, pp. 59–67).

In 1911, Mikhail was delegated by the Coptic Congress and the Coptic Society to go to London, where with the assistance of Louis Fānūs, a Coptic political personality, he established an Egyptian Information Bureau. This was the beginning of a new phase in his career as he published articles supportive of the Coptic cause in the English press. During 1911 Mikhail wrote *Copts and Moslems Under the British Control.* A. J. Butler reported that the tone of the book was "admiringly calm and temperate, and the author has been obviously careful to avoid any expressions to which a Muslim reader may take exception" (Mikhail, 1914, p. 13).

It was about this time when the Nationalist Party (Al-Ḥizb al-Waṭanī) was founded, and its leaders were outspoken in their hostility to the Coptic cause. These party leaders were exiled in Europe in 1911–1912, and they "found another target for abuse in the visit of Kyriakos Mikhail, the young Coptic journalist, to London, where he was endeavouring to seek redress for certain grievances of his people" (Alexander, 1911, p. 369). Mikhail asserted that the Copts "have asked for justice and equality with other Egyptians" (Mikhail, 1911, p. 19). He accused Prime Minister Riyāḍ Pasha of siding with the Muslim Congress in Cairo and with its fanatic newspaper, *Al-Ahālī*, published in Alexandria. The paper repudiated the Coptic claims voiced by the COPTIC CONGRESS OF ASYŪṬ (Mikhail, 1911, pp. 32–35; Baḥr, 1979, pp. 67–71).

When Mikhail founded the bureau in London, he used it to address business and political issues until the outbreak of World War I. He was able to combat the views of a certain member of Parliament named Robertson, who in a series of articles in the *Times* defended Commissioner Gorst's colonial policy in Egypt.

In 1912 he decided to start his own newspaper in Egypt, but his request was rejected by the Egyptian government. Consequently, he published *Freedom of the Press in Egypt* (1914), in which he attacked restrictive laws on the press as well as discrimination against Coptic organs. Shortly before Egypt was declared an English protectorate in 1914, Mikhail protested this expected action in an article in the *Westminster Gazette.*

During World War I, he was not allowed to leave Britain and so made a living by writing and lecturing on Egyptian politics, society, and history at Birmingham and Oxford universities, as well as at the Egyptian Christian Club in London. During that period, Egyptians in Britain were threatened with arrest as Ottoman subjects, but a debate in the House of Lords led by Lord Cromer contested any such action, thus enabling Mikhail to retain his freedom. With the end of World War I, the English merchant marine replaced Egyptian workers with Englishmen back from war. The dismissed Egyptians faced many difficulties, but through Mikhail's efforts, Parliament convinced the government to extend financial aid to them until they left for Egypt six months later. Mikhail also led the Egyptian workers out of Cardiff during the riots against non-English colored workers in 1918. To make both ends meet, he wrote articles and opened the Redline Bookstore, which proved to be a principal supplier of literature on the Middle East. This was a successful financial venture, but was closed in November 1919 at the time of his deportation from Britain.

With the emergence of Saʿd Zaghlūl, a leader in the modern history of Egypt, and his exile to Malta on 8 March 1919, Mikhail wrote approximately a hundred articles in the English press and submitted numerous memoranda to British members of Parliament in defense of the nationalistic Wafd party and its exiled leader. After Zaghlūl's release from exile and the departure of the Wafd to Paris, Mikhail assumed the role of informing the English public of Egyptian affairs. His involvement in Anglo-Egyptian relations intensified with the issuance in November 1919 of his *Egyptian Newsletter,* which was intended for members of Parliament. This was censored by the authorities, who also accused him of meddling with the opposition Labour Party and leading an Egyptian student demonstration in London. His position was discussed in Parliament, and he was accused of working against British interests. His residence, office, and bookstore were searched by the police. On 9 December 1919 he was arrested and incarcerated, pending his final deportation from Britain.

On his arrival in Egypt in late December 1919, though he had been instructed by the authorities to refrain from discussing politics, he was received by the public as a national hero in Alexandria and Cairo. In January 1920 Mikhail was elected a member of the central committee of the Wafd Party.

With the normalization of relations with Britain and Egypt's declaration of independence in 1922 Mikhail returned to London, where his residence became a focal point for the Wafd politicians and many governmental missions visiting England. He also helped incoming students obtain higher education in that country.

In 1950 he was recruited for participation in the Wafd negotiations with Ethiopia concerning the regulation of the Nile waters, on account of his personal friendship with Emperor HAILE SELASSIE, which had grown during the imperial exile to London in 1936. After Mikhail died in London, his body was taken back to Egypt and buried in his native village.

BIBLIOGRAPHY

Alexander, J. R. *The Truth About Egypt.* London, 1911.

Mikhail, K. *Copts and Moslems Under British Control: A Collection of Facts and a Resume of Authoritative Opinions on the Coptic Question.* London, 1911.

———. *Freedom of the Press in Egypt.* London, 1914.

Muḥammad Sayyid Kīlānī. *Al-Adab al-Qibṭī.* Cairo, 1962.

RAGAI N. MAKAR

MĪKHĀ'ĪL ʿABD-AL-SAYYID, noted nineteenth-century teacher of English in the Coptic College founded by CYRIL IV. He is one of three Copts who under concealed identity were admitted to al-Azhar, the oldest Islamic university in Cairo. There he studied Arabic language and literature.

More significant in his career was his founding in 1877 of the Coptic daily newspaper *al-Waṭan.* This was a forum in which the Copts expressed their views, not only on Coptic matters but also on national problems of constitutional importance. One of the burning discussions of the day was the parliamentary representation of the Copts as a special group. Though the subject was not accepted for inclusion in the constitution, the role of *al-Waṭan* in the discussion was remarkable. *Al-Waṭan* ceased publication as a Coptic organ in 1930.

BIBLIOGRAPHY

Tawfīq Iskarūs. *Nawābigh al-Aqbāṭ fī al-Qarn al-Tāsiʿ-ʿĀshar.* Cairo, 1910.

Ramzī Tadrus. *al-Aqbāṭ fī al-Qarn al-ʿIshrīn.* 5 Vols. Cairo, 1911–1919.

MOUNIR SHOUCRI

MĪKHĀ'ĪL AL-BAḤRĀWĪ (or al-Naḥrāwī, since the manuscript has no diacritical point), known only as the owner of the oldest and finest manuscript of the *Summa Theologica* (known as *Majmūʿ Uṣūl al-Dīn; Vatican Library, Arabic 103);* written by Mu'taman al-Dawlah ibn al-ʿAssāl (chaps. 1–21 only), copied in Egypt during the author's lifetime. An unpublished autograph note on folio 208v, dated A.M. 1198/A.D. 1482, indicates this.

BIBLIOGRAPHY

Samir, K. "Date de composition de la Somme Théologique d'ibn al-ʿAssāl." *Orientalia Christiana Periodica* 50 (1984):94–106.

KHALIL SAMIR, S.J.

MĪKHĀ'ĪL IBN BUṬRUS, *protopsaltis* of the Greek Orthodox patriarchate of Alexandria in 1790. This position as "first singer" corresponds to the "precentor," who directs the two choirs during the liturgical services (cf. Clugnet, 1895, p. 132).

This was the position he occupied when he copied a manuscript containing the psalter and the biblical hymns, probably for the use of the patriarchal church of Alexandria (Sinai Arabic 42). The colophon (fol. 172b) tells us of his position and the date on which he completed the copying, 4 September 1790.

BIBLIOGRAPHY

Atiya, A. S., and J. N. Youssef. *Catalogue raisonné of the Mount Sinai Manuscripts*, p. 96. Alexandria, 1980.

Clugnet, L. *Dictionnaire grec-français des noms liturgiques en usage dans l'église grecque.* Paris, 1895.

KHALIL SAMIR, S.J.

MĪKHĀ'ĪL IBN GHĀZĪ, Melchite priest known only from the manuscript he copied in Cairo and completed on 12 February 7204 of Adam/A.D. 1696 under the Melchite patriarch of Alexandria, Gerasimus II Palladas (1688–1710).

The manuscript he copied is now the Sinai Arabic 59, which contains the Psalter including Psalm 151, the biblical odes, and the *Kathismata*.

BIBLIOGRAPHY

Atiya, A. S., and J. N. Youssef. *Catalogue raisonné of the Mount Sinai Manuscripts*, pp. 117–18. Alexandria, 1980.

Nasrallah, J. *Histoire du mouvement littéraire dans l'église melchite*, Vol. 4, pt. 1, pp. 174–75. Louvain and Paris, 1979.

KHALIL SAMIR, S.J.

MĪKHĀ'ĪL IBN YA'QŪB 'UBAYD AL-MIṢRĪ, copier of the manuscript Sinai Arabic 223, a liturgical collection of 142 pages, including the office of communion, evening and morning prayers, and the eucharistic liturgies attributed to JOHN CHRYSOSTOM, BASIL THE GREAT, and Gregory the Theologian. He completed it on 21 November 1774.

This Melchite from Cairo is quite different from the two Mīkhā'īl 'Ubayd mentioned by G. Graf in *Geschichte der christlichen arabischen literatur* (Vol. 3, p. 351; and Vol. 3, p. 474), who were both Maronites, the first of whom lived in the mid-seventeenth century.

BIBLIOGRAPHY

Atiya, A. S., and J. N. Youssef. *Catalogue raisonné of the Mount Sinai Manuscripts.* Alexandria, 1980.

KHALIL SAMIR, S.J.

MĪKHĀ'ĪL JIRJIS, MUʿALLIM (1873–1957), master chanter of the Cathedral of Saint Mark in Cairo and described as the figure in whom the Coptic church's vocal music was preserved and from whom its immortal chants were transmitted through his pupils. He was a blind man whose intense sensitivity for Coptic chanting and church hymnology impressed upon his inborn musical genius the fullest record of traditional Coptic musicology as he had heard it from the older priestly masters of that art. This evolved especially from the ancient monasteries where unbroken conservative traditions handed the singing of liturgical texts from generation to generation.

From his early youth he showed an outstanding aptitude to learn the tunes in which only two chanters specialized before him: Mu'allim Armāniyūs and Mu'allim Ṣalīb. Hence he is considered as the channel through which church tunes in their pure ritual form were transmitted intact from ancient and medieval times to the modern era.

He was brought up in his early childhood like the majority of Coptic children, joining the Coptic *kuttāb*, or lowest elementary school, of Abū al-Sa'd, in the Azbakiyyah quarters. There he remained for two years, from 1879 to 1881 during which time he studied the Psalms and hymns as well as the Coptic and Arabic languages. Later he joined the Coptic Clerical College, which was then under the administration of Yusuf Manqariyūs. He graduated in 1893 and was appointed teacher of church music there.

In 1895 he was asked to teach church ritual, religion, Coptic, and Arabic in the school for the blind, set up at Zeitoun, a suburb of Cairo. He used the Braille method in teaching Arabic, and designed the Coptic alphabet after the same method for teaching Coptic.

He was chosen by CYRIL V as church singer of the cathedral and as teacher of church music at the Clerical College. When the Higher Institute for Coptic Studies was founded in 1954, he collaborated with Rāghib Muftāḥ, head of the department of Coptic music at the Institute.

His most important achievement was the translation of the Coptic service into Arabic, in collaboration with the *qummuṣ* PHĪLŪTHĀWŪS IBRĀHĪM, who was a priest at the cathedral under CYRIL V.

His legacy continued with his pupils, some of them blind like himself, who attended his classes of religious cantors. His task extended from Coptic vocal music to Coptic elocution where he had to rectify the pronunciation of a language long dead and largely forgotten.

SULAYMĀN NĀSĪM

MĪKHĀ'ĪL AL-MIṢRĪ, a monk at the MOUNT SINAI MONASTERY OF SAINT CATHERINE at the end of the thirteenth century. He is known from a note he left at the end of an Arabic Pentateuch (Sinai Arabic 4, copied by Jibrīl ibn Mūsā al-Kātib in A.H. 353/A.D. 963). This note (on fol. 281b) reads, "The servant of the servants of the Word of God, Mīkhā'īl al-Miṣrī, read from this holy Pentateuch in the holy monastery of Ṭūr Sīnā, this being in the year 701 of the Hijrah. May the Lord God grant pardon to him who prays for him." This date corresponds to the year 1301–1302. This Melchite monk came from Cairo (Miṣr) as his ethnic surname indicates.

This monk may well be the same one who was present at the armistice between the king of Egypt, Manṣūr Qalāwūn, and the Republic of Genoa on 14 May 1290. This armistice stated that the Genoan signatories swore on the Gospel in the presence of Peter, the Melchite bishop of Miṣr, of Arsenius the abbot of the Melchite monastery of al-Quṣayr near Cairo, of the deacon Mattā, and of Mīkhā'īl, monk of Sinai. The treaty was made at Cairo. A copy of this document is found in an anonymous work recounting the life of Manṣūr Qalāwūn (Brockelmann, 1949, Vol. 1, p. 551).

Mīkhā'īl al-Miṣrī should not be confused with Mīkhā'īl ibn Ya'qūb ibn 'Ubayd al-Miṣrī, who in 1774 copied the two liturgies of JOHN CHRYSOSTOM and BASIL THE GREAT contained in Sinai Arabic 223 (Atiya and Youssef, 1980, p. 414).

BIBLIOGRAPHY

Atiya, A. S., and J. N. Youssef. *Catalogue raisonné of the Mount Sinai Manuscripts,* pp. 28–29 and 414. Alexandria, 1980.

Brockelmann, C. *Geschichte der arabischen Literatur,* 2nd ed., Vol. 1. Leiden, 1949.

Nasrallah, J. *Histoire du mouvement littéraire dans l'église melchite du Ve au XXe siècle,* Vol. 3, pt. 2, p. 56, n. 97. Paris and Louvain, 1981.

KHALIL SAMIR, S.J.

MĪKHĀ'ĪL SHĀRŪBĪM (1861–1918), Coptic historian. At the age of seven he enrolled in the Coptic school of Ḥārit al-Saqqāyīn, where he became proficient in Arabic, English, French, and the elements of Coptic. In his early youth, he began to write interesting stories in Arabic, and at the age of fourteen he was employed as a redactor in foreign languages in the ministry of finance. He was later moved to the post of private secretary to Ismā'īl Pasha Ṣiddīq until the death of his employer in 1876. Afterward he was transferred to the customs department in Alexandria, where he remained until 1880, the date of his return to Cairo. For two more years, he was recalled for service under English and French heads of departments owing to his language skills. Then he was selected by Muḥammad Sulṭān Pasha to establish a new department to deal with all matters connected with the British occupation army. After the suppression of that department, he returned to the ministry of finance as a translator. In 1884 he moved to a judicial capacity for the region of the east Delta comprising the provinces of Daqahliyyah and Sharqiyyah as well as the governorates of Damietta, Port-Said, and al-'Arīsh.

Because of his steady progress in the administration, the khedive conferred the title of bey on him, and he was also decorated by the Greek monarch, the shah of Persia, and the king of Spain.

In 1888, he decided to retire from service, owing to differences between him and the minister Riyāḍ Pasha. Then he devoted his life and energy to agricultural pursuits and to the writing of his monumental history of Egypt entitled *al-Kāfī,* with which he became identified.

In 1894, he was solicited by the minister of finance, Aḥmad Mazloum (Pasha), and his English under-secretary to return to government service as director general of the important survey department. He remained in service until 1903 shuttling from one department to another. During that period, he was decorated by the Ottoman sultan and by the Ethiopian emperor. At this point, he was eager to resume his historical writing of *al-Kāfī* that he had begun five years before. He thus prevailed upon his superiors to accept his resignation from public office and devoted his remaining years to caring for his property in the provinces of Giza and Banī Suef and to the completion of his history.

He was able to publish four volumes. The first comprised ancient history to the end of Roman domination and the advent of the Arab conquest. The second deals with the medieval period and rule of the Islamic dynasties until the emergence of the Turks and Selim II's Ottoman conquest of Egypt in 1517. The fourth treats the modern history of Egypt with the French Expedition leading to the establishment of the MUḤAMMAD 'ALĪ DYNASTY, which he followed down to the reign of the khedive Tawfīq Pasha. He spent the remaining years of his life in preparation of materials for the fifth volume, which unfortunately was left unpublished. His library was donated to the Coptic Museum, and his notes for the fifth volume are in the process of being published.

AZIZ S. ATIYA

MILLET, corruption of the Arabic term *millah* (religion or rite). The word has come to signify the people or community of a non-Muslim protected religion—that is, the Jews and the Christians, *ahl al-kitāb* or *ahl al-dhimmah* (people of the book [the Bible], and people entrusted to Islam).

AZIZ S. ATIYA

MĪNĀ I, or Menas I, forty-seventh patriarch of the See of Saint Mark (767–774). Mīnā was a monk of Dayr Anbā Maqār, when he became associated with and acted as a disciple of his predecessor, KHĀ'ĪL I, who was a monk in the same monastery. The bishops and the clergy of Alexandria, together with the Coptic archons, do not seem to have had any trouble in coming to full unanimity about the election of the monk Mīnā as the worthy successor of Khā'īl, and they faced no difficulty in securing the governor's approval, which was followed by Mīnā's peaceful consecration. The state of the Copts during his reign was totally different from what it had been under his predecessors. Peace and prosperity seemed to return to Egypt, and the community of the faithful suffered no extraordinary financial imposts.

Nevertheless, that peaceful atmosphere was disturbed by a strange internal incident, so different from the former persecutions that the community had suffered from the ruling class. A monk named Buṭrus, of the same monastery as Mīnā, was an ambitious but vicious person. He asked the patriarch to make him a bishop, but his request was refused because he was considered unfit for that ecclesiastical office. So he withdrew from his monastery and went to Antioch, where he submitted false patriarchal letters of introduction to the Antiochene patriarch, George, who welcomed him as a representative of his colleague and brother, the patriarch of Alexandria. He further wrote to the bishops of his diocese to treat the visitor kindly and offer him all the help he might need. Consequently, Buṭrus was able to collect great amounts of money, which enabled him to reach the capital and meet the caliph, to whom he reported that the patriarch of Alexandria was a magician and able to transform with chemical ruses much metal into gold, to be used in filling his churches with gold sacramental cups. The Abbasid caliph, Abū Ja'far al-Manṣūr (754–775), was hard-pressed for funds and listened to the impostor, who prevailed upon him to issue a decree making Buṭrus patriarch instead of Mīnā, on the condition that he would cede the accumulated gold of the church to the caliph. Armed with that decree, he returned to Egypt and requested its governor, 'Abd al-Raḥmān ibn Ḥudayj (769–772), to carry out the caliphal order. Consequently, Ibn Ḥudayj summoned Anbā Mīnā and confronted him with the royal decree, which he meekly accepted. But the congregated bishops were furious and refused to accept the impostor, who had openly abused Anbā Mīnā. Two of the bishops, Mīnā of Ṣanabū and Anbā Moeses, bishop of Awsīm, pounced on Buṭrus, seized his cap, and threw it down. They reported to the governor that their churches had only glass and wooden utensils for sacramental use, and that they possessed no gold or silver utensils, since they had already been plundered by former governors in times of persecution. Apparently the matter ended when Buṭrus threatened the governor that he would take his complaint to the higher authority of the caliph's administration in the capital, because of the governor's rather lenient treatment of the patriarchal party. This infuriated the governor, who arrested Buṭrus and placed him in prison for three years, during which time the situation was again normalized and Mīnā could exercise his patriarchal authority in peace. Evidently, Buṭrus was freed and returned to his native village, where he was rejected and disowned by his own family for his treachery.

Mīnā seems to have spent the remaining period of his reign in peace and harmony with the Islamic administration of the country, and the Copts in general did not suffer from the persecutions and financial imposts that had been customary under the rule of former governors. He died peacefully in 774, after the completion of seven years on the throne of Saint Mark.

BIBLIOGRAPHY

Hanotaux, G., ed. *Histoire de la nation égyptienne,* 7 vols. Paris, 1931–1940.

Lane-Poole, S. *A History of Egypt in the Middle Ages.* London, 1901.

______. *The Mohammadan Dynasties.* Paris, 1925.

SUBHI Y. LABIB

MĪNĀ II, sixty-first patriarch of the See of Saint Mark (956–974). Mīnā was a native of the village of Ṣandalā. He became a monk in the monastery of Saint Macarius (DAYR ANBĀ MAQĀR). He was a docile youth and his parents married him to a relative against his will. So when he joined his wife in seclusion, he preached to her the virtues of chastity and a godly life, which she accepted. After they had lived together for three days, without physical contact, she allowed him to silently withdraw to Wādī Habīb. There he became the disciple of a saintly old monk, to whom he revealed his situation and his chastity in the seclusion of his cell. Consequently, his spiritual father accepted him for monastic life and instructed him in all religious traditions. Mīnā was thus concealed for three years, during which he proved his sanctity.

When the sixtieth patriarch, THEOPHANES, died, the bishops and clergy of Alexandria became aware of the old and saintly monk of Saint Macarius, whom they asked to succeed the deceased pope. But he declined on account of his advanced years and directed them to a younger person, his disciple Mīnā, whom they readily accepted and carried against his will in iron fetters to Alexandria for consecration. While touring the diocese with his bishops, he went to his village of Ṣandalā, where a native divulged to the bishops that Mīnā was a married man. Mīnā confessed the marriage and told them to call on his wife for their secret. The revelation of their nominal marital relation and their purity appeased the bishops, and Mīnā began one of the most important patriarchal reigns, during which momentous events in the history of Egypt took place.

Nominally, Egypt was still a province of the moribund Abbasid caliphate in Baghdad. Al-Muṭīʿ (946–974) was the Abbasid caliph, but Egypt, which had almost secured independence under the Tulunid dynasty, passed to the kingdom of the Ikhshids. The governor of the country was Abū al-Qāsim Ūnjūr ibn Muḥammad al-Ikhshīd ibn Ṭughj (946–960). But neither Abū al-Qāsim nor his brother and successor, Abū al-Ḥasan ʿAli ibn al-Ikhshīd (960–966), was in real command of the government of Egypt, for their father, al-Ikhshīd ibn Ṭughj, had placed them under the tutelage of an Abyssinian slave and eunuch by the name of Abū al-Misk Kāfūr, whom he had bought for ten dinars. Observing the unusual talents of Kāfūr, he appointed him regent over his two young sons, who cared only for the life of luxury and their stipend of 400,000 dinars a year. Neither of them was aware of what was happening in the church or the patriarchate. They were equally unaware that their regent had employed a Copt by the name of Abū al-Yumn Quzmān ibn Mīnā as his vizier. In these circumstances, the Copts, their church, and the patriarchate had a breathing space and a period of relative peace and security, providing they rendered the KHARAJ tax. The last of the Ikhshids, Abū al-Fawāris Aḥmad ibn ʿAlī (968–969), had a short reign, during which the Shiʿite caliphate of al-Muʿizz in the west was biding its time for a fateful attack on the Sunni Abbasid regime in the east. In 969 al-Muʿizz dispatched his able general, Jawhar al-Siqillī (the Sicilian), apparently an Islamized Christian from the island of Sicily, with an army for the invasion of Egypt.

After establishing permanent peace in the provinces of northwestern Africa, al-Muʿizz had his eyes on Egypt. Along the littoral of the Mediterranean toward Alexandria, he began to prepare the road for the imminent invasion by digging wells and by constructing rest houses for his army. In February 969, headed by Jawhar, his troops began to move from Qayrawān toward the Egyptian capital. The situation in Egypt was full of confusion and discontent. A man from the inner Sunni circles and a descendant of the Prophet himself, Abū Jaʿfar Muslim, hastened to meet Jawhar outside Alexandria and offer capitulation of the city for a promise of amnesty for all the population, both Muslims and Copts alike. With little or no resistance, his armies reached Giza in July of the same year. In little time, with a white flag, Jawhar's heralds were marching along the streets of al-Fusṭāṭ (Cairo), announcing total amnesty for all who surrendered without resistance (Lane-Poole, 1901, p. 102). The depressed Copts had nothing to lose by the change of masters. On the contrary, their prospects looked better with the advent of a more lenient regime.

However, according to the HISTORY OF THE PATRIARCHS, there was resistance in Tinnīs from a band of a thousand Muslim youths, who seem to have closed the gates of their city and fought the enemy resolutely. The Coptic majority of the population, pressed by the siege of their city and the depletion of drinking water, contacted al-Mu'izz, who sent a representative by the name of Mash'alah to deal with the situation. Negotiations with the rebels and the promise of ten dinars and a robe of honor for each of their hundred leaders ended the strife, and the gates of the city were opened. Subsequently, over food and drink, the rebels celebrated with the enemy for three days, after which the soldiers descended upon their drunken hosts, killed most of them outright and crucified the rest.

With peace and security established in the country, Jawhar started the founding of the new capital, al-Qāhirah (the Victorious), to the northeast of al-Fusṭāṭ. The new capital was made ready for the triumphant entry of the Shi'ite caliph and his dynasty. The immense construction projects offered the native craftsmen, both Muslims and Copts alike, infinite opportunities, and people's attention was concentrated on productivity rather than disaffection or rebellion. The new caliph was sympathetic toward the Coptic natives, who seem to have enjoyed more security than under the Umayyad or the Abbasid regimes.

During the events mentioned above, Mīnā lived outside Alexandria in a village called Maḥallat Dāniyāl in the region of Tīdā between Sakhā and Nastarūh, where a rich old Coptic woman named Dīnā took care of his needs. By then, many dioceses had lost their bishops and some were incorporated in others less populated. These included Tarnūṭ, Arwāṭ, Nastarūh, Anḥalū, Iṣṭaf, Ḥaryūṭ, Abū Shuwā, Abū Rashā, Daqahlah, and Nikiou. Before he died, Mīnā founded a church in the name of Saint Mark at Maḥallat Dāniyāl, to which he carried the chrism and celebrated his liturgies.

The *History of the Patriarchs*, despite the peace that reigned in the land, records that the country suffered from natural calamities for the first seven years of Fatimid rule. The first year, the land became desiccated because the Nile was low, and people's provisions were depleted. The second year, the Nile flooded and the land became irrigated and produced ample crops, which swarms of rats and vermin consumed. The third year, strong winds spoiled the fields. The fourth year, a plague of locusts consumed the crops. The following three years, famine continued and wheat had to be imported from Palestine. In the end, however, the situation was ameliorated, and people began to prosper under Fatimid rule in the latter years of Mīnā, who died with peace and prosperity around him.

BIBLIOGRAPHY

Amélineau, E. *La Géographie de l'Egypte à l'époque copte.* Paris, 1893.

Lane-Poole, S. *History of Egypt in the Middle Ages.* London, 1901.

______. *The Mohammadan Dynasties.* Paris, 1925.

Parise, F., ed. *The Book of Calendars.* New York, 1982.

SUBHI Y. LABIB

MĪNĀ, SAINT. *See* Menas the Miracle Maker, Saint.

MĪNĀ TOGO. *See* Togo Mina.

MINSHAH, AL-. *See* Pilgrimages; Pshoi.

MINŪF AL-SUFLA. *See* Mahahhat Minuf.

MINŪF AL-'ULYAH, old Arabic name of a city in the Western Delta now known simply as Minūf. Located in the province of Minufiyyah, the city lies about 15 miles (24 km) west of Banhā. Minūf al-'Ulyah was known in Greek as Ὄνουθφις (Onothphis) and in Coptic as ⲁⲛⲟⲩϥⲉ or ⲟⲛⲟⲩϥⲉ.

Minūf al-'Ulyah was a bishopric by the middle of the fourth century as evidenced by the attendance of Bishop Adelphios of Onouphis at a synod in Alexandria in 362 (Munier, 1943, p. 8). Though we cannot be certain because there are some periods for which we have no records, it appears that the city has had a bishop for most of the time since that century. The seat of the present bishop of Minūf al-'Ulyah is Shibīn al-Kom, located about 8 miles (about 13 km) northeast of the city.

Saint Abraham (see ABRAHAM OF MINŪF) was from Minūf al-'Ulyah as was the martyr Simeon (see SAINTS, COPTIC), who was put to death in the Arabic period.

There is still a Coptic church in Minūf, the construction date of which is unknown.

BIBLIOGRAPHY

Munier, H. *Recueil des listes épiscopales de l'église copte.* Cairo, 1943.

Timm, S. *Das christlich-koptische Ägypten in arabischer Zeit,* pt. 4, pp. 1575–85. Wiesbaden, 1988.

RANDALL STEWART

MINYĀ, city located on the west bank of the Nile in Middle Egypt and the capital of the province of Minyā. The city was known in Coptic as ⲧⲙⲱⲛⲏ (Tmone). Before the late nineteenth century, Minyā was known in Arabic as Banī Khaṣīb after al-Khaṣīb ibn ʿAbd al-Ḥamīd, the financial administrator of Harūn al-Rashīd. The city was a bishopric by the early fourteenth century, as evidenced by the attendance of a Bishop Yūsāb of Minyā at the preparation of the holy CHRISM in 1330 (Munier, 1943, p. 40).

BIBLIOGRAPHY

Maspero, J., and G. Wiet. *Matériaux pour servir à la géographie de l'Egypte.* Cairo, 1919.

Munier, H. *Recueil des listes épiscopales de l'église copte.* Cairo, 1943.

RANDALL STEWART

MINYA AL-QAMH. *See* Pilgrimages.

MIṢĀ'ĪL, SAINT, ascetic. The principal source for his life is the notice for 13 Kiyahk in the SYNAXARION of the Copts from Lower Egypt; the Synaxarion from Upper Egypt does not refer to him.

The name Miṣā'īl is evidently a borrowing from the Bible, frequent in the Byzantine period, when the cult of the THREE HEBREWS IN THE FURNACE was very popular. Nothing is said of the childhood of this saint. We learn only that his birth was miraculous and that at the age of twelve he entered the monastery of al-Qalamūn, very probably the one in the south of the Fayyūm. We learn the rites customary for the reception of a candidate. His parents having died when he was still small, the bishop of the place (who is not named) took care of his education. The superior of the monastery was called Anbā Isḥāq, but there is nothing to identify him with Isaac, author of the life of Samuel, the famous founder of the monastery of al-Qalamūn. Miṣā'īl protected the monastery in a time of famine, which he had predicted to the abbot, against the assaults of the surrounding peasants. Finally, thanks to his inheritance, which Bishop Athanasius (probably of al-Bahnasā) administered for him after the death of his parents, he caused a church to be built (perhaps at al-Qalamūn), which Bishop Athanasius and others consecrated, and which was known by Miṣā'īl's name.

BIBLIOGRAPHY

Baumstark, A. "Die liturgischen Handschriften des jakobitischer Markusklosters in Jerusalem." *Oriens Christianus* N.S. 1 (1911):103–115; 286–314.

Budge, E. A. W. *The Book of the Saints of the Ethiopian Church,* 4 vols. Cambridge, 1928.

Gascou, J. "Notes de papyrologie byzantine (II)." *Chronique d'Egypte* 59 (1984):333–45.

Muyser, J. "Le culte des trois saints jeunes gens chez les Coptes." *Les Cahiers coptes* 6 (1954):17–31.

Till, W. *Datierung und Prosopographie der koptischen Urkunden aus Theben.* Österreichische Akademie der Wissenschaften, Philosophisch-Historische Klasse, Sitz-berichte 240, pt. 1. Vienna, 1962.

RENÉ-GEORGES COQUIN

MISBĀḤ AL-ẒULMAH WA-ĪḌĀḤ AL-KHIDMAH (The Luminary of Church Services), theological encyclopedia that is the principal written work of Abū al-Barakāt IBN KABAR. Its aim was to transmit to future generations the knowledge of the doctrine proclaimed by the first apostles and their successors, to pass on the practices of public worship, and to protect church doctrine from deviations and distortions. It does this by treating the whole range of ecclesiastical and theological subjects in essays and in reviews and summaries of the contents of other works. The listing of the sources reviewed and summarized makes this work especially valuable for the history of Christian literature written in Arabic.

According to G. Graf (1947), the dogma of the oneness and threeness of God and the incarnation of the Logos is given first, with the deviating doctrine of the Melchites and Nestorians outlined and a list of seventeen older heresies also given. Then there is biographical information on the first apostles and the seventy disciples, along with a list of the Alexandrian patriarchs. A list with a description of the contents of the compendiums of ecclesiastical law follows. An introduction to the Scriptures, with a presentation of the biblical canon and pedagogical notes on the individual books, is next. Chapter 7 has a valuable catalog of Christian writers and works in Arabic, giving the sources of church tradition. The remainder treats rites and ritual, church architecture and furnishings, consecrations, cloister life, baptism, weddings, burial, prayer, holy days, and the ecclesiastical calendar.

It is most easily accessible in Villecourt's French translation (1928).

VINCENT FREDERICK

MISR. *See* Press, Coptic.

MISSIONARIES IN INDIA, COPTIC. The story of the first Christian missionaries in the southern part of the Indian subcontinent is associated with the apostle Thomas. According to the apocryphal *Acts of Thomas* (Judas-Thomas in the Syriac version), written by Bardesanes, a famous author in Edessa, Syria, in the late second or early third century, Gondophernes, king of Malabar on the south coast of India, sent messengers to Jerusalem to search for an architect to build a palace for him. Thomas agreed to undertake this task and went to India. He had in mind a celestial, not an earthly, palace, and when he started spending the king's money on the poor, Gondophernes seized him and put him in prison. At that time the king's brother Gad died, but at his burial he came to life and recounted the miraculous visions he had witnessed in heaven. Consequently, the king released Thomas and with his brother allowed Thomas to baptize him. The apostle then committed the nascent church to a deacon named Zenophus or Xanhippus and proceeded to preach Christianity in other areas of India. He was martyred, and his body was taken back to Edessa by a fellow Christian.

When a son of Gondophernes became seriously ill, the king sought the relics of the deceased saint to heal his ailing child. Though Thomas' body was gone, the miracle of healing the prince was performed in absentia by the saint. Consequently, the royal family adopted the new religion; thus Christianity became established in the Malabar kingdom.

Though the story is apocryphal, the historicity of the introduction of Christianity in India is not without foundation. The trade routes between Syria and western India had long existed via the Red Sea and the Persian Gulf, and there was an active trade in pepper between the two countries. A colony of Jews, Greeks, and Syrians is known to have existed at Muziris-Cranganore on the Malabar Coast, and we must assume that Thomas joined that group. The descriptions of the court of Gondophernes in the *Acts of Thomas* fit a maharajah's household rather than a Parthian royal household, and the general climatic conditions are identical with those of the area under consideration. The numismatic evidence also confirms the existence of King Gondophernes around the middle of the first century.

Even if we choose to overlook the legendary and apocryphal nature of the *Acts*, certain other data offer testimony to the ancient and apostolic character of Malabar Christianity and its relationship with the Coptic church and its Syrian sister church. First, PANTAENUS, the first head of the CATECHETICAL SCHOOL OF ALEXANDRIA (on the authority of the historian EUSEBIUS OF CAESAREA), "was appointed as a herald for the Gospel of Christ to the heathen in the East, and was sent as far as India." Consequently Pantaenus must have reached the Indian subcontinent before the end of the second century and have found that other preachers of the new religion had preceded him and had left the Indians "the writing of Matthew in Hebrew letters, which was preserved until the time mentioned."

Second, the earliest reference to Indian Christianity appeared in official records of the First Council of NICEA in 325 when "Bishop John the Persian of the whole of Persia and India" appeared at that ecumenical assembly with a delegation of East Syrian bishops from Edessa and Nisibis. It is quite possible that that delegation included Theophilus the Indian.

Third, the most authoritative statements accepted by historians about Malabar Christianity occur in the records of COSMAS INDICOPLEUSTES, a famous early medieval traveler from the MOUNT SINAI MONASTERY OF SAINT CATHERINE. His seafaring adventures between 520 and 525 were recorded in his *Christian Topography*. He states that he found a Christian church established in interior India, with Indian clergy and a considerable congregation of believers. At its head was a bishop of "Kalliana," which must be identified as Quilon in Travancore. In the thirteenth century, Marco Polo confirmed the existence of that church when he visited the south Indian subcontinent on his way to China.

At that time a new missionary enterprise from Roman Catholicism was launched by Pope Innocent III, whose emissary to the Far East, John of Monte Corvino, spent a year (1291) in Malabar. He was followed by a Dominican friar named Jordanus, who reached India in 1319 and 1328 and was ordained Roman bishop of Quilon by the Avignonese pope John XXII. Gradually, Malabar Christianity was drawn within the pale of Roman Catholicism. In fact, Roman Catholicism in Malabar emerged in the face of preexisting Orthodox communities as well as a number of Nestorian families. The arrival of the Portuguese explorer Vasco da Gama in the fifteenth century led to the inauguration of a new chapter in the story of Malabar Christianity.

With the advent of Islam and the Arabs in Egypt during the Middle Ages, the missionary spirit among the Copts died. The weight of Muslim persecutions deflected the church from international projects to deal with immediate problems at home.

BIBLIOGRAPHY

Browne, L. W. *The Indian Christians of St. Thomas.* Cambridge, 1956.

Dahlmann, J. *Die Thomas-Legende.* Freiburg, 1912.

Fortescue, A. *The Lesser Eastern Churches.* London, 1913.

Medlycott, A. E. *India and the Apostle Thomas.* London, 1905.

Pothan, S. G. *The Syrian Christians of Kerala.* New York, 1963.

Winstedt, E. O., ed. *The Christian Topography of Cosmas Indicopleustes.* Cambridge, 1909.

AZIZ S. ATIYA

MISSORIA. *See* Metalwork, Coptic.

MIT DAMSIS. *See* Pilgrimages.

MITER. *See* Liturgical Vestments.

MODALISM. *See* Monarchianism.

MODERN EGYPT, COPTS IN. Following the withdrawal of the French in 1801, Copts fell on bad times, as they were adherents of the same religion as the departing enemy. Conditions improved four years later with the emergence of MUḤAMMAD ʿALĪ in 1805, to whom the Copts proved indispensable in carrying out his reform plans, thus keeping up the Islamic administrative tradition since the beginning of the early Middle Ages. Several eminent Copts stood in his favor for rendering him services in finance and administration. The most notable among them was al-Muʿallim GHĀLĪ, who carried out a survey of the whole country and divided it into provinces, each with its own capital and smaller subdivisions for the purpose of efficient revenue assessment.

It is also believed that Ghālī suggested to Muḥammad ʿAlī the idea of linking the Mediterranean and the Red Sea by means of a canal, a project to be financed principally by Egyptian capital. Yet, as in the case of a few other people close to the viceroy, he fell victim to a campaign of intrigue that resulted in Muḥammad ʿAlī's twice exiling him and twice reinstating him, until he was eventually killed in 1821. His son BASILIUS succeeded him as auditor general of accounts, and had the title of bey conferred upon him, thus becoming the first Copt to achieve this position.

BUṬRUS AGHĀ ARMĀNIYŪS, who had previously been governor of the province of Jirjā in Upper Egypt during the French occupation, was appointed governor of Wādī Bardis and given a free hand to restore law and order. Faraj Aghā and Makram Aghā were assigned similar offices in Fashn and Iṭfiḥ, respectively. As a result of the Copts being more qualified, many distinguished themselves as administrators, engineers, surveyors, accountants, scribes, and translators. In recognition of their services and cooperation in implementing reform projects, Muḥammad ʿAlī issued various decrees authorizing Copts to have new churches built and older ones restored.

ʿAbbās I, however, was not as tolerantly or favorably disposed toward the Copts as his father. Upon his accession, many Copts lost their positions of influence. It is believed that at one time he considered the idea of deporting all Copts to the Sudan, and asked the then *shaykh* of Al-Azhar, Ibrāhīm al-BAJŪRĪ, to prepare the necessary legal opinion, but the latter declined.

The reign of ʿAbbās, however, witnessed the start of the infiltration of various missionary movements into Egypt. Roman Catholic societies established a foothold in Jirjā, and Protestant groups in Banī Suef, Minyā, and Asyūṭ.

Under Saʿīd, the Copts fared better. In 1855 they were given equal rights of citizenship with the abolition of the poll tax imposed on Christians and Jews ever since the ARAB CONQUEST OF EGYPT in 640. In 1856 they were conscripted to the army for the first time. When Saʿīd decided to purge the army of Turkish and other foreign elements, the Copts were quick to respond and enlist.

With his European education and upbringing, Khedive ISMĀ'ĪL followed a totally uninhibited policy of goodwill and tolerance. His 1866 decree gave generous financial help to Coptic schools, and when he invited heads of state to the inauguration of the Suez Canal in 1869, he impressed Empress Eugenie by taking her on a round of visits to wealthy Coptic families in Upper Egypt. He also gave 1,500 *feddans* of land as a religious endowment to the Copts, and an annual grant of £200 in acknowledgment of their services in the education of both Coptic and Muslim children. Copts continued to hold important executive, legislative, and judiciary positions, and when the parliament was first established Ismā'īl prescribed the inclusion of a Coptic member among the representatives of each province.

The Copts did not deny 'Urābī their moral or material support in his struggle to free the country from the oppressive rule of both the Ottoman sultan and Khedive Tawfīq. "Under 'Urābī a Copt was promoted to be sub-Minister of Justice, a post which carried with it the superintendence of the Qāḍī's courts and the necessary minor appointments for the courts" (Leeder, 1914).

With the British occupation in 1882 the number of Copts in senior official posts was significantly diminished as a result of the enforcement of a so-called policy of British justice that was aimed at redressing the balance in favor of the majority, and giving the impression that such was the will of the Muslim government in power. In due time this gave rise to a situation where Copts and Muslims were mutually suspicious.

During the reign of Muḥammad 'Alī, domestic and foreign trade was almost completely in the hands of Copts and Maronite Syrians, and when various services were franchised, Copts became agents for foreign commercial firms. Some also acted as consuls on behalf of various countries. Thus many Copts showed great entrepreneurial skill and made immense fortunes. At the turn of the century, there were many Coptic landowners in the provinces of Minufiyyah, Daqahliyyah, and Gharbiyyah, and by mid-century their numbers had greatly increased in Upper Egypt where a large section of the population were Copts.

When Nasser introduced his socialist measures in the early 1960s, many enterprises exclusively or largely owned by Copts were nationalized, especially those connected with local transport, as were investments in major banks and companies. Many thousands of *feddans* were expropriated under agrarian reform laws, not only from wealthy Coptic families but also from endowments belonging to the patriarchate and the monasteries. All dispossessed land was subdivided among peasants, but few Copts benefited from that action.

The number of Copts in government posts steadily decreased in the second half of the twentieth century due to a dramatic increase in the Muslim population. At the beginning of the century, Copts occupied 40 percent of the government posts. In 1927 they occupied 9 percent. At present it is taken for granted that there are certain leadership and government positions to which Copts are not entitled.

[*See also:* Muḥammad 'Alī Dynasty.]

BIBLIOGRAPHY

Baer, G. *A History of Landownership in Modern Egypt,* p. 63. London, 1914.

Cromer, Lord. *Modern Egypt,* Vol. 2, pp. 208–212. London, 1908.

Leeder, G. *Modern Sons of the Pharaohs,* pp. 332–34. London, 1914.

Wakin, Edward. *A Lonely Minority: The Modern Story of Egypt's Copts.* New York, 1963.

SAMIRAH BAHR

MONARCHIANISM, a movement in the trinitarian controversy in the early church that denied the distinction of Persons in the relationship between Father and Son within the Godhead. It became a heresy.

There were two quite separate groups of Monarchians. Modalist Monarchians claimed that God was a single and differentiated being whose monarchy was nothing else than *singulare et unicum imperium,* "a singular and unique empire," as Tertullian expressed it about 213 in refuting Praxeas, a modalist teacher in Rome. This meant that the Son and the Holy Spirit had no individual existences but were simply "modes" or aspects of the Father.

The Adoptionist or Dynamic Monarchians stood at the opposite end of the theological spectrum. They claimed, according to their opponent, the Roman presbyter HIPPOLYTUS, in his refutation "that Jesus was a mere man (*psilos anthrōpos*), born of a virgin according to the counsel of the Father. After he had lived a life common to all men and had become preeminently religious, he received at his baptism "the Christ" in the form of a dove. This gift enabled him to manifest miraculous powers, which he had not shown before, and after his death he was "adopted" into the Godhead. Jesus was therefore entirely human, though controlled by the Spirit. He was to be revered as the greatest of all the prophets, but whether he was to be worshiped "as God" was questionable.

Though some traces of Modalist Monarchianism may be found in teachers denounced by Justin Martyr, the doctrine first attracted serious notice in Rome about 200 through a school of Christians from western Asia Minor, of whom Noetus, Polemon, and Praxeas were the most prominent. According to Hippolytus, Noetus proclaimed openly that "Christ was the Father himself, and that the Father himself was born, suffered and died." Another orthodox writer, Epiphanius of Salamis, affirmed about 380 that when challenged, Noetus protested, "What harm am I doing in glorifying Christ?" The objection to these ideas, apart from inherent absurdity, was that they destroyed the concept of the Trinity. As Tertullian summed up in his reply to Praxeas, Praxeas "did two bits of the devil's business in Rome. He banished the Paraclete and crucified the Father."

Nevertheless, two early third-century bishops of Rome, Zephyrinus and Calixtus, tended to favor a Modalist Monarchian form of Christology. Modalist monarchianism was refined by Sabellius the Libyan about 220 (see SABELLIANISM), and in this form played its part in the Trinitarian controversies of the third century, as well as in the disputes in the half-century following the First Council of NICAEA (325). It influenced the attitude of the Roman church toward both the Nicene Creed, with its assertion that Christ was "of one substance with the Father," and the Christological definition of Chalcedon.

As was to be expected, the two Roman bishops strongly opposed the Dynamic Monarchians, who were influential in Rome at about the same time as the Modalists. The Dynamic group were also Greek-speaking Christians, such as Theodotus, a tanner from Byzantium, and Theodotus, a banker. They were criticized as "atheists" by the Roman presbyter Gaius, who pointed out, according to the historian Eusebius, that the language of the evangelists and the worship of the church treated Christ as divine. Despite excommunication, the Dynamic Monarchians held their ground. One of their number, the confessor Natalius, was consecrated bishop and received a stipend of 150 denarii a month, the first firm evidence for a paid clergy. Around 230 a certain Artemon was continuing their tradition in Rome.

In Egypt, ORIGEN denounced both forms of Monarchianism in his development of the doctrine of the Logos, though he reserved his angriest comments for the Adoptionists, for "denying the divinity of Christ" (*Dialogue with Heracleides,* p. 439). Origen also disputed with Beryllus, bishop of Bostra in the province of Arabia, who, according to Eusebius, was charged with holding Modalist Monarchian views.

Modalism, in the form of Sabellianism, took root in Cyrenaica, North Africa, in the mid-third century, where it was controverted by DIONYSIUS THE GREAT, bishop of Alexandria. He, however, used terminology that suggested that Christ, far from being an aspect of the Godhead, was "creature," and part of the created order. An appeal by the Cyrenaicans to Rome brought Dionysius bishop of Rome into an indecisive exchange of letters with his fellow bishop in Alexandria about 263, according to J. F. Bethune-Baker.

The bishop of Alexandria demonstrated the strongest opposition of his see to what he interpreted as the "Adoptionist" views of Paul of Samosata, bishop of Antioch. The tendency of the church in Alexandria, through its acceptance of the *Logos-sarx* ("Word-flesh") interpretation of Jesus' relationship to the Godhead, was toward Modalist Monarchianism. Suspicion of this view underlay the doctrinal objections of the majority of the Eastern bishops to Saint ATHANASIUS, bishop of Alexandria, and to his uncompromising adherence to the Nicene Creed. The Easterners feared that Monarchianism would lead the church back toward Judaism. Saint BASIL THE GREAT of Caesarea wrote about 375 to a group of lay notables in Caesarea (*Letter* 210. 5): "For it is indispensable to have a clear understanding that, as he who fails to confess the community of essence or substance falls into polytheism, so he who refuses to grant the distinction of the hypostases ["individualities"] is carried off into Judaism." Only when the Creed of Constantinople (381) chose forms of words that safeguarded the separate individuality of the Persons of the Trinity did the fear of monarchianism as a hidden danger to Christian orthodoxy fade.

BIBLIOGRAPHY

Athanasius. *De decretis Niceanis.* In PG 25, cols. 415–476. Paris, 1884.

______. *Epistula de synodis.* In PG 26, cols. 681–794. Paris, 1887. Bardy, G. "Monarchianism." In *Dictionnaire de théologie catholique,* Vol. 10, pt. 2, cols. 2193–2209. Paris, 1929.

Bethune-Baker, J. F. *An Introduction to the Early History of Christian Doctrine to the Time of the Council of Chalcedon*, 9th ed., chaps. 7, 8. London, 1951.
Harnack, A. von. *History of Dogma*, Vol. 3, chap. 1. New York, 1958.
Kelly, J. N. D. *Early Christian Doctrines*, 5th ed., chap. 5. London, 1978.
Kidd, B. J. *History of the Church to A.D. 461*, Vol. 1, pp. 359–71. Oxford, 1922.

W. H. C. FREND

MONASTERIES, ECONOMIC ACTIVITIES OF. Despite schisms, persecutions, occasional devastation by the barbarians, and the Persian and Arab conquests in 619 and 641, respectively, the history of the Egyptian monasteries from the fourth to the eighth centuries constitutes a whole. The period was one of expansion and material prosperity. Various categories of sources—literary, papyrological, and archaeological—indicate this. This is not the place to analyze them or to appraise their value. It is enough to say, by way of delineating the limits of the present essay, that they do not allow of a rigorous, objective, quantified grasp of the facts. Hence, the way in which the subjects broached here have been treated is largely impressionistic.

Institutional and Legal Bases of the Monastic Economy

According to the times and places, Egyptian monastic economy varied with regard to individual liberty and hierarchical centralism—at times leading to collectivism. Nor is this simply a reflection of the well-known opposition between the lifestyles of the hermit and the cenobite.

Throughout the fourth to eighth centuries, an important element of monasticism wholly escaped the framework of the monasteries. These were the ascetic extremists who had withdrawn into the desert places and were completely isolated, but it also involved an entire urban and village population of both sexes, such as the *remnuoth* spoken of by Saint Jerome with disdain (*Epistle* 22.34), or those women who "withdrew" into their own houses (cf. Rémondon, 1972, p. 260), or semi-tramps like Mark the Mad (Clugnet, 1900, pp. 60–62), not to mention the itinerant monks, or *gyrovagues*. These people kept body and soul together as circumstances permitted or their own desires suggested, sometimes in little informal groups, working, trading, or living on their income. In these instances, the monastic economy was indistinguishable from a private domestic economy.

Within organized monasticism, economic individualism played a significant part; the monasteries displayed some reticence about taking in people who were in financial difficulty. This was to prevent encumbering their own finances and especially to test vocational genuineness. Thus, many monks at the beginning of an ascetic career were in easy circumstances (cf. Cadell, 1967, pp. 195–201 for the papyrological examples, and Martin, 1979, pp. 14f., for the literature). When they entered a monastery, they were entirely at liberty to get rid of their wealth (*Sancti Pachomii Vitae Graecae*, Vita prima, 80) if they thought that by doing so they were doing good works. But generally they held on to it and thereby their full economic and legal capacity. They continued to manage their property in their own way (cf. Cadell, 1967). Moreover, they had at their disposal the products of their labor and what it brought in.

During their time in the monastery, they entered into all sorts of contractual negotiations, whether with their "brother" ascetics or with civil society. Thus, one finds recorded loans (Rémondon, 1972, p. 259, notes in this connection that the monks most frequently figure as creditors), sales, the leasing of houses or lands (cf. Cadell, 1967), and the emancipation of slaves "to redeem their sins." The cells (*kellia*) and the monasteries themselves were often the property of their lay or ecclesiastical founders. These assets could give rise to security arrangements or mortgages. They could be passed on to one's heirs, as in the case of the monastery of the renowned ABRAHAM OF HERMONTHIS (Armant). Despite the protests of the emperor JUSTINIAN, the Egyptian monasteries could be sold even to lay people. For example, the Melitian establishment of Labla (Hawwārah) and that of Abbā Kopreous at Oxyrhynchus were both sold in this way. To sum up, the institution of monasticism often seems weak and insubstantial in the face of all the private interests involved in it, and in these instances one might hesitate to speak of a monastic economy. However, historically the trend appears to have reinforced the institution in two ways: the establishment of a specific economic administration going beyond the individual actions of the monks or regulating them, and the working out of protective legal, constitutional rules.

As to the first point, the Pachomian cenobites may have provided an example to follow. In this environment, the economic primacy of the institution was a question of principle. The ways of putting this into practice are well known: an authoritarian division and planning of the work, specialization in the houses, careful bookkeeping, the early institution of local *oeconomi,* or stewards, and of the general stewardship of the order (*Sancti Pachomii Vitae Graecae,* Vita prima, 28, 59, 83). Outside the Pachomian world, and probably matching the increase in the monasteries' own wealth and the varied developments in economic and commercial links with civil society, the same tendencies reveal themselves, but without such extreme results. Everywhere one can find some evidence of *diakoniai,* "general" and "special stewards," and *dioikētai,* or special funds, though one cannot always define exactly how these words were understood, other than that they related to the management of the common finances and the common property (Kahle, 1954, Vol. 1, pp. 30–40, Vol. 2, fol. 312r). Sometimes there appears to be a confusion of the superior with the steward, and in all sorts of ways the spiritual director of an establishment carried significant responsibilities of a material and financial nature, especially as regards taxes. In this connection, one must note that the interests of the superior are distinguished on the bookkeeping level from those of the rest of the community. This position was open to purchase at a very high price—up to fifty-three golden solidi. This sum served as caution money for good management (cf. Schmidt, 1932, pp. 60–68; Kahle, 1924, Vol. 2, fol. 312r).

Parallel to the preceding, there developed legal safeguards, with legal personality (*dikaion*) embodied in the person of the superior and legal competency—early attested—to receive legacies and consequently to make a settlement of an estate *in propria persona.* From the sixth century, many monasteries with assets held the status of foundations of public law, comparable to that of the imperial *domus divina* or of the bishops' churches. Consequently these assets were *res extra commercium* and thus, in principle, inalienable and not subject to distraint or attachment. Justinian's anger on learning that Egyptian monasteries were sometimes put up for sale demonstrates that in his mind this status must already have been the norm. No trace has been preserved of the legal measures that could enforce it, but one can, without the slightest doubt, gauge their effects. Thus, life leases or long leases were practiced by certain monasteries. These are instances of direct borrowing from the system of public land grants and implied sizable restrictions on the right to transfer property, in conformity with the general rule expressed in Justinian's Novella 7.1. Also typical of this system, which had a sacralizing effect, was the use of fiscal terminology (e.g., the word *demosion*) to refer to monastic income (cf. the well-known record of the *Kinderschenkungen* [children given as gifts] from western Thebes). Levies on long leases were themselves assimilated to a form of tax (Gascou, 1985, pp. 14–15).

Resources of the Monasteries

A monastery's resources came first and foremost from the monks' work. On this point Egypt gives an example to the rest of the world (Cassian *De institutis coenobiorum* 10.22). However, work in the monastery was not seen as an economic activity but as a form of ascesis, of high moral and religious value, and necessary for mental stability (cf. Guillaumont, 1979, pp. 117–26). Over all, work was divided into "tasks" and "trades." By the former is meant activities connected with subsistence and with the wellbeing of the communities. Cooking, baking, weaving, shoemaking, working the fields and the gardens and local mineral resources such as salt, building cells, and the like were often done by the monks themselves. The more manual aspects of these forms of work seem to have been the responsibility sometimes of special staff of relatively low standing, such as the novices or penitents.

The purpose of the trades was the production of goods that could be exchanged. On this point the monasteries specialized very clearly in basketmaking and ropemaking. Evidence for this comes from an abundant literature and from papyrological documentation. The raw material, palms and reeds, was easily obtained. This simple, mechanical, repetitive activity, which did not require much intellectual concentration and could be accomplished in the seclusion of one's cell, was regarded as well adapted to spiritual discipline. Thus, in the long run, the monasteries ended up by virtually monopolizing a good proportion of Egyptian production of baskets, mats, and ropes. These articles could be exchanged—MACARIUS THE EGYPTIAN thus obtained bread from the guards at the nitreworks of Scetis—but above all, they were sold. Selling could be the responsibility of the community, of lay wholesalers, or of the workers themselves. The marketing outlets could be very distant; thus, the Pachomians went from Pbow to Alexandria to trade their mats. A legal text preserves a request for a passport submitted to the Arab authorities in the name of Theban monks who wished to go to the Fayyūm to sell ropes. On some occasions the customers came to the monastery (e.g., the sailors spoken of in Orlandi, 1975, pp. 66–67).

One of the best-attested trades is weaving. Documentation comes primarily from the "Holy Mountain of Djeme" at western Thebes. There one finds archaeological traces of the installation of weaving looms in the cells, and the written sources give detailed information on the raw materials, palm fibers and flax (so much sought after that some Alexandrian monks came to the Thebaid to look for it), and production standards. A whole manufacturing organization, which had an influence on civil society, had developed around DAYR EPIPHANIUS and required the aid of employees. The establishment supplied the neighborhood with linen and cloths. Some monks contracted with the peasants for the production of tow.

Of course, other trades were practiced, too, but these occupations are much less well documented than the foregoing. However, one must mention at Scetis and in the Fayyūm work done in the fields for a wage, (18), painting, and the copying of books.

Income from work in principle allowed everyone to cater to his own needs and to save a little. In weaving it was even possible to grow rich (up to one hundred solidi, according to Jerome, *Epistle* 22.33). Thus, economically speaking, the work of the monks was in no way either a token performance or a marginal activity.

Very soon, and above all among the Pachomians, the monasteries came to control other, very powerful resources. It is correct to say that to a great extent they owed these to their own endeavors and ingenuity, for instance, in the Tabennesiote Nile flow transport business that was so characteristic of this milieu; likewise, they owed it to their toil, for instance, in clearing land or working mines at Qalamūn. Many acquisitions of land or items of equipment were financed from the communities' own funds or from the "portions" contributed by the monks. Here one must mention banking as contributing to gains in this category. Individually, but also as a body, the monks indulged in the giving of credit. Credit—which is to say usury—was veiled by sales on delivery, a type of transaction several times attested in the archives of the Hermopolis Monastery of Abbā Apollos of Titkoïs (cf. Harrauer and Sijpesteijn, 1982, pp. 296–302), relating to wine and grain.

It would, however, appear that the chief road to wealth was by way of assistance from the outside world, the diocesan ecclesiastical hierarchy, the upper echelons of the administration, and the laity. This aid was not always spontaneous. The monks would canvass, soliciting from door to door. A letter sent by an Oxyrhynchus community to a lay potentate illustrates this: "We beg your Lordship to ordain that we be sent the liberality which it is the custom of your illustrious house to bestow on us, so that we may give your Lordship our thanks and, sinners as we are, may send up to heaven our customary prayers for the health of your Lordship and for the prosperity of your illustrious house" (Rémondon, 1972, p. 272). The import of this text lies in its indication that the "consideration" that lay people preoccupied with their salvation were entitled to expect was prayers. This concern was paramount when a person was "at the article of death"; thus, some donations to the monasteries are in the nature of funerary foundations. In 570, Phoibammon, the principal physician of ANTINOOPOLIS, bequeathed to a Monastery of Apa Jeremiah an inalienable plot of vineyard "as an eternal memorial for the rest of his soul" and for the expense of his perpetual commemorative mass (prosphora). His body was to be buried in the monastery, and his name recorded in the register of deaths. The preferred location of monasteries on the *jabal* (mountain), the traditional site of the cemetery, predisposed them to carry out the service of taking charge of corpses.

It is hard to list the entire range of oblations. These could be occasional gifts or bounties in kind, in cash, in precious articles, or even in the form of servants with the standing of oblates, which would be left behind by visitors or pilgrims, or left in their wills by pious people thinking of their approaching demise, or fulfilling a vow. They could also be acts of patronage, like that of Caesarius, who built or restored the church of DAYR ANBĀ SHINŪDAH, or the White Monastery (cf. Monneret de Villard, 1925–1926, Vol. 1, pp. 18–20). Oblations were frequently presented in the form of regular annual payments, which was of particular economic advantage: thus, a widow of Oxyrhynchus provided the Monastery of ṢAMŪ'ĪL OF QALAMŪN annually with three measures of oil (van Cauwenbergh, 1914, p. 117). Other offerings were more substantial: the consul Apion II, around 565, was sending annually two hundred double measures of low-quality wine to an establishment of Abba Jeremias. Archbishop John the Almoner maintained the monasteries that he had founded with the income from lands that he possessed in his native township of Amathonta. Finally, one should mention that the emperor Zeno ordained that the monks of Saint Macarius of Scetis be provided with all they required in the way of corn, wine, and oil, and all they needed to equip their cells.

Many a gift boiled down in the end to a capital endowment: ships, cattle, workshops, agricultural lands, and, above all, real estate. Thus the monasteries, despite the apprehensions of Theodorus (*Sancti Pachomii vitae graecae,* Vita prima, 146), quickly found themselves in charge of substantial patrimonies.

The surviving information about the management of patrimonies relates primarily to wealth in the form of land. Latifundia (large landed estates) were a rarity. Rather, because of the chance nature of oblations and acquisitions, one finds references to numerous lots, often small and isolated and quite far from the monastic centers themselves. Thus the lands of the renowned Dayr Anbā Shinūdah are scattered about in the village of Aphrodito, 31 miles (50 km) to the north, in the Panopolis, and in the Hermopolis and Antinoopolis areas. In Panopolis one finds analogous cases with the Monastery of Zmin or Smin, which is the Tesmine of the Pachomian corpus. This parceling out and geographical dispersion explain in part why the most valued method of cultivation was tenant farming. Thus the monasteries were content to pocket the rents in cash or in kind that were made available from their tenants, who were treated with neither more nor less harshness than by lay proprietors. They did not intervene in agricultural or industrial production. These revenues could give rise to resale. Bishop Theodorus of Pentapolis purchased fifteen hundred knidia of wine from the Tabennesiote monastery of Pouinkoris (Hermopolitan), and a curious little Coptic text in the John Rylands Museum relates the resale of cucumbers belonging to the Monastery of Saint Phoibammon.

It is difficult to measure the scope of land acquisitions. According to a fiscal roll dating in all probability from the beginning of the eighth century it is clear that the Monastery of Saint Jeremias of Saqqara was one of the biggest taxpayers in the region of Memphis. This enables one to gauge its wealth indirectly. The land register of Aphrodito from the beginning of the sixth century, relating to a quarter of the ground area of this village, shows that 33 percent of the lands were already in the hands of the local or neighboring monasteries. There are reasons for thinking that for the other three quarters, the proportion hardly differed. On the level of villages like Aphrodito, the monasteries were therefore powers to be reckoned with and were standards of economic measurement, as indicated by the texts where the total amount of income is calculated in accordance with the bushel (*metron*) "of the mountain," "of the monastery," or "of the monk" (Drew-Bear, 1979, pp. 291ff.).

Only one monastery out of the twenty at present known appears in a list of the principal taxpayers of Oxyrhynchus, for a very modest payment. There is none in a comparable contemporary list. The records from Hermopolis and Antinoopolis, attesting to the existence of more than forty monasteries, in no way leads one to think that there was a significant concentration of landed property in their hands, though it is true that the Bāwīṭ archives are unpublished. Actually, given the available information, which includes no data of consequence for Lower Egypt (Alexandrian groups, Nitria, Kellia, and Scetis), it does not look as if the wealth of the monasteries in landed property had developed to the extent of that of the patriarchate, the imperial crown, the various bishops' churches, or the lay dignitaries, such as the Apions. As far as can be judged, the monasteries were reasonably well-to-do, but the distribution of their wealth was very uneven, for the road to riches depends on numerous circumstances that not every monastery could compass.

Geographical position was very important. It is, for instance, certain that the riches of the Pachomians owed much to their care not to settle their establishments too far from civil centers or waterways. The proximity of a city like Alexandria or Antinoopolis *a fortiori* favored the inflow of oblations. Allowance must be made for ability in popularizing the cult of a saint, establishing a bishop's residence (e.g., DAYR AL-BAHRI), and, in times of schism, maintaining trusting relations with the "Melchite" archbishop or the imperial power. It was simply a question of good management of their affairs, for there are examples of monasteries in difficulties, stripped of everything, burdened with debt or victimized by dishonest monks. Thus one finds an extreme variety of cases, from the richest to the poorest.

Outlays

Monastic wealth and income basically provided for internal consumption and various redistribution purposes.

Despite their ideals of autarchy and hard work, the monks were not always in a position to be wholly self-sufficient. Receipts in kind helped directly, and income in the form of money served for the procurement of goods or services. For example, the stylites of Antinoopolis had a contractual arrangement for their supply of water with a professional ass-driver. The monks of the Oktokaidekaton purchased oil and wheat at Alexandria. Part of the receipts had to be used for the maintenance of the buildings, especially places of worship, for which nothing was too fine, as evidenced in the excavations at Bāwīṭ and Saqqara. Divine service, with its multiplicity of funerary masses and festivals, certainly also involved sizable expenses for the sacramental species (wheat and wine) and for the lighting (oil). But clearly it was in redistribution activities that the monasteries swallowed up the best part of their surpluses.

Both the literature and the papyri forcefully proclaim that one of the first duties of the monks is to aid the weak and especially the poor, though it is not clear what was meant by this at that period. Almsgiving was practiced on an individual basis by drawing on income from work or in the name of the community itself. Internal services and special funds were expressly dedicated to this purpose, subsidized by the monks' personal surpluses or by foundations. Thus these establishments were enabled, for example, to undertake food distributions. The White Monastery and the Monastery of Samū'īl of Qalamūn were well known for their generosity. People who were in difficulties either begged directly from the establishments or used third parties, by way of written recommendations, in sufficient numbers to discern a "routine" for charity. One may justly assume that on such occasions many unfair advantages and injustices must have crept in. The "weak" also included those in prison, whom the monasteries were much exercised to feed and to assist. The redemption of captives also constituted part of the good works that certain donors wished to ensure was done.

Not very different from charity was the welcome afforded to travelers, pilgrims, or monks on the move. This involved sizable expenses. The monastic inns (*xenodochia*) could make a profit. In Nitria, hospitality without a consideration in return was afforded only for a week.

These budgets, already severely encumbered, had to bear the additional burden of "gifts" to the bishop's church, which were never spontaneous but were demanded on certain feast days. Even the bishop seems to have carved out for himself the lion's share of the income of the religious establishments (Wipszycka, 1972, p. 130).

In the Byzantine period, the monasteries paid taxes because of their landed estates. It was for tax purposes that their lands were entered in the land register, and in fact, many monasteries are found among payers in the Hermopolis fiscal codices of the beginning of the seventh century. Under the Umayyads there was to be added the personal tax, which was rather heavy. In this field the financial liability lay on the superior. The monasteries also provided their fiscal guarantee to any taxpayer who was in distress, and this meant that sometimes they had to pay.

The Monasteries and the General Economy of Egypt

For lack of overall data, this part of the subject is the most delicate and the most difficult to handle in an objective manner. A. H. M. Jones (1986, Vol. 2, p. 933) is slightly patronizing in his description of a "huge army of clergy and monks" as "idle mouths, living upon offerings, endowments and state subsidies." It is quite true, in line with Jones, that in certain respects the monasticism of the late empire, and especially in Egypt, represented a burden and a high economic and social expense.

Reliable figures as to the population of the Egyptian monasteries, both in detail and in general, are lacking, but there is every indication that it must have been in the tens of thousands of men and women (see the summary of the literary sources in Johnson and West, 1949, pp. 67f.). But as there is no acceptable means of estimating the total Egyptian population, one may jib at speaking of the monks as a "huge army." On the basis of the archives, the impression is that civil society did not find monasticism importunate or burdensome. Nevertheless, the monks did represent a significant population that was withdrawn from the function of reproduction and established in the often very difficult conditions of the desert fringes of the valley or of the interior desert, and was that much more difficult to feed, clothe, house, and care for. Also these regions were insecure, being the first to be exposed to the incursions of Libyan and Saracen tribes, and this involved costs for their protection. The pilgrim known as Antoninus of Piacenza thus saw in Wādī Feiran in Sinai part of the local civil population organized into territorial militias that drew their provisions and uniforms from Egypt and whose purpose it was to defend the monasteries and the hermits against the Arabs (Geyer, 1964, p. 150). Sometimes the army was quartered in the monastery, as at Pbow under Justinian. It is known that the upkeep of personnel was a burden on the budgets of the neighboring municipalities of Antaeopolis and Apollinopolis Parva.

One cannot mitigate the drawbacks associated with the monks by citing the multiplicity of their humanitarian activities, for despite their high social and moral value, they were sterile in a strictly economic sense. There are, however, certain subtle aspects to this reproach of sterility that cannot be ignored. Demographically speaking, although it is true that the monasteries took in very young people and sometimes even children and thus withdrew them from the generative cycle, it is also true that many a monk was the father of a family but found in the monasteries the opportunity for an honorable retirement after a very full life. This was so in the case of the *protokometes* (headman) Apollos, father of the poet DIOSCORUS OF APHRODITO. As to the cost of the monks' upkeep, it should be remembered that even without its reaching the excessive degree of privation related in the literature and without its being basically different from that of present-day Egyptian peasants, their lifestyle was most frugal: no meat and little in the way of genuinely cooked food. Moreover, there is every reason to think, as shown above, that the tasks and trades that occupied the monks covered in large measure the costs of their upkeep.

What is more, it can be argued that monasticism offered a certain number of clear economic advantages for society and the state in Byzantine Egypt. In the first place, the monasteries were centers of population and, as such, developed regions normally given over to solitude or to burial grounds, like the fringes of the desert, or else abandoned by the civil populations. Sometimes the Pachomians installed themselves near deserted villages. By their activities in clearing the ground and in mining, the monks of Qalamūn restored to life the site south of the Fayyūm. Dayr Abū Līfā maintained a human presence to the north of Lake Qarūn, whereas the corresponding civil site, Soknopaïounēsos, had long since returned to the desert (Munier, 1937, pp. 1–5). Regular links, commercial intercourse, and pilgrimages became established between these advanced positions of Egyptian society and the Nile Valley. The defense of the country acquired there a strategic depth that made up for the military costs.

Furthermore, the monasteries stimulated production, directly by their own activities, trades, and involvement in activities related to the surrounding world (e.g., Pachomian boat transportation) and indirectly by their role in banking (providing loans for putting ground under cultivation) and, above all, by developing safe economic areas through subinfeudation. For example, long-term leases created tenures that were more advantageous than private property. For a relatively modest annual levy, the lessee obtained on a transmissible life basis an asset that was immune from seizure but open to transfer of rights, if necessary, and was tax-free, as the levy took the place of the taxes. It was thus possible to devote one's attention with every confidence to improvement of the estate.

If truth be told, many private fortunes must have been built up at the expense of the monasteries. One may instance those of the prosperous agricultural entrepreneurs such as Phoibammon, son of Triadelphos, a farmer of the White Monastery and of the Monastery of Apa Sourous (cf. Keenan, 1980, p. 151), or those of many lay people who protected their wealth by using it wholly or partly to found or endow a monastery, reserving the right of managing it on the material side by various expedients. An assured example of these slightly questionable foundations exists in the *diakonia* of the Holy Apostles of Aphrodito, established by Apollos, the rich yeoman, whose son Dioscorus later became curator.

Trusteeship by lay curators, which was an economic and financial administration, seems to have been widespread at the time. It could, moreover, be requested by the monks themselves as a remedy for material difficulties or as insurance against insecurity. There was what appears to be the beginning of a contract of trusteeship entered into by the Apions of Oxyrhynchus with an unknown monastery, showing the range of responsibilities granted to these potentates. The result is as described by Rémondon (1972, p. 274): "On the one hand, the monastery is transformed into a production center, a workshop operating for a powerful family; on the other hand, into a distribution center for their personal alms, i.e., into a pressure or propaganda tool. Thus in P. Oxy. [16.]1952 is found the injunction from the illustrious house (of the Apions) to the most holy Pamouthios, archimandrite of the Monastery of the Consubstantiality, to distribute 600 loaves to the people of Tarouthinon, viz. 200 persons." These extreme examples show the monasteries operating to the advantage of the lay world and in a position of total subordination.

Finally, the state profited, not only in fiscal terms but also by the multiplicity of services demanded. Thus very soon Pachomian boat transportation—that of the Tabennēse monastery in this instance—had to take its share in the *navicularia functio* (naval operation), in the transportation of the wheat tax. In the sixth and seventh centuries this service was still weighing on the Pachomians, in this case the renowned Alexandrian establishment of the Metanoia, whose boatmen sailed throughout Egypt. In the Arab period, the authorities continued to require the services of the monasteries for public transportation work: the Monastery of Qalamūn thus had to lend out its camels to take wheat to Clysma. It is also known that the Byzantines deposited their fiscal receipts in the White Monastery, using it as a kind of bank.

To sum up, the Egyptian monasteries gave back to the civil world a good portion of what they had cost it, by the guarantees, the instances of patronage, and the various services and opportunities for profit that they provided.

BIBLIOGRAPHY

Amélineau, E. *Monuments pour servir à l'histoire de l'Egypte chrétienne.* Mémoires publiés par les membres de la Mission archéologique française au Caire 4. Paris, 1895.

Bagnall, R. S. "Price in 'Sales on Delivery.'" *Greek, Roman, and Byzantine Studies* 18 (1977):85f.

Cadell, H. "Papyrologica." *Chronique d'Egypte* 42 (1967):189–208.

Cauwenbergh, P. van. *Etudes sur les moines d'Egypte.* Paris and Louvain, 1914.

Clugnet, L. "Vie et récits de l'Abbé Daniel de Scété." *Revue de l'Orient chrétien* 5 (1900):49–73, 254–71, 370–90; see also 391–406, 535–64, and 6 (1901):51–87.

Cotelier, J. B., ed. *Apophthegmata Patrum.* PO 65. Paris, 1864.

Drew-Bear, M. "Deux Documents byzantins de Moyenne Egypte." *Chronique d'Egypte* 54 (1979): 285–303.

Gascou, J. "Les Grands Domaines, la cité et l'état en Egypte byzantine (recherches d'histoire agraire, fiscale et administrative)." *Travaux et mémoires* 9 (1985):1–90.

Guillaumont, A. *Aux origines du monachisme chrétien: Pour une phénoménologie du monachism.* Bégrolles en Mauges, Maine-et-Loire, 1979.

Harrauer, H., and P. J. Sijpesteijn. "Verkauf von Wein gegen Vorauszahlung." *Chronique d'Egypte* 57 (1982):296–302.

Johnson, A. C., and L. C. West. *Byzantine Egypt: Economic Studies.* Princeton, N.J., 1949.

Jones, A. H. M. *Later Roman Empire, 284–602: A Social Economic and Administrative Survey.* 2 vols. Norman, Okla., 1964; repr. Baltimore, 1986.

Judge, E. A. "The Earliest Use of *Monachos* for Monk (P. Coll. Youtie 77) and the Origins of Monasticism." *Jahrbuch für Antike und Christentum* 20 (1977):72–89.

Judge, E. A., and S. R. Pickering. "Papyrus Documentation of Church and Community in Egypt to the Mid-fourth Century." *Jahrbuch für Antike und Christentum* 20 (1977):47–71.

Kahle, P. E. *Bala'izah: Coptic Texts from Deir el-Bala'izah in Upper Egypt,* 2 vols. London, 1954.

Keenan, J. G. "Aurelius Phoibammon, Son of Triadelphus: A Byzantine Egyptian Land Entrepreneur." *Bulletin of the American Society of Papyrologists* 17 (1980):145–54.

Les Ermitages chrétiens du désert d'Esna, 4 vols. Fouilles de l'Institut français d'Archéologie orientale. Cairo, 1972.

Martin, A. "L'Eglise et la khôra égyptienne au IVe siècle." *Revue des études augustiniennes* 25 (1979):3–26.

Monneret de Villard, U. *Les Couvents près de Sohag (Deyr el-Abiad et Deyr el-Ahmar),* 2 vols. Milan, 1925–1926.

Munier, H. "Le Deir Abou-Lifa." *Bulletin de la Société d'archéologie copte* 3 (1937):1–5.

Orlandi, T., ed. and trans. *Vite dei monaci Phif e Longino.* Milan, 1975.

Rémondon, R. "L'Eglise dans la société égyptienne à l'époque byzantine." *Chronique d'Egypte* 47 (1972):254–77.

Schmidt, C. "Das Kloster des Apa Mena." *Zeitschrift für ägyptische Sprache und Altertumskunde* 68 (1932):60–68.

Wessely, C. "Die Vita S. Theodorae." In *Fünfzehnter Jahresbericht des K.-k. Staatsgymnasiums in Hernals,* pp. 24–44. Vienna, 1889.

Winlock, H. E., and W. E. Crum. *The Monastery of Epiphanius at Thebes.* New York, 1926; repr. 1977.

Wipszycka, E. *Les Ressources et les activités économiques des églises en Egypte du IVe au VIIe siècle.* Brussels, 1972.

JEAN GASCOU

MONASTERIES, NUBIAN. *See* Nubian Monasteries.

MONASTERIES IN AND AROUND ALEXANDRIA. Very few monasteries in the city of Alexandria are mentioned in the texts besides those of Brucheum, of Paul the Leper, and of the Tabennesiotes if, indeed Tabennesiotes was located in Alexandria itself. Most were at the town gates or some distance away. To the northeast was the Monastery of the Metanoia, on the ancient site of Canopus; to the east Saint Mark's Monastery (if this is not the same as the one designated DAYR ASFAL AL-'ARḌ in the Middle Ages), and the DAYR QIBRĪYŪS, whose location remains doubtful. In the west, there were the Lithazomenon, the Monastery of the Forty Saints, the patriarchal residence of Metras, a second Monastery of Saint Mark, and then, on the tongue of land between the Mediterranean and Lake Maryūṭ, the monasteries whose names were linked to the milestones near which they had been built: Pempton, Enaton, (medieval Dayr al-Zujāj), Oktokaidekaton, and Eikoston with the laura of Qalamūn and the cenobium of Maphora.

Here are listed only those monasteries whose memory is preserved by short references only. The better known monasteries covered in separate entries.

The Monastery of Brucheum is also the name of a very old part of the town, situated near the sea, to the east, mentioned by Saint JEROME in his life of Saint Hilarion, a hermit.

The Monastery of Paul the Leper held the relics of the Prophet Elisha according to the *Chronographia* of Theophanes compiled between 810 and 814. On 11 May 463, Elisha's relics were transferred to the Monastery of Paul the Leper in Alexandria. Later, they were supposed to have been moved to Constantinople to the Church of the Holy Apostles. According to the Coptic sources, since the patriarchate of THEOPHILUS (385–412), these relics had been in the martyrium of John the Baptist and Elisha.

The Monastery of the Tabennesiotes was, perhaps, in Alexandria itself on part of the site of the Serapion, a Pachomian monastery; or else, simply, Tabennesiote monks served the Church or the Martyrium, or both at once, of John the Baptist and Elisha.

A traveler, Bernard the Wise, about 870 indicates "outside the East Gate, Saint Mark's Monastery, where there are monks near the church where the saint himself rested." He adds that a short time before Venetians had carried off the saint's body to Venice.

The same Western traveler tells of having seen "outside the Western Gate, the so-called Monastery of the Forty Saints, where monks also live." No other source mentions this monastery.

On the same western side but near the sea, Abū al-Makārim cites a Monastery of Saint Mark, unfortunately without any other detail. It is not possible for this monastery to be identical with the one placed by Bernard the Wise outside the East Gate, where as many sources attest, the Martyrium of Saint Mark stood.

H. G. Evelyn-White has made a case for the existence of a Monastery of the Mother of God "at Gazarta, near Alexandria" (1932, p. 371, n. 1, and p. 447). A certain Samuel Bar Cyriacus, a Syrian Stylite monk, between 1081 and 1101 copied several Syriac manuscripts originating from the DAYR AL-SURYĀN. But the Syriac *be gazarta* is not the proper name of a place; it means "in the island [of the Banī Naṣr]." Moreover, one of the colophons of which Evelyn-White speaks says explicitly "in the island [*be gazarta*] called Niqiyūs." This copyist must therefore be identified with the Syrian hermit of whom the HISTORY OF THE PATRIARCHS speaks at that same period, as being at Azarī, in the Jazīrat Banī Naṣr.

BIBLIOGRAPHY

Evelyn-White, H. G. *The Monasteries of the Wadi'n Natrūn*, pt. 2. *The History of the Monasteries of Nitria and Scetis.* New York, 1932.

Wright, T. *Early Travels in Palestine.* London, 1848

Wright, W. *Catalogue of the Syriac Manuscripts in the British Museum.* London, 1870–1872.

RENÉ-GEORGES COQUIN
MAURICE MARTIN, S.J.

MONASTERIES IN THE BEHEIRAH PROVINCE.

Few monasteries or hermitages are attested in this province of the west of the Delta. Apart from the great communities of the KELLIA and NITRIA, one may really mention only Dayr Ams.

This place name is quoted as a village toward 1180 (Toussoun, 1925, Vol. 1, pp. 215, 223). It is also mentioned in the *al-Tuḥfah al-Saniyyah* (A.H. 715/A.D. 1315; trans. Sacy, p. 664). It was in the *markaz* (district) of Abū Ḥummuṣ, therefore to the northwest of Damanhūr.

BIBLIOGRAPHY

Al-Baghdādī Abd al-Latif ibn Yūsuf. *Al-Tuḥfah al-Saniyyah.* Trans. by Silvestre de Sacy as in *Relation de l'Egypte.* Paris, 1810. "L'Etat des provinces" is translated in an appendix.

Toussoun, O. *Mémoire sur l'histoire du Nil,* 3 vols. Cairo, 1925.

RENÉ-GEORGES COQUIN
MAURICE MARTIN, S.J.

MONASTERIES IN AND AROUND CAIRO.

Several monasteries that earlier were outside Cairo are today swallowed up by the development of greater Cairo.

To the north, there was a village called Damanhūr Shūbrā or Damanhūr Shahīd (Dayr Yuhannā), and not far from there but outside Cairo in the Middle Ages, DAYR AL-KHANDAQ, which contained several churches.

Within Cairo there were two convents of nuns near the residence of the patriarch, called Dayr al-Rāhibāt, the first dedicated to Saint Mary the Virgin and the second dedicated to Saint Theodorus. One of these two monasteries is in ḤARIT ZUWAYLAH and the other in ḤARIT AL-RŪM. There is no text to help fix the date of these convents, but it is probable that they are as ancient as the patriarchal residence situated near the first of them, which dates from the pontificate of the patriarch MACARIUS II (1102–1128).

To the south in the ancient Miṣr outside Cairo is the Monastery of Saint Mercurius or DAYR ABŪ SAYFAYN. This monastery was reconstructed under the patriarch CYRIL V (1874–1927). A passage between the churches of Anbā Shinūdah and Abū Sayfayn at first appears to be a cul de sac, but leads to the convent of nuns (Jullien, 1891, p. 225). A certain number of objects worthy of mention are here (Coquin, 1974, pp. 58–59).

Inside the QAṢR AL-SHAM' is DAYR AL BANĀT, mentioned by travelers from the seventeenth and eighteenth centuries on and by the HISTORY OF THE PATRIARCHS. Mention should be made of a wooden door of the Fatimid period (Coquin, p. 151).

Two groups of churches still bear the name of Dayr: Dayr Babilūn al-Daraj and Dayr Tadrus (Coquin, pp. 181f.).

Farther to the south is the Dayr Mīkhā'īl al-Qiblī. This is today no more than a church that is mentioned at several places by the *History of the Patriarchs* (the texts are conveniently collected in Coquin, pp. 205ff.). The oldest mention of this church appears to be from 1210.

We must also mention the two monasteries called DAYR AL-ṬĪN and Dayr al Nuzhah, as well as DAYR AL-NASṬŪR.

BIBLIOGRAPHY

Coquin, C. *Les Edifices chrétiens du Vieux Caire*. Bibliothèque d'etudes coptes 11. Cairo, 1974.

Jullien, M. *L'Egypte, souvenirs bibliques et chrétiens*. Lille, 1891.

Vansleb, J. M. *Nouvelle relation en forme de journal d'un voyage fait en Egypte en 1672 et 1673*, p. 241. Paris, 1677. Transl. as *The Present State of Egypt*. London, 1678; repr. Farnborough, 1972.

RENÉ-GEORGES COQUIN

MONASTERIES IN CYPRUS. The earliest mention of Copts in Cyprus comes from a traveler, Iohann van Kootwyck, who writes that they arrived following the capture of Jerusalem by Salāḥ al-Dīn in 1187 (Burmester, 1942, pp. 11–12). A letter of benediction dated from Christmas A.M. 1225/A.D. 1508 from the ninety-fourth patriarch of Alexandria, JOHN XIII (1484–1524) gives a list of the bishops submitting to his jurisdiction. There was then an Anbā Mīkhā'īl, metropolitan of Cyprus and afterward of Rhodes (Muyser, pp. 161–63). This presupposes a fairly large Coptic community on the island.

In a census taken by the Turks in 1777, Copts were conspicuously absent and presumably did not then form part of the island's population. The latest mention of the Coptic community occurs in 1646 in a colophon of an Arabic commentary on the last three books of the Pentateuch that was copied in Cyprus and now is in possession of the Coptic Patriarchate. Between 1646 and 1777, therefore, the Coptic community of Nicosia, the capital city, disappeared for an unknown reason.

The Coptic monasteries of Cyprus include the following:

Monastery of Saint Antony at Famagusta (fourteenth century) The oldest attestation of the presence of Coptic monks in Cyprus comes from a Spanish Dominican, Alphonse Bonhome (or Buenhombre), who discovered an Arabic Life of Saint ANTONY at a Coptic monastery at Famagusta. In the dedication that he added to his Latin translation and dated 1342, he stated that a Coptic monastery was present in the upper part of the town of Famagusta in the southeastern part of the island. Bonhome unfortunately does not specify the origin of the convent, nor the number of monks.

An act of WAQF (religious donation of land) for the benefit of the Church of Saint Antony at Famagusta very probably deals with the same convent (undated Egyptian manuscript with fourteenth-century writing; Troupeau, 1972, p. 58).

Monastery of Saint Macarius of Klima (sixteenth century) An act of *waqf* for the benefit of the monastery of Saint Macarius of Klima in Cyprus is preserved in a manuscript dated 1526. It is not possible to say whether this convent is identical with the following one (Troupeau, 1972, p. 85).

Monastery of Saint Macarius at Platani (sixteenth century) The historian Etienne de Lusignan in 1573 writes of a Coptic monastery called after Saint Macarius that was situated outside Nicosia toward the north, near the village of Platani. It belonged to the Armenians. It is very probably the convent of Surp Magar (Saint Macarius), which still exists today, 16 miles (26 km) northeast of Nicosia in the mountains near the village of Halevka. It still belongs to the Armenian community (Burmester, 1972, pp. 10–11; Keshishian, 1967, pp. 178–79).

Monastery of Saint Antony at Nicosia (seventeenth century) A manuscript of biblical commentary of the Coptic Patriarchate of Cairo, according to the colophon of the second part, was written "in the island of Cyprus, the well-guarded, in the God-loving town of Levkosia [Nicosia], in the monastery of the great saint, our father, Anbā Anṭūniyūs, father of all monks"; this note is dated 7 Bābah A.M. 1363/A.D. 1646.

Three or four Coptic monasteries are therefore attested in the island of Cyprus from the fourteenth to the seventeenth centuries. It is not possible to say when and how they have disappeared.

BIBLIOGRAPHY

Burmester, O. H. E. "The Copts in Cyprus." *Bulletin de la Société d'archéologie copte* 7 (1942):9–13.

Halkin, F. "La Légende de saint Antoine traduite de l'arabe par Alphonse Bonhome, O.P." *Analecta Bollandiana* 60 (1942):143–212.

———. "Un Monastère copte à Famagouste au XIVe siècle." *Le Muséon* 59 (1946):511–14.

Keshishian, K. K. *Romantic Cyprus*. Nicosia, 1967.

Muyser, J. "Contribution à l'étude des listes épiscopales de l'église copte." *Bulletin de la Société d'archéologie copte* 10 (1944):115–76.

Troupeau, G. *Catalogue des manuscrits arabes*, pt. 1: *Manuscrits chrétiens*, Vol. 1. Paris, 1972.

RENÉ-GEORGES COQUIN
MAURICE MARTIN, S.J.

MONASTERIES IN THE DAQAHLIYYAH PROVINCE.

This province occupies the northern part of the Delta between the Mediterranean, the Suez Canal, and the so-called Damietta Branch of the Nile. The monastic settlements attested in this region by literary evidence are fairly numerous. We distinguish them by the actual *markaz* (district) in which they were situated.

Nawasā and al-Dayr (*Markaz* of Ajā)

The village of Nawasā is situated near the Nile to the north of Mīt Samannūd. The Life of the Patriarch CHRISTODOULOS (1047–1077) mentions a recluse of saintly fame named Shenuti who lived there in a cell toward the end of this patriarch's reign. This village, which still exists, is indicated as the seat of a bishopric under the following patriarch, CYRIL II. A map prepared by Guest (1912, opposite p. 980) shows its medieval situation.

A village still bears the name of al-Dayr. In A.H. 933/A.D. 1526–1527, it was called Kafr al-Dayr because, writes Ramzī, there was a Christian convent there.

Tmuis (*Markaz* of al-Sinbillāwayn)

According to John CASSIAN (*Collationes* 14.4 and 16.1), there was in the neighborhood of Tmuis (today near Timay al-Amdīd, northeast of al-Sinbillāwayn), a large cenobium (Amélineau, 1893, pp. 500–501; Maspero and Wiet, 1919, pp. 59–60).

Ṭambūq (*Markaz* of al-Manṣūrah)

When Daniel, the famous superior of Scetis, refused to subscribe to the *Tome* of Pope LEO, which the Emperor JUSTINIAN wanted to impose on the Egyptian monks, he fled with a disciple to Ṭambūq and there built a small monastery, to the west of the village, where he lived until Justinian's death (565). When the barbarians invaded Scetis at the end of the sixth or the beginning of the seventh century, Daniel returned to Ṭambūq, where he died and was buried (Guidi, 1900, pp. 562–64). H. G. EVELYN-WHITE doubts the authenticity of the episode of the *Tome* of Leo at Scetis, but appears to admit Daniel's exile and death at Ṭambūq (1932, pp. 246–50). Cauwenbergh considers this event authentic; it is indeed in conformity with what is known of Justinian's religious policy from 535 onward (1914, pp. 25, 28, 85). Ramzī thinks that it is the village known today as al-Danābīq.

Panephysis, Heracleopolis Parva, Tūnah, and Barbiyyah (*Markaz* of al-Manzalah)

The town of Panephysis may have been situated on the site of the present day al-Manzalah, or it may have been farther north, if we are to believe John Cassian's report that it was submerged by the rising of the waters of Lake al-Manzalah following an earthquake (*Collationes* 7.26 and 11.3). He locates there a cenobium of more than a hundred brothers and a convent of virgins; in the neighborhood there were many anchorites. The site is mentioned several times in the APOPHTHEGMATA PATRUM.

Heracleopolis Parva was the ancient Sethron, situated, no doubt, farther east than Panephysis before the Suez Canal was built. It is also referred to in the *Apophthegmata Patrum* as a place inhabited by anchorites.

In Lake al-Manzalah, the island of Tūnah is mentioned by ABŪ AL-MAKĀRIM, who locates there a monastery dedicated to Saint Pachomius belonging to the Melchites. It was destroyed by the Ghuzz in 1168. The date given by Abū al-Makārim is that of Shīrkūh's expedition against Egypt (Lane-Poole, 1925, p. 179ff.; see also Amélineau, 1893, pp. 502–503).

In his list of the churches and monasteries of the twelfth to fifteenth centuries, F. 'Awaḍ (1932, p. 218) indicates between Tinnis and Damietta, although it had been destroyed, a monastery of the Trinity belonging to the Melchites, in a place which he writes as Bazqiyyah. The source of this information is without any doubt the work of Abū al-Makārim, but the publisher (1984, p. 134) has printed Barbiyyah, without specifying the location.

Monastery of Pamin (*Markaz* of Dikirnis)

Abū al-Makārim indicates in the neighborhood of the small town of Ashmūn Ṭanāḥ (today called Ashmūn al-Rummān) a monastery where Pamin the Confessor lived. The author has perhaps confused him with the saint of the same name who was a monk near al-Ashmūnayn in Middle Egypt.

Monastery of Saint George at Shaṭā (*Markaz* of Fāriskūr)

Abū al-Makārim mentions at Shaṭā a large monastery and a church with the name of Saint George; the latter was destroyed by the Muslims and transformed into a mosque because the Franks had landed there at the time of Salāḥ al-Dīn's victory in 1177. On Guest's map (1912, opposite p. 980), Shaṭā is to the east of Damietta and very near the town.

Monastery of Jeremiah (Governorate of Damietta)

A monastery of Jeremiah (Dayr Apa Jeremiah) is situated by Abū al-Makārim in the Island of Damietta. Its lofty buildings could be seen from Damietta, but during the reign of the Fatimids, they were lowered because of the advanced position of this convent, and the provisions that were kept there for fear of a siege were removed to Damietta.

The HISTORY OF THE PATRIARCHS notes that this convent belonged to the Melchites and was one parasang (between 3 and 3½ miles) from Damietta, to the north, on the west bank. On 9 May 1211, the Franks landed there in force to attack Damietta. No doubt it was destroyed at the same time as old Damietta.

BIBLIOGRAPHY

Amélineau, E. *La géographie de l'Egypte à l'époque copte*. Paris, 1893.

Cauwenbergh, P. van. *Etude sur les moines d'Egypte*. Paris and Louvain, 1914.

Evelyn-White, H. G. *The History of the Monasteries of Nitria and of Scetis*. New York, 1932.

Guest, R. "The Delta in the Middle Ages." *Journal of the Royal and Asiatic Society* (1912):941–80.

Guidi, I. "Vie et récits de l'abbé Daniel de Scété." *Revue de l'Orient chrétien* 5 (1900):535–64; 6 (1901):51–53.

Lane-Poole, S. *History of Egypt in the Middle Ages*. London, 1925.

Maspero, J., and G. Wiet. *Matériaux pour servir à la géographie de l'Egypte*. Mémoires publiés par les membres de l'Institut français d'Archéologie orientale 36. Cairo, 1919.

Muḥammad Ramzī. *Al-Qāmūs al-Jughrāfī lil-Bilād al Miṣrīyyah*, 2 vols. in 5 pts. Cairo, 1953–1963.

RENÉ-GEORGES COQUIN

MAURICE MARTIN, S.J.

MONASTERIES OF THE EASTERN DESERT. "Eastern desert" refers to all of Egypt between the fertile valley of the Nile and the Red Sea. Perhaps because the watering places and the regular caravan routes are less numerous there, the hermitages and monasteries are few. Two centers should be pointed out: one to the north formed by DAYR ANBĀ ANṬŪNIYŪS and DAYR ANBA BŪLĀ with the hermitages that cluster or clustered around them. The wādīs that debouch on the Wādī 'Arabah where the Dayr Anbā Anṭūniyūs is situated—the Wādī Natfah and the Wādī Hanneba, which come down from the Jabal al-Jalālah al-Baḥriyyah, at 'Ayn Bardah and Bīr Bakhīt (sometimes called Abū Khīt)—were inhabited by hermits. 'Ayn Bardah is situated near a well, as its name (the cold spring) indicates, halfway between the valley of the Nile and the monastery of Saint Antony.

The best known is the group of hermitages with its center, a small monastery called DAYR ABŪ DARAJ, situated on the road that runs along the Red Sea about 42 miles (68 km) south of Suez.

The second monastic center in the eastern desert is farther south and near the Red Sea, not far from the road that today links the town of Qena to the Red Sea, the Mons Porphyrites, so called in the

Hellenistic period because of its prophyry quarries, today called the Jabal Abū Dukhkhān (mountain of the father of smoke) and quite close to the JABAL QAṬṬĀR. Leading to the first and its porphyry quarries is the Wādī Qaṭṭār, which still retains traces of its occupation by Christian hermits, of which numerous texts speak.

BIBLIOGRAPHY

Bissey, F., and R. Chabot-Morisseau. "Notes de voyage sur l'ouadi Arabah. Ruines de constructions chrétiennes dans les branches est et ouest de l'ouadi Hanneba." *Bulletin de la Société d'etudes historiques et géographiques de l'Isthme de Suez* 5 (1953–1954):155–60.

Fontaine, A. L. "Exploration dans l'ouadi Arabah, Ayn Barda, ses vestiges d'habitats anciens." *Bulletin de la Société d'études historiques et géographiques de l'Isthme de Suez* 5 (1953–1954):59–86.

———. "Le monachisme copte et la montagne de St. Antoine." *Bulletin de l'Institut d'etudes coptes* 1 (1958):3–30.

Fourteau, R. "Voyage dans la partie septentrionale du désert arabique." *Bulletin de la Société de géographique d'Egypte* 5 (1900):517ff.

RENÉ-GEORGES COQUIN

MONASTERIES OF THE EASTERN DESERT OF THE DELTA AND SINAI.

A number of places are mentioned in the ancient sources as the abodes of monks in this vast region.

Pelusium is today called Tall al-Faramā, and is 2 miles (3 km) from the Mediterranean coast and 14 miles (23 km) east of the al-Tīnah station on the railway line that links Port Said and al-Ismā'īliyyah. It is cited several times as the center of an area in which anchorites lived.

ABŪ ṢĀLIḤ THE ARMENIAN writes that in his time (thirteenth century) there were numerous churches and monasteries in ruins in this place. He attributes its destruction to the Persians (619–629) and the Arabs.

Kasios or Mount Casios, today Katīb al-Qals, was about 50 miles (75 km) east of Port Said, on the north edge of Lake Bardawil. It was the site of a monastery of Saint Romanos, where JACOB BARADAEUS, the restorer of the Monophysite hierarchy, died on 30 July 578.

Ostracine was at the eastern extremity of Lake Bardawil. Some identify it with the village called KHIRBAT AL-FILŪSIYYAH, others with the hamlet of Zananīq; J. Clédat excavated a fortress-monastery there. More recently another monastery has been discovered but not excavated (Figuéras, 1982).

Rhinokorua is generally identified with the present al-'Arish: this was the first town in Egypt when one came from Syria.

The Greek historian Sozomen (*Historia ecclesiastica* 6.31) names three anchorites at this place. Two brothers, Melas and Solon became bishops of the town, one after the other; the first was exiled by the Arian emperor Valens (364–378) and died in 375. The third ascetic, Dionysius, built for himself a hermitage to the north of the town. Sozomen specifies that all three were autochthonous, which no doubt means that they originated from the bedouin tribes of the peninsula.

[*See also:* Clysma; Pharan; Raithou.]

BIBLIOGRAPHY

Amélineau, E. *La Géographie de l'Egypte à l'époque copte.* Paris, 1893.

Ball, J. *Egypt in the Classical Geographers.* Cairo, 1942.

Clédat, J. "Fouilles à Khirbet al-Flousiyeh." *Annales du Service des Antiquités de l'Egypte* 16 (1916):6–32.

Figuéras, P. "Le Christianisme au Nord-Sinai." *Le Monde de la Bible* 24 (May-July 1982).

Kugener, M. A. "Récit de Mar Cyriaque." *Revue de l'Orient chrétien* 7 (1902):197–217.

Maspero, J., and G. Wiet. *Matériaux pour servir à la géographie de l'Egypte.* Mémoires de l'Institut français d'archéologie orientale, Vol. 36. Cairo, 1919.

RENÉ-GEORGES COQUIN
MAURICE MARTIN, S.J.

MONASTERIES OF THE FAYYŪM.

In the notice about the patriarch KHĀ'ĪL I (744–767), the HISTORY OF THE PATRIARCHS indicates that there were then thirty-five monasteries in the Fayyūm. ABŪ ṢĀLIḤ THE ARMENIAN repeats the same information, which he seems to relate to the same period; he names or describes only eight of them. Al-Nābulsī cites thirteen. A certain number of these monasteries still exist today: DAYR ABŪ ISḤĀQ (or Dayr al-Ḥammām), DAYR ABŪ LĪFAH, DAYR AL-AZAB, DAYR AL-MALĀK GHUBRĪYĀL (Naqlūn), DAYR ANBĀ SAMŪ'ĪL OF QALAMŪN, DAYR MĀR JIRJIS OF SIDMANT, and some hermitages in the Wādī al-Rayyān. Monasteries that have disappeared are well enough known from various documents: DAYR ABĪRŪN, the two DAYR AL-'ADHRĀ' and DAYR AL-

IKHWAH at Sayalah, the monastery of al-Hamūlī, the scriptoria of TUṬŪN.

For many others, on the contrary, we have no more than sporadic mention of their existence, here and there among the writers Abū Ṣāliḥ and al-Nābulsī and from other sources.

Abū Ṣāliḥ mentions two monasteries at Aflaḥ al-Zaytūn, in the Fayyūm: one named after a Saint Theodorus the Martyr on the al-Manhā canal (i.e., the Baḥr Yūsuf, which rules out the place of the same name al-Zaytūn to the north of Banī Suef) and the other called that of the Apostles.

He mentions another monastery, Dayr al-Ṣalīb, in the district of Fānū, to the north of Madīnat al-Fayyūm, also attested, although without indication of the name, by al-Nābulsī, who places it to the west of the town (Salmon, 1901, p. 54).

Al-Nābulsī mentions the following monasteries, most often only indicating the nearest town or village and the direction in which the monastery is situated in relation to them: Dayr Anbā Shinūdah, south of Minshat Awlād 'Arafah (today Ma'ṣarat 'Arafah), southwest of Madīnat al-Fayyūm (Salmon, 1901, p. 66); Dayr al-'Āmil, south of al-'Idwah, northeast of Madīnat al-Fayyūm (Salmon, 1901, p. 46); Dayr Bamwiyyah, east of the town of the same name, in the north of the Fayyūm near Sanhūr (Salmon, 1901, p. 56); Dayr Dimūshiyyah, south of the town of this name, south of Madīnat al-Fayyūm (Salmon, 1901, p. 64; Muḥammad Ramzī thinks that this monastery is the same as Dayr al-'Azab, Vol. 1, p. 253; Vol. 2, pt. 3, p. 95); Dayr Dhāt al-Ṣafā, south of this borough; Dayr Disyā, north of the town (Salmon, 1901, p. 62); and Dayr Sannūris, west of the town, northwest of Madīnat al-Fayyūm (Salmon, 1901, p. 51).

Seven monasteries are mentioned in other sources. Dayr Abū Ja'rān is mentioned only by *al Tuḥfah al-Saniyyah* (trans. Sacy, 1810, p. 682, no. 58). According to M. Ramzi, it was about 5.5 miles (9 km) west of Iṭsā (Vol. 1, p. 260). Dayr al-'Ajamiyyīn is indicated in the *Book of the Hidden Pearls* (Daressy, 1917, p. 206), near the village of this name in the north of the Fayyūm, in the district of Ibshawāy. Dayr al-Banāt is also mentioned by the *Book of the Hidden Pearls*, but the author has perhaps confused it with the Qaṣr al-Banāt to the southwest of Lake Qārūn (Daressy, 1917, p. 200). Under the Greek name Labla, several Greek papyri of the sixth century mention two monasteries "in the mountain called Labla" (Barison, 1938, pp. 69–72; the reader will find in this nomenclature other references to several monasteries in the Fayyūm). At Madīnat Ghurān, west of Madīnat Māḍī, excavations have brought to light a small Coptic monastery backing on to a small Ptolemaic temple (Jouguet, 1901, p. 305). Dayr Shallā is mentioned at the same time as Dayr al-Naqlūn (Dayr al-Malāk Ghubriyāl) in a deed of gift of the tenth century (Abbott, 1937, pp. 19–20). It should not be very distant from the latter: al-Maqrīzī speaks of this locality, overhung by the mountain of Naqlūn (*al-Khiṭaṭ*, Vol. 2, p. 505). Dayr al-Zakāwah is mentioned only as ruins in the *Description de l'Egypt* (Vol. 16, p. 52; atlas, fol. 19) southeast of Madīnat al-Gharaq (south of the Fayyūm).

BIBLIOGRAPHY

Abbott, N. *The Monasteries of the Fayyūm.* Studies in Ancient Oriental Civilization 16. Chicago, 1937.

Amélineau, E. *La Géographie de l'Egypte à l'époque copte.* Paris, 1893.

Baghdādī, Abd al-Laṭif ibn Yūsuf al-. *Al-Tuḥfah al-Saniyyah (état des provinces et des villages de l'Egypte: 715 H/1315 A.D.).* Trans. Silvestre de Sacy in *Relation de l'Egypte par 'Abd-Allatif.* Paris, 1810.

Barison, Paola. "Ricerche sui monasteri dell Egitto bizantino ed arabo secondo i documenti dei papiri greci." *Aegyptus* 18 (1938):29–148.

Daressy, G. "Indicateur topographique du "Livre des perles enfouies et du mystère précieux.'" *Bulletin de l'Institut français d'Archéologie orientale* 13 (1917):175–230; 14 (1918):1–32.

Jouguet, P. "Fouilles du Fayoum. Rapport sur les fouilles de Medinet-Madi et Medinet Ghoran." *Bulletin de correspondance hellénique* 25 (1901):379–411.

Muḥammad Ramzī. *Al-Qāmūs al-Jughrāfī lil-Bilād al Miṣrīyyah* (geographical dictionary of Egyptian towns), 2 vols. in 5 pts. Cairo 1953–1954, 1963.

Salmon, G. "Répertoire géographique de la Province du Fayyoum d'après le Kitab al-Fayyoum d'an-Naboulsi." *Bulletin de l'Institut français d'Archéologie orientale* 1 (1901):29–77.

RENÉ-GEORGES COQUIN

MONASTERIES IN THE GHARBIYYAH PROVINCE. Testimonies are relatively numerous concerning the monasteries of this province, which occupies the north of the Delta between the two branches of the Nile, that of Damietta (Dumyāṭ) and that of Rosetta (Rashīd). Mentioned are the sites of Diolkos and hermitages at Naqīzah and Sinjār. To the north near the salt marshes are found a group of four monasteries: DAYR AL-ʿASKAR, DAYR AL-MAYMAH, DAYR SITT DIMYANAH, and DAYR AL-MAGHṬIS; to the southwest are the hermitage of AZĀRĪ and Dayr Mār Mīnā at Ibyār. In addition, brief accounts refer to other monasteries or hermitages.

In the west of this province at Fuwwah the presence of monks is attested by a letter from CYRIL I of Alexandria, in which the patriarch addresses them about being on guard against Origenist doctrines (Honigmann, 1953, pp. 52–53). It is, however, possible that φουά (*phoua*) is a copyist's error for φαοῦ (phaou), that is, Pbow, the motherhouse of the Pachomians, some of whose monks appear to have been attracted by ORIGEN's ideas (Lefort, 1943, pp. 352–56).

Ibn Duqmāq mentions a Dayr Shubrā Kalsā in the center of the Gharbiyyah, which was in the present district of Kafr al-Shaykh. It is also mentioned under the name of Diyarb Shubrā Kalsā by the fourteenth-century writer ʿAbd al-Laṭif.

Abū al-Makārim notes a walled monastery named Saint Michael at Misīr southeast of Kafr al-Shaykh.

Abū al-Makārim also mentions two monasteries to the north of this town at Damrū al-Khammārah (formerly called Damrū al-Kanā'is), which recalls the importance of this small town in the history of the Coptic patriarchate in the eleventh century in the district of al-Maḥallah al-Kubrā. One, for monks, adjoins the church of Saint THECLA. The other was for nuns, whose superior (A.D. 1177), called Qumriyyah, was celebrated for her asceticism, her holiness, and her learning. Abū al-Makārim dates the destruction of the numerous churches (he does not speak of monasteries) to 1177–1178 in the period of Ṣalāḥ al-Dīn, and attributes it to the Frankish king of Jerusalem, Baldwin (al-Barzānī).

Abū al-Makārim also speaks of a Dayr Abū Hurmus situated near Abūsīr, in the district of al-Maḥallah al-Kubrā. ʿAbd al-Laṭif knows of a Hūrīn Buhurmus, sometimes called simply Buhurmus, which could be the same place. Ramzī (Vol. 1, p. 472) locates it northwest of al-Maḥallah al-Kubrā. Abū al-Makārim indicates that Ṣā, son of Miṣrā'im, the grandson of Ham, who was the son of Noah and said to be the founder of the town of ṢĀ (Sais), was buried there.

To the east of the province in the district of Ṭalkhā there is still a village called Dayrayn (lit. "two monasteries"). This locality is already pointed out by Ibn Duqmāq, but Abū al-Makārim does not mention any monastery there.

In the district of Ṭanṭā, a monastery in the name of some martyrs is mentioned by Abū al-Makārim at the place called Būrīj. There, he says, lived a monk named Macarius the Painter, who later became patriarch under the name of MACARIUS II (1102–1128). The Lewata, a Berber tribe, destroyed the monastery and maltreated Macarius. This occupation of the Delta by these Lewatis is related in the HISTORY OF THE PATRIARCHS OF THE EGYPTIAN CHURCH. They were repulsed in A.D. 1074 by Badr al-Jamālī. According to Abū al-Makārim, the village called Ikhnāway al-Zallāqah was built on the ruins.

To the north of Ziftā, and near the Damietta branch of the Nile, at Sunbāṭ, Abū al-Makārim calls attention to a monastery for men and another for women near the Church of Saint George. They are said to have been founded by Marqus ibn Qanbar (d. 1208). ABŪ ṢALIḤ THE ARMENIAN in his excursus on this personage, in fact, indicates that he had asked that a church should be attributed to him at Sunbāṭ in 1186.

BIBLIOGRAPHY

ʿAbd al-Laṭif ibn Yūsuf. *Al-Tuḥfah al-Saniyyah*. Trans. Silvestre de Sacy in *Relation de l'Egypte*. Paris, 1810. "L'Etat des provinces" is translated in an appendix.

Honigmann, E. *The Monks of Fua, Adressees of a Letter from St. Cyril of Alexandria*. Patristic Studies, Studi e Testi 173). Vatican City, 1953.

Lane-Poole, S. *A History of Egypt in the Middle Ages*. London, 1925.

Lefort, L. T. *Les vies coptes de saint Pachôme*. Bibliothèque du Muséon 16. Louvain, 1943.

RENÉ-GEORGES COQUIN
MAURICE MARTIN, S.J.

MONASTERIES OF THE LOWER ṢAʿĪD.

This region, which nearly corresponds to the Arcadia of the Byzantine period, was very rich in monasteries, as is shown by the papyri.

The Left Bank

The ancient monastery of DAYR NAHYĀ is also called Dayr al-Karrām. The monastery of Apa Harūn may have been near Giza. It may be the monastery of Apa Harūn mentioned in the Life of ABRAHAM AND GEORGE OF SCETIS (Amélineau, 1893, p. 54). Attention should also be paid to the group of monasteries of DAYR AL-AḤMAR, DAYR ABŪ SAYFAYN (Tamwayh), and DAYR AL-SHAMʿ.

Between the pyramids of Giza and the pyramids of Abūsīr at Zawyat al-ʿIryan, excavations have brought to light a small monastery the name of which is unknown (Barsanti, 1906, p. 110). To the north of Saqqara, on the remains of a temple of Nectanebo II destroyed by the Christians, Emery discovered a monastery composed of cells ranged along the length of a street, a church, and communal halls (Emery, 1969, p. 34; 1970, p. 5). To the south of Saqqara was the important DAYR APA JEREMIAH.

Near Dahshūr a monastery existed and had already disappeared at the time of ABŪ ṢĀLIḤ in the thirteenth century; with the disappearance of "good people," the church was transformed into a mosque.

In the mountain adjoining the village called Bamhā, monks and hermits lived about 640–650 (Menas, *Life of Isaac*, Porcher, ed., PO 11, p. 318; Amélineau, 1893, pp. 297–98; Evelyn-White, 1932, p. 283, n. 3). A little more to the south of the famous pyramid of Licht was the DAYR AL-MUHARRAQAH. Near the Nile and near the village called Būsh, farms were built relating to the two monasteries of the Red Sea, DAYR ANBĀ ANṬŪNIYŪS and DAYR ANBĀ BŪLĀ. Not far from there was the monastery called Takinash, where the road for Dayr Anbā Samū'īl of Qalamūn began. Near the Nile was the monastery of al-Nūr, according to Abū Ṣāliḥ, who is the only one to mention it. Its church was dedicated to the archangel Gabriel. There was also a monastery at Aqfahs, an important Christian center.

Farther to the south was the town of Ṭanbidā, where Abū Ṣāliḥ located a monastery consecrated to the martyr Tarnīmah not otherwise known; the martyr's body was preserved in this monastery. The HISTORY OF THE PATRIARCHS indicates there a monastery named for Apa Epima, with his relics. AL-MAQRĪZĪ mentions a monastery there, named for the Holy Virgin, outside the town and containing only one monk. A little more to the south, in the village of Ishnīn al-Naṣarā, al-Maqrīzī also draws attention to a monastery in the name of the Virgin Mary. Abū Ṣāliḥ mentions simply a church. Still farther to the south, the village of al-Jarnus remained famous because of the passage of the Holy Family.

Farther to the south, the *State of the Provinces* (fourteenth century; ed. Sacy, 1810, p. 689) points out a Dayr al-Qaṣanūn and also a DAYR ATIYYAH. To the west of al-Bahnasā, the place-name Saba' Banāt may bear witness to a monastery now disappeared. At the limits of the province, beyond al-Bahnasā, was Dayr Sanquriyyah.

The Right Bank

Going back up the Nile, DAYR AL-ʿADAWĪYYAH is the first monastery encountered. Farther on, on the mountain, are Dayr Quṣayr and Saint George of Ṭurah, and the one that received the popular nickname DAYR AL-FAKHŪRĪ (monastery of the potter). It was attested by Abū Ṣāliḥ, who says it was dedicated to Saint Mercurius. *The History of the Patriarchs* also speaks in the same terms of this monastery. Farther south is DAYR SHAHRĀN. Recent excavations have uncovered the remains of a monastery at Hulwān.

Farther south is evidence of a small monastery, DAYR AL-QAṢRĪYYAH, near Iṭfīh; the ancient site consecrated to Saint Antony, DAYR AL-MAYMŪN; and Bayaḍ al-Nasārā, where there was a monastery. Opposite Fashn is evidence for DAYR AL-ḤADĪD. Sharūna preserves some Christian remains.

Sites Not Identified

The HISTORIA MONACHORUM IN AEGYPTO indicates that the region of Oxyrhynchus was full of monks. We should have some faint idea from the preceding enumeration, but we can complete it by the data from the Greek papyri for this region. Bataille's manual (1955) lists the editions of the relevant texts.

BIBLIOGRAPHY

Amélineau, E. *La Géographie de l'Egypte à l'époque copte*. Paris, 1893.

Barsanti, A. "Lettre de M. Barsanti sur la découverte des restes d'un petit couvent copte près de Zaouyet al-Aryān." *Annales du Service des Antiquités* 7 (1906):110.

Bataille, A. *Les papyrus*. Traité d'études byzantines 2. Paris, 1955.

Drew-Bear, M. *Le nome Hermopolite. Toponymes et sites*. American Studies in Papyrology 21. Missoula, Mont., 1979.

Emery, W. B. "Preliminary Report on the Excavations at North Saqqâra." *Journal of Egyptian Archeology* 56 (1970):5–11 and pl. 1–20.

Evelyn-White, Hugh G. *The Monasteries of the Wādi n'Natrūn*, pt. 2: *The History of the Monasteries of Nitria and of Scetis*. New York, 1932.

Muḥammad Ramzī. *Al-Qāmūs al-Jughrāfī lil-Bilād al Miṣrīyyah*, 2 vols. in 5 pts. Cairo, 1953–1963.

Sacy, S. de., ed. *'Abd al-Latīf*. Paris, 1810. Appendix includes translation of "L'Etat des provinces" of 1375–1376.

RENÉ-GEORGES COQUIN
JEAN GASCOU

MONASTERIES OF THE MIDDLE ṢAʻĪD. The Greek geographers and the Arab historians of the Middle Ages identified this province of Egypt as beginning south of al-Bahnasā (OXYRHYNCHUS) and ending at AKHMĪM (Panopolis).

Left Bank

To the south of al-Bahnasā, going up the Nile, lies the site of Dayr al-Juʻ, followed by Dayr Abū Bifām, where there was a monastery dedicated to Saint PACHOMIUS. *The Churches and Monasteries of Egypt* noted a Dayr al-ʻAsal south of Minyā, which has now disappeared. The next site is the ancient Hermopolis Magna (al-Ashmūnayn). In this province the two monasteries of Nawāy and Kahyor were founded by Theodorus, the successor of Saint Pachomius. Beyond doubt, the first is located in the village of Nawāy, which still exists. The second was probably near the river, according to the Life of the Pachomian martyr Hamay.

ABŪ ṢĀLIḤ mentioned Dayr Abū Nūb to the north of al-Ashmūnayn. Near the so-called Libyan mountain between the Nile and the Red Sea and close to the present village of Hūr is situated the famous DAYR ABŪ FĀNAH. Al-MAQRĪZĪ called attention to a church resembling a monastery outside Dayrūṭ al-Sharīf, which was then called Dayrūṭ Sarabam[on] or Dayr Abū Sarabām.

Near the village of Rayramūn was the monastery of the archangel Michael. The large village called Dayr Mawās perhaps still preserves the name of a vanished monastery. Some texts mention vanished monasteries around Ṣanabū. Abū Ṣāliḥ spoke in the past tense of a monastery of Saint Onophrius near Daljah, which was then on the right bank of the Baḥr Yusūf. Al-Maqrīzī places a Dayr Marqūrah to the east of Daljah in its *ḥajir* (stony region at the edge of the desert). To the south, near the Libyan mountain, was the celebrated monastery of Bāwīṭ. A little farther to the south, some tombs from ancient Egypt, situated in the necropolis of Meir, were occupied by hermits. Still farther to the south is the great Monastery of al-Muḥarraq; nearby is the Monastery of the Abyssinians. To the east of DAYR AL-MUḤARRAQ is the village of Būq, where J. VANSLEB said he saw the Monastery of the Angel Gabriel. A little farther on, to the south of the village of al-Jawlī, then called al-Jawliyyah, there was, according to al-Maqrīzī, a monastery dedicated to Saint MERCURIUS, of which a church surrounded by a necropolis survives.

Al-Maqrīzī mentioned a Monastery of the Angel Gabriel near Manfalūṭ, at Banī Kalb. Near Old Manqabad some rock tombs were occupied by hermits and retain reminders of their presence.

Next is the region of Asyūṭ, rich in Christian memorials. The cliff of the Libyan mountain was occupied by cemeteries of the pharaonic period. They are successively Dayr al-ʻIẓām, Dayr al-Muṭṭin, and Dayr Durunkah; and nearby the ruins of Dayr Anbā Sawīrus. Then comes Dayr Rīfah and, closer to the Nile, Dayr Abū Mūsha and Dayr al-Zāwyah. Farther down is DAYR AL-BALA'IZAH and, in Wādī Sarjah, Dayr Thomas. Finally come the two neighboring monasteries, Dayr Abū Maqrūfah and Dayr al-Ganadlah.

Farther on and forming part of the district of Abū Tīj are the ruins of al-Duwayr and, nearer to Ṭimā, the Monastery of Abū Bifām. To the south of Abū Tīj and opposite Qāw al-Kibīr (the ancient Antaeopolis) was Dayr Anbā Abshāy, the ruins of which Vansleb could still see. Abū Ṣāliḥ wrote of a Dayr al-Malāk Mīkhā'īl near the town of al-Marāghah. Farther south and near Suhāj is first of all Dayr al-Aḥmar, so called because of its construction in red bricks and dedicated to its founder Anbā Bishoi. Near it, some 6 miles (10 km) from Suhāj, is Dayr al-Abyaḍ, or Dayr Anbā Shinūdah. This marks the southern limit of this province.

Right Bank

Going up the left bank of the Nile one first sees the quarries of Shaykh Ḥasan, which were occupied by the hermits; then opposite Samālūt, Dayr al-ʻAdhrā rises on the summit of Jabal al-Ṭayr. The neighboring mountain, called Achoris in the Byzantine period, was inhabited very early by anchorites (Tihna al-Jabal in Minyā).

Opposite Minyā lies Dayr Apa Hūr at Sawādah and then the village of Zāwiyat al-Mayyitīn, which still preserves some Christian remains. Farther to the south, the Speos Artemidos, like all the Arabian mountain, or, as it is called, Libyan Mountain, has been fitted up with monastic habitations (Banī Ḥasan).

Near the ancient town of Antinoopolis are several monasteries: Dayr al-Dīk, Dayr al-Naṣārā, Dayr Sunbāṭ, Dayr Abū Ḥinnīs, Dayr al-Barshah. The tombs of Shaykh Saʻīd were inhabited by hermits, as at TALL AL-ʻAMARNAH. Next comes the massif of Jabal Abū Fūdah, where from north to south there are Dayr Tādrus, Dayr al-Quṣayr, Dayr Mārī Mīnā, and Dayr al-Jabrāwi.

One thus arrives at the right bank of ASYŪṬ, or rather at the basin of Abnūb, for the Nile, turning aside from the Arabian mountain, delimits by its windings two important basins where monasteries were established.

In the basin of Abnūb are, from north to south, Dayr Buqṭur of Shū, then Dayr al-ʿAdhrāʾ, Dayr Abū Isḥāq, and Dayr Biṣrah. In the basin of Badāri are first the Monastery of al-ʿAwanah, then Dayr Tāsā, and last Dayr Harmīnā.

Near Akhmīm, to the north in the Wādī bīr al-ʿAyn, is found Dayr al-Madwid, Dayr Apa Thomas, Dayr Bakhūm, and Dayr al-Qurqās.

To the east of Akhmīm are Dayr al-Malāk Mīkhāʾīl, Dayr al-Shuhadā, and finally Dayr al-ʿAdhrāʾ, and there ends the province of the Lower Thebaid.

Sites Not Located

Several monasteries mentioned by Abū Ṣāliḥ or al-Maqrīzī are difficult to identify, particularly in the region of Asyūṭ. Abū Ṣāliḥ spoke of the Monastery of Abū Ṣurrah, which is perhaps a corruption of the name Theodorus. He also named a monastery called Hanādah, which he placed at Rīfah. He also mentioned two monasteries dedicated to the Holy Virgin, the first named for Azilun and the second for Abū Ḥārith. He cited a Monastery of Culluthus and a Monastery of Ibsidiyyah at Rīfah. He located Dayr Philemon as being south of Aqfahs.

Similarly al-Maqrīzī named a Monastery of Abū al-Surra, but put it under the name of Saint George. He also spoke of a Monastery of Saint George Khammas, a Monastery of Isaac on the left bank dedicated to the Holy Virgin, and the Monastery of the Holy Apostles or of the Tamaris.

[For further information, see under individual monasteries.]

RENÉ-GEORGES COQUIN

MONASTERIES IN THE MINŪFIYYAH PROVINCE.

This province occupies the southern part of the Delta between the two principal branches of the Nile, that of Rosetta to the west and that of Damietta to the east.

The traces of and witnesses for monastic establishments here are very few in number, for we can cite only Atrīs and Malīj.

Malīj is situated a few miles north of Shibīn al-Kom (Amélineau, 1893, p. 503). ABŪ AL-MAKĀRIM (1984, pp. 72–73) mentions very briefly a monastery with a church dedicated to Saint John the Baptist.

BIBLIOGRAPHY

Amélineau, E. *La Géographie de l'Egypte à l'époque copte*. Paris, 1893.

RENÉ-GEORGES COQUIN
MAURICE MARTIN, S.J.

MONASTERIES IN THE QALYŪBIYYAH PROVINCE.

This province is situated in the southeast of the Delta, between the Eastern Desert and the Damietta branch of the Nile. Monastic traces here are few. In addition to the two important sites of Atrīb and Dayr Apa Hor of Siryāqūs, we may note the Dayr Nujtuhur and Kafr al-Dayr.

Perhaps the name of Dayr Nujtuhur bears witness only to the existence of a monastery at one time in this place. Today simply called al-Dayr, it is situated in the district of Ṭūkh. Muḥammad Ramzī notes that the name varies in the ancient documents. In fact, we find it under the names of Dayr Awlād Khatʿam or Dayr Banī Ḥarām. The name of Dayr Najtuhur appears to be the oldest.

A small town in the district of Shibīn al-Qanāṭir bore the name Kafr al-Dayr, which may come from the presence of a monastery there at one time. Today it is simply called al-Dayr.

BIBLIOGRAPHY

Muḥammad Ramzī. *Al-Qāmūs al-Jughrāfi*. Cairo, 1953–1963.

RENÉ-GEORGES COQUIN

MONASTERIES OF THE SHARQIYYAH PROVINCE.

This province occupies the central part of the eastern Delta between the Suez Canal and the Damietta branch of the Nile, hence between Qalyūbiyyah to the south and Daqahliyyah to the north.

Monastic establishments in this region appear to have been few in number, for apart from the DAYR MART MARYAM near Bilbays we can cite only the Dayr Baḥṭīṭ, the Dayr al-Kharbah, and Kafr al-Dayr.

The *Book of the Hidden Pearls* speaks of a Dayr Baḥṭīṭ at Bilbays (Kamāl, 1907). Daressy (1917, p. 200) believes that this is an error for DAYR ʿATIYYAH. Dayr ʿAṭiyyah, however, is in the province of Minyā, while there is indeed a village still called Baḥṭīṭ near Bilbays, formerly in the district of al-Zaqāzīq and today in that of Abū Ḥammād. This monastery does not seem to be attested elsewhere, at least under this name.

The place-name Dayr al-Karbah is mentioned in the *Book of the Hidden Pearls.* Daressy (1917, p. 203) thought that this *dayr* was in the region of Akhmīm, but al-Karbah is the vanished but well-attested name of a town in the Delta.

A township bears the name Kafr al-Dayr in the district of Minyā al-Qamh. The presence of a monastery at one time is attested by the monks' cemetery, which is still visible near the church dedicated to Saint Michael. This is the object of a pilgrimage on the occasion of the summer feast of Saint Michael on 12 Ba'ūnah (Viaud, 1979, pp. 73–74).

BIBLIOGRAPHY

Aḥmad Kamāl. *Le Livre des perles enfouies et du mystère precieux,* 2 vols. Cairo, 1907.

Daressy, G. "Indicateur topographique du 'Livre des Perles enfouies et du mystère précieux.'" *Bulletin de l'Institut français d'Archéologie orientale* 13 (1917):175–230; 14 (1918):1–32.

Muḥammad Ramzī. *Al-Qāmūs al-Jughrāfī lil-Bilād al Miṣrīyyah,* 2 vols. in 5 pts. Cairo, 1953–1963.

Viaud, G. *Les Pèlerinages coptes en Egypte d'après les notes du Qommos Jacob Muyser.* Bibliothèque d'études coptes 15. Cairo, 1979.

RENÉ-GEORGES COQUIN
MAURICE MARTIN, S. J.

MONASTERIES OF THE UPPER ṢA'ĪD.

The upper Ṣa'īd encompasses the southern third of the Nile Valley, according to its division (from Cairo to Aswan) into three sections by the ancient Greek geographers and their Arabic imitators (see Grohmann, 1959, pp. 21, 27).

Left or West Bank

The first site is at Abydos, which was greatly renowned in ancient Egypt; here are found the two monasteries of Moses (Dayr Abū Mūsā or Misās) and DAYR ANBĀ BĀKHŪM (Pachomius). Farther up comes BAKHANIS, the name of which perpetuates a foundation of Pachomius. A little farther on, the large town of Farshūṭ recalls the memory of Abraham who was born there and, driven from Pbow by the Emperor Justinian's police, founded two monasteries near the town, one for men and the other for women. It is a short distance to the town of Bahjūrah, where DAYR ANBĀ BĪDABĀ still stands; about 6 miles (10 km) away was situated the ancient Diaspolis Parva (today Hiw), to the south of which is DAYR MĀR MĪNĀ. The left bank is void of Christian remains as far as Qena, where on the island of al-Ḥamidāt remains a memory, perhaps legendary, of a convent of nuns. Up as far as DAYR AL-BALLĀṢ and from Naqādah to Qamūlah there are no fewer than eight monasteries over a strip of some 6 miles (10 km), six of which are on the edge of the desert: DAYR AL-MALĀK MĪKHĀ'ĪL, DAYR AL-ṢALĪB, DAYR ABŪ AL-LĪF, DAYR AL-MAJMA', DAYR ANBĀ PISENTIUS, the celebrated bishop of Qifṭ in the seventh century, DAYR MĀR BUQṬUR, and finally Dayr al-Malāk Mīkhā'īl) to the west of Qamūlah. Two other notable sites are the rock churches of Elias and al-Sanad, which in contrast with the monastery churches were no more than places of assembly for hermits who lived in the neighborhood.

The region of Thebes is celebrated among tourists for its Valleys of the Kings and Queens and for temples that preserve traces of their occupation by Christian hermits. First, to the north, as its name indicates, is DAYR AL-BAKHĪT, then DAYR APA PHOIBAMMON (also called Dayr al-Bahri), then quite close DAYR EPIPHANIUS and Dayr Kyriakus. There is also the temple of Hathor, which was transformed into a monastery called DAYR AL-MADĪNAH, a name it has retained to this day. Not far away, on the hill of QURNAT MAR'Ī are the ruins of a hermitage recently excavated. Behind MADĪNAT HĀBŪ the small DAYR AL-AMĪR TADRŪS still remains, and at the beginning of the Valley of the Queens rises the site today called DAYR AL-RŪMĪ (Greek monastery), although it is not known whence the name comes. A little farther on can be noted a small pharaonic temple of the Ptolemaic period, called Dayr al-Shalwīt (the remote monastery). Near Armant at the bottom of a deep gorge are the remains of a *topos,* which is wrongly called Dayr Phoibammon. This region of Armant contains numerous sites: DAYR AL-NAMŪS (or al-Misaykarah), DAYR AL-NASĀRĀ (of the Christians, for the original name has been lost), DAYR POSIDONIOS, DAYR AL-MAṬMAR (or Dayr al-Abyaḍ, the White Monastery, not to be confused with that at Suhāj), and finally DAYR AL-SĀQIYAH (also called the topos al-Qiddis Yuḥannis, although which Saint John is concerned is not clear).

In the neighborhood of Isnā, near the village of al-Dimiqrāṭ, is DAYR MĀR JIRJIS; nearer Isnā is the celebrated DAYR AL-FĀKHŪRĪ, near the ancient Aṣfūn. To the southwest of the town of Isna is DAYR AL-SHUHADĀ', and beside it the ruins of DAYR APA ISḤĀQ. Approaching Idfū, Dayr al-Malāk Mīkhā'īl (also called Dayr Anbā Bākhūm) still bears witness to the planting of Christianity in this region. Farther along, the valley narrows at a place named JABAL AL-SILSILAH (mountain of the chain), which preserves traces of hermits who lived there. Nearer the town of Aswān are DAYR AL-KŪBĀNIYYAH and the Dayr Qubbat al-Hawā. Above Aswān are the imposing ruins of the DAYR ANBĀ HADRĀ. The island of Philae perhaps preserves some monastic souvenirs at the gate of Nubia, of which it was sometimes considered the capital.

Right or East Bank

Somewhat curiously, the monasteries are much less numerous here, perhaps because the Left Bank was traditionally the region of the dead, and the hermits took up their abode in the ancient tombs. The expression "to pass to the west" was equivalent to "become a monk."

Going up the Nile, on leaving Akhmīm near the Nile, is DAYR MĀR JIRJIS AL-ḤADĪDĪ, and, opposite al-Minshāh Psoi (Ptolemais Hermiou), DAYR ANBĀ BISĀDAH, which commemorates and preserves the relics of an ancient bishop of Psoi, Bisādah (PSOTE). A little farther on lie the ruins of Dayr Yuḥannis (John, although we do not know which John). Still farther on, opposite the town of Jirjā, a church still bears witness to a small monastery, the DAYR AL-MALĀK MĪKHĀ'ĪL. Farther south, to the east of al-Khiyām and inside a village called Najʿ al-Dayr (village of the monastery), a small monastery dedicated to Saint Philotheus still exists. Then begins the JABAL AL-ṬĀRIF, celebrated for its tombs where the famous Nag Hammadi Gnostic papyri are said to have been discovered. Beginning from the village of QAṢR AL-ṢAYYĀD and as far as Qina, the Nile flows from east to west. The area is celebrated for the first foundations of Saint PACHOMIUS. Near the present village of Qaṣr al-Ṣayyād is Dayr Anbā Palaemon and not far away DAYR AL-MALĀK; then a little above the village of Fāw al-Qiblī, which preserves the memory of the second foundation of Pachomius, Pbow. The first and most celebrated cenobitic foundation, that of Tabennēsē, is supposed to have been situated not far away but near the river. It is necessary to go up as far as QŪṢ to come upon a monastery still in existence, DAYR ABŪ SAYFAYN (of Anbā Bākhūm) at Ḥijāzah, to the south of Qūṣ. In the Theban region are Dayr Anbā Bākhūm near al-Madāmūd, Karnak (famous for temples that preserve important traces of their occupation by the monks), and to the south of Luxor, east of the town of al-Ṭūd, the monastery called DAYR ANBĀ ABSHAY, where a quantity of blocks deriving from the neighboring temple of Montou were reused. Finally, shortly before arriving at the height of Isnā, come the ruins called DAYR AL-RŪMĀNIYYAH (Greek monastery, although why it was given this name is not known).

Monasteries Not Precisely Located

The papyri give some names of monasteries that cannot be placed on a map; Barison's study (1938, pp. 128–34) lists several. In the Thinite nome (the region of Jirjā) was the Dayr Apa Jeremiah. In the nome of Dandarah was the monastery of Pampane, which is perhaps that of al-Ballāṣ, near the village of al-Dayr. In the nome of Apollonopolis Minor (today Qūs) was the monastery of Apa Agenios, which is no doubt the name of the founder. In the nome of Diaspolis Magna (the modern Karnak and Luxor), the following monasteries should be noted: that of Pisentius, probably from the name of its founder, was situated in the Castrum Memnonium, hence on the left bank; that of Saint Phoibammon no doubt designates the monastery established in the temple of Hatschepsut; another monastery was situated near the Castrum Memnonium, but its name is not known.

At Apollonopolis Magna (today Idfū) there were several monasteries, that of the abbot Agenes, that of Bawlos, and that of the abbot Patois; these were in the village of Tanaithis, the site of which is known, although because of the provenance of the papyri it may have been in the nome of Apollonopolis Magna. Near this same town (today Idfū), Remondon thinks that formulae in documents of the sixth to eighth centuries "for Saint Stephen" and "for Saint Cyriacus" designate churches or perhaps monasteries (1953, pp. 208–9), Dayr Mār Stefanos and Dayr Mār Kyriakos.

Adding to the testimony of the Greek Lives of Pachomius, the *Vita prima* mentions a foundation (hence a Pachomian monastery) near Armant under the generalship of Theodorus and therefore at the end of the fourth century. The information is also given by the *Vita tertia* (ed. Halkin, 1932, pp. 84 and 388); the Coptic Lives do not give this indication.

ABŪ ṢĀLIḤ THE ARMENIAN at the beginning of the thirteenth century mentions several monasteries for which there is no other attestation and which cannot be located. In the region of Qena he notes two monasteries of Saint Colluthus and of Saint Michael without giving any further details (1895, p. 281), but he remarks that in his time they were already in ruins. In the district of Qifṭ he indicates seven monasteries, that of the Virgin, that of Anbā Shinūdah, that of Saint Victor (DAYR MĀR BUQṬUR near

Qamūlah), that of nuns dedicated to Saint George, two monasteries of Saint Theodorus, and one of Saint Antony, Dayr Anbā Antūniyūs (p. 281). In the town of Qūṣ he points out three monasteries: of the archangel Michael, of Anbā Shinūdāh, and of Saint Pachomius (p. 280); in the region near Qamūlah he notes two monasteries, that of Apa Nob and that of Saint Theodore, without specifying whether they were within the town of Qamūlah or outside of it; near Qamūlah and close to a village named (A)bū Ḥarūq, today disappeared, he points out a monastery named for Saint Michael (p. 284).

The *State of the Provinces* (A.H. 777/A.D. 1375–1376) mentions (Sacy's translation, p. 703) a Dayr Qaṭṭān in the province of Qūṣ, for which Ramzī suggests seeing the survival in the village of Naj' Qurquṭān (Vol. 1, p. 261). It is between Danfīq and Qamūlah, hence on the left bank.

Some monasteries are named in Coptic documents and are cataloged by Crum (1926, Vol. 1, pp. 108–115). These are Colluthus in the diocese of Qifṭ, at Ape, Karnak; Apa Sergius and the *topos* (perhaps a simple church) of Apa Papnute, at Jeme (today Madīnat Habu); Patermuthius, Menas, the *topos* (see above) of Apa Psote; and Saint Victor. They also indicate in the *kūla* (a regional word designating a hill) of Djeme the monastery of Saint Apa Paul. Finally they mention at Armant the *topos* (perhaps monastery) of the forty Martyrs (Dayr al-Arba'īn Shahīd) or of Saint Theophilus (Dayr Theophilus).

The Sahidic recension of the SYNAXARION of the Copts (twelfth, thirteenth centuries) mentions in the region of Armant two monasteries, Dayr Anbā Daryūs and Dayr Ghubriyāl, without further detail.

One of the letters received by Bishop Pisentius in the seventh century makes mention of the monastery of Apa or Papas (i.e., priest) Macarius (son) of Patoure, opposite (P)Shanhūr, hence to the south of Qūṣ (Revillout, 1900, pp. 146–47).

BIBLIOGRAPHY

Barison, P. "Ricerche sui monasteri dell'Egitto byzantino ed arabo secondo i documenti dei papiri greci." *Aegyptus* 18 (1938):29–148.

Grohmann, A. *Studien zur historischen Geographie und Verwaltung des frühmittalalterlichen Ägypten.* Österreichische Akademie der Wissenschaften philologie—historische Klasse. Denkschriften 77, Vol. 2, Abhandlungen. Vienna, 1959.

Halkin, F. *Sancti Pachomii vitae graecae.* Subsidia hagiographica 19. Brussels, 1932.

Muḥammad Ramzī. *Al-Qāmūs al-Jughrāfī,* 2 vols. in 5 pts. Cairo, 1953–1963.

Rémondon, R. *Papyrus grecs d'Apollonos ano.* Documents de fouilles de l'Institut français d'Archéologie orientale 19. Cairo, 1953.

Revillout, E. "Textes coptes extraits de la correspondance de Saint Pésunthius." *Revue égyptologique* 9 (1900):146–47.

Sacy, S. de, trans. and ed. *Relation de l'Egypte de 'Abd al-Latīf.* Paris, 1810. "L'Etat des provinces" is translated in an appendix.

Winlock, H. E., and W. E. Crum. *The Monastery of Epiphanius at Thebes,* 2 vols. New York, 1926.

RENÉ-GEORGES COQUIN

MONASTERIES OF THE WESTERN DESERT. In the western desert, also called the Libyan massif because it is near Libya, the oases are numerous and well known. Since the watering places and the frequency of the caravans provided regular provisioning, the monastic centers were numerous here.

It is convenient to distinguish first of all the "great" oasis, the one today called Kharjah (the outer), the largest and the best connected to the Nile Valley by a road starting from Asyūṭ. Here were several hermit centers, first on the edge of the depression, to the west, the Dayr al-Ghanāyim, then toward the second oasis, that of Dākhlah (the inner), 'AYN 'AMŪR, still on the edge of the depression. To the northwest of the capital of Khargah, not far from the Christian necropolis of al-Bagawāt, is the DAYR MUṢṬAFĀ KĀSHIF; in the same sector we have the JABAL AL-ṬAYR.

In the oasis of Dakhlah, a single site bears the name of Dayr (Dayr al-Ḥajar), but this is in reality a temple of the Ptolemaic period. A village perpetuates by its name (al-Qalamūn) the existence of a marsh planted with reeds and perhaps the presence of Christian hermits, for these made great use of them (*kalamon* in Greek).

In the oasis of al-Farāfrah, in the latitude of Asyūṭ, traces remain of occupation by one or more Christian hermits at the place called 'AYN JILLĀW.

Still farther to the north, in the oasis of al-Baḥariyyah (that of the north), are the ruins of a church called al-Dayr, which may preserve the memory of a monastery or a hermit center. Besides, nearby some ruins are said to be those of the monastery of al-Rīs.

Farther north, in the middle of the present desert road from Cairo to Alexandria is the famous Wādī al-Naṭrūn with its four still active monasteries. To the west is the Khashm al-Qu'ūd, excavated in 1932 by Omar Toussoun; he identified the site, however, as being the KELLIA.

Finally, not far from the oasis of Siwa, al-ʿAraj perhaps preserves traces of occupation by Christian hermits, while a traveler at the beginning of the twentieth century notes vestiges of a monastery in the oasis of Siwa itself.

It is appropriate to mention, following the *History of the Patriarchs,* a "mountain called Jabal Jarād, which was perhaps near the Wādī al-Natrūn; we must point out, although no trace of it remains, the monastery that was near the milestone marking the twentieth mile from Alexandria" (the *Eikoston*).

As can be seen, the traces of monasticism in the western desert are numerous. We must also mention, although the exact site is not known, a monastery of the inhabitants of the oasis, probably Kharjah, attested by papyri and then dependent on the province of Aphrodito (today the town of Kom Ishqāw).

BIBLIOGRAPHY

Barison, P. "Ricerche sui monasteri dell'Egitto bizantino ed arabo secondo i documenti dei papiri greci." *Aegyptus* 18 (1938):29–148.

RENÉ-GEORGES COQUIN

MONASTERY. *See* Dayr.

MONASTERY OF THE ETHIOPIANS. *See* Dayr al-Muḥarraq.

MONASTERY PAINTINGS, COPTIC.

The Egyptian desert was a nurturing ground for monasteries, some of which have been occupied almost continuously since their founding. Others, abandoned and buried in sand through the centuries, have been uncovered only in recent years. Still others, mentioned in Arabic texts or in accounts of European travelers, await excavation.

Those monasteries occupied at present are those in Wādī al-Naṭrūn, in the Western Desert, the Monastery of Upper Ṣaʿīd, and DAYR ANBĀ BŪLĀ in the Eastern Desert. They actually reveal very little information concerning their primitive decor. The monastery churches, extensively decorated, have undergone many alterations and repairs. Their paintings are juxtaposed or superimposed, and often only the most recent stages are now visible. The cells and common buildings have conserved but few painted items, which are barely perceptible to the naked eye.

In those compounds abandoned between the ninth and twelfth centuries, the situation is reversed; there is little information about the churches but an abundance of data about the other buildings (e.g., see KELLIA, ABŪ MĪNĀ, DAYR APA JEREMIAH, BĀWĪṬ, and ISNĀ). A few general observations may be made. The paintings are placed in the same edifices: churches, common rooms such as the refectory at the Monastery of Saint Jeremiah at Saqqara, and the monks' cells. In the beginning, a cell comprised at least a vestibule, an oratory, and a dwelling room. Most often the floor was covered only with plaster, but in rare instances, a carpet design was painted in dark red (there are numerous examples at Kellia). The majority of the paintings were to be found in the vestibule and, above all, in the oratory.

Everywhere the wall decoration is distributed in two registers. The lower register (approximately 3 feet [1 m] high) may simply be painted with a uniform layer of dark red, occasionally topped with a band of geometric and/or floral motifs. In other cases, the lower register consists of a succession of frames painted with lines or dots, whose design is reminiscent of stone, marble, or porphyry, such as those at Abū Jirjā in MAREOTIS and at Kellia. Or they are composed of skillful arrangements of geometric forms imitating intarsia (inlaid work) as in Saqqara and Bāwīṭ. The subjects are thereby related to those that decorate mosaic pavings in North Africa and Syria: birds within squares and/or segments of circles (Abū Jirjā, Kellia), mattings (Kellia, ʿALAM SHALTŪT), plaited crowns (ʿAlam Shaltūt), or sets of intertwined geometric designs (Saqqara, Bāwīṭ).

The upper register portrays human figures: monks, hermits, and founders of monasteries; saints (mainly local); and occasionally biblical scenes. It is the choice of motifs that gives each site its originality.

The composition in two registers is directly descended from the Greco-Roman world. In Egypt such examples are to be found at Tūnah al-Jabal and Luxor, where above the base, which evokes intarsia, scenes from pharaonic or Greek mythology (at Tūnah) or from Roman life (at Luxor) are depicted.

The eastern wall of the cell is pierced with niches, often three in number. The smaller, or secondary, niches contained liturgical objects and were most often left undecorated. The larger, principal niche was emphasized by pillars or columns that supported an archivolt that was sculpted, or stuccoed and painted. Inside this niche were depicted special themes, objects of devotion, and cult objects of the cell's inhabitant.

Isnā

In the hermitages of Isnā, the ornamentation is simple, homogeneous, and very limited in the choice of subjects. At times a dark red stripe outlines the angles of the rooms and the contours of the doors, windows, stairs, and niches. These niches may be emphasized by motifs, either floral or geometric (torsades mainly). On the walls and inside the niches, numerous crosses were painted—Greek, Latin, straight, or potent enclosed in circles. The arms of these crosses were occasionally ornamented with garlands or torsades. Classical subjects were also depicted in the paleo-Christian art: birds face-to-face (peacocks and doves mostly) and, more rarely, boats. Personages also adorn the walls: pagan figures (dancing girls, soldiers, desert animals sometimes grappling with a man); founders of monasteries (Paul, Saint MACARIUS THE GREAT, JEREMIAH, Abū Mīnā); famous monks (Paphnutius, Moses); illustrious saints (Victor, Phoibamon, George); as well as the Virgin and seraphim. The eastern niches basically contain crosses and birds facing each other.

Kellia

At Kellia, extremely varied and abundant flora and fauna fill the walls. There are also cavaliers, boats, and most frequently, crosses of all types: simple, with torsades, studded with precious stones, bearing garlands, unadorned or framed by birds, and even occasionally accompanied by a boat. Note that all these crosses have one point in common—the staff upon which they rise; they are all processional crosses. The personages derive most often from Christian iconography (Pantokrator, saints, monks) and sometimes from the pagan world (a god, river, warrior).

Dayr Apa Jeremiah

At Dayr Apa Jeremiah at Saqqara, monks and local saints, among whom are the founders of the monastery (Paphnutius, ONOPHRIOS, Saint Macarius, Alexandrinus, APOLLO OF BĀWĪṬ), constitute the basic mural decoration. However, one should also note the presence of a boat, the virtues of the spirit, crosses, and the theme of the three Hebrews in the furnace. Biblical themes are extremely rare at Saqqara. Along with the three Hebrews, however, the sacrifice of Abraham, painted on one of the refectory walls, should be mentioned.

The motifs decorating the oratory niches are repeated: Virgin and Child framed by the archangels Michael and Gabriel, and occasionally by the founders; Christ in Majesty adored by angels and/or carried by bodiless beasts. These two subjects are sometimes associated, in which case Mary and Jesus are then pictured on the walls, and the Christ in Majesty in the conch of the apse.

Monastery of Apollo

At the Monastery of Apollo at Bāwīṭ, contrary to what is seen in the great monasteries described above, there are frequent scenes from the Old and New Testaments: the story of the Three Hebrews in the Furnace, the grand exploits of David, events in the life of Mary (the Annunciation, Visitation, Nativity) and the life of Christ (massacre of the innocents, baptism by John the Baptist, various miracles, the Last Supper). Elsewhere in this monastery at Bāwīṭ, as at Kellia and Saqqara, various monks and saints adorn the walls, with a predilection shown for the cavalier saints (Claudius, Sisinnios, Mercury, Phoibamon). It must also be noted that among these Christian scenes there are allegories (virtues of the spirit, seasons) as well as secular subjects (gazelle and hippopotamus hunts, and Orpheus taming the wild beasts). The oratory niches, exactly like those at Saqqara, contain the Virgin and Child and Christ in Majesty. But here at Bāwīṭ the two themes are almost always found together. Moreover, Christ is very often depicted according to the apocalyptic vision, enthroned in a chariot with fiery wheels drawn by the tetramorph (a winged figure), and the Virgin is occasionally surrounded by the Twelve Apostles. These never appear at Saqqara.

This brief survey of a few monastic institutions indicates a certain homogeneity as to the location of the paintings but also a great individuality in the choice of themes, such as the adoration of the Cross at Isnā and Kellia, the Christ in Majesty and the Virgin at Saqqara and Bāwīṭ, and the numerous evocations of the Old and New Testaments at Bāwīṭ.

As for style, monastic painting is sometimes lively, as in the hunting scenes from Bāwīṭ or the animals devoured alive from Kellia, sometimes static, as in the long lines of hieratic saints. It may sometimes be elegant and sure, as with plants and clothing; sometimes rapid and schematic, as evidenced in certain boats or figures reduced to their simplest expression.

BIBLIOGRAPHY

Meinardus, O. *Monks and Monasteries of the Egyptian Desert.* Cairo, 1961.

Walters, C. C. *Monastic Archaeology in Egypt.* Warminster, 1974.

MARGUERITE RASSART-DEBERGH

MONASTERY OF SAINT JOHN. *See* Dayr al-Sāqiyah.

MONASTERY OF SAINT JOHN THE BAPTIST. *See* Holy Land, Churches of the.

MONASTERY OF SAINT SIMEON. *See* Dayr Anbā Hadrā.

MONASTICISM, EGYPTIAN. Numerous theories, which have given rise to an abundant literature, have been advanced since the end of the nineteenth century to explain the origins of monasticism in Egypt. Some explanations appeal to a revival of the way of life of the Therapeutae described by Philo, those Jewish ascetics who lived in the neighborhood of Alexandria in the first century; to a survival of certain practices of the ancient Egyptian religion (recluses of Sarapis); to the influence of the Manichaean missions that reached Egypt from the third century; and more recently, since the discovery of the Nag Hammadi texts, to the influence of the Gnostic sects.

None of these explanations is convincing. The very beginnings of the monastic movement are obscure. Normally Saint ANTONY is considered to be "the father of the monks," but the Life of Antony bears witness that when he was converted to the ascetic life in 270, there were already ascetics who withdrew from the villages. The new feature with Saint Antony—unless he was preceded in this way of life by PAUL OF THEBES—is that, instead of remaining near the village as the other ascetics did, he went into the interior of the desert and practiced there an ANACHORESIS that grew ever greater. This anachoresis is, in fact, what characterizes monasticism properly so called.

One cannot relate this monastic anachoresis, as certain historians have done, with the "anachoresis" of the peasants who fled from their villages to escape fiscal burdens. But certain circumstances could have furthered it, notably the persecutions, which drove some Christians to the desert. Such was precisely the case, if we believe Saint Jerome, with Paul of Thebes himself, who took refuge in the desert during the Decian persecution (249–250) and remained there permanently, embracing by free choice a way of life that necessity had at first imposed upon him.

The monastic anachoresis has an essentially religious motive, arising from the ideals of the Christian ascetics of the first centuries. Before designating the monk who lived in the solitude of the desert, the Greek word *monachos*, according to its earliest attestations, described the ascetic who was a "solitary" because he renounced marriage in order to have no other concern but the service of the Lord (cf. I Cor. 7:32–35). By separating himself from the world through anachoresis, the monk realized in an effective way that renunciation of the world that is the fundamental element of Christian ascesis. This distancing from the world, realized in material terms, was felt to be all the more necessary after the conversion of the Roman empire to Christianity, when the "world," in the Johannine sense of the term, invaded the church itself. Thus the monk appeared as the successor of the martyr, a witness to the incompatibility of the world and Christian faith.

In its beginnings, monasticism was anchorite. PACHOMIUS himself began by living as an anchorite, under the guidance of the anchorite PALAEMON. It was only after disciples had come to him and he had learned by experience that it was necessary to organize their way of life that he created monasteries. Each monastery contained a number of "houses," and the whole body of the monasteries constituted the Pachomian *koinonia* or congregation. Each house, each monastery, and the congregation itself had at its head a superior, and was under rigorous material organization. The monks had everything in common: prayer, meals, work. Written rules regulated the life of the community down to its slightest details. Communities of the same type—designated by the name of cenobitism—multiplied in Upper Egypt in the course of the third century, in particular in the church that issued from the Melitian schism. The most celebrated, after those of Pachomius, are those in the region of Akhmīm in the fourth and fifth centuries that were dominated by the powerful personality of SHENUTE.

In Lower Egypt, under the more or less direct influence of Antony, monasticism developed especially in the form of semi-anchoritism. This occurred in particular in the celebrated deserts of

SCETIS, NITRIA, and the KELLIA. There the solitary and the communal life balanced one another. The monks lived alone, each in his cell during the week, and came together on Saturdays and Sundays in the church, where they took together a meal called the *agape* and participated in the eucharistic liturgy, celebrated by monk priests. Living as hermits, the monks were divided in a rather free fashion, it appears, into congregations, each of which had its church. One of the priests assisted by a council of the elders exercised a certain authority. At Scetis, where there were four congregations in the fifth century, the whole body of the monks was under the authority of one of them, considered "the father of Scetis." But this authority was more moral and charismatic than judicial. In the early period, the life of the monks in these deserts was not subject to any written rule. It was regulated above all by the traditional teaching of the elders, transmitted orally.

Two features are strongly characteristic of this monasticism—work and residence in a cell. Manual work was an obligation, each monk having to provide for his needs—at Scetis the majority of the monks devoted themselves to basket-making. This work was to be as far as possible continual, like prayer itself, which consisted not only in the recitation of the office at appointed hours but also in what was called *melete* (meditation), the recitation of texts from scripture, chiefly from the psalms. The monks were constrained to residence in their cells, which was called *hesychia,* a term borrowed from the Hellenic tradition. In Egypt, and particularly in the region of Oxyrhynchus, legendary traits and factual description are inextricably mixed in stories that tell of monks who led an itinerant life. But in general Egyptian monasticism did not show itself very favorable to this form of asceticism, which was much in favor in Syrian monasticism. "Remain seated in your cell" is the counsel that unflaggingly recurs in the APOPHTHEGMATA PATRUM in reply to the young monk who asks an older one how he will be saved. "Remain seated in your cell," is the very definition of *hesychia.* The word implies, at the same time, solitude, silence, quiet reflection, but above all the steadfastness in one's cell that is the condition of the rest.

Monk inside a monastery. *Courtesy Aziz S. Atiya collection.*

The monks rapidly became very numerous. From the time of the earliest documents, high figures are given, the accuracy of which is difficult to judge. The author of the HISTORIA MONACHORUM IN AEGYPTO speaks of an abbot Serapion in the Fayyūm who was at the head of a community of about 10,000 monks; elsewhere he affirms that in the town of Oxyrhynchus the monastic population was in his time (end of the fourth century) more numerous than the civilian population—5,000 monks. Palladius declares that towards 390 there were about 5,000 monks in Nitria and 600 in the Kellia, and that when Pachomius was alive, the Pachomian congregation comprised 3,000 monks; toward the end of the fourth century 7,000 monks—1,300 in the monastery of Tabennēsē alone—lived according to the Pachomian rules (chap. 32, p. 93). In the preface to his translation of the Rules of Saint Pachomius, Saint Jerome reports a clearly exaggerated figure of 50,000 monks as having attended at the chapter general of the congregation every year (Boon, 1932, p. 8). According to the Arabic Life of Shenute, the monks who found themselves under the authority of this archimandrite were 2,200 (Amélineau, 1907, p. 143). John Moschus, the Palestinian author of the *Pratum Spirituale,* reports that an abbot, John of Petra, told him that when he was at Scetis in his youth toward the beginning of the sixth century, there were then in this desert about 3,500 monks. This figure is not improbable, but what the fifteenth-century historian al-MAQRĪZĪ affirms on the faith of ancient historians, that at the time of the Arab conquest 70,000 monks from Scetis betook themselves to meet ʿAmr ibn al-'Āṣ (trans. in Leroy, 1908), cannot be accepted. If all these figures are not trustworthy, it is nevertheless certain that the monastic population of Egypt before the coming of Islam was extremely numerous. Thereafter it diminished greatly. According to the HISTORY OF THE PATRIARCHS there were in Scetis in the eleventh century only 712 monks, divided among seven monasteries (Evelyn-White, 1932, p. 360).

It is appropriate to add to this male monastic population the nuns, who according to the ancient documents were also very numerous. From the beginning there were women in the church who dedicated themselves to virginity, but continued to live at home. It is not certain that the virgins to whom Saint Antony entrusted his young sister in about 270 when he was converted to the ascetic life (Life of Antony 3) were already living in a community (Garitte, 1961). An interesting testimony about the creation of a monastery for women is furnished by Palladius, who relates how an ascetic named Elias gathered together some virgins who until then had lived separately, and founded a monastery for them in the town of Atrīb. It is known that Pachomius founded two monasteries for women, and a third was established by his successor Theodorus. The first that Pachomius founded for his sister and her companions is probably the one described by Palladius in chapters 33 and 34 of his *Historia lausiaca* (Butler, 1904, pp. 96–100). It was at Tabennēsē itself, where the first monastery for men had been established, but on the other side of the river. A strict regulation forbade any passage from one monastery to the other. Only a priest and a deacon might go to the women's monastery on Sunday to celebrate the Eucharist. Four hundred nuns were then in residence there. Palladius affirms besides that there were twelve monasteries of women at this same period in the single town of Antinoopolis in the Fayyūm. Later, 1,800 lived under the authority of Shenute, according to the testimony of the Arabic Life (Amélineau, 1907). There were women who condemned themselves to RECLUSION, like the virgin Alexandra who, according to Palladius, shut herself up in a tomb in the environs of Alexandria. But it is not very likely that there were women hermits. The desert and the monks who lived there did not welcome women. The desert was characterized as the place where there are no women (*Apophthegmata Patrum*, Sisoes 3, Migne: *Patrologia Graeca* 65, 392D). Stories of women living incognito in a cave lost in the depths of the desert and being discovered only when they are on the point of dying (Verba Seniorum, John III, Migne: *Patrologia Latina* 73, 1008 A.B.) probably belong more to hagiographic romance than to real history.

Egypt has long been considered the motherland of monasticism. Born in Egypt, the monastic movement was thought to have spread from there throughout the Christian world. In reality, it is now established that the movement appeared almost simultaneously and in independent fashion in other countries, notably in Palestine, Syria, and Mesopotamia. But Egypt was the favorite land of monasticism. Probably in no other country was the monastic population so numerous. Egyptian monasticism very early enjoyed an almost universal celebrity, thanks to the literary works devoted to it, which met with an extraordinary diffusion. There were biographies such as the Life of Saint Antony by Saint ATHANASIUS or the Lives of Saint Pachomius; travel narratives like the *Historia Monachorum in Aegypto* and the *Lausiac History* of Palladius; and above all the *Apophthegmata Patrum* which, compiled in Greek and translated not only into Latin but into all the languages of the Christian Orient, made the teaching and the way of life of the monks in the deserts of Nitria and Scetis known everywhere. Through the Latin translation of the Rules of Pachomius made by Saint Jerome, and the *Conferences* and *Cenobitic Institutes* of John CASSIAN, the example of the Egyptian monks exercised a profound influence on the origins of the Western and Benedictine monastic tradition.

Thus Egyptian monasticism took on an exemplary and normative significance. Everywhere people sought to take as their model the Egyptian masters, and it was through them that they came to be initiated into the monastic life. Rufinus and Melania the Elder, on their way to found monasteries in Jerusalem, stopped and sojourned among the monks of Nitria toward 374. Some twenty years earlier Saint Basil, who laid down the laws for monasticism in the Greek world, had made a journey among the monks of Egypt before himself withdrawing into solitude at Annesoi in Pontus. It is said of numerous monks in Mesopotamia that at the beginning of their monastic life they too went to visit the monks of Egypt, as, for example, did Abraham the Great, founder of the great monastery of Mount Izlā, in the sixth century. The prestige and authority that

Egyptian monasticism enjoyed were such that fictitious tales were circulated, the aim of which was to give local monasticism Egyptian origins, in order to confer upon it a greater nobility. Such is the aim of the legend of Mâr Awgên who, an Egyptian by birth and in his youth a disciple of Pachomius, is said to have imported monasticism into the region of Nisibis in the fourth century. The Life of Hilarion, written by Saint Jerome at Bethlehem toward 390, arose even earlier from the intention of attaching Palestinian monasticism to Saint Antony and the monasticism of Egypt.

Monasticism left a profound mark on Coptic Christianity in its piety, its ethics, and its institutions. With few exceptions, down to our own day the patriarch is chosen from among the clergy who come from the monastic milieu. But Egyptian monasticism, through the immense influence it exercised outside of Egypt, has set its stamp no less profoundly upon the church universal, in the West as well as in the East. This is certainly the most considerable legacy Egypt has left to Christianity.

BIBLIOGRAPHY

Amélineau, E. *Oeuvres de Schenoudi,* Vols. 1 and 2. Paris, 1907.

Boon, A. *Pachomiana latina.* Bibliothèque de la Revue d'histoire ecclésiastique 7. Louvain, 1932.

Cauwenbergh, Paul van. *Eutde sur les moines d'Egypte depuis le concile de Chalcédoine (451) jusqu'à l'invasion arabe (640).* Paris and Louvain, 1914.

Chitty, D. J. *The Desert a City: An Introduction to the Study of Egyptian and Palestinian Monasticism under the Christian Empire.* Oxford, 1966.

Colombàs, G. M. *El monacato primitivo,* Vols. 1 and 2. Madrid, 1974–1975.

Evelyn-White, H. G. *The History of the Monasteries of Nitria and of Scetis,* Pt. 2, *The Monasteries of the Wadi'n Natrun.* New York, 1932.

Farag, R. F. *Sociological and Moral Studies in the Field of Coptic Monasticism.* Leiden, 1964.

Garitte, G. "Un Couvent de femmes au IIIe siècle? Note sur un passage de la vie grecque de S. Antoine." In *Scrinium Lovaniense. Mélanges historiques E. Van Cauwenbergh.* Louvain, 1961.

Guillaumont, A. *Aux origines du monachisme chrétien. Pour une phénoménologie du monachisme.* Spiritualité orientale 30. Abbaye de Bellefontaine, 1979.

Heussi, K. *Der Ursprung des Mönchtums.* Tübingen, 1936.

Iris Habib, El-Masri. "A Historical Survey of the Convents for Women in Egypt up to the Present Day." *Bulletin de la Société d'archéologie copte* 14 (1950–1957):63–111.

Leclercq, H. "Cénobitisme." *Dictionnaire d'archéologie chrétienne et de liturgie,* Vol. 2, cols. 3047–3248. Paris, 1910.

Leroy, L. "Les couvents des chrétiens. Traduction de l'arabe d'Al-Makrizi. *"Revue de l'orient chrétien"* (1908):33–46, 192–204.

Meinardus, O. "The Nestorians in Egypt." *Oriens Christianus* 51 (1967):112–29.

Ranke-Heinemann, U. *Das frühe Mönchtum. Seine Motive nach den Selbstzeugnissen.* Essen, 1963.

Schiwietz, S. *Das morgenländische Mönchtum,* Vol. 1. Mainz, 1904.

Vergote, J. "L'Egypte, berceau du monachisme chrétien." *Chronique d'Egypte* 17 (1942):329–45.

Weingarten, H. "Der Ursprung des Mönchtums im nachconstantinischen Zeitalter." *Zeitschrift für Kirchengeschichte* 1 (1877):1–35.

ANTOINE GUILLAUMONT

MONASTICISM, PACHOMIAN. The word *koinonia* (community) is at the heart of the cenobitic form of monasticism developed by Saint PACHOMIUS in the fourth century. In Coptic as well as in Greek, it became, at a very early stage, the technical term to designate what L. T. Lefort called the Pachomian Congregation, that is, the large community formed by all the Pachomian monasteries. There were nine of them (plus two convents of women) at the time Pachomius died. At that time there were 5,000 monks, more or less, in the *koinonia.*

At the head of the *koinonia* were a father and a second. They were responsible for making the necessary appointments of local superiors—and most of all for visiting all the monasteries, comforting the brothers, and preaching the Word of God to them. Pachomius, who had gathered that *koinonia,* was its father until his death. He was succeeded in that office by PETRONIUS, who died a few months after him, then by HORSIESIOS, and finally by THEODORUS, who had been his assistant for many years but had been discharged. Horsiesius was father of the *koinonia* again for a number of years after the death of Theodorus. We know very little about the *koinonia* following Theodorus' death. One of the most famous Pachomian monks in the next generation was SHENUTE, but he was the father of one of the Pachomian monasteries, not the father of the *koinonia.*

Also at the head of the *koinonia* was the great

steward, who was responsible for the material organization of all the monasteries. The local superiors had to report their needs and the fruit of their work to him.

Every year two meetings assembled all the brothers at the central monastery of PBOW. The first was for the holy PASCHA, which they celebrated in fasting and in the Word of God, at the end of which they baptized all the catechumen monks. The other general meeting, in the month of Misrā at the end of the Coptic year, originally probably had a practical purpose: to bring the accounts of the material administration to the great steward and to receive the various appointments. But at a later time it was also the occasion for a collective remission of sins and offenses.

Each monastery had its own father and its second as well. All the brothers of the monasteries were divided into houses or wards of about forty monks each, a specific service being assigned to each house (such as care of the sick, reception of visitors, or preparation of food). A monastery could have up to thirty or forty such houses, and each one had its master and his second.

The responsibility of all these various superiors was both material and spiritual. Apart from comforting the brothers in times of trials and difficulties, their pastoral role consisted mainly in the frequent instructions or catecheses they had to give on the Word of God.

The Word of God was at the heart of the life of the Pachomian monk. He learned it by heart as soon as he arrived at the monastery, in order to be able to recite it during all his various occupations throughout the day. He also must make every effort to understand it well, since it was his rule of life.

Twice a day, morning and evening, the monks of a monastery gathered for common prayer. But what they did then was what they did the rest of the day. They recited the scripture by heart or listened to a brother reciting it, in order to let it penetrate their hearts.

The whole life of the Pachomian monk was therefore centered on union with God in prayer, which was expressed by a constant recitation of His Word. But Pachomius, being an experienced man, knew very well that such a union with God could not be realized without renouncing everything that is not God: sin, the world, one's family, and, most of all, self-will. All these forms of renunciation constitute the essence of monastic conversion.

The monk came to the monastery in order to realize a continuous conversion. The awareness of the need for personal conversion often gave the prayer of the Pachomian monks accents of intensity and of ardor that are surprising for the period. Although their prayer was rooted in the recitation of scripture, it had at times very personal and moving accents.

This life of prayer and conversion was lived within a community of brothers who considered themselves responsible for one another. They also considered themselves collectively responsible for maintaining a lifestyle in which such a life of prayer and conversion could be realized, under the direction of superiors who were their shepherds after Christ, taking care of all their material and spiritual needs.

The community also expressed itself in an integral sharing of material goods; everything was held in common, and all received an equal share. Special needs were taken into consideration, and the sick in particular were the object of great attention and care.

Communion in prayer and in conversion, as well as in material possessions, the *koinonia* was also a communion in mutual forgiveness among men who were all limited human beings. And, finally, the Pachomian monks were firmly convinced that the bonds that had been established between them on earth would be maintained in heaven, where the great family of Pachomius would be reunited around him in glory.

BIBLIOGRAPHY

Bacht, H. "L'Importance de l'idéal monastique de s. Pachôme pour l'histoire du monachisme chrétien." *Revue d'ascétique et de mystique* 26 (1950):308–326.

______. "La Loi du 'retour aux sources.' (De quelques aspects de l'idéal monastique pachômien)." *Revue Mabillon* 51 (1961):6–25.

______. "Zur Typologie des koptischen Mönchtums. Pachomius und Evagrius." *Christentum am Nil*, pp. 142–57. Internationale Arbeitstagung zur Ausstellung "Koptische Kunst." Recklinghausen, 1964.

Büchler, B. *Die Armut der Armen. Über den ursprünglichen Sinn der mönchischen Armut*. Kösel, 1980.

Cranenburgh, H. van. "Nieuw licht op de oudste kloostercongregatie van de christenheid: De instelling van Sint-Pachomius." *Tijdschrift voor geestelijk leven* 19 (1963):581–605, 665–90; 20 (1964):41–54.

———. "Actualiteitswaarde van het pachomiaanse kloosterleven." *Tijdschrift voor geestelijk leven* 24 (1968):233–57.

Deseille, P. *L'esprit du monachisme pachômien, suivi par les moines de Solesmes.* Spiritualité Orientale 2. Bellefontaine, 1968.

Ladeuze, P. *Etude sur le cénobitisme pachômien pendant le IVe siècle et la première moitié du Ve.* Louvain and Paris, 1898; repr. 1962.

Ruppert, F. *Das pachomianische Mönchtum und die Anfänge klösterlichen Gehorsams.* Münsterschwarzacher Studien 20. Münsterschwarzach, 1971.

———. "Arbeit und geistliches Leben im pachomianischen Mönchtum." *Ostkirchliche Studien* 24 (1975):3–14.

Tamburrino, P. "*Koinonia:* Die Beziehung 'Monasterium'—'Kirche' im frühen pachomianischen Mönchtum." *Erbe und Auftrag* 43 (1967):5–21.

Veilleux, A. "Pachomian Community." In *The Continuing Quest for God. Monastic Spirituality in Tradition and Transition,* ed. W. Skudlarek. pp. 51–60. Collegeville, Pa., 1982.

———. "Asceticism in Pachomian Cenobitism." In *The Continuing Quest for God. Monastic Spirituality in Tradition and Transition,* ed. W. Skudlarek, pp. 67–70. Collegeville, Pa., 1982.

ARMAND VEILLEUX

MONASTIC VESTMENTS. *See* Costume of the Religious.

MONDE COPTE, LE, illustrated quarterly journal devoted to the study of Coptic culture, founded in Paris in 1979 by a retired architect of Orthodox faith, Pierre de Bogdanoff. The journal enjoys the sponsorship of an international committee including a number of names well known both in politics and in Coptology.

This publication is intended to link the Western world with Coptic culture in a form free from the forbidding aspect of academic reports, in order to be accessible to nonspecialists. As a popular magazine, it is open to studies in all branches of Coptic humanities, concentrating on subjects connected with the church as well as the modern Coptic community.

A. I. SADEK

MONENERGISM (Monergism), a movement that developed in the early part of the seventh century from an attempt by Emperor Heraclius I (610–641) to find a formula that would reconcile the Monophysites with neo-Chalcedonian orthodoxy.

The dramatic success of Heraclius against the Persians, culminating in the triumphant restoration of the True Cross to Jerusalem in 630, gave what proved to be a final chance of reconciling the two beliefs with the political framework of the Byzantine empire. The Monophysites were in a commanding position in Armenia and in the provinces of Syria and Egypt reconquered by Heraclius, and their loyalty had to be retained.

The idea that in Christ the Divine Logos and manhood were separate natures but activated by a single human-divine activity had been held on both sides of the Monophysite-Chalcedonian division and had its place in Coptic theology (Hatch, 1926, pp. 372–81). It was also the view of Sergius, patriarch of Constantinople (611–638), and by 622 Heraclius had been won over to it.

Between 630 and 634, with the ending of the Persian Wars, Heraclius pressed monenergism successively on Ezr, catholicus of the Armenian Church; on Athanasius, the Monophysite patriarch of Antioch; on the east Syrian church at Edessa; on the Copts; and finally on Pope Honorius I (625–638). Everywhere he gained striking initial success. A national synod of the Armenian church at Erzerum accepted the "one activity" formula, and in the spring of 631 a series of conferences was held at Maboug in Mesopotamia; there Heraclius and Patriarch Athanasius attempted to reach an agreement that in the two natures of Christ there was one will and one activity "according to Cyril" (Michael the Syrian *Chronicon* 11.3). However, agreement was, as so often previously, thwarted by the issue of the status of the Council of CHALCEDON; and when Athanasius died in July 631, the prospect of success was lessened further. Meanwhile, opposition to the monenergist formula was starting to grow in Palestine, where the majority of the monks were pro-Chalcedonian. This opposition found a champion in an aged and learned monk named Sophronius.

Heraclius realized that Egypt would provide the decisive test for his attempted compromise with the Monophysites. In the autumn of 631 he sent his friend and adviser Cyrus, bishop of Phasis in Colchis (eastern Black Sea), to be patriarch of Alexandria. This proved to be a twofold error. First, Cyrus was a "foreigner" (Cyrus "the Caucasian," he was called by the Copts) who never won the confidence of the Egyptians. Second, in making this appointment he ignored the presence of BENJAMIN, the Coptic (Monophysite) patriarch who had been elected in 622.

Nonetheless, Cyrus was able to hold a synod of Egyptian bishops in 633 at which nine articles were drawn up, the seventh of which confessed that "there was one and the same Christ and Son activating the godly and human through one divine-human energy." Chalcedon, however, was not mentioned. Even so, the Tome of Union was signed by a considerable number of clergy including, claimed Cyrus, "all the clergy of the party of the Theodosians" (perhaps strict followers of Severan monophysitism, of which Patriarch THEODOSIUS I [535–567] was accepted as representative). On 3 June 633 Cyrus celebrated his success by a solemn *Te Deum* and sent an enthusiastic report of events to Sergius at Constantinople.

Had Cyrus been more trusted by the Copts, he might have succeeded, for nearly all the Monophysite phraseology concerning Christ had been conceded in the Tome, and many Egyptians accepted "one activity" as automatically involving "one nature." But trust was what he could not achieve, and the Copts stayed loyal to Benjamin.

Meantime, the monenergist position was being attacked by Sophronius, who became patriarch of Jerusalem early in 634. His protests first to Sergius, and then to Pope Honorius, were rebuffed. Honorius supported Sergius, and was even more explicit than he in his assent to monenergism. "Inasmuch," he wrote, "as the Humanity was naturally united with the Word, and Christ is therefore One, we acknowledge one will of our Lord Jesus Christ" (i.e., not merely "activity").

External events now began to play their part. In April 634 the Arabs began to raid Palestine and Syria in earnest. Henceforth, the emperor's energies were increasingly devoted to the losing struggle to maintain the empire. In 638, after the loss of Syria with the fall of Antioch to the Arabs, he published an "exposition of faith" (the ECTHESIS) in the hope of rallying the provincials to the empire. The *Ecthesis* forbade discussion on the subject of the unity or duality of the "activities" of Christ, and laid down that the Catholic faith demanded the acknowledgment of only one will in Christ. With this, the monenergist movement merged with MONOTHELITISM and the ultimate refinement of Christology, the monothelite controversy, began.

The *Ecthesis* thus follows the HENOTIKON of Zeno and "The Second Henotikon" of Justin II as an effort by an emperor to bridge the gap between the pro- and anti-Chalcedonians in the empire. It was too little and, in this case, too late.

It came as near success as possible in the circumstances of the seventh century, and it had the added merit of not alienating the papacy. However, once more personal antagonisms, especially the irreconcilable hostility between Cyrus and Benjamin, and the popular fear of Chalcedon prevented settlement. Cyrus, instead of being the great conciliator between Monophysites and Chalcedonians, went down in history as the oppressor of the Copts. The arrival of the Arabs on Egyptian soil in December 639 allowed the emperor and his advisers no further chance of conciliation.

BIBLIOGRAPHY

Bréhier, L. "La Nouvelle crise religieuse. Juifs, monoénergisme, Islam (632–639)." In *Histoire de l'église*, ed. A. Fliche and V. Martin, Vol. 5, *Grégoire le Grand, les états barbares et la conquête arabe (590–757)*, pp. 103–130. Paris, 1947.

Duchesne, L. *L'Eglise au VIe siècle*, chap. 11. Paris, 1925.

Frend, W. H. C. *Rise of the Monophysite Movement*, 2nd ed., chap. 9. Cambridge, England, 1979.

Hatch, W. H. P. "A Fragment of a Lost Work on Dioscorus." *Harvard Theological Review* 19 (1926):372–81.

Hefele, C. J., and H. Leclercq. *Histoire des conciles*. Paris, 1909. See Vol. 3, pt. 1, pp. 339–41, for the text of the tome of unity.

Tixeront, J. *Histoire des dogmes*, Vol. 3, pp. 160–177. Paris, 1928.

W. H. C. FREND

MONK, someone who lives apart from the world in an all-male community, devoting himself to prayer, contemplation, and the performance of religious duties. He may prefer to live as a hermit, dwelling alone and meeting other members of the community only occasionally, as in church and at mealtime in the monastery refectory. A cenobitic monk, on the other hand, lives in a cloistered community and follows a strictly organized pattern of daily life.

The Four Main Aspects of Monastic Life

1. Isolation from the world and withdrawal from human companionship. In the solitude of his own cell the monk finds solace in prayer and the study of the scriptures and devotional literature. Accord-

ing to Saint ANTONY, the first monk and the father of monasticism, "just as a fish would die out of water, a monk would perish if he tarried long away from his cell."

It appears that in the early ages, some monks followed this rule without exception and declined to renew contact with even their closest family relations. A monk, however, may absent himself from his monastery for a limited period and a specific purpose, such as some service beneficial to his monastery or the church in general. We know that Saint Antony interrupted his stay in the desert on two occasions: he visited Alexandria at the height of persecution to comfort the victims and again during the Arian heresy to strengthen and encourage the faithful.

2. Chastity, which by mortifying the body helps a monk to attain a purer and more dedicated spiritual life (see 1 Cor. 7:7, 38; Is. 56:3–9; Mt. 19:10–12; 22:30). In the words of Saint Jerome (c. 342–420), "It is a mark of great faith and of great virtue, to be the pure temple of God to offer oneself a whole burnt-offering, and, according to the apostle Paul, to be holy both in body and in spirit" (*Adversus Jovinianum* 1.12).

3. Obedience and readiness to comply with and submit to the guidance and commands of his abbot, not only when he is still a neophyte but throughout his life. Among Coptic monks, Saint John the Short (see JOHN COLOBOS) is considered a paragon of virtue and obedience. It is related that his mentor Saint POEMEN once handed him a dry and withered branch asking him to water it regularly. Though water was not easily available, John continued to look after it until the tree flourished and gave fruit. Poemen offered its fruit to the monks saying, "Eat the fruit of obedience."

4. Voluntary poverty in fulfillment of Christ's teaching, "sell what you have, and give to the poor, and you will have treasure in heaven; and come, follow me" (Mk. 10:21; see also Mt. 19:29).

To be accepted as a neophyte, a candidate must be over seventeen years of age and supply a recommendation from a priest who is usually his father confessor. He has to undergo a period of probation extending from one to three years.

A Monk's Daily Life

A monk's day usually begins at midnight, after he has slept during the first half of the night, with the service of the midnight psalmody and its prayer, followed by readings from the Scriptures until daybreak. He attends the Liturgy (if celebrated), and engages himself in the particular vocation to which he is suited or which has been assigned to him, be it carpentry, gardening, cooking, baking, copying, or other communal service. Throughout he is supposed to be silently praying or attending other prayers according to the time of the day. "Pray continually," Saint Antony ordered his monks, "avoid vainglory; sing psalms before sleep and on awaking; hold in your heart the commandments of Scripture."

While sitting at their meals, monks do not engage in conversation about worldly or social topics, but eat silently, listening to a fellow monk read to them passages from *Bustān al-Ruhban* (Paradise of the Monks) and similar works of edification.

Monasticism has experienced a revival in the second half of the twentieth century. The monks who now take their vows are young people who are mostly university graduates. Their skills or professions (medical doctors, for example) have benefited their monasteries and the communities around them. By special order of the patriarch they serve in churches in Egypt and abroad, when needed, as priests or helpers to a priest. They have not abandoned meditation and prayers. They still live under very rigid monastic rule. Monasticism is not disappearing but some aspects of a monk's life have had to be modified to fit modern times. Monks today choose their way of life through true faith and conviction, not as an escape from the world.

BIBLIOGRAPHY

Banūb Ḥabashī, et al. *Al-Rahbanah al-Qibṭiyyah.* Alexandria, 1948.

Evelyn-White, H. G. *The Monasteries of Nitria and Scetis,* 3 vols. New York, 1933.

Kīrullus al-Anṭūnī, Hegumenos. *Kawkab al-Barriyyah, al-Qiddīs al-Anbā Anṭūniyūs.* Cairo, 1950.

Risālat Mār Murqus. Alexandria, 1948.

Riyād Sūryāl. *Al-Mujtama' al-Qibṭī fī al-Qarn al-'Ishrīn.* Cairo, 1984.

ARCHBISHOP BASILIOS

MONNERET DE VILLARD, UGO (1881–1954), Italian archaeologist and Orientalist. He studied engineering first, but became interested in medieval architecture and later in Oriental studies. His first visit to Egypt was for the purpose of making a study of the pharos of Alexandria. He later conducted a long series of excavations in Upper

Egypt between 1921 and 1934. He was able to demonstrate that Coptic art was in the Hellenistic tradition and made a special study of the monasteries near Suhāj. Christian art in Nubia formed but one of a large number of subjects in which he was interested, covering areas as far apart as Persia and Sicily. He died in Rome.

BIBLIOGRAPHY

Dawson, W. R., and E. P. Uphill. *Who Was Who in Egyptology*. London, 1972.

Kammerer, W., comp. *A Coptic Bibliography*, pp. 205–206. Ann Arbor, Mich., 1950; repr. New York, 1969.

AZIZ S. ATIYA

MONOPHYSITISM, the doctrine that the incarnate Christ is one Person and has one divine nature as opposed to the orthodox doctrine that he is one Person and has two natures, one human and one divine. The rift between the Monophysites, including the Coptic, Syrian, Ethiopian, and Armenian churches, and the Orthodox Church has divided Eastern Christianity since the sixth century. It emerged slowly after the Council of CHALCEDON in 451. The Monophysites hold firm to the main Christological tenant of Saint CYRIL I, early fifth-century patriarch of Alexandria, that the two natures of Christ were united at the Incarnation in such a way that the one Christ was essentially divine, although he assumed from the Virgin THEOTOKOS the flesh and attributes of a man.

The Period Before Chalcedon (325–451)

The distant origins of the Monophysite position can be found in John 1:14 ("The Word became flesh and dwelt among us"), but no theological issue arose until after the First Council of NICAEA in 325, at which it was agreed that Christ was to be acknowledged as "of one substance with the Father." If, however, He was of one substance (HOMOOUSION) with the Father, how was His humanity to be understood? The long duration of the controversy over ARIANISM, which denied that Christ was divine, masked the problem, but during the 370s Apollinaris of Laodicea, an anti-Arian and a lifelong friend of Saint ATHANASIUS I, patriarch of Alexandria, set out a radical and uncompromising solution (see APOLLINARIANISM). "The supreme point in our salvation," he argued, "is the incarnation of the Word. We believe therefore that with no change in his Godhead, the incarnation of the Word took palce for the renewal of man." "We confess therefore," he told the bishops of Syria at Diocaesarea, "that [the] Word of God . . . has become flesh without having assumed a human mind, i.e., a mind changeable and enslaved to filthy thoughts, but existing as a divine mind, immutable and heavenly." Therefore, "We confess that . . . the one Son is not two natures, one to be worshipped and one without worship, but one incarnate nature of God the Word to be worshipped with His flesh in one worship" (Lietzmann, 1904, pp. 178, 250).

Apollinarius' ideas struck an immediate response throughout the East, and though they were condemned as unorthodox at the First Council of CONSTANTINOPLE in 381, a large number of tracts setting out his views were circulating at the end of the century under the names of orthodox theologians, including Pope Saint Julius I and Athanasius. These "Apollinarian forgeries" had an enormous effect on the development of monophysitism, not least in contributing toward the formation of Cyril of Alexandria's concept of the Person of Christ.

Cyril's Christology was influenced by both genuine and false Athanasian writings, and as his controversy with the Antiochene monk NESTORIUS, patriarch of Constantinople, quickened, the Monophysite element came increasingly to the fore. In his third letter to Nestorius, who held that Christ was two separate persons, he spoke of "the One Hypostasis ["Person"] Incarnate of the Word"; and in the third of the Twelve Anathemas appended to this letter he declared anathema "anyone who divides the hypostases after the union." There was "One Lord Jesus Christ," according to the Scriptures.

The Council of EPHESUS in 431 condemned Nestorius but did not declare Cyril's anathemas canonical. Two years later, in April 433, Cyril was obliged to come to terms with the Antiochenes and in the formula of reunion to accept the orthodoxy of those who spoke in terms of "two natures." This was a victory for Antiochene theology and a reverse for the Alexandrians. Cyril's successor, DIOSCORUS I, was determined to restore Alexandria's now traditional status as "city of the orthodox." In Constantinople he found an ally in the archimandrite EUTYCHES. The latter, however, pushed his fear of two-nature Christology further than Cyril would have allowed, asserting that the flesh of Christ was God-made, so that Christ could in no sense be "consubstantial with us." Eutyches was deposed on 22 November

448 by a synod presided over by Flavian, archbishop of Constantinople.

Eutyches appealed to the councils of the other archiepiscopal sees and to the church in Ravenna (the imperial residence in the West) against his sentence. Annoyed by the quarrel between Flavian and Eutyches, and fearing a revival of Nestorianism, Emperor Theodosius II, who was now strongly Cyrilist in his theology, convoked the Second council of Ephesus in 449 to judge the case of Eutyches and to decide whether his deposition by Flavian had been just. Dioscorus was to preside. Once again, the Apollinarian forgeries played a crucial part in channeling doctrinal views in the East toward a one-nature Christology. Eutyches produced texts, accepted at Ephesus in 431 as genuine, of documents written ostensibly by Pope Julius and Gregory the Wonderworker to support his case. The council was entranced. "Two natures before the union, and one afterward. Is that not what we all believe?" asked Dioscorus. A long epistle from Pope LEO THE GREAT, known to history as the *Tome* of Leo, written to support Flavian, asserted exactly the opposite view. It was left unread. The council vindicated Eutyches and condemned as troublemakers Flavian and the archbishop of Antioch, Domnus, who had attempted to innovate statements of the Council of Nicaea. The sentence was confirmed by Theodosius.

The emperor's sudden death on 28 July 450 transformed the situation. His successor, Marcian, married Theodosius' pro-Roman sister PULCHERIA, and in the autumn of 451 they summoned another ecumenical council, this one at Chalcedon. It had two aims: to define the faith in a way that would restore communion between Rome and the other patriarchates and to vindicate the position of the see of Constantinople vis-à-vis all other sees in the East, particularly that of Alexandria.

The council achieved both objectives. Dioscorus was excommunicated and deposed—not, however, for doctrinal heresy but for ecclesiastical indiscipline. The Definition of Chalcedon was accepted, a statement of faith declaring that Jesus Christ was "made known to us in two Natures, unconfusedly, unchangeably, indivisibly, inseparably: the difference of the natures being in no way removed because of the Union, but rather the properties of each nature being preserved and concurring into one Prosopon and one Hypostasis. . . ." Though the framers of the Definition intended a careful balance between opposing Christologies, the wording favored the *Tome* of Leo and the Antiochene cause. While Pope Leo accepted the Definition, he rejected Canon 28 of the council, which restated the primatial rights of Constantinople as the "New Rome." Rome objected to the omission in the canon of any reference to the apostolic and Petrine character of the see of Rome and was never prepared to concede patriarchal status to its sister see of New Rome (Constantinople). This canon, however, was all-important to Constantinople, and for this reason, it could never entirely renounce the Council of Chalcedon.

The arrogant behavior of Dioscorus had created a rift among the seventeen Egyptian bishops who accompanied him to Chalcedon. While the majority stood by their archbishop out of fear and loyalty, four sided with the majority at the council, accepted the Christological definition, and took part in the consecration of the archpriest Proterius as successor of Dioscorus.

From Chalcedon to the *Henoticon* of Zeno (451–482)

Although the Definition of Chalcedon was well received in Rome, Constantinople, Antioch, and throughout the European provinces of the empire, there was deep disquiet elsewhere. Clergy and laity alike found it difficult to understand how opinions accepted by 135 bishops only two years before Ephesus II should now be regarded as heretical, and why Dioscorus should have been excommunicated by many of the same bishops who previously had applauded him. There were serious riots in Alexandria and in Jerusalem, where Bishop Juvenal, an ally of Dioscorus who had abandoned him at Chalcedon, was forced to flee the city (Zacharias Rhetor, 3. 2; Liberatus, 14. 99; Evagrius, 2. 5). Something of the intensity of popular feeling in many parts of the East against Chalcedon has been caught by JOHN OF MAYUMA in his *Plerophoria* (Witnesses), compiled about 512, in which he branded as traitors and apostates those who had supported Chalcedon.

Although imperial troops suppressed the riots and Juvenal returned to Jerusalem, Proterius failed to gain support in Egypt. Opposition to Chalcedon coalesced around one of the priests of Dioscorus, Timothy Aelurus ("the Cat") (later TIMOTHY II AELURUS) and the deacon Peter Mongus ("the Hoarse One") (later Peter II Mongus), both future patriarchs. As soon as the news of the death of Marcian reached Alexandria, there was a popular uprising against Proterius. Timothy was consecrated bishop on 16 March 457 or 458, and on 28 March Proterius was lynched. There was now a schism between Chalcedonians and anti-Chalcedonians in Egypt.

The schism lasted until 482. In 459 Timothy Aelurus was ordered into exile in Kherson in the Crimea by the new emperor, Leo I, who was responding to episcopal opinion throughout the rest of the empire (see Zacharias Rhetor, 4.5–7, Brooks ed., pp. 121–24; and Schwartz, 1914, 2.v.). In 460 the Proterians elected as successor to Proterius, who had died, the Pachomian monk TIMOTHY SALOFACIOLUS ("Wobble Cap"). The death of Leo in January 474 gave Timothy Aelurus his chance. Leo's son, Leo II, died in November, and his successor, Zeno, was unpopular. Timothy took advantage of Basiliscus' revolution against Zeno, in January 475, to leave his place of exile and make for Constantinople. There he was favored by the usurper and restored as patriarch of Alexandria. Basiliscus published an encyclical condemning the *Tome* of Leo and all things of Chalcedon that "innovated against the holy creed of the 38 holy fathers [of Nicaea]" (Evagrius, 3.4, 3.7). Up to this point, neither the Alexandrian opponents of Chalcedon nor their allies elsewhere, the *Diakrimonenoi* (Hesitants), contemplated a division in the church. Their aims were the acceptance by the empire of Cyril's teaching in its fullness, the denunciation of the *Tome* of Leo, and the reduction of the status of Chalcedon to that of a disciplinary synod (like Ephesus II) anathematizing Nestorius and Eutyches. Basiliscus had been ready to comply.

Basiliscus fell, largely owing to the opposition of Acacius, patriarch of Constantinople, who was supported by the people of the capital and spurred on by Daniel the Stylite (Evagrius, 3.7). Zeno returned in triumph in August 476, but he recognized that the empire must come to terms with ever increasing anti-Chalcedonian feeling in Egypt, parts of western and southern Asia Minor, and now in Syria, where, opponents of the council had found a leader in Peter the Fuller. After the death of Timothy II Aelurus, and of his rival in February 482, the emperor and his patriarch addressed a letter to "the bishops, monks and laity of Alexandria, Egypt and Cyrenaica" with the aim of achieving an acceptable compromise.

The HENOTICON (Instrument of Unity) of 28 July 482 went as far as possible to conciliate the anti-Chalcedonians without explicitly denouncing Chalcedon (for the full text, see Schwartz, 1927, pp. 924–27). The safety of the Roman world was asserted to rest on a universal acceptance of the Nicene Creed confirmed by the Council of Constantinople (381). Eutyches and Nestorius were condemned, but the Twelve Anathemas of Cyril were upheld, and Christ incarnate from the Virgin was to be acknowledged "as one and not two, for we say that both His miracles and His sufferings which He willingly underwent in the flesh are of one person. Every person, who has thought or thinks anything else now or at any time either in Chalcedon or in any other synod whatever, we anathematize."

Though in form the emperor had merely written a letter to the patriarchate of Alexandria, the *Henoticon* marks another important step in consolidating the emperor's role as divinely appointed governor of all Christians. For the next thirty-five years the *Henoticon* was accepted as a statement of belief by the churches in the East. Constantinople, Antioch, Jerusalem, and Alexandria were again in communion.

The Acacian Schism

The Eastern patriarchates were not, however, on good terms with Rome. A quarrel developed between Pope Simplicius and Acacius, patriarch of Constantinople (see ACACIAN SCHISM), not over the *Henotican* but because Acacius accepted Peter Mongus as patriarch of Alexandria, although he had previously denounced him to the pope as a "son of darkness" and unfit even for his original office as deacon (Simplicius to Acacius, *Epistulae;* see also Frend, 1972, pp. 181–83).

The issue between Rome and Constantinople was primarily disciplinary, but the *Henoticon* added fuel to the fire and to the Acacian schism, which lasted until 519. In this period pro- and anti-Chalcedonian sentiment in the empire gradually crystallized. By about 500 the majority of the clergy and people of Constantinople and the European provinces of the empire were Chalcedonian, together with northern Asia Minor, western Syria (where the influence of the Greek cities was strong), and Palestine (where the monks were of various national origins and needed the emperor's military support for their survival against Saracen marauders and Jewish and Samaritan enmity). Egypt, Antioch, eastern Syria and Mesopotamia, and the provinces of Isauria and Pamphylia in southern Asia Minor were anti-Chalcedonian. Western Asia Minor with Ephesus was sharply divided. Emperor Anastasius, though personally inclined to monophysitism, steered a middle line by insisting on unreserved respect for the *Henoticon*.

In 508, however, a new situation began to develop with the arrival in Constantinople of the Monophysite monk Severus, on mission from the monastery of Mayuma near Gaza, to appeal to the emperor against harassment by Elias, the pro-Chalcedonian patriarch of Jerusalem. Severus gained the ear of Anastasius. In 510, as a result of a dispute between Patriarch Flavian II of Antioch and his metropolitan, Philoxenus of Mabboug (Hierapolis) in Mesopotamia, the emperor promulgated the Formula of Satisfaction. This document, while explicitly accepting the *Henoticon* as the basis of orthodoxy, denounced the *Tome* of Leo and the acknowledgment of the incarnate Christ "in two natures," and downgraded Chalcedon to the level of a disciplinary synod (or, according to some sources, denouncing the Definition of Chalcedon altogether). For good measure, it condemned the works of the Antiochene theologians Diodorus of Tarsus and THEODORUS OF MOPSUESTIA. Then in August 511 came the deposition, largely through the influence of Severus, of Macedonius, patriarch of Constantinople, and, early in 512, mainly through the intrigues of Philoxenus, of Flavian II. On 6 November 512, Severus was consecrated patriarch of Antioch. The empire had taken a long step toward accepting monophysitism as its faith.

Severus of Antioch and the Consolidation of Monophysite Theology (510–530)

The activities of Severus as patriarch mark the transition between anti-Chalcedonianism and monophysitism. He provided opponents of Chalcedon with a clear-cut alternative theology that justified rejection of the *Tome* and the council. His organizing ability resulted, even against his will, in a rival Monophysite hierarchy challenging that of the Chalcedonians in many parts of the empire.

Severus is one of the great figures in the religious history of the eastern Mediterranean. He was born into a wealthy landowning family in Sozopolis in Pisidia, in Asia Minor, about 465. His grandfather had been among the 200 bishops who had deposed Nestorius at Ephesus. Severus, however, showed little inclination to follow any profession other than law until 488, when he met the famous anti-Chalcedonian ascetic and leader Peter the Iberian and was converted by him to a life dedicated to the service of Christ. After a stay at the monastery of Romanus in the Palestine wilderness near Elentheropolis, he went about 500 to Peter's monastery at Mayuma. He became, if not leader, spokesman of the anti-Chalcedonian cause.

The theology of Severus, as revealed in his letters and treatises (largely in the *Patrologia Orientalis* and *Corpus Scriptorum Christianorum Orientalium*), was based on that of Cyril. In a moment of enthusiasm, Severus wrote that every utterance of Cyril should be regarded as canonical (*Select Letters* 1.9, p. 45). At the same time, he guided the anti-Chalcedonian cause away from support of Eutyches, and he criticized Dioscorus as "contentious" and prone to "fighting unnecessarily about words" (*Ad Nephalium*, ed. Lebon, 1949, p. 9 of translation). His Christological beliefs, repeated time and again, might be summed up thus: "The Fathers have taught us that God the Word, the Unique One begotten by his Father without beginning, eternally, impassibly, and incorporeally, did in the last times for our salvation take flesh of the Holy Spirit and of the Holy *Theotokos* and ever-Virgin Mary, flesh consubstantial with us, animated by an intelligent and reasoning soul" (Severus *Philalèthe*, p. 107). It was obvious, Severus went on, "that the same being is at once God and man, consubstantial with the Father according to His divinity and with us men according to His humanity" (p. 113). Christ was united "with the flesh of our nature" (Epistle 65, PO 14, p. 30). This was "the royal road" of truth from which no deviation was permissible.

Severus was not hostile to the Roman see; indeed, he praised Pope Julius for his sane and orthodox views. But he was irrevocably opposed to Pope Leo and his *Tome*. In his view, Leo not only had divided the natures of Christ but also had made each nature quote Scripture against the other, one declaring "I and my Father are one" and the other, "the Father is greater than I." Such teaching he considered fallacious and heretical (*Liber . . . grammaticum* 3.1.5, ed. Lebon, pp. 49–50 of translation). Elsewhere he denounced the *Tome* as "Jewish" (Epistle 46, PO 12.2, p. 321), and Leo himself, for accepting the orthodoxy of the Antiochene theologians Ibas and Theodoret as a "Nestorian" (Epistle 31, PO 12.2, p. 265). The Council of Chalcedon, by adopting the "two natures" formula, was in error and had "innovated" the ever sacred Nicene Creed (Epistle 34, PO 12.2, p. 272). This was the theologian who became patriarch of Antioch in November 512. During a reign of less than six years his tireless energy propagated the anti-Chalcedonian faith from one end of the vast diocese to the other.

In this effort, Severus was aided powerfully by Philoxenus of Mabboug, whose monophysitism differed from his. Philoxenus was Syriac in speech and culture, and the mold in which his ideas were formed was Syriac, not Greek. Some aspects of his Christology approximated the Antiochene views, which he abominated. Thus, he believed in the complete and individual manhood of Jesus, emphasizing that He came under the law who "had become by his will a man who served the law" (Vaschalde, 1961, p. 184). He criticized the Apollinarians, using the same argument as the Cappadocian fathers, that if the Word did not assume a human mind, the human mind could not be saved.

How, then, did Philoxenus avoid acceptance of the Chalcedonian position? Emotion played its part, but on analysis, his theology, if somewhat forced, was consistent. Christ is God the Word, who, however, existed in two modes of being simultaneously: as God by nature and as man by a miracle. The manhood was added to the Godhead so as to preserve the true features of man and at the same time retain the nature of the Word. Through faith one appreciated the resulting single hypostasis of the incarnate Christ. By analogy man, by nature human, was born a son of God by receiving the Spirit in baptism (Vaschalde, p. 120). The emphasis on baptism, the source of newness and salvation for Christ as well as for ordinary men, was also Antiochene in inspiration. Metaphysical concepts had less place in Philoxenus' system than in that of Severus, but he was at one with Severus in his opposition to the *Tome* and Chalcedon.

The years of the patriarchate of Severus were stormy. Though he and Philoxenus engineered the removal of Elias, patriarch of Jerusalem, on 1 September 516, opposition increased among the Greek cities of western Syria, while the passion of Severus for doctrinal "accuracy" began to dismay his followers. In 517 a rift, not the last, appeared between the Severan and Alexandrian Monophysites, DIOSCORUS II of Alexandria showing himself less anxious than Severus formally to denounce Chalcedon (see Severus Epistles 49–50, PO 12.2, pp. 323–25). At the end of the same year, 207 monks from monasteries in western Syria, led by Alexander, presbyter and archimandrate of Maro, wrote to Pope Hormisdas, attacking Severus for his "daily denunciation of Chalcedon" (Epistle 139). Conflict was growing throughout the patriarchate of Antioch when Emperor Anastasius died in July 518. The reaction against Severus was immediate. In September 518 he left Antioch to find refuge in Alexandria, never to return.

The Chalcedonian Reaction (518–532)

The accession of Emperor JUSTIN I brought a complete change of direction in the religious policy of the empire. Justin came from the residual Latin-speaking provinces, and he aimed to restore communion between the "two Romes" on the basis of mutual acceptance of Chalcedon and the removal, so far as possible, of traces of the Acacian Schism. At the emperor's urgent request, papal legates arrived on 25 March 519 in Constantinople, where they were rapturously received. On 28 March, the long dead anti-Chalcedonian leaders in Alexandria and Antioch "and their followers," as well as Acacius and his four successors as patriarch of Constantinople and the emperors Zeno and Anastasius, were struck from the diptychs. The papal victory, however, turned out to be less complete than it seemed, for the initiative remained with the emperor, and Rome had received no satisfaction over Canon 28 of the Council of Chalcedon.

Justin had no intention of allowing his patriarch to be humiliated. He aimed simply at restoring the status quo ante Acacium, and he largely succeeded. The end of the Acacian Schism, however, entailed close collaboration between Rome and Constantinople and consequently heavy pressure against the followers of Severus. Between 519 and 522, no fewer than fifty-five bishops suspected of Monophysite leanings were deposed—some, like Philoxenus, to die in exile.

For the Monophysites, the reign of Justin and the first years of that of his nephew JUSTINIAN were important for two developments—a quarrel between Severus and his fellow exile JULIAN, bishop of Halicarnassus, in Caria; and the taking of the first steps to establish a hierarchy loyal to the one-nature Christology and, hence, out of communion with the Chalcedonians. In the quarrel the Julianists held that while Christ was indeed consubstantial with man, this related to His assumption of Adam's nature before the Fall. Therefore, the flesh of the incarnate Christ was not mortal. This Severus denied (Epistle 35 to the Eastern monks, PO 12. 2, p. 290), but Julian's views made headway in Egypt and were to influence the Monophysite missionary movement.

The move to establish a hierarchy favoring one nature was the result of popular pressure in Syria on Severus. Sixty years later, the Monophysite historian John of Ephesus described how the first ordinations came about. In his Life of John of Tella, who had ordained him deacon, he wrote:

> At the end of ten years of persecution [i.e., 529/530] the faithful who remained in diverse places began to be concerned about ordinations and consulted the faithful bishops; but these latter feared to bring down on themselves even fiercer flames of persecution, and they refused to make ordinations openly, but only some in secret. Then

> complaints of the faithful persecuted arose from all sides against the blessed bishops because of the great deficiency of clerics and they wrote and besought the bishops to make ordinations of the faithful for the matter was urgent [*Lives of the Eastern Saints*, pp. 515–16].

Severus and his colleagues in Alexandria bowed to John's arguments. The effect was sensational. Hundreds sought ordination from him. According to John of Ephesus, "Every day fifty, a hundred and sometimes as many as two hundred or three hundred men, came to him for ordination." It was like a "flooded river that had burst its banks." Postulants came from all over the Eastern Roman Empire—from Cappadocia, Phoenicia, and the Persian frontier. Though no episcopal consecrations had been carried out, the Monophysite church had now come into being.

Another Monophysite biographer of John of Tella, Elias, writing after 542, claims that the success of John's mission persuaded Emperor Justinian to stay the persecution begun by Justin and attempt to heal the widening rift between the Chalcedonians and their opponents by means of a conference. Recently discovered Syriac material relating to the conference that Justinian summoned in 532 suggests the truth of this estimate (see Brock, 1980, pp. 219–28).

The conference took the form of a series of meetings in Constantinople between six representatives from each side and extended over "a year or more" (Zacharias Rhetor, 9.15, p. 84), probably February 532 to March 533. Severus did not attend. Quite rightly, he expressed distrust of Justinian, but he sent a long memorandum to the emperor emphasizing his own loyalty and that of his colleagues and arguing for the acceptance of the one-nature Christology as the religion of the empire. One phase of the discussions, recorded by Innocentius of Maronia of the Chalcedonian delegation, shows how the Chalcedonians were able to entangle their opponents in their inconsistent attitude toward Eutyches but could not prove that Cyril would have accepted Chalcedon. On matters of faith, the two sides were very near agreement on the Theopaschite formula put forward by Justinian himself: that both the miracles and the sufferings of Christ were to be attributed to one and the same being, and thus "he who suffered in the flesh was one of the Trinity." But the disciplinary issue (as in most ecclesiastical disputes) proved insurmountable. Justinian insisted on acceptance of Chalcedon in some form (but not of the *Tome* of Leo), and this the followers of Severus were not prepared to give.

Severus' Last Triumph and Condemnation (534–538)

The edict that Justinian published on 15 March 533 condemned Eutyches, Apollinaris, and Nestorius but not Severus and his colleagues. In Alexandria, conflict between Severus and the supporters of Julian of Halicarnassus increased, while in Constantinople, Empress THEODORA, her influence enhanced after the Nika Riot in January 532, worked for the Monophysites. In the winter of 534/535, Severus accepted an invitation from the emperor, instigated by the empress, to come to Constantinople (Zacharias Rhetor *Historia*, 9.15). In the summer of 535, Severus persuaded the new patriarch of Constantinople, Anthimus, of the rightness of the Monophysite cause. For a few months the sees of Alexandria and Constantinople were reunited in communion and theological outlook. Once again, however, the counterattraction of the bond between Constantinople and Rome proved too strong. Pope Agapetus, on a visit to Constantinople on behalf of King Theodahad, the Gothic ruler of Italy, deposed Anthimus for having accepted translation from his original see of Trebizond, contrary to Canon 15 of the Council of Nicaea. On 13 March Agapetus consecrated Anthimus' successor, the Alexandria-born Menas. A letter signed by Justinian and Agapetus reemphasized the orthodoxy of the two-nature Christology. In May–June 536 an impressive local synod convoked by Menas condemned both Anthimus and Severus as heretics. The emperor confirmed the decision and on August 6 published an edict (Justinianus, 42, no. 56) accusing Severus of waging "undeclared war" and setting the churches against each other. His writings were proscribed. From then on, efforts to reunite Chalcedonians and Monophysites were doomed. The years 536–538 saw another severe persecution of Monophysite clergy. Among the victims was John of Tella.

The Monophysite Missions (542–565)

Justinian followed up the condemnation of Severus by another blow at the Monophysites, the restoration of the Chalcedonian succession in Egypt. Toward the end of 537, he summoned Saint THEODOSIUS I, patriarch of Alexandria, who had successfully beaten off a Julianist challenge on his accession in 535, to Constantinople and declared him deposed. Theodosius was imprisoned at Derkos in Thrace. Thereupon the emperor had a Pachomian monk named Paul consecrated as patriarch of Alexandria by Menas. When Paul proved unsatisfactory, he was succeeded by a Palestinian monk named Zoilus (c. 540). Thanks largely to Theodora, the Monophysites were able to reply effectively. First, the empress secured the return of Theodosius to Constantinople, where he established a Monophysite presence under her patronage in the palace of Hormisdas. In 541, taking advantage of a request by the powerful ruler of the Ghassanid confederation of Arab tribes on Rome's southeastern frontier for an "orthodox bishop," the empress persuaded Theodosius to consecrate JACOB BORADAEUS, an east Syrian, as metropolitan of Edessa, and Theodorus as bishop of Bostra, the capital of the Roman province of Arabia.

Jacob Baradaeus (James Bar 'Adai) will always be associated with the consolidation of monophysitism in Syria and Mesopotamia. In fact, his original mission was not confined to these provinces or identified with them. He was vested with authority "over all countries not only of Syria and the whole of Armenia and Cappadocia" but also over Isauria, Lycia, Phrygia, Cyprus, and the islands. His was to be a roving commission devoted to the maintenance of individual Monophysite congregations, wherever they might be. The enormous energy of Jacob and his dedication to his task transformed the situation. Between 542 and 578 he moved from place to place: "sometimes travelling thirty or forty miles a day, never staying long in any one district, he added to the numbers of believers in every place, both Greeks and Syrians" (John of Ephesus, LIVES OF THE EASTERN SAINTS, Vol. 18, col. 693; cf. col. 695). He consecrated bishops as well as lower clergy, "causing the priesthood to flow like great rivers over the whole world of the Roman domains." His successes, especially in eastern Syria, indicated both the underlying anti-Chalcedonian sentiment of the mass of the people and their readiness, at least in matters of belief, to oppose the will of the emperor. Constantinople, however, remained the center of the movement and Patriarch Theodosius its focus.

Similar trends can be seen in the second great Monophysite missionary saga, the conversion of the Nobatian kingdoms (see NOBATIA) south of the Roman frontier in Egypt. Christianity had spread into NUBIA by the mid-fifth century (Michalowski, 1970, p. 12), but the conversion of the Nobatian court and kingdom was the work of Monophysite missionaries sent by Theodora in 542 under the presbyter Julian. The Nobatian king (not Silko—as once thought [see Skeat, 1977, pp. 159–70; Rea, 1979, pp. 147–50]) was converted to monophysitism and defied the later efforts of the orthodox envoys sent by Justinian to change his mind. "We accept the gift of the king of the Romans," he is reported to have said, "but his faith we will not accept. If we deserve to become Christians we will follow after the Pope Theodosius, whom because he would not accept the evil faith of the king he expelled and ejected." Julian had done his work of conversion well.

Though MAKOURIA, the middle of the three Nobatian kingdoms, was converted to Chalcedon about 567, this was a temporary phase; by the time of the Arab invasions, the vast majority of the populations of Nobatia, of Egypt, and of Ethiopia were Monophysite. Parts of southern Arabia and the kingdom of Armenia were also Monophysite.

From the early eighth century on, the Nobatian kingdoms produced a brillant Christian art, of which FARAS has provided the most splendid examples (see Michalowski, 1974). Fragments of a handsomely produced manuscript of the liturgy of Saint James and manuscripts of the Greek *Acta Mercurii* and *Acta Georgii* have been found in the cathedral church at Qaṣr Ibrīm.

Relations with the Empire up to the Arab Conquests (536–641)

Justinian's condemnation of Severus in 536 marked a watershed in the history of monophysitism. Up to then the Monophysites had aimed at converting the empire to their view within the framework of a united church. Now they were obliged to accept the fact of schism whose healing would require the abrogation of a conciliar decision against Severus, as well as denunciation of the *Tome* and Chalcedon. Moreover, with the capture of Rome, on 9 December 536, by the Byzantine general Belisarius, the Roman bishops became the emperor's subjects once more, and their influence in Constantinople correspondingly increased. Finally, in Monophysite-dominated areas, the *Tome* and Chalcedon had become objects of popular dislike. When, near the end of Justinian's reign, Bishop Abraham bar Kaili tried to proclaim the decisions of Chalcedon at the fortress town of Amida, the people shouted, "We will never accept the synod and the *Tome*," and they rioted against the bishop and the magistrates. Chalcedon had become a name of ill omen.

Despite these factors making for continued schism, the personal relations between leading Monophysites and Justinian and his two immediate successors, Justin II and Tiberius II, remained reasonably friendly. A striking example is Justinian's use in 542 of John of Ephesus as a missionary to surviving pockets of paganism in western Asia Minor. John was so successful that it was recorded that 70,000 converts were baptized, and ninety-eight churches and twelve monasteries were built for their use. This success, however, did not prevent his being a prolific propagandist for monophysitism and becoming Monophysite archbishop of Ephesus in 558. In addition, Sophia, the consort of Justin II, was a friend of the Monophysites at court.

After 536, however, all efforts to heal the breach had a depressing similarity of high hopes succeeded by failure and disillusion.

First, the "Three Chapters" controversy and the Second Council of Constantinople in 553 were less concerned with monophysitism than with the relations between Constantinople and Rome. While the writings of Theodorus of Mopsuestia, the works of THEODORET, bishop of Cyrrhus, against Cyril's Twelve Anathemas, and the letter of Ibas to the presbyter Maris criticizing Cyril's theology were condemned, the key Monophysite tenet that "out of the two natures" there resulted "one" was also anathematized. Orthodoxy was now enthroned on neo-Chalcedonian principles. Monophysitism had been overtaken by new orthodox thought pioneered by Leontius of Byzantium (see Meyendorff, 1975, pp. 74–85).

Second, at the Conference of Callinicum in 568, the Monophysites were offered a compromise by Emperor Justin II. The sole faith was that of the Nicene Creed. Christ was to be confessed as "out of two natures one hypostasis and one persona," the "Three Chapters" were to remain condemned, and the edict against Severus would be abrogated. Jacob Baradaeus was ready to accept, but his and other leaders' efforts to persuade the monks of the orthodoxy of the statement without the explicit condemnation of Chalcedon failed.

Third, the second *Henoticon*, of 571, was the final attempt by Justin II to secure agreement with the Monophysites on the basis of acknowledgment of Christ as "one Son, one person, one subsistence, both God and man together," and the confession of "one incarnate nature of the God-Logos" But again, since there was no denunciation of Chalcedon, it failed.

The reign of the emperor Maurice, beginning in 582, saw a renewal of persecution of the Monophysites, especially in Syria. When Maurice was murdered by Phocas, who became emperor in 602, and the Persians invaded the empire, Monophysite opposition to the imperial government began to harden. The seventh-century chronicler JOHN OF NIKIOU commented on the disasters that befell the empire: "This chastisement has befallen the earth owing to the heresy of the emperor Maurice." Though the Persians were no light taskmasters, the Monophysites found it was possible to retain religious liberty under a foreign power, not least because the policy of Chosroes II was to give them the status of a majority religion in the Roman territory his armies occupied.

This policy was wise, for during the sixth century economic changes had been taking place in Egypt and Syria that had enormously increased the influence of the monasteries over the lives of the rural population. In northern Syria, where monophysitism was already strong, fieldwork by French archaeologists has established that areas once dominated by large landed proprietors had in the sixth century been transformed into villages where land was held by individual families engaged in olive culture closely associated with monasteries. In Egypt, monastic lands were even more extensive, and the dependence of the peasants on the monasteries was accordingly greater. Tradition preserved in the HISTORY OF THE PATRIARCHS speaks of an area near Alexandria where "there are 600 flourishing monasteries, all inhabited by the orthodox," and their cultivators "all held the true faith." This was the rock on which all attempts by Justinian and his successors to convert Egypt to Chalcedonianism foundered.

The victory of the emperor Heraclius over the Persians in 627–630 gave the empire a final chance of settling with the Monophysites. The emperor's acceptance of the Monenergist creed, that in Christ there was one source of activity or *energeia* (see MONENERGISM), came as near success as any of Justinian's and Justin II's efforts, especially in Syria. In Egypt, however, incipient goodwill was gradually eroded and then destroyed by the high-handedness and duplicity of Cyrus, the emperor's choice for civil governor and patriarch. When in 634 Heraclius was forced to withdraw his project of unity on the basis of Monenergism owing to the opposition of Pope Honorius and Sophronius, patriarch of Jerusalem, the last hope of accord ended. Cyrus the Caucasian's arbitrary rule alienated the Copts: "Sullen gloom descended on the land" (Butler, 1902, p. 191). By 639, when the Arab armies arrived in Egypt, they were ready to change masters.

Monophysitism must be regarded mainly as a religious dispute within the framework of Byzantine Christianity. No social cleavage divided its adherents from those of Chalcedon. Families rather than clans were divided. Regional identities, except in Egypt, were slow to form. While eventually monophysitism served as a focus for discontent with the imperial government, it was far from being the Byzantine equivalent of North African DONATISM. The key to its territorial consolidation in both Egypt and Syria is to be found in the great influence of the Monophysite monasteries on the lives of the ordinary people, especially on the land. The combination of popular religious devotion and economic changes that favored the growth of vast monastic estates contributed to the victory of monophysitism in Syria and Egypt in the sixth century. Thus the dispute "over a single letter" (Evagrius, 2.5), the difference between HOMOOUSION (of one substance) and HOMOIOUSION (of like substance), ultimately proved insoluble.

BIBLIOGRAPHY

Atiya, A. S. *A History of Eastern Christianity*. London, 1968.

Baynes, N. H., and E. Dawes, trans. "St. Daniel the Stylite." In *Three Byzantine Saints*. Oxford, 1948.

Brock, S. P. "The Orthodox-Oriental Orthodox Conversations of 532." In *Hellenikè Perilepsé*. Leukosia, Cyprus, 1980.

Butler, A. J. *The Arab Conquest of Egypt*. Oxford, 1902.

Chesnut, R. C. *Three Monophysite Christologies*. Oxford, 1976. Useful bibliography.

Dvornik, F. *Byzantium and the Roman Primacy*. New York, 1979.

Ebied, R. Y., and L. R. Wickham. "A Collection of Unpublished Syriac Letters of Timotheus Aelurus." *Journal of Theological Studies* n. s. 21 (1970):321–69.

Frend, W. H. C. *The Rise of the Monophysite Movement*, 2nd ed. Cambridge, 1979.

Grillmeyer, A., and H. Bacht, eds. *Das Konzil von Chalkedon, Geschichte und Gegenwart*, 3 vols. Würzburg, 1951–1953.

Halleux, A. de. *Philoxène de Mabbog, sa vie, ses écrits et sa théologie*. Louvain, 1963.

Hardy, E. R. "The Patriarchate of Alexandria. A Study of National Christianity." *Church History* 15 (1946):81–100.

———. *Christian Egypt: Church and People*. New York, 1952.

Harnack, A. von. *History of Dogma*, Vols. 4 and 5. Boston, 1905; New York, 1958.

Honigmann, E. "La hiérarchie monophysite au temps de Jacques Baradée (542–578)." In *Evêques et évechés monophysites d'Asie au Ve siècle*. CSCO 126–127, *Subsidia*, Vol. 2.

———. *Le Couvent de Barsauma et le patriarcat jacobite d'Antioche et de Syrie*. CSCO 146, *Subsidia*, Vol. 7.

Jones, A. H. M. "Were Ancient Heresies National or Social Movements in Disguise?" *Journal of Theological Studies*, n.s. 11 (1959):280–98.

Jugie, M. "Monophysisme." In *Dictionnaire de théologie catholique*, Vol. 20, cols. 2216–51. Paris, 1905.

———. "Julien d'Halicarnasse et Sévère d'Antioche." *Etudes orientales* 24 (1925):129–62, 257–85.

Krüger, G. "Monophysiten." In *Realencyclopädie für protestantische Theologie*, ed. J. J. Herzog, Vol. 13. Leipzig, 1896–1913.

Lebon, J. *Le Monophysisme sévérien*. Louvain, 1909.

Lietzmann, H. *Apollinaris von Laodicea und seine Schule*. Tübingen, 1904.

Macmullen, R. "Nationalism in Roman Egypt." *Aegyptus* 44 (1964–1965):177–99.

Meyendorff, J. *Christ in Eastern Christian Thought*. New York, 1975.

Michalowski, K. *Kunst und Geschichte Nubiens in christlicher Zeit*, ed. E. Dinkler. Recklinghausen, 1970.

———. *Faras*. Warsaw, 1974.

Moeller, C. "Le Type de l'empereur Anastase." In *Studia Patristica* 3. Berlin, 1961.

Raabe, R. *Petrus von Iberien*. Leipzig, 1895.

Rea, J. "The Letter of Phonen to Aburni." *Zeitschrift für Papyrologie und Epigraphik* 34 (1979):147–50.

Richard, M. "Le traité *De sectis* et Léonce de Byzance." *Revue d'histoire ecclésiastique* 35 (1939):695–723.

Schwartz, E. "Publizistische Sammlungen zum acacianischen Schisma." *Abhandlungen der bayerischen Akademie der Wissenschaften*, Philosophisch-historische Abteilung, n. s. 10, no. 4 (1934).

———. "Zur Kirchenpolitik Justinians." *Sitzungsberichte der bayerischen Akademie der Wissenschaften*, Philosophisch-historische Abteilung 2 (1940).

———. *Roman State and Christian Church: A Collection of Legal Documents to A.D. 535*, Vol. 3. London, 1966.

Sellers, R. V. *The Council of Chalcedon: An Historical and Theological Study*. London, 1961.

Tchalenko, G. *Villages antiques de la Syrie du nord*. 3 vols. Paris, 1953–1958.

Tixeront, J. *Histoire des dogmes*, Vol. 3. Paris, 1928.

Vaschalde, A., ed. *Tractatus tres de Trinatate et incarnatione*. CSCO 9.

Vasiliev, A. A. *Justin the First: An Introduction to the Epoch of Justinian the Great. Dumbarton Oaks Studies* I (1950):136–60.
Vööbus, A. *A History of Asceticism in the Syrian Orient.* CSCO 184, 197, *Subsidia,* Vols. 14, 17.
Wigram, W. A. *The Separation of the Monophysites.* London, 1923.
Woodward, E. L. *Christianity and Nationalism in the Later Roman Empire.* London, 1916.

W. H. C. FREND

MONOTHELITISM. For Egypt and the Coptic church, monothelitism may be taken simply as a continuation of the monenergist crisis with which imperial power in Egypt ended. At CONSTANTINOPLE, two councils in 638 and 639 accepted the ECTHESIS of Emperor Heraclius (610–641). As in other efforts over the previous two centuries to find agreement on a formula reconciling the divergent views held in Alexandria, Constantinople, and Rome concerning the Person of Christ, the attempt to define this as to be acknowledged in two natures moved by a single activity (*energeia*) failed.

With the death of Sophronius, patriarch of Jerusalem, in 638, the leadership of the opposition to the emperor's creed passed to a monk, Maximus the Confessor. There followed a long and embittered controversy that involved the surviving Byzantine province in North Africa as well as the Roman see. The climax came with the debate between Maximus and Pyrrhus, former patriarch of Constantinople, at Carthage in 645, which resulted in a victory for Maximus and condemnation of the view that in Christ there was one activating principle (*energeia*) and one will (*thelema*). The papacy also turned against Constantinople, though largely on the grounds of ecclesiastical discipline, in that Pyrrhus had been called *sanctissimus,* a title to which Pope Theodore I considered he had no claim.

In 648 Emperor Constans II (642–668) replaced the *Ecthesis* with a new document known as the *Typos.* In this he rejected both the monothelitic and the dyothelitic ("two wills") formulas and forbade their use. At Rome, Pope Theodore summoned a council of 150 bishops at the Lateran Palace in 649, and there the monothelite doctrine was condemned. Both "the most impious *Ecthesis*" and "the damnable *Typos*" were denounced, and the existence of two wills in Christ associated with His two natures was proclaimed.

The long wars between the Byzantines and Arabs distracted the attention of successive emperors from the issue, and the controversy was not settled until the Third Council of Constantinople (sixth general council), which met in 680–681. It was agreed after long debate that in Christ there were indeed two wills, human and divine, perfectly united.

While the issues in the monothelite controversy closely resembled those of MONOPHYSITISM, Egypt had come under Arab occupation in 645 and was only marginally affected.

BIBLIOGRAPHY

Bréhier, L. "L'Ekthesis, la fin du règne et la succession d'Héraclius (638–641)" and "Le démembrement des chrétientés orientales et le schisme monothélite (641–668)." In *Histoire de l'église,* ed. A. Fliche and V. Martin, Vol. 5, *Grégoire le Grand, les états barbares et la conquête arabe (590–757).* Paris, 1947.
Grumel, V. "Recherches sur l'histoire du monothélisme." *Echos d'Orient* 27 (1928):6–16, 257–77; 28 (1929):19–34, 272–82; 29 (1930):16–28.
Jugie, M. "Monothélisme." In *Dictionnaire de théologie catholique,* Vol. 10, pt. 2, cols. 2307–2323. Paris, 1929.

W. H. C. FREND

MORENZ, SIEGFRIED (1914–1970), German Egyptologist and Coptologist. He studied theology under Johannes Leipoldt and Egyptology under W. Wolf in Leipzig. He was professor of Egyptology and history of religions in Leipzig (1952–1970); director of the Egyptian Museum in Berlin (1952–1958); and professor of Egyptology and history of religions at Basel (1961–1966). He was a member of the Saxon Academy of Sciences and the Bavarian Academy of Sciences. In 1959 he was awarded an honorary doctorate of theology at Tübingen. Among his books and articles are important contributions to Coptic philology and literature, and to Hellenism.

BIBLIOGRAPHY

Irmuscher, J. "S. Morenz als Koptologe." *Berliner byzantinistische Arbeiten* 45 (1974):19–28.

MARTIN KRAUSE

MOSES, bishop of Aw Sīm (c. 750) in the time of Patriarch KHĀ'ĪL (744–767). He promoted the election of Khā'īl and, along with him and other laity and bishops, endured repeated incarceration for resistance to taxes (see TAXATION and FUGITIVES). He worked zealously in protracted discussions between the Coptic and the Melchite church leaders at Alexandria, while advising a peaceful resolution. He was considered a blessed, spiritual man, endowed with the gift of prophecy. Under the succeeding patriarch, Mīnā (767–774), he appears as a defender of the holy places against official encroachment. He was the comforter of his fellow sufferers in confinement and acted in a pastoral capacity by writing a letter to the patriarch and all the members of his church in which he admonished them to keep the Sabbath holy.

VINCENT FREDERICK

MOSES OF ABYDOS (feast day: 25 Abīb), fifth–sixth-century monk. The SYNAXARION of the Copts and the *Synaxarion* of the Ethiopians give no information about Moses of Abydos, but only allude to him in the brief commemoration of MACROBIUS, "the son of Abū Mūsā, head of the monastery of al-Balyanā," for 7 Baramūdah. No Arabic manuscript of his life has been accounted for. At the White Monastery (DAYR ANBĀ SHINŪDAH), however, he was celebrated on 25 Abīb, as the *typika* testify: "Moses, archimandrite of Ebōt [Abydos/Afūd]," and fragments have been preserved of three codices containing his life and no doubt an encomium (Campagnano, 1978, pp. 227–30). A certain number of these leaves were published by E. Amélineau (1886–1888, pp. 680–706), W. Till (1935–1936, Vol. 2, pp. 48–60), and H. Munier (1916, pp. 53–54). Eighteen others are unpublished. These fragments correspond roughly to half the original work. Two other sources give some information: the Life of his disciple Macrobius, founder of a community to the south of Asyūṭ (Lycopolis), preserved in a Coptic fragment (Museum of Antiquities, Leiden, MS 30) and an Arabic version (two manuscripts indexed), and that of ABRAHAM OF FARSHŪṬ, archimandrite of Pbow, deposed by JUSTINIAN.

According to the author of the Life of Moses, SHENUTE is reported to have announced shortly before his death the birth of Moses at Abydos. The latter would put an end to the pagan sacrifices and destroy the temples, which Shenute had been unable to do. This would place the birth of Moses in the second half of the fifth century. His parents, Christians, were called Andrew and Tshinoute. Before the birth of Moses, they had three sons, Paul, Joseph, and Elias, and two daughters, Mary and Theodota. Impressed by the stature of the prophet Moses, they made a vow to God to consecrate to him the son whom he should give them, and call him Moses, which shortly after came about. The priest of the village, Theophanes, had a vision at the moment of immersing the child in the baptistery: he saw a dove on his head, and then a hand of light on his mouth when he gave him communion. At the age of five, Moses was offered to the church by his parents and entrusted to the priest. He learned by heart the four Gospels, which one day he recited to an astonished bishop, who in a vision the following night saw the child clothed in the monastic *schema* and surrounded by a multitude of monks.

The beginnings of the monastic life of Moses are missing in the fragments we possess. Thus it is not known where or by whom he was initiated. We learn, however, that he persuaded his three elder brothers Paul, Joseph, and Elias, his younger brother Andrew, and his nephew Abraham to become monks with him. Some people of the neighborhood laid a trap for them, but Joseph learned of it and warned his brothers. Later Moses by his prayer provoked the destruction of the temple of Apollo (? Horus) at Abydos. Thirty pagan priests were overwhelmed, and other temples collapsed. The monastery established by Moses appears to have been near a place called Pehke. Overwhelmed by the crowds attracted by his cures, Moses preferred to depart into the mountains toward the south, but a heavenly voice commanded him to return to Pehke. So Moses and his followers returned toward the north. An angel stopped them a mile from Pehke and traced for Moses the site of the monastery enclosure. They were helped in the construction of the monastery by Serēnēs, the steward of a patrician named Komēte. They dug two wells and built several "houses," one called "the house of Apa Moses" and another that "of the calligraphers," later a third called that of Apa Elias, and a fourth of Apa Andrew. This information about houses suggests that Moses founded a community of the Pachomian type. The text speaks of a journey by the patrician Komēte to Constantinople, where he praised Moses and his monks to the emperor and his court and obtained for the monastery at Abydos annual revenues of wheat, no doubt part of the *embolē*, an imperial gift attested by papyri for the monastery of the METANOIA. This event must be placed in 518 before the death of Anastasius, who was favorable to the anti-Chalcedonians.

The Life indicates that Moses prophesied the interview with the emperor at Constantinople of Anthimus, Severus, and THEODOSIUS, archbishops respectively of Constantinople, Antioch, and Alexandria. By their discourse "God brought back the heart of the emperor to the orthodox faith." This meeting is attested by the historians and must be placed at the end of the summer of 535. The emperor of whom the life of Moses speaks is Justinian, but contrary to what the Coptic text says, Severus had to return to exile in Egypt, Anthimus was deposed by Pope Agapetus and banished, and Theodosius was driven out of Alexandria in 538.

The story also relates various miracles of Moses, and several prophecies. He drove out a demon that lived in the temple of Bes, north of the monastery, which may correspond to the temple of Osiris, and he smote the people with various infirmities. Moses took seven brothers with him and spent the night in the temple to strive against the demons, whom he succeeded in driving out. The author speaks also of numerous conversions, and of the construction by Apa Reuben of a church for the nuns dedicated to Mary which presupposes a community of women under the direction of Moses.

Here the biographer of Moses places the visit of the patriarch SEVERUS at a place named Pkorks. Also mentioned in the life of Macrobrius, Moses and three brothers came to welcome him there. The patriarch of Antioch stayed ten days at the monastery. Probably this visit by Severus must have taken place at the beginning of his exile in Egypt, starting in September 518. After his journey to Constantinople in 535, Severus lived at Xois (Sakhā), where he died on 8 February 538. However, the Panegyric of Saint Claudius, attributed to Severus of Antioch, says that he stayed in the monastery of Abydos with Theodosius, patriarch of Alexandria (elected in 535), pursued by Justinian's police.

The Life of Moses speaks also of a patrician who wished to please the emperor and joined the partisans of the COUNCIL OF CHALCEDON. He received the command of the Thebaid, which presupposes an emperor of Byzantium favorable to the Chalcedonians, no doubt Justin or Justinian; but this patrician later lost all his goods and was reduced to beggary. The author, to show the saint's gift of prophecy, mentions also the announcement by Moses of a raid by the Blemmyes as far as Antinoopolis, through the interior of the desert.

In a vision, Moses is warned that he will soon die and will have to leave the direction of his community to his brother Paul. On 7 Abīb, the day of the feast of Shenute, Moses is warned that death is near. On the 10th he falls ill, and on the 25th, in the morning, he assembles his disciples, entrusts them to his brother Paul, and dies at the third hour of the day, a Friday. He is buried at the tenth hour near the tomb of Apa Sabinos, according to his wish. The Life then relates some miracles wrought at his tomb.

The Life of ABRAHAM OF FARSHŪṬ reports that the latter, archimandrite of Pbow, was driven out by Justinian (527–565) at the beginning of his reign because when summoned to Constantinople, he refused to adhere to the definitions of Chalcedon. Thereafter he lived first at Atrīpe, in the monastery of Shenute, where he copied the latter's rules and had them taken in sealed vessels to the monastery of Apa Moses, then at Farshūṭ, where he founded a monastery for men and another for women. The formula "monastery of Apa Moses" very probably relates to that at Abydos, and it seems indeed that at that time Moses was already dead.

Did Moses of Abydos found a community of the Pachomian type? His Life does not speak of any relations with Pbow. Some indications, however, allow us to answer in the affirmative. The mention of different "houses," so characteristic of the Pachomian monastery, in the monastery at Abydos is remarkable. The author's care to have the birth of Moses announced by Shenute, and the quotations from Shenute that Moses makes in his letters (see below) should also be noted. The same is true of the links between Abraham of Farshūṭ and the monastery of Apa Moses. The silence on life in regard to Pbow, the motherhouse of the Pachomian congregation, may be explained by the presence of Chalcedonians, of whom Moses must have disapproved.

On the other hand, there is no indication in the life that hermits living in the neighborhood of Abydos were under the direction of Moses, as described in the life of his disciple Macrobius. But archaeology offers some additional information. There is at Abydos a Dayr Abū Mūsā to the west of the temple of Osiris and the ruins of another monastery called DAYR ANBĀ BAKHUM, according to C. Sicard; but Dayr al-Rūm, according to G. Lefebvre (1911, pp. 239–40), are to the south of the temple of Seti I (Strabo's Memnonium). Coptic inscriptions with invocations to Apa Moses show that a community of women lived in this temple. Hermitages were also fitted up in the tombs of the pharaonic necropolis to the south of the temples, but we cannot say whether these hermits were dependent on Moses' monastery.

Some fragments of five letters addressed to nuns have been preserved—numbered from 15 to 18 by "Moses the archimandrite." The author is very probably Moses of Abydos. He frequently quotes Shenute and also the treatise *De virginitate* attributed to ATHANASIUS. These letters deal especially with purity and relations with the laity, the entry of young people into the monastery, reading, and manual work. The texts were published by Amélineau (1886–1888, pp. 693–701).

The leaves also preserve the end of the "Canon of our father Moses the archimandrite." This is an exhortation to monks, dealing with charity, renunciation, and fasting, and commending the merits of one Apa Andrew, perhaps the brother of Moses (Coquin, 1988).

BIBLIOGRAPHY

Amélineau, E. *Monuments pour servir à l'histoire de l'Egypte chrétienne aux IVe, Ve, VIe et VIIe siècles.* Mémoires publiés par les membres de la mission archéologique francaise au Caire, Vol. 4. Paris, 1886–1888.

Campagnano, A. "Monaci egiziani fra V e VI secolo." *Vetera Christianorum* 15 (1978):223–46.

Cauwenbergh, P. van. *Etude sur les moines d'Egypte depuis le concile de Chalcédoine (451) jusqu'à l'invasion arabe (640).* Paris, 1914.

Coquin, R.-G. *Moïse d'Abydos.* Etudes Coptes 2 = Cahiers de la bibliothèque copte 3, pp. 1–14. Strasbourg, 1986.

______. "La 'Règle' de Moïse d'Abydos." In *Mélanges Guillaumont,* pp. 103–107. Cahiers d'orientalisme 20. Geneva, 1988.

Godron, G. *Textes coptes relatifs à Saint Claude d'Antioche.* PO 35, pt. 4 [no. 166], pp. 399–692.

Lefebvre, G. "Egypte Chrétienne." *Annales du service des antiquités de l'Egypte* 11 (1911):238–50.

Munier, H. *Manuscripts coptes.* Catalogue général des antiquités égyptiennes du Musée du Caire, Vol. 74. Cairo, 1916.

Stein, E. "Cyrille de Scythopolis, à propos de la nouvelle édition de ses oeuvres." *Analecta Bollandiana* 62 (1944):170–86.

______. *Histoire du Bas-Empire.* Paris and Bruges, 1949 and 1959.

Till, W. *Koptische Heiligen- und Märtyrerlegenden (OCA 102 and 108).* Rome, 1935–1936.

RENÉ-GEORGES COQUIN

MOSES THE BLACK, SAINT (d. 407), anchorite and martyr and the most famous of the monks called Moses (feast day: 24 Ba'ūnah). He was a former black slave who had been dismissed by his master "because of his immorality and acts of highway robbery." When he became a monk at Scetis, he was subjected to violent assaults by demons, but he triumphed over these with the advice and encouragement of Abbā Isidorus. His progress in virtue was so rapid that he was soon reckoned among the greatest of the old men and was ordained a priest. Above all else he was distinguished by his compunction, his gentleness, and his humility. He was so gracious and welcoming that he no longer had a moment's peace. On the advice of MACARIUS he withdrew to greater solitude at Petra. His death at the hands of the Mazices was thus the bloody death he had predicted and wished for as the just punishment for his former crimes. Most of the collections of apothegms contain in various forms "seven chapters sent by the abba Moses to the abba Poemen," possibly representing something in the nature of a summary of what Moses taught his disciples. Among the latter, the most famous is fairly clearly ZACHARIAS, who died a godly death before his master's very eyes.

Moses is very popular among the Copts. His remains are venerated in the main church of DAYR AL-BARĀMŪS of Scetis.

BIBLIOGRAPHY

Butler, C. *The Lausiac History of Palladius,* Vol. 2, pp. 58–62, 197f. Cambridge, 1904.

Chitty, D. J. *The Desert a City,* pp. 53, 60, 66f. Oxford, 1966.

Cotelier, J. P., ed. *Apophthegmata Patrum.* PG 65, cols. 281–89. Paris, 1856.

Evelyn-White, H. G. *The Monasteries of the Wadi'n Natrūn,* pt. 2. *The History of the Monasteries of Nitria and of Scetis.* New York, 1932.

LUCIEN REGNAULT

MOUNT SINAI MONASTERY OF SAINT CATHERINE, fortified monastery built in the sixth century by the Byzantine emperor JUSTINIAN I. It lies in the Wādī al-Dayr below a shoulder of Mount Sinai and near the center of the Sinai Peninsula. To the west is the Plain of al-Raḥā, the traditional campground of the Israelites while Moses communed with God on the summit of the mountain. Since the fourth century, this mountain, Jabal Mūsā, has been generally accepted as the veritable Mount of the Decalogue. Likewise the spot where the monastery now stands has been revered since that time as the site of the burning bush, out of which God had called to Moses and had given him the mission to lead hither the children of Israel, after God had delivered them from pharaoh's power. Until the Middle Ages a growing bush firmly believed to be the original one stood in a small courtyard adjoining the apse of Justinian's church. But by the thirteenth century, the growing bush had been replaced by a marble plaque on the floor of a

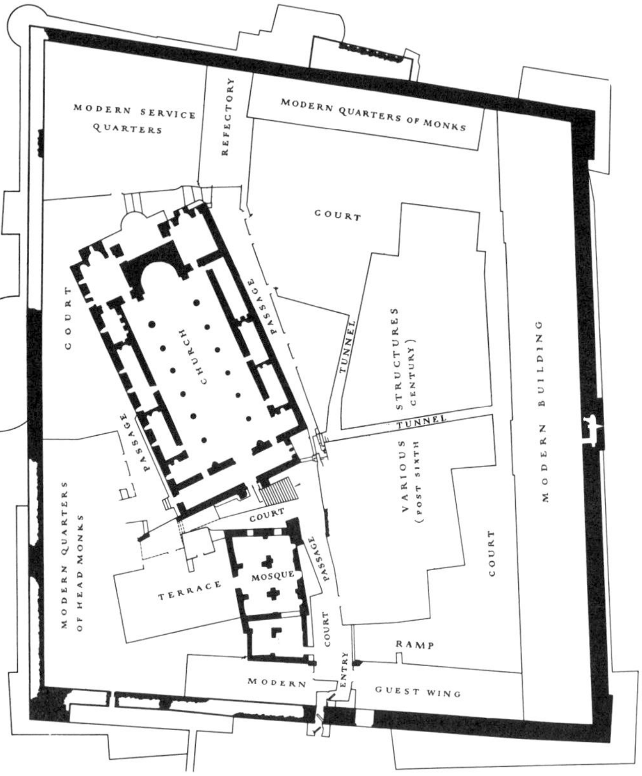

Mount Sinai Monastery of Saint Catherine. Modern plan. Sixth-century elements in heavy outline. Drawing by George H. Forsyth. Photo courtesy Michigan-Princeton-Alexandria Expedition to Mount Sinai.

new chapel that replaced the small courtyard and perpetuates the traditional sanctity of the spot.

Prior to the construction of the monastery, a loosely organized laura of hermits inhabited nearby caves and tended the bush in a garden with an adjoining church. They also welcomed pilgrims attracted to so sacred a spot. Since the construction of the monastery, the hermits have been superseded by a strict monastic organization under the rule of an archbishop-abbot, which occupies a carefully articulated architectural complex designed to accommodate monks and pilgrims to the bush, within a frontier fortress of Justinian's empire. According to a contemporary historian, PROCOPIUS OF CAESAREA, its purpose was to prevent the barbarian peoples in that desert region from making "inroads with complete secrecy into the lands of Palestine proper."

The monastery is a key monument in the history of early Byzantine military and religious architecture. Its outer wall can be traced through its entire perimeter, under later remodelings and superstructures, and on three sides it rises to its original height. In many places its original battlements are still in position. Its surface is enlivened by decorative carved panels, also from the sixth century, which are set above slit windows. The main entrance, which was located at the center of the northwest wall, was a double one consisting of a large and imposing portal, now closed in. A postern to the left of it is now preceded by an eighteenth-century porch. The portal was crowned by a flat arch and must have been closed by a massive door.

In the part of the monastery that is to the right of its main portal as one enters, an open space may have been reserved as a courtyard. No trace of early structures is found in that area. As a pilgrimage center, the monastery was in part a caravansary and may well have included within its sheltering walls an open area for all the multitudinous activities of arriving and departing groups of pilgrims. The area is now occupied by more recent buildings largely of a service nature, and by irregular courts.

Relative to neighboring structures, the church appears to be sunk deeply in the ground. Actually, the ground level within the monastery, unlike the level outside its walls, has changed little. The site of the bush, in the lowest corner of the monastery, determined the floor level of the church, nearly 13 feet (4 m) below the portal of the monastery. A flight of steps leads down to the narthex of the church.

As originally planned, the church was to be entered through three small doors opening into the nave and aisles. During construction, the narthex was added and the center door was widened on one side, so as to afford a full view of the nave from the narthex. The nave retains its simple monumentality in spite of later additions (pulpit, chandeliers, ceiling panels and coves, crucifix, icons, iconostasis, episcopal throne, marble floor, and furniture). The ceiling panels conceal the original thirteen roof trusses, previously visible from the floor. The unique preservation of these trusses, which formerly carried a lead roof, is due to the dry climate. Their sixth-century date is proved by carbon-14 tests. Three of their horizontal beams bear inscriptions on the vertical sides, which were originally visible from the floor but are now concealed by the later panels. They are invocations on behalf of Justinian, his empress Theodora, and the architect of the church, Stephanus.

Since the first inscription implies that Justinian was still alive, and the second indicates that Theodora was already dead, the church was commissioned between the years in which each died, that is, between 548 and 565. The bottom surfaces of the beams, not being covered by the later panels, remain visible from the floor. These surfaces retain their original sixth-century carvings of floral ornament and of animals, river scenes, and sea creatures, all of them rendered realistically and with animation. On one beam is a Nilotic scene with men rowing a boat, a threatening crocodile, an enraged bull and, surprisingly, two tritons swimming with crosses in their arms. Similar carvings of floral ornament and animals appear on the great wooden door that opens from the narthex into the nave. They all formed part of the original decor of the church, as do the two marble panels flanking the main altar on each of which is carved a cross between two deer confronted in a heraldic composition.

To the right and left of the sanctuary are original bronze doors opening into two large chapels, which flank the apse and give access to the medieval Chapel of the Burning Bush. It replaced the small courtyard on the same spot wherein grew a bush, believed by earlier pilgrims to be the original. They would have visited this goal of their pilgrimage by passing outdoors through a formal doorway at the north end of the narthex and thence along the north flank of the church to its far end, where grew the bush in the small courtyard, probably enframed by a chancel rail, perhaps supporting a small colonnade, like the choir enclosure in a church. After construction of the new chapel closed the circuitous outdoor route, pilgrims would have passed from the narthex along the aisles of the church and through the bronze doors into the former chapels, converted from their original liturgical purpose to antechambers of the new chapel. The piety of pilgrims was satisfied by services said at the site of the bush, which had gained further reverence through its association with the Virgin Mary. The new routing also took them past the renowned tomb of Saint Catherine of Alexandria whose body, miraculously revealed to the monks on nearby Mount Saint Catherine, spread the fame of her monastery far and wide from the time of the Crusades.

Saint Catherine's tomb is on the south side of the sanctuary, adjoining the south aisle. The sanctuary itself and the apse are little altered since the sixth century. The great marble altar table stands at the center under an eighteenth-century domical structure. The apse retains its original veneer of matched marble panels encircling the marble throne of the abbot, which is flanked by a triple tier bench of marble (behind later marquetry) for the clergy.

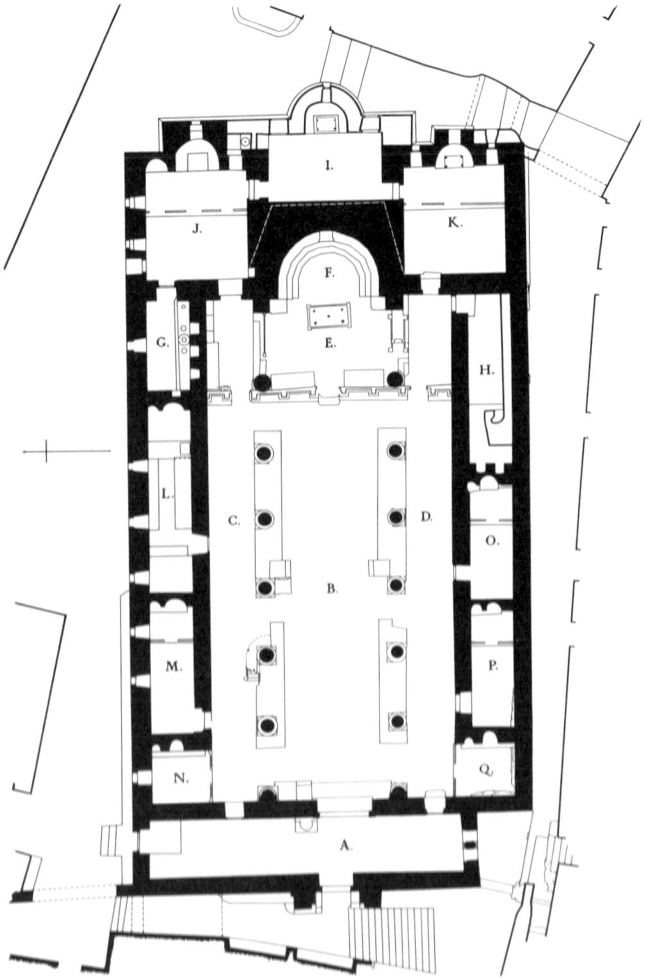

Mount Sinai Monastery of Saint Catherine. The Church. Modern plan showing sixth-century elements in heavy outline. Drawing by George H. Forsyth. Photo courtesy Michigan-Princeton-Alexandria Expedition to Mount Sinai. Key: A. Narthex. B. Nave. C. North aisle. D. South aisle. E. Sanctuary. F. Apse. G. Sacristy. H. Storeroom; Chapels in Church. I. Burning Bush (medieval). J. St. James the Less. K. Forty Martyrs (Holy Fathers). L. St. Antipas. M. SS. Constantine and Helen. N. St. Marina. O. SS. Anne and Joachim. P. St. Simeon Stylites. Q. SS. Cosmas and Damian.

Two panels of the original enclosure of the sanctuary are still in place (one below the tomb) and in the half-dome of the apse and on the wall above it are magnificent sixth-century mosaics, including the Transfiguration and Moses at the Burning Bush receiving the Law. On the flat marble surfaces that flank the apse were painted, at a somewhat later

Monastery of Saint Catherine from the East. Mount Sinai rises to the left. *Photo courtesy Michigan-Princeton-Alexandria Expedition to Mount Sinai.*

date and in encaustic, the Sacrifice of Isaac on the left and the Sacrifice of Jephthah's Daughter on the right (behind Saint Catherine's tomb). There is no evidence that the nave or aisles ever had any figurative decoration.

In plan, the core of the church is a normal three-aisled basilica with a single eastern apse. Flanking that core is an alignment of six chapels plus a sacristy and a long room that may have been another sacristy or a treasury. These flanking elements are not later additions but are parts of the original plan and are incorporated into it like the outer aisles of a five-aisled church. They have not been altered; their small apses with adjoining service niches are original; and they were roofed by continuous flat decks on both sides, just below the aisle windows. Such an organic incorporation of secondary chapels in this sixth-century plan appears to be a precocious example of a development in the Byzantine rite toward a "private" liturgy in addition to the traditional liturgy at the main altar. The two eastern chapels are also "private," being connected to the church interior only by small entrances closed by bronze doors. These chapels originally may have had a liturgical function in relation to the burning bush relic accessible from both of them.

A notable feature of the church is the loftiness of its proportions. The vertical effect of its nave, originally enhanced by the open work ceiling above it and by the abnormally high pitch of its roof, is exceptional in contemporary Byzantine basilical churches. It serves to offset the relatively inferior location of the church. The two original facade towers, which have no obvious practical use, may have had a similar intention of elevating the church's silhouette.

Before the front entrance of the church stands another important structure, a three-story building that has been largely absorbed into more recent constructions but is contemporary with the church. Its middle story, which is at the level of the nearby portal of the fortress, consists of an entrance foyer opening into a reception hall of six bays separated by piers carrying great arches of a scale comparable to the arches in the church. Above this formal hall was a suite of six chambers, later destroyed. Below it was another, smaller, arcaded room that connected with other arcaded rooms at the same subterranean level, so as to form a vast adjoining storage dungeon. Such a combination of a monumental reception hall suitable for official appearances, with a private suite of rooms above it suggesting an official residence, and with huge storage facilities below it as if to withstand a siege, resembles the keep of a fortress. This building was surely the headquarters of the military commander, in the tradition of the Roman *praetorium*. Its juxtaposition to the church completes the double Byzantine con-

Mount Sinai, Monastery of Saint Catherine. Mosaic on half-dome of apse. Transfiguration. Sixth century. *Photo courtesy Michigan-Princeton-Alexandria Expedition to Mount Sinai.*

cept of a stronghold as equally under the protection of church and state.

In the Fatimid period the monks, in a fine show of religious amity, authorized conversion of the outmoded headquarters building to a mosque with minaret, for use of local bedouins who staffed the monastery. The bell tower on the church was a gift from Russia in 1871.

Most of the secondary structures necessary to maintain the complex practical functions of the monastery, so isolated and dependent on its own resources, can still be traced beneath later alterations. Along the outer wall on its southeast side and partly built on top of that wall is a long modern dormitory consisting of small single rooms behind a verandah that overlooks the nearby church. This dormitory is now occupied by monks. Since it adjoins a latrine tower, no longer used but of sixth-century origin, and since it is above an extensive complex of sixth-century kitchens and related storage rooms in the basement, apparently this eastern area of the monastery has always been reserved as the residence of the monks. The opposite western area adjoining the main portal of the monastery was reserved for the military and for pilgrim guests. Above that portal is another modern dormitory with verandah, which is now allocated to guests and probably replicates a sixth-century guest dormitory at the same place. Along the inner face of the outer wall, on its northeast side, are the modern quarters of the head monks and an alignment of flimsy modern service structures, partly destroyed in a fire. Beneath them is an imposing sixth-century arcade that may be the ground floor of military barracks originally built against the outer wall and next to the storage dungeon and near to the military headquarters building. On the southwest wall of the monastery there is a huge and ungainly domed structure erected in the 1930s as a dormitory for pilgrims. Since the sixth-century wall below it also has rows of windows in its outer face, although smaller, a sixth-century dormitory, whether monastic or military, probably preceded the present one.

Although located on Egyptian soil, the monastery does not much resemble contemporary Coptic monasteries. It has retained its Greek Orthodox character, as indicated by the design of its church, which has numerous features in common with contemporary Syrian and Palestinian churches but has little resemblance to contemporary Coptic churches.

BIBLIOGRAPHY

Atiya, A. S. *Monastery of St. Catherine in Mt. Sinai.* Cairo, 1950.

Drewer, L. J. "The Carved Wood Beams of the Church of Justinian, Monastery of St. Catherine,

Mount Sinai." Ph.D. diss., University of Michigan, 1971.

Forsyth, G. H. "The Monastery of St. Catherine at Mount Sinai: Church and Fortress of Justinian." *Dumbarton Oaks Papers* 22 (1968):3–19.

Forsyth, G. H.; K. Weitzmann; et al. *The Monastery of St. Catherine at Mount Sinai: Church and Fortress of Justinian*. Ann Arbor, Mich., 1973.

Mathews, T. F. "Private Liturgy in Byzantine Architecture: Toward a Re-appraisal." *Cahiers archéologiques* 30 (1982):125–38.

Mayerson, P. "Procopius or Eutychius on the Construction of the Monastery of Mount Sinai: Which Is the More Reliable Source?" *Bulletin of the American Schools of Oriental Research* 230 (1978):33–38.

McClure, M. L., and C. L. Feltoe, eds. *The Pilgrimage of Etheria*, pp. 1–11. London, 1920.

Rabino, M. H. L. *Monastère de Sainte-Catherine du Mont Sinai*. Cairo, 1938.

Sevcenko, I. "The Early Period of Sinai Monastery in the Light of Its Inscriptions." *Dumbarton Oaks Papers* 20 (1966):255–64.

Tsafrir, Y. "St. Catherine's Monastery in Sinai: Drawings by I. Dunayevsky." *Israel Exploration Journal* 28 (1978):218–29.

Weitzmann, K. "The Jephthah Panel in the Bema of the Church of St. Catherine's Monastery on Mount Sinai." *Dumbarton Oaks Papers* 18 (1964):341–52.

______. "The Mosaic in St. Catherine's Monastery on Mount Sinai." *Proceedings of the American Philosophical Society* 110 (1966):392–405.

______. *Studies in the Arts at Sinai*. Princeton, 1982.

Wilson, C. W., and H. S. Palmer. *Ordinance Survey of the Peninsula of Sinai*, Vol. 1. Southampton, 1869.

GEORGE H. FORSYTH

MOURNING IN EARLY CHRISTIAN TIMES. As Spiegelberg's comparison with the Egyptian sources (pp. 32f.) has shown, the description of mourning given by Herodotus (1893, p. 118, no. 85) is both graphic and correct: "When in a house a respected inmate dies, all the female occupants smear their heads or faces with mud, leave the corpse lying in the house, and run through the town with bared breasts, smiting themselves; all the female relatives join them. The men too smite themselves, and have their garment tied fast below the breast." The Copts mourned their dead in the same manner. In contrast with their attitude toward MUMMIFICATION, however, theologians and monks in Egypt turned against the continuance of the old Egyptian mourning rites in the Christian period. A dictum of SHENUTE has been preserved (*Mémoire de la mission*, IV.27), according to which Christians ought not to weep and mourn over faithful Christians, but over those who have died godless. In the cenobite monasticism of the fourth and fifth centuries, the Egyptian church replaced mourning with prayers and psalm-singing, as the sources show. After the death of a monk, all the monks in the monasteries of Pachomius (Lefort, 1965, Vols. 99 and 100, pp. 87ff.) and Shenute (Leipoldt, 1903, 134) assembled round the mortal shell of the dead man, to sing psalms and to pray.

The arrangement of having the burial of nuns carried out by monks probably goes back to the observation that the women clung more than the men to the old customs. But despite all admonitions, the Christians continued to mourn their dead. On a gravestone from ANTINOOPOLIS the dead man, a deacon, invites the visitor to the grave to mourn: "All who would weep over those who have died from among them, let them come here, to speak a lamentation" (Hall, 1905, 400). At synods mournings were forbidden, and those who offended had the church's ban imposed upon them (Riedel, 1900, 191). But even these penalties could not dislodge the firmly rooted mourning of the dead. The Coptic church saw itself constrained not only to tolerate mourning but also to accept it into the funeral liturgy (Tuki, 1763, p. 499). At the beginning of this liturgy, as on the Antinoopolis gravestone, people are summoned to lamentation: "Gather you all with me, ye men skilled in speech, and let us together mourn in a great lamentation."

There are also representations of mourning in Coptic book illustrations (Cramer, 1964, pl. 17). Even in the twentieth century Blackman noted ancient Egyptian mourning at a Coptic funeral among fellahin in Upper Egypt. In the case of mourning, the old customs of the country won out over the prohibitions of the church.

[*See also:* Burial Rites; Funerary Customs.]

BIBLIOGRAPHY

Amélineau, F. *Monuments pour servir à l'histoire de l'Egypte chrétienne aux IVe, Ve siècles, Texte copte publié et traduit*. Mémoires de la Mission archéologique française au Caire 4. Paris, 1888.

Blackman, W. *The Fellahin of Upper Egypt. Their Religious, Social and Industrial Life To-day with Special Reference to Survivals from Ancient Times*. London, 1927.

Cramer, M. *Die Totenklage bei den Kopten. Mit Hinweisen auf die Totenklage im Orient überhaupt.* Sitzungsberichte der Akademie der Wissenschaften in Wien, Philosophisch-historische Klasse 219,2. Vienna, 1941.
______. *Koptische Buchmalerei.* Recklinghausen, 1964.
Hall, H. R. *Coptic and Greek Texts of the Christian Period from Ostraca, Stelae, etc. in the British Museum.* London, 1905.
Herodotus. *The History of Herodotus,* Vol. 2, ed. George Rawlinson. New York, 1893.
Krause, M. "Das Weiterleben ägyptischer Vorstellungen und Bräuche im koptischen Totenwesen." In *Das römisch-byzantinische Ägypten. Akten des internationalen Symposions 26.–30. September 1978 in Trier,* ed. G. Grimm, H. Heinen, and E. Winter. Aegyptiaca Treverensia 2, pp. 85–92. Mainz, 1983.
Lefort, L. T. *S. Pachomii vitae sahidicae scriptae.* CSCO 99 and 100. Louvain, 1965.
Leipoldt, J. *Schenute von Atripe und die Entstehung des national ägyptischen Christentums.* Leipzig, 1903.
Riedel, W. *Die Kirchenrechtsquellen des Patriarchats Alexandrien.* Leipzig, 1900. Reprinted Aalen, 1968.
Spiegelberg, W. *Die Glaubwürdigkeit von Herodots Bericht über Ägypten im Lichte der ägyptischen Denkmäler.* Orient und Antike 3. Heidelberg, 1926.
Tuki, R. ⲡⲓϫⲱⲙ ⲛⲧⲉ ϯⲙⲉⲧⲣⲉϥϣⲉⲙϣⲓ ⲛⲛⲓⲙⲩⲥⲧⲏⲣⲓⲟⲛ ⲉⲑⲩ ⲛⲉⲙ ϩⲁⲛϫⲓⲛϩⲏⲃⲓ ⲛⲧⲉ ⲛⲓⲣⲉϥⲙⲱⲟⲩⲧ ⲛⲉⲙ ϩⲁⲛϫⲓⲛϩⲱⲥ ⲛⲉⲙ ⲡⲓⲕⲁⲧⲁⲙⲉⲣⲟⲥ ⲛⲁⲃⲟⲧ (pijōm nte tmetrefshemshi nnimystērion ethy nem hanjinhēbi nte nirefmōout nem hanjinhōs nem pikatameros nabot). Rome, 1763.

MARTIN KRAUSE

MU'AQQUB, AL-, Arabic term, meaning "the repeated," used for a metrical rhymed Coptic composition called ⲉⲣⲙⲏⲛⲓⲁ (ermēnia) or ⲉⲣⲙⲉⲛⲓⲁ (ermenia), a TAFSĪR, or explanation, attached to the Saturday THEOTOKIA. It is so called because each stanza begins by repeating the last line of the preceding stanza. Each stanza is composed of four lines. The first three lines rhyme, and the fourth line is repeated as the first verse of the following stanza and rhymes with the two succeeding lines, as in the following:

ⲁⲓⲛⲁϩⲱⲥ ⲛⲁⲕ ⲡϭ̅ⲥ̅ ⲛⲟⲩⲛⲁⲓ:
ⲁⲓⲕⲱϯ ⲛ̀ⲥⲁ ⲡⲉⲕⲟⲩϫⲁⲓ:
ⲙⲁⲕⲁϯ ⲛⲏⲓ ⲕⲁⲧⲁ ⲡⲉⲕⲛⲁⲓ:
ϫⲱ ⲛⲏⲓ ⲉⲃⲟⲗ ⲛ̀ⲧⲁⲙⲉⲧⲁⲧϩⲏⲧ.

ϫⲱ ⲛⲏⲓ ⲉⲃⲟⲗ ⲛ̀ⲧⲁⲙⲉⲧⲁⲧϩⲏⲧ:
ⲁⲣⲓⲟⲩⲱⲓⲛⲓ ⲙ̀ⲡⲁϩⲏⲧ:
ⲉⲑⲣⲓϫⲱ ⲙ̀ⲙ̀ⲧⲁⲓⲟ ⲛ̀ⲧⲉ ⲧⲁⲓϣⲉⲗⲉⲧ:
ϯⲁⲑⲱⲗⲉⲃ ⲛ̀ⲥⲉⲙⲛⲉ.

ainahōs nak pčs nounai:
aikōti ǹsa pekoujai:
makati nēi kata peknai:
jō nēi ebol ǹtametathēt.

jō nēi ebol ǹtametathēt:
ariouōini m̀pahēt:
ethrijō m̀ptaio ǹte taishelet:
tiathōleb ǹsemne.

A *mu'aqqab,* like the Saturday theotokia, is composed of nine sections. An alphabetical order is followed in the beginning of each section. Thus, the first section of a *mu'aqqab* begins with the letter ⲁ (a/alpha), the second with the letter ⲃ (b/bēta), and so on.

A *mu'aqqab* is sung together with the other *tafāsīr* at the Saturday *theotokia* in the PSALMODIA before the service of the evening offering of incense performed on Saturdays in the month of Kiyahk and optionally during Lent.

BIBLIOGRAPHY

Kitab al-Absalmūdiyat al-Muqaddasat al-Kiyah-Kiyah (Psalmody for the Month of Kiyahk). Cairo, 1911.
O'Leary, De L. *The Coptic Theotokia.* London, 1923.

EMILE MAHER ISHAQ

MUBĀSHIRŪN, title of the leading Coptic officials in the Egyptian tax administration during the French occupation of Egypt (1798–1801).

"*Mubāshirūn*" (sing. *mubāshir,* steward) and *katabah* (sing. *kātib,* secretary), were names given in Mamluk and Osmanli Egypt to employees in the *ruznāmah* (state financial administration) and in the domain of the Mamluk and native ruling class. In the second half of the eighteenth century, these posts were held predominantly by Copts. In particular, the Mamluk beys employed Copts as agents. Usually they had a whole staff of secretaries. At their head was the *ra'īs al-kataba* (chief secretary) or *kātib awwal* (first secretary). There was, as a rule, beside him a *kātib yadd* as chief assistant. In addition there was a *kātib al-'alīq* (secretary for fodder), who had the task of providing for the horses in the stables of the Mamluk household, a *kātib al-makhlah* (bookkeeper), in charge of disbursements within the house, a *kātib al-khazīnah* (secretary of the exchequer), who kept watch on the treasury, and a special *ṣarrāf* (money changer) competent for all calculations and questions of money. To these were added the employees who worked in the assessment and collection of taxes on the bey's estates, among them the *ṣayārif* (sing. *ṣarrāf*, tax collector) or *jubāt* (sing. *jābī*, tax collector), the *massāḥūn* (sing. *massāḥ*, surveyor), and the *'ummāl* (sing. *'āmil*, agent).

The first secretaries of the leading Mamluk beys attained considerable political, economic, and social influence in the second half of the eighteenth century; above them all was the *kātib* of the ruling *shayk al-balad* of Cairo, the bey, who de facto exercised authority over Egypt. This Coptic secretary was at the same time head of the corporation of all Coptic secretaries and tax collectors. He was designated as *ra'īs al-katabah al-aqbāṭ bi-Miṣr* (chief of the Coptic secretaries of Egypt) or *kabīr al-mubāshirīn bi-al-diyār al-miṣriyyah* (chief of the administrative officials of Egypt). As an influential member of the Coptic upper class, he was generally treated as political representative of the Copts as a whole, and also simply called *kabīr* or *ra'īs al-aqbāṭ* (leader of the Copts). In the second half of the eighteenth century the holders of this post were *Mu'allim* (master) Rizq, the *kātib* of 'Alī Bey al-Kabīr (1755–1772), IBRĀHĪM AL-JAWHARĪ, and his brother JIRJIS AL-JAWHARĪ, both secretaries of Ibrahim Bey (1775–1798). With the increasing control over the sultan's financial administration that the Mamluk beys secured for themselves, the Coptic secretaries also gained access to these key posts in the administration of Egypt. (The office of the *kabīr al-mubāshirīn* is not to be confused with that of the *ṣarraf bāshī* or chief money-changer, the leader of the corporation of the public money-changers, to which native Christians and Muslims belonged as well as many Jews.)

When the French occupied Egypt in 1798 and expelled the Mamluks, they could easily dispense with the Osmanli personnel of the *ruznāmah*, who for the most part had taken flight, because they had available in the Coptic secretaries administrators familiar with the secrets of Egyptian tax and financial administration and ready to cooperate. Napoleon left to this corporation the calculation and collection of taxes on agriculture, which made up the major part of Egyptian tax income, and appointed Jirjis al-Jawharī as *intendant général.* This title from the French administration of the Ancien Régime was considered an equivalent of *kabīr al-mubāshirīn.*

The complete administrative staff of the comptroller general comprised some 100 employees: thirteen provincial comptrollers, four of them at the rank of comptroller general, each of whom had as assistants two chief secretaries and four other tax collectors, and some collaborators in the central office of the comptroller general in Cairo. These official employees, paid by the treasury, used to employ further collaborators and subordinates at their own expense. They paid them from the side income which they were accustomed to make in the collection of taxes, although the French for the most part regarded this as illegal.

Jirjis al-Jawharī held the position of responsible leader of the tax administration until the treaty of al-'Arīsh came into effect in February 1800. After the failure of this agreement and the reconquest of Egypt, Jirjis al-Jawharī lost his status of pre-eminence to Ya'qūb Ḥannā. However, he remained one of the five comptrollers general, alongside Ya'qūb Ḥannā and his colleagues, Filtā'ūs Malaṭī and Anṭūn Abū Ṭaqiyyah. It is not known whether his function as *ra'īs al-katabah* also passed to Ya'qūb. Since the latter left Egypt with the French, Jirjis al-Jawharī in time regained his former prominent position in the Egyptian tax and financial administration.

BIBLIOGRAPHY

Boustany, S., ed. *The Journals of Bonaparte in Egypt 1798–1801,* 10 vols. Cairo, 1971–1977.

Estève, R. X. "Mémoire sur les finances de l'Egypte, depuis sa conquête par le sultan Selym Ier, jusqu'à celle du général en chef Bonaparte." In *Description de l'Egypte, Etat moderne,* Vol. 1, pt. 1, pp. 299–398. Paris, 1809–1826.

Girard, P. S. "Mémoire sur l'agriculture, l'industrie et le commerce de l'Egypte." In *Description de l'Egypte, Etat moderne,* Vol. 2, pt. 1, pp. 491–714. Paris, 1809–1826.

Lancret, M. A. "Mémoire sur le système d'imposition territoriale et sur l'administration des provinces de l'Egypte dans les dernières années du gouvernement des Mamlouks." In *Description de l'Egypte, Etat moderne,* Vol. 1, pt. 1, pp. 233–60. Paris, 1809–1826.

Marcel, J. J. *Contes du cheykh el-Mohdy,* Vol. 3, p. 336. Paris, 1835.

Motzki, H. *Dimma und Egalité. Die nichtmuslimischen Minderheiten Ägyptens in der zweiten Hälfte des 18. Jahrhunderts und die Expedition Bonapartes* (1798–1801). Bonn, 1979.

Shaw, S. J. *Ottoman Egypt in the Age of the French Revolution.* Cambridge, Mass., 1964.

HARALD MOTZKI

MUFAḌḌAL IBN MĀJID IBN AL-BISHR, AL-, also known by the name of Ibn al-Bishr al-Kātib (the secretary), a famous Coptic physician who lived during the mid-thirteenth century. M. Steinschneider suggested that he was a Jew, and C. Brockelmann, following that example, gave Mufaḍḍal the name of al-Isrā'īlī. In most manuscripts, however, he is simply called al-Qibṭī.

He authored a medical treatise, written in verse, totaling nearly 3,500 verses, called *Naq' al-Ghalal/ wa naf' al-'alal* (Treatise on How to Quench Thirst [for Medical Knowledge]). The work opens with various definitions, discusses different medicines, and ends with the subject of poisons.

We possess the autographed manuscript written by al-Mufaḍḍal himself in A.H. 667/A.D. 1268/1269 (National Library, Paris, Arabe 2997, 137 sheets with 13 lines per page).

The text remains unedited, and for its identification we quote the incipit:

"Al-ḥamdu li-llāhi al-ladhī abda'a-l-bashara nār^{an} wa-mā'^{an} wa-hawā'^{an} wa-madara!" which may be translated "Praise be to God who created man,/ Fire, water, air and earth!"

Besides the autograph manuscript mentioned above, at least five others are known under his name.

BIBLIOGRAPHY

Brockelmann, C. *Geschichte der arabischen Literatur,* Vol. 1, pp. 492, 493; (no. 35); 2d ed., vol. 1, p. 649 (no. 35). Leiden, 1949. Supplement 1, p. 890 (no. 35). Leiden, 1936.

Cheikho, L. "Catalogue raisonné des manuscrits de la Bibliothèque Orientale de l'Université Saint-Joseph." *Mélanges de l'Université* 8 (1922):419, no. 308.

Sbath, P. *Al-Fihris (Catalogue de manuscrits arabes),* Vol. 1. pp. 63f., no. 516. Cairo, 1938.

———. "Manuscrits arabes d'auteurs coptes." *Bulletin de la Société d'archéologie copte* 5 (1939): 159–73, especially p. 168, no. 64.

Slane, W. McGuckin baron de. *Catalogue des manuscrits arabes de la Bibliothèque nationale,* pp. 533, 534. Paris, 1883–1895.

Steinschneider, M. *Die arabische Literatur der Juden. Ein Beitrag zur Literaturgeschichte der Araber grossenteils aus handschriftlichen Quellen,* p. 239. Frankfurt am Main, 1902; repr. Hildesheim, 1964.

KHALIL SAMIR, S.J.